The Purposeful Writer

A RHETORIC WITH READINGS

The Purposeful Writer

A RHETORIC WITH READINGS

Donna Gorrell

St. Cloud State University

Allyn and Bacon

Boston   London   Toronto   Sydney   Tokyo   Singapore

Executive Editor: Joseph Opiela
Production Administrator: Rowena Dores
Editorial-Production Service: Editorial Inc.
Text Designer: Pat Torelli
Cover Administrator: Linda Dickinson
Composition and Manufacturing Buyer: Louise Richardson

Library of Congress Cataloging-in-Publication Data

Gorrell, Donna.
    The purposeful writer : a rhetoric with readings / Donna Gorrell.
      p.   cm.
    Includes index.
    ISBN 0-205-12659-6
    1. English language—Rhetoric.   2. College readers. I. Title.
PE1408.G629   1991
808′.042—dc20
                                    90-19806
                                        CIP

 This textbook is printed on recycled, acid-free paper.

Credits

Page 7. Neil Postman, from *Amusing Ourselves to Death*. Copyright © 1985 by Neil Postman. Reprinted by permission of Viking Penguin, a division of Penguin Books USA Inc.

Credits continued on page 477, which constitutes an extension of the copyright page.

Printed in the United States of America
10 9 8 7 6 5 4 3 2 1   95 94 93 92 91 90

Contents

PART II The Practice of Purposeful Writing   111

6 *To Reflect: Writing with Emphasis on the Writer*   *112*

12   *To Explain: Writing with Emphasis on the Subject*   *331*

Checklists

Preface

I believe that writers—authors of books and stories and essays—are the best teachers of writing. They're always available, always instructive, always right on track, always supportive. They are always ready with examples of excellent writing, often demonstrative of problems writers have in expressing ideas. They show how words go together to make up sentences, how sentences join to make paragraphs, how paragraphs contribute to the development of a central idea. They show how writers like themselves achieve coherence and a tone appropriate to a given situation. They show the many ways they have of developing an idea and the multitude of purposes they might have for writing.

Experienced writers know that they can learn from other writers, and they know how to *read as writers* in order to learn from other writers—how to read for style and structure as well as how to read for meaning. They are so experienced at such reading, in fact, that they usually do it unconsciously. But writers of less experience have often not acquired this skill, and some are even ineffectual in reading as readers. They read, but not actively and critically. Many college students have not yet come to understand that reading for what a writer *does* as well as for what a writer *says* can increase both comprehension of content and skill in writing.

This book is based on the premise that our common goal—that college students become mature, capable writers—can be aided if they become active readers. In learning how to learn from other writers, such as what to look for to discover how a writer achieves coherence and tone or develops an idea—that is, to use reading to learn writing—students can acquire that sense that tells them when a phrase is right, when it's time to begin a new paragraph, and when other judgments that must be made in writing are right for the occasion. Realizing that most writing textbooks do not truly bring together reading and writing, in this book I have attempted a genuine integration that uses reading to illustrate and model the purposes of writing and what writers do to attain those purposes.

Purpose is a key term in this book. Writers write for particular purposes: to inform someone, to entertain, to reflect, to record, and so on. How they develop their ideas—such as by classification, comparison, or cause-and-effect analysis—depends on what they need in order to achieve their purposes. So purpose has been my organizing principle, with methods of invention, development, and revision being treated within the context of writing. My selection of purposes may differ from those of other teachers, but any book can present only a selection. My selection relies in part on James Moffett's categories of recording, reporting, informing, and generalizing (or explaining, as I term it), plus extensions to other kinds of writing that student writers do: summarizing, responding, and showing what they know. Wanting to do more than concentrate on school writing, and preferring to treat writers holistically, I've included purposes for writing other than those usually required in school, such as reflecting, personal corresponding, entertaining, and praising.

The chapters are arranged sequentially in that reflection, composing close to the self, comes before the two chapters on writing with special emphasis on the audience. The remaining chapters present writing emphasizing the subject, beginning with subject-emphasis writing close to the self, recording, and proceeding through reporting, informing, and explaining. The remaining three subject-emphasis chapters are not particularly sequential but present purposes for writing that student writers may sometimes encounter: instructing, praising or censuring, and summarizing and responding. Despite their somewhat sequential arrangement, any of the chapters can be used in any order. When I used an early draft of the book, I began with Chapter 1 as an introduction, then moved to one of the Part II chapters, and from there on continued to integrate chapters in Part I with assignments in Part II. In using the book according to their own purposes, teachers and students alike may rely on the glossary, the index, and cross-referencing for access to discussions of particular aspects of writing. Coherence, tone, and methods of development, for example, are treated here and there throughout the text.

Part I establishes the position that writing and reading are related inseparably. Addressing students as writers and readers, Chapter 1 discusses a variety of writing processes and the number of ways that readers read, according to their purposes and experience. The chapter makes specific suggestions for developing active reading and encourages students to read as writers. Chapter 2 presents an overview of the rhetorical principles applied to writing. Students frequently have negative attitudes toward rhetoric, thinking that altering roles to fit situations is artificial and that adapting appeals to suit audiences is dishonest; however, because rhetoric is part of everyday life, a knowledge of its principles can make us more informed as both readers and writers. Moreover, by applying the principles to specific rhetorical situations, we can see that, in many cases, the varying roles are real and the appeals are only a consideration for the needs and interests of the audience.

Chapters 3, 4, and 5 then examine the writing process—not that there is a single process and not that it occurs in the order presented: prewriting, drafting, and revising. My position on this issue is that the writing process may be recursive, all at once, sequential, linear—whatever, depending on the writer's purpose for writing and the familiarity with the subject. But for instructional purposes the parts must be separated and may indeed be called *stages*, considering that stages are not necessarily linear, allow for backtracking, and may even be conflated. Chapter 3 discusses methods of invention; Chapter 4 methods of development and arrangement; and Chapter 5, methods of revision—all with the understanding that invention may occur at any point, as may drafting and revision. Each chapter in Part I is illustrated with examples for student and professional writing and has exercises to augment the discussion.

Part III puts into practice the principles discussed in Part I. Except for Chapter 15, these chapters all follow a pattern: a discussion of the writing purpose and then several pieces of writing illustrating specific aspects of that purpose, accompanied by questions, discussion, exercises, and writing assignments. Reading and writing are closely integrated, but in such a way that teachers can adapt the arrangement to their own teaching style and local constraints. It's possible, for example, to assign several readings within a chapter and only one writing, to skip entire chapters, or to permit students to select a writing from a chapter in which some of the readings have been considered in class. The exercises are coordinated with the reading and writing, inviting students to explore ideas rather than arrive at pat answers. Almost all the exercises require some writing. Many of them work well for class or group discussions, and most of them are appropriate for journal writing.

The readings suit the type of discourse covered in the chapter. The specific purposes they illustrate are not exhaustive, and most readers can undoubtedly think of other specific purposes beyond those included here. I realize too that most writing has more than one purpose—not just to inform, for example, but to entertain as well, not just to reflect but also to persuade and inform. I ask teachers and students to understand, where I have not called attention to the multiplicity of purposes, that very seldom do writers have a single purpose.

Most of the readings are short enough to function as examples and models. Because most have not previously been anthologized, many of them are fresh and challenging. When preparing this book, I asked my students what kind of writing interested them, and they said topics that are relevant to them, humorous, and timely. Acknowledging the aging of the average college student, I've tried to select themes of interest to students of whatever age; consequently I've included essays on nature and the environment, drugs, the Vietnam War, abortion, the family, and holocaust, to name a few. My students also wanted examples of writing by their peers, so I have included numerous student essays. These essays show that students are capable of interesting, sometimes enormously powerful and moving writing. Because these writings are not overly polished, they still read as if they were written by students.

Acknowledgments

Readers familiar with scholarship in rhetoric will recognize themes and echoes from various camps and theorists. I am reluctant to name them, however, because of the alterations the ideas may have undergone before appearing here. James Moffett, for example, would hardly lay claim to the transmutation of his theories as they appear in this book. Even Frank Smith, to whom I am indebted for his compelling ideas on reading as a writer, would no doubt be reluctant to receive attribution for my treatment of such reading. I'm not claiming that my discussions are Aristotelian, Kinneavyan, Brittenist, Vygotskyan, Burkean, or whatever, but the influences are there, in altered form.

There are some people, however, who must be acknowledged because of their direct influence on the outcome of this book. I owe a tremendous debt to the colleagues who took the time and trouble to review early drafts and offer encouragement and specific suggestions for revisions: Kathleen Bell, Old Dominion University; Patrick Bizzaro, East Carolina University; Charles Dodson, UNC-Wilmington; Theresa Enos, University of Arizona; Patricia Graves, Georgia State University; Stephen Hahn, William Paterson College; C. Jeriel Howard, Northeastern Illinois University; Robert Inkster, St. Cloud State University; Mary McGann, Rhode Island College; George Miller, University of Delaware; James Porter, Purdue University at Fort Wayne; Robert Schwegler, University of Rhode Island; Christopher Thaiss, George Mason University; Nancy Walker, Southwest Missouri State University; Irwin Weiser, Purdue University; and Richard Zbracki, Iowa State University. At Allyn and Bacon, many people were actively involved in getting this book into print. I especially want to thank Joe Opiela, Series Editor; Amy Capute and Rebecca Dudley, Editorial Assistants; and Bob Davis, Production Editor at Editorial Inc. Closer to home, let me acknowledge my students—for encouraging me at each stage of production and especially for creating some lively, thoughtful writing and then allowing me to use it. Finally, I thank Ken, who, while I labored at crafting a book in my workroom, worked in his woodshop crafting objects at least as functional— the degree of function depending on one's purpose, of course.

PART I

The Principles of Purposeful Writing

CHAPTER 1

The Writer/Reader

Everyone who becomes a competent writer uses authors in exactly the same way. . . . They must read like a writer in order to learn how to write like a writer. There is no other way in which the intricate complexity of a writer's knowledge can be acquired.

—*Frank Smith*

You are a writer. Any time you put pen to paper or compose at the word processor, you are a writer. You may think you're just a student in a college writing class, doing assignments to get a grade and fulfill a requirement. You may think school writing is not real writing, not what professional writers do. There may even have been times when you would have *liked* to think of yourself as a "real" writer, maybe not in the company of Ernest Hemingway or Alice Walker, but a writer all the same. Or perhaps you *do* like to think that doing school writing makes you a writer but are hesitant to call yourself one. Whether or not you want to be a writer or have ever thought of yourself as one, you *are* one. In writing your assignments, you do some of the things professional writers do, and you think in some of the ways all writers think.

Being a writer means that you, like other writers, work with ideas. Your ideas may originate outside yourself—say in a lecture, something you've read or observed, or a discussion with friends. Then your mind does something with those ideas: bounces them around, turns them upside down, looks at them in different ways, relates them to and compares them with other ideas, sorts them out, takes them apart and looks at the components, questions what they mean. You may talk about these ideas with other people. And you put them down on paper. Eventually they get to a reader.

Paths Writing Takes

Writers have various ways of getting their thoughts on paper, ready for readers. These differences depend somewhat on the writer's preferences, but often they are decided more by the subject and purpose of the writing. When you are working with new ideas or new ways of looking at ideas, or in other ways striking out into uncharted territory, you can't map the plan in advance. First you explore; then you draw the map. But when the writing is familiar or routine, perhaps with its own structure, such as the narration of an incident, you already have an idea of what you're going to say. Picture these different approaches to writing as walks through the woods, sometimes slow and meandering, sometimes direct.

The Discovery Route

You take the slow discovery route when you don't know precisely what you want to say. With just a general idea in mind, you start writing about your thoughts, developing them as you go, not worrying about where you're heading because you can always go back and mark the path later, or take another path, or take a shortcut. At this stage you're not interested in following a map, such as an outline of some sort. You're interested only in exploring, to see where your ideas will take you, where you will end up, or whether you have to go back and start over. You're *discovering* now.

Only later, when you start thinking about an audience—someone who needs to follow you—do you begin to mark your path clearly. Then you write a thesis sentence as an overall guide to where your paper is going, you make your paragraphs coherent and complete, you add details as necessary, you delete irrelevant side trips, you add transitional sentences to connect paragraphs, and you write a concluding paragraph that clearly tells your readers, "Here we are, you and I; we've made it through the woods together, and this is what we've seen."

The Direct Route

At other times, you do mark your path before you begin. You've been over this territory before and know the quickest way of getting to your destination. You know how to avoid pitfalls, obstructions, and wrong turns. You stay on familiar paths. When faced with this kind of writing, you engage in considerable thinking; you make an outline; you plan your examples, details, and arguments; you think about who your audience is and what you need to say to satisfy that audience. When you begin to compose, you follow your plan, making adjustments if necessary but for the most part using it as your guide. When you finish, your work is in decent order; it may need some revisions at the sentence level and some additions of overlooked details, but you don't have to move parts around or delete large chunks of unrelated material.

The Combination

Probably most of your writing combines the discovery and direct routes. You've been in these woods before, written this kind of paper before, but not by this path. Before you write, you think about what you are going to say and why you want to say it. You explore your ideas, either in your head or on paper, informally or through specific strategies. You may do some reading to find out what others have said. But at some time you feel the need to mark a plan for your ideas. As you write you do more discovering, because new ideas and new ways of looking at ideas come during composition. And you may revise your plan. Some of your writing goes quickly and easily, because you know what you want to say, and some of it is a struggle, because you're still working with your ideas.

EXERCISE

Here are three writing assignments on the general topic breakfast. *Write a short paragraph on each one and identify your method of writing each paragraph as (a) discovery route, (b) direct route, or (c) combination.*

1. Describe what you ate for breakfast this morning.
2. Compare the breakfast you ate this morning with the kind of breakfast you usually had as a child.
3. Discuss the relative merits of eating breakfast and skipping the meal.

Whatever your process for producing a piece of writing, being a writer means that at least at some stage—at the beginning, at the end, or all the way through—you think about your readers and order your thoughts so that your readers know where you are going, won't take any wrong turns, and won't get lost or frustrated along the way. As a writer, then, you must *revise*, not just correcting and polishing but standing back and seeing the piece of writing again, through a reader's eyes, and making whatever changes are necessary— adding details, transitions, explanations; deleting unnecessary repetitions and empty words; working with awkward sentences; rearranging paragraphs that are not in logical order; substituting words, sentences, and new ideas.

All this work and more is what it means to be a writer. And you are a writer.

Ways to Read

You're also a reader. This is not news to you; in your lifetime you've read assignments too numerous to count, and here you are, on the fifth page of this book, having just read about being a writer and what that means. You probably also know that there is more than one way of reading—of looking at those black-and-white marks on a page and making sense of them. You don't read a college textbook in the same way as you read a romantic novel. If you did, you would probably fail the exam. Nor do you read a letter from the telephone company telling you that your account is a month overdue in the same way as you read a letter from a good friend. If you did, you would probably have your telephone disconnected.

The way you read, like the way you write, is determined by your purpose. If you read for artistic appreciation when you need to remember and understand facts, you may overlook some of those facts. If you read for appreciation or facts when you need to proofread, you may overlook errors. When you read a news article in the newspaper, you seek information, and you expect it to be accurate and objective. But when you turn to the editorial page, you seek opinions on the news; the facts may be accurate here too, but the writer may have been strongly biased in selecting them, and you know you can disagree. Much of your reading, like writing, is probably done with a combination of purposes; when you read a poem, for instance, you no doubt have some desire to appreciate its artistry but surely also to understand what it has to say. Readers always have a purpose for reading, and they read according to their purpose and the requirements of the situation.

Reading for Meaning

If your purpose for reading is to prepare for an exam, then you read closely for a particular kind of meaning. You want to understand and remember everything that might be important and might be on the exam. You pay close attention to facts, charts, boldfaced type, and other clues to what is significant. You try to relate facts to ideas, so that they're more meaningful to you and therefore more likely to stick in your memory. If, in contrast, your purpose for reading is to enjoy a story, just to relax and forget about your own world, you read fast, and in your eagerness to find out what the characters do next you may pass quickly over whatever seems insignificant. When you finish, you can vividly recount the plot and describe the characters, because you've just shared their experience of life, but when it comes to specific facts you have nothing to say. You skipped them.

Meaning Making Is Individual

Reading for meaning is a complex activity, more than just decoding marks on the page. Each time you read, whatever you read, you bring to that reading your own knowledge and experience, and your own purpose. To make meaning of the marks you see, you relate them to what you already know. If, for example, you were to read "The day was frustrating from start to finish," you would remember the frustrating days you've known. You might think of missed buses, rain pouring down when you forgot your umbrella, long lines at the bookstore, or other unfortunate times when everything went wrong. But what *you* see in the words is not quite the same as what someone else—a classmate also reading the book, perhaps—sees. You and other readers all envision different frustrating days. And none of them may be what the writer had in mind.

The writer is responsible for giving you more information than is presented in that sentence, and for doing so as clearly and explicitly as possible. In fact, as a reader you would *expect* the writer to tell you more. If the writer is careful in describing the frustrating day, you and other readers may be able to imagine a frustrating day that is similar to the one the writer intended. Your responsibility as a reader is to read the words in their context and not to make something else of them.

Active Reading

When reading for information or someone else's opinions, you need to read actively and critically, searching for the information you want, getting involved in what the writer is saying, but not allowing yourself to be swayed by faulty appeals to your emotions. To understand what writers are saying, active readers ask themselves questions like these:

Questions for Active Reading

1. What is the writer's purpose in writing?
2. What is the writer's main point?
3. Does the writer imply more than he or she is saying?
4. Is the information accurate?
5. Are the explanations clear?
6. Is the writer biased?
7. Does the writer suppress or overlook some important information?
8. Does the writer attempt to pass off opinions as facts?
9. What is the writer's attitude toward the subject?
10. Is the writer an expert on the subject—or just pretending to be one?

(These types of questions are discussed and illustrated in Part II. See in particular Chapter 7, To Persuade.)

If you are naturally skeptical, you probably already—perhaps unconsciously—question whatever you read. If you tend not to question what people say, you will find that you learn more about what you read if you actively seek answers to questions like these. You might also ask questions about the writer's relationship with the audience, like those listed on page 25.

EXERCISE

Read the following paragraph carefully and critically, asking the questions for active reading *and preparing to discuss your answers in class.*

There is an evangelical preacher on television who goes by the name of Reverend Terry. She appears to be in her early fifties, and features a coiffure of which it has been said that it cannot be mussed, only broken. Reverend Terry is energetic and folksy, and uses a style of preaching modeled on early Milton Berle. When her audiences are shown in reaction shots, they are almost always laughing. As a consequence, it would be difficult to distinguish them from audiences, say, at the Sands Hotel in Las Vegas, except for the fact that they have a slightly cleaner, more wholesome look. Reverend Terry tries to persuade them, as well as those "at home," to change their ways by finding Jesus Christ. To help her do this, she offers a "prosperity Campaign Kit," which appears to have a dual purpose: As it brings one nearer to Jesus, it also provides advice on how to increase one's bank account. This makes her followers extremely happy and confirms their predisposition to believe that prosperity is the true aim of religion. Perhaps God disagrees. As of this writing, Reverend Terry has been obliged to declare bankruptcy and temporarily halt her ministrations.

—Neil Postman, *Amusing Ourselves to Death*

Reading as a Writer

Sometimes when you read, your primary purpose is not to make meaning of the words and marks on the page. Instead of directing your attention to what the marks represent, you scrutinize the marks themselves. The most obvious example of this purpose is proofreading your own writing for error. With this kind of reading, you pay attention to every word, dot, and squiggle you've written, so that you can find any mistakes you might have made in typing or copying. If you don't notice the errors and correct them, you may be giving your readers false signals. On a broader scale, you read your own writing for the purpose of revising: to determine whether your sentences are phrased clearly, to assess the accuracy and adequacy of your details, to see whether you've supported your thesis and whether you've gone off your topic, and so on. Reading to revise is essential for writers. (This kind of reading is discussed in greater detail in Chapter 5.)

Another purpose for reading that is not mainly to gain information is reading what others have written just to see how they express their thoughts. *You read as a writer.* This is a second kind of critical reading, in which you read not only for meaning but for style and structure as well. You notice how other writers organize their ideas, how they arrange words in their sentences, what words they use, how they fill up their paragraphs and then shift to new paragraphs, how they connect their paragraphs and sentences, how they begin, and how they end. This kind of reading is especially common to experienced writers, because they, like all other writers, struggle with their writing and want to know how others have solved similar problems. You too need sometimes to read as a writer, learning writing from other writers.

Reading as a writer is often an unconscious act, done as an aside while reading for meaning. But it is an acquired way of reading; people can learn how to do it. The following list gives examples of questions readers ask when they read as writers. Try applying these questions to essays, chapters, newspaper and magazine articles, and anything else you read.

Questions for Reading as a Writer

1. How does the writer begin?
2. How does the writer end?
3. Where does the writer state the main idea of the whole piece (thesis)?
4. How long are the writer's paragraphs?
5. Where does the writer express the main idea (topic sentence) of each paragraph?
6. How does the writer support ideas (examples, explanations, statements of authorities [testimony], statistics, comparisons, analogies, and so on)?
7. How does the writer use long sentences?
8. How does the writer use short sentences?
9. How does the writer connect ideas?
10. What kind of repetition does the writer use?
11. Does the writer repeat any grammatical structures (parallelism)?
12. Does the writer use any figurative language (metaphors, similes, and so on)?
13. Does the writer use any unusual words?
14. How does the writer use commas and other punctuation marks?

EXERCISE

Here is a paragraph by Henry David Thoreau. Reading it as a reader, *you would ask questions like the* active reading *questions on page 6—in other words, you would want to know What does he say? When you read it as a* writer, *however, you ask How does he say it?: How does he connect related ideas? How does he emphasize important ideas? How does he begin and end? And so on. Read the paragraph first as a* reader *to determine what Thoreau says. Then read it as a* writer *to determine how he has written his ideas. After your second reading, answer the questions that follow.*

I went to the woods because I wished to live deliberately, to front only the essential facts of life, and see if I could not learn what it had to teach, and not, when I came to die, discover that I had not lived. I did not wish to live what was not life, living is so dear; nor did I wish to practise resignation, unless it was quite necessary. I wanted to live deep and suck out all the marrow of life, to live so sturdily and Spartan-like as to put to rout all that was not life, to cut a broad swath and shave close, to drive life into a corner, and reduce it to its lowest terms, and, if it proved to be mean, why then to get the whole and genuine meanness of it, and publish its meanness to the world; or if it were sublime, to know it by experience, and be able to give a true account of it in my next excursion. For most men, it appears to me, are in a strange uncertainty about it, whether it is of the devil or of God, and have *somewhat hastily* concluded that it is the chief end of man here to "glorify God and enjoy him forever."

—Walden

1. Writers emphasize their main ideas through repetition. How many times does Thoreau repeat *life* and related words? How many additional times does he refer to life by means of the pronoun *it?*
2. Writers connect related ideas by means of parallel structures. What ideas are connected by the parallel infinitives in sentence 1—*to live, to front, see, discover?*
3. Writers sometimes use figurative language in the form of similes, metaphors, or analogies to make their writing vivid. "Suck out all the marrow of life" is one example of figurative language. Find other figures in this paragraph.
4. Writers often begin directly, plunging into the heart of the matter. What does Thoreau's direct beginning tell you about the main idea of this paragraph?

In the chapters in Part II you are asked to read both ways: as a reader and as a writer.

Learning Writing

This book is based on the assumption that reading aids writing. People who have studied writing know that effective writing can be achieved in three ways:

1. Through writing
2. Through instruction and feedback
3. Through reading

Improvement in writing requires all three techniques; one or two of the three is not enough. To write well, you need (1) plenty of writing; (2) someone to tell you how other writers write, what you're doing well, and how you can make your writing better; and (3) the special kind of reading just discussed—reading as a writer.

Writing

Much can be said for native ability. The best tennis players probably start out with an inherited predisposition for muscular coordination, strength, and build, together with mental alertness and speed. But the presence of these characteristics is not enough. If John McEnroe and Martina Navratilova had depended only on their inherited abilities, they would never have been good enough to play professional tennis. Only when inherited predispositions are developed through use can physical potential become physical prowess. Furthermore, and this is good news for the rest of us, even people whose genes don't make them the strongest or fastest or best coordinated can develop the characteristics they did inherit. They may not become the next Wimbledon champions, but with practice they can become skilled enough to enjoy an occasional game of tennis.

As with physical prowess, some people seem to be born with an inclination toward writing ability. They have an active imagination, an excellent memory for detail, and a sense of order and arrangement. They may start writing stories while they're still in elementary school, and in secondary school they may enter essay contests—and win. They get A's on their papers. They may become professional writers. But they, like athletes, must exercise their abilities if they want to use them well. The mental activities involved in writing, like physical skills, can be improved with use or can deteriorate with disuse. Even the less skilled writer can become skilled enough to enjoy writing. But there are no shortcuts. To write well, you must write and write and write.

It's not easy. It's not easy to be a very good tennis player, and it's not easy to be a very good writer. Both require work. And the difficulty of that work is not equally distributed. You may find some writing tasks relatively easy and others quite hard, while what's easy for you may be difficult for someone else. Very few people find all writing tasks easy. Some find all writing tasks hard. Analytical writing is almost always difficult, because it requires close reading, an open yet skeptical mind, comprehension, a critical response, and the skill for conveying this response to an audience. Narration of a personal experience, in contrast, is frequently easier, because it requires mainly remembering the experience and making sense of it for a reader.

Writing is difficult because it is a complex activity, involving many mental processes that are all tied up with knowledge and experience, attitudes toward subjects and audiences, and even physical ability to get words on the page. And to complicate matters, ideas and attitudes change even as we write. No one really knows everything that happens when someone writes. But we do know that through practice we can exercise the skills required for writing.

Instruction and Feedback

Tennis players need trainers and coaches—people to tell them how to handle the racquet and move their feet, what happens when a play doesn't work, what is getting better, what is good about their style, what still needs improvement. This instruction and feedback is meant to develop natural ability and to assist practice and training.

Writers too need instruction and feedback. Just writing, practicing the skills, isn't enough. You need someone to help you see when an idea doesn't come across clearly, which details could be added and which ones omitted, how your sentences might be improved, what is strong and good about your writing style, and so on. In this way you learn to look critically at your own writing. For student writers, this kind of feedback usually comes from the teacher or from classmates.

Everybody seems to fear criticism. We all want to think that what we've done is perfect and couldn't possibly be improved on, so, when other people tell us that they don't see how our third paragraph relates to our thesis, or that our conclusion is weak, or that other aspects of our writing are faulty, we're defensive. But criticism is part of writing. Remember that criticism can be favorable too. Doesn't it make you feel good when someone tells you what he or she really likes about something you've written? And even if the criticism is negative, isn't it better to get that feedback while you can still make changes, rather than after your work is completed? Writing always has readers, and reading is a matter of comprehending not only *what* writers say but *how* they say it. When the *how* is done well, readers are less conscious of it and concentrate more on the *what*. When writing is done poorly, the inaccuracies stand in the way of meaning, and readers notice the *how* instead of the *what*.

Don't underestimate the value of your classmates' opinions, and don't be afraid to ask for their feedback. Also, consider asking for criticism from other willing readers—roommates, parents, friends. Finally, learn to be your own best critic. Don't read your writing as if it's already perfect and the best you can do. Instead, look at it as something like a lump of wet clay on a potter's wheel. With a light touch here and there, or sometimes with a heavy hand, you can form a vase, then alter its style, redesign its shape, clarify your intentions—change the vase from just a pot to one that is both functional and lovely.

Reading

One way of learning to look at your writing as others might see it is to look critically at what others have written. As we have discussed, there are two kinds of **critical reading:** asking *what* the writer has said and asking *how* the writer has said it. Both can happen at the same time, while you are reading for meaning. You may have noticed when reading poetry that your attention focuses on both meaning and style, and that meaning, in fact, depends on style. This dual reading occurs at other times too, most often unconsciously. You may not even be aware that the style of a piece of writing has affected you as you read it. For example, read these sentences:

I began to read everything I could lay my hands on.

I began to read everything I could get.

In reading the first sentence, you probably paid no notice to the phrase "lay my hands on," yet your reading of the phrase affected your understanding of the sentence. When you read the second sentence, however, your attention was no doubt drawn to the word *get* simply because it is what makes the second sentence different from the first. Then you probably began thinking about any difference in meaning the change may have brought about. You shifted from unconscious to conscious perception of style; you were looking at *how* and *how well*.

When you read critically, you make the unconscious act of analysis a conscious one. You observe that something was said particularly well, or badly, and you pause to notice the phrasing. You come across a word you have never seen in print, and you observe how it's spelled and how it fits the context. Your attention is drawn to a single-sentence paragraph, and you stop for a second to wonder why it's so short. Maybe you've never read in this way before, but that's not to say you can't do it. It's not something you want to do every time you read, because it does slow your reading. But you will find that, as you practice being a conscious critical reader, your unconscious analytical powers will increase. At the same time, your appreciation of good writing will increase. When you analyze the work of other writers, trying to understand not only *what* they have said but *how* they have said it and *how well* they have said it, you have become a critical reader.

You can learn to apply this kind of critical reading to your own writing, to step back and look at *how* you've written as well as *what* you've written—to be your own, your first, critical reader.

Reading, Writing, and Thinking

What do you know about how you write? If you've ever written about your process of writing, the chances are good that you went into great detail on early stages (brainstorming, outlining, or whatever you do when you begin), and you devoted some time to what you do with a completed draft (how you revise). But what about the part in the middle? Can you describe what happens while you compose your draft? Many people, when asked, can't. They may know what they do before they start composing, and they can often describe how they revise, but they usually leave a big gap in between.

Reading this book will help you understand that part of the procedure. When you write, something tells you which words to use, how to combine your words in phrases, when to end a sentence, and so on. Something told Loren Eiseley to say, in the example sentence on page 12, "lay my hands on" instead of "get" or something else. And something tells you when you need an example to illustrate your point or when you're getting off your topic. Something tells you when your conclusion is not right. Where does this "something" come from? On what basis do you make all these decisions? What happens while you compose?

The easy way for you to describe your composing is to observe and record your actions, or to have someone else watch you as your pen moves across paper or your fingers tap keys on the word processor, producing words and sentences and other little marks on the paper or screen. This kind of observation usually reveals periods of fast composing, letters and words easily turning into sentences, sentences into paragraphs. It also reveals pauses, both long and short ones, in which you might stare out the window, pick at your fingernails, get up and walk around, sometimes even pack it up for the day. It reveals deletions, additions, substitutions. These are all observable aspects of composing.

But what is it that tells your fingers to make the letters? How do those fingers even know what a letter is? How do they know which letters go together to make particular words? (And even if you're a poor speller, remember that your fingers get *most* of your words right.) How do those words combine to make sentences? Why those words and not others? Why those sentences and not others?

It is your mind, of course, that propels your fingers, but how does your mind make those decisions? Somehow the mind works on ideas and ways of stating those ideas. It looks for relationships between what has been said and what is yet to be said. The mind asks: Can I say this? Is it true? It it right? Is it accurate? Is it clear? Then: How can I say this to make it clear? The mind looks for words and arrangements of words and for examples and analogies to illustrate the idea. And when the going gets really difficult, the mind backs off, takes a break, observes the caterpillar inching across the windowsill or goes to the kitchen to inspect the contents of the refrigerator. The mind is not really off the task; it's just resting.

But still unanswered are the questions about how the mind knows what letters and words to choose and how to arrange them. How does a writer decide to say, as in the paragraph preceding the last one,

But what is it that tells your fingers . . . ?

Why not

But what is telling your fingers . . . ?

The second sentence is the way it read before revision. You may not even like the revised version; you may prefer the original. Or you may prefer still another version:

But what tells your fingers . . . ?

All three ways are grammatically correct and say essentially the same thing, so why bother changing the sentence? How can we explain the final choice?

The mind makes its decisions on the basis of past experience. It weighs the truth and accuracy of a statement on the basis of what it has known to be true and accurate. It bases grammatical and stylistic decisions on what it has seen and done before: on *reading* and *writing*. Experience in reading and writing is what informs the decisions writers make. The more experienced the writer, the better informed the decisions.

This is where reading as a writer enters in. When you observe how other writers write, whether consciously or unconsciously, you amass knowledge that you can draw on when you yourself write. You don't copy what other writers have done, but, because you have read those ideas and stylistic choices, you are able to use them to inform your own decisions. When you know many ways to start a sentence, you can select the one that seems to give the emphasis, tone, and stylistic rhythm that you want. Take another look at the three example sentences, and see that even though the grammar is correct in all three and the meaning almost exactly the same, the emphasis, tone, and rhythm are different. Choices on such matters, where there are no rules, can be made only with knowledge gained from reading and from practice in writing.

Being a Reading Writer

This chapter carries the idea that reading is purposeful. You may read for various reasons, such as for information, for pleasure, for revising and correcting, and, as suggested here, for learning from other writers. The chapters in Part II of this book are designed to help you to be a *reading* writer, analyzing how other writers have met specific purposes in writing, and then to be a *writing* writer, writing to meet similar purposes. You will read the ideas of other writers as a means of generating new ideas. You will study how those writers express their ideas in writing, and perhaps you'll learn from their experience.

The remaining chapters in Part I will give you some background on what writing is and what writers do. Chapter 2 introduces purposes for writing and illustrates how purpose influences the emphasis of the writing. Chapters 3 through 5 investigate the process writers engage in as they write: prewriting in Chapter 3, drafting in Chapter 4, and revising in Chapter 5.

EXERCISES

1. Read the following autobiographical excerpt. As you read, ask the questions for active reading on page 6. In addition, be prepared to discuss these questions:
   a. What does Eiseley say about reading?
   b. What does he say about writing?
   c. What do you learn about his parents?
   d. What do you learn about Eiseley?
   e. What do you think is his opinion on the see-John-run sort of books?
   f. Eiseley recounts two vows he made as a child. What were they?

2. After reading "How I Learned to Read," write a brief account of the circumstances of your learning to read. Consider when it happened, where it occurred, who taught you, the first stories you remember reading, how you felt about reading, problems you had, or something else you recall about the experience. Choose the most interesting aspect and focus on that. Prepare to discuss your experience in class.

3. Write several sentences that describe *how* Eiseley tells his story. Do not focus on content; rather, discuss what Eiseley *does* with the content. Here are some questions to help you focus your analysis:
   a. How does Eiseley use direct quotations? What is their effect?
   b. Eiseley's first sentence is packed with information. List at least five things he tells you in it.
   c. How does Eiseley handle chronology? What does paragraph 3 tell you about when he learned to read? Where does he tell the year of his parents' decision not to send him to kindergarten?
   d. List the words that seem unusual to you. Are they clear in context?
   e. Consider sentence length. Paragraph 1 consists of two long sentences separated by a short one. In paragraph 2, notice the different sentence patterns. Count the sentences and the words in this paragraph. Divide the second number by the first to get an average sentence length. What is the effect of the short sentences in this paragraph?

How I Learned to Read

Loren Eiseley

It so happened that when I was five years old my parents, in a rare   1
moment of doting agreement, looked upon their solitary child and decided
not to pack him off to kindergarten in that year. One can call them feckless,
kind, or wise, according to one's notions of the result. Surprisingly, I can
remember the gist of their conversation because I caught in its implications
the feel of that looming weather which, in after years, we know as life.

"Let him be free another year," they said. I remember my astonishment   2
at their agreement. "There'll be all his life to learn about the rest. Let him be
free to play just one more time." They both smiled in sudden affection. The
words come back from very far away. I rather think they are my mother's,
though there is a soft inflection in them. For once, just once, there was total
unanimity between my parents. A rare thing. And I pretended not to have
heard that phrase "about the rest." Nevertheless when I went out to play in
the sunshine I felt chilled.

I did not have to go to kindergarten to learn to read. I had already   3
mastered the alphabet at some earlier point. I had little primers of my own,
the see-John-run sort of thing or its equivalent in that year of 1912. Yes, in
that fashion I could read. Sometime in the months that followed, my elder
brother paid a brief visit home. He brought with him a full adult version of
Robinson Crusoe. He proceeded to read it to me in spare moments. I lived for
that story. I hung upon my brother's words. Then abruptly, as was always
happening in the world above me in the lamplight, my brother had departed.
We had reached only as far as the discovery of the footprint on the shore.

He left me the book, to be exact, but no reader. I never asked mother   4
to read because her voice distressed me. Her inability to hear had made it
harsh and jangling. My father read with great grace and beauty but he
worked the long and dreadful hours of those years. There was only one
thing evident to me. I had to get on with it, do it myself, otherwise I would
never learn what happened to Crusoe.

I took Defoe's book and some little inadequate dictionary I found about   5
the house, and proceeded to worry and chew my way like a puppy through
the remaining pages. No doubt I lost the sense of a word here and there, but
I mastered it. I had read it on my own. Papa bought me *Twenty Thousand
Leagues Under the Sea* as a reward. I read that, too. I began to read everything
I could lay my hands on.

Well, that was a kind of vow made to myself, was it not? Not just to   6
handle ABC's, not to do the minimum for a school teacher, but to read
books, read them for the joy of reading. When critics come to me again I
shall say, "Put Daniel Defoe on the list, and myself, as well," because I kept

the vow to read *Robinson Crusoe* and then to try to read all the books in the local library, or at least to examine them. I even learned to scan the papers for what a boy might hopefully understand.

That was 1912 and in the arctic winter of that year three prisoners   7
blasted their way through the gates of the state penitentiary in our town. They left the warden and his deputy dead behind them. A blizzard howled across the landscape. This was long before the time of the fast getaway by car. The convicts were out somewhere shivering in the driving snow with the inevitable ruthless hunters drawing a narrowing circle for the kill.

That night papa tossed the paper on the table with a sigh. "They won't   8
make it," he said and I could see by his eyes he was out there in the snow.

"But papa," I said, "the papers say they are bad men. They killed the   9
warden."

"Yes, son," he said heavily. Then he paused, censoring his words care-   10
fully. "There are also bad prisons and bad wardens. You read your books now. Sit here by the lamp. Stay warm. Someday you will know more about people out in the cold. Try to think kindly, until then. These papers," he tapped the one he had brought in, "will not tell you everything. Someday when you are grown up you may remember this."

"Yes, papa," I said, and that was the second vow, though again I did not   11
know it. The memory of that night stayed on, as did the darkness and the howling wind. Long after those fleeing men were dead I would re-enter that year to seek them out. I would dream once more about them. I would be— Never mind, I would be myself a fugitive. When once, just once, through sympathy, one enters the cold, one is always there. One eternally keeps an appointment with one's self, but I was much too young to know.

—All the Strange Hours

CHAPTER 2

The Writer's Purposes

*Purpose in discourse is all important. The aim of a discourse
determines everything else in the process of discourse.*
—*James L. Kinneavy*

Chapter 1 establishes that readers have various purposes for reading, including gaining information, seeking pleasure, revising and correcting, and learning from other writers. In this chapter we investigate purposes for *writing*. Because you are both a reader and a writer, you should be aware of both kinds of purposes.

Writing always has a **purpose.** Think about it: Do you ever write when you don't have a reason for doing so? Even if you're just writing a shopping list or a diary entry, you have a purpose—to remember what to buy or to record thoughts or events. You may not always know what your purpose is; you may think you're writing to inform when your essay ends up being a piece of persuasion. In fact, most times when you write you probably have more than one purpose. The readings in Part II illustrate how writers often have multiple purposes. Jonathan Kozol in Chapter 11, for example, gives a lengthy list of facts about illiteracy ostensibly to inform the reader about its extent, but, in wanting to inform the reader, Kozol very likely wants also to persuade the reader to take action.

Your purpose in writing is related to three other components of the writing situation: the **writer,** the **audience,** and the **subject**—or the *I*, the *you*, and the *it*. Your purpose determines which of the three is being emphasized. When you write a shopping list to remember to buy certain things, the emphasis is on the subject, *it*. But when you write an entry in your diary to express your thoughts, with no intention of letting anyone else read what you've written, the emphasis is on the writer, *I*. By contrast, when you write a humorous essay intending to entertain, the emphasis is on your audience, the *you*.

What we're considering is **rhetoric,** a term that has many definitions. Some definitions of this word are negative, as a result of people using rhetoric for deception. But others are more neutral. One of the clearer definitions comes from a modern rhetorician, Donald C. Bryant: Rhetoric is "adjusting ideas to people and people to ideas." This definition assumes our three components: a subject, "ideas"; an audience, "people"; and a writer or speaker, the person doing the adjusting. Every piece of writing evolves from a **rhetorical situation.**

The Flexible Triangle

Think of the rhetorical situation as a triangle made of a rubber band, with each angle representing a component. The rubber band itself is the writer's purpose, and the area it encloses is the piece of writing: an essay, a story, a journal entry, a grocery list, a book report, and so on. If all angles and sides of the rhetorical triangle are equal, no one component is emphasized. Visualize it as in Figure 2-1. But the equilateral triangle is probably more common in geometry than in rhetoric. In rhetoric, the triangle is usually pulled in one direction or another, because the purpose generally emphasizes one component. Visualize it as one of those in Figure 2-2.

EXERCISE

Each of the following passages illustrates writer-emphasis, audience-emphasis, or subject-emphasis writing. Read each passage to decide which component of the rhetorical situation is dominant and how the other two components enter in. Be prepared to discuss your decisions in class and support them with evidence from the passages.

1. "What's wrong with your language behavior? Have you said the wrong thing one too many times? When your back's against the wall, will you know what to say? In this book, best-selling author Dr. Elgin will show you how to develop verbal and nonverbal communication skills to control your language behavior and trigger positive responses from listeners."—From back cover of Suzette Haden Elgin, *The Last Word on the Gentle Art of Verbal Self-Defense*
2. "Without warning, in the middle of my thirties, I had a breakdown of nerve. It never occurred to me that while winging along in my happiest and most productive stage, all of a sudden simply staying afloat would require a massive exertion of will. Or of some power greater than will.

   "I was talking to a young boy in Northern Ireland where I was on assignment for a magazine when a bullet blew his face off. That was how fast it all changed."—Gail Sheehy, introduction to *Passages*

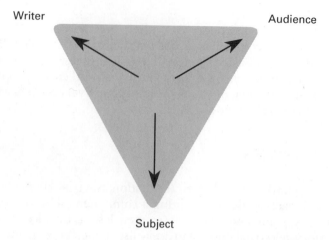

Figure 2-1. Rhetorical Triangle with Equal Emphasis on Components.

Figure 2-2. Rhetorical Triangles with Emphasis on Various Components.

3. "On May 23, 1987, the *New York Times* ran a long obituary of Archie Carr, a zoologist who spent his entire fifty-five-year career studying the giant sea turtle. I had never heard of Professor Carr, but I enjoyed reading the story of his life. Operating mainly from a field camp in Costa Rica, he reestablished turtle populations in many countries where they had been almost exterminated for their food, developed tagging techniques that partly solved the mystery of their breeding cycle and their 1,200-mile migrations, and wrote eleven books that created a popular understanding of the work he and his colleagues were doing to save the species."—William Zinsser, *Writing to Learn*

In each passage in the exercise, you could probably identify writer, audience, or subject as the dominant feature. You may also have been aware of the other components. Now let's examine each component of the rhetorical situation in greater detail.

Writer-Emphasis Writing

The writer is always present in a piece of writing. As its originator, he or she must be there. Sometimes the writer's presence is barely discernible, as in most scientific and technical writing. In writer-emphasis writing, however, the *I* is dominant. Some instances of this writing may be like Gail Sheehy's paragraphs, being *about* the writer and intended for an external audience. Others may be *for* the writer, with no other audience intended.

Writing in which the writer is the initial intended audience is often called *reflective* writing, because it looks into the writer's thoughts. In Chapter 6 Mark Baker examines evil as it is encouraged in warfare, and two student writers reflect on growing up with alcoholic parents. These writers first used a personal style to explore their topics, then revised their drafts for another audience.

Another example of writer-emphasis writing is journal writing, in which the writer records experiences and impressions for personal purposes: to set down ideas for future reference, to think through confusing issues, to work out emotional reactions, and so on. Like the explorative type of reflective writing, journal writing sometimes yields topics than can be rewritten for an external audience. You can read more about reflective writing and journal writing in Chapter 6.

Autobiography and Credibility

As a reader, you will sometimes encounter entire pieces of autobiographical writing, writing *about* the writer that was intended for an audience other than the writer. More often, you will find such writing in introductions, where writers establish *credibility*, or their authority to write on a given subject. For instance, in her paragraphs on page 20, Gail Sheehy introduces herself and an experience that propelled her into the writing of her book. A few pages later she announces, "It was this experience that made me eager to find out everything I could about this thing called *midlife crisis.*" As in much writing, she found it necessary first to clarify her relationship to her subject.

Writers establish their credibility primarily by being informed about their subjects. If you don't know about cataloging library books, you don't write about it. But if you are an accomplished swimmer, you can give authoritative instructions on how to do the backstroke. Given that you know your subject, you can increase your believability by projecting a role appropriate for the rhetorical situation.

Writer's Roles

People have many legitimate roles. You are probably not quite the same person in the classroom as you are when you're out with your friends or at home with your family. Depending on the situation, you present various facets of your character. You do this by the language you use, your tone of voice, the way you laugh and what you laugh at, the way you listen, even the clothes you wear. And though these facets of your character are all different, they are all valid; they're all you.

The same is true in writing. The facet of your character that presents a formal report is not quite the same as the part of you that writes an entry in your journal. In fact, the facet of your character that writes a paper for an English class is different from the one that writes a lab report. And as the role changes, the expression of it—the voice—changes too. Like your spoken voice, your written voice changes with your role. You would no more write an English paper the way you write a letter to a friend than you would talk in a classroom the way you would talk at a party. This is not to say that the role or the language in the classroom is better than at the party, just different.

Why is the role different? Because the other components of the rhetorical situation are different. The writer's role changes according to the audience and the subject. You are casual with friends, more formal with teachers. You can be frivolous at a party but must be serious in writing a paper.

Roles in Academic Writing

The features of the writer's role in academic writing are similar to those in writing for an employer or in any formal writing. When you write a paper, at school or on the job, you assume a **voice** that shows you are serious about your subject and respectful of your audience. You avoid slang and colloquial expressions, use vocabulary befitting the situation, and carefully edit errors. To appear informed about your subject, you try to be thorough and specific. To give the impression of an orderly mind, you organize your writing logically.

Your role as a writer is evident, then, in your vocabulary, grammar, style, tone, organization, treatment of details, and subject. This formality is not a fake role—no more than the *you* in dress clothes is any less real than the *you* in faded blue jeans and ragged sweatshirt. The more formal *you* is simply appropriate for the more formal situation.

These adjustments are often unconscious. Before beginning a piece of writing, you probably don't sit down and decide what role you need to assume. But when you write you do need to consider consciously the total rhetorical situation. Many inexperienced writers begin by considering only their subject, overlooking their own roles as writers, their audiences, and their purposes for writing. But what you say and how you say it are determined at least as much by the audience you're saying it to and your relationships with that audience and with your subject as they are by the subject itself.

EXERCISE

Use the following information to write two paragraphs, the first in your English classroom role, the second in another role of your choice, one that seems to you decidedly different from the first. By vocabulary, grammar, style, tone, organization, and selection and treatment of details, express your role in the appropriate voice. Use as much information as you need and whatever order suits your purpose.

1. The copyright law of 1790, 1831, and 1909 was amended in 1976.
2. The amended law came into effect on January 1, 1978.
3. Copyright law gives ownership to authors of books, periodicals, computer programs, and other literary works; musical compositions, dramas, pantomimes, motion pictures, videotapes, and sound recordings.
4. With a few exceptions, the owner of a copyright has exclusive rights to reproduce the copyrighted work.
5. To declare a copyright, the author affixes a notice on the work by means of the letter *c* in a circle, the word *copyright,* or the abbreviation *copr.,* plus the date and the name of the owner of the copyright. Example: Copyright 1990 John Doe.
6. Owners may register their copyrights with the U.S. Copyright Office, The Library of Congress, Washington, DC 20559.

Audience-Emphasis Writing

Audience-emphasis writing tends to be more consciously persuasive in purpose than some other kinds of writing. The writer appeals to characteristics of the reader's personality and background to move that reader to believe as the writer does. The first passage in the exercise on page 20 appears on the back cover of the book it advertises, appealing to the bookstore-browsing reader to purchase the volume. Reading this sales pitch, you might suddenly remember all those embarrassing moments when you said the wrong thing.

Some audience-emphasis writing is written strictly for entertainment. Like persuasive writing, writing for entertainment makes certain assumptions about its readers: that they share experiences and knowledge upon which humor or pleasure can be based.

EXERCISE

Read the following paragraphs and determine what shared knowledge they depend on.

Take the experience of the couple from Lorain [Ohio] who bought a   1
house trailer and went on a vacation trip to Florida. All went well until the

return trip home. The husband grew weary after many hours at the wheel and finally abdicated the driver's seat in favor of his wife, while he went back to the trailer and fell asleep.

It was a nervous sleep, to be sure. He had never before trusted his wife 2 at the wheel, and he was naturally uneasy over the risks involved. When the vehicle suddenly came to an abrupt, screeching stop, he immediately assumed the worst and leaped out of the back of the house trailer to see what had gone wrong.

All that had happened, actually, was that a traffic signal suddenly had 3 turned red and the wife had found it necessary to slam on the brake. By the time the husband, dressed only in his underwear, made his exit to the street and in his slow, sleep-fogged way sized up the situation, the light had turned green and the wife blithely drove away, leaving him in the middle of the intersection in his underdrawers. That's where a police cruiser came upon him a few minutes later.

"I can explain it all, officer!" said the husband to the policeman as his 4 shivering shanks were hustled into the cop car. No doubt he did, in time, but the explanation could not possibly have been an easy one.

—George E. Condon, *Cleveland Plain Dealer*

If your purpose is to persuade or to entertain, your audience will be the most important consideration, and knowing something about your readers will be essential; at the very least, you should be able to make reasonable guesses about their character and preferences. (You will find writing for persuasion and entertainment treated in more detail in Chapters 7 and 8.)

Audience Considerations

Whatever the rhetorical situation, writers need to consider their audience. What you write will most likely be read by people who have backgrounds, experiences, and perceptions of your subject that are quite different from yours. As noted in Chapter 1, a writer must give readers enough information to allow them to read as the writer intended. To know what information is necessary, you need to know something about your readers.

Here are some questions you might ask as you write—while you're exploring the subject, while you're composing, and as you revise.

Questions about Audience for Writing

1. Who is my audience?
2. What does my audience know about my subject?
3. What does my audience know about me?

Questions *(continued)*

4. What is my relationship to my audience?
5. How interested is my audience in my subject?
6. How can I stimulate audience interest?
7. What is my audience's attitude toward my subject?
8. What is my audience's attitude toward me?
9. Do I want to change what my audience knows or how it feels about me and my subject?
10. What experiences and knowledge do I share with my audience?
11. How can I use those experiences and that knowledge to present my subject?
12. How does my audience perceive the rhetorical situation in which I am writing: reflective, persuasive, informative, or something else?
13. What does my audience expect of my grammar, style, and vocabulary?

Answers to questions about your audience—these or others you may ask—can help you make decisions about your approach to your subject, what details to include and omit, how to organize your material, what words to use, what level of formality is appropriate, and so on. You won't always have answers to all your questions, but ask them anyway (even if your audience is "just" your teacher) and *guess* the answer. You'll probably be close to right, and that's better than not considering the audience at all.

Questions about audience are useful for reading as well, whether we're analyzing our own writing or that of other people. Use them along with the questions for active reading on page 6. When you are reading someone else's writing, turn the questions around.

Questions about Audience for Reading

1. Who is the intended audience? Am I among that group?
2. What does the writer assume the audience knows about the subject?
3. What does the writer seem to know about the audience?
4. What is the writer's relationship to the audience?
5. How interested am I, as audience, in the subject?
6. What does the writer do to stimulate my interest?
7. What is my attitude toward the subject?
8. What is my attitude toward the writer?

> ### *Questions* (continued)
>
> 9. Does the writer want to change what I know or how I feel about the writer and the subject?
> 10. What experiences and knowledge does the writer assume we share?
> 11. How does the writer use those experiences and that knowledge to present the subject?
> 12. How do I perceive the rhetorical situation of this piece of writing: reflective, persuasive, informative, or something else?
> 13. What assumptions does the writer make about my expectations of grammar, style, and vocabulary?

Answers to these questions can give you insights into the relationship writers establish with their audiences.

EXERCISE

Read the following column, being particularly sensitive to the writer-audience relationship. Then answer the questions about audience for reading. Be prepared to discuss your answers in class, supporting them with details from the column.

Medicine That Purrs

Ellen Goodman

Not long ago, I read a small story about a cardiac study in Baltimore and filed it away in my mind under the heading "Pets Heal Broken Hearts." 1

The story was about a biologist, Erika Friedman, who had studied ninety-two heart patients for a year after they left the hospital. She wanted to see whether there were any special social reasons why some of them did better than others. 2

It turned out that there was something called a Pet Factor. Only three of the fifty-seven patients with pets died during that year, compared to eleven of the thirty-nine without pets. 3

I am, by habit, wildly skeptical about the sort of studies that end up in pop form. Their authors are usually found a few months later jogging through *People* magazine in expensive terrycloth shorts, followed by their children and their paperback rights. So I have no idea whether the American Heart Association should start filling out prescription pads for budgies and beagles. 4

Nevertheless, the study piqued the curiosity I've had about people and pets since I bought my first turtle at my first circus. It has often occurred to me that pet owning is not a two-way relationship, but is, rather, two one-way relationships.

I currently live under the same roof with two large, black dogs that eat mail in lieu of the mailman. In my life as a dog owner, I have grown to realize that people and pets do not really have very much in common except each other. I have to give credit for this thought to William James, who once said: "Take our dogs and ourselves, connected as we are by a tie more intimate than most and yet . . . how insensible each of us is to all that makes life significant for the other—we to the rapture of bones under hedges, or smell of trees and lamp posts, they to the delights of literature and art."

The truth is that we have hung out together for lo these million years out of convenient mutual needs. The need of a pet for a person is as clear-cut as a bowl of food. The only true love song uttered by a dog in the entire history of Anthropomorphism is the one Snoopy howls called "Suppertime." The chorus goes like this: "Suppertime, suppertime, suppertime. . . ."

The average dog or cat will do almost anything to reinforce human supper-giving behavior. Ogden Nash once glowingly wrote:

> I marvel that such
> Small Ribs as These
> Harbor such a
> Desire to Please.

But to the less romantic among us, this behavior is a matter of thousands of years of natural selection. The dogs that did not "desire to please" ended up in dog pounds that stretched from the Fertile Crescent to the Golden Gate.

But the need of a person for a pet is something entirely different. Except for Doberman pinschers, the average urban-suburban pet owner is looking for a living thing that (1) needs him and (2) can't talk back.

In short, we seek an uncritical constant companion that can never spill the beans. Millions of dog owners commit themselves to a lifetime of walking in the rain simply because the animal on the other end of the leash will never sue . . . for malparenting. Thousands prowl the streets of Manhattan with scoopers and paper bags in order to have something wagging its tail when they get home. Millions more become devoted to kitty litter so that they can lecture something which will only come back with a purr, and never say, "You're neurotic."

I'm not talking about the crazies, the 141-cat-ladies, and people who build monuments to their Welsh terriers and leave trust funds to their Siamese. They always knew that one dog was worth ten doctors.

We are in this case talking about your better-basic-hamster owner, the full professor who talks baby-talk to his schnauzer and the bureaucrat who worries if he has to leave his bunny at a strange kennel.

This study suggests, just suggests mind you, what we may need for our   13
health. "Taking care" may be as important as taking digitalis. A loyal and
friendly companion may be a perfect pacemaker. We all seem to need to be
needed, and we thrive on a dose of uncritical companionship. If we can't get
it on two legs, we'll take it on four. We'll even take it on the wing.

Subject-Emphasis Writing

Most writing emphasizes the subject. In academic writing, as in business,
technical, and other nonfiction writing, the primary purpose is to convey
information—to compile it and transmit it, to show you have learned it, to
learn it through writing it, sometimes even to show that you know the
conventions of conveying it. If you think of most of the school writing you've
done, you'll probably realize that the emphasis was not on you, the writer, or
on your intended audience. Rather, the emphasis was on the subject—again
with the qualification that the writer and audience components of the
rhetorical situation were present. Refer to the paragraph by William Zinsser
in the exercise on page 20. There you see an emphasis on the subject,
Professor Carr, for the purpose of informing the reader about Zinsser's
newly discovered knowledge about him. Note that even though the passage
has a subject emphasis, Zinsser includes a bit of himself: "I had never heard
of Professor Carr, but I enjoyed reading the story of his life."

In much school writing, not only is the subject emphasized but it is
determined by someone else. You write a sentence, a paragraph, or an essay
in response to a teacher's question. By so doing you show what you know
about the subject, and you often learn something new about it. Or you read
about an assigned subject and then summarize and/or respond to what
you've read, showing that you have done the reading and understand it. In
such assignments, you don't need any means of discovering a subject. In
other cases, though, you have to find your subject, especially in writing
classes when your teacher assigns a particular kind of writing (for example,
a narrative essay) or a particular purpose (such as telling someone how to
make something). Whether the subject is assigned or not, you need ways of
exploring it, generating ideas related to it, and deciding what you will say
about it. (Writers have many ways of exploring ideas, some of which will be
discussed in Chapter 3 under "Discovering Ideas" and "Invention." In
addition, each chapter in Part II suggests things you can do to discover what
you have to say.)

People have many **purposes** for conveying information. Some of these
are *to record, to report, to inform, to explain, to instruct, to praise or censure, to
summarize and respond,* and *to ask and answer questions.* This chapter takes a
brief look at these purposes; each one is explained and illustrated in more
detail in Part II.

Subject-emphasis purposes for writing overlap a great deal. In this book the essays illustrating recording as a purpose can generally be viewed as telling *what is happening;* for example, saying, "By exercising, you are reducing the cholesterol in your blood." In contrast, the essays illustrating reporting look back on *what happened;* you might say, "You reduced the cholesterol in your blood by exercising." The essays illustrating informing tell *what happens* under given circumstances; they generalize about events. For example, you might say, "Exercise reduces cholesterol in the blood." Two other subject-emphasis purposes, explaining and instructing, tell *why something happens or happened* and *how something is done or how to do it:* why exercising reduces cholesterol in the blood and how to exercise to reduce cholesterol in the blood.*

To Record

Writers **record** something as it happens for the purpose of preserving the information: "The temperature is 96°F." "The committee agrees to hear the petition." Your class lecture notes and lab notes are records, as are notes you make on your reading. You may record individual and group activities, for later summarizing and reporting. Records are often informal, telegraphic, and fragmented. When they are prepared for another audience, however, as for a teacher or a supervisor, they are rewritten in a more complete form.

The following paragraph records the end of a tennis match. Notice in its terminology the assumptions it makes about the audience's knowledge. Notice too the present tense of verbs and the relative absence of the writer's opinions.

> Taylor lobs. Laver runs back, gets under the bouncing ball, kneels, and drives it into the net. He is now down 1-5. He is serving. He wins three points, but then he volleys into the net, again he volleys into the net, and again he volleys into the net—deuce. He serves. He moves forward. He volleys into the net. Advantage Taylor—match point. The sound of the crowd is cruel. "Quiet, please!" the umpire says. Laver serves, into the net. He appears to be trembling. He serves again. The ball does not touch the ground until it is out of the court beyond the base line.
> —John McPhee, *Pieces of the Frame*

No writing can be totally objective. It can represent information only as the writer perceives it. In this paragraph, the sentences "The sound of the crowd is cruel" and "He appears to be trembling" record the writer's impressions of what he observes. (Chapter 9 has further examples of writing to record.)

---

*I am loosely borrowing from and amplifying James Moffett's *Teaching the Universe of Discourse* (Boston: Houghton Mifflin, 1968).

To Report

Reporting is related to recording in that something that is reported may first be recorded. In other words, a thing is *recorded* as it happens; it is *reported* after it happens. Reporting is also related to informing in that most reports convey information.

School writing, as well as much business and scientific writing, requires a great deal of reporting. You might do book reports, lab reports, news reports, reports of library research, and reports of individual or group activities. In much of this kind of writing, the personality and opinions of the writer are not important or relevant. Moreover, the audience is assumed to be interested, so there is often no need to appeal to its preferences. It is important, however, to know who the audience is and what its level of expertise on the subject is, because this knowledge will determine your vocabulary and selection of details. The subject is presented as clearly and directly as possible, using as much detail as is necessary for the audience. The style is usually formal, but not extremely so. The verbs are mainly in the past tense.

In Chapter 10, Rachel L. Carson reports objectively on conditions in the Sargasso Sea, but when student writer Janice Anderson reports an experience at the state fair, she includes her reactions. The following paragraph concentrates on the subject, telling you little about the writer's opinions.

> Ominous black clouds boiled up into the afternoon sky over eastern Iowa one day in September 1972, and shortly before 2 P.M. a tornado touched down northeast of Cedar Rapids. It was a giant twister. It plowed through the countryside for 66 miles, staying on the ground six times longer than the average tornado and leaving a mile-wide swath of destruction.
>
> —*Wall Street Journal*

(Chapter 10 has more examples of writing that reports.)

To Inform

In writing that focuses on the subject, **informing** may be the most common purpose. Much of what is written in magazines and books is for the purpose of passing on information to an audience, sometimes with an ancillary aim of entertaining. Your textbooks are written to inform and to instruct. Many of the essays you write in an English class are for informing, with the additional purpose of improving your writing. In practice, informing can incorporate almost every other subject-emphasis purpose, and even purposes with an emphasis on the writer or the audience. Writing that informs may also report, explain, instruct, praise, and so on.

The writer of a magazine article not only wants to inform and entertain you, she also may want to persuade you, as well as to make money and become known as a writer. You write an essay in class not just to inform your reader and summarize an assigned reading but to get a grade as well. So, when you think of informing as your purpose for writing, you might well probe a little deeper and see what submerged purposes you have. If, for example, persuasion is one of your aims, you will need to give a different kind of attention to your audience than if you want only to inform. In careful reading, too, you ought to be aware of the writer's possible multiple intentions.

Audience is always a consideration in informative writing. To inform successfully, you must make some guesses about what the audience knows. Otherwise you risk boring your readers with something they already know or frustrating them by saying too little. With informative writing, you should always have answers to questions like those on page 25. In the following example, the audience is assumed to be student writers who might want to learn from professional writers.

> Professional writers begin by trying to interest readers. They never start by saying, "How can I avoid making mistakes?" They ask themselves this question instead: "How can I make people pay attention to what I am saying and take my writing seriously?" Good writers want to be correct. They know that if they use incorrect spelling, sloppy punctuation, erratic grammar, and rough syntax they will destroy the effect of their writing—just as a pianist who hits a few wrong notes will destroy the effect of a Beethoven concerto. But professional writers never assume that correctness is enough in itself. They want to engage readers and keep them engaged.
>
> —Richard Marius, *The Writer's Companion*

This paragraph borders on instruction, as well it might since it comes from a textbook. You may find that much writing to inform has instruction as a secondary purpose. But compare this paragraph with the example in the section "To Instruct" to see how instruction as a primary purpose influences writing. (You will find more examples of informative writing in Chapter 11.)

To Explain

Although explaining is similar to both informing and instructing, **explaining** tells *why* something is the way it is or works the way it does. Sometimes it analyzes *how* something works. Explaining may intend to justify actions, for example why you missed class. It aims for understanding through analysis of parts or causes. In Chapter 12, Judith Viorst explains, through classification analysis, how she perceives friendships, Jonathan Schell explains, by causal analysis, what the consequences of the detonation of a one-megaton bomb would be, and Elie Wiesel explains, or justifies, why he writes. (Other essays in Chapter 12 further illustrate explaining as a purpose for writing.) Here's a brief example that explains how lie detectors work:

As I understand it, a human being cannot tell a lie, even a small one, without setting off a kind of smoke alarm somewhere deep in a dark lobule of the brain, resulting in the sudden discharge of nerve impulses, or the sudden outpouring of neurohormones of some sort, or both. The outcome, recorded by the lie-detector gadgetry, is a highly reproducible cascade of changes in the electrical conductivity of the skin, the heart rate, and the manner of breathing, similar to the responses to various kinds of stress.

—Lewis Thomas, "The Lie Detector"

To Instruct

You may think that much of what you read in school has been written for the purpose of instruction, and in a way that's true. However, the distinction here is between instructing *that* and instructing *how*. Instructing *that*—relating facts, information, conjectures, and so on, or analyzing causes, actions, or relationships—falls more within our categories of informing or explaining as a purpose. **Instructing** as a purpose of writing in this book means instructing *how*. This kind of writing usually addresses the reader directly, while concentrating on the subject. In Chapter 13, Campbell Morris discusses how to make a smooth-flying paper airplane, and Garrison Keillor tells how to write a personal letter. Here is a brief example of instruction:

Don't ever hesitate to imitate another writer—every artist learning his craft needs some models. Eventually you'll find your own voice and shed the skin of the writer you imitated. But pick only the best models. If you want to write about medicine, read Lewis Thomas; if you want to write literary criticism, read Edmund Wilson and Alfred Kazin.

—William Zinsser, *On Writing Well*

In this paragraph, the imperative mood ("don't ever hesitate") and the pronoun *you* speak directly to the reader, telling *how* to write. (You will find other examples of instruction in Chapter 13.)

To Praise or Censure

Praising and **censuring** are more common in writing outside school. But even in school you know their effects: You read biographies, sometimes book length or essay length but more often short pieces describing an author, a scientist, a diplomat, and so on. Often these pieces are more than information; they extol the individual. And you may be familiar with the necessity of having letters of recommendation, highlighting your good points and, you hope, omitting your weaknesses. On the other side, there is censure—

less common than praise and certainly less welcome. In Chapter 14, a student criticizes a former teacher and Tom Wolfe takes a cynical look at people who want to be like everyone else.

You probably remember Marc Antony's speech in Shakespeare's *Julius Caesar* that begins

> Friends, Romans, countrymen, lend me your ears;
> I come to bury Caesar, not to praise him.
> The evil that men do lives after them,
> The good is often interred with their bones;
> So let it be with Caesar.

Then Antony does just the opposite of what he proposes: He praises Caesar, as well as censures Brutus, inciting the crowd against Brutus and the other traitors. This speech shows how both praise and censure can be effective. You'll find other examples of praise and censure in Chapter 14.

To Summarize

Although **summarizing** usually accompanies other kinds of writing, it also stands alone as a primary aim in both student writing and writing on the job. Summarizing is an essential skill. It is a component of reporting: You summarize lecture or lab notes, reading assignments, articles you've read in your library research, and individual or group activities. Summarizing is also integral to reviewing or responding to reading. Your teachers sometimes assign summaries of required reading because they know that the act of summarizing will aid both your remembering and your understanding. Abstracts, which are a type of summary, and executive summaries are almost always parts of business and other professional reports, serving to focus the reader's attention and save valuable time.

To summarize well, go to the heart of the matter first, then add other essential information—not quoted sentences and phrases—from the original. In the following opening paragraph of summary, you can see that the writer makes an overall statement of what the summarized book is about.

> The newly single man has the reputation of being lucky: freed from the old ball and chain at last, he can pursue his every whim. But divorced and widowed men suffer and often suffer alone, as Jane Burgess explains in *The Single-Again Man. . . .* Burgess describes how these men cope with their feelings and their children and how they readjust.
> —Pamela Black, *Psychology Today*

(Chapter 15 gives you an opportunity to work on your summarizing skills.)

To Respond

Response, a common purpose, is a companion to summary. Think of the millions of letters and memos written every day in response to other letters and memos. Think of all the requests for information which bring about responses that furnish the information (in which case a secondary purpose is to inform). People also respond to arguments, with the added purpose of persuasion. Book and article reviews are a type of response that includes summary. Response can be either information or opinions, sometimes a statement of the writer's opinion based on evidence or authority.

Here is a very brief book review that includes both summary and response:

> Mr. Dovlatov's "Russian Family Album" consists of ironically deadpan sketches of his relatives. That is, he claims the characters are his relatives, but he uses them to present a satirical picture of Soviet society in its more pretentious and irrational aspects. This small book is tart, funny, and maliciously deflative.
> —Phoebe-Lou Adams, review of *Ours* by Sergei Dovlatov, from *The Atlantic*

(Chapter 15 also covers response.)

To Ask Questions

Students are often thought of as the ones who *answer* questions, but serious students learn to *ask* them too. You have probably known times when you realized that to ask the right question you had to be informed. In class, for example, your questions and the way you frame them reveal that you've read the assignment. When you ask an informed question, you not only show what you know but also get more information. You see a remarkable increase in your learning simply by doing your assignments and then asking questions about what you don't understand. In writing too, asking informed questions is appropriate. Questions are common in the business world, where letters and memos are written to elicit information and clarify points.

In writing, asking questions is a way of beginning essays and ending them, a way of responding to required reading, a way of looking at the implications of research. Sometimes writers use questions as the organizing principle of an entire piece of writing. Here is the way Sydney J. Harris opens one of his essays:

> If there should be, on Christmas night, a second coming, would there not be soon a second crucifixion?
>
> And this time, not by the Romans or the Jews, but by those who proudly call themselves Christians?
>
> I wonder. I wonder how we today would regard and treat this man with His strange and frightening and "impractical" doctrines of human behavior and relationships. Would we believe and follow, any more than the masses of people in His day believed and followed?

> Would not the militarists among us assail Him as a cowardly pacifist because He urges us not to resist evil?
>
> —"If Christ Returned on Christmas"

Harris continues asking questions that begin "Would not," and he ends the essay with the quizzical statement "I wonder." Though such extensive use of questions is rare, it does happen. These questions are not so much to solicit answers as to stimulate thought. For this reason, they are effective at the beginning and end of an essay.

To Answer Questions

Paired with asking questions is answering them. This purpose for writing appears to be informing; however, there is a fundamental difference between the two. When you inform, you assume that the audience doesn't know what you know. But when you answer questions *to show what you know,* as in exams, your audience knows more than you do and will evaluate your learning on the basis of what you write. That's not a very desirable writing situation, and it's not as much fun as most other kinds of writing, but it's a fact of school life (and often of business and professional life) and a valid aim for writing. When you are in this situation, you must

1. focus on the larger picture to show that you understand the information,
2. add supporting details to show that you can handle the facts,
3. use vocabulary appropriate to the subject or field,
4. organize carefully, again to show that you understand your material, but also to make the reading easier,
5. edit for gross errors that will impede reading.

Essay examinations are a specialized type of writing in which answering questions is the major purpose.

You might say that showing that you know a subject well is an aspect of all writing, because you never want to appear uninformed when you write. But in those cases your main purpose is something else, and you probably know more about your subject than your reader does. (Essay-examination writing is discussed in more detail in Chapter 15.)

A Rhetorical Blend

Writer emphasis, audience emphasis, subject emphasis—these are some of the important purposes for writing. This chapter has established that all writing has a rhetorical situation: a writer, an audience, and a subject, all of which are affected by the purpose for writing. We have concentrated on each component separately and described the related purposes. Yet it is important to remember that, even when writing emphasizes one of the components, the other components are present. You always have your role as a writer; you have an audience, usually other readers but sometimes yourself; and you have something to write about, your subject. It may be the presence of all three components that accounts for writers often having more than one purpose when they write. As you will see in Part II, multiple purposes are common, even while one purpose is dominant. In the next chapter we will begin looking at what writers do to produce a piece of writing.

EXERCISE

Read the following short essays and prepare to discuss these questions in class:

1. What is the purpose of the essay? Can you find secondary purposes?
2. Is the emphasis of the essayist on the writer, the audience, or the subject?
3. What role does the writer seem to assume?
4. What is the writer's attitude toward the subject?
5. Whom does the writer seem to assume as audience?
6. What do you see as the main idea of the essay? Write that idea in a single sentence.

Banning Butts

If you're a smoker, you can take a simple test to see whether quitting could be a snap or a drag for you. Just hold your breath for as long as possible and time yourself.   1

In a study of 56 people who entered a stop-smoking clinic, psychologist Peter Hajek of the Institute of Psychiatry in London and colleagues found that the people who successfully quit were able to hold their breath much longer than those who started smoking again.   2

Successful quitters were able to hold their breath for 38 seconds, on average, while failures could do so for only 26 seconds. People were considered successful short-term quitters if they stayed off cigarettes the entire last week of the four-week course. Two-thirds were able to quit for at least a week.   3

The researchers believe the successful quitters may have more endurance and capacity to withstand discomfort. People who can hold their breath longer may be more persistent personalities in all areas of life. "Breath-holding endurance might well reflect the type of persistence necessary for resisting withdrawal discomfort," the researchers write in *Addictive Behaviors* (Vol. 12, pp. 285–288).   4

—Vincent Bozzi, *Psychology Today*

Writers at Work

Kenneth Roberts' working methods and ours differ so widely it is hard to realize we are in the same line of business. We've just been looking through his book "I Wanted to Write" and marvelling at his stamina and his discipline. The thought of writing apparently stimulates Roberts and causes him to sit upright at a desk, put in requests to libraries, write friends, examine sources, and generally raise hell throughout the daylight hours and far into the night. He works at home (where his privacy is guarded), writes in longhand, counts the words, keeps a record of moneys received, and gets a great deal done. Now turn for a moment to your correspondent. The thought of writing hangs over our mind like an ugly cloud, making us apprehensive and depressed, as before a summer storm, so that we begin the day by subsiding after breakfast, or by going away, often to seedy and inconclusive destinations: the nearest zoo, or a branch post office to buy a few stamped envelopes. Our professional life has been a long, shameless exercise in avoidance. Our home is designed for the maximum of interruption, our office is the place where we never are. From his remarks, we gather that Roberts is contemptuous of this temperament and setup, regards it as largely a pose and certainly as a deficiency in blood. It has occurred to us that perhaps we are not a writer at all but merely a bright clerk who persists in crowding his destiny. Yet the record is there. Not even lying down and closing the blinds stops us from writing; not even our family, and our preoccupation with same, stops us. We have never counted the words, but we estimated them once and the estimate was staggering. The only conclusion we can draw is that there is no such thing as "the writing man," and that after you have waded through a book like "I Wanted to Write" you still don't know the half of it, and would be a fool to try and find out.

—E. B. White, *The Second Tree from the Corner*

Sick of Slipping and Sliding on Icy Streets?

1   Imagine walking across all of the thin, slick patches of ice on sidewalks and streets without the worry of slipping and falling. A revolutionary product is now available which will save you the pain and embarrassment of slipping on ice and packed snow. Shoe chains.

2   Sure, you may feel a little strange at first to be the only person walking down the street with chains on the bottom of your shoes or boots, but once others realize how carefree you are when you walk across the icy sidewalks, they'll want shoe chains too.

3   Shoe chains are designed to give traction the same way tire chains work for cars. Just slip them around your shoes and you're ready to tackle the ice and snow without worry. Shoe chains don't weigh down your feet and will last many snowy, slippery winters. They come in three sizes made to fit all shoes.

If you are ready to give up all the needless worry of an embarrassing fall   4
on the ice, just fill out the enclosed order form, which includes a size chart
to help you determine your shoe chains size. For only $10.00 you can
abandon the hassle of slippery sidewalks and streets. Order shoe chains for
friends and family as Christmas gifts and save $2.00 on every additional pair.

If you are in need of traction and stability for winter walking, shoe   5
chains are for you!

—Michele (student writer)

CHAPTER 3

The Writing Process: Prewriting

The teacher may demonstrate the technique of systematic questioning, but the students must apply the technique for themselves if they are really to learn its usefulness.
—*Richard L. Larson*

There is no single writing process. The way you write a report is probably very different from the way you write a persuasive piece. Writing a letter to your girlfriend is different from writing a letter to your employer. Your process of writing is determined by who you are as a writer, who your audience is, what you're writing about, and what your purpose is for writing.

Whatever your procedure for producing a piece of writing, you decide what to write, *prewriting;* get it down in words, *drafting;* and make some changes, *revising.* When you write a lengthy report, you may spend much of your time searching for, reading, and sifting information. By the time you are ready to begin your first draft, you may already have a thick stack of note cards, a thesis sentence, an outline, and an odd assortment of jottings. After you've composed your first draft, you revise carefully and repeatedly to produce a paper that represents your best work. When you write a friendly letter, by contrast, you may start writing as soon as the paper is in front of you, you discover your ideas as you write, one idea leads to another, and you cross out and substitute words as you go, so that whatever revisions you make are done while you are composing.

Most writing, however, is somewhere between these extremes. You start with some kind of prewriting or planning, then do your drafting, then work on revising. Even with the friendly letter, you are likely to begin thinking about what you want to say before you get the paper out and then to read over and correct what you've written before you fold it up and drop it in the mail. Thinking in advance is part of the writing process just as surely as forming the words on the page or crossing out and revising are.

The scale of this process is not necessarily the entire essay or letter. More likely, the scope is smaller, such as a paragraph or even a sentence. The "stages" of writing may occur within a single sentence, as when you pause to decide what you want to say in your next sentence, draft the sentence, then reread and revise it, or when you plan and revise even while composing the sentence. Prewriting, then, to look at it literally, is what you do before you draft, and revising is what you do after there's something to revise, either in your thoughts or on paper. All the decisions you make before you write are **prewriting.**

Discovering Ideas

Ideas for writing may originate in the middle of a conversation when a word or an idea opens up a flood of new thoughts, or in a sensory impression when a particular scent or sight evokes half-forgotten images. Ideas may begin in class discussions or something you hear on radio or television. Some of your best ideas occur quite unconsciously while you're reading: What another writer says spurs you to begin looking at a thing in a fresh way. If you pursue those thoughts, you may discover something you want to say or write: new insights into a familiar subject, an opinion you want to share, knowledge that someone else could use.

Sometimes, though, ideas do not originate unless you make a conscious effort to stir them up. You may have to prod your mind until you discover something that you realize you can write about. Discovering is not as simple as pulling ideas out of a file drawer. It's more like starting a fire. Although some fires erupt spontaneously (like some ideas), most of the time a good fire requires careful preparation of combustible materials (reading, study, and experience) and a spark to ignite them. Even after the fire is started, it may need some fanning and poking for the flame to keep going. While the fire is burning, it is *active*. Like ideas, it *does* things. It generates heat and light. In so doing, a fire, like ideas, can be immensely destructive. But fires and ideas are also capable of generating untold benefits.

Prewriting may be a spoken or written effort to explore ideas (such as freewriting, listing, or questioning), or it may be the mulling over of thoughts as you go about other business. Some of the best prewriting is done while the writer is doing something else: driving the car, riding the bus, taking a walk, running, or washing the dishes. The methods described in the next section can assist you in discovering an idea and in exploring your thoughts once you have a topic in mind. You can use these methods in three ways:

1. In writing, by discovering ideas on paper;
2. In speech, by talking out a subject with someone else;
3. In your mind, by talking out a subject with yourself.

Invention

Prewriting uses methods of **invention:** ways of discovering and exploring ideas and how to express them. As you read about these methods, bear in mind that you discover and explore at all points in your writing, while you're drafting and revising as well as while you're planning. While you draft, you use some type of invention when you pause to consider what to write next; while you revise, the methods of invention are particularly useful in discovering how to rethink. Writing is inventing. In this chapter, ten of the common methods of invention are described, and some of them recur in Chapter 5 on revising. Then in Part II you can apply invention to specific writing assignments. You will probably find the methods of invention most productive when you combine two or more for a single writing project.

Reading

In your search for ideas, you may overlook an obvious source: **reading.** Consider the wealth of ideas residing between the covers of books and magazines and on the pages of newspapers, on microfilm and microfiche, and in computer data banks. Much of what is written is based on what someone else has already written. When you read, you think not only of what the writer has said but also of something the writer has not said, a new angle, a new application. In other words, you are an *active reader.* When you ask questions like the active reading questions in Chapter 1 (page 6), you may discover new things to say. Here are some additional questions you might ask:

Questions for Discovering Ideas in Reading

1. Do I agree with what the writer is saying?
2. How might this idea be expressed better?
3. How does this information relate to what I know?
4. How can I apply this information to what I know?
5. What could I add to what this writer has said?
6. How do I feel when reading this piece of writing?
7. What does this writing contribute to my experience?
8. How significant is this writing to my experience?
9. What new idea does this writing give me?

These questions are similar to those in Chapter 1, but they probe deeper into what the writing might mean to you.

Ideas may come serendipitously, as unexpected gifts, while you're reading for another purpose, or you may deliberately pursue a topic to learn more about it. When you're looking for information on a topic, you can use your library's card catalog or on-line catalog and indexes. If you're just casting around for something that interests you, you can browse in your library or your own bookshelves or magazine rack, skimming until you find something that appeals to you. Then read; if you read actively, the ideas you gain are likely to engender new thoughts. To explore these thoughts further, you can take up another method of invention. Next you might return to reading, to fill in the gaps you discover in your knowledge.

When you get around to writing, you may need to credit the other writer for his or her ideas. In so doing you will also give your reader information on how your ideas developed, and your statements will be based not only on your own credibility but on the authority of the other writer as well. Here's an example of how reading leads to new thoughts. First is the reading, a portion of an article in *The Atlantic* about dolphins ensnared in tuna nets, then the new writing. Note how the second writer credits the ideas of the first.

Reading

The beaks of Sam LaBudde's first dolphins strained against the net that   1
had formed a canopy over them. Their flukes churned the ocean white. They thronged at the surface, desperate to force slack in the net sufficient to free their blowholes for a breath. Their shrieks and squeals began high in the hearing range of humans and climbed inaudible scales above. LaBudde wanted to scream himself.

The net was brailed, or hauled in. Its red mesh was scarcely visible, and   2
the dolphins snagged in it seemed to levitate from the sea. High above the deck the great spool of the power block, turning by fits and starts, raised and gathered the seine, conveying the dolphins—some drowned, some still struggling feebly—up toward the block's tight aperture. The net passed through the block, crushing the dolphins, and then slowly descended to the deck. LaBudde stepped forward with his shipmates and began disentangling dead and dying dolphins from the mesh. The dying trembled in their death throes. The dead stared with eyes wide open. LaBudde noticed that the hue of the iris was different in each animal—dolphins are individuals even in death. He noticed his own red arms. A dolphin, the first he had ever touched in his life, had left him bloody to the elbows.

Months later, on land, Sam LaBudde's sleep would be troubled by a   3
recurrent dream in which injured dolphins spoke in cryptic tongues. He might have spared himself the dream, perhaps, had he given vent to his feelings at sea. He could not. LaBudde was not what he seemed—just another crewman on a Panamanian purse seiner in the eastern tropical Pacific. LaBudde was a spy.

—Kenneth Brower, "The Destruction of Dolphins"

The second writer, stirred by the emotional impact of Brower's description of such wanton killing of dolphins ensnared in tuna nets, decides to write on human disregard for all nonhuman life.

Writing based on reading

Perhaps the wrong species has been given dominion over the creatures of the earth. We seem to think that "subduing" them means killing off whatever we want or whatever gets in our way. Kenneth Brower in "The Destruction of Dolphins" shows in graphic terms how indifferent we are to the lives of other creatures. Instead of fishing in ways that catch only the tuna they want to catch, fishermen use purse seines that entrap not only the tuna but the dolphins that travel with the tuna. As a result, when the nets are drawn in, sometimes hundreds of dolphins, intelligent creatures that Brower describes as "individuals even in death," are crushed, dismembered, and killed (37).

The parenthetical number following the quotation refers to the page number in Brower's article. If she had not included his name in her paragraph, the second writer would also have named the author within the parentheses, like this: (Brower 37). At the end of her paper, this writer cited the article as follows:

Work Cited

Brower, Kenneth. "The Destruction of Dolphins." *The Atlantic,* July 1989: 35–58.

Questions about Audience

Sometimes asking **questions about audience**—to establish who your audience is and what it knows about your subject—provides ideas for writing and helps you know what sort of details you need to use. If, for example, you want to persuade people who do not use seat belts that they should buckle up, you might decide to collect statistics about accident victims who were not wearing seat belts or to paint a picture of the traumatic effects on the families of accident victims whose lives might have been saved had they been buckled. Refer again to the questions about audience for writing in Chapter 2 (page 25). Answers to questions such as Who is my audience? How interested is my audience in my subject? and What experiences and knowledge do I share with my audience? can be a big help in determining what to say and what you need to find out.

Listing or Brainstorming

One of the simplest ways to prewrite is to **list,** or **brainstorm.** One dictionary defines brainstorming as "a disturbance in the brain." As a method of invention, brainstorming is an intense prodding for the purpose of uncovering memories, thoughts, and images and making new relationships among them, leading to new ideas. The brain becomes "disturbed," stirred up, and remembers forgotten ideas and details. When you brainstorm or list, you begin with a given topic and write down everything that occurs to you on that topic, whether it seems related or not. You try to work fast.

When you've finished, you go back over the list and strike out unlikely ideas, group according to similarities those that are left, and brainstorm again to fill in gaps. As an alternative, choose one item, and from it start a new list. This method works well in collaboration with one or more other people. You can work together on building a list, or, after you have brainstormed alone for a while, you can ask someone else for input.

Here's a sample brainstormed list on the topic "human disregard for all nonhuman life":

killing of dolphins
killing of baby seals
Greenpeace
Marine Mammal Fund
tuna fishing
veal production
chicken houses
vivisection

The writer got this far in her list and decided that she would rather explore "human disregard for dolphin life." So she proceeded from her first item:

killing of dolphins
tuna fishing
Greenpeace
Marine Mammal Fund
laws—U.S.
international law
numbers of dolphins killed
intelligence of dolphins
inhumanity of killing intelligent creatures
fishermen's point of view
need for tuna

This writer could have gone on, but she realized from the items she already had that she would need more information. She read the rest of the *Atlantic* article and went to her library to search for information on dolphins, the tuna-fishing industry, and relevant laws.

Mapping or Clustering

A variation of listing is **mapping,** or **clustering,** a discovery technique borrowed from instruction in reading. Again, you start by jotting down everything that occurs to you on a topic. The difference is that you write the ideas in clusters and then map out related thoughts, as in Figure 3-1. The topic is in the center, double-circled; it is the starting place. From there, related thoughts are jotted down and circled, then connected to associated ideas by lines.

Mapping allows you to see how parts of your topic relate to the whole. The writer of this map could see a pattern developing, in that every cluster seems to lead to the costs of drought, so he underlined each type of cost. His next step would be to explore that thought further and develop it as a controlling idea, stating it as a thesis (see pages 54–58). The clustering might evolve into an outline like the ones on pages 53–55.

Try mapping on any topic you want to explore. If no clear idea emerges from your first exploration, you might, as with listing, choose one thought and begin mapping again.

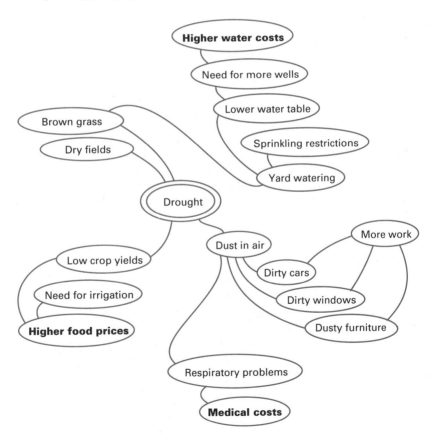

Figure 3-1. Mapping, or Clustering.

EXERCISE

Use mapping, or clustering, as a discovery technique for reading comprehension. After reading the following essay, write the main idea in the center of a sheet of paper and circle it. Then jot down supporting and related ideas, circle them, and connect associated ideas to one another by lines. In class, compare your map with those of your classmates. The maps will be different, because you each will have read the essay out of your own experience. But your sense of the main idea will probably be similar.

The hot-spot hypothesis was put forward in the early nineteen-sixties by   1
J. Tuzo Wilson, of the University of Toronto, as a consequence of a stopover in Hawaii and one look at the islands. The situation seemed obvious. James Hutton, on whose eighteenth-century "Theory of the Earth" the science of geology has been built, understood in a general way that great heat from deep sources stirs the actions of the earth ("There has been exerted an extreme degree of heat below the strata formed at the bottom of the sea"), but no one to this day knows exactly how it works. Heat rising from hot spots apparently lubricates the asthenosphere—the layer on which the plates slide. According to theory, the plates would stop moving if the hot spots were not there. Why the hot spots are there in the first place is a question that seeks its own Hutton. For the moment, all Jason Morgan can offer is another shrug and smile. "I don't know," he says. "It must have something to do with the way heat gets out of the lower mantle."

From very deep in the mantle (and perhaps all the way from the core)   2
the heat is thought to rise in a concentrated column, and for this reason is alternatively called a plume. Its surface features are not proof in themselves that they are the product of some plant-stem phenomenon that is (or was) standing in the mantle far below. The chemistry of hot-spot lavas suggests that the rock is coming from below the asthenosphere, but there is no direct evidence of fixed hot spots in the mantle. They exist on inference alone. There is no way to sample the mantle. It can only be sensed—with vibrational waves, with viscosity computations, with thermodynamic calculations of what minerals do at different temperatures and pressures. Sound waves move slowly in soft rock, and some modes of the sound can be stopped completely when the rock is molten. The speed and patterns of seismic waves tell the story of the rock. Seismology is not quite sophisticated enough to look through the earth and count hot spots, but it approaches that capability, and when it gets there hot spots should appear on the screen like downspouts in a summer storm. If they don't, that may be the end of the second-greatest story in the youthful explorations of geological geophysics.

—John McPhee, *Rising from the Plains*

Journalist's Questions

Another variation of list making is using questions to assist your brainstorming. Sometimes known as the five *W*'s and an *H,* these interrogatory words will start your **journalist's questions:** *who, what, where, when, why,* and *how.* Use each word as often and as many times as you can. You'll be amazed at how many answers you'll get. On the topic of drought, for example, you might start by asking questions like these:

Who is affected by drought?
How are people affected by drought?
Where is drought most serious?
What is drought?
Why is there drought?
How does drought begin?
When do people first notice a drought?
What can be done about drought?
How is my neighborhood affected by drought?
How is my state affected by drought?
Why is insufficient rainfall a problem?

The first round of questions could go on for another page or two, or you could take one question, such as "How is my neighborhood affected by drought?" and ask further questions along that line. For example:

How is my neighborhood affected by drought?
Who seems to be the most affected?
Why are those people affected the most?
What are they doing about insufficient rainfall?

You go on until a controlling idea begins to emerge and you're ready to write a tentative thesis sentence. The next step would be to organize your ideas under that thesis sentence or to begin focused freewriting using the ideas you have generated so far. The outline on pages 54–55 shows how one writer developed an essay on drought.

EXERCISE

The journalist's questions can be used to discover ideas in reading. Using these questions will make you an active reader, and, if you apply them to much of your reading, they may help you discover ideas for your writing as well. As you read the following paragraph, ask questions that begin with who, what, where, when, why, and how: like Who is the writer? Who is he writing about? What is he saying? When do the events take place?

For those who fought, the war had other features unknown to those who looked on or got the war mediated through journalism. One such feature was the rate at which it destroyed human beings—friendly as well as enemy. Training for infantry fighting, few American soldiers were tough-minded enough to accept the full, awful implications of the term "replacement" in the designation of their Replacement Training Centers. (The proposed euphemism "reinforcement" never caught on.) What was going to happen to the soldiers they were being trained to replace? Why should so many "replacements"—hundreds of thousands of them, actually—be required? The answers came soon enough in the European theater, in Italy, France, and finally Germany. In six weeks of fighting in Normandy, the 90th Infantry Division had to replace 150 percent of its officers and more than 100 percent of its men. If a division was engaged for more than three months, the probability was that every one of its second lieutenants, all 132 of them, would be killed or wounded. For those being prepared as replacements at officer candidate schools, it was not mentally healthy to dwell on the oddity of the schools' turning out hundreds of new junior officers weekly after the army had reached its full wartime strength. Only experience would make the need clear. The commanding officer of the 6th King's Own Scottish Borderers, which finally arrived in Hamburg in 1945 after fighting all the way from Normandy, found an average of five original men remaining (out of around 200) in each rifle company. "I was appalled," he said. "I had no idea it was going to be like that."

—Paul Fussell, "The Real War, 1939–1945," *The Atlantic*

Classical Probes

The ancient rhetoricians knew that people have a great deal more knowledge than they usually use. To draw out what they knew about a specific topic, the rhetoricians devised six specific categories called the **classical probes:** *identification, comparison and contrast, classification, causes and effects, process analysis,* and *exemplification.* These categories, they thought, coincide with ways the mind collects and stores information. People want to know how? and why? and what? So under each category the rhetoricians asked related questions. Here are some of the questions you can ask when exploring a topic:

Identification
What is it?
What does it look like?
What does it feel like?

Comparison and contrast
How is it like other things?
How is it different from other things?

Classification
What are its parts?
How does it relate to other things?
How are its parts interrelated?

Causes and effects
What are its causes?
What are its effects?

Process analysis
How does it operate?
How is it produced?

Exemplification
What are some examples of it?

As with other methods of exploring ideas, this one can feed itself. You can take the answer to any question and ask additional questions about that idea.

EXERCISE

Working by yourself or with a partner, use the classical probes to explore the topic greenhouse effect *(or another topic of your choosing). Here are some questions to begin a probe on* greenhouse effect. *Answer these and compose further questions that fit the topic. You may find that your questions begin to center on one or two probes.*

What is the greenhouse effect? (*identification*)
Is the greenhouse effect like anything else I know? (*comparison*)
How is the greenhouse effect different from normal climatic features?
    (*contrast*)
What causes the greenhouse effect? (*cause*)
What effects does it bring about? (*effect*)
Can the causes of the greenhouse effect be described in groups?
    (*classification*)
How does the greenhouse effect operate? (*process analysis*)
What are some examples of the greenhouse effect? (*exemplification*)

Cubing

Related to the classical probes is **cubing,** a strategy that allows you to visualize prewriting. Imagine your topic or problem enclosed in a cube—a six-sided square box—in which each side represents a way of looking into your topic or problem (See Figure 3-2). Here are some sample cubing questions to ask about your topic:

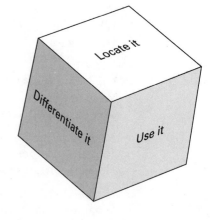

Figure 3-2.   Cubing.

Classify It	*Describe It*	*Analyze It*
To what group does it belong?	What does it look like?	What are its parts?
How is it like others in the group?	What is its shape?	What is it made of?

Differentiate It	*Locate It*	*Use It*
What makes it different from other things?	Where can I find it?	What is it good for?
		What does it do?

Your process of discovery can continue to add related questions. In other words, as you discover ideas, keep turning the cube so that other sides face your topic. As with the classical probes, one or two aspects of the cube may be the most helpful for a particular topic. The advantage of cubing is that you can objectify your topic, putting it in front of you and examining it from all sides. If you're a visually oriented person, this may be an especially useful strategy for you. Once you have uncovered ideas, you can proceed to another prewriting strategy—devising a tentative thesis, outlining if you have a structured topic and thesis, freewriting (see page 51), or reading if you're still exploring.

You can also use the cubing strategy to discover a topic. In this case, you examine the assignment. Here are examples of the kinds of questions you might ask:

Classify It	*Describe It*	*Analyze It*
How is it like other assignments?	How does it look rephrased in my own words?	What are its parts?

| *Differentiate It* | *Locate It* | *Use It* |
| How is it different from other assignments? | Where can I find more information on this assignment? | What can I learn from this assignment? |

Finally, cubing is a strategy for active reading. To comprehend a reading assignment thoroughly, think of it as a cube and examine it from all sides by asking questions similar to those in the six categories.

EXERCISE

Use cubing for an active reading of the following paragraph. Imagine the paragraph enclosed in a cube, and, as you view the paragraph through each of the cube's six sides, beginning anywhere,

Classify it—How does this information relate to what I already know about the subject?

Describe it—What is the subject?

Analyze it—What is the main point, and how does the author support it?

Differentiate it—How is it different from other information on the subject?

Locate it—Where would I expect to find information like this?

Use it—How can I apply this information?

These implacable costumes, male and female, reflected the prevailing credo as to the relations between the sexes. The ideal woman was the sheltered lady, swathed not only in silk and muslin but in innocence and propriety, and the ideal man, whether a pillar of rectitude or a gay dog, virtuously protected the person and reputation of such tender creatures as were entrusted to his care. If unmarried, a girl must be accompanied by a chaperone whenever she ventured out to an evening's entertainment in the city. If she were a daughter of the rich, a maid might take the place of the chaperone; it was never quite clear, under these circumstances, who was supposed to protect the maid's virtue. Eleanor Roosevelt has recorded in her autobiography her relief when, at the age of twenty or so, she found that her friend Bob Ferguson was considered close enough to the family to be permitted to escort her home from evening parties at the studio of Bay Emmet the painter. "Otherwise I always had to have a maid wait for me—that was one of the rules my grandmother had laid down." And James W. Gerard has added his testimony as to the iron code which still governed New York Society in that period. "Even when I was thirty years old," wrote Gerard in his old age, "if I had asked a girl to dine with me alone, I would have been kicked down her front steps. If I had offered her a cocktail, I

would have been tossed out of Society for my boorish effrontery." Needless
to add that a woman must never be seen in a bar—or even a smoking car.
—Frederick Lewis Allen, *The Big Change: America Transforms Itself, 1900–1950*

Freewriting

One way of exploring ideas that involves neither making lists nor answering questions is focused **freewriting.** You just write on a particular topic,
without stopping, without planning, without making corrections or worrying about what word to use or how to spell it. Like most methods of
invention, freewriting is based on the classical notion that people accumulate a wealth of knowledge and may need a strategy for tapping that knowledge.
It also derives from the modern theory that people learn—generate ideas—
by writing. That is, when you freewrite you not only draw information from
your memory bank but you also *do* something with that information: analyze
it, compare it, combine it with other information, actually *engender new
thoughts* as you write.

Sometimes freewriting is used without a focusing topic. In such a case,
you begin writing whatever is on your mind. If nothing comes, or until
something comes, just write "I can't think of anything to write" or "I wonder
what will come of this" or anything else that keeps your pen moving across
the paper or your fingers tapping on the keyboard. Sooner or later, something emerges—perhaps not a usable idea, but then again it may be one that
leads to something better.

EXERCISE

Freewrite on the general topic freedom *or on one of the ideas suggested by the
readings on pages 46, 48, or 51. Write fast for ten minutes without stopping or
correcting errors, putting down whatever occurs to you. If the ideas you generate look
usable, apply another invention strategy to explore them further and possibly develop
a paper from them.*

Imitation

Imitation is an old practice enabling less experienced writers to learn
from the more experienced. One form focuses on acquiring stylistic variations. You may be asked to write in the style of Ernest Hemingway, for
example, so you would write a series of short sentences and a few that seem
to go on and on with clauses joined by conjunctions. Or you may be asked to

imitate sentences that have features you often write incorrectly. Many writers, for example, have trouble with compound sentences in which two clauses must be separated by a semicolon, so they imitate such sentences, patterning correct writing instead of remedying mistakes. At other times, writers imitate entire essays to acquire a sense of essay components: thesis sentences, for example, or paragraph development and methods of achieving coherence. There are many ways of using imitation for improving style and structure.

Another, often overlooked, feature of imitation is that, by imitating the writing of others, the writer discovers new ideas. As you write that paragraph imitating Hemingway's style, your own ideas come to you. If you study a model essay and then write an essay patterned on it, you find that while you concentrate on the form of the original you discover ideas of your own. You find something that fits. Once you have begun to generate ideas, you can depart from the pattern and write an essay that is not only your own ideas but your own pattern.

EXERCISE

Write an imitation of the following paragraph, substituting another action, something you know, like building a house, decorating a room, or moving to college. Choose your own topic. "Millions of years ago" can be "several days ago" or "a score of years ago." Sample first sentence: "Several months ago my twelve-year-old brother built a tree house in the crotch of an old maple tree."

Millions of years ago, a volcano built a mountain on the floor of the Atlantic. In eruption after eruption, it pushed up a great pile of volcanic rock, until it had accumulated a mass a hundred miles across at its base, reaching upward toward the surface of the sea. Finally its cone emerged as an island with an area of about 200 square miles. Thousands of years passed, and thousands of thousands. Eventually the waves of the Atlantic cut down the cone and reduced it to a shoal—all of it, that is, but a small fragment which remained above the water. This fragment we know as Bermuda.

—Rachel L. Carson, *The Sea Around Us*

If you like the idea that develops, explore it further with other invention strategies—freewriting, perhaps, or the journalist's questions.

Outlining

As a method of exploring ideas, **outlining** is last in this discussion because it works best after you have used other methods. In fact, after employing one or two other methods of invention you may not even need an outline. Your list, cluster, or whatever may be all you require as a guide for writing. Or you may be one of those people who prefer to use outlining as a next step. Outlining systemizes the thoughts you have generated with other methods. It has the advantage of forcing you to clarify distinctions by means of parallel and subordinate categories.

Some people almost always use some kind of outline when they write; others rarely use one. Most people probably use one only part of the time, as, for example, with a complex subject, a large amount of material, or a very formal paper. Here is a conventional pattern for formal outlines:

I. Main topic
   A. First subtopic of I
   B. Second subtopic of I
      1. First subtopic of B
      2. Second subtopic of B
         a. First subtopic of 2
         b. Second subtopic of 2
            (1) First subtopic of b
            (2) Second subtopic of b
               (a) First subtopic of (2)
               (b) Second subtopic of (2)

Each level has at least two items, since subcategories *divide* the preceding item; however, a level may have as many more items as necessary. Most outlines go no further than the fourth level, designated by lowercase letters (*a, b*).

Here is a formal topic outline based on the ideas generated in the drought cluster on page 45:

I. Introduction
   A. "Greenhouse effect"
      1. Increased carbon dioxide in the atmosphere
      2. Higher average temperatures
      3. Lack of rainfall
   B. Definition of drought
   C. *Thesis: Drought is everybody's business because it escalates the cost of living*
II. Costs from the farm
   A. Dry fields
      1. Need for irrigation
      2. Expense of water and equipment

    B. Lower yields

       1. Higher costs for farmers

       2. Higher food prices

III. Costs from technology

    A. Lower water tables—quote statistics

    B. Need to drill more wells

    C. Higher water bills

IV. Medical costs

    A. Respiratory problems

       1. Dust in the air

       2. Pollen in the air

    B. Need for medical care and medicine

V. Conclusion

    A. Other effects

       1. Dry lawns

       2. Dirty houses and cars

    B. Need for concern and understanding

This outline has three levels, the first represented by roman numerals, the second by capital letters, and the third by arabic numerals. The items at each level are parallel. In drafting, the section under each roman numeral would probably represent a paragraph, filled in with supporting details.

    In a sentence outline, each item in the topic outline would be rephrased as a complete sentence. Here is section I:

  I. Changes in the earth's climate are making the periodic occurrence of droughts a very real possibility.

    A. Some people call these changes the "greenhouse effect" and attribute them to misuse of our environment.

       1. We pour excessive carbon dioxide into the atmosphere.

       2. The result is a warming of the earth.

       3. Warmer temperatures contribute to lack of rainfall.

    B. Drought can be defined as a severe lack of rainfall that results in low crop yields, burned up lawns, dead trees and shrubs, lowered water tables and lakes, reduced flow in rivers and streams, and dust everywhere.

    C. *Thesis: Drought is everybody's business because it escalates the cost of living.*

Often a working outline, no more than a list of items in the order in which you will use them, is enough. But because a formal outline is a guide not only to the order of development but to the relationships among items as well, you should know how to make one so that you can use it with facility when you need it. Note how Chapter 5 suggests outlining as a revision strategy.

Developing a Thesis Sentence

The preceding formal outline includes a thesis sentence: "Drought is everybody's business because it escalates the cost of living." A **thesis sentence** states the main idea of an essay. It is not just a statement of subject: not just "This essay is about drought" or "The purpose of this essay is to discuss the drought situation." These are both statements of subject only—despite the wording of the second one implying purpose.

In stating the main idea of an essay, a thesis sentence (1) declares the subject and (2) asserts what is being said about the subject. It sometimes also (3) states the method of development. Purpose is implied. The thesis sentence in the preceding outline declares the subject ("drought") and makes an assertion about it ("is everybody's business"). The thesis sentence also states the method of development.

Subject: "drought"
Assertion: "is everybody's business"
Development: "because it escalates the cost of living"

The main idea of this proposed essay is that drought is everybody's business. The essay would be developed casually, showing why drought is everybody's business (because it escalates the cost of living), and the purpose would be to inform and persuade.

Thesis sentences often develop during prewriting. In exploring a subject, you may discover that you have something to say, that you are forming an attitude toward your subject, and that you are taking a position on it. Knowing what you want to say beforehand and stating your assertion in your thesis makes your drafting easier than beginning with only a vague idea. In fact, a well-phrased thesis sentence is sometimes the only guide necessary for writing a short essay, a business memo or letter, or some other uncomplicated composition with a single subject. However, there are no doubt times when you do not have a thesis until after you have done some drafting, when you discover your thesis as you write. The result is that, after drafting, you must carry out extensive revision to make your draft support your thesis. You delete irrelevant material, add details, work on coherence, adjust your phrasing, and so on. (Chapter 5 deals with revision.)

Sample Thesis Sentences

Thesis sentences are as varied as are subjects for writing. Read the following thesis sentences and note how they state both subject and assertion, or point, with the purpose implied.

To understand how your paper airplane flies is a step in making your plane fly well.

—Campbell Morris

Subject: how a paper airplane flies
Assertion: understanding helps you to fly your plane well
Purpose: to inform readers about flight theory

We haven't yet developed a clear idea of the ethics of picture-taking.

—Ellen Goodman

Subject: ethics of picture taking
Assertion: we haven't yet developed a clear idea
Purpose: to persuade readers to develop an ethical position

We must learn the rules, courtesies, and etiquette of attending a concert or recital.

—Lynette Frohrip (student writer)

Subject: the rules, courtesies, and etiquette of attending a concert or recital
Assertion: we must learn them
Purpose: to instruct readers

Despite this tragic object lesson, we seem bent on repeating precisely the same mistake in the handling of drugs.

—Milton Friedman

Subject: the handling of drugs
Assertion: we seem bent on repeating a mistake
Purpose: to persuade to a different action

At Mr. Duggleby's I nearly landed in the biggest trouble of all.

—James Herriot

Subject: a barely averted trouble
Assertion: it was the biggest trouble
Purpose: to entertain and inform

Writing Workable Thesis Sentences

Writers sometimes compose thesis sentences that hinder writing instead of aiding it. Theses that are broad, general, or mixed present problems. In constructing your thesis, concentrate on making it *limited*, *specific*, and *unified*, as these examples illustrate.

> *Limited.* "There are still barriers to political action. Let me discuss five of them."—Senator Albert Gore. Of all the barriers to political action on the environment, Gore will discuss five.
>
> *Specific.* "Thousands of balloons released at sporting events may be a deceptive threat to wildlife."—*Audubon*. As opposed to a general thesis, such as "Balloons are a problem," this thesis states what the problem is in particular terms.
>
> *Unified.* "As Mickey's personality softened, his appearance changed." —Stephen Jay Gould. Main ideas are stated in *main clauses*. Gould will write about Mickey Mouse's appearance, not his personality. Had he written his thesis as two main clauses ("Mickey's personality softened, and his appearance changed"), his main idea would not have been clear.

Placement of Thesis Sentences

In academic writing and in most business writing, the thesis, or point, is stated explicitly. These statements usually occur in the introduction—often at the end of the introduction, after background or related information has been given. An alternative location is at the end of the piece of writing. This arrangement occurs frequently in narrative writing, in which the writer recounts a story before declaring its significance. Sometimes the writer who holds the statement of thesis till the end will begin by asking a question, which is answered when the thesis is stated. As an example, in "Why I Write: Making No Become Yes" (Chapter 12), Elie Wiesel begins by asking "Why do I write?" and he concludes, "Why do I write? To wrench those victims from oblivion. To help the dead vanquish death."

At times, the thesis is left unstated. Such usage occurs especially in some professional writing, where the writer is able to maintain tight control over the essay development without an explicit statement. In such writing, readers are generally able to identify the controlling idea because the entire essay supports it.

(Additional discussions of thesis sentences and their development accompany the readings in Part II.)

Increasing Your Options

This chapter has presented ways of discovering and exploring ideas. You may have been familiar with some of them before reading, but now you can expand your prewriting options by trying others. In Chapters 4 and 5, you will see how the same invention techniques that assist your prewriting are useful also in drafting and revising.

EXERCISES

1. Identify subjects and assertions in the following thesis sentences. Be prepared to discuss your decisions in class.

   a. "The Big Bang is the earliest event about which we have any record."

       —Carl Sagan

   b. "The wind is the most fundamental fact of life in Patagonia."

       —George Gaylord Simpson

   c. "Consider these varieties of friendship."

       —Judith Viorst

   d. "Probably the most vexing new question for writers is what to do about the 'he-she' pronoun."

       —William Zinsser

   e. "If you become one of the nearly two million taxpayers audited by the Internal Revenue Service, here are a few things to keep in mind."

   f. "We now know that "Sesame Street" undermines what the traditional idea of schooling represents."

       —Neil Postman

   g. "One such superstition is the belief that black magic is all powerful."

       —Virginia Buckmire (student writer)

2. Select a partner in class and agree on a topic for joint exploration. With your partner, use three methods of invention to explore that topic. Work together on two methods, like brainstorming and clustering, and individually on one, for example freewriting. Then compare notes and together write a thesis sentence and/or an outline.

CHAPTER 4

The Writing Process: Drafting

> *Thought is not merely expressed in words; it comes into existence through them.*
>
> *—Lev Vygotsky*

Drafting is what many people think of as writing: putting the pen to the page, the fingers to the keyboard. Drafting is working your way through a writing project, getting your ideas down and creating new ones as you go, arriving at the last period, when you can breathe a sigh of relief and take a well-earned rest before you start purposeful revising.

Drafting, or composing, is more than choosing words. It's more than developing and arranging your ideas. In fact, you can be composing even when your pen and fingers are still. When you stare out the window, thinking about how to phrase your next sentence, you are composing. When you stretch out on your bed to think through your next paragraph, you are composing—just as truly as when you're tapping keys on the word processor or pushing your pen across the page. Drafting is so closely tied to prewriting and to revising that it's difficult to separate it, for purposes of discussion, from the entire process of writing. This chapter will treat drafting as the portion of writing that concerns putting ideas on the page: matters of paragraphing, developing and arranging ideas, and beginning and ending essays. At the same time, it will be based on the assumption stated in Chapter 3: that prewriting, drafting, and revising may be as close together as the composition of a single sentence.

How People Write

When you develop a guide in prewriting—a list, a cluster, an outline, a thesis sentence, or maybe just some first thoughts—you probably try to follow it as you write, changing that plan as necessary as your ideas develop.

60

Think of your plans as controls against getting bogged down in irrelevancies or losing your sense of direction, not as rigid road maps that prevent you from staying a little longer on one idea or skipping another that you realize doesn't require your attention.

While composing your first drafts you probably work alone. You may have consulted other people as you were exploring ideas, and you may ask someone to give you feedback when you're ready to revise, but while drafting you're on your own. You're the one to make decisions about how to arrange your ideas, how to illustrate and explain your points, what words to use, how to frame your sentences, and so on. Drafting is a private act and a very personal one, even while you consider your future audience.

The way people write is determined by the specific rhetorical situation: the purpose, the role of the writer, the audience, and the subject. Yet people write in their own ways. Some people are *fast* writers, and some proceed at an agonizingly *slow* pace. Some might be termed *inch-at-a-time* writers, pausing after every sentence or phrase to get it right; others are *chunk-at-a-time* writers, writing whole paragraphs or essays before looking back. Some require a working outline *before* they begin, and others write an outline as part of their revising.

You probably know people who are *planners* when they write, who spend hours and days deciding what they will say, how they will explain their main ideas, who their likely audience will be, and what characteristics of that audience are significant for the writing. They outline their ideas or use some other means of arranging them, and, when their first draft is completed, it may require very little revision. You probably have other acquaintances who are *revisers*. They do very little planning, choosing instead to draft their ideas quickly and then spend hours and days rearranging, adding, deleting, and substituting. They need to identify a controlling idea in their drafts and then revise to support it. Finally, you may know people who are *drafters*. They sit down to write with little apparent prewriting, and, except for reading over their drafts to correct spelling and punctuation, they do no revising either. Most writers, including most professional writers, can't write this way. To develop their ideas with the depth and insight necessary to make their writing worth reading, they need to plan and revise as well as to draft.

EXERCISE

Here are three writers' accounts of how they write. Two are by student writers and one by a professional writer. As you read these accounts, try to characterize each writer's process. Are the writers planners, revisers, *or* drafters? *Are they* inch-at-a-time *writers or* chunk-at-a-time? Fast *or* slow? Outliners *before or after* drafting? *You may find more than one characteristic for each person. After characterizing the processes, compare them—in writing or as a group project in class.*

For me, the process of writing is the same, regardless of the piece. I tend   1
to meditate or think about my topic for a long, long time before I sit down
to write even the first draft. Sometimes it seems like I write the entire piece
in my mind, so when I finally sit down to write, the first draft comes fairly
easily and is normally pretty good. I do have a tendency to dwell on a
particular sentence for long periods of time, until I get it right. Getting it
right basically amounts to expressing the idea in the exact way in which I
want it to be received, taking into account word choice, sentence structure,
and tone. I love to experiment with a variety of sentence structures. This
doesn't come easily because I am extremely critical of my own work.

I spend a lot of time reading my piece out loud when I am writing and   2
also when I am revising. I look for consistency in tone, variety in sentence
arrangement, rhythm, parallelism, wordiness, spelling, verb tense, and
repetitive word choice. Then I work on my transitions and organization,
making sure that the piece is clear, well-directed toward my purpose, and
flows smoothly. Finally, I try to come up with a title. This is usually the most
difficult part for me.

I've found that there is always room for revision, and what I like one day   3
may not be what suits me the next. Generally, I am very satisfied with a piece
before I read it to anyone or turn it in to an instructor. I am very pleased
with my final drafts of "A Pain in the Name" [see Chapter 8] and "We
Celebrated Chanukah and Christmas" [see Chapter 12]. I am also very
satisfied with the titles. "A Pain in the Name" took a bit more work than "We
Celebrated," probably because it dealt with humor, which I found challenging—I hate bad humor!

"We Celebrated" is of particular importance to me. I read the piece to   4
my mom and dad, and both were very emotionally moved by it. When I
read the piece, I am even moved by it. It seems that I said exactly what I
needed to say, sincerely and effectively. My writing seems to reflect a very
strong voice, which is evident in "We Celebrated."

—Terry Splett (student writer)

When I initially get an idea for a paper, I am usually in some inconve-   1
nient place like in the bathtub soaking, in my car driving, or in a classroom
where I am supposed to be actively participating or taking notes. I have
learned that no matter how inconvenient it is, I must obtain a piece of paper

and a writing implement (pen, pencil, or crayon) and write the idea down. If I don't, I will either forget the concept or spend the entire time thinking about the idea without paying attention to what I am doing.

The second step, although a relatively subconscious act at first, is to think. Writers have called this pre-thinking; for me it is more like day-dreaming. I generally come up with a blockbuster title that I seldom use, because by the time I am finished with my pre-thinking, the title does not apply anymore.   2

When I first began to take writing seriously, I would use the clustering method, which consists of a small circle which contains the central idea, with spider-like lines emerging from the outer rim. Attached to these lines are additional lines relating to the central theme. Spawning from these circles are supporting ideas and tidbits of information. The next step was to decide which direction I was going and eliminate ideas which were not supportive of the direction I had taken. Finally I would write the paper in longhand, type it, and submit it for acclaim or condemnation. Sometimes the work was good and the revisions were few; often it was my tenses which needed help. Rewrite, rewrite, and, one day, I had a paper worth reading.   3

After a time, I found that I was eliminating the clustering on paper and replacing it with mind clustering. It became more efficient for me to do additional pre-thinking and then type my thoughts. I use a computer, so it is easy to reword as I reread and to change paragraphs and sentences before I turn in the finished product.   4

I found that as I developed my typing skills, I eventually could keep up with my racing mind. For me it is imperative that I get my ideas down before I forget them, and if I think too much about the structuring I lose the flavor of what I am writing.   5

The first paragraph is the most important to me, because it is there that I capture my readers and seduce them into reading further. I spend more critical time on the first paragraph than I do on the rest of the paper, generally speaking. Conclusions or ending paragraphs are second to me in importance, because I want the readers to be satisfied that I have ended and not left them hanging.   6

—Susan Wollack (student writer, "The Poetry of Sister Margarete" in Chapter 14)

Interviewers: Is the act of writing easy for you?   1

[James] Thurber: For me it's mostly a question of rewriting. It's part of a constant attempt on my part to make the finished version smooth, to make it seem effortless. A story I've been working on—"The Train on Track Six," it's called—was rewritten fifteen complete times. There must have been close to 240,000 words in all the manuscripts put together, and I must have spent two thousand hours working at it. Yet the finished version can't be more than twenty thousand words.   2

Interviewers: Then it's rare that your work comes out right the first time?   3

Thurber: Well, my wife took a look at the first version of something I   4
was doing not long ago and said, "Goddamn it, Thurber, that's high-school
stuff." I have to tell her to wait until the seventh draft, it'll work out all right.
I don't know why that should be so, that the first or second draft of
everything I write reads as if it was turned out by a charwoman. I've only
written one piece quickly. I wrote a thing called "File and Forget" in one
afternoon—but only because it was a series of letters just as one would
ordinarily dictate. And I'd have to admit that the last letter of the series, after
doing all the others that one afternoon, took me a week. It was the end of the
piece and I had to fuss over it.

Interviewers: Does the fact that you're dealing with humor slow down   5
the production?

Thurber: It's possible. With humor you have to look out for traps.   6
You're likely to be very gleeful with what you've first put down, and you
think it's fine, very funny. One reason you go over and over it is to make the
piece sound less as if you were having a lot of fun with it yourself. You try to
play it down. In fact, if there's such a thing as a *New Yorker* style, that would
be it—playing it down. . . .

Interviewers: Does it bother you to talk about the stories on which   7
you're working? It bothers many writers, though it would seem that particularly the humorous story is polished through retelling.

Thurber: Oh, yes. I often tell them at parties and places. And I write   8
them there too.

Interviewers: You write them?   9

Thurber: I never quite know when I'm not writing. Sometimes my wife   10
comes up to me at a party and says, "Dammit, Thurber, stop writing." She
usually catches me in the middle of a paragraph. Or my daughter will look
up from the dinner table and ask, "Is he sick?" "No," my wife says, "he's
writing something." I have to do it that way on account of my eyes. I still
write occasionally—in the proper sense of the word—using black crayon on
yellow paper and getting perhaps twenty words to the page. My usual
method, though, is to spend the mornings turning over the text in my
mind. Then in the afternoon, between two and five, I call in a secretary and
dictate to her. I can do about two thousand words. It took me about ten
years to learn.

—James Thurber, *Writers at Work*, First Series

WRITING EXERCISE

*Write an essay that explains your usual method of writing an essay. Consider questions
like these:*

Which portion of the process gets your primary attention: prewriting,
    drafting, or revising?

How do you handle each part?
Where do your ideas come from?
How do you develop your ideas?
What do you do about titles?
Do you use an outline?

Paragraphs

Essays usually develop as a series of interconnected paragraphs, all supporting a single main idea expressed (or sometimes unexpressed) in a thesis sentence. The way the paragraphs develop is sometimes established by the thesis sentence, as Chapter 3 explains. In the following thesis sentence, for example, the method of development is included with the statement of subject and the assertion about the subject:

> The art of ditch diving is in the elegance with which you perform three distinct actions.
>
> —Tom Bodett, "Ditch Diving"

Here the subject is ditch diving and the assertion is that to make ditch diving an art you need to perform three actions elegantly. In reading this essay, you expect to read not only about something called ditch diving but also about three actions that are important to it.

A paragraph is a unit of writing, an unspecified number of sentences that focus on a central idea. The central idea is often expressed in a topic sentence—sometimes appearing at the beginning of the paragraph, sometimes at the end, and sometimes in the middle. When you develop your essay from an outline, especially a sentence outline, your topic sentence and its support will derive from a major section of the outline. When you develop your essay from freewriting, you may end up with one long unit that you need to examine to determine where your paragraph shifts occur. In revising, you may need to add topic sentences to assist your reader in seeing how your paragraphs are connected to your thesis sentence.

EXERCISE

Here is an essay in which the paragraph breaks have been removed. Read it through and then go back and mark (¶) the places where you think natural paragraph divisions should occur. Some paragraphs may have topic sentences and some may not, but all paragraphs should concern a central idea. When you have made your decisions, compare your paragraphing with your classmates' and try to explain whatever disagreements you discover.

Youngster's Goosefish Catch Remains as a Vivid Memory

[1]I snagged the prehistoric-looking goosefish when I was ten years old. [2] I caught it on my new fishing pole. [3]I miss the times when I could claim any fish that was caught on my fishing pole simply because it got hooked on my pole. [4]Did it matter that my dad hauled in the fish most of the way? [5]No. [6]The catch was still mine, because it liked my worm better—and I didn't even put it on the hook. [7]The Massachusetts inlet called Cape Cod Bay was where I hooked swimmers such as flounder, striped bass, bluefish, tautog, skates, and eels. [8]I spent every early June of my childhood in Truro with my family. [9]And every June I claimed nearly every fish. [10]And there was Dad. [11]He'd prepare the lines, bait the hooks, reel in the fish, remove the hooks, clean the fish . . . and allow me to take the credit, as I so often did. [12]Most years we stayed with the Bardwells, a transplanted family from my home-town of Emden, Illinois. [13]"Doc" Bardwell had delivered me and been my doctor for my first few years. [14]Doc is a cigar-puffing, pipe-smoking man of many expletives. [15]He'd complain plenty as we tried to get out the door to go fishing, wondering if we had all the equipment, or enough to eat. [16]But despite all the hassle, he was always more than willing to take Dad and me on little fishing excursions on his boat. [17]On one of the these trips, I caught the most exotic fish I had ever snagged before the goosefish. [18]I hooked a dogfish—I had a knack for catching the fish with other animal names attached to them. [19]Of course, a dogfish looks nothing like a dog. [20]It's actually a small shark, and this one was small—a couple feet long at the most. [21]But the goosefish. . . . [22]I had heard of it, probably from Dad and Doc. [23]Dad had read that a fisherman found seven whole ducks in one gutted goosefish. [24]"Sure," I thought. [25]That morning we were jigging for mackerel to use as trolling bait for bluefish. [26]But I preferred to fish for the familiar flounder, which usually camp out on the ocean floor. [27]So Dad had rigged my line and I'd set it deep. [28]Doc caught a squid, which he decided to keep for bait. [29]As he was poking at it, trying to get it to squirt its cloaking substance, I saw my pole dip. [30]I thought the largest flounder on record must've been at the end of my line. [31]I attempted to reel it in, but I barely even budged the line. [32]Good ol' Dad stepped in once again. [33]The goose-fish broke the water. [34]All I saw was a mouth—at least a foot wide. [35]And teeth. [36]Teeth upon teeth. [37]"What is that? [38]What d'ya' got there?" Doc bellowed. [39]"Geez, is that a goosefish? [40]Hold on," he said as he killed the engine and grabbed the gaff hook. [41]As Doc swung the hook toward the angered monster, the fish snapped and broke the line. [42]The goosefish slowly settled to its dark underwater home. [43]That fish was by far the ugliest, scariest-looking creature I'd seen in my life. [44]And I'd only seen the mouth. [45]I owe my clear image of it now to a book of fish I looked at. [46]The goosefish is brown, two to three feet long, and can weigh up to 50 pounds. [47]I wish I could've just weighed it. [48]I'm sure we would have had no intention of keeping the thing. [49]But if I had known then what I know

now . . . . [50]The goosefish is also called a monkfish, in restaurants anyway. [51]Supposedly it's quite tasty, very similar to lobster. [52]If people only knew how that creature really looks. [53]Of course, lobsters aren't the most friendly looking seafood either. [54]But then, you wouldn't find seven whole ducks inside a lobster.

—Louisa Gorrell, *Milwaukee Sentinel*

How Writers Develop and Arrange Ideas

Some writers arrange their thoughts by making an outline or list and using it as a guide (see Chapter 3, "Outlining"). They feel that they work better if outlining is part of their prewriting. Some kinds of writing work especially well with this method—for example, research papers, reports, and other papers with circumscribed formats. Other writers prefer to let the form develop from their ideas. They discover what they mean to say through freewriting and rough drafting, then arrange and rearrange their ideas through extensive revision. This strategy can work well when writers are still exploring a topic and when they know the forms that a particular kind of writing conventionally takes. For inexperienced writers, letting the form develop without conscious effort can result in a piece of writing that is disorganized, with parts off the topic and no controlling idea. Whenever you begin your writing without a plan, think of it as freewriting and the resulting piece of writing as a rough draft, one that will require extensive revision.

Knowledge of conventional forms is useful at all stages of writing: prewriting, drafting, and revising. Consciously or unconsciously, writers need to know answers to such questions as these:

What makes a group of sentences a paragraph?
Where are thesis sentences commonly located?
How are paragraphs developed?
How are essays concluded?

One way of acquiring knowledge of this sort is to have someone *tell* you what essays and other pieces of writing are supposed to look like: "Thesis sentences frequently occur at the end of the introduction" or "Don't introduce any new information in your conclusion."

But learning by being told is much less efficient than learning by observing, imitating, and practicing. Think of how you learned to speak. It was not so much by having someone *tell* you how as by listening to other people speak. When you first learned to repeat a sound you had heard your mother say, something like "Da Da," and found that your father was exceedingly pleased when you uttered it, you continued making the sound. You had learned a word. Later on, as your family read you stories, you learned certain things about stories, such as the way they begin: phrases like "Once upon a time" or "There was once" or "Long ago in a faraway land." And when you wrote your first stories, you used these phrases. Throughout your education, you have used imitation, perhaps more than you realize.

You can also learn how other writers arrange their ideas through these processes. By practicing methods of arrangement similar to those of other writers, you learn some of the limitless variations of language. Writers learn from other writers. This kind of learning works with both a structured and an unstructured approach. The writing assignments in Part II call for a kind of reading that draws your attention to the way other writers use ideas and words. For a quick overview of the most common methods of developing and arranging ideas for writing, read the next section.

Methods of Developing and Arranging Paragraphs and Essays

In most writing, ideas are developed and arranged in a variety of patterns. Used singly or more often in combination, these patterns develop individual paragraphs or entire essays. You can use them as an aid to both reading and writing. In writing, you can use them in prewriting, drafting, and revising.

In your *reading,* you can increase your comprehension and retention, and perhaps even improve your reading speed, with an understanding of the writer's method of organization and idea development. If you know, for example, that a paragraph, an essay, or a textbook chapter is arranged by cause and effect, you will read actively for effects and causes. By relating the information in a causal way, you will make more sense of it and thus remember it better.

In your *writing,* these methods of development and arrangement can assist you not only in organizing your ideas but in developing, or discovering, them as well. You will notice similarities to the invention strategies suggested in Chapter 3. You can examine a topic *spatially,* for example, discovering details and relationships, and you can *compare* a new topic with something you are familiar with, examining similarities and differences and drawing conclusions. If you observe in your prewriting that you are asking mainly *when* questions, you may need chronology for arranging your ideas; if you are asking mainly *why* questions, you may need cause and effect. Taking advantage of the relationship between methods of development and arrangement and methods of invention can make your writing easier.

Sometimes the arrangement of ideas evolves as one writes. Topics and thesis sentences often determine the arrangement. In Chapter 11, for example, John McPhee sets out to explain the burning of a fireplace fire, and his ideas develop *chronologically.* If, after drafting the essay, he wanted to check the completeness and clarity of his details, he could read the draft chronologically to see if he had omitted anything or had events out of order.

The common methods for developing and arranging ideas are explained in the following sections.

Chronology or Sequence

Narrations of events and explanations of how things are done are arranged chronologically. **Chronology** is a simple time order. Here is an example:

> Four men lay snoring in the bamboo cabin while Torstein sat clicking with the Morse key and I was on steering watch. Just before midnight I caught sight of a quite unusual sea which came breaking astern of us right across the whole of my disturbed field of vision. Behind it I could see here and there the foaming crests of two more huge seas like the first, following hard on its heels. If we ourselves had not just passed the place, I should have been convinced that what I saw was high surf flung up over a dangerous shoal. I gave a warning shout, as the first sea came like a long wall sweeping after us in the moonlight, and wrenched the raft into position to take what was coming.
>
> —Thor Heyerdahl, *Kon-Tiki*

Did you notice that you read each occurrence as it related to the previous one? Heyerdahl gives you clues to the chronology: "Just before midnight," "as the first sea came." As you consider *space* in the next section, reread this paragraph for its spatial development.

Kon-Tiki, a book-length account of Heyerdahl's rafting adventure across the Pacific, is entirely narrative. More often, narratives are only a portion of a longer piece of writing, sometimes introductions. Jonathan Kozol, for example, introduces his essay on illiteracy with a narrative account of a day in the life of an illiterate man (see Chapter 11). In "Thinking Like a Mountain" (Chapter 6), Aldo Leopold supports his point about the extinction of wolves by narrating a hunting incident from his own life.

Space

Descriptions are often arranged **spatially,** usually from a single perspective. The object may be described vertically, horizontally, circularly—whatever is appropriate for the situation. In the following paragraph, note how the writer describes Sable Island, an ark of sand in the North Atlantic "where no land should be" and consequently a graveyard for sailors and ships.

> If reminders of death are everywhere on Sable, one realizes that he is also in the midst of great fecundity. Anytime I cast my eye around, seals

were feeding in the water or sunning on the beach, horses were grazing in the marram [grass] or galloping beside the surf, seabirds were filling the air with shrill sound. Sable is sanctuary as well as graveyard. Oppressive in light of human history, it is nevertheless a majestic natural place.

—Harry Thurston, "The Devil's Work Is an Ark of Sand"

In Chapter 14, student writer Susan Wollack spatially describes a teacher as she makes her point of disapproval. In Chapter 10, Rachel L. Carson uses spatial development to describe the Sargasso Sea, and George Gaylord Simpson the Patagonian wind.

EXERCISE

In Thurston's paragraph, arranged spatially, identify the topic sentence and the details that develop it. What is the function of the final sentence?

Classification

Some topics are arranged according to how they are **classified.** An essay on computer printers, for example, might be arranged by the method of printing: dot matrix, daisy wheel, laser, and others. The following paragraph introduces a chapter on the uses of computers in education:

The uses of computers can be categorized in many arbitrary ways. I shall focus on five of their most visible contemporary functions, as (1) game-playing devices, (2) information sources, (3) teaching machines, (4) creative tools, and (5) communication links. Most of my opening comments will focus on negative aspects of computers, but I shall end on a more optimistic note.

—Frank Smith, *Joining the Literacy Club*

Senator Albert Gore uses classification in "What Is Wrong with Us?" in Chapter 7, as he explains what he sees as five barriers to effective political action on the global environment. Judith Viorst in Chapter 12 classifies friends.

Comparison

Arrangement by **comparison** is called for when an essayist considers two or more subjects. This method has several subcategories. With it you might show similarities and differences, or advantages and disadvantages. You might first show similarities and then differences, or alternate between the two. Focusing on description of each item, you might first describe one item then the other, or alternate in describing two (or more) items. Comparison is a complicated arrangement to follow because you are dealing with more than one subject and you must treat each fairly.

The following paragraphs from an essay entitled "How to Get Rich Quick" explain, tongue in cheek, how to "get rich" by refraining from buying high-ticket items. After saving $150,000 a year by not renting an expensive apartment, the author saves more money by not buying a Mercedes-Benz.

> A short time later, while my wife and I were still just *nouveaux riches,* I saw one of those Mercedes-Benz station wagons. It was parked in front of the liquor store. The car was so new that it still had the dealer's price sticker in the window. Do you know what the manufacturer's suggested retail price was? It was almost $50,000.
>
> I was shocked. My wife and I have a station wagon, but it's just one of the normal brands. It has a front seat, a back seat, and a "way back," just like the Mercedes, and it cost only about a quarter as much. I did some on-the-spot arithmetic and decided not to trade up—a deal that left roughly $35,000 on the table for my wife and me.
>
> —David Owen, "How to Get Rich Quick"

The comparison arrangement here is simple: In the first paragraph Owen describes the Mercedes, and in the second he compares the couple's station wagon with it. Another example of comparison is the essay "We Celebrated Chanukah and Christmas" in Chapter 12, in which Terry Splett, a student writer, shows how a Judeo-Christian family celebrated the two holidays.

EXERCISE

In magazines or other reading, find an example of comparison *and one of* classification *as methods of development and bring them to class. With a partner, discover what features your comparisons have in common and what features your classification samples share. Then discuss what makes the comparisons different from the classification samples.*

Analogy

As a method of developing and arranging ideas, **analogy** has some similarities to comparison, but its function is different. In contrast to comparison, which focuses on two or more subjects somewhat equally, analogy concentrates on one subject, explaining it with references to the second. In "Senses" in Chapter 11, for example, George R. Harrison describes the eye by means of the terminology for cameras. Analogy takes the form "Subject A is like Subject B," in which the writer is focusing on Subject A, an unknown or difficult concept, and relating it to Subject B, a familiar concept or object.

In the following paragraph, Mark Twain only apparently describes knowledge of a New York City street. He is really using this description to present a pilot's knowledge of the Mississippi River, since his readers are more likely to know about walking urban streets, be they in New York or any large city, than to know about navigating the Mississippi.

> One cannot easily realize what a tremendous thing it is to know every trivial detail of twelve hundred miles of river and know it with absolute exactness. If you will take the longest street in New York and travel up and down it, conning its features patiently until you know every house and window and lamppost and big and little sign by heart, and know them so accurately that you can instantly name the one you are abreast of when you are set down at random in that street in the middle of an inky black night, you will then have a tolerable notion of the amount and exactness of a pilot's knowledge who carries the Mississippi River in his head. And then, if you will go on until you know every street-crossing, the character, size, and position of the crossing-stones, and the varying depth of mud in each of these numberless places, you will have some idea of what the pilot must know in order to keep a Mississippi steamer out of trouble. Next, if you will take half of the signs in that long street, and *change their places* once a month, and still manage to know their new positions accurately on dark nights, and keep up with these repeated changes without making any mistakes, you will understand what is required of a pilot's peerless memory by the fickle Mississippi.
>
> —*Life on the Mississippi*

Analogy is useful in explaining. Use it with caution, however, bearing in mind that analogous things are never alike in all ways. City streets and the Mississippi River, for example, have obvious differences.

EXERCISE

Take Twain's analogy a little further, trying to uncover other ways in which a river is like a city street. Find additional examples of analogies in your reading.

Cause and Effect

A very common method of arrangement is **cause and effect**—common because it answers questions that begin Why? Writers using this method sometimes begin with a single cause, like lack of rainfall, and then discuss several effects, like decreased crop yields, lower water tables, and increased respiratory illnesses. Or they may begin with an effect and discuss causes—for example, several causes of increased respiratory illnesses.

Here is a paragraph that begins with a single cause, sodium cyanide—called "magic" by its Filipino fish collectors—and ends with its effects:

> A squirt into the coral, and all the fish hiding there come out spinning and jerking. Any angelfish, triggerfish, squirrelfish, or blue tangs the diver catches in his hand. Most of the rest are unmarketable and left spiraling and fluttering amid poisoned corals. For every fish captured alive by cyanide, nine die, by the estimate of Steve Robinson of the International Marinelife Alliance. "Magic" is black magic. Cyanide fishing is an effective method in the short term, disastrous in the long. The chemical is bad for the health of the divers, who suffer skin lesions and hair loss and sometimes fatally poison themselves; bad for the longevity of the cyanide-shocked fish; and fatal for the coral upon which the aquarium-fish business—and millions of Filipinos—depend.
>
> —Kenneth Brower, "State of the Reef"

A more complicated cause-and-effect arrangement is a causal chain, in which the writer starts with either a cause or an effect and then works backward or forward with related causes and effects. Figure 4-1 starts with a cause, lack of rainfall, and traces related causes and effects. In this chain, each effect becomes the next cause. The first cause, lack of rainfall, results in the ultimate effect, higher water costs.

In Part II you will see additional examples of development by causes and effects. In Chapter 6, student writer Lorrie Anderson explains the effects of a father's alcoholism and Vietnam veteran Mark Baker shows effects of the evils of war. In a Chapter 10 essay, George Gaylord Simpson describes the Patagonian wind by showing its effects, and in Chapter 11 a short article from *Audubon* magazine informs readers on the effects of releasing helium-filled balloons.

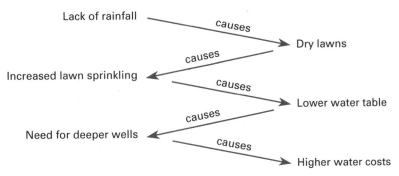

Figure 4-1. Causal chain.

EXERCISE

List the effects of cyanide poisoning detailed in the paragraph by Kenneth Brower. Find other examples of cause-and-effect development in your reading.

Exemplification

Much writing is developed by **examples.** In the following paragraph, a specific illustration explains the topic, or first, sentence:

> Here and there we find dramatic illustration of the fact that the tides affect the whole ocean, from its surface to its floor. The meeting of opposing tidal currents in the Strait of Messina creates whirlpools (one of them is Charybdis of classical fame) which so deeply stir the waters of the strait that fish bearing all the marks of abyssal existence, their eyes atrophied or abnormally large, their bodies studded with phosphorescent organs, frequently are cast up on the lighthouse beach, and the whole area yields a rich collection of deep-sea fauna for the Institute of Marine Biology at Messina.
>
> —Rachel L. Carson, *The Sea Around Us*

This paragraph shows how methods of development are often combined: Most of the paragraph *exemplifies* the topic sentence—through *description*. In addition, the topic sentence implies cause and effect, so the descriptive sentences show the effects brought about by the ocean tides. You will find development through exemplification throughout this book.

Definition

Definitions of terms are frequently necessary in writing. Sometimes you encounter an entire essay devoted to definition, but more frequently you find paragraphs clarifying terms. Any time you use terms that your readers may not understand—whether the terms are totally unfamiliar or are unfamiliar only in the way you are using them—you need to define them. In the following paragraph, the author takes a familiar term and tells his readers how he is using it:

> "Now . . . this" is commonly used on radio and television newscasts to indicate that what one has just heard or seen has no relevance to what one is about to hear or see, or possibly to anything one is ever likely to hear or see. The phrase is a means of acknowledging the fact that the world as mapped by the speeded-up electronic media has no order or meaning and is not to be taken seriously. There is no murder so brutal, no earthquake so devastating, no political blunder so costly—for that

matter, no ball score so tantalizing or weather report so threatening—that it cannot be erased from our minds by a newscaster saying, "Now . . . this." The newscaster means that you have thought long enough on the previous matter (approximately forty-five seconds), that you must not be morbidly preoccupied with it (let us say, for ninety seconds), and that you must now give your attention to another fragment of news or a commercial.

—Neil Postman, *Amusing Ourselves to Death*

Definitions often use methods of development other than telling what a term means. In "Taste," in Chapter 11, William Zinsser defines an intangible subject, taste in writing, mainly through exemplification—giving examples of taste in clothing and in the arts, plus examples of what he calls timeless taste. In "A Third of the Nation Cannot Read These Words," also in Chapter 11, Jonathan Kozol uses a narration (chronology) and specific details (exemplification) to define illiteracy.

Question and Answer

Writers sometimes like to lead into their subjects by asking questions. They then develop the paragraph or essay with answers. Here is such a paragraph:

Have you ever stopped to wonder what it would be like to see two completely different visions simultaneously, one with each eye? That, of course, is what fish do. Our eyes focused on the same object report a single merged image to the brain; the fish's brain receives two images at once, for its eyes face in opposite directions and cannot focus simultaneously on the same object.

—Eugenie Clark, *Lady with a Spear*

The writer, a noted ichthyologist, then devotes several more paragraphs to answering her question, asking another challenging question along the way: "Can a fish remember with its left eye something it has learned with its right?"

Beginning a paragraph or an essay with a question assists the reader in sharing the writer's interest in the subject. It focuses the subject for both writer and reader. In Chapter 15, Peter F. Drucker asks, "What can you learn in college that will help you in being an employee?" Because the answers to introductory questions are not readily discovered, readers will read on.

EXERCISE

Rewrite the Rachel L. Carson paragraph on page 74 to begin with a question. What changes do you notice accompanying the changes in phrasing? Consider features such as emphasis, audience attention, and style.

Problem and Solution

The **problem and solution** method of development is similar to the question and answer method, except that it sets up a problem instead of asking a question. Here is an example:

> It's Friday afternoon, and you have almost survived another week of classes. You are just looking forward dreamily to the week end when the English instructor says: "For Monday you will turn in a five-hundred-word composition on college football."
>
> Well, that puts a good big hole in the week end. You don't have any strong views on college football one way or the other. You get rather excited during the season and go to all the home games and find it rather more fun than not. On the other hand, the class has been reading Robert Hutchins in the anthology and perhaps Shaw's "Eighty-Yard Run," and from the class discussion you have got the idea that the instructor thinks college football is for the birds. You are no fool. You can figure out what side to take.
>
> —Paul Roberts, "How to Say Nothing in Five Hundred Words"

The problem is established: trying to please the teacher with an essay. In the remainder of the essay, the author attempts a solution.

Like question-and-answer development, problem and solution challenges the reader to contemplate a situation with the writer. The introduction to Terry Splett's essay on Chanukah and Christmas in Chapter 12 sets up the problem of how a Judeo-Christian family celebrates the December holidays, beginning with the children trying to understand the family's Sunday morning habit of the children going off to Sunday school while their father stays home and makes breakfast for them. Splett's readers are thus involved in a situation they may not have considered previously.

Emphasis

The **emphatic** method of arrangement is based on the idea that the most notable positions in a piece of writing are the beginning and the end. Writers therefore may start with the most important point and work to the least important, or start with the least significant and move toward the strongest point. In this example, the writer saves his emphasis for the end:

> When I was seven I was playing dodgeball on a warm March day at the school playground next to my house. A huge, cloudy icicle hung from the school roof, three stories up. It was a seven-foot dagger that heroically withstood a daily cannonade of snowballs as my playmates and I tried to pick off icicle after icicle.
>
> I stood beneath Fang, poised in case the ball was thrown my way. Suddenly, the guy who was "it" whirled and flung the ball at my head. I

ducked, scooted to my right, then instinctively flinched as I heard a monstrous, growling explosion. Ice was skidding everywhere. Fang had fallen—right where I had been standing.

—Gary Legwold, "The Crystalline Challenge"

John McPhee uses emphasis in his description of fire in "Firewood," Chapter 11. Though he is using chronology to explain the process of burning, he saves for his last sentence his identification of the burning compounds.

EXERCISE

Now that you know where Gary Legwold was going with his narrative about the giant icicle, reread his paragraphs and identify words and phrases that set you up for the ending. Then rewrite the paragraphs so that you state at the beginning the fact that the icicle fell. Notice the change in emphasis and use of details.

General to Specific and Specific to General

Two related ways of arranging ideas are from general to specific and from specific to general. A writer using the **general to specific** method would start with a thesis or topic sentence and develop it with specific statements and illustrations. A writer using the **specific to general** method would accumulate illustrations and specific statements, finally arriving at a statement of thesis or topic. The following paragraph is developed from general to specific, beginning with a topic sentence followed by specific statements that develop the topic:

Wherever climate has permitted it, men have evaporated salt from sea water for many centuries. Under the burning sun of the tropics the ancient Greeks, Romans, and Egyptians harvested the salt men and animals everywhere must have in order to live. Even today in parts of the world that are hot and dry and where drying winds blow, solar evaporation of salt is practiced—on the shores of the Persian Gulf, in China, India, and Japan, in the Philippines, and on the coast of California and the alkali flats of Utah.

—Rachel L. Carson, *The Sea Around Us*

This next example is developed from specific to general. The paragraphs have the specific statements first, with the final sentence stating the topic.

Given a paycheck and the stub that lists the usual deductions, 26 percent of adult Americans cannot determine if their paycheck is correct. Thirty-six percent, given a W-4 form, cannot enter the right number of exemptions in the proper places on the form. Forty-four percent, when given a series of "help wanted" ads, cannot match their qualifications to the job requirements. Twenty-two percent cannot address a letter well enough to guarantee that it will reach its destination. Twenty-four percent cannot add their own correct return address to the same envelope. Twenty percent cannot understand an "equal opportunity" announcement. Over 60 percent, given a series of "for sale" advertisements for products new and used, cannot calculate the difference between prices for a new and used appliance. Over 20 percent cannot write a check that will be processed by their bank—or will be processed in the right amount. Over 40 percent are unable to determine the correct amount of change they should receive, given a cash register receipt and the denomination of the bill used for payment.

From these and other forms of evidence, the APL* concludes that 30 million men and women are now "functionally incompetent." Another 54 million "just get by." This total of 84 million far exceeds all other estimates that we have seen.

—Jonathan Kozol, *Illiterate America*

These two methods of arrangement, plus emphasis, are usually used with another type of development. Carson's paragraph, for example, uses *exemplification,* naming specific examples of salt harvests. The Kozol paragraphs likewise use *exemplification,* piling up statistical evidence of illiteracy. In addition, each example presents an *effect* of illiteracy. (In Part II you will find other examples of arrangement by general to specific and specific to general.)

These, then, are some of the common methods of developing and arranging ideas in writing: chronology, space, classification, comparison, analogy, cause and effect, exemplification, definition, question and answer, problem and solution, emphasis, and general to specific and specific to general. They may be used to develop and organize paragraphs and entire essays, and, as we have seen, they often are used in combination.

You may be thinking that usually when you read you are unconscious of the writer's method of development, just as you are unconscious of grammar and punctuation. When the form and conventions are what you expect, you don't notice them. If you sometimes read *as a writer,* however, you *will* notice how other writers develop and arrange their ideas and possibly give yourself more options when you write.

---

*Adult Performance Level: A study carried out in 1973 at the University of Texas to identify how many adults were unable to cope with the responsibilities of everyday life.—D.G.

Introductions, Conclusions, and Titles

Introductions, conclusions, and titles are often the most troublesome parts of writing. Whether you are writing essays for school, letters for business or personal communication, or reports, if you're like many writers you may tell yourself that you'll be fine if you can just get started. Then when you get to the end, you're stumped all over again: How can you finish it up?

Introductions

Here are several introductory paragraphs from essays in Part II. Read them and see what you anticipate happening in the essays.

A deep chesty bawl echoes from rimrock to rimrock, rolls down the mountain, and fades into the far blackness of the night. It is an outburst of wild defiant sorrow, and of contempt for all the adversities of the world.
—Aldo Leopold, "Thinking Like a Mountain"

I had a little puppy for a while in Vietnam. For a period of three days, I would take this little puppy and squeeze it until it would yelp. Or twist its little paw.
—Mark Baker, "The Taste of Evil"

When I announced I was running for President, I said the greenhouse effect, the depletion of the ozone layer, and the global ecological crisis will, by the end of this election year, be recognized as the most serious issue facing this country and the world. Three days later, a George Will column ridiculed the naiveté of a politician who could imagine that issues of this kind would be politically salable.
—Albert Gore, "What Is Wrong with Us?"

Appearing at times as if an artist has splashed paint on tree trunks and across the faces of rocks, lichens present a display as vibrant as wildflowers. Yet most people know very little about these exotic plants. Striking in variety as well as in color, lichens are useful to humans and serve as excellent reminders of both nature's fragility and its resilience.
—Kathleen Almy, "Lichens: Nature's Paintbox"

If a neatly adjusted time machine could take you back to the Main Street of an American town in 1990, to look about you with your present-day eyes, your first exclamation would probably be, "But look at all those horses!"
—Frederick Lewis Allen, "The Way It Was"

We shy persons need to write a letter now and then, or else we'll dry up and blow away. It's true. And I speak as one who loves to reach for the phone, dial the number, and talk. I say, "Big Bopper here—what's shakin', babes?" The telephone is to shyness what Hawaii is to February, it's a way out of the woods, *and yet:* a letter is better.

—Garrison Keillor, "How to Write a Personal Letter"

Life is filled with things that are assumed to be true because they are "obvious" or "self-evident." It's always a shock to learn that one of those things is not true at all. It gives you a chance to imagine what it was like to hear from the town crier that the world was round rather than, as was obvious and self-evident, flat.

—Suzette Haden Elgin, "Telephone Listening"

One fairly clear observation from these introductory paragraphs is that there are many right ways to begin an essay. For instance, Frederick Lewis Allen's essay describes town life in 1900, so his introduction sets the scene. Garrison Keillor's essay is mildly serious, and so is his introduction. Each introduction is appropriate for its essay.

Your introductions may be easier to write if you think of them as temporary placeholders. They don't have to be perfect before you get on with the essay. After you find out what your essay actually says, you can always revise your beginning to tell your reader what to expect. At that time you can see that your introduction is appropriate for your essay. Sometimes writers even postpone writing an introduction until after they have composed the essay. Each of the preceding introductions begins a *revised* essay. For the *reader,* then, your revised introductions should have five features. They should

1. Be consistent with the purpose of the essay,
2. Be interesting,
3. Usually present the subject and your position on it (thesis),
4. Establish the essay's tone,
5. Establish a relationship between you and your audience.

The introductions quoted here are consistent with the purposes of the essays they introduce. They employ some of these means of heightening interest:

Attention-getting statements
Curiosity-arousing details
Background statements
Humor
Challenging statements
Questions
Quotations
Statistics
Narratives

They also establish a **tone** for their essays, perhaps one of these: humorous, serious, objective, cynical, sad, contentious, or angry. Tone in writing is comparable to the sound of your voice. The way you sound in writing reflects your attitude toward your subject and your audience. Tone should be established in your introduction and be consistent throughout your essay.

EXERCISE

What is the tone of each of the example introductions? How do the writers establish their voices? What do their voices, or tones, tell you about their attitudes toward their subjects and audiences?

The common location for thesis sentences is the introduction; the thesis sentence is often the final sentence of the introduction. But, as noted in Chapter 3, theses sometimes occur in the conclusion, as with an essay arranged from specific to general, and sometimes are even left unstated, being implied instead. The accepted convention for academic writing, however, is that theses be stated.

(The essays in Part II illustrate other ways in which writers introduce their essays.)

Conclusions

The easiest way to write a **conclusion** is to reread your entire essay, then concentrate on the introduction, in particular the thesis sentence, and write something that finishes what you started. Restate your thesis, answer a question you asked, refer to an anecdote you began with, or summarize your solution to the problem you introduced. If you don't write your essay at the last minute, you can let it rest for a while, then reread it later, when a conclusion may easily occur to you. Conclusions usually do not present new information, examples, or opinions. They are usually only a few sentences long.

Titles

Unless you have a great idea for a **title** before you begin an essay, save its composition for last, because you will have a much better idea of how to describe your essay *after* you've written it. Titles should be descriptive: "The Eyes of Fishes," "Basic Flight Theory." They should also be short; in fact, they're usually fragments: *Illiterate America,* "The Decline of Heroes," "Command Performance." And they should be interesting, for it is usually the title that convinces a reader to pay attention to what you've written: "Bringing Back the Beast of Lore," "Pondering the Personal Pronoun Problem."

Do not underline the title of your essay or enclose it in quotation marks. Just center it near the top of your first page.

Completing the First Draft

Drafting is more than arranging ideas. When you write you examine your knowledge in new ways, and you *make new ideas*. Through the complex activity of engaging in composition, you not only communicate with a reader; you also sometimes surprise yourself with new insights by the time you get to your final period and your first draft is finished. You have probably already done some revising, but you still have much ahead of you. Chapter 5 discusses some techniques.

EXERCISE

Read the following paragraphs and identify examples of these methods of development and arrangement:

Chronology
Space
Classification
Comparison
Analogy
Cause and effect
Exemplification
Definition
Question and answer
Problem and solution
Emphasis
General to specific and specific to general

You are likely to find more than one method for most paragraphs. In what other ways might each paragraph be developed and arranged?

1. "Now that *Ms.* has made it, we're going to have to settle the problem of the masculine pronoun's taking charge when the gender is undetermined, as in "Each member should supply *his* own utensils." Today, a great many people are laboriously conscientious in saying things like "his or her own utensils" or "his/her own utensils." In the

past few years, I've received dozens of suggestions for new pronouns to cover both genders. The most recent was from Thomas S. Jackson, a Washington, D.C., lawyer, who says that the use of "him or her," "he or she," and so on, "is both awkward and wasteful." He suggests some new pronouns."

—Thomas H. Middleton, "Pondering the Personal Pronoun Problem"

2. "Until recently, seeking has been done primarily by boys and merging by girls. Girls could seek scholarship so long as it didn't interfere with popularity. It was fine to take a summer job, but not to embark on a serious career. They could train their talents in dance lessons, drama clubs, piano recitals, church choirs, any of which would suit them well for a lifetime of pleasing. Unless—and this apprehension lurked always in the back of the mind—they turned out to be gifted. For then they would be forced to make a painful choice: either marriage or mastery of their art. Most of them gave up the lessons."

—Gail Sheehy, *Passages*

3. "If direct taxes upon the wages of labour have not always occasioned a proportionable rise in those wages, it is because they have generally occasioned a considerable fall in the demand for labour. The declension of industry, the decrease of employment for the poor, the diminution of the annual produce of the land and labour of the country, have generally been the effects of such taxes. In consequence of them, however, the price of labour must always be higher than it otherwise would have been in the actual state of the demand: and this enhancement of price, together with the profit of those who advance it, must always be finally paid by the landlords and consumers."

—Adam Smith, *The Wisdom of Adam Smith*

4. "I used to worry that computers would become so powerful and sophisticated as to take the place of human minds. The notion of Artificial Intelligence used to scare me half to death. Already, a large enough machine can do all sorts of intelligent things beyond our capacities: calculate in a split second the answers to mathematical problems requiring years for a human brain, draw accurate pictures from memory, even manufacture successions of sounds with a disarming resemblance to real music. Computers can translate textbooks, write dissertations of their own for doctorates, even speak in machine-tooled, inhuman phonemes any words read off from a printed page. They can communicate with one another, holding consultations and committee meetings of their own in networks around the earth.

—Lewis Thomas, "The Corner of the Eye"

5. "The Pilgrims were not nineteenth century pietists, or quietists. They were not pale plaster saints, hollow and bloodless. They were men— and women, too—of courage and conviction, strong and positive in their attitudes, prepared to sacrifice much for their principles, even their very lives. Far from being Victorians, they were children of another and a greater age, the Elizabethan, and in their lives reflected many of the qualities of that amazing age—its restlessness and impatience with old ways, its passionate enthusiasms, its eager curiosity and daring speculation in all fields, its boldness in action, its abounding and apparently inexhaustible energies."

—George F. Willison, *Saints and Strangers*

CHAPTER 5

The Writing Process: Revising

*Revision is, indeed, re-seeing and it goes on continually in the
composing process.*

—Ann Berthoff

Writers **revise.** They want to make their meaning clearer, more explicit,
self-explanatory. They want to see if they have said everything they intended to
say, if they have said anything they want to retract or rephrase before
someone else reads it, and if they have made all the necessary connections.
They want to make their style clear, direct, precise, concise, and appropriate
to the situation—taking into account their readers, the subject and purpose
of the writing, and their roles as writers. Writers want to avoid offending or
confusing their audiences. They want to speak with authority. They want to
say everything necessary for clarity but no more than necessary. They want
to use the right words, spell them correctly, arrange them in their sentences
to prevent awkwardness, avoid inappropriate usage, have smooth and logical transitions between sentences and paragraphs, relate all their paragraphs to their thesis sentences, give appropriate signals with punctuation,
and so on.

This is what revising is. It's not just correcting spelling and punctuation,
though correcting is part of revising. It's not just replacing words with
synonyms, though it is that too. Nor is it just searching for sentence fragments or faulty verbs or dangling modifiers, though revision does include
those chores. It's not even just checking organization or coherence or
thought development. Revising is more like *reconsidering, rethinking,* and
reseeing. James Thurber, a noted humorist whose thoughts on writing are
quoted in Chapter 4, admits that his writing often does not take shape until
the seventh draft.

In writing your school papers, you probably don't have time to complete
seven drafts. But you do have time to revise. If you use your available time

well and understand revising thoroughly, you can produce papers unlike Thurber's first drafts that his wife calls "high-school stuff." Remember that revising occurs at all stages of writing. You may revise while prewriting—altering your plans even before you begin drafting, adjusting your outline or thesis, deleting thoughts you decide are no longer important, considering and reconsidering how you will begin, and so on. And, like most people, you probably also revise while drafting—adding or deleting sentences, rearranging words, correcting typing errors, and making all the other changes writers make when, pausing to consider what to say next, they go back and reread what they have just written.

But even with the adjustments you make as you compose, the writing is likely not perfect when you have finally put down your last period. You may know now what you want to say, but your draft is not ready for a reader. This first draft is often called a "rough draft," and sometimes not even a "first" but a "zero" draft, after which counting begins; sometimes writers call it a "discovery" draft, a "writer-based" draft appropriate only for the writer's eyes, or "speculative" draft. Call it what you will, it can be improved.

Revising, like drafting, is something only the writer can do. Other people can give you suggestions, but only you, the writer, can make the changes. Only you know what details you can add, how you planned to connect two ideas, which ideas are irrelevant, and whether rephrasing a sentence alters the meaning you intended. Revising, like drafting, is making and discovering meaning, clarifying thoughts by putting them into words and adjusting those words. When you write something, you discover what you mean to say and your purpose for saying it. Because others may read for different meanings and purposes, they may not see what you intended. At the same time, however, audience response is crucial information for a writer, since the main point of writing is to get an idea across. So ask for and accept the feedback of other readers; then weigh their criticisms with your own intentions and clarify your writing as necessary.

This chapter will show you some ways of reconsidering, rethinking, and reseeing your writing. We will look mainly at *reading as a reader, using invention questions, mapping or outlining, applying a checklist,* and *getting feedback from others.* The chapter treats revision as that part of the writing process usually needed after drafting; however, bear in mind that revision occurs anywhere in the procedure. The end of the chapter will treat two related parts of writing: *editing* and *proofreading.*

Reading as a Reader

Chapter 1 recommends that you read as a *writer* to develop a sensitivity to how other writers express their ideas. This chapter now advises you, when reading what *you* have written, to read as a *reader*—to put yourself in your reader's place. Whatever method you use for revising your writing, you have to go back and reread. You are, after all, your first reader. If you don't like or understand what you read, you can probably assume other readers won't either. Novelist William Styron, discussing his writing process, says, "Every day I pick up the story or whatever it is I've been working on and read it through. If I enjoy it as a reader then I know I'm getting along all right." *Enjoyment* is his criterion for criticism. "The writer," he says, "must criticize his own work as a reader" (*Writers at Work*, 1st series, 278).

Can you put some distance between yourself and your drafts and read them as a reader, not as their writer and creator? Your readers are limited to the words you put on a page; they can't read your mind, and they can't ask you questions. So if, when you set out to revise, you read your drafts critically as a *reader*, you may discover that you have omitted some details or that you did not make all your connections clear. As a *writer*, you know what those details are, and to you everything seems to flow logically. Reading as a reader, you see what is missing and unclear.

When you reread your first draft, you will probably find parts that you enjoy and others that are too rough for even you to appreciate. These parts you pause to tinker with, trying to clarify your sentences and paragraphs so that they say what you meant to say. *Meaning* is undoubtedly the major object of criticism. If your writing doesn't say—directly and unambiguously—what you intended, then it must be revised. With your first draft, ask questions like these:

> Does my main idea come through clearly?
> Do my details lend sufficient support to that central idea?
> Is it clear how all parts of my essay are connected to one another?

Revising Is Changing Meaning

Anything you do to change the meaning of your writing is revising. You can alter meaning in four ways:

> Adding   Substituting
> Deleting   Rearranging

These four actions operate on a number of levels. You can **add** a paragraph or a whole section, significantly building on your meaning, or you can add a brief example, even an adjective, a comma, a transition, or an underline. You can **delete** a paragraph, a sentence, a comma, or a conjunction, eliminating wordiness and repetition and combining sentences to achieve conciseness and variety. You can **substitute** a verb, a phrase, an example, a paragraph, a sentence. And you can **rearrange** a paragraph, some examples, the spelling of a word, words in a sentence.

Let's examine more closely how changes such as these qualify as changes in meaning. Correcting spelling is usually thought of as editing, something anyone, even a computer, can do because meaning is not involved. Adjusting punctuation, too, is often thought of as editing. Changing meaning, then, is thought of as occurring on a global scale, affecting the entire essay: revising a thesis sentence, adding or omitting a paragraph, altering one's writing voice. These are significant revisions, to be sure. However, sometimes just adding a comma or changing spelling alters meaning. Consider what happens when you add commas to this sentence:

My brother who is still in elementary school won a new Mazda in a raffle.

My brother, who is still in elementary school, won a new Mazda in a raffle.

In the second version, the meaning is different. The first version implies more than one brother, with the *who* clause identifying which one; the second implies a single brother, and the *who* clause supplies additional information about him. Since only the writer is likely to know how many brothers are involved, only the writer can revise such a sentence; only the writer knows what changes can be made without saying something other than what was meant. Unless the writer makes those changes, the reader may be misled.

When you revise, you do change the meaning—sometimes slightly, sometimes a great deal. If you revise "dirty cars" to "dust-covered cars," you've changed the meaning a little, yet significantly. If you correct your spelling from "hop" to "hope," you've changed the meaning more significantly. And if you change the order of your paragraphs so that they read from least emphatic to most emphatic instead of the other way around, you have made a greatly significant change.

Read your essay as many times as necessary to get it in shape for a reader. At some point you may need to make a fresh, preferably typed, copy because the original is getting too messy. Then continue revising. On one of your readings, read your essay aloud so you can listen for awkward phrases and sentences.

Revising with a Word Processor

If you do your composing on a word processor, revising is easier in many ways than it would be with typed or handwritten copies. You can add or delete on the screen and still have a clean, readable text. You can rearrange easily, moving large chunks from one part of your text to another. In an overtype mode, you can substitute words and sentences without deleting the originals. But the process of drafting and revising on the word processor has features that you should guard against. Because of the ease of revision, you might muddy your writing by making unnecessary additions and substitutions. Through deletion you could lose some sentences you wish you had kept; perhaps you can retrieve them, perhaps not. In moving your paragraphs around, you may undo your original connections.

Here are some tips for revising on the word processor:

1. Unless your word-processing program saves automatically, *always* save your composition before printing a paper copy. The best of us make mistakes or encounter power failures. While drafting or revising, save text every few minutes.
2. Always print a paper copy to refer to while you are revising; then work with both the paper copy and the screen.
3. Look for repetitions and inconsistencies that occurred as a result of your having before you only a screen at a time while you composed.
4. Look for digressions and irrelevancies that might have occurred because composing is so easy on the word processor.

You are more likely to achieve the distance you need for reading as a *reader* when you revise from your paper draft than when you read from the screen, where you have been the writer. Also, with a paper draft you can more readily conceptualize your paper as a whole and avoid inconsistencies in structure and development; you can see how well you have connected sections and can detect unnecessary repetitions.

EXERCISE

Here are the first four drafts of a paragraph that introduces an essay about the advantages of low-intensity workouts. Read each draft and decide how the writer uses (1) addition, (2) deletion, (3) substitution, and (4) rearrangement. Then ask, How does the writer discover meaning through revising?

First Draft

Most people think exercise is too much work. They're too busy or it makes them too tired. They're satisfied being couch potatoes. They tried working out and pushed themselves to the limit. Finally they become frusturated and used one of the many excuses to drop out: too busy, too tired, sick or injured and unable to continue.

Second Draft

Many people don't get enough exercise because they think it's too much work. They're satisfied being couch potatoes. When they tried working out, they pushed themselves to their limits, telling themselves, "No pain, no gain." Finally they became frustrated and used one of the many excuses for dropping out: too busy, too tired, sick or injured and unable to continue. Instead, a low-intensity workout may be the answer.

Third Draft

Many people don't get enough exercise because they think that exercising is too much work. They tried working out once or twice, even signed up for sixteen weeks of Nautilus, telling themselves, "No pain, no gain," but they finally became frustrated. They didn't see any improvement in their health or appearance, and they were tired of being tired and sweaty. So they used one of the many excuses for dropping out: too busy, too tired, or sick or injured. What they didn't know was that a low-intensity workout provides the same benefits of improved health and appearance but at a more enjoyable pace.

Fourth Draft

Are you one of the many people who don't get enough exercise because you think that exercising is too much work? Perhaps you've tried working out once or twice or even signed up for sixteen weeks of Nautilus, exercising at a high intensity and telling yourself all the time, "No pain, no gain." But then you became frustrated. You didn't see any improvement in your health or appearance, and you were tired of being tired and sweaty. You finally dropped out, using one of the many excuses: too busy, too tired, sick, or injured. Well, here's the good news: you can improve your cardiovascular fitness, lose weight, and increase muscle mass with a low-intensity workout.

Using Invention Questions

If you're sometimes at a loss as to how to proceed with revision, try applying the methods of invention discussed in Chapter 3. Since these methods are ways of discovering ideas, they can be particularly useful for revealing incompletely developed thoughts and for discovering information that should be added to clarify your meaning. Here we'll consider the journalist's questions, the classical probes, and questions about audience, but you might find some of the other invention methods useful as well, particularly cubing and brainstorming.

Journalist's Questions

Try asking the **journalist's questions,** the five **W's** and an **H:** *Who? What? Where? When? Why?* and *How?* Asking these questions about the ideas you've put down can tell you whether you've explained yourself adequately. If you were the writer of the paragraph in the preceding exercise, you could ask questions such as these about your essay:

Who will read this?
Who exercises?
How do people exercise?
Why do people not exercise?
What are the benefits of exercise?
What is harmful about exercise?

What kind of exercise is best?
Where can people get exercise?
When is a good time to exercise?
Why should people exercise?

Questions like these could reveal a wealth of details for enriching the paragraph and the essay that it introduces. Using these interrogatory words can help you to see what you are saying and what you are not saying.

Classical Probes

Another way of asking questions about your draft is to use the **classical probes:** asking questions about *identification, comparison and contrast, classification, causes and effects, process analysis,* and *exemplification.* For example:

What is exercise? (*identification*)
What kinds of exercise do I discuss? (*classification*)
How do I say exercise improves health and fitness? (*process analysis*)
What do I say are the effects of intense workouts? low-intensity workouts? (*causes and effects*)
How do I compare intense workouts with low-intensity workouts? (*comparison*)
What examples of intense workouts do I use? What examples of low-intensity workouts do I use? (*exemplification*)

This type of questioning might continue until you are sure your draft includes answers to all the questions you consider important for developing your point. As with using the classical probes during prewriting, you might find you are concentrating on one or two probes, for example asking a number of comparison questions if your essay compares two subjects, as the one on exercises seems to do.

Questions about Audience

Even though in prewriting you establish who your intended audience is and how much you know about it, you might find it useful to ask some **questions about audience** after you have a draft in front of you. Here are the audience questions from Chapter 2, rephrased for revision. For a given essay, ask as many as apply.

Questions about Audience for Revising

1. Who is my intended audience?
2. What does my audience know about my subject?

> *Questions* (continued)
>
> 3. Do I establish my credibility in relation to my subject?
> 4. Do I establish my relationship with my audience?
> 5. What do I say to interest my audience in my subject?
> 6. Do I say anything that promotes positive attitudes toward my subject?
> 7. Do I say anything that promotes positive attitudes toward me?
> 8. Do I want to change audience attitudes toward my subject or me?
> 9. Do I establish ties with my audience by means of shared experiences and knowledge?
> 10. Do I use shared experiences and knowledge in presenting my subject?
> 11. How will my audience perceive the rhetorical situation in which I am writing: reflective, persuasive, informative, or something else?
> 12. How will my audience react to my grammar, style, and vocabulary?

EXERCISES

1. Select two methods of invention to use for revising a draft of your writing. Apply these methods to your draft to see if there is anything you should add, delete, substitute, or rearrange.

2. Here is the rough draft of a student's letter to the president of his university. When his teacher read this draft, she told him that his argument was weak and needed more thought and development. Apply the journalist's questions, the classical probes, and the questions about audience from a reader's perspective to discover how the writer might strengthen his case. If you were the university president receiving this letter, how would you react and what else would you want to know?

Dear Mr. Campbell:

The parking problem at this university is becoming a big problem   1
because there is nowhere to park. I was advised by other older students to take early classes to prevent the problem of parking. But even students with 9:00 A.M. classes have to walk five or six blocks and sometimes even farther to get to class. This is a real problem when the temperature is below 0. It is frustrating to go to school and not find a close parking spot. The only way is to go to school a couple of hours before class.

Another problem with the parking tickets. A lot of students are receiv- 2
ing parking tickets because they have to park in illegal places so they don't
have to walk far to classes. The parking tickets are a disadvantage to the
students who live off campus. These students should be able to go to school
knowing that they can find a parking spot a couple of blocks from school.

I hope you will take this problem into consideration and try to have 3
something done.

I would like to see something done so students wouldn't face this 4
problem in the future. Maybe the school could pay for a parking lot or ramp
close to school. There is not enough parking for the students who attend
this university so something has to be done.

Sincerely,
John Martinez

Outlining or Mapping

Although invention questions are useful for revealing omissions, outlining your draft helps you check for irrelevant information and faulty organization, as well as omissions. Outlining or mapping a completed draft is a
good idea especially for writers who compose without an outline, who begin
instead by freewriting or following a loose mental plan. You may produce an
outline only when a teacher requires you to submit one; legitimize it now as
a part of your writing process.

Outlining

To **outline** your rough draft, state the main idea of each paragraph in a
sentence, using a roman numeral for each paragraph. These should be your
topic sentences, whether you expressed them explicitly in your essay or not.
Use sublevels to show the development of each paragraph. When you are
finished, you should be able to see the connections between all your topic
sentences. You should also be able to see whether each paragraph is adequately developed and whether it has irrelevant information. (Refer to
"Outlining" in Chapter 3 for a fuller discussion.)

Mapping

Mapping, as described in Chapter 3, is a method of listing and visually
organizing ideas. A visual map of your paper may help you revise it. To **map**
your rough draft, place the main idea of your essay, or the thesis, in the
center of a sheet of paper and enclose it in a double circle. Then around that
circle write the main ideas of your paragraphs, circle them, and add your
supporting information. Draw lines to connect related information. If you

end up with an idea you haven't been able to connect to anything else, it may be irrelevant to this essay. If it is truly unnecessary to your essay, discard it. It may, however, be critical information that needs more development. If so, go back to some kind of invention questions to discover how to develop that idea.

EXERCISE

Here's the student essay on exercise, followed by a partial outline of its organization and development. Each roman numeral in the outline represents a paragraph in the essay. Complete the outline, using the essay and the filled-in outline items as guides. Note that the outline has some flaws; however, these are clues to flaws in the essay's organization. As you complete the outline and study it, you will discover undeveloped ideas and ineffective organization. Be prepared to discuss in class needed revisions in development or organization of the essay.

ALTERNATE EXERCISE

Read the student essay on exercise and check its organization and development with mapping.

No Pain, No Gain?

(student writer)

Are you one of the many people who don't get enough exercise because you think that exercising is too much work? Perhaps you've tried working out once or twice or even signed up for sixteen weeks of Nautilus, exercising at a high intensity and telling yourself all the time, "No pain, no gain." But then you became frustrated. You didn't see any improvement in your health or appearance, and you were tired of being tired and sweaty. You finally dropped out, using one of the many excuses: too busy, too tired, sick, or injured. Well, here's good news: you can improve your cardiovascular fitness, lose weight, and increase muscle mass with a low-intensity workout.

A common misconception is that the greater the exercise intensity, the more fat burned. In reality, fat can only be utilized when oxygen is present. For fat to be converted into energy it must be converted into energy by being broken down to fatty acids. This is done when the fat molecule combines with oxygen. It is only possible in an aerobic workout. Intense workouts are anaerobic, therfore, they can only use carbohydrates and protein for sources of energy. If you think about it the process is logical. When the body is working at a high intensity, it naturally uses its most efficient fuel, carbohydrates. When working at lower intensities, the body can afford to fall back on its less efficiently burned caloric sources, such as fat.

A similar misconception is that exercising at higher intensities burns   3
significally more fat. In fact it does not. Kath and McCardle cite the following in their book *Nutrition, Weight Control and Exercise*. "A 150 pound person
expends about 110 kilocalories while jogging one mile in twelve minutes. If
the same person runs the mile in five and a half minutes, only about 130
kilocalories are expended."

You may be surprised to learn that only twenty additional calories were   4
expended by exercising twice as hard. Are you willing to exercise that hard
and triple your chance of injuring yourself or dropping out? An ideal
exercise program is one that is low enough to use fat as an energy source,
but high enough to elicit a cardiovascular training effect.

One example would be walking instead of running. If you run you   5
should run at a pace where you can still talk comfortably. In chosing an
exercise you should pick one that you enjoy, and remember that variety is
the spice of life. If you enjoy your workouts you will look forward to each
session. It has always been easier for people to find time in their busy
schedules to do activities they enjoy. Aerobic exercise should be done three
times a week for at least thirty minutes. Thes advice has become the first
commandment of phsical fitness—the requirement needed by the body to
keep the heart and lungs healthy.

The important factor to remember when developing a fitness routine is   6
that duration of exercise, not the intensity, is the critical factor for burning
more calories. And longer duration is acheived by lowering the intensity. As
you maintain an exercise program year after year, a healthy lifestyle will
come more and more naturally and you will keep looking and feeling
healthier.

Outline

I. Introduction of the subject

   A. Audience and exercise

   B.

   C.

   D. Thesis: You can improve your cardiovascular fitness, lose weight, and
      increase muscle mass with a low-intensity workout.

II. Common misconception that intense workouts burn more fat

   A. Reality: fat utilized in presence of oxygen

     1. Broken down into fatty acids

     2.

     3. Anaerobic workouts

   B. Logical process

III. Similar misconception that intense workouts burn more fat

   A. Kath and McCardle quotation

IV. Difference in caloric expenditure

   A.

   B. Ideal exercise program

      1.

      2.

 V. Example of ideal exercise program

   A. Advice on exercise

      1.

      2.

      3.

      4.

VI. Conclusion: duration not intensity as critical factor

   A.

   B.

Applying a Checklist

Every revision is specific to a piece of writing, so no revision checklist applies to all situations. There are general guides, however. As just discussed, the invention questions can be adapted to revisions of many pieces of writing; outlining and mapping can also often apply. In addition, you might try a checklist such as this one:

> ### Revision Checklist
>
> 1. Is my *purpose* apparent throughout the essay?
> 2. Does my *thesis sentence* state both the point of my essay and my subject?
> 3. Are all *paragraphs* clearly related to my thesis?
> 4. Is each *paragraph* developed fully enough that my readers aren't left with unanswered questions?
> 5. Do I have any *paragraphs* that should be combined? any that should be separated?
> 6. Are my *paragraphs* clearly connected to one another?

Revision *(continued)*

7. Does my *introduction* appeal to the interests of my audience, and does it prepare my audience for what I am about to say?
8. Does my *conclusion* end with the point I stated in my thesis?
9. Do I have a clear, authoritative *voice* that is appropriate for my subject, my audience, and my purpose?
10. Is there anything I should delete to avoid inappropriate *repetition or inconsistencies?*
11. Is there anything I should add to *clarify my position?*
12. Do the *grammar and usage* in my sentences clearly express my meaning?
13. Have I used *words* that convey my meaning accurately and unambiguously, without bias, pretensions, and unintended connotations?
14. Have I shown how the parts of my essay *relate* to my thesis and *connect* to one another?
15. Does my *title* both describe my subject and interest my audience?

A checklist like this points out that revision goes on at several levels: essay, paragraph, sentence, and word. At all levels you look for clarity and completeness, for connections between parts, for unity and consistency. Revision usually does not concentrate on one level at a time—say, working at the essay level before looking at sentences and words—and the preceding checklist reflects this roving of the revising eye. Some writers even prefer to do some editing—correcting spelling or usage errors—before beginning their larger revising projects, just so these errors won't distract them. In practice, you will probably revise and edit (see "Editing") at the same time.

Essay-Level Revisions

Applying the revision checklist at the essay level, use questions 1, 2, 7, 8, 9, 10, 13, and 14. At this level, look for a coherent whole: Do all parts relate to a thesis that states your central idea clearly and precisely? Is your purpose or are your purposes for writing apparent and consistent throughout the essay? If your purpose is to report a factual occurrence, for example, is it appropriate for you to speculate? Is your tone, or voice, consistent, and does it coincide with your purpose? Lapsing into humor or cynicism is not appropriate for a serious report. Does your conclusion reiterate the central idea you began with—by summary, restatement, or some other means? (Chapter 4 has more on conclusions.) Is your title consistent with the whole essay, reflecting your central idea in an interesting way—as does the title for the essay on exercise, "No Pain, No Gain?"?

Paragraph-Level Revisions

In analyzing your paragraphs, use questions 3, 4, 5, 6, and 13. In a well-written essay, all the paragraphs relate to the main idea (expressed in the thesis sentence) and connect to one another. If all these connections are made, your essay has *coherence*. (For a discussion of coherence, see pages 305–306). Paragraphs sometimes are not developed and sometimes do not focus on a single idea. Sometimes they are excessively long and need to be divided, but at other times the essay would be easier to follow if two paragraphs were combined.

Sentence-Level Revisions

At this level, see that your sentences follow one another smoothly, that you are not omitting details and connections. Grammar and usage should not stand in the way of the ideas you want to express; your usage should be like what you find in published writing of the same type. To develop a style that employs conventional sentence patterns and usage, study the sentences of other writers. Read some of the essays in Part II to gain a sense of usage, voice, and level of formality for expository writing. Try to make your sentences sound like written, not spoken, sentences you have encountered. Questions 8, 9, and 11 can assist you on this level.

Word-Level Revisions

Question 12 directs your attention to the words you use. If any word stands out as a little odd, give it a close look. Does it express your meaning accurately? *Flout* and *flaunt,* for example, have very different meanings. In the context of your essay, could a word have a double meaning? For example, in the phrase "exercise more naturally," does *more* relate to *exercise* or *naturally?* Could a word you use give the impression that you are biased, such as the pronouns *he, his,* and *him* refer to persons of both sexes? Is a word pretentious, such as *endeavor* instead of *try,* or *deem* instead of *think?* Does a word convey meanings that you didn't intend because of the connotative baggage it carries—*gloomy* rather than *dim,* for example? Mark Twain said that the "difference between the right word and the almost-right word is the difference between lightning and a lightning-bug." You are the best judge of what is the right word for your essay, so you must revise for the exactly right word.

EXERCISE

Apply the revision checklist to John Martinez's letter in exercise 2 on page 92. Does the checklist yield information that you did not get with the invention questions?

Getting Feedback from Others

As noted earlier, your first drafts are probably not the sort of thing you want someone else to read. They express the thoughts you had while you were still discovering what you wanted to say. First drafts may have irrelevant material, gaps where explanations are necessary, unclear pronoun references, shifts in focus. You revise your writing so readers will understand what you mean and think well of you. There may be times, however, when, to see clearly what changes you should make, you need to let someone else read your draft, with all its inaccuracies and imprecisions.

When you ask other people for **feedback,** tell them how you want them to read your writing, what you want them to look for. If you're concerned about focus, tell your readers to consider whether your essay concentrates on a central idea or seems to slip off at times. If you think your examples might not be concrete enough, tell your readers you want them to give close attention to how you illustrate your points. If you want an overall assessment, you might ask your readers to use the revision checklist questions in the previous section.

Sometimes you voluntarily request feedback, and sometimes it is an assigned part of a course. For whatever reason you get reader response, and whether it's from teacher or peers, you'll probably need to moderate your natural sensitivity to criticism. If you're like most writers, you feel as if your writing's an extension of yourself, as if criticism of your writing is criticism of you. However, suggestions for improvement of early drafts can be thought of as collaborative aids, as helpful pointers that can make your final draft better. This is why you *want* feedback from others.

A readily available and often overlooked kind of feedback is what you can get from other writers. Published writers are always available, through their writing, for guidance and instruction. If you have questions about how to revise your introduction, observe how other writers begin their essays. Do you want to know how to lead into an example? See how other writers do it. Writers can show you how to connect paragraphs, how to subordinate less important information in your sentences, how to use transitional words and phrases, how to conclude your essays, and so on. They don't *tell* you; they *show* you in their own sentences and paragraphs and essays. All you need to do is apply the principles to your own writing.

EXERCISES

1. Exchange recent drafts of an essay with a classmate and give each other feedback on ways to revise them. Discuss what is troubling you about your paper, where you think the problems are, what kind of response you want. Use the revision checklist questions on pages 96 and 97 if you want an overall response.

2. Working with a partner in class, apply the revision checklist (page 96) or the questions about audience for revision (page 91) to the student essay "No Pain, No Gain?" on page 94. What advice on revision would you give its writer?

Editing

Related to revising is **editing.** Unlike revising, editing can often be done by other people as well as by the writer, although the writer ought to be the *first* editor (and the *last*). Sometimes teachers are editors, sometimes classmates, sometimes friends, sometimes people called *editors* who prepare writing for publication. Editing is preparing a revised draft for presentation to other people. It usually does not change meaning, at least not significantly. When writers edit, they correct spelling and punctuation and make other changes so that their writing conforms to conventional standards. Editing is therefore one of the last steps in writing. Still, many writers do some editing as they draft and revise. If when rereading their drafts they see a misspelled word or a misplaced comma, they correct it so that it doesn't distract them while they concentrate on the broader issues.

The way to edit is to look for the kinds of errors that usually crop up in your writing. If you commonly write sentence fragments, look for fragments. If pronoun reference is a problem, make sure that every time you use a pronoun (for example, *it, this, they, he, she*) the noun it refers to is absolutely evident. If you have a problem with the forms of your verbs, read your essay through once looking only at verbs. You probably can't get your editing done in one pass through. Most writers need to go over their writing repeatedly to make all the corrections they have to make. At some point in your editing, type a clean copy; then continue to read carefully for errors and faulty phrasing.

Checklists are sometimes helpful as reminders of what to look for when you edit. Each writer and each writing situation requires a particular kind of editing, but you can use the following checklist as a guide, adapting it for each piece of writing you edit.

Editing Checklist

1. Does my *punctuation* follow conventional usage?
2. Should I check the *spelling* of any of my words?
3. Does every *verb* agree with its subject, especially in sentences where subjects and verbs are widely separated?

> ### *Editing* (continued)
>
> 4. Are the *tenses* of my verbs consistent with the way I want to use them?
> 5. Does every *pronoun* (particularly *it, this, they, he, she*) clearly refer to a noun or another pronoun?
> 6. Does every *modifier* have an obvious connection to the word I want it to modify?
> 7. When I have used *coordinating conjunctions* (*and, but, or, nor, for, so, yet*), are the sentence parts they connect equivalent in grammar and in meaning?
> 8. Do I use *capitals, abbreviations, numbers,* and *underlines* according to conventional usage?
> 9. Do I have unnecessarily *wordy constructions,* such as those that begin *there are* or those that have a verb plus a noun, or a verb plus an adjective, when a verb will do ("they *took notice of*" instead of "they *noticed*" and "they *are desirous of*" instead of "they *want*").
> 10. Do I have any *clichés,* overworked figures of speech such as "rat race" and "to top it off"?

Editing with a Word Processor

If you have drafted with a word processor, begin your editing on the screen. Word processors make editing so easy that it's no problem to pass through an essay or other piece of writing several times to correct errors. If you have a spelling checker, use it, remembering that you need to watch for words it doesn't flag—homonyms like *to/too/two,* for example. If you tend to overuse or misuse words such as *there* or *this,* use your "search" function to locate them; then decide whether each usage is appropriate. Before considering your editing ended, print a paper copy and continue reading for errors and inappropriate usage. Mark your corrections with a red pen so you won't miss any when you transfer them to your word-processing disk.

EXERCISE

Edit the following paragraph, applying the editing checklist as appropriate and writing a clean copy.

The wolf is an often mis-understood creature. It's reputation paints a picture of a cold blooded killer but in fact the wolf is a very important part of natures ecolgical balance. For instance as depicted in the movie *Never Cry*

Wolf the wolf was thought to be a major contributer to the decline of the great caribu heards. Research proved however, that the wolf packs only hunted to survive, and to provide for the young pups. The decline of the caribu came from overkill from man, and disease within the heard. The wolfs while hunting, would single out the young, old, and weak caribu; therefore letting the strong, healthy caribu move on to mate again. By hunting only out of necessiry and survival, the wolves actually contributed to the propagation of the caribu heard.

Proofreading

Also related to revising is **proofreading,** which, like editing, can be done by either the writer or someone else. Ultimately, however, the responsibility is the writer's. The errors that go under your name are *yours,* no matter who the typist or proofreader is. Proofreading is done on the final copy, to make sure it conforms to conventional standards—that there are no errors in typing, spelling, or punctuation, no unintentionally omitted or repeated words, no strikeovers or smudges—in other words, that the copy is clean and ready for presentation to a reader.

Proofreading is difficult to do, because reading is usually for meaning, and this kind of reading is precisely what writers must *not* do when proofreading. When you proofread, you must read for *error,* and nothing else. When reading for meaning, a person's eyes take in two or three words at a time, focusing on one of them and giving the outlying words only scant attention. You can appreciate the implications for proofreading, especially for the words at the beginnings and ends of lines. Here are some tips for meticulous proofreading:

Proofreading Tips

1. Look at every word and punctuation mark.
2. Resist the temptation to overlook the first and last words on a line.
3. Read aloud; doing so slows your reading.
4. Point at each word as you read.
5. Read backward from the end of the essay.

Do whatever you need to in order to avoid reading fast and for meaning. Catch all your final errors, because whatever errors remain are *yours.* Teachers often think it is a shame when a student spends hours writing a paper and then submits it with errors that could have been eliminated by careful proofreading.

Proofreading on a Word Processor

If you have composed with a word processor, always proofread your final paper copy. To prevent a possible need for reprinting, however, give your document a careful last reading on your screen. If you generally read too fast, keep the line you are proofreading at the *bottom* of your screen, and scroll to the next line only after you've read the last word on the line you're reading. If you still skip words, move the cursor to each word as you read. Reading with the cursor is tedious, though, and you will have to train your eyes to slow down.

A Final Word

Revising is a lot of work, often requiring a great deal of time. But the payoff is a piece of writing you can be proud of as a representation of you. It expresses your thoughts to another person, in words and a style that you have made as good as you can. To know when to quit revising, you might follow the practice of novelist John Dos Passos: "I usually write to a point where the work is getting worse instead of better. That's the point to stop."

EXERCISES

1. Apply two methods of revision to the draft of your essay on your writing process or some other essay to see if there is anything you should add, delete, substitute, or rearrange.
2. Apply the editing checklist on page 100 to John Martinez's letter in exercise 2 on page 92.
3. With a partner, observe how your eyes move when you read. First, read paragraph 1 in this exercise for *meaning* (there are no errors). Have your partner count the number of times your eyes stop as you read each line. Compare the number of stops with the number of words per line. Then observe as your partner reads. Next, read paragraph 2 for errors, and have your partner count the stops your eyes make; compare the number of stops with the number of words per line. Then reverse with your partner. Your findings will fall in these categories:

   a. Eye stops equal number of words.
   b. Eye stops are fewer than the number of words.
   c. Eye stops are more than the number of words.

   Don't be surprised if your eyes also make backward movements. Discuss the implications of your findings with your partner and your class.

The cold late October air was biting my arms, legs, and face. My uniform, consisting of a pair of cotton shorts and a t-shirt, wasn't enough to keep anyone warm in October, especially on such a chilly day. The athletic socks covering my arms to my elbows made me pretend that my fingers weren't as numb as my frozen toes. I didn't even notice the numbness of my nose because my concern was for my lungs, which ached from the cold, brisk air. Yet the heavy breath billowing from my lungs was warm enough to create steam when it escaped through my mouth.

—Deneen Young, student

We're not good enouhg to be on a leauge team, Buzz always ends up getting too drunk and starts goofing off. He likes to see how far he can throw his ball using an overhand delivery the league guys do'nt like that. Besides, you have to have your own bowling shoes to be on a team. I'll be damned if I'll pay 25 bucks for a pair of shoes I can only wear on Wendsday nites. We do'nt even rent bowling shoes, we tell Jerry that we all have enormous feet—size 17. He does'nt have any rentals that big so he let's us bowl in our socks.

4. Here is the final draft of "No Pain, No Gain?" Compare it with the rough draft on page 94 and answer the following questions.

   a. Did the writer reconcile her problems with organization?
   b. Did her revisions clear up problems with development?
   c. Does her essay as revised develop her thesis as revised?
   d. What problems still remain?

   Now apply the revision checklist (page 96) to the revised essay and be prepared to discuss in class whatever revisions you think should be made.

No Pain, No Gain?

(student writer)

Are you one of the many people who don't get enough exercise because you think that exercising is too much work? Perhaps you've tried working out once or twice or even signed up for sixteen weeks of Nautilus, exercising at a high intensity and telling yourself all the time, "No pain, no gain." But then you became frustrated. You didn't see any improvement in your health or appearance, and you were tired of being tired and sweaty. You finally dropped out, using one of the many excuses: too busy, too tired, sick, or injured. Well, here's good news: you can improve your cardiovascular fitness and lose weight with a low-intensity workout.   1

A common misconception is that the greater the exercise intensity, the more fat burned. In reality, fat can be utilized more efficiently in low-intensity workouts. For fat to be converted into energy it must be broken   2 down to fatty acids. This can be achieved only in the presence of oxygen, because the fat molecule must combine with oxygen. This conversion is possible only in an aerobic, low-intensity workout, which promotes the body's ability to utilize oxygen. Because anaerobic workouts are less likely to circulate oxygen throughout the body, they can only use carbohydrates and protein for sources of energy. When the body is working at a high intensity, it naturally uses its most efficient fuel, carbohydrates. When working at lower intensities, the body can afford to fall back on its less efficiently burned caloric sources such as fat.

A similar misconception is that exercising at higher intensities burns significantly more fat. In fact it does not. According to Katch and McArdle in their book *Nutrition, Weight Control, and Exercise,* a 150-pound person expends about 110 kilocalories while jogging one mile in twelve minutes, but if the same person runs the mile in five and a half minutes, only about 130 kilocalories are expended. You may be surprised to learn that only twenty additional calories were expended by exercising twice as hard. Are you willing to exercise that hard and increase your chance of injuring yourself or dropping out? 3

An ideal exercise program is one that is low enough to use fat as an energy source but high enough to elicit a cardiovascular training effect in which heart, lungs, and circulatory system utilize increased oxygen. Good examples are swimming, rowing, walking, cycling, and running. Because walking allows exercise over a longer period, it has an advantage over running. If you run, you should run at a pace that allows you to still talk comfortably. In choosing an exercise, pick one that you enjoy. If you enjoy your workouts you will look forward to each session. It has always been easier for people to find time in their busy schedules to do activities they enjoy. 4

Aerobic exercise should be done three times a week for at least thirty minutes—the requirement for keeping the heart and lungs healthy. If you want to burn more calories, the important factor to remember when developing your fitness routine is duration of exercise, not the intensity. And longer duration is achieved by lowering the intensity. As you maintain an exercise program year after year, a healthy lifestyle will come more and more naturally and you will keep looking and feeling healthier. 5

Work Cited

Katch, Frank I., and William D. McArdle. *Nutrition, Weight Control, and Exercise.* Boston: Houghton, 1977.

5. Here's Chapter 2 of British author Joyce Cary's *The Horse's Mouth* (New York: Harper, 1944), a novel about a talented but slightly disreputable painter. Just released from prison for "uttering menaces," Gulley Jimson returns to the old boathouse where he had left a massive unfinished painting. Read the chapter first for the enjoyment of getting to know this old rascal; then read it for what it says

about revision. Be prepared to discuss your responses in class. What does the chapter tell you about

a. Reseeing a creative work after a period of rest?
b. Response from other people?
c. What an artist (or writer) can do with responses from others?
d. "Big holes" and "little holes" in creative work?
e. The artist's (or writer's) attitude toward revision?

from *The Horse's Mouth*

Joyce Cary

I could see my studio from where I stood, an old boathouse down by the water wall. A bit rotten in places, but I had been glad to get it. My trouble is I get big ideas. My last one was the Fall, twelve by fifteen, and you can't get room for an idea like that in a brick studio under two hundred pounds a year. So I was glad to get the boathouse. It had a loft. I took the planks off the beams at one end and got a very nice wall, seventeen foot high. When I had my canvas up, it was two foot off the floor, which just suited me. I like to keep my pictures above dog level. **1**

Well, I thought, the walls and roof are there still. They haven't got blown away yet. No one has leant up against 'em. I was pleased. But I didn't go along in a hurry. One thing at a time. Last time I was locked up, in thirty-seven, I left a regular establishment behind. Nice little wife, two kids, flat and a studio with a tin roof. Watertight all round. North light. Half-finished picture, eight by twelve. The Living God. Cartoons, drawings, studies, two painter's ladders, two chairs, kettle, frypan, and an oil stove. All you could want. **2**

When I came back, there was nothing. Wife and kids had gone back to her mama. Flat let to people who didn't even know my name. And the studio was a coal store. As for the Living God, my drawings, cartoons, ladders, they'd just melted. I hadn't expected to see the frypan and kettle again. You can't leave things like that about for a month in any friendly neighbourhood and expect to find them in the same place. But the Living God with his stretchers and stiffeners weighed a couple of hundredweight. When I came back from gaol even the smell had gone. Coker said that someone said the landlord took it for the rent. The landlord swore he had never seen it. I daresay he had hidden it somewhere in an attic telling himself that it might be worth thousands as soon as I was dead, and the more I was worried, the sooner that would be. **3**

The top of my boathouse suddenly nodded its head at me, as if saying, "That's it, old man." Then I saw that a couple of kids were taking a plank off the roof. More patrons, I thought. When they saw me coming, they slid off the roof and ran. But not far. Crouching round like a couple of wolves **4**

waiting for the old horse to drop. I didn't need to unlock the door. Somebody had done it for me by knocking off the hasp of the padlock. And when
I opened it, two more kids got out of the window on their heads. "Don't
hurry," I said, "there's plenty of time before dinner."

There was nothing inside except a lot of pools on the floor from last   5
night's rain. And the picture. I got another surprise. A big one. It was still
there. Why, I thought, it's not bad in places. It might be a good thing. The
serpent wants to be a bit thicker, and I could bring his tail round to make a
nice curl over the tree. Adam is a bit too blue, and Eve could be redder—to
bring up the blues. Yes, yes, I thought, getting a bit excited, as I always do
when I come back to work after a holiday, I've got something there. Adam's
right leg is a gift, whatever you may say. Nobody has done that before with
a leg. What a shape. I must have been tight or walking in my sleep when I
knocked that off. And yet it's leggy all right. If that limb could speak, it
would say, "I walk for you, I run for you, I kneel for you. But I have my
self-respect."

Just then a stone came and knocked out the last window-pane that   6
wasn't broken already. And I heard a voice, "Ya, mister, how did you like
chokey?" Those kids had had a fright and they were getting their own back.

Next minute I heard a different kind of yell, and when I went to the   7
window I saw them making for the street with young Nosy on their tails.

He came in two minutes later, blowing, with the sweat on his nose and   8
his cap falling off the back of the head. "It's a shushame, Mr. Jimson. I hope
they haven't done any damage."

"Not to speak of. There's quite a lot left. And it's an expensive canvas.   9
Make a good floorcloth for any scullery." "Why, it's all f-full of holes, and
they've cut a piece out."

For somebody had been shooting at the birds with an air-gun and there   10
was a piece about a foot square cut out of Adam's middle with a blunt knife.
"What a shushame," said Nosy, and his nose turned pink. "You ought to tell
the po-police." "Well," I said, "Adam hadn't got a bathing-dress." "It's
disgusting." "So he was, and somebody has made him respectable. Some
mother, I expect. Anxious about her children. There's a lot of very good
mothers in this district. You'd be surprised." "But the p-picture's ruined."
"Oh no, I can easily put in a patch. It's the little holes are the nuisance. Are
you going to school yet?" for I wanted to get rid of him. I wanted to get on
with my work. "Nun-no," he said, "it's dinner-time." "Don't you do any
work in your dinner-time?" "S-s-sometimes." "If you want to get that scholarship and go to Oxford and get into the Civil Service and be a great man
and have two thousand pounds a year and a nice clean wife with hot and
cold and a kid with real eyes that open and close and a garage for two cars
and a savings' book, you'll have to work in your dinner-time. All the good
boys round here work in their dinner-time."

"They've been writing names all over Eve, Mr. Ji-jimson. It's b-beastly,   11
b-beastly." "Yes, they seem to have appreciated my picture a whole lot." "I

wonder you can go on pa-painting, Mr. Jijimson, for such people." "I like painting. That's been my trouble all my life." "I wuwish I could paint." "Now, young chap, you go home quick; before you catch anything." And I chased him out.

6. Here is a draft of an assigned paper that a student asked both a classmate and his teacher to read and respond to before he revised it. He wanted to know if they felt his organization was right, if they detected any irrelevancies, if they saw any problems in his tone, and if there was any information he should add. Finally, he wanted an overall revision check. Put yourself in the place of his classmate, and write a response to assist him in his revision. Answer his questions, and tell him what your major problems are as a reader of this paper.

The Dive

Jason Fisher (student writer)

Staring above me, watching the bubbles, I find myself in another world.   1
A trance, damned to be reality, a joy beyond belief. Floating like a leaf, anxious to be part of the deep blue, I dive deeper and deeper into the ocean.

Being so excited to dive, I became part of the ocean. Swimming as if I   2
was one of the underworld creatures, a small tear formed inside my mask. Little did I know an incident frightning beyond reason was about to take place. This incident brought me so close to death, I swore never to this type of dive again. If I had the power to change anything in my life, I would remove this incident.

On this particular dive, we were doing wreck dives off the northern   3
coast of the Grand Cayman. In a wreck dive, you find a sunken ship and search the rooms for artifacts. In this case, I was in training to become a diving instructor. I had to go alone into the wreck. To fully grasp the horror of diving into a wreck alone, you must first realize that as soon as you hit the water you are disorientated. If I was to swim ten feet away from the boat, unless I knew the surroundings very well, I would need to do a complete turn or use a compass to find my way back to the boat. Therefore, in a sunken ship, amongst unknown surroundings, it is easy to become lost. There are precautions to take, tieing a rope to a belt around your waist which is connected to the boat is an easy way to find your way out of the wreck.

As I sat on the boat, getting my gear ready for an important and   4
dangerous dive, I gazed through the blue water that surrounded us. Forgetting all possible danger, I was mesmerized by the silent world below. After a careful check of my gear, I rolled backwards off the boat. Only to make a nightmare reality. Desending into the light blue at a resonable

speed, I found the wreck. The wreck was located at sixty-four feet below surface. I swam towrds it, pulling the rope behind me. Following through the welcoming door, I turned my flashlight on. Looking around, I proceeded into the heart of the ship. Only to find darker and darker rooms.

In confused realization, I discovered a horrible aspect about myself. At least it was horrible to find out about it now. I discovered that I am claustrophobic. As the room got darker and darker, and smaller and smaller, I felt as though I would be flattened inside the room. In all the anxiety and panic, I kicked the rope from my belt. The room began to crush me, so I quickly swam in and out of rooms, only to find smaller rooms. I felt as though I had to squeeze my way through minute chambers. Finally, grabbing hold of myself, I remembered the rope. Not knowing that I had kicked it off about six rooms back. I was scared and lost in sixty-four feet of water. In all dives your tank holds 3000psi, whick basically means you have 20–40 minutes of diving, depending on the dive and depth. At 1000psi, the amount of air you have is questionable. At 500psi, you could only have 20psi, because SCUBA gauges cannot read below that level. Although, most tanks come equipt with 3000psi.

In fifteen short minutes I had drained my tank from 3000psi to 1200psi, and was breathing as if I had just ran a marathon. In my nine years of diving which accumulated 125 dives, not including my dives to become an instructor, I never dreamed that the ocean could hurt me. I looked at my gauge which now read 900psi, and I began to panic. Swimming furiously through the wreck, I gave up. I sat to quietly die. During my last outrage I found out later, I kicked the rope. Which made the rope move in a straight line. At this point I was laying on the floor watching my gauge drop from 900psi to 500psi. I saw a light flash through the room. A diver was looking for me! He helped me up and we slowly proceeded out of the wreck. To my surprise, before we reached the door to leave, my tank ran dry, as my gauge read 430psi. We buddy breathed out of the wreck and to the surface. When you buddy breathe you share the rig, which releases air from the tank. Later I found out that they were worried about me, because my rope had not moved for a considerable amount of time. Then, when it did, it moved abruptly in one direction. I thank God they came to find me. If not, when approximately two more minutes passed, my breathing aparatus would have stopped disprsing air.

Still today I love the ocean. Nothing will ever be able to change that. The ocean, in all its power, beauty, and might, is the most unpredictable creation in this world. I had the idea in my head that nothing would ever hurt me when I was below. Now I know that is not true. Although this is an incident I would like to forget and remove from my life, I respect the ocean a quite deal more because of it. The scariest part of my incident, was at the edge of death, as I layed watching my last pockets of air rise to the surface, I felt a comfort in death.

PART II

The Practice of Purposeful Writing

CHAPTER 6

To Reflect: Writing with Emphasis on the Writer

Until writing, most kinds of thoughts we are used to thinking today simply could not be thought.

—Walter Ong

Reflection is something people usually do for themselves rather than for an audience. Usually it doesn't even get onto paper, occurring instead in the mind. **Reflection** is careful, deliberate thought prompted by a specific circumstance, a purposeful consideration of a particular subject. A reflection tends to be philosophical, seeking meaning to one's environment. Here is an illustration, a poem by William Wordsworth prompted by the sight of a rainbow:

> My heart leaps up when I behold
>   A rainbow in the sky:
> So was it when my life began;
> So is it now I am a man;
> So be it when I shall grow old,
>   Or let me die!
> The Child is father of the Man;
> And I could wish my days to be
> Bound each to each by natural piety.

In this verse, the poet's view of a rainbow recalls similar instances in the past, leading to contemplation on the continuity within a life span.

Reflections also explore and express emotions—sometimes only in the mind but at other times in writing. Love letters are a common type of reflective writing. Whatever their end, whether sent to the object of love or left to languish in a drawer, the writer probably feels better for having written them. People experiencing bereavement sometimes seek an outlet for their emotions by writing about the experience, working through the anger, grief, discouragement, and the entire complex of emotions that accompany it. People overcome by emotions that are difficult to handle may keep a notebook in which they record feelings and their immediate causes, with the hope of achieving control over them.

Even though reflection occurs most commonly as a mental act, it is sometimes done best in writing. Some thoughts are just too complex to hold in one's mind. Writing assists reflective thought for the same reason that some arithmetic problems must be done on paper—the limits of the short-term memory. For example, it is likely that you can multiply 7 times 6 in your head by relying on your memory; you can probably even multiply 7 times 68 without pencil and paper, if you force yourself a little. But multiplying 87 times 96 probably exceeds the limits of your ability to carry out all the steps and to hold the numbers in your mind while you work with them.* Similarly, if you want to analyze a complicated chain of events, you might need to take some notes instead of trying to remember and connect each incident. Also, you are more likely to remember and comprehend much of your school-work if you use writing in addition to your reading.

The Journal

Some people keep a regular record of their reflections and activities in a special notebook for the purpose, commonly called a **journal.** Because journals record reflections as they occur, many writers find them a tremendous source of ideas for writing. You may already be one of those people. If not, now is a good time to start. Get yourself a notebook: some writers prefer a spiral composition book, some a loose-leaf binder, some a lined tablet, and others a pocket folder with loose lined paper. Set aside a special portion of your day for journal writing; if you don't reserve a certain time, you will forget to write. Then *use* your journal. Here are some ways some people use journals.

Ways to Use a Journal

1. Record thoughts, observations, activities and impressions you want to remember.
2. Analyze your feelings about certain events.
3. Explore problems that need solutions.

---

*This idea is explained by Richard Young and Patricia Sullivan in "Why Write? A Reconsideration," *Essays on Classical Rhetoric and Modern Discourse,* ed. Robert J. Connors, Lisa S. Ede, and Andrea A. Lunsford. Southern Ill. U. Press, 1984.

Ways (continued)

4. Ask questions that need answers.
5. Summarize class lecture notes.
6. Summarize reading assignments.
7. Analyze or compare reading assignments.
8. React to books you've read, plays you've seen, music you've heard.
9. Respond to newspaper commentaries and editorials.
10. Begin drafts of writing assignments.
11. Analyze the dynamics of a conversation.

(Academic journals are also discussed under "Notes" in Chapter 9.)

In a journal, you write for yourself. Journal entries sometimes lead to public writing with an intended audience and purpose; at other times they remain informal and private. Here are some examples of student journal entries. Do you see any possibilities of their leading to writing that is more formal and public? Do you see any evidence that the writers of these samples thought they would be read by someone else?

Hajimemashite . . . How do you do. Watashi wa hima o arimasen . . . I have no free time. The Japanese language has got to be the hardest foreign language to take. My roommate has Russian. The amount of homework he is putting into the class and receiving a passing grade is slightly between one or two minutes a week. The only time he practices is when he says "Nyet" and that's only when I'm into his food.

Smell the air. It's fresh and cool with a touch of autumn. The only thing on my mind today is hunting. Hunting is more than killing. Picture yourself in camouflaged garments, a twelve-gauge at your side. Black lab, ammo, duck call, bologna sandwiches and sunflower seeds. It's a cloud-covered day and the grass is tan. Trees of October have started to appear. The dry grass rustles like a snare drum crescendoing over the rolling hills. I lie in the grass, tired but spirited. The grass has a distinct smell like a barn full of sweet hay mixed with a little breeze of fresh air and evaporating dew. I let my head rest on the cushion of grass and watch the clouds turn different shades of grey as they move on towards tomorrow.

9-18. Since my grandmother died eight days ago, life just isn't the same. My parents said, "She got to see so many things: the four oldest grandchildren graduate and her granddaughter's wedding. But what are we going to do with Grandpa?"

9-19. I am wondering how lonely my grandpa is to be married sixty years and then lose what he was living for. The last time I talked to him he said, "I'll be with her soon." This just makes me crumble inside.

9-22. All of a sudden I feel someone tapping me on my shoulder. It is my sister, crying. "I tried calling but the phone was busy. Grandpa died last night." I've never felt so helpless in my life.

9-25. The day of the funeral. I was just here two weeks ago, doing the same thing, feeling the same way. It's like I could feel part of my grandpa leave me. The worst part was when they played taps, and the flag was presented to my dad. It was only the second time I've seen my dad cry.

If you keep a journal regularly, making entries three or four times a week, you will inevitably incur benefits. Writing may become easier for you. You will have a source of ideas for formal writing needs. And you are likely to have a greater understanding of the coursework and other subjects you summarize and analyze. You will probably, though, have ambivalent feelings toward your journal: disliking to sit down to write in it even while appreciating the advantages that derive from doing so.

Journals Made Public

Henry David Thoreau kept a journal for years. His sixteen published volumes are examples of journal writing that began as personal records, sources of ideas for lectures and essays, but gradually became more refined in style, as if he thought they might someday have other readers. Regarding journal writing, he wrote: "Of all strange and unaccountable things this journalizing is the strangest. It will allow nothing to be predicated of it; its good is not good, nor its bad bad" (*Journal*, I, January 29, 1841). He seems to be asking, What can one say about a journal? And answering, One can simply say, it exists. One of Thoreau's journal entries, "A Fire in the Woods," is included in this chapter.

Like Thoreau, Annie Dillard took a secluded house and kept a journal for recording her reflections on nature, life, and whatever else occurred to her. In *Pilgrim at Tinker Creek* we find private reflections prepared for a public audience. Here are a few excerpts to further illustrate what journal writing can be: recollections of childhood, wonderings on paper, records of dreams. What ideas do they give you for your journal?

Like the bear who went over the mountain, I went out to see what I could see. And, I might as well warn you, like the bear, all that I could see was the other side of the mountain: more of same. On a good day I might catch a glimpse of another wooded ridge rolling under the sun like water, another bivouac. I propose to keep here what Thoreau called "a meteorological journal of the mind," telling some tales and describing some of the sights of this rather tamed valley, and exploring, in fear and trembling, some of the unmapped dim reaches and unholy fastnesses to which those tales and sights so dizzyingly lead.

When I was six or seven years old, growing up in Pittsburgh, I used to take a precious penny of my own and hide it for someone else to find. It was a curious compulsion; sadly, I've never been seized by it since. For some reason I always "hid" the penny along the same stretch of sidewalk up the street. I would cradle it at the roots of a sycamore, say, or in a hole left by a chipped-off piece of sidewalk. Then I would take a piece of chalk, and, starting at either end of the block, draw huge arrows leading up to the penny from both directions. After I learned to write I labeled the arrows: SURPRISE AHEAD or MONEY THIS WAY. I was greatly excited, during all this arrow-drawing, at the thought of the first lucky passer-by who would receive in this way, regardless of merit, a free gift from the universe. But I never lurked about. I would go straight home and not give the matter another thought, until, some months later, I would be gripped again by the impulse to hide another penny.

I wonder how long it would take you to notice the regular recurrence of the seasons if you were the first man on earth. What would it be like to live in open-ended time broken only by days and nights? You could say, "it's cold again; it was cold before," but you couldn't make the key connection and say, "it was cold this time last year," because the notion of "year" is precisely the one you lack. Assuming that you hadn't yet noticed any orderly progression of heavenly bodies, how long would you have to live on earth before you could feel with any assurance that any one particular long period of cold would, in fact, end? "While the earth remaineth, seedtime and harvest, and cold and heat, and summer and winter, and day and night shall not cease": God makes this guarantee very early in Genesis to a people whose fears on this point had perhaps not been completely allayed.

I had a curious dream last night that stirred me. I visited the house of my childhood, and the basement there was covered with a fine sifting of snow. I lifted a snow-covered rug and found underneath it a bound sheaf of ink drawings I had made when I was six. Next to the basement, but unattached to it, extended a prayer tunnel.

The prayer tunnel was a tunnel fully enclosed by solid snow. It was cylindrical, and its diameter was the height of a man. Only an Eskimo, and then only very rarely, could survive in the prayer tunnel. There was, however, no exit or entrance; but I nevertheless understood that if I—if almost anyone—volunteered to enter it, death would follow after a long and bitter struggle. Inside the tunnel it was killingly cold, and a hollow wind like broadswords never ceased to blow. But there was little breatheable air, and that soon gone. It was utterly without light, and from all eternity it snowed the same fine, unmelting, wind-hurled snow.

EXERCISE

Write a journal entry on (1) a recollected childhood incident, (2) something you wonder about, or (3) a remembered dream. Think of it as writing for yourself that you might eventually revise for an audience.

Shared Reflections

Dillard's reflections, Wordsworth's poem, and the other readings in this chapter are evidence that people sometimes want to share their thoughts with others. Reflections that we write for ourselves are sometimes very personal. The thoughts may be incomplete, undeveloped, disorganized, and characterized by digressions and irrelevancies. In form, they may be fragmentary, loosely punctuated, unparagraphed, with vague and incomplete references. They may have doodles and drawings made during writing pauses.

Writing for others, however, is usually organized in some logical way, its ideas developed enough for readers to understand them as the writer intends and connected so that readers can see how they are related. Shared reflections are revised with the reader outside the self in mind. Here's an example of a reflective paragraph before it was revised for a reader:

> Bart and I went to the lake today. We backed the car out of the garage carefully and then drove over to Robert's and picked up him and Charles. When we got to the lake, we discovered that Mr. Ciatti's boat had come unmoored, so we spent the rest of the day tying up the boat and repairing the damage.

While this paragraph may be perfectly clear to the writer, as a reader you probably have a few questions. For instance, who is Bart? And who are Robert and Charles and Mr. Ciatti? What lake? Why did they go to the lake? Is there something significant in backing the car out of the garage *carefully?* How badly was the boat damaged? How does the writer feel about the incident? Here's a revision that answers some of these questions. The new parts are italicized.

> *My Brother* Bart and I went to Lake *Kenilworth* today, *as we usually do on the Fourth of July, to do a little fishing off the boat of our dad's boss, Mr. Ciatti. Since Mr. Ciatti was out of town on a business trip, he asked us to use his boat so that someone would be keeping track of it. Excited about the prospect of spending the*

day on Mr. Ciatti's cabin cruiser, we hopped into our dad's new Oldsmobile and drove off to pick up *our friends* Robert and Charles. *We were beginning to count our fish already and were making bets about who would catch the biggest. Little did we know that we would not be doing any fishing that day.* When we got to the lake, we discovered that Mr. Ciatti's boat had come unmoored. *Though the damage was slight,* we had to spend the rest of the day getting it tied up again and repairing the damage.

In the revised paragraph, the writer provides more details as well as the significance of certain details.

EXERCISE

Rewrite your journal entry from the preceding exercise, adjusting it for an audience other than yourself by adding or deleting details that may increase understanding of the incident, reflection, or dream.

The essays in this chapter represent reflective writing written or revised for readers. They illustrate reflections on nature, on evil, and on student pressures, for purposes of exploring, discovering, and comprehending.

Reflecting in a Journal Entry

Journals are a familiar form of reflective writing. Reflections in journals are usually written for the self for the purpose of exploring ideas or recording events and the writer's reactions to them. Academic journals have the specific purpose of recording, summarizing, and analyzing school-related lectures and reading. At times, writers will revise their journals or portions of them to make them public. Before reading the journal entry below, read the discussion of journals on pages 113–116 in this chapter.

Reading

"A Fire in the Woods" is a disturbing entry in Henry David Thoreau's journal that records a thoughtless act which leads to a potentially dangerous fire, loss of property, and cooperative fire-fighting efforts. In writing about the fire, Thoreau seems to be trying to work out his own feelings concerning it. He begins recording the incident, just narrating the events as they occurred, but then finds himself reacting to the incident, trying to discover meaning in it and his feelings toward it.

As you read this entry, think about whether Thoreau intended for an audience to read it. On what features do you base your decision? How does Thoreau feel about the fire?

A Fire in the Woods

Henry David Thoreau

I once set fire to the woods. Having set out, one April day, to go to the sources of Concord River in a boat with a single companion, meaning to camp on the bank at night or seek a lodging in some neighboring country inn or farmhouse, we took fishing tackle with us that we might fitly procure our food from the stream, Indian-like. At the shoemaker's near the river, we obtained a match, which we had forgotten. Though it was thus early in the spring, the river was low, for there had not been much rain, and we succeeded in catching a mess of fish sufficient for our dinner before we had left the town, and by the shores of Fair Haven Pond we proceeded to cook them. The earth was uncommonly dry, and our fire, kindled far from the woods in a sunny recess in the hillside on the east of the pond, suddenly caught the dry grass of the previous year which grew about the stump on which it was kindled. We sprang to extinguish it at first with our hands and feet, and then we fought it with a board obtained from the boat, but in a few minutes it was beyond our reach; being on the side of a hill, it spread rapidly upward, through the long, dry, wiry grass interspersed with bushes.

"Well, where will this end?" asked my companion. I saw that it might be bounded by Well Meadow Brook on one side, but would, perchance, go to the village side of the brook. "It will go to town," I answered. While my companion took the boat back down the river, I set out through the woods to inform the owners and to raise the town. The fire had already spread a dozen rods on every side and went leaping and crackling wildly and irreclaimably toward the wood. That way went the flames with wild delight, and we felt that we had no control over the demonic creature to which we had given birth. We had kindled many fires in the woods before, burning a clear space in the grass, without ever kindling such a fire as this.

As I ran toward the town through the woods, I could see the smoke over the woods behind me marking the spot and the progress of the flames. The first farmer whom I met driving a team, after leaving the woods, inquired the cause of the smoke. I told him. "Well," said he, "it is none of my stuff," and drove along. The next I met was the owner in his field, with whom I returned at once to the woods, running all the way. I had already run two miles. When at length we got into the neighborhood of the flames, we met a carpenter who had been hewing timber, an infirm man who had been driven off by the fire, fleeing with his axe. The farmer returned to hasten more assistance. I, who was spent with running, remained. What could I do alone against a front of flame half a mile wide?

I walked slowly through the wood to Fair Haven Cliff, climbed to the   4
highest rock, and sat down upon it to observe the progress of the flames,
which were rapidly approaching me, now about a mile distant from the spot
where the fire was kindled. Presently I heard the sound of the distant bell
giving the alarm, and I knew that the town was on its way to the scene.
Hitherto I had felt like a guilty person—nothing but shame and regret. But
now I settled the matter with myself shortly. I said to myself: "Who are these
men who are said to be the owners of these woods, and how am I related to
them? I have set fire to the forest, but I have done no wrong therein, and
now it is as if the lightning had done it. These flames are but consuming
their natural food." (It has never troubled me from that day to this more
than if the lightning had done it. The trivial fishing was all that disturbed me
and disturbs me still.) So shortly I settled it with myself and stood to watch
the approaching flames. It was a glorious spectacle, and I was the only one
there to enjoy it. The fire now reached the base of the cliff and then rushed
up its sides. The squirrels ran before it in blind haste, and three pigeons
dashed into the midst of the smoke. The flames flashed up the pines to their
tops, as if they were powder.

When I found I was about to be surrounded by the fire, I retreated and   5
joined the forces now arriving from the town. It took us several hours to
surround the flames with our hoes and shovels and by back fires subdue
them. In the midst of all I saw the farmer whom I first met, who had turned
indifferently away saying it was none of his stuff, striving earnestly to save his
corded wood, his stuff, which the fire had already seized and which it after
all consumed.

It burned over a hundred acres or more and destroyed much young   6
wood. When I returned home late in the day, with others of my townsmen,
I could not help noticing that the crowd who were so ready to condemn the
individual who had kindled the fire did not sympathize with the owners of
the wood, but were in fact highly elate and as it were thankful for the
opportunity which had afforded them so much sport; and it was only half a
dozen owners, so called, though not all of them, who looked sour or
grieved, and I felt that I had a deeper interest in the woods, knew them
better, and should feel their loss more, than any or all of them. The farmer
whom I had first conducted to the woods was obliged to ask me the shortest
way back, through his own lot. Why, then, should the half-dozen owners
[and] the individuals who set the fire alone feel sorrow for the loss of the
wood, while the rest of the town have their spirits raised? Some of the
owners, however, bore their loss like men, but other some declared behind
my back that I was a "damned rascal;" and a flibbertigibbet or two, who
crowed like the old cock, shouted some reminiscences of "burnt woods"
from safe recesses for some years after. I have had nothing to say to any of
them. The locomotive engine has since burned over nearly all the same
ground and more, and in some measure blotted out the memory of the
previous fire. For a long time after I had learned this lesson I marvelled that
while matches and tinder were contemporaries the world was not consumed;

why the houses that have hearths were not burned before another day; if the flames were not as hungry now as when I waked them. I at once ceased to regard the owners and my own fault—if fault there was any in the matter—and attended to the phenomenon before me, determined to make the most of it. To be sure, I felt a little ashamed when I reflected on what a trivial occasion this had happened, that at the time I was no better employed than my townsmen.

That night I watched the fire, where some stumps still flamed at midnight in the midst of the blackened waste, wandering through the woods by myself: and far in the night I threaded my way to the spot where the fire had taken, and discovered the now broiled fish—which had been dressed—scattered over the burnt grass.   7

Questions

1. Recount the progress of the fire and the fire-fighting efforts. What does this account tell you about chronological development?

2. Trace Thoreau's changing reactions to the fire. How does he feel at the beginning of the fire? at its end? How does he feel about the fire at the time of writing the journal entry? What do you think is his primary attitude toward the fire?

3. What were the effects of the fire? Which did the fire affect most, land or people?

4. Do you see any evidence of Thoreau's intending to have an audience read this journal entry? Explain your answer.

Discussion

Thoreau's journal entry begins with his story about how the fire started: "I once set fire to the woods." He describes the circumstances and the setting, what he and his companion did to try to extinguish the fire, the progress of the fire, and the actions aimed at putting it out. In describing the incident, he also explores his attitudes to it, being a concerned citizen, assessing fault, being curious, and so on.

Development. Thoreau's *narrative* of the fire's development is *chronological,* one event following another: first he and his companion catch some fish for their dinner, but their cooking fire ignites the dry grass surrounding the stump on which they've kindled it, and suddenly the fire is out of control. Thoreau's entry also uses *cause and effect analysis.* From the first cause, the spread of the cooking fire, he recounts a number of effects.

EXERCISE

In your journal, write an entry about fire.

Writing

Use your journal entry about fire or the one you wrote for the exercise on page 117 and expand it into an essay. Do some brainstorming or use the classical probes (see Chapter 3) to discover additional details and ideas to make this reflective piece interesting for an audience. To assist you in making this mainly private writing public, ask the Questions about Audience for Writing on (page 24). Also, ask yourself how you feel about your subject, since your reactions will tell the audience why you are writing.

Because this essay is largely reflective writing, you can expect to be using the personal pronoun *I*. However, if you discover as you revise that the pronoun is recurring too frequently—for example, every sentence or so—try revising your sentences to eliminate some of the incidences. Note how the following sentences are revised:

> *I* was crying as *I* got into the backseat with my brother. *I* reached for the box of tissues that my mother had had the foresight to bring. *I* was thinking about the silence in the car as we set out for the funeral service. For some reason *I* could not explain, *I* was remembering my grandmother's Swedish meatballs and the way *I* used to watch *The Sound of Music* with her.

> *Revised: I* was crying as my brother and *I* got into the backseat. Fortunately, my mother had had the foresight to bring a box of tissues, and in silence *I* reached for them as we set out for the funeral service. For some unexplained reason, *I* was remembering my grandmother's Swedish meatballs and the way we used to watch *The Sound of Music* together.

The revised passage has four *I*'s as opposed to seven in the original version. The passage is still personal, relating one writer's thoughts on the death of her grandmother, but the repetition no longer calls attention to itself.

Reflecting on Nature

Quality of life is inextricably tied to environment. Yet the evidence is clear that the greatest enemy to the global environment is the species with the most intelligence and sensitivity for maintaining it—humankind. Witness denuded mountains, rain forests stripped bare, parklands burned off by careless campfires, topsoil washed into the sea, species decimated and endangered. Environmentalists are often charged with standing in the way of progress, and frequently they are as strident in expressing their convictions as are those who would replace clean water and air with pollution or kill dolphins along with tuna or cut down trees to build more houses.

At the same time, there is the quiet voice of reflection. People sit on the dock and watch the incoming waves as the sun sets; they walk through the park and listen to the ripple of leaves or the unremitting call of the wren; they run along the footpath and feel on their faces the refreshing morning air; they are surprised by a rainbow and pause to admire it. There is much to appreciate about nature. Often our reflections do not get onto paper; the moment passes and the thoughts are gone. Occasionally we remember how good the air felt or how we glowed on sighting the rainbow; we may tell someone about the experience, or we may keep it to ourselves. Times like these give us reasons for carrying a pocket-size journal, for recording our thoughts while they are fresh.

Reading

Aldo Leopold recorded his reflections on nature in a widely read book, *A Sand County Almanac*. In the excerpt here, he reflects on the fate of wolves—and deer and mountains—in a world controlled by humans. As you read, note his attitude toward his subject and how he acquired that attitude. Observe also how a reflective, or personal, piece of writing can be intended for an audience other than the self, and how as public writing it can be powerfully persuasive; it acquires a more decisive purpose upon publication.

Thinking Like a Mountain

Aldo Leopold

A deep chesty bawl echoes from rimrock to rimrock, rolls down the mountain, and fades into the far blackness of the night. It is an outburst of wild defiant sorrow, and of contempt for all the adversities of the world. 1

Every living thing (and perhaps many a dead one as well) pays heed to that call. To the deer it is a reminder of the way of all flesh, to the pine a forecast of midnight scuffles and of blood upon the snow, to the coyote a promise of gleanings to come, to the cowman a threat of red ink at the bank, to the hunter a challenge of fang against bullet. Yet behind these obvious and immediate hopes and fears there lies a deeper meaning, known only to the mountain itself. Only the mountain has lived long enough to listen objectively to the howl of a wolf. 2

Those unable to decipher the hidden meaning know nevertheless that it is there, for it is felt in all wolf country, and distinguishes that country from all other land. It tingles in the spine of all who hear wolves by night, or who scan their tracks by day. Even without sight or sound of wolf, it is implicit in a hundred small events: the midnight whinny of a pack horse, the rattle of rolling rocks, the bound of a fleeing deer, the way shadows lie under the spruces. Only the ineducable tyro can fail to sense the presence or absence of wolves, or the fact that mountains have a secret opinion about them. 3

My own conviction on this score dates from the day I saw a wolf die. We were eating lunch on a high rimrock, at the foot of which a turbulent river elbowed its way. We saw what we thought was a doe fording the torrent, her breast awash in white water. When she climbed the bank toward us and shook out her tail, we realized our error: it was a wolf. A half-dozen others, evidently grown pups, sprang from the willows and all joined in a welcoming mêlée of wagging tails and playful maulings. What was literally a pile of wolves writhed and tumbled in the center of an open flat at the foot of our rimrock. 4

In those days we had never heard of passing up a chance to kill a wolf. In a second we were pumping lead into the pack, but with more excitement than accuracy: how to aim a steep downhill shot is always confusing. When our rifles were empty, the old wolf was down, and a pup was dragging a leg into impassable slide-rocks. 5

We reached the old wolf in time to watch a fierce green fire dying in her eyes. I realized then, and have known ever since, that there was something new to me in those eyes—something known only to her and to the mountain. I was young then, and full of trigger-itch; I thought that because fewer wolves meant more deer, that no wolves would mean hunters' paradise. But after seeing the green fire die, I sensed that neither the wolf nor the mountain agreed with such a view. 6

Since then I have lived to see state after state extirpate its wolves. I have watched the face of many a newly wolfless mountain, and seen the south-facing slopes wrinkle with a maze of new deer trails. I have seen every edible bush and seedling browsed, first to anaemic desuetude, and then to death. I have seen every edible tree defoliated to the height of a saddlehorn. Such a mountain looks as if someone had given God a new pruning shears, and forbidden Him all other exercise. In the end the starved bones of the hoped-for deer herd, dead of its own too-much, bleach with the bones of the dead sage, or molder under the high-lined junipers. 7

I now suspect that just as a deer herd lives in mortal fear of its wolves, so does a mountain live in mortal fear of its deer. And perhaps with better cause, for while a buck pulled down by wolves can be replaced in two or three years, a range pulled down by too many deer may fail of replacement in as many decades. 8

So also with cows. The cowman who cleans his range of wolves does not realize that he is taking over the wolf's job of trimming the herd to fit the range. He has not learned to think like a mountain. Hence we have dust-bowls, and rivers washing the future into the sea. 9

We all strive for safety, prosperity, comfort, long life, and dullness. The deer strives with his supple legs, the cowman with trap and poison, the statesman with pen, the most of us with machines, votes, and dollars, but it all comes to the same thing: peace in our time. A measure of success in this is all well enough, and perhaps is a requisite to objective thinking, but too much safety seems to yield only danger in the long run. Perhaps this is behind Thoreau's dictum: In wildness is the salvation of the world. Perhaps this is the hidden meaning in the howl of the wolf, long known among mountains, but seldom perceived among men. 10

Questions

1. What does Leopold mean by "thinking like a mountain"?

2. What does the mountain understand that the deer, the coyote, the cowman, and the young hunter Leopold do not?

3. What does the "fierce green fire" that died in the eyes of the wolf tell the young hunter Leopold about nature?

4. How did you feel when you read the essay? What aspects of the story affected you as you read?

5. Is Leopold advocating a prohibition on killing wolves? What does he mean in paragraph 8 when he says, "so does a mountain live in mortal fear of its deer"?

6. What do you understand in Leopold's indirect quotation from Thoreau in paragraph 10: "In wildness is the salvation of the world"?

7. In your own words, state Leopold's persuasive purpose for publishing this reflective essay.

Discussion

Leopold's reflections begin with hearing the call of a wolf. He reflects on the "hidden meaning" of the call and then remembers how he came to understand that meaning himself, ending with "thinking like a mountain." In reflecting on the change in his attitude toward killing wolves, Leopold urges the reader to change with him: to witness the death of the old wolf and to understand the implications of senseless extermination of a species. When he says in paragraph 7 "Since then I have lived to see state after state extirpate its wolves," he clearly regards this destruction as a mistake.

This position is echoed by another writer, Ted Williams, who, in an article called "Bringing Back the Beast of Lore," chronicles how thoroughly humans have eliminated wolves:

> For centuries we trapped them, poisoned them, shot them, and burned their pups alive in their dens. In 1905 we even tried biological warfare, infecting them with mange. Ten years later Congress passed a law requiring their elimination from federal lands. We had cleansed Yellowstone Park by 1926. It hasn't been easy, but finally we have won against the wolf.

Williams reports barely a thousand of the animals still living in the late 1980s in the contiguous forty-eight states. Though openly informative in purpose, his article, like Leopold's essay, is strongly persuasive about the wanton destruction of natural species.

Rather than use historic facts as William does, Leopold attempts to persuade by recounting a personal story about the death of a mother wolf and her family. Reflecting on his change of attitude and quoting another naturalist, Henry David Thoreau, Leopold invites the reader to participate in tolerance for nature.

Thesis

As a piece of reflective writing, this essay does not have an explicitly stated *thesis*. Yet it does have a controlling idea—an unstated thesis that makes the piece a coherent whole, holding its parts together and determining what the author includes and what he omits. In fact, it may have two theses, one *informative* and one *persuasive*. The informative thesis might be phrased something like this: "The mountain understands the balance of nature." Leopold develops his informative thesis by narrating his hunting story and explaining how nature maintains its own balance.

If we understand Leopold's purpose to include persuasion, we will express the thesis differently, perhaps "People should allow nature to maintain its own balance." Leopold's final sentences would seem to support such a thesis.

EXERCISE

Leopold uses mostly familiar words and moderate-length sentences (twenty to twenty-five words). Such a style enables reading at a comfortable pace with a high degree of comprehension. But a few words in this essay may have been unfamiliar to you or used in an unfamiliar way, impeding your comprehension. From the context, you probably guessed at their meaning. List those words now and look them up in a dictionary, searching for a meaning suitable to Leopold's essay. Then write sentences that use these words in what you perceive to be the same way Leopold uses them.

Writing

Reflect on an aspect of nature. Like Leopold, concentrate on an incident you've observed or experienced that contributed to an insight. Look around you. Even in urban settings you will find a natural world: pigeons and squirrels if not wolves and deer; sunsets and clouds and trees and rain showers. Thoreau once wrote about ants, John Steinbeck about a turtle.

Begin with a first draft that is truly a personal reflection, intended only for your own reading. If you are keeping a journal, you may want to use one of your journal entries or to begin this assignment as a new journal entry. Explore the natural incident in detail, including your feelings and thoughts when it occurred. At this point, don't give a great deal of attention to vocabulary, sentence style, or even thesis. Because your essay is personal, it may start out loosely structured, digressive, and disconnected.

As a controlling idea begins to emerge, you can develop it by adding details and eliminating irrelevant information. Your finished essay will still be reflective in tone—highly personal, and not instructive or argumentative.

But it will be a coherent whole, organized and developed around a specific thesis or controlling idea. It will explain and illustrate your reflections in enough detail that they will have meaning for an audience other than yourself.

Reflecting on Human Weakness

Everyone has a darker side—an aspect of our personalities that we're not proud of, one that we've learned we must keep in check. We may remember beating up on a younger brother or sister and recall with discomfort how we enjoyed it, knowing that that urge is still with us. Behind the wheel of a vehicle, the personalities of many people change from placid sociability to aggressive competitiveness. People lie sometimes when they don't want to acknowledge the truth; they cheat, slander, torment, and insult.

People ordinarily try to refrain from such behavior and even from admitting that they indulge in it. When our reflective writing brings to the fore the unpleasant aspects of our personalities and the acts they have caused, we usually don't want to reveal such admissions. Sometimes, however, we realize that others can learn from our experience, and we make our darker thoughts public.

Reading

The essay that follows is a reflection of how warfare encourages and thrives on humanity's darker side and how the prompting of this evil affects the soldiers, who are encouraged to be ruthless. The author, Mark Baker, is a Vietnam veteran recounting the stories of other Vietnam veterans. As you read this essay, which is an introduction to one of the chapters in his book *Nam: The Vietnam War in the Words of the Men and Women Who Fought There,* try to discover Baker's attitude toward warfare's encouragement of expressions of evil. Does he have a purpose for writing other than reflection?

The Taste of Evil
Mark Baker

"I had a little puppy for a while in Vietnam. For a period of three days,   1
I would take this little puppy and squeeze it until it would yelp. Or twist its little paw.

"I knew what I was doing. I knew that I was transferring something to   2
this little puppy. Somebody or something had to suffer for all the pain inside of me, and it was going to be the puppy.

"I was so horrified by my behavior that I gave the puppy to someone   3
else. I had to get it out of my sight. I don't think I would have killed it, but

I didn't quite know where this spark of sadism was going to lead me. It went against the grain of who I thought I was. I had a sense of being split in two."

It rises like a wave of nausea in your throat, out of nowhere, uncontrolled, the dry, bitter taste of evil. You're walking the dog and in canine goofiness he insists on sniffing one empty square of sidewalk, holding his ground until you jerk the leash so hard the choke chain almost cuts his windpipe in two. A child says "No" at just the wrong time and you swallow hard when you find yourself towering over your own flesh and blood with murder in your eye. You actually slam on the brakes, jump out of the car, and run back to rip the throat out of the tailgater behind you before he can roll up his windows. An uneasy joke escapes from the knot of petty viciousness inside you and you seem to stand outside yourself as you watch it metamorphosize to malicious teasing. Suddenly you're tormenting some other human being— usually someone you love—until he's ready to take a wild swing at you. 4

The feeling passes quickly leaving you shaking with every thump of your heart, wondering where in this sane and ordered world a psycho like that comes from. But that psycho was you, the other you, the darker side, the one who knows all the nasty things you've done or thought in the privacy of your mind, the flipside of your conscience that hoards the merest slights and demands revenge no matter how petty, how misdirected. 5

No eighteen-year-old kid went to Vietnam thinking, "Oh boy, now I'm going to be evil." But most of them met their darker sides face to face in that war. A few of them had an adolescent meanness which blossomed ugly, nurtured by the circumstances they found in Vietnam. Many of them indulged the ruthlessness they discovered as part of the instinct to survive. 6

For all the glory words like duty, honor, and valor, war runs best on evil, a breeder reactor that vomits out a hell full of pain for the little spark of sadism people feed into it. Evil was encouraged with rewards of medals, time off from the horror, a hot meal. How else can you convince boys to kill one another day after day? And when the darker side grabs the upper hand, takes control, how else can it be excused? 7

Vietnam veterans do not have the luxury of dismissing evil as a momentary aberration in an otherwise civilized world. They have seen the ugliness humans are capable of inflicting—that they themselves are capable of inflicting. 8

The brutal stories are delivered with a nervous chuckle, dirty jokes from another world that don't quite survive translation. "I guess you had to be there." But there is no enjoyment in the telling. The hesitant laughter is self-defense, a shaky feint to keep the evil at arm's length. If the mortal slapstick can be kept in a cartoon life, maybe the shadow of inhumanity can be denied a little longer, the personal pain can be buried a little deeper. 9

Questions

1. What is your first reaction upon reading the essay? What does Baker do to promote your reaction? What is his attitude toward his subject?

2. How does audience reaction relate to Baker's purpose in writing?

3. What *persuasive* purpose might Baker have had for writing?

4. What does Baker say about evil in the final four paragraphs?

5. What does he say about people's ability to control their baser instincts in situations where those instincts are encouraged?

6. What sentence might be regarded as Baker's thesis?

Discussion

"The Taste of Evil" is not meant to be pleasant reading. It reflects on an undesirable aspect of human nature. One of Baker's purposes may be to inform readers about a burden that Vietnam veterans brought home with them and about the horrors of war. But his foremost purpose seems to be to reflect on the nature of evil and how it figures into warfare. While reflections are first of all personal, the philosophical insights that derive from them can achieve other purposes when they are shared with an audience.

Development

In developing his essay, Baker begins by quoting a veteran's experience with a puppy and the veteran's horror at his behavior. Baker then attempts in paragraphs 4 and 5 to define the "dry, bitter taste of evil" with examples, getting the reader directly involved through use of the second-person *you:* "You're walking the dog," "you seem to stand outside yourself," "that psycho was you." The effect of these paragraphs might have been different if Baker had used third person: "Someone is walking the dog," "people seem to stand outside themselves," "that psycho was someone's best friend."

Baker devotes the remainder of the essay to the Vietnam experience. "War," he says, "runs best on evil," and Vietnam veterans know firsthand what evil and ugliness people, themselves included, can inflict. After his introductory *narrative* (paragraphs 1–3) and his *definition* of evil with examples (paragraphs 4–5), Baker applies his definition to specific circumstances (paragraphs 6–9). The first sentence of paragraph 8 seems to sum up the various parts of the essay—the definition of evil, the relating of war and evil, the specific references to Vietnam. Given his persuasive purpose, this sentence might also be viewed as Baker's *thesis.*

Style

Consider Baker's use of *passive voice.* In paragraph 7 he says, "Evil was encouraged with rewards of medals, time off from the horror, a hot meal." The passive verb *"was encouraged"* does not say who did the encouraging. Would you prefer that the writer name the encourager? Again, in paragraph 9, Baker writes, "The brutal stories are delivered with a nervous chuckle." Would the sentence have been better if he'd said, "The veterans deliver the brutal stories with a nervous chuckle"? Writers ordinarily use active voice—as in this proposed revision naming the persons doing the delivering—unless they have a reason for using passive voice. In active voice, the subject of the sentence performs the action of the verb ("veterans deliver"). In passive voice, the performer of the action follows the verb, usually in a *by* phrase, or is not included, as in the two examples just quoted.

Ordinarily, writers want to tell who is performing the action of their verbs. Sometimes, however, as in these four circumstances, they do not:

When the performer is not known ("The window was broken")
When the performer is not important ("The program was printed")
When the writer wants to conceal the identity of the performer ("The money was embezzled")
When the writer has stylistic reasons, such as to keep subjects consistent in a series of sentences or to shift the emphasis in a sentence

The two sentences quoted from Baker's essay illustrate stylistic reasons for using passive voice. In both, Baker has placed in subject position the topical subjects. The first sentence is about evil, the second about brutal stories. By using passive voice, Baker emphasizes evil and brutality, the focus of his essay. The best rule to follow about passive voice is to use it if you have a good reason; otherwise avoid it.

EXERCISES

1. Baker's final paragraph has another sentence with passive voice. Find the sentence and rewrite it to make the passive verbs active. Add subjects as necessary, but do not otherwise change the meaning. Then compare your revised version with the original. How has the effect changed?
2. Examine a piece of your own writing for occurrences of passive voice. Consider your reasons for writing in the passive, and revise if you think that doing so would improve the sentences.

Writing

Reflect on a common human weakness, one that requires training and constant attention to keep it in check—perhaps

- Rudeness
- Prejudice

- Lying
- Procrastination
- Greed

Reflection can take many paths when it explores a subject. The classical probes (see Chapter 3) are especially useful tools for prompting reflective thoughts: *identify* the subject, *compare* it with similar things, *classify* it, *analyze* its *causes and effects,* tell how it works (*process*), and give some *examples* of it.

As you revise your reflections for an audience, you may choose to organize your essay as Baker does, begin with a narrative illustration, then define your subject with examples, and finally relate your subject to a specific circumstance. Remember that reflections revised for an audience include details and explanations that may be unnecessary when the writer is the only reader.

Remembering a Painful Experience

We've all had painful experiences. They may have been caused by other people, been brought on by our own actions, or just happened. We may have unwittingly caused a fire, as Thoreau remembers in his journal entry, or caused someone mental or physical anguish. Recalling such occurrences often brings remorse and a wish that we could undo our actions. Some of our recollections concern the hurtful actions of other people, and in recalling the pain we also try to make sense of these incidents. Such recollections may come to the surface almost against our wills when we write reflectively in our personal journals.

Reading

"Whimpering Puppies," written by a college student, recalls a painful childhood experience. Like Baker's "The Taste of Evil," this essay explores the effect of unchecked evil, but from the perspective of a recipient of abusive behavior. This essay, though, is somewhat narrower in scope than Baker's, focusing on a personal experience and the writer's understanding of it. On the basis of the title, what do you think the writer's purpose is?

Whimpering Puppies
Lorrie Anderson (student writer)

For years I never fully realized anything had been wrong with my   1
childhood. I only knew one thing: I thought I was going crazy. I felt different from everyone else. I couldn't seem to have close relationships with people. I didn't have many close friends. None of my social relationships

lasted longer than a few days or a couple of weeks at the most. I felt insecure and unsure of myself in social situations and at school. I really didn't know what self-esteem was at that time, but I knew I lacked confidence in my abilities. I honestly didn't think I was good at anything. My parents seemed to confirm this thought by their constant badgering and insults. My father was an alcoholic, and his illness affected us all.

One of my most vivid memories was of one of my father's alcoholic ram-   2
pages when I was in about fifth grade. My parents had been fighting, which usually happened whenever my father had been drinking. As their voices grew louder, their tone became more abusive. I was huddled in a bedroom with two of my sisters, neither of whom acknowledged that there was anything wrong. I prayed that the fight would not involve any of my brothers or sisters.

Suddenly I heard louder noises and screaming. It sounded as if some-   3
one was being killed. My mother had been on the receiving end of my father's temper many times. Now I was afraid she was being hurt . . . no, I was actually afraid my father was going to kill her. I raced out of the bedroom to stop the fight.

When I came into the kitchen, I saw what had caused all the noise. My   4
father had thrown a cupboard full of pots and pans all over the kitchen. He was screaming at my mother, who just stood there taking his abuse and not trying to stop him. I jumped between them trying to shut out the verbal beating my father was giving me.

"Stop it, just stop it!" I yelled, I think at both of them. My father grabbed   5
my arm in a drunken rage. My mother tried to protect me and grabbed onto my other arm. They pulled at me from opposite directions, and my father screamed: "Okay, who do you love?"

This sort of abuse occurs in alcoholic families. My father would get   6
drunk and would start fighting with my mother. He would tire of her as a target, and then the kids would be involved. That's why my brothers and sisters and I would disappear as quickly as we could whenever fighting started. We were like puppies, cowering under the bed or in a closet or whimpering in a corner until our angry master passed out or tired of his rampage.

Questions

1. Do you agree with the writer's analogy of whimpering puppies? Does it seem an appropriate way to describe the reactions of the children to their father's drunken behavior?

2. How does the analogy connect to the lack of self-esteem the writer describes in her introductory paragraph?

3. How did you react to the narrative when reading it?

4. What does this incident tell you about children dealing with parental alcoholism?

5. What kind of reader does the essay seem to be written for—one who has not grown up in an alcoholic family, one who has had no contact with alcoholic families, or one who has experienced alcoholism?

6. What do you think is Anderson's purpose for making this experience public?

Discussion

This is a reflective essay—a writer's recollections about a painful childhood experience, one incident to illustrate her point about an unhealthful family situation. Notice her personal reactions to the incident:

I was huddled in a bedroom.

I prayed that the fight would not involve any of my brothers or sisters.

I was afraid [my mother] was being hurt.

The details about the incident are specific, and the reactions are clear. But the writer says nothing about the causes of her father's alcoholism or treatments for alcoholism, because that is not her purpose.

Purpose and Thesis

The first sentence in paragraph 6—"This sort of abuse occurs in alcoholic families"—seems to indicate a purpose other than reflection, an audience other than the writer. However, it is the only sentence in her essay that generalizes beyond the writer's specific situation. The generalized statement seems to be more *informative* than persuasive, in that it does not require action from the reader. Consider the likelihood of the statement as the essay's *thesis.* A narrower, more specific sentence occurs at the end of paragraph 1: "My father was an alcoholic, and his illness affected us all." Do you feel that this is a more likely thesis sentence? Does it sum up the subject and point of the essay?

EXERCISE

Anderson does not answer the question screamed by her father: "Okay, who do you love?" Write a paragraph in which you assume the writer's role and try to answer this question. Make it a paragraph that would be appropriate inserted before the final paragraph in the essay and would resolve the problems posed in the first paragraph.

Writing

Reflect on an experience that was difficult or painful for you—one that, like the one in "Whimpering Puppies"—was caused by another person, or one that was a result of accidental occurrences or your own carelessness. Since this is a personal experience, connect it to something you've learned about yourself.

When you revise for your audience, delete information that you don't want others to know and add details that an interested audience would like to read. Your readers will want to know not only what happened but also how you reacted.

Reflecting on Human Folly

Every now and then, people begin to contemplate how foolish we all are. Isn't it folly to build magnificent new skyscrapers while the homeless wander on the streets below? Isn't it idiocy to pump water out of the eons-old aquifers beneath the earth's surface in order to maintain lush green lawns for a season? And we continue to pump oil out of the earth at a furious pace to keep up with our insatiable energy demands. We continue to use chlorofluorocarbons even though we know they are destroying the ozone layer that protects us from the sun's harmful ultraviolet rays.

Pick up any newsmagazine or newspaper and you will find writers decrying human folly. Such writings are usually informative or persuasive in purpose, intended to effect change. Sometimes, however, we turn to the foolish ways of humankind in our reflections. We reflect on what the world will be like for our children: are we damaging the earth so irreparably that living as we know it now will be impossible for them? Will there be space and resources on this earth for the generations to come? Such reflections, like informative writings, may have persuasion as a purpose, especially when the writers make them public.

Reading

In "Late Night Thoughts on Listening to Mahler's Ninth Symphony," Lewis Thomas asks if it is not irresponsible to build bombs and missiles when what we want to achieve is a world for our young people to grow up and grow old in. A noted scientist, a physician, and a widely published writer, Thomas also enjoys fine music. In this essay, he records reflections on how his listening has changed over the years. As a result of nuclear armament, he can no longer assume that the earth will endure, and this thought affects the way he hears music. Perhaps you listen to music as Thomas does—in part tuned in to the music, in part absorbed in your own thoughts, with the result that music and thoughts blend into a new way of hearing the music and a fresh insight that would not have occurred without the music's input. As you read, note how the strains of the symphony prompt Thomas's contemplation.

Note also the persistent use of *I*. As a record of the writer's own thoughts, the first-person pronoun is appropriate. At the same time, this essay has been published, so we can assume that Thomas intended it for an audience beyond himself.

Late Night Thoughts on Listening to Mahler's Ninth Symphony

Lewis Thomas

I cannot listen to Mahler's Ninth Symphony with anything like the old melancholy mixed with the high pleasure I used to take from this music. There was a time, not long ago, when what I heard, especially in the final movement, was an open acknowledgment of death and at the same time a quiet celebration of the tranquillity connected to the process. I took this music as a metaphor for reassurance, confirming my own strong hunch that the dying of every living creature, the most natural of all experiences, has to be a peaceful experience. I rely on nature. The long passages on all the strings at the end, as close as music can come to expressing silence itself, I used to hear as Mahler's idea of leave-taking at its best. But always, I have heard this music as a solitary, private listener, thinking about death.

Now I hear it differently. I cannot listen to the last movement of the Mahler Ninth without the door-smashing intrusion of a huge new thought: death everywhere, the dying of everything, the end of humanity. The easy sadness expressed with such gentleness and delicacy by that repeated phrase on faded strings, over and over again, no longer comes to me as old, familiar news of the cycle of living and dying. All through the last notes my mind swarms with images of a world in which the thermonuclear bombs have begun to explode, in New York and San Francisco, in Moscow and Leningrad, in Paris, in Paris, in Paris. In Oxford and Cambridge, in Edinburgh. I cannot push away the thought of a cloud of radioactivity drifting along the Engadin, from the Moloja Pass to Ftan, killing off part of the earth I love more than any other part.

I am old enough by this time to be used to the notion of dying, saddened by the glimpse when it has occurred but only transiently knocked down, able to regain my feet quickly at the thought of continuity, any day. I have acquired and held in affection until very recently another sideline of an idea which serves me well at dark times: the life of the earth is the same as the life of an organism: the great round being possesses a mind: the mind contains an infinite number of thoughts and memories: when I reach my time I may find myself still hanging around in some sort of midair, one of those small thoughts, drawn back into the memory of the earth: in that peculiar sense I will be alive.

Now all that has changed. I cannot think that way anymore. Not while those things are still in place, aimed everywhere, ready for launching.

This is a bad enough thing for the people in my generation. We can put up with it, I suppose, since we must. We are moving along anyway, like it or not. I can even set aside my private fancy about hanging around, in midair.

What I cannot imagine, what I cannot put up with, the thought that keeps grinding its way into my mind, making the Mahler into a hideous noise close to killing me, is what it would be like to be young. How do the young stand it? How can they keep their sanity? If I were very young, sixteen or seventeen years old, I think I would begin, perhaps very slowly and imperceptibly, to go crazy.

There is a short passage near the very end of the Mahler in which the   7
almost vanishing violins, all engaged in a sustained backward glance, are edged aside for a few bars by the cellos. Those lower notes pick up fragments from the first movement, as though prepared to begin everything all over again, and then the cellos subside and disappear, like an exhalation. I used to hear this as a wonderful few seconds of encouragement: we'll be back, we're still here, keep going, keep going.

Now, with a pamphlet in front of me on a corner of my desk, published   8
by the Congressional Office of Technology Assessment, entitled *MX Basing*, an analysis of all the alternative strategies for placement and protection of hundreds of these missiles, each capable of creating artificial suns to vaporize a hundred Hiroshimas, collectively capable of destroying the life of any continent, I cannot hear the same Mahler. Now, those cellos sound in my mind like the opening of all the hatches and the instant before ignition.

If I were sixteen or seventeen years old, I would not feel the cracking of   9
my own brain, but I would know for sure that the whole world was coming unhinged. I can remember with some clarity what it was like to be sixteen. I had discovered the Brahms symphonies. I knew that there was something going on in the late Beethoven quartets that I would have to figure out, and I knew that there was plenty of time ahead for all the figuring I would ever have to do. I had never heard of Mahler. I was in no hurry. I was a college sophomore and had decided that Wallace Stevens and I possessed a comprehensive understanding of everything needed for a life. The years stretched away forever ahead, forever. My great-great grandfather had come from Wales, leaving his signature in the family Bible on the same page that carried, a century later, my father's signature. It never crossed my mind to wonder about the twenty-first century; it was just there, given, somewhere in the sure distance.

The man on television, Sunday midday, middle-aged and solid, nice-   10
looking chap, all the facts at his fingertips, more dependable looking than most high-school principals, is talking about civilian defense, his responsibility in Washington. It can make an enormous difference, he is saying. Instead of the outright death of eighty million American citizens in twenty minutes, he says, we can, by careful planning and practice, get that number down to only forty million, maybe even twenty. The thing to do, he says, is to evacuate the cities quickly and have everyone get under shelter in the countryside. That way we can recover, and meanwhile we will have retaliated, incinerating all of Soviet society, he says. What about radioactive fallout? he is asked. Well, he says. Anyway, he says, if the Russians know they can only destroy forty million of us instead of eighty million, this will deter them. Of course, he adds, they have the capacity to kill all two hundred and twenty million of us if they were to try real hard, but they know we can do

the same to them. If the figure is only forty million this will deter them, not worth the trouble, not worth the risk. Eighty million would be another matter, we should guard ourselves against losing that many all at once, he says.

If I were sixteen or seventeen years old and had to listen to that, or read   11 things like that, I would want to give up listening and reading. I would begin thinking up new kinds of sounds, different from any music heard before, and I would be twisting and turning to rid myself of human language.

Questions

1. What two specific occurrences alter the nature of Thomas's thoughts?
2. Locate instances in the essay that express Thomas's changes in attitude toward death and toward Mahler's symphony.
3. Who do you think Thomas's intended audience is? Does his final paragraph assume a youthful audience, sixteen- or seventeen-year-olds? Explain your answer with evidence from the essay.
4. Can you think of any reason for Thomas to select "sixteen or seventeen" for his "If I were" statements?
5. Are Thomas's personal reflections generalizable? In other words, do his thoughts on listening to Mahler relate to you and other readers?

Discussion

One of the primary themes of Thomas's essay seems to be thoughts of death—how he once thought of death and how he thinks of it now. For years, Thomas listened to Mahler's symphony contemplating only his own death. But, after reading the graphic descriptions in the congressional pamphlet *MX Basing,* he could think only about global death and destruction. With this alteration in focus came a change in attitude toward death and toward the symphony.

Thesis

Thomas's *thesis* is in his very first sentence: "I cannot listen to Mahler's Ninth Symphony with anything like the old melancholy mixed with the high pleasure I used to take from this music." This thesis states his subject, his assertion about his subject, and his method of development:

Subject: Listening to Mahler's Ninth Symphony
Assertion: I cannot listen as I did in the past.
Method of development: Contrast of present with past

Development

As implied in his thesis, Thomas's reflections develop along the lines of *comparison/contrast.* He contrasts the present with the past, the "now" with the "not long ago." Beginning with the past, he relates how he once listened to Mahler's symphony; then in paragraph 2 he presents a contrast with "now," relating his thoughts while listening. Paragraph 3 shifts again to past contemplations, then back to "now" in paragraphs 4 through 6. In paragraph 7 Thomas again relates the "used to" of his listening, contrasting in paragraph 8 with a specific occurrence that prompted his new thoughts. Paragraph 9 shifts back to the past, and the remainder of the essay addresses the full import of Thomas's present reflections. The pattern looks like this:

Not Long Ago	*Now*
Paragraph 1	Paragraph 2
Paragraph 3	Paragraphs 4–6
Paragraph 7	Paragraph 8
Paragraph 9	Paragraphs 10–11

The essay is a combination of philosophical *reflection, reminiscence,* and a *record* of the present. In part Thomas states his beliefs and ideas, and in part he records events and actions. Paragraphs 1 through 7 and 11 are mainly statements of beliefs and ideas, whereas paragraphs 8 through 10 primarily relate events and actions.

Purpose and Audience

Look again at the concluding paragraph. Its opening clause, "If I were sixteen or seventeen years old," repeats the opening of paragraph 9, in which Thomas remembers what it was like to be sixteen, and his first reference in paragraph 6: "If I were very young, sixteen or seventeen years old, I think I would begin, perhaps very slowly and imperceptibly, to go crazy." The "If I were" statement seems to be a thread that ties the essay together. Imagine Thomas writing this reflective essay: listening to Mahler's symphony, his thoughts roaming, recalling past reflections, being sixteen or seventeen, the civil defense official on television, the pamphlet on his desk, the symphony and thoughts of death, what life was like when he was sixteen or seventeen, how the world has changed, worldwide death and destruction, what life will be like for people who are sixteen or seventeen now. Reflections are often tied by recurring thoughts: the symphony, death, a particular time in life.

Thomas's first audience for this reflective essay was undoubtedly himself and his purpose only to reflect—to record his thoughts while listening to Mahler's Ninth Symphony. In making his reflections public, however, his audience broadened—probably including sixteen- and seventeen-year-olds but not limited to them. And his purpose? Reflections intended for an audience usually have purposes beyond the exploration of ideas. If we study Thomas's final paragraph, we might decide that his purpose, other than to record reflections, is to *persuade* readers to work toward nuclear disarmament, to *explain* how awareness of the nuclear age alters even the small things in life, or perhaps only to inspire further *reflections* in his readers.

EXERCISES

1. In your journal or elsewhere, write an exploration of why Thomas would select sixteen or seventeen years of age as the basis for his reflections. Are these just ages picked out of the air? Since you are closer to sixteen or seventeen years old than Thomas is, do you think his reactions to nuclear armament are appropriate and helpful?
2. For Thomas, reflecting while listening to music yielded important insights. Try it yourself. Turn on some music that you enjoy listening to, and while you listen do a freewriting (see Chapter 3) on whatever thoughts occur to you. If you're keeping a journal, do the writing in your journal and keep it as a source of ideas. Or use this exercise as prewriting for the following writing assignment.

Writing

Reflect on a change in attitude, a difference in how you look at something now from how you viewed it in the past. Here are some ideas:

- Studying
- Reading
- A kind of music
- Parental rules
- A place

First do a freewriting, possibly accompanied by music, concentrating on "now" and "not long ago," exploring your change in attitude, and establishing what caused the change. Through your reflections you may discover some things about how you have changed and why, and about how these insights might relate to what's important to other people.

Your comparisons are likely to end up, like Thomas's, as a balanced essay of contrasting paragraphs. As you revise, insert the cause of the change where appropriate, and bring in enough reminiscence, records of present actions, and philosophical insights to interest and inform an audience about the change. While reflective essays sometimes rely on an implicit thesis or controlling idea (Leopold's, page 123) and others state the thesis at the end

(Baker's, page 127), for this essay consider *beginning* with a thesis sentence that sets up your comparison. Because this essay will report *your* experiences and reflections, incidents from your own life are appropriate.

ADDITIONAL READINGS FOR DISCUSSION

Reading

This essay was written by Jidit, a student at Seminar Hakibutzim, while she was studying the Jewish Holocaust in Kibbutz Lohamei Haghetaot in Israel. The essay was translated from Hebrew by an instructor at the seminar, Dorka Sternberg. Because you are more familiar with English than Dorka was, you will undoubtedly find her translation not quite idiomatic. Try to overlook the oddities as you read for the message.

6,000,000

Jidit

(Translated by Dorka Sternberg)

Six million. A number. Since I was a child I tried to imagine. I closed my eyes and tried to see. I ordered people in rows, so I could count them, but it was impossible. The more I pressed them the less I succeeded to fill in a thousand people before the picture became a grey and black spot.   1

Then I decided to count. Every night before falling to sleep. I counted till the minute before I fell asleep. I put a notebook under my pillow in which I wrote exactly the number I had arrived to. The second night I continued to count from the number where I had stopped last night. After a week I reached 5,000. I learned that if I should continue in such a system it would take me a year to arrive at 240,000 and almost five years to the first 1,000,000. I decided to increase the speed of counting and took my notebook with me and counted also at school during class and while walking in the street, but at the end I gave up.   2

I sank in reading—diaries, stories, songs. I identified, cried, and admired the power that those children had in them. I didn't have the strength to give each and every one of them one second of counting . . . not more. Then I tried to imagine a book that contains 6,000,000 songs: I tried to multiply this number with the number of the diaries, stories, and struggles of the moment, and again I was lost. I couldn't grasp.   3

Later, when I was a soldier, Jeremy died and I started visiting the cemetery. Many times I went through the same city of the white rectangles set in perfect order among the cypress trees and pathways. Only there I   4 succeeded to feel the huge quantity of people who lost their lives during the wars in order to have a country, even though I was in the silent city only. Once, in a memory day, I tried to imagine a cemetery for the Holocaust victims: a whole country of white rectangles stretched out from horizon to horizon. Still I tried to realize the same number, 6,000,000, to give a personal sign to each and every one of them. But still without success.

Questions

1. Jidit tries to comprehend tangibly the extermination of 6 million Jews during World War II. In what ways does she attempt to represent the number?

2. What is the point of the fact that she repeatedly fails to realize this number?

3. What effect does the language of this translation have on your reading? Is it distracting? What about it disturbs you most? How does the language enhance the writer's communication efforts?

4. Which phrases in the essay seem unidiomatic to you? Revise them to read more naturally.

5. Think of some ways, other than those represented here, of trying to comprehend the enormity of the Holocaust.

Reading

Campus life is often stressful, full of pressures such as parental expectations, the difficulty of keeping grades up, balancing work and studies, learning to be responsible for one's own life, and so on. In this essay, a student writer reflects on those familiar pressures.

Holding On

Kim (student writer)

The trip went too fast. I was home before I knew it. Even though I'd been away three weeks, nothing had changed. Well O.K.!, maybe the house was cleaner. I am sure my parents never stopped noticing that. It was cleaner because I was gone.

No one was around. I knew where Mom was. She was at school. Besides working fifty-plus hours a week with an hour drive both ways, she still insisted that she go to school. So she took classes at a college almost three hours away every other weekend. She always wanted more.

After I searched the house for my father, I ventured outside to find out what kind of job he would be doing. Did I mention it was Saturday? My dad was pulling weeds out of the lawn with his bare hands. He could have gone to the drugstore and got some weed killer, and the job could have been done in less than half the time. But no! I mentioned the word *job* on purpose. Although it was Saturday, you still could not be just relaxing—you must be working.

Then I knew it was my turn. I didn't dare go in the house and plop   4
down in an easychair. What kind of work would I do? It would have to be somewhat involved—it couldn't just be homework. Well, I figured out what I would do. I decided to begin reading one of my textbooks, but I also threw in doing some laundry.

Every minute of studying sent my mind wandering off even more.   5
Nothing had changed. Even my cat was as mean as ever. They don't understand! I am not like they are! Just what is important to me? This is a question my parents are always asking. What is important to me? Maybe it is not so much what is important as what can I handle? The scary part is that I seem capable of handling less and less each day. Work with its unbreakable schedules, school with its constant work, home with my insensitive parents, and friends who don't understand that you need them too sometimes—all are pressures, each seeming to multiply the others.

I knew I had to concentrate on my reading. Just as I got settled in, the   6
dryer buzzer went off. The clothes were not dry. "Damn!" Nothing was going right. The day ended with little conversation between my dad and me. We each kept to our own area of the house, each doing our own work.

Sunday morning church seemed so early at 8:00 A.M., but you can't   7
sleep in until ten o'clock church because you would waste half the day. There were things to be done. I wondered what they would do all day. I hadn't seen Mom in weeks. I knew I would see her at breakfast.

Breakfast was uneventful. Just the same old questions. "How are your   8
classes?" "How are your roommates?" "How are your instructors?" I handled them in the usual manner—"Fine!"

The ride home from Perkins Restaurant was no more eventful than I   9
expected. It was the same old story: "You need to organize your finances." "A student loan isn't the answer." "Move back into the dorms; it's cheaper."

I felt as if I were losing my grip. I wanted to scream, but all I could   10
manage to do was cry. Don't they understand that is not the problem? The problem is their expectations. Sixteen credits, 3.5 G.P.A. or better, and still work. Don't they understand! I can't do it! I am tired all the time. I know people can do it. I guess that is why I still try. The more I try, however, the farther behind I become. It is hard to get up when you are down.

We finally got home, and the first thing I did was call my ride back to   11
school. "I am ready to go back." My parents didn't understand why I had to go back so soon; after all, it was only eleven o'clock in the morning. I made up some excuse. Don't they understand? It is them!

I sank into the car seat and settled in for the three-hour ride back to   12
school. This time the ride couldn't go fast enough. It felt good to pull onto the highway. I knew my problems didn't go away, but it did feel good to be closed up in a car, far away from everyone else.

As I burst into the doorway of my apartment, my roommates welcomed   13
me home. I knew I would be O.K.

Questions

1. What pressures of student life does Kim identify in this essay?
2. Characterize how Kim sees her relationship with her parents.
3. Why does she feel better when she returns to school?
4. Do you think Kim would want her parents to read this essay? What reasons might she have for wanting them to read it? for not wanting them to read it?
5. Write a note to Kim advising her on how she might revise this essay before slipping it under her parents' door.

Reading

In this essay, a nontraditional student writer reflects on the effects of growing up in an alcoholic home. As you read the essay and speculate on the problems it presents, you might compare it with "Whimpering Puppies" earlier in this chapter.

Epitaph for a Childhood

Lorna Marro

It was during my turbulent childhood that the Viet Nam War raged in   1
a land I had never known existed. It meant nothing more to me than a few glimpses on the "Evening News" and hushed conversations between adults. I could not fathom the fear, anger, and horror that shrouded all those involved in the fighting; I could not feel it; it was not real to me. I was struggling to survive in another war. A war that had live combat, P.O.W.'s, and excessive cruelty; a war that crushed all hope of peace like a bug under a heel of a boot; a war where the dark, incessant nights held no faith that a renaissance of a new day would dawn; a war where I lay eternally on the verge of sleep welcoming the exhaustion that would block out the pain of reality; a war where the closing of the garage door was enough to jolt me back into the truth to tell me that now it would begin again; a war that was called alcoholism.

Some soldiers hid in foxholes and trenches; I hid under my bed. Those   2
same men prayed to God to spare their lives; I could only pray to end mine. They spoke in whispers—the enemy was near; I could not speak at all—the enemy was here. The Nation mourned for the sons who had given their lives to fight the "Communist Enemy"; no one grieved for the death of a little girl's childhood given in sacrifice to a bottle of "Russian Vodka."

I was a prisoner in my own house, and I spent hours staring out the   3
window of the cell that was assigned me for sleeping. From the loneliness of
that room I watched the unaware world go by, leaving me behind. I felt the
weight of the universe crushing, crushing, crushing my young shoulders
until all my feelings and emotions lay dead around my feet. The only thing
that kept me behind those invisible bars, and from shouting my rage to the
four corners of the earth, was the binding, unspoken code of an alcoholic
home: at all costs I must protect the secret sickness that thrives within the
family; I must tell no outsider what is going on; I must pretend, lie, or make
excuses if someone questions me; I must not ask friends over to play because
they might see something that is forbidden; I must not go out and play with
them because there is no one to protect my mother.

This was the burden of a child. The hours my mother spent crying; the   4
angry shouts and curses that echoed through the night; the Antarctic cold
that permeated every fiber of everything living and non-living in our
house; the all-consuming fear that enveloped me like layers of clothing on
a winter day—these were the only things that I could rely on. Too afraid to
speak the truth, I silently begged visitors with my eyes to look past the
facade; to look past the frozen smiles; to look into—the child that hovered in
the background. The people saw, but didn't see; the people heard, but didn't
hear; and through it all I drifted alone. I had no survival training; I had no
weapons; I could not fight the unseen enemy inside my father. Alcoholism:
the killer of whole families that pledges to maim and wound without leaving
the home. It knows no gender, age, race, or creed; it shows no prejudice.

As an adult not able to cry since childhood, I received the news of my   5
father's death with numbness mixed with anger. Looking down upon his face
for the last time, I saw him as he really was—an angry, old man consumed
by a disease and tortured with the memories that tormented all of his family.
I felt my throat constrict as the first of a universe of bottled-up tears slowly
slid down my cheeks. I understood in those few moments what my hate had
hidden for a lifetime—I still loved my father. The healing had begun.

Questions

1. Lorna Marro's reflective essay began as a journal entry, one she felt she had to
   write for her own self-discovery. But she also felt it was something that had to be
   said to an audience, so she spent hours revising and refining the essay, through
   it all discovering more about herself and her subject. As a reader you bring your
   own experiences to reading, and they affect your reading. The writer of
   "Whimpering Puppies" would read this essay one way, the writer of "Holding
   On" another way. What is your reaction to the essay?

2. Marro uses repetition and parallel structure extensively. What uses did you
   find particularly effective? Are there any places where she overuses these
   stylistic devices?

3. How does Marro's use of analogy contribute to the effectiveness of the essay?

4. How does she achieve emphasis?

CHAPTER 7

To Persuade: Writing with Emphasis on the Audience

> *Wherever there is persuasion, there is rhetoric. And wherever there is "meaning" there is "persuasion."*
> —*Kenneth Burke*

To **persuade** is to use various means for changing someone else's beliefs or opinions or for moving someone to a particular action. You live with persuasion every day. Advertising companies try to persuade you to buy their clients' products. Television networks and stations want you to watch their programs. Colleges and universities want you to enroll in their classes. Fund-raisers of all kinds ask you to contribute to their projects. At the same time, you are daily in the role of persuader: "Let's watch this program." "My absence from class was unavoidable." "Will you give us an extra day to complete this assignment?"

Most language uses are at least partly persuasive in intent. Even though you may have another primary purpose when you write, persuasion cannot easily be separated from that purpose. While you inform or praise, for example, you may also be trying to persuade. Moreover, when your primary intention is to persuade, you also have other purposes: informing, praising, reporting, or something else. Many of the readings in this book have purposes that are persuasive in addition to their other purposes. In this chapter the essays are primarily persuasive, but as you read you will notice other purposes as well.

Persuasive Appeals

There are three basic ways to persuade, and they overlap. One of the most famous rhetoricians, Aristotle, said that people persuade by the *appeal* of their own good character (ethos), by an *appeal to the minds and emotions of their audience (pathos)*, and by an *appeal based on logical reasoning (logos)*. Let's examine each of these appeals.

Appeal of Character (Ethos)

Persuasion is sometimes thought to assume an adversarial relationship between writer and reader; that is, persuasion is necessitated by opposing viewpoints. Once the audience is confronted and persuaded, and its views have become similar to those of the writer, the adversarial relationship is ended. But thinking of your readers as adversaries may not be the most effective attitude if you want to persuade. More effective is to *identify* with them. Appeal to things you have in common. Show how you are on their side. Try to see things the readers' way. Demonstrate how your ideas could benefit them.

Candidates for political office never give the impression that their constituents are their adversaries; rather, they try to be seen as being on the voters' side by shaking hands, holding babies, wearing windbreakers and baseball caps, and so on. And they offer benefits—new highways, cleaner environment, more scholarship money, higher employment, no new taxes. Identification wins votes.

It also sells products. An automobile manufacturer says that buying its cars is "A great way to teach your kids the value of the dollar." The beef industry boasts of "Real food for real people." A cleansing tissue "feels just wonderful next to your skin." A typewriter is "the simplest typewriter in memory." All these slogans identify with the audience by promising some kind of benefit: a good buy, a great taste, a good feeling, and something easy to do. At the same time, they're just ambiguous enough that they don't commit the manufacturer. The "simplest typewriter" ad, for example, has a double meaning for the word *memory:* the audience's memory and the typewriter's. How can the manufacturer be held to one or the other?

But this kind of deception is identification gone awry, and such manipulation gives persuasion a bad name. When you know that an advertiser or a political candidate is trying to manipulate you, you become skeptical, distrusting. When as a critical reader you discern that a writer is trying to persuade you, you react accordingly, judging the merits of the case instead of being mindlessly swayed. Persuasion is not intrinsically a bad thing. Manufacturers must sell their wares, political candidates must be elected, actions must be taken. But when the persuaders are not truthful, they lose what they need most: respect and credibility in the long term.

The Greek rhetorician Aristotle had a word for the **appeal of character: ethos.** Think of a person you respect and trust. What do you admire about that person? What has that person done that makes you so trustful? Ordinarily, the people who are the most believable are those who have earned respect for their honesty, integrity, fairness, wisdom, self-control, and concern for others. We respect them because of past behaviors that have shown they keep their word. They have made right decisions, have weighed the facts intelligently, and have acted for the good of others, not purely out of self-interest. This kind of credibility is difficult to achieve. At the same time, it's extremely easy to lose. One lie or exaggerated truth will do it. As Cicero, a noted Roman orator, observed, "We give no credit to a liar even when he speaks the truth." Honesty increases credibility, and credibility improves persuasion.

Respect and trust must be earned in writing as well. Credible writers support their opinions with facts, check the truth of their facts, and use emotional appeals with restraint. They know their subject well, and they understand and identify with their audience. They maintain a tone that is calm and reasoned, not sarcastic or angry. They write carefully, using conventional grammar and punctuation. Credible writers do not falsify or invent facts. Nor do they misrepresent facts and twist them to suit their own purposes. They do not represent the ideas of other people as their own. In other words, they do not attempt to deceive their audience.

Careful readers test writers' credibility by looking for clues in how they handle both their facts and their relationship with their audience. In "What Is Wrong with Us?" an essay in this chapter, Senator Albert Gore establishes his credibility in the first two paragraphs by noting his professed concern for the "global ecological crisis" and his failure to win the 1988 presidential nomination as a result of the apparent unpopularity of that interest. He thus establishes his authority as an environmentalist-politician. In an essay in Chapter 6, "The Taste of Evil," author Mark Baker establishes his authority, as a Vietnam veteran to write about Vietnam. Readers generally want to know where the writer derives the authority to discuss a given subject.

Appeal to the Minds and Emotions of the Audience (Pathos)

To identify with an audience, you must first understand it. To persuade an audience to your point of view, first try to find out what you have in common, what beliefs, interests, and values you share. If you want to write a letter to the campus newspaper in response to a recent editorial on legalized abortion, for example, you should remember that some people in your audience are strongly opposed and some strongly in favor, that some have had abortions and some have carried unwanted pregnancies to term, and, though you can't identify with everyone in your audience, your effectiveness will be increased with the amount of identification you can achieve. Considering your audience should give you insight into how to begin a persuasive essay, how to develop your points, what assumptions and fears you may have to allay, and so on. Answering the Questions about Audience for Writing on page 24 may help.

An appeal to the audience's minds and emotions (Aristotle called it *pathos*) is a valid part of persuasion. However, both writers and readers approach emotional appeals with care. Children who are good at persuading their parents have acquired just the right balance of tears and attempts to hide them. But when a television evangelist or a speaker of the House of Representatives openly weeps before the cameras while repenting his sins, the audience, like parents deluged by a superabundance of tears, backs off, unconvinced. There's a term for tears like those: *crocodile tears.* Impassioned expressions, like crocodile tears, beg for sympathy and agreement: "My fellow Americans," "the blessing of God," "unjust laws." Other loaded terms evoke fear or anger: "redneck," "Fascist," "broken promise," "grim existence." These are like pouring on the tears, and they generally get agreement only from people who already agree.

Appealing to an audience's minds is also an effective means of persuasion. Senator Gore appeals to his audience by sharing a concern for the environment and a frustration over the difficulties of saving it. Using the first-person plural *we* throughout his essay, he conveys a sense of urgency and appeals to his audience's desire to act now. In another essay in this chapter, "What 'Sesame Street' Teaches," Neil Postman, a parent as well as an educator, appeals to parents' concern for the well-being of their children. He explains how both children and parents "embraced" "Sesame Street" and why children "loved" it. While both writers probably have more differences than commonalities with their audiences, they share with them the common ground of their subjects, and they use emotional appeals that will be acceptable to those audiences.

Appeal of Logical Reasoning (Logos)

Mutual interest can be stimulated by the way the writer handles the subject matter. When you begin reading something on a subject you previously had no concern for, what sort of thing keeps your interest? a stimulating narrative? telling statistics? forcefully worded opinions backed by facts? You might not have known or cared about a lost clause in the Declaration of Independence before reading "High Cost of Compromise" (in "Additional Readings for Discussion"), in which Sydney J. Harris tells what that clause provided and presents it as a missed opportunity for changing the course of history. Your readers, likewise, may have had no previous interest in a subject you choose to write about—until you stimulate their interest.

An **appeal of logical reasoning** (Aristotle called it *logos*) depends on an **arguable proposition,** or thesis, and evidence to support it. Let's examine the proposition first. A proposition is arguable if it represents a difference of **opinion.** Statements of **fact** are not arguable. The following sentences are verifiable statements of fact and therefore not arguable:

> There are more teenage pregnancies now than ever before. [Could be verified with statistical reference works.]
> Communications in business have undergone many changes in the past few years. [Could be verified by observation, encyclopedia entry, and so on.]

"This is not a copy of the original Declaration as written by Thomas Jefferson."

—Sydney J. Harris [Could be verified by comparison.]

"He has kept among us in times of peace, Standing Armies without the Consent of our legislatures."

—Declaration of Independence [Could be verified by observation and historical accounts.]

Neither are statements of personal preference, such as these, arguable:

The smell of cigarette smoke reminds me of burning trash. [My distaste for cigarette smoke may not be yours.]

I don't like walking in the cold from a parking lot five blocks away. [A reader can't dispute your dislikes.]

Opinions that can be supported by facts, however, *are* arguable and therefore qualify as propositions for logical reasoning. Here are six examples:

If we continue our present actions, we will destroy our environment.

Every public school should educate children about AIDS.

We could solve the drug problem by legalizing marijuana.

"We are at an environmental boiling point right now."

—Albert Gore

"Television educates by teaching children to do what television-viewing requires of them."

—Neil Postman

To avoid the potential for child abuse, parents should not spank their children.

Statements like these can serve as thesis sentences.

EXERCISE

Read the following statements and decide which are arguable.

Political action committees favor incumbent members of the House of Representatives over their challengers.

The campaign to clean up America's waterways has many names
—Project Mayfly, Adopt-a-Stream, River Watch, and others.

The World Bank is one of the most secretive institutions in Washington.

Hong Kong symbolizes imperialist power in the Far East.

We hold these truths to be self-evident, that all men are created equal.

Supporting the Arguable Proposition

Since facts are not arguable, they are forceful support for the arguable proposition, or supportable opinion. Types of facts you might encounter in your reading and can find useful in making your own arguments are examples, testimony, statistics, and historical evidence.

Types of facts

Examples

An **example** illustrates or explains a point. You might draw examples from your personal experience, from the experience of people you know, or from your reading and observations. A single example is usually less effective than several examples or an example used with other kinds of facts. A type of example is the analogy, in which the writer uses a familiar example to illustrate something less familiar—for instance Albert Gore's reference to a science experiment with frogs to illustrate the world's response to the environmental crisis, or a description of the atmospheric ozone layer in terms of a blanket.

Testimony

Quotations, or **testimony,** from experts are powerful support for an argument, particularly for a novice writer whose credibility needs bolstering. Quoting an environmental biologist from the University of California at Davis, for example, makes you more than a first-year college student urging environmental safety; you are backing your position with that of an expert. Choose your "experts" well, however; they must be recognized authorities on the subject you are writing about. If you find that they are quoted by other people writing about the same subject, you can probably safely assume their authority.

Statistics

If they are reliable, meaningful to an audience, and applicable to the subject at hand, **statistics** are effective support for an argument.

Writers rarely depend on statistics alone, however. Even Jonathan Kozol's essay "A Third of the Nation Cannot Read These Words" (in Chapter 11), which makes abundant use of statistics, uses a narrative example too.

Historical Evidence

Things happen. The nuclear power plant at Chernobyl melted down. Mount St. Helens exploded. Nazi Germany invaded Poland in 1939. Kareem Abdul-Jabbar was born Ferdinand Lewis Alcindor in New York City. Thomas Jefferson drafted the Declaration of Independence at the Second Continental Congress. Such facts are historically verifiable and can be useful in supporting arguments. To be effective, the facts must be true and must relate to the argument.

Other Types of Support

In supporting their arguable propositions, writers of persuasive essays sometimes find it necessary to *define* terms that are unfamiliar to the audience or that they are using in an unfamiliar way. A volatile term like *gun control,* for example, must be defined as the writer is using it, as must the specialized use of a common term such as *feedback.* Definitions are often cleared up in an introduction, especially if their clarity requires several sentences, as in this definition of "China Syndrome":

> The "China Syndrome" refers to the possibility that a reactor might lose its primary coolant and then its emergency core cooling system and backup systems for some reason might also not function, while the temperature of the core continues to increase. In the usual scenario, the core becomes molten and then melts way down through the bottom of the containment vessel, continuing on into the ground where presumably it eventually cools off. Radioactivity would then be released to the atmosphere and perhaps also to the ground water. This event could indeed be disastrous and could lead to many deaths.
> —Jack J. Kraushaar and Robert A. Ristenen, *Energy and Problems of a Technical Society*

Sometimes definitions are accomplished briefly when the term occurs, inserted in the sentence and set off with parentheses, commas, or dashes; here is an example:

> Radon gas *(a naturally occurring radioactive gas)* may be the cause of 5,000 to 20,000 lung cancer deaths each year.

In addition to supporting their arguments with facts, writers rely on relevant *opinions*. Testimony, for instance, is often the opinion of a recognized authority, as shown in these sentences about the prospect of the extinction of elephants:

> Such a prospect truly alarms Richard Leakey, the world-famous paleontologist who heads Kenya's wildlife department. Says he: "The elephant has been around a long time and has given much pleasure to so many and has the potential to give such pleasure to so many more. Should we allow it, through our inaction, greed, and perhaps cowardice to become an exotic on this continent?"
>
> —Ted Gup, "Trail of Shame"

More frequently, writers support their arguments with their own considered opinions, as in this example:

> The deepest change may be a planetary intuition that military war is pointless. Except in atavistic places like the Middle East and Ireland, conquering territory is a fruitless and counterproductive exercise. Why conquer land? The Soviets have more trouble than they can manage with their nationalities. The new world's battlegrounds are markets and ideas. The Japanese and Germans, having learned their military lessons the hard way, reentered the war by other means.
>
> —Lance Morrow

Any good argument, of course, will be based on facts as well as thoughtful opinions.

Generally weak forms of support are personal *likes and dislikes* and personal *beliefs*. To say that a movie is bad because you don't like science fiction does not convince an audience not to see the movie. To say that abortions should be illegal because you believe a human life begins at conception does not convince the person who believes otherwise. While beliefs often form a portion of an argument, they are usually its weakest portion and must be supported by facts and fact-based opinions.

In supporting their propositions, writers are wise to avoid biased statements and stereotypical characterizations, since references of this type will probably have a negative effect on all but a like-minded audience. Words such as *feebleminded, bigoted, muscle-bound, silly, shifty, lazy, prudish,* and *sexy* insensitively describe people according to our own biases. Such prejudicial terms are not based on knowledge nor do they promote it; therefore they are avoided in careful writing.

Unexpressed Assumptions

Arguable propositions usually have **unexpressed assumptions** that both writer and reader should be aware of. The proposition "If we continue our present actions, we will destroy our environment" assumes that our present actions are destructive to the environment. "Every public school should educate children about AIDS" assumes that if children are educated about AIDS they will be able to avoid contracting the disease. "We could solve the drug problem by legalizing marijuana" assumes that we want to solve the drug problem.

Sometimes the unexpressed assumptions don't require support, as when readers agree with them. This agreement of course depends on who the audience is—one more reason for writers to be sensitive to their audience. A writer might be able to assume audience agreement that the drug problem must be solved. Agreement on AIDS education as a solution to the spread of the disease would be less likely. An argument is weakened when a writer doesn't recognize unexpressed assumptions or presumes that the audience agrees with them.

EXERCISE

Examine the following arguable propositions for their unexpressed assumptions. Then decide whether these assumptions need to be supported or not. Discuss your views, as well as the implications of any differences in views, with your classmates.

To avoid the potential for child abuse, parents should not spank their children.

"We are at an environmental boiling point right now." —Albert Gore

"Television educates by teaching children to do what television-viewing requires of them."—Neil Postman

Blaming violent crime on society's shortcomings is easier than attributing it to the lack of the perpetrators' moral character.

The NCAA needs rules aimed at reducing criminal misconduct by college athletes.

Fallacies

Errors in logic are called **fallacies;** they are unsound or incomplete reasoning. Whenever they are present, they weaken an argument. Try to avoid them in your writing and watch for them in your reading. Here are the most prominent fallacies:

Broad generalization—a claim that extends beyond what the evidence will support: "Elderly people are poor drivers."

Oversimplification—a statement that tries to make a complex issue seem uncomplicated: "Gasoline prices have gone up because of the oil spill on the West Coast."

Question begging—an argument based on an unproven statement: "Pointless courses like the general education requirements should be eliminated." (The pointlessness of the courses has not been proven.)

Either-or reasoning—an assumption that there are only two positions and only one of them is right: "If we don't increase the number of land-based missiles, we're sure to have war."

Post hoc cause—an assumption that because one event occurs before another, the first causes the second: "If we plan a barbecue, it will rain; it always does when we have one."

Ad hominem—an attack on persons rather than issues: "Because Johnson had a child out of wedlock, she should not be elected to Congress."

Persuasive writing employs the principles discussed in Part I for all writing—probably because almost all writing is in part persuasive in purpose. Persuasion does make particularly evident the writer's necessity to be sensitive to his or her own credibility and to the beliefs, interests, and values of the audience, as well as to possess adequate knowledge of the subject and competence in writing.

Here is a summary checklist of the special considerations of persuasive writing:

Checklist for persuasive writing

1. Be honest and accurate in your representation of facts.
2. Maintain a calm and reasoned tone.
3. Identify your audience, and then identify *with* it on the strength of beliefs, interests, and values you share.
4. Use restraint with emotional appeals, restricting yourself to those you know your audience will accept.
5. Build your persuasion on a thesis sentence that is an arguable proposition—an opinion supportable by facts.
6. Present a reasoned argument supported with examples, testimony, statistics, and historical evidence, plus carefully considered opinions.
7. Be aware of the unexpressed assumptions of your argument, and support them if necessary.
8. Check your argument for fallacies.

As we have seen, you can find persuasion in almost every piece of writing. This chapter has a collection of essays that are primarily persuasive.

They are representative of what you might find as you read magazines and books. And they are representative of the kinds of writing you may at times be inclined to do. Look for persuasive purposes in all the reading you do. Examine magazine and newspaper articles, advertisements, even your textbooks for purposes other than reporting, informing, or the like. Be an active, critical reader, seeking evidence of the writer's credibility; sensitivity to the beliefs, interests, and values of the audience; and quality of the logical appeal.

Persuading about a Common Cause

In the 1960s there was talk about "Spaceship Earth," an analogy that put all of humankind together in one vehicle moving through the universe. On the journey we travelers have only the water and air that accompany us, only the food we can produce with the supplies we take with us, only the inhabitable area on our spaceship's outer surface that is not covered with water. We cannot get off the spaceship, and we cannot take on fresh supplies. The supplies we take with us are renewable only if we manage them carefully— not wasting them, not polluting them, not consuming them too quickly.

In recent years, much has been written about the earth's environment. We read about "the global village." We are warned about oil spills in our oceans, pesticides running into our lakes and streams, smoke and gases polluting the air we breathe, population outpacing our resources, our protective ozone layer being destroyed. We deal with predictions of more skin cancer, more deaths by respiratory diseases, higher ocean levels and consequent flooding of coastal cities, and so on. In short, people are writing about the environment.

The environment may be the most common of causes, because wherever we live we are a part of it. But we do have other common causes: the societal destruction brought on by drugs and other substance abuse, the modern-day plague called AIDS, the escalating cost of education, the charges of decreased learning in education, the reproach of increased homelessness, the perpetual threat of wanton terrorism, the dangers of being on the streets at night, and so on. Common causes are always topics for persuasive writing.

Reading

In the summer of 1988, Senator Albert Gore of Tennessee, chair of the Senate Subcommittee on Science, Space, and Technology, met with scientists, administrators, and political leaders from five continents in a conference to explore environmental issues with the hope of discovering solutions. The essay "What Is Wrong with Us?" is excerpted from his address to that group and was published in a special environmental issue of *Time* magazine. As you read the essay, note how Gore establishes his credibility; how he identifies with, and appeals to, his audience; and how he supports his argument with examples, testimony, statistics, and historical evidence.

What Is Wrong with Us?

Albert Gore

When I announced I was running for President, I said the greenhouse effect, the depletion of the ozone layer, and the global ecological crisis will, by the end of this election year, be recognized as the most serious issue facing this country and the world. Three days later, a George Will column ridiculed the naiveté of a politician who could imagine that issues of this kind would be politically salable.   1

I guess he was partly right and partly wrong. I was right in that the issue has, during this year, attained enormous importance and new recognition. But he was right, since it didn't do me any good politically. There are still barriers to political action. Let me discuss five of them.   2

Number one, there are areas of uncertainty about the greenhouse effect and the dire nature of the ecological crisis we face, which are seized upon as excuses for inaction. This is a psychological problem common to all humanity. If strong responses are needed and yet there is some residual uncertainty about whether you are going to have to make those responses, the natural psychological tendency is to magnify the uncertainty and say, "Well, maybe we won't really have to face up to it."   3

But the fact that we face an ecological crisis without any precedent in historic times is no longer a matter of any dispute worthy of recognition. And those who, for the purpose of maintaining balance in debate, take the contrarian view that there is significant uncertainty about whether it's real are hurting our ability to respond.   4

The second barrier to political action is an unwillingness to believe that something so far outside the bounds of historical experience can, in fact, be occurring. To put it another way, this set of problems sounds like the plot of a bad science-fiction movie. People automatically assume it can't be real.   5

The third political barrier is the assumption that it will be easier and more sensible to adapt to whatever climate change occurs than it will be to prevent the crisis. But the change could come so swiftly that adaptation will be all but impossible.   6

The fourth barrier is the lack of widespread awareness among the peoples of the world about the nature of the problem. Most political leaders, let alone their public, are unaware of what is happening and how severe it is. That must be changed.   7

The fifth barrier to political action is the knowledge that many of the ultimate solutions are almost unimaginably difficult.   8

And since they are harder than anything we have done before, and the   9
efforts may all come to naught anyway, why mess with them? Why not
conserve our energy and just not even try? That is a formidable barrier, not
least because the solutions require international cooperation on a scale that
is totally unprecedented in history.

Those five barriers must be overcome before the political system reacts.   10
The role of leadership is critical in spreading awareness, in framing solutions, in offering a vision of the future we want to create, as well as a vision
of the nightmare we wish to avoid.

There is an old science experiment in which a frog is put into a pan of   11
water, and the water is slowly heated to the boiling point. The frog sits there
and boils because its nervous system will not react to the gradual increase.
But if you boil the water first and then put the frog in it, it immediately
jumps out.

We are at an environmental boiling point right now. Is the destruc-   12
tion of one football-field's worth of forest every second enough to make
the frog react and jump out of the pan? What will it take? If, as in a
science-fiction movie, we had a giant invader from space clomping across
the rain forests of the world with football field–size feet—going boom,
boom, boom every second—would we react? That's essentially what is
going on right now.

We saw the two whales trapped in the Arctic ice, struggling for air, and   13
the world responded. The United States and the Soviet Union cooperated.
Yet we see 40,000 babies starving every day, and we don't react. What is
wrong with us?

There used to be a debate in the '70s about appropriate technology.   14
Now the question is: Did God choose an appropriate technology when he
gave human beings dominion over the earth? The jury is still out. And the
answer has to come in our lifetime from the political system.

There are precedents. We made human sacrifice, once commonplace,   15
obsolete. We made slavery obsolete. These things, just like changes in
weather patterns, took a long period of time. But now, just as climate
changes are telescoped into a very short period of time, changes in human
thinking of a magnitude comparable to the changes that brought about the
abolition of slavery must take place in one generation.

We know how to solve the problem. It will be unimaginably difficult.   16
The cooperation required will be unprecedented. But we know what to do.
What is required is a change in thinking and a change in the equilibrium of
the world's political system.

Right now the political equilibrium is characterized by short-term   17
policies at the expense of long-term policies. It is characterized by actions to
confer national advantage at the expense of actions designed to promote
global advantage. It is characterized by preparations for war, ignorance,
and starvation.

Our challenge as political leaders is to come up with an agenda of   18
solutions, which we are doing. But the larger challenge for all of us is to shift
the world's political system into a new state of equilibrium, characterized by
more cooperation, global agendas, and a focus on the future. As General
Omar Bradley said at the end of World War II, "It is time we steered by the
stars and not by the lights of each passing ship."

Questions

1. Gore positions himself as an environmentalist-politician addressing the issue of politics and the environment. What evidence do you see of his authority on his subject? How does he establish his credibility?

2. This essay addresses other political leaders. What does Gore propose they do in addition to coming up with a plan for attacking the problem?

3. Given the five "barriers to political action," how possible do you think change is? Which of the barriers do you think is the most formidable?

4. What audience might Gore have besides world political leaders?

5. What does Gore's analogy of the giant and the rain forests tell you about the environmental problem? about Gore? about the knowledge he assumes his audience shares?

6. Examine Gore's essay for other kinds of support. Does he use any statistics? testimony—statements from experts? examples other than the analogies? historical evidence? opinions? Does he appeal to the beliefs, interests, and values of his audience? What would you say is the most effective support for his argument? Speculate on his choice of kinds of evidence.

Discussion

Gore establishes his credibility in the initial two paragraphs, first by reminding his audience that he had just run for nomination as a candidate for president of the United States and lost and then by declaring himself an environmentalist. In linking the two, observing that his environmental interest did not aid his political aspirations, he introduces the major point of his essay: that politics is not ready to deal with environmental problems.

Audience and Purpose

Even though Gore's essay was addressed to world political leaders for the purpose of influencing them to bring about a change in the world's political system, it has other *audiences*. When it was published in *Time* magazine with Gore's permission, it acquired as its audience all *Time*'s subscribers. When it entered this textbook, it gained still another audience—college students who own the text. Do you think the *purpose* of a piece of writing changes as the audience changes? Think first of Gore's purpose for addressing the political leaders, which he makes clear in his final paragraph. Then think of *Time*'s purpose for publishing the article in a special environmental issue, which featured on its cover a globe wrapped in knotted ropes as its "Planet of the Year." You might assume that *Time* shares Gore's concern, though the purpose undoubtedly broadened with the wider audience. What reactions might *Time* expect from its readers? Would you say that the essay has the same purpose here in your textbook as it did in *Time* and at the environmental conference?

These are not easy questions, and there are probably no right answers to them, but if you understand what these questions are asking you probably have a good sense of how all aspects of a *rhetorical situation*—writer, audience, subject, and purpose—overlap and interrelate. One change in the triangle of writer, audience, and subject may have a notable effect on the purpose. Though a piece of writing remains the same, its purpose may change as its audience does. You can apply this principle to college writing. If you submit a paper to one teacher according to that teacher's expectations, you may receive an A for it, but when you use the same paper for another class you get a C. Why? Because the rhetorical situation—in this case the teacher's expectations—was different.

Development

Gore uses *analogies* to illustrate his argument graphically. First with the frog and the boiling water and then with the giant and the rain forests, he tells us something about the environment and our attitude toward it. Analogies are often regarded as a weakness in arguments, because readers can question their validity. Boiling frogs and clomping giants, after all, have very little to do with the environment. At the same time, analogies can be powerfully illustrative. The problem in using them lies in relying too strongly on them, letting them carry the argument.

But Gore uses other methods of developing his argument. After establishing his credibility as a politician who has committed himself to preserving the environment, he divides and *classifies* the problem into what he sees as the major barriers to political action. He thus identifies the issues that must be dealt with. These statements are *informed opinions,* based on *historical evidence* and Gore's political experience dealing with the issues. By examining his essay, you can find other opinions to support his argument. Gore also uses *examples:* He contrasts the international efforts to save two whales with the inaction to save starving babies (using also a *statistic,* the number of starving babies), and he compares the present need for change with precedents, the abolition of human sacrifice and slavery. Finally, he quotes General Omar Bradley, applying Bradley's words to the present context.

EXERCISES

1. Imagine a piece of your own writing—from an essay to something as simple as a shopping list or a telephone message. *Without being changed itself in any way,* how would the message change in purpose if it had a different audience? Discuss your perceptions with your classmates.

2. Brainstorm (see Chapter 3) a list of common causes to discover where your interests lie. Let your list lead you to explore a specific issue. Then write a journal entry that speculates on that issue's impact on you and your world.

Writing

What common causes interest you? Do you agree with Senator Gore about the environment? Do you see barriers to political action other than those he names? Are you concerned about a specific aspect of the deteriorating global environment—perhaps something in your own neighborhood? Common causes can have local as well as global implications. Your interest may be as specific as people walking on grass instead of sidewalks or the need for students to collect recyclable containers. You may be concerned about drug use by students at your school. Or racial or sexual discrimination where you work or go to school. Or ethics in government—local, state, or federal.

Select a subject you are familiar with so you can establish your credibility. Using your journal entry from the preceding exercise as a starting point, think of something you want to say that would persuade others to think or act as you do. You will need to select a realistic audience: fellow students, perhaps, or parents of young children. Related to your selection of audience is your purpose: to convince other students to stay on the sidewalks, to persuade parents to teach recycling habits to their children, and so on. If you like, address your essay to the editor of your school newspaper or some other newspaper, or even write it as a letter to someone who might be able to bring about change—a senator or congressional representative, for example.

Base your persuasion mainly on facts and opinions, using examples, testimony, statistics, and analogies as appropriate. Maintain a reasonable tone, avoiding anger and undue appeals to destructive emotions such as fear and hatred. Use sarcasm only if you are familiar enough with your audience to know it will take your tone as you intend it. To convince your audience, try to see its point of view.

Challenging Common Assumptions

Say that you are in a parking lot, waiting at a respectable distance as another car backs out of a parking place, and, before you can pull in, someone coming from the other direction slips in ahead of you. You're incensed; you were there first and had a right to the spot. Or say that, after coming in late Saturday night, you want to sleep in on Sunday morning—till 10:30 or so. But at 8:00 A.M. your next-door neighbor is revving up his lawn mower under your window. You're furious; doesn't he know that people don't mow their lawns at eight o'clock on Sunday morning? In each case, the basis of your right is assumption, not law. And that assumption is founded on social conventions.

Our lives are simplified because of the assumptions we make about the world we live in. Because we assume that other automobile drivers will obey the rules of the road—stay on their side of a two-lane highway, stop at red lights, drive with their headlights on at night, and so on—we dare to venture out in our own cars. Because we assume that attending college will provide us with an education to increase our job opportunities and enrich our lives, we commit four or more years to attaining that education. We assume that friends will be loyal, that family will support us through difficult times, that television and newspaper reports of current events are accurate, if not complete.

Our assumptions are not always correct, however. Occasionally people drive on the wrong side of the road, speed through red lights, and drive without their headlights on at night—making life dangerous for us if we happen to be driving by at the time. Friends sometimes betray us, family sometimes is uninterested in our problems, news reports are exaggerated for effect. And the enhancement of our lives from a college education depends more on how much we take than on how much is given.

We can't go about our lives without assumptions based on trust in our fellow human beings. Yet we don't have to be totally trusting. We are alert to other drivers not obeying the rules of the road. We do some research before deciding on a college and question courses and teachers and schools that do not seem to be providing the education we expected. We judge the integrity of our friends and the television news reports.

Persuasive essays sometimes challenge our assumptions. They challenge a university president who assumes he can spend millions to refurbish his official residence, a school system whose students score below the norm on standardized tests, a television evangelist who solicits donations to support missions, a newspaper reporter whose "facts" seem to be invented. Student writers question the value of a textbook, the necessity of grades, the need for gender-free language.

This section has two essays that challenge assumptions, the first concerning what people expect from television, the second concerning what people consider their public rights.

Reading

How much do the media (television, newspapers, magazines, radio) have to do with what you do and think? Does television news decide what you will know about world events? Do the television cameras and newspaper commentaries elect our presidents? Do television commercials and printed advertisements influence you to buy certain products? Do soap operas decide what you're going to do during lunch hour and how you're going to schedule your classes? Media, both print and electronic, are a considerable aspect of our lives—like it or not. And as with most things that are prominent, the media come in for their share of criticism, television perhaps most of all.

Neil Postman is a critic, writer, educator, parent, and communications theorist. One of his books, *Amusing Ourselves to Death: Public Discourse in the Age of Show Business,* exposes everything on television—even news, educational shows, and religious programs—as show business. "The problem," he says, "is not that television presents us with entertaining subject matter but that all subject matter is presented as entertaining, which is another issue altogether." The essay that follows is part of his chapter "Teaching as an Amusing Activity." Read it to discover what assumptions he challenges concerning "Sesame Street," and weigh his position with your own experience. Note his tone and how he supports his argument.

What "Sesame Street" Teaches
Neil Postman

There could not have been a safer bet when it began in 1969 than   1
that "Sesame Street" would be embraced by children, parents, and educators. Children loved it because they were raised on television commercials, which they intuitively knew were the most carefully crafted entertainments on television. To those who had not yet been to school, even to those who had just started, the idea of being *taught* by a series of commercials did not seem peculiar. And that television should entertain them was taken as a matter of course.

Parents embraced "Sesame Street" for several reasons, among them   2
that it assuaged their guilt over the fact that they could not or would not restrict their children's access to television. "Sesame Street" appeared to justify allowing a four- or five-year-old to sit transfixed in front of a television screen for unnatural periods of time. Parents were eager to hope that television could teach their children something other than which breakfast cereal has the most crackle. At the same time, "Sesame Street" relieved them of the responsibility of teaching their pre-school children how to read—no small matter in a culture where children are apt to be considered a nuisance. They could also plainly see that in spite of its faults, "Sesame Street"

was entirely consonant with the prevailing spirit of America. Its use of cute puppets, celebrities, catchy tunes, and rapid-fire editing was certain to give pleasure to the children and would therefore serve as adequate preparation for their entry into a fun-loving culture.

As for educators, they generally approved of "Sesame Street," too. Contrary to common opinion, they are apt to find new methods congenial, especially if they are told that education can be accomplished more efficiently by means of the new techniques. (That is why such ideas as "teacher-proof" textbooks, standardized tests, and, now, micro-computers have been welcomed in the classroom.) "Sesame Street" appeared to be an imaginative aid in solving the growing problem of teaching Americans how to read, while, at the same time, encouraging children to love school.

We now know that "Sesame Street" encourages children to love school only if school is like "Sesame Street." Which is to say, we now know that "Sesame Street" undermines what the traditional idea of schooling represents. Whereas a classroom is a place of social interaction, the space in front of a television set is a private preserve. Whereas in a classroom, one may ask a teacher questions, one can ask nothing of a television screen. Whereas school is centered on the development of language, television demands attention to images. Whereas attending school is a legal requirement, watching television is an act of choice. Whereas in school, one fails to attend to the teacher at the risk of punishment, no penalties exist for failing to attend to the television screen. Whereas to behave oneself in school means to observe rules of public decorum, television watching requires no such observances, has no concept of public decorum. Whereas in a classroom, fun is never more than a means to an end, on television it is the end in itself.

Yet "Sesame Street" and its progeny, "The Electric Company," are not to be blamed for laughing the traditional classroom out of existence. If the classroom now begins to seem a stale and flat environment for learning, the inventors of television itself are to blame, not the Children's Television Workshop. We can hardly expect those who want to make good television shows to concern themselves with what the classroom is for. They are concerned with what television is for. This does not mean that "Sesame Street" is not educational. It is, in fact, nothing but educational—in the sense that every television show is educational. Just as reading a book—any kind of book—promotes a particular orientation toward learning, watching a television show does the same. "The Little House on the Prairie," "Cheers," and "The Tonight Show" are as effective as "Sesame Street" in promoting what might be called the television style of learning. And this style of learning is, by its nature, hostile to what has been called book-learning or its handmaiden, school-learning. If we are to blame "Sesame Street" for anything, it is for the pretense that it is any ally of the classroom. That, after all, has been its chief claim on foundation and public money. As a television show, and a good one, "Sesame Street" does not encourage children to love school or anything about school. It encourages them to love television.

Questions

1. What assumption about "Sesame Street" does Postman challenge? How does he establish his authority to challenge assumptions?

2. What harm does Postman see in the "Sesame Street" style of education?

3. Evaluate Postman's assumptions about classroom learning. Which of these would you challenge for accuracy?

4. On the basis of your experience, support or refute Postman's statement that children reared on "Sesame Street" and other educational programs on television expect to be entertained in school.

5. Postman's tone is somewhat sarcastic, especially when he is accounting for the success of "Sesame Street." Which group—children, parents, or educators—receives the worst of Postman's sarcasm?

6. Examine Postman's essay for fallacies in his argument. Which are unacceptable and acceptable in the context?

Discussion

"Sesame Street" has "taught" the nation's children for years. You may have watched it as a child and grown familiar with Big Bird and Cookie Monster and other friendly creatures that inhabit the fabled street. Your parents might have thought that watching the show was educational for you, because you were learning your ABC's and your numbers. But Postman charges that "Sesame Street" educates children only toward television-style learning. He does not say that it is a bad program, nor does he say that it is not educational. Postman says that the program teaches children to want their learning to be entertaining. At the end of the chapter from which this essay is excerpted, Postman tells how television's education as entertainment will affect children:

> Mainly, they will have learned that learning is a form of entertainment or, more precisely, that anything worth learning can take the form of an entertainment, and ought to. And they will not rebel if their English teacher asks them to learn the eight parts of speech through the medium of rock music. Or if their social studies teacher sings to them the facts about the War of 1812. Or if their physics comes to them on cookies and T-shirts. Indeed, they will expect it and thus will be well prepared to receive their politics, their religion, their news, and their commerce in the same delightful way.

Think of your own experience regarding television. Is Postman correct in his assumptions about the medium? Is he right in challenging those assumptions?

Thesis and Purpose

Postman states his *thesis* in the fourth paragraph: " 'Sesame Street' undermines what the traditional idea of schooling represents." This is his *arguable proposition.* It has two *unexpressed assumptions:* (1) that "Sesame Street" is something like school, and (2) that traditional schooling is a desirable norm. Unless an audience agrees upon the underlying assumptions of an argument, those assumptions must be supported. Postman supports his first assumption in his first three paragraphs, showing how children, parents, and educators view the television program as similar to school. How does he support the second assumption? And how critical to his argument is his audience's agreement with that assumption?

Think about Postman's purpose for writing this essay. Does it seem that he wants parents to forbid their children to watch "Sesame Street" and other educational-entertainment programs? In this section of his book, at least, he does not seem to be calling for such action. Instead, it seems more likely that he wants to persuade readers to view so-called educational programs as he does—as entertainment. In that case, his thesis may be tied to his final sentence: "It encourages them to love television." In other words, "Sesame Street" and programs like it are acceptable if they're viewed as entertainment, not as education.

Development

As we have seen, Postman's first three paragraphs support the unexpressed assumption of his thesis that " 'Sesame Street' has been considered educational. After these paragraphs on why the program was widely accepted, paragraph 4 begins the challenge: "We now know. . . ." This paragraph may be Postman's strongest statement on his argument that " 'Sesame Street' undermines what the traditional idea of school represents." In his final paragraph he explains the problem with such programs. Here is a rough outline of the essay's structure:

I. Assumptions about "Sesame Street"

    A. Children love it because it's entertaining.

    B. Parents embrace it because it relieves them of teaching their children.

    C. Educators approve of it because it appears to help them do their jobs.

II. The challenge

    A. Compared with classrooms, "Sesame Street" is more attractive.

    B. The problem with "Sesame Street" is that it undermines traditional schooling.

Postman's argument is based mainly on *informed opinions* and *historical evidence.* The first three paragraphs are mostly opinions. It would be difficult to prove a statement that children accepted "Sesame Street" as a type of commercial, with which they were already familiar, or that parents embraced the show because it was a convenience for them—a baby-sitter, a substitute for their own teaching. This sentence in paragraph 2, "Parents were eager to hope that television could teach their children something other than which breakfast cereal has the most crackle," sounds like a statement of fact, but we have no evidence of its truth, and because of its sarcasm we're not sure if Postman intends it as fact. Postman wants his readers to add support to his argument by recalling their own experiences. In paragraph 4, he develops his contrast of television school with traditional school by a series of "whereas" sentences. These supportive statements are factual and accurate—common knowledge perhaps, but observations that the audience may not have made. The last sentence of the paragraph, however, is opinion again: "Whereas in a classroom, fun is never more than a means to an end, on television it is the end in itself."

You may be able to find some *fallacies* in Postman's argument, *broad generalization,* most notably. In paragraph 3, for example, he says that educators acclaimed "Sesame Street" as an "imaginative aid," which seems to imply that all teachers thought "Sesame Street" was a great idea. In paragraph 1, he states, "Children loved it because they were raised on television commercials," again a broad generalization that assumes all members of the group share the characteristic.

Postman's final paragraph stresses his argument that "Sesame Street" is educational, just as any entertainment is educational, and that it encourages children to love television, not school. In this paragraph in particular, he appeals to the values of his readers to see so-called educational programming for what it is—entertainment.

Tone

The *tone* of Postman's essay might be read as sarcastic. Consider the tone of the following sentence, for example: "Parents were eager to hope that television could teach their children something other than which breakfast cereal has the most crackle." Here, as throughout the essay, Postman satirizes the ready acceptance of "Sesame Street" as entertaining education for children. Do you think the sarcastic tone is appropriate for Postman's purpose? Considering his treatment of the children who grew up with "Sesame Street," the parents who encouraged them to watch it, and the educators who welcomed it as an "imaginative aid," who do you suppose is Postman's intended audience?

EXERCISE

Write a series of "whereas" sentences like Postman's in paragraph 4. Take a stance either in favor of or against "Sesame Street" or some other television program in which you can make a series of comparisons. In each of your sentences, contrast the program and something not on television, such as books.

Reading

Do you have the right to snap a few photographs of derelicts standing in a doorway, or Mexicans at work, Irish dancers at a local celebration, Indians at a reservation store? When is it appropriate to take pictures of other people? Consider another case: spending the evening with friends, you politely sit through their home slide show with pictures of "natives" watching the affluent Americans point cameras at them. How do you feel? There is no law that prohibits the practice, but when there is no law to govern the exercise of rights, assumptions regarding social conventions must take over.

Social interchange runs on assumptions. Occasionally, however, people challenge those assumptions, as Ellen Goodman does in "Protection from the Prying Camera." As you read, try to determine what Goodman suggests in place of the assumption that we have a right to take pictures of one another. How does she support her argument? Do you note any fallacies? What is her tone?

Protection from the Prying Camera
Ellen Goodman

Maybe it was the year-end picture roundup that finally did it. Maybe it was the double exposure to the same vivid photographs. Or perhaps it was the memory of three amateur photographers carefully standing in the cold last fall, calculating their *f* stops and exposures with light meters, trying to find the best angle, pointing their cameras at a drunk in a doorway. Or maybe it was simply my nine-year-old cousin playing Candid Camera at the family gathering. 1

But whatever the reason, it has finally hit me. We have become a nation of Kodachrome, Nikon, Instamatic addicts. But we haven't yet developed a clear idea of the ethics of picture-taking. We haven't yet determined the parameters of privacy in a world of flash cubes and telescopic lenses. 2

We "take" pictures. As psychologist Stanley Milgram puts it, "A photographer takes a picture, he does not create it or borrow it." But who has given us the right to "take" those pictures and under what circumstances? 3

Since the camera first became portable, we have easily and repeatedly aimed it at public people. It has always been open shooting season on them. With new technology, however, those intrusions have intensified. This year, someone with a camera committed the gross indecency of shooting an unaware Greta Garbo in the nude—and *People* printed it. 4

This year, again, Ron Gallela "took" the image of Jacqueline Onassis and sold it as if it belonged to him. This year, we have pictures of a crumpled Wayne Hays, an indiscreet Nelson Rockefeller, and two presidential candidates in every imaginable pose from the absurd to the embarrassing. 5

We have accepted the idea that public people are always free targets for   6
the camera—without even a statute of limitations for Jackie or Garbo. We
have also accepted the idea that a private person becomes public by being
involved in a public event. The earthquake victims of Guatemala, the
lynched leftists of Thailand, the terror-stricken of Ireland—their emotions
and their bodies become frozen images.

The right of the public to know, to see, and to be affected is consid-   7
ered more important than the right of the individual to mourn, or even
die, in privacy.

What happens now, however, when cameras proliferate until they are   8
as common as television sets? What happens when the image being "taken"
is that of a butcher, a baker, or a derelict, rather than a public figure? Do we
all lose our right to privacy simply by stepping into view?

Should we be allowed to point cameras at each other? To regard each   9
other as objects of art? Does the photographer or the photographed own
the image?

Several years ago, *Time* photographer Steve Northup, who had covered   10
Vietnam, and Watergate, took a group of students around Cambridge
shooting pictures. He quietly insisted that they ask every pizza-maker, truck
driver, and beautician for permission. His attitude toward private citizens
was one of careful respect for the power of "exposure." In contrast to this,
the average camera bug—like the average tourist—too often goes about
snapping "quaint" people, along with "quaint" scenes: See the natives smile,
see the natives carrying baskets of fruit, see the native children begging, see
the drunk in the doorway. As Milgram wrote, "I find it hard to understand
wherein the photographer has derived the right to keep for his own purposes the image of the peasant's face."

Where do we get the right to bring other people home in a canister?   11
Where did we lose the right to control our image?

In a study that Milgram conducted last year, a full 65 percent of the   12
people to whom his students talked in midtown Manhattan refused to have
their pictures taken, refused to be photographed. I don't think they were
camera shy, in the sense of being vain. Rather, they were reluctant to have
their pictures "taken."

The Navahos long believed that the photographer took a piece of them   13
away in his film. Like them, we are coming to understand the power of these
frozen images. Photographs can help us to hold on to the truth of our past,
to make our history and identity more real. Or they can rip something away
from us as precious as the privacy which once clothed Greta Garbo.

Questions

1. Which of Goodman's examples did you find most convincing? which least
   convincing?
2. What alternative does Goodman suggest to the willy-nilly snapping of pictures?

3. What fallacies do you detect in Goodman's argument?

4. How do you feel about being included in Goodman's statement about how "we" feel about picture taking?

5. What facts does Goodman use to support her argument? How does she use examples, testimony, statistics, or historical evidence?

6. Goodman quotes the statistic that 65 percent of people surveyed refused to have their pictures taken. She also wonders whether we may all "lose our right to privacy simply by stepping into view." What is your attitude toward taking pictures of people without permission?

Discussion

Even though Goodman's essay was written in 1977, you should have little trouble recalling parallel current instances. Think of public people who have been "exposed" by telephoto lenses of victims of calamities whose sufferings are laid open to public view. Families of accident victims are interviewed on television. Cameras show drowning victims being pulled from the water. Are these instances all part of the public's right to know? Do you agree with Goodman's challenge to the assumption that we have a right to take whatever pictures we want? Do you think it's acceptable under some circumstances to take pictures of other people? Is there a difference, for instance, between using a telephoto lens to photograph someone in her backyard and snapping someone at a public event?

Thesis

Goodman states her *thesis* in the form of questions:

"Do we all lose our right to privacy simply by stepping into view?"
"Should we be allowed to point cameras at each other?"
"To regard each other as objects of art?"
"Does the photographer or the photographed own the image?"
"Where do we get the right to bring other people home in a canister?"
"Where did we lose the right to control our image?"

Her answers to all her questions are the same: that we do not have the right to "take" pictures of other people without permission. Her *arguable proposition* is implied in the examples she presents.

Development

Goodman uses the pronoun *we* to present the assumptions she challenges:

"We have become a nation of Kodachrome, Nikon, Instamatic addicts. But we haven't yet developed a clear idea of the ethics of picture-taking."

"We have accepted the idea that public people are always free targets for the camera."

"We have also accepted the idea that a private person becomes public by being involved in a public event."

By *we* Goodman evidently means you and me, as well as all her other readers. Might this phrasing be regarded as the *fallacy* of *broad generalization?*

While her assumptions and some of the support for her argument are her own considered *opinions,* Goodman also rallies some *facts.* She employs *testimony* several times, quoting psychologist Stanley Milgram and *Time* photographer Steve Northup and reporting a Navaho belief about picture taking. She also includes a *statistic,* that "65 percent of the people to whom [Milgram's] students talked in midtown Manhattan refused to have their pictures taken." And she has *examples* of public people whose private lives have been exposed by the camera.

Tone

Goodman's *tone* seems to be somewhat confrontational. Rather than identifying with her audience, she seems to regard the audience as an adversary. For, even though she says "we," she seems to have separated herself from the rest of the camera bugs ("it has finally hit me"); she might just as well be saying "you." Would the tone be less contentious if she had used third person: "People haven't yet developed a clear idea of the ethics of picture-taking"? Perhaps her confrontational tone is necessary in an essay that challenges assumptions.

EXERCISE

Experiment with how tone changes by rewriting the following sentences using third-person nouns and pronouns instead of we *and changing other words that seem too harsh. Then rewrite the sentences again using second-person pronouns:* you. *Which version sounds least confrontational? which most confrontational?*

1. We have become a nation of Kodachrome, Nikon, Instamatic addicts.
2. But we haven't yet developed a clear idea of the ethics of picture-taking.
3. We haven't yet determined the parameters of privacy in a world of flash cubes and telescopic lenses.
4. We "take" pictures.
5. Since the camera first became portable, we have easily and repeatedly aimed it at public people.

6. We have accepted the idea that public people are always free targets for the camera.
7. Where do we get the right to bring other people home in a canister?

Writing

Write a persuasive essay that, like Postman's "What 'Sesame Street' Teaches" and Goodman's "Protection from the Prying Camera," challenges a common assumption. Like Postman, you might examine an assumption about media—television, radio, newspapers, or magazines—such as one of these:

- Television—not news but entertainment
- Soap operas—not pulp but therapy
- Docudramas—not truth but lies
- Newsmagazines (or television newsmagazines)—not news but unethical sensationalism

Or consider challenging a custom built into societal interchanges, such as one of these ideas:

- It's all right to dig through other people's trash cans.
- "Finders keepers"—it's all right to keep what you find.
- It's all right to break a date if a better one comes along.
- It's all right to cheat on tests as long as you don't get caught.

Examine your thesis for unexpressed assumptions that may need to be supported. In developing your essay, specify what common assumption you are challenging and then state your challenge, using appropriate evidence. You may want to present a new idea of the ethics concerning your subject or another way of viewing it. If you think you can handle a sarcastic or confrontational tone, try it; or write in a straightforward, serious tone. Give some thought to who your audience will be, and try to identify with that audience.

ADDITIONAL READINGS FOR DISCUSSION

Reading

Perhaps the most famous persuasive document in the United States is the Declaration of Independence, written primarily by Thomas Jefferson and adopted by the Second Continental Congress on July 4, 1776. This document presented reasons why the thirteen American colonies should declare themselves politically independent of Great Britain. As you read, examine its tone and look for types of evidence: examples, testimony, statistics, historical facts, and informed opinions.

The Declaration of Independence

Thomas Jefferson et al.

In Congress, July 4, 1776. The unanimous Declaration of the thirteen united States of America,

When in the Course of human events, it becomes necessary for one 1
people to dissolve the political bands which have connected them with another, and to assume among the powers of the earth, the separate and equal station to which the Laws of Nature and of Nature's God entitle them, a decent respect to the opinions of mankind requires that they should declare the causes which impel them to the separation.—

We hold these truths to be self-evident, that all men are created equal, 2
that they are endowed by their Creator with certain unalienable Rights, that among these are Life, Liberty, and the pursuit of Happiness.—

That to secure these rights, Governments are instituted among Men, 3
deriving their just powers from the consent of the governed,—

That whenever any Form of Government becomes destructive of these 4
ends, it is the Right of the People to alter or to abolish it, and to institute new Government, laying its foundation on such principles and organizing its powers in such form, as to them shall seem most likely to effect their Safety and Happiness. Prudence, indeed, will dictate that Governments long established should not be changed for light and transient causes; and accordingly all experience hath shown, that mankind are more disposed to suffer, while evils are sufferable, than to right themselves by abolishing the forms to which they are accustomed. But when a long train of abuses and usurpations, pursuing invariably the same Object evinces a design to reduce them under absolute Despotism, it is their right, it is their duty, to throw off such Government, and to provide new Guards for their future security.—

Such has been the patient sufferance of these Colonies; and such is now 5
the necessity which constrains them to alter their former Systems of Government. The history of the present King of Great Britain is a history of repeated injuries and usurpations, all having in direct object the establishment of an absolute Tyranny over these States. To prove this, let Facts be submitted to a candid world.—

He has refused his Assent to Laws, the most wholesome and necessary 6
for the public good.—

He has forbidden his Governors to pass Laws of immediate and 7
pressing importance, unless suspended in their operation till his Assent

should be obtained; and when so suspended, he has utterly neglected to attend to them—

He has refused to pass other Laws for the accommodation of large   8 districts of people, unless those people would relinquish the right of Representation in the Legislature, a right inestimable to them and formidable to tyrants only.—

He has called together legislative bodies at places unusual, uncomfort-   9 able, and distant from the depository of their public Records, for the sole purpose of fatiguing them into compliance with his measures.—

He has dissolved Representative Houses repeatedly, for opposing with   10 manly firmness his invasions on the rights of the people.—

He has refused for a long time, after such dissolutions, to cause others   11 to be elected; whereby the Legislative powers, incapable of Annihilation, have returned to the People at large for their exercise; the State remaining in the mean time exposed to all the dangers of invasion from without, and convulsions within.—

He has endeavoured to prevent the population of these States; for that   12 purpose obstructing the Laws for Naturalization of Foreigners; refusing to pass others to encourage their migrations hither, and raising the conditions of new Appropriations of Lands.—

He has obstructed the Administration of Justice, by refusing his Assent   13 to Laws for establishing Judiciary powers.—

He has made Judges dependent on his Will alone, for the tenure of   14 their offices, and the amount and payment of their salaries.—

He has erected a multitude of New Offices, and sent hither swarms of   15 Officers to harrass our people, and eat out their substance.—

He has kept among us in times of peace, Standing Armies without the   16 Consent of our legislatures.—

He has affected to render the Military independent of and superior to   17 the Civil power.—

He has combined with others to subject us to a jurisdiction foreign to   18 our constitution, and unacknowledged by our laws; giving his Assent to their Acts of pretended Legislation:—

For quartering large bodies of armed troops among us:—   19

For protecting them, by a mock Trial, from punishment for any Mur-   20 ders which they should commit on the Inhabitants of these States:—

For cutting off our Trade with all parts of the world:—   21

For imposing Taxes on us without our Consent:—   22

For depriving us in many cases, of the benefits of Trial by Jury:—   23

For transporting us beyond Seas to be tried for pretended offences:—   24

For abolishing the free System of English Laws in a neighbouring   25 Province, establishing therein an Arbitrary government, and enlarging its Boundaries so as to render it at once an example and fit instrument for introducing the same absolute rule in these Colonies:—

For taking away our Charters, abolishing our most valuable Laws, and altering fundamentally the Forms of our Governments:— 26

For suspending our own Legislatures, and declaring themselves invested with power to legislate for us in all cases whatsoever.— 27

He has abdicated Government here, by declaring us out of his Protection and waging War against us.— 28

He has plundered our seas, ravaged our Coasts, burnt our towns, and destroyed the lives of our people.— 29

He is at this time transporting large Armies of foreign Mercenaries to compleat the works of death, desolation, and tyranny, already begun with circumstances of Cruelty & perfidy scarcely paralleled in the most barbarous ages, and totally unworthy the Head of a civilized nation.— 30

He has constrained our fellow Citizens taken Captive on high Seas to bear Arms against their Country, to become the executioners of their friends and Brethren, or to fall themselves by their Hands.— 31

He has excited domestic insurrections amongst us, and has endeavoured to bring on the inhabitants of our frontiers, the merciless Indian Savages, whose known rule of warfare, is an undistinguished destruction of all ages, sexes, and conditions. 32

In every stage of these Oppressions We have Petitioned for Redress in the most humble terms: Our repeated Petitions have been answered only by repeated injury. A Prince, whose character is thus marked by every act which may define a Tyrant, is unfit to be the ruler of a free people. 33

Nor have We been wanting in attentions to our Brittish brethren. We have warned them from time to time of attempts by their legislature to extend an unwarrantable jurisdiction over us. We have reminded them of the circumstances of our emigration and settlement here. We have appealed to their native justice and magnanimity, and we have conjured them by the ties of our common kindred to disavow these usurpations, which, would inevitably interrupt our connections and correspondence. They too have been deaf to the voice of justice and of consanguinity. We must, therefore, acquiesce in the necessity, which denounces our Separation, and hold them, as we hold the rest of mankind, Enemies in War, in Peace Friends.— 34

We, therefore, the Representatives of the united States of America, in General Congress, Assembled, appealing to the Supreme Judge of the world for the rectitude of our intentions, do, in the Name, and by Authority of the good People of these Colonies, solemnly publish and declare, That these United Colonies are, and of Right ought to be, Free and Independent States; that they are Absolved from all Allegiance to the British Crown, and that all political connection between them and the State of Great Britain, is and ought to be totally dissolved; and that as Free and Independent States, they have full Power to levy War, conclude Peace, contract Alliances, establish Commerce, and do all other Acts and Things which Independent States may of right do.— 35

And for the support of this Declaration, with a firm reliance on the   36
protection of divine Providence, we mutually pledge to each other our
Lives, our Fortunes, and our sacred Honor.

Questions

1. When Jefferson says "we," as in paragraph 2, who does he mean?
2. After careful reading, who do you think was the intended audience for the Declaration?
3. What is the purpose of the Declaration?
4. What is the purpose of including the long list of abuses committed by Great Britain in the person of King George III?
5. Considering the audience and purpose of the Declaration, what is the reason for including paragraphs 3 and 4 on the legality of governments?
6. How is the credibility of the signers established?
7. What is the tone of the document? Name some specific determinants of its tone.
8. What type of evidence is most common in the Declaration? What other types of evidence lend support? Give examples.

Reading

In the essay that follows, newspaper columnist Sydney J. Harris reveals a little-known aspect of the Declaration of Independence—an excluded clause that might have altered the course of history had it not been deleted in a political compromise.

High Cost of Compromise

Sydney J. Harris

Schoolchildren who are taken on visits to Washington generally tour   1
the Library of Congress. There, in a glass cage, they can see a copy of the
Declaration of Independence. But this is not a copy of the original Declaration as written by Thomas Jefferson.

The original sheets, which have been seen only by officials and scholars,   2
are kept in a safe, and they contain a clause which was omitted from all later
copies. No reference is ever made to it in history classes.

In this clause, Jefferson denounces King George and the British gov-   3
ernment for acquiescing in slavery and the slave trade. The clause was
knocked out by pressure groups from the South, who agreed to accept
other parts of the Declaration only if this part were deleted.

Nobody knows, of course, what history "might have been," but it seems   4
reasonable to assume that the whole social pattern of our country would
have been different if the clause against the slave trade had remained in the
Declaration, putting the new nation on record as favoring its abolition,
along with the other civilized nations of the time.

We would have abolished slavery when it was comparatively easy to do   5
so, and the whole tragic and inconclusive episode of the Civil War would
have been averted—an episode for which America is still paying a heavy
price today.

This is the terrible paradox of politics—that, by its very nature, it is   6
incapable of solving basic political problems. For the essence of politics is
compromise, and Jefferson was forced to compromise his ideals and his
good sense in order to obtain the requisite signatures on the Declaration.

But political compromise usually defers, rather than resolves. It closes   7
its eyes to the deeper causes of a problem, in order to treat its symptoms—
and meanwhile, since the causes go unchecked, the disease breaks out in
more virulent form in the future.

The delegates from South Carolina and Georgia, who pressured Jef-   8
ferson to delete the slavery clause, were also politicians fighting for what
they thought were their regional advantages. But slavery actually dragged
down the South in the long run, and the Civil War engendered only
bitterness and revenge. Slavery deformed the Negro, denigrated the South,
and dragged its evil consequences into the Twentieth Century.

All political issues, if they are fundamental, are at bottom moral issues.   9
They cannot be settled at the political level, and certainly not at the military
level. Yet we cannot work out our moral problems outside the political
process, outside the give-and-take of practical compromise. That is why
genuine progress is so slow. As a man, Jefferson knew slavery was wrong; as
a politician, he had to condone it. And we pay the price.

Questions

1. What clause does Harris say was omitted from the Declaration of Independence for political reasons?

2. What does Harris identify as implications of this political compromise?

3. The development of Harris's essay is basically cause and effect. What are the actual effects, and what are the conjectural ones?

4. Explore the following implications and extend them as far as you can:
   a. Civil War averted
   b. Negro slavery ended

5. Read "I Have a Dream" by Martin Luther King, Jr., on page 211, particularly paragraphs 3 and 4, and relate them to Harris's essay.

Reading

Milton Friedman wrote "Prohibition and Drugs" in 1972. With some updating on types of drugs available and their sources, the essay still is timely. Drugs are even more of a problem now than they were then, and legalization is still occasionally presented as a solution. Friedman's major support for his proposal to legalize drugs is an analogy with the prohibition of alcohol. As you read, ask yourself if this analogy is valid.

Prohibition and Drugs
Milton Friedman

"The reign of tears is over. The slums will soon be only a memory. We will turn our prisons into factories and our jails into storehouses and corncribs. Men will walk upright now, women will smile, and the children will laugh. Hell will be forever for rent." 1

This is how Billy Sunday, the noted evangelist and leading crusader against Demon Rum, greeted the onset of Prohibition in early 1920. We know now how tragically his hopes were doomed. New prisons and jails had to be built to house the criminals spawned by converting the drinking of spirits into a crime against the state. Prohibition undermined respect for the law, corrupted the minions of the law, created a decadent moral climate—but did not stop the consumption of alcohol. 2

Despite this tragic object lesson, we seem bent on repeating precisely the same mistake in the handling of drugs. 3

On ethical grounds, do we have the right to use the machinery of government to prevent an individual from becoming an alcoholic or a drug addict? For children, almost everyone would answer at least a qualified yes. But for responsible adults, I, for one, would answer no. Reason with the potential addict, yes. Tell him the consequences, yes. Pray for and with him, yes. But I believe that we have no right to use force, directly or indirectly, to prevent a fellow man from committing suicide, let alone from drinking alcohol or taking drugs. 4

I readily grant that the ethical issue is difficult and that men of goodwill may well disagree. Fortunately, we need not resolve the ethical issue to agree on policy. *Prohibition is an attempted cure that makes matters worse—for both the addict and the rest of us.* Hence, even if you regard present policy toward drugs as ethically justified, considerations of expediency make that policy most unwise. 5

Consider first the addict. Legalizing drugs might increase the number of addicts, but it is not clear that it would. Forbidden fruit is attractive, particularly 6 to the young. More important, many drug addicts are deliberately made by pushers, who give likely prospects their first few doses free. It pays the pusher to do so because, once hooked, the addict is a captive customer. If drugs were legally available, any possible profit from such inhumane activity would disappear, since the addict could buy from the cheapest source.

Whatever happens to the number of addicts, the individual addict would clearly be far better off if drugs were legal. Today, drugs are both incredibly expensive and highly uncertain in quality. Addicts are driven to associate with criminals to get the drugs, become criminals themselves to finance the habit, and risk constant danger of death and disease. 7

Consider next the rest of us. Here the situation is crystal-clear. The harm to us from the addiction of others arises almost wholly from the fact that drugs are illegal. A recent committee of the American Bar Association estimated that addicts commit one-third to one-half of all street crime in the United States. Legalize drugs, and street crime would drop automatically. 8

Moreover, addicts and pushers are not the only ones corrupted. Immense sums are at stake. It is inevitable that some relatively low-paid police and other government officials—and some high-paid ones as well—will succumb to the temptation to pick up easy money. 9

Legalizing drugs would simultaneously reduce the amount of crime and raise the quality of law enforcement. Can you conceive of any other measure that would accomplish so much to promote law and order? 10

But, you may say, must we accept defeat? Why not simply end the drug traffic? That is where experience under Prohibition is most relevant. We cannot end the drug traffic. We may be able to cut off opium from Turkey— but there are innumerable other places where the opium poppy grows. With French cooperation, we may be able to make Marseilles an unhealthy place to manufacture heroin—but there are innumerable other places where the simple manufacturing operations involved can be carried out. So long as large sums of money are involved—and they are bound to be if drugs are illegal—it is literally hopeless to expect to end the traffic or even reduce seriously its scope. 11

In drugs, as in other areas, persuasion and example are likely to be far more effective than the use of force to shape others in our image. 12

Questions

1. Update paragraph 11 with more recent details.
2. We are still unable to refute Friedman's statement in paragraph 11, "We cannot end the drug traffic." Cite some other statements in the essay that are still true.
3. How analogous are drugs and alcohol? Consider also the validity of the analogy relating the present era to the time of Prohibition.
4. In addition to his major analogy, how does Friedman support his argument?

5. Friedman makes a number of statements that border on fallacies; for example, in paragraph 10, "Legalizing drugs would simultaneously reduce the amount of crime and raise the quality of law enforcement." Find other statements that are not adequately supported.

Readings

Here are two essays about hunting, the first by *Time* magazine contributor John Skow and the second by Universal Press Syndicate writer James Kilpatrick. You will find that these writers, while viewing hunting from opposite sides, have some common ground. Both also take a satirical stance, but notice how satire can have a variety in tone.

Heroes, Bears, and True Baloney

John Skow

Let's say that I am the benevolent and enlightened despot of my 1
exasperating homeland, the U.S.A., and can eliminate any stupidity or foolishness by waving my hand. I have already banished basketball coaches, light beer, and neckties. Now, on the third or fourth day of hand waving, will I decide to ban hunting? My local newspaper, the Concord, N.H., *Monitor*, reports that black bears have migrated southward in our state. I knew this already. I haven't had the luck to see one, but a few weeks ago a neighbor saw three of them, presumably a female and two cubs, at the edge of a pond a few hundred feet from my house in central New Hampshire. We can all rest easy, however, because the state's fish and game commission has opened a five-week bear-hunting season in our county. Since October 1, the hairy-eared fellows who keep two big-game rifles racked in the back windows of their pickups fifty-two weeks each year, in case World War III starts, have been blasting away at the hairy-eared invaders.

The *Monitor* story told of a local farmer who had been pestered by bears 2
getting into his feed corn. Had to shoot two last year, he said. A fish-and-game-commission biologist said, "Rather than have farmers kill the bears, we would rather have sportsmen utilize the resource." You get used to blood-sport bureaucratese; "utilize," or "harvest," is what you do when you get something fuzzy and four-footed in your sights. As in most states, New Hampshire's fish and game policies often seem to be caught in a time warp, perhaps in the decade of the 1820s, when subsistence hunting was an important food source for most families. Bears, these days, behave like large raccoons. They are smart, cute, hungry corn thieves and garbage raiders, happy in the suburbs and virtually harmless. Last year the state paid less than $7,000 to corn farmers because of bear damage. This is a tolerable

figure. It would cost more to keep a bear in the zoo. A citizen determined to be grumpy might reflect that while the last recorded human fatality from a bear attack in New Hampshire was in the 1700s, the last recorded human death from a hunter's blunder was last week.

The fact is that in New Hampshire, it is hunters, not bears or deer or 3
moose, that are troublesome pests. For most of the fall, shooting of some kind is legal, and while I am willing to risk a peppering of bird shot, I don't want to be hulled by the antitank ammunition used for bear or moose (fifty-nine moose no longer menace us as the result of a recent three-day shooting season). So most of us stay out of the woods during the year's most beautiful season. Once, during deer season, I rounded a turn on a logging road while running with my dogs. A couple of heroes were sitting in a pickup truck, drinking beer. One had his rifle trained on my midsection. If he had killed me, he would have received a severe talking-to from the authorities. No one I mentioned this to was surprised. They all had similar stories.

So here I sit, leafing through *Meditations on Hunting* by José Ortega y 4
Gasset, who never jumped deer from a pickup truck. His book is a classy volume that hunters like my friend George Butler give, with wry smiles, to nonhunters like me. Butler is a gifted documentary filmmaker (*Pumping Iron* and *Pumping Iron II: The Women*) who was raised in Somalia and Kenya when hunting was a natural way of living in the great, broad grassland. His new documentary, called *In the Blood* and shot in Tanzania, is about hunting. The action builds toward a scene in which his eleven-year-old son Tyssen shoots his first buffalo and is "blooded"—his forehead is smeared with the animal's blood—by a celebrated hunter, Robin Hurt. "Today you were part of nature," Hurt tells the boy. "It is also a sad occasion . . ." This is baloney, of course, but it is true baloney, like the guff about climbing a mountain because it is there. I am not so sure about another remark in the film, that killing is a way of taking responsibility for what you eat. I can take responsibility for eating meat without hunting, or spending my vacation hacking up beef quarters at an Armour plant.

Still, Hurt is a serious man who believes that Kenya's decision to ban 5
hunting in 1977 has led to the near extinction of elephants there. In the old days his clients and those of other hunters killed about 200 bulls a year, from an elephant population of about 160,000. When the hunters were forced out and game officials no longer patrolled the bush, gangs of ivory poachers moved in from Sudan and Somalia. Hurt is not optimistic about the future of animals or hunters in East Africa. "I don't think we're there for long," he says. But never mind Africa; it's truth time at home: Do I wave my despotic hand and ban hunting in the United States? (Silence. More silence; the despot is thinking hard.) At last, the answer is: no.

It is a glum, unconfident no. The fact is that hunters are pests. Their 6
blather about improving wildlife is mostly self-serving (though the effective Ducks Unlimited effort to preserve wetlands is both self-serving and environment-serving, which is fair enough). But we all need true baloney,

even the armed innocents from Massachusetts who drive up here, see three trees standing together in my side yard, and think they have discovered the Big Woods. Their fantasy is bloody and obsolete, but hunting gives them something they can't get watching golf on the tube. Theodore Roosevelt wrote of the hunting life that "when it is gone, there can be no substitute." Probably true, for good or not.

And the bears? Ah, the bears. They have put up with people for a long time. Hunters will kill them, and fish and game will close the season next year. And five or ten years from now, with luck, they will again begin to repopulate central New Hampshire. Maybe then I will see one.

7

Some Hunting Protesters Are Overzealous Hypocrites
James Kilpatrick

The hunter who appeared on the television screen a few days ago was doing a great job of holding his temper. He was being badgered by a willowy fellow with long hair whose purpose was to spoil the hunter's day. Looking at the screen, I kept hoping the hunter would punch this milksop zealot in the snoot.

1

It appears that people who profess to be animal lovers are waging a concerted effort this year. In Hawaii they are mad about dolphins as swimming companions. Elsewhere they are out to ruin the lives of trappers who depend upon the fur trade for a living.

2

The particular game this season appears to involve the provocative harassment of law-abiding sportsmen in the field. Having alerted local TV stations, the animal lovers turn up on public lands where hunting is permitted. There they ring cowbells or take to bullhorns, the better to frighten game. They chase wildly after hunters, asking insipid questions, and the TV cameramen chase wildly after the troublemakers. All this is supposed to preserve wildlife.

3

One young woman pronounced that "we have as much right as the hunters to do what we please on public lands." Up to a point, this is true. But no one has a constitutional right to interfere physically with the lawful conduct of another. Free speech has its limits, and the animal lovers, so-called, are breaching them.

4

I say "so-called," because one wonders about those who agitate in the name of animal rights. It seems unlikely that all of them are barefoot vegetarians. More probably they eat meat now and then. They may have enjoyed turkey for Thanksgiving. Their diet may include fish, lobster, and crab. If so, then the weight of their hypocrisy must be a terrible weight to bear.

5

Dan Matthews, director of the anti-fur campaign of People for the Ethical Treatment of Animals, finds it morally wrong for people to wear fur. Does the gentleman wear shoes? Does he hold up his pants with a leather belt? Does he find it morally wrong to have bacon with his eggs? If not, why

6

not? The moral distinction between shooting a deer in the wild and slaughtering a pig in a plant is not immediately apparent.

In the television incident that involved the Gucci-Pucci pest and the   7
hunter, the ostensible object was to prevent the killing of deer. Let me tell you something about deer. I have lived for twenty-four years in the Blue Ridge Mountains of Virginia. In these parts we are overrun with deer. The animals can destroy a vineyard or devastate a young apple orchard overnight. They are a positive menace on rural roads. Every year hunters take 120,000 deer in Virginia, and the deer population is not affected at all. State wildlife biologists place the deer population at between 750,000 and 1 million.

Most of the deer hunters in my county are local hunters. It seems not to   8
have occurred to the Gucci-Puccis that in our low-income area, a deer represents 80 pounds of dressed meat in the freezer. Mountain men are feeding their families. They hunt as a way of life, as their fathers and grandfathers hunted before them.

A personal word: I do not hunt. The only gun on our farm is an ancient   9
double-barreled .410 that belonged to my father-in-law. He was a self-taught naturalist who loved and respected all of God's creatures and treated them with respect, and he taught me his values. I fought for adoption of the Endangered Species Act; I have defended snail darters, sea turtles, dune mice, and spotted owls. The abuse of animals in laboratory experiments arouses me to fury.

But fanaticism in any form has small appeal, and the thought will not go   10
away that the pro-animal nuts are as offensive as the pro-gun nuts. They are equally nuts. And when it comes to the supposed evils of hunting, let it be said for the record that hunters do more toward the preservation of wildlife than whole battalions of publicity-seeking pantywaists have ever done.

Since enactment of the Pitman-Robertson Act of 1937, wild game   11
hunters have provided more than $2 billion toward the care and propagation of wild animals. Through the duck stamp program, other hunters have preserved wetlands and developed breeding grounds for waterfowl that otherwise would have been lost. These are the true lovers of nature.

The thought will not go away that in harassing the deer hunters, the   12
willowy boys and the earnest girls are not wholly concerned with prolonging the life of a deer. Their companion purpose lies in preventing the pleasure of the hunter. It is a new Puritanism, as selfish and censorious as the old.

Questions

1. In your own words, state the thesis, or position on hunting, of each writer.

2. What is the occasion that instigated each essay?

3. Compare the two essays for support. How do they use examples, testimony, statistics, and opinion?

4. What points do Skow and Kilpatrick agree on? On what do they disagree? On what do they seem to disagree most strongly?

5. Compare the essays' tone. What is the tone of each? How does each essayist establish his tone?

6. How does each writer establish his credibility on the subject of hunting? How credible is each?

7. In "Thinking like a Mountain" in Chapter 6, Aldo Leopold makes a point similar to Kilpatrick's, that unhunted deer herds destroy vegetation. Yet, with similarities to Skow's essay, he regrets having killed wolves when he was younger. Where do you stand on hunting? Is it destructive or constructive? Should wild animals be killed for sport? for their meat? How should hunting be regulated?

8. What other questions does the hunting issue raise?

Reading

The following student essay expresses a persuasive viewpoint on a subject that Lewis Thomas reflects on in Chapter 6: both writers wonder how children growing up today can handle the threat of nuclear war.

Nuclear Children

Holly Sue Anderson

The truth is simple; the saddest and by far the scariest aspect of nuclear war is that we're emotionally killing each other, and especially our children, before doomsday has even a chance to arrive. 1

Now, I realize that nuclear war is a global problem that does exist and must be acknowledged, but I'm not comfortable with letting life stop in the meantime; children have to experience childhood if they are to grow to be emotionally healthy adults. Can they do so if they are preoccupied with death; if, in response to concerns thrust upon them by misguided parents and the media that they worship, they place the fear of nuclear disaster before every other concern in their lives? 2

"What is it like to grow up without believing that you will?" This question, raised by an April 1984 issue of *Psychology Today* in response to interviews done on grade-school children, has a lot to say. For the interviews, classes were chosen that had not previously discussed nuclear weapons. Three out of five teachers warned investigators that their students knew nothing about nuclear weapons, did not think about the threat of nuclear war, and would have nothing to say about it. They were wrong. Some examples to ponder include the fears of a six-year-old boy who said that each time he heard a plane overhead he wondered if it was "the war plane." Another remarked, "I always keep thinking I'm going to grow up to be an 3 astronaut, but I think I'm never going to be one." In response to a question asking what the world would be like in five years, one student replied, "How are we supposed to know? There could be a war tomorrow and blow us all off the face of the Earth."

How sad! In childhood we should be consumed with thoughts of   4
puppies and butterflies, mudpies and mischief; why then are we condemning our children to thoughts of hell?

Irene Petteys, a free-lance writer, wife, and mother, in an editorial   5
published in the December 17, 1984, issue of *Newsweek*, states:

> Heaven only knows, it's hard enough being a kid today without having your parents or teachers confront you with issues that even they have difficulty comprehending. Young children have enough fears to deal with without being supplied with more. Most parents know the difficulty of consoling a child who fears the "witch under the bed" or the "bogyman in the closet." . . . What must it be like for the child who fears going to bed without a light if his parents are telling him that all the lights may go out forever?

But it's not just parents and educators who are corrupting our youth,   6
but society and the mass media in particular. Even if we protect young people from such gruesome documentaries as *The Day After,* have you taken time to sit down and view a so-called "cartoon" lately? One example that stands out in my mind is a strip called *Thundar, the Barbarian;* each episode is introduced by explaining that the modern world destroyed itself and Thundar evolved and reigns over the new barbaric state that survives. The cinema has also capitalized on the nuclear situation, and production such as *Wargames* and *Spies Like Us* go out of their way to show the government as a bunch of raving idiots and nuclear disaster as only a human error away.

Supposed experts like Dr. Helen Caldicott, founder of Women's Action   7
for Nuclear Disarmament, don't help the situation either. In a recent speech to a group of children in Maine, she asserted that if the nuclear arms race doesn't stop, "you aren't going to grow up." This was certainly not the thing to say to instill hope in children. Whatever happened to innocence?

Try to remember back when you were six. What were you doing? Were   8
you playing dress-up, building castles in the sand, picnicking with imaginary friends, jumping rope—or jumping each time the network tested the Emergency Broadcast System, a plane flew overhead, or you heard a loud noise?

Now, I am not advocating a "head in the sand" approach to so impor-   9
tant an issue; I simply agree with Irene Petteys when she says:

> A child develops intellectually and emotionally as he grows physically. We don't encourage hang gliding by two-year-olds or teach calculus in the first grade, nor should we tell a six-year-old that his uncertain future includes the possibility of the death of everyone dear to him and the end of his own short life as well. Children should not be subjected to activities, information, or problems that are beyond their comprehension.

Along with songwriter Whitney Houston, I believe that "the children 10 are our future," because I believe that there is a future. If we teach them well, they will have the ability to lead. Exposing them to the pressure of trying to cope with the enormity of nuclear war will not mold them into the leaders of the next generation. More likely than not, these frightened kids will stand out as a group for their lack of accomplishments. They will have trouble sorting out their own problems, let alone national ones. If we show them their internal beauty, they will learn to see things from a healthy perspective. If we raise them to feel loved and secure, they will become adults who approach problems with confidence and take pride in intelligent decisions. If our babes aren't paralyzed by fear, they can hug a puppy out of pure joy and wrestle in the autumn leaves with the abandon of youth. The memories of simple pleasures will give them a beautiful reverence for life.

Instead of making our children the victims, we should concentrate on 11 making them our saviors. Maybe, if the people in power in our presently chaotic world were urged to watch their children—how they greet the morning, or the glow that lights up their eyes at Christmas, or the way they dream of their futures—we could finally see the light at the end of the tunnel. Maybe if we first let the children laugh, we could take Whitney Houston's advice and "let the children's laughter remind us how we used to be"—innocent and hopeful.

Questions

1. What action is Anderson urging? Is such an action possible in today's world? Explain your answer.

2. Anderson seems to assume an audience of parents or, like her, future parents. Do you agree with her assumptions about that audience? How does her message relate to the world as you know it?

3. How does Anderson support her position? What evidence do you think is the most convincing? Can you think of anything else she might have said?

4. What do you remember about the threat of nuclear war as you were growing up? What effect did such knowledge have on you?

5. While Anderson discusses how frightening the nuclear threat is for children, Lewis Thomas, in "Late Night Thoughts on Listening to Mahler's Ninth Symphony" (Chapter 6) wonders what it would be like to be sixteen years old and have to deal with government officials calmly discussing the killing of millions of people. What effect does the knowledge of stockpiled nuclear weapons have on you today?

6. In a particularly grim description in "A Description of the Effects of a One-Megaton Bomb" (Chapter 12), Jonathan Schell considers the effects of a nuclear bomb dropped on New York City. How old do you think children should be before reading such intense details or being told other possibilities of nuclear war?

7. If you were to write an essay of advice to present or future parents, what would you say about the nuclear threat?

Readings

Here are two short essays by the same student writer. The first takes a pro-life stance on the abortion issue, the second a pro-choice stance. It was particularly difficult, Cindy Johanek says, to write these essays and be fair to each side. As you read, observe how she uses words and details to support whichever position she is taking.

The Decline of Morality

Cindy Johanek

Legalized abortion is indeed the clearest indication of moral decay in   1
the United States. The very fact that the United States Supreme Court could justify the killing of an unborn child is sending this message: murder is OK. Although the pro-abortion position argues that life does not begin at conception, it has been made clear through women's testimonies that the presence, development, and life of the baby are strongly felt shortly after conception.

The baby, at this point, has a soul and is a child of God. Murdering the   2
baby for the sake of convenience, financial gain, and other selfish reasons is similar to allowing premeditated murder for the sake of similar convenience, financial gain, and selfish reasons. The baby is not a "part" of the mother but is a person in the eyes of God. The pro-abortion position treats the baby as a parasite that attaches itself to an unwilling victim.

In our highly technical society, medical advances have offered us sev-   3
eral safe methods for preventing pregnancy. These methods should be used. Abortion is too often used as a form of birth control, encouraging unwanted pregnancies in the future.

The Constitution, according to the pro-abortion position, protects the   4
life of the individual and guarantees individual freedoms. This, of course, is true. However, the pro-abortion side forgets that an unborn baby is also an individual and should be protected under the Constitution, especially since this innocent victim is particularly vulnerable.

A Matter of Faith

Cindy Johanek

It is difficult to imagine anyone wanting to take away individual rights,   1
especially when our Constitution emphasizes the rights of individuals in the United States. The anti-choice position on the abortion issue is attempting to eliminate individual freedom in arguments that often focus on what they call "morality" and "personhood." Although the concepts of morality and

personhood are governed by an individual's religious affiliation, anti-choice supporters use the very argument of religion to overturn a guaranteed constitutional right, religious freedom.

If the anti-choice position gains power in the United States, its supporters will define "personhood," and the right to define personhood will no longer rest with the individual. The anti-choice argument regarding personhood is this: life begins at conception. In other words, the cells that congregate at conception form a "person," or a "baby." Certainly, some religious beliefs hold that this "cluster of cells" is a person; other beliefs, however, do not. Accordingly, if the United States makes abortion illegal, the message will be that only certain religious beliefs will be upheld as morally right in a court of law.

A person, by Webster's definition, is a "human being," a personality or self, or the human body. The human body as we know it has arms, legs, feet, hands, eyes, ears, and so on. A cluster of cells, then, can only be a cluster of cells—in no fashion is it a human body unless one's religious belief expressly declares it to be. The bottom line in the abortion debate is, in fact, the right to express individual religious beliefs. The Constitution has never attempted to persuade the United States of which denomination is morally right; however, the anti-choice people are trying to do just that.

Questions

1. Johanek's arguments deal with two major issues: individual rights and morality. The pro-life argument is that babies are killed in abortions, an immoral act; the pro-choice argument is that a court judgment against abortion imposes one set of religious beliefs on the nation in place of individual rights. Which of Johanek's essays do you think is stronger? What makes it more convincing?

2. Select several words that appear in both essays, such as *babies,* and contrast how Johanek uses them and how their meaning changes.

3. In the essays, which appeal do you find most dominant: the appeal of the writer's character, an appeal to the emotions of the audience, or an appeal based on logical reasoning? Explain your answer. What other appeals might Johanek have used?

4. What kinds of evidence does Johanek use for developing each essay: examples, testimony, statistics, or informed opinions? Refer to the essays in explaining your answer.

5. What influence did the ordere of Johanek's essays have on your reading? How might your response have changed if "A Matter of Faith" had preceded "The Decline of Morality"?

CHAPTER 8

To Entertain and Move: Writing with Emphasis on the Audience

> If we arouse in someone an attitude of sympathy toward something, we may be starting him on the road towards overtly sympathetic action with regard to it.
>
> —Kenneth Burke

Entertaining and moving are related purposes for writing. **Moving** stirs the emotions of readers, sometimes to encourage some kind of action, sometimes to engender empathy for others. People may be moved to pity, anger, fear, a whole host of emotions. **Entertaining** moves an audience too. It moves to pleasure—with humor, for example, or with a good story and a harmonious combination of word sounds. Both entertaining and moving thus appeal to the emotions of the audience. They usually accompany other purposes for writing, such as persuasion or information.

Shared Experiences

To achieve the aim of entertaining or moving, the writer's primary need is to understand the audience. A writer must know what is important to and what interests the audience. The writer must actually be, or give the impression of being, at one with the audience, sharing similar backgrounds. Entertaining and moving, more even than informing and persuading, depend on common ground.

People who care about animals are more likely to be moved by a statement about the pain and suffering that minks and other animals undergo so someone can wear their fur. Similarly, since most people care about

188

children, emotional descriptions of starving, abused, or drug-dependent children move most people to pity. But, of course, allusions to a shared worldview make sense only if the audience knows what the writer is referring to. Many people are familiar with the Bible, so quotations from that book and allusions to its stories will often put an audience in a favorable frame of mind. Most people in the United States celebrate Christmas in some way, so allusions to Santa Claus, the Wise Men, or the Nativity draw upon common images and emotions.

For cartoons, jokes, and other humor to be funny, an audience must understand what a writer means by any allusions. Writer and audience must share knowledge about particular people, say the vice president of the United States, or television or film personalities, or television commercials, makes of cars, and so on. A writer can make a humorous parody of the tale of the three little pigs only if the audience knows the original story.

One of the facts of writing humor, then, is that a single piece of humor probably won't appeal to every audience. Humor is often topical, issue-oriented, and thus bound by time. Satires about the current vice president won't be funny a decade from now. Humor based on current events will be outdated next year. Some humor, however, is timeless. Such humor is based on common human experiences: eating, working, paying taxes, raising a family, living with pets, and so on. While not all entertainment is meant to be humorous, all entertainment, like the specialized type humor, provides relief from daily routine and stress.

Style

Both entertaining and moving rely on an exaggerated style. Parody and satire, for example, depend on controlled **exaggeration,** or hyperbole. *Parody* mimics the style and tone of another piece of writing, often to ridicule. In the following excerpt from a piece called "Across the Street and into the Grill," E. B. White parodies Ernest Hemingway's style and manner of telling a story:

> This is my last and best and true and only meal, thought Mr. Perley as he descended at noon and swung east on the beat-up sidewalk of Forty-fifth Street. Just ahead of him was the girl from the reception desk. I am a little fleshed up around the crook of the elbow, thought Perley, but I commute good.
>
> He quickened his step to overtake her and felt the pain again. What a stinking trade it is, he thought. But after what I've done to other assistant treasurers, I can't hate anybody. Sixteen deads, and I don't know how many possibles.

After the manner of Hemingway, White alludes to people and events as if the reader ought to know about them: "the girl from the reception desk" (what girl? what reception desk?); "felt the pain again" (what pain?); "sixteen deads" (dead whats?). And, like Hemingway's, White's sentences rely heavily on coordinating conjunctions: *and* and *but*. If you know Hemingway's writing, you are more likely to appreciate the humor than if you don't.

Satire uses exaggeration too, often with the intent of ridicule or derision. Newspaper columnists sometimes use satire to point out the folly of elected officials and other public figures. In this brief excerpt from a Dorothy Parker story, "From the Diary of a New York Lady," a type of person is satirized. Judge for yourself what the point of the satire is.

> Wednesday. The most terrible thing happened *just this minute*. Broke one of my finger nails *right off short*. Absolutely *the* most horrible thing I ever had happen to me in my life. Called up Miss Rose to come over and shape it for me, but she was out for the day. I do have *the* worst luck in the *entire* world. Now I'll have to go around like this all day and all night, but what *can* you do? *Damn* Miss Rose.

Parker's use of italics further enhances the exaggeration.

Writing for the purpose of moving employs exaggeration too. For example, exaggerated **repetition** draws on the reader's sense of rhythm. Poetry often evokes an emotional response because of its repetitive rhythm, as do some essays and speeches. Notice how Martin Luther King, Jr., a master of rhythmic repetition, employs the technique in this excerpt from his "I Have a Dream" speech:

> So let freedom ring from the prodigious hilltops of New Hampshire. Let freedom ring from the mighty mountains of New York. Let freedom ring from the heightening Alleghenies of Pennsylvania. Let freedom ring from the snowcapped Rockies of Colorado. Let freedom ring from the curvaceous peaks of California.
>
> But not only that. Let freedom ring from Stone Mountain of Georgia. Let freedom ring from Lookout Mountain of Tennessee. Let freedom ring from every hill and molehill of Mississippi. From every mountainside, let freedom ring.

No doubt about it: this is exaggerated repetition. As a piece of writing, "I Have a Dream" relies in part on readers drawing on the *sound* of words. If you have heard recordings of the speech, you probably actually hear King's voice as you read the words. Speeches by their nature rely more heavily on repetition than do essays meant to be read. They appeal to the ear as well as to the eye. The balance between the unexpected, or surprise, and the expected, gained by repetition and other devices, varies between speech and writing. In writing, entertaining and moving are often achieved with a controlled exaggeration, avoiding too frequent repetition and the incidence of a joke or emotional appeal every line. Humorist James Thurber gives this advice about control:

> With humor you have to look out for traps. You're likely to be very gleeful with what you've first put down, and you think it's fine, very funny. One reason you go over and over it is to make the piece sound less as if you were having a lot of fun with it yourself. You try to play it down.

Surprise is difficult to achieve when humor and emotional appeal are unremitting. If you study humorous essays, you will find that they often have breaks in the humor, to prepare readers for the next incidence. Much of moving and entertaining, especially humor, depends on surprising the audience. Surprise is often balanced with fulfilled expectations. In the E. B. White parody, you are first surprised to discover Hemingway's style, but, once you realize what White is doing, you expect additional similarities and enjoy finding them.

The essays in this chapter represent entertaining and moving as purposes for writing. Even though these two purposes are often widely divergent in their ends—laughter as opposed to sympathy, for example—they employ similar means. Both rely on common experiences and worldviews, balancing the expected with the unexpected, using both controlled exaggeration and surprise. As purposes for writing, both entertaining and moving are usually paired with additional purposes—to inform, perhaps, or to persuade. Read these essays to study technique, to gain enjoyment, and to determine their secondary purposes.

Entertaining with Humor

People who make their living by writing humorous essays and books write about everyday things—subjects they know well. James Thurber wrote "The Night the Bed Fell" (on his father), "University Days," and "The Dog That Bit People," the family Airedale, named Muggs. Erma Bombeck writes about *Motherhood: The Second Oldest Profession,* including chapters called "So You Want to Be a Mother!" and "Who Are Harder to Raise—Boys or Girls?" Such writers say that it's much easier to be funny about something you're familiar with; it's easier to exaggerate a known humorous situation, they say, than to invent something funny.

The two essays in this section are about things that are ordinary, usually serious, and often unpleasant: names and punctuation. By exaggeration the writers make their subjects funny. The writers also depend on shared backgrounds with their audiences: everyone has a name and may have had some unpleasant experiences with it, and every reader has had some encounters with punctuation.

Reading

Student writer Terry Splett is pregnant for the first time and has begun to think about names for the expected baby. Not wanting to burden the child with a ridiculous or an intolerable name, she considers her options. As you read, notice how she relies on common backgrounds and how she uses exaggeration, repetition, and surprise to create humor. What point might she be making with this humorous essay?

A Pain in the Name

Terry Splett

I once worked with a man named Daniel Boone. When I came across   1
his name for the first time on a time card, I thought the guys in the warehouse were just pulling my leg, but when I investigated I found out that it wasn't a joke. Daniel Boone did, in fact, work the night shift, and he even had a union card. I wonder what provoked his mother and father to name him Daniel Boone.

I went to school with a Ben Hur and a Mary Hartman. I remember   2
when a thoughtless teacher calling roll in an auditorium class yelled "Mary Hartman, Mary Hartman" just like on the TV show, and I'll never forget the look in that poor ninth grader's eyes, or the laughter that echoed through the auditorium that day. I wonder what provoked her parents when they named her.

I also know a Roman Rowan, a Becky Beckman, and a Delana Dalei-   3
den. I wonder why parents wreck perfectly good last names with rhyming and clashing first names. Don't they know that children get teased and scorned because of their names?

As my husband and I, first-time parents-to-be, discuss names for our   4
baby, we are well aware of this fact. We know from experience that it's especially hard for kids whose last names aren't so hot to begin with, and parents have to be especially careful.

My family name was Nat, like short for Natalie, N-A-T. As I grew up,   5
there were constant remarks regarding my ancestors, the g-n-a-t gnats, especially at picnics and baseball games. I used to receive mail addressed to Terry Net, Terry Not, Terry Nut, and Terry Nate. Very rarely was my mail addressed to Terry Nat. No one was able to get my name right, which seemed odd because it was so short. At restaurants, when asked for my name, I used to say N-A-T, and the reservationists would stand there as if they expected ten more letters. Even the bank screwed up. When I went to

pick up my title card after paying off my first car loan, I found that the car belonged to Terry National. Did they really think that I abbreviated my last name when I signed for the loan?

I guess that even despite all the jokes and confusion, the name Terry 6 Nat wasn't really that bad, and after talking with Mom I knew that it could have been much, much worse. She told me how careful she had been when naming all of us kids, and how she rejected many of the names that she liked the best, for our sake. I'm forever grateful to Mom for the fact that none of us was named Nanette Nat, Nick Nat, Pat Nat, or Zack Nat! For some reason she wasn't provoked like some parents are.

When I was growing up, I always thought that when I got married my 7 name problems would be over, and that when I had kids I would be able to name them anything in the world, within reason. What I didn't know then was that I'd marry a man named Splett. It was a real dilemma choosing between Nat and Splett. I had to choose because there was no way that I was going to hyphenate my name and live the rest of my life as Terry Nat-Splett, so I became a Splett.

Almost immediately I began to receive mail addressed to Terry Split, 8 Terry Spit, and Terry Spleet. Reservations are still a problem. If the reservationists don't think I'm spitting when I say the name Splett, they mispronounce it. In fact, a girlfriend and I once missed our reservations altogether because I had no idea that when they repeatedly called "Spell-it" over the intercom they were referring to me.

Oh, well, if I lived with Nat for twenty-six years I could certainly live 9 with Splett. It's my kids that I'm concerned about though. I guess I'm in the same spot as Mom was because I can't name them Nanette Splett, Pat Splett, or Zack Splett either, no matter how much I like the names. Nothing in the world could provoke me to do that to them. To make matters worse, because my first name is Terry and my husband's is Gary, we both agree that there won't be another "airy" in our family: no Cheri or Larry or Mary or Harry. And because both of us have the same middle name, Lynn is out too.

Even though our choices seem limited, I imagine that there are still 10 several names that don't rhyme with "airy" or that don't clash with Splett. We could choose Andrew, Emily, or Christine. They'd work. Yet I can't help praying for a little girl. Little girls grow up and get married, and I have a plan for our daughter. When she's old enough to date, age twenty-one or so, I'll screen the young men like most parents do, not according to age, intentions, or looks, but according to last names, of course. I'll see to it that she marries a man named Anderson or Jones or Johnson, and she'll be grateful to me forever. She won't have to worry about naming her children as I had to do. She'll be able to name them anything in the world, within reason.

Questions

1. In what ways does Splett use exaggeration in developing her essay?
2. What is the effect of her repetitive use of the word *provoked?*

3. In paragraph 2, Splett assumes that readers have heard of the television soap opera "Mary Hartman, Mary Hartman." What other common knowledge does she assume in developing her essay?

4. Name some details that surprised you and be prepared to explain in class why they did.

5. What did you learn about Splett's personality as you read her essay?

6. Splett uses this humorous essay to make a point about names. What is it?

Discussion

Writers establish contracts with their readers as to the nature of a piece of writing. Readers want to know from the beginning how to read the piece. They are often turned away if writers pretend to be sharing information or offering a service when in fact the primary purpose is persuasion to buy a product or support a cause. Readers are often similarly annoyed when a piece of writing turns out to be humorous after a serious beginning or when it purports to be fact but is in reality mainly fiction. In "A Pain in the Name," Splett tells her readers with her title that she is playing with words and that she will be presenting something other than a serious discussion. Her first sentence continues in this vein, as does the second paragraph.

The humor becomes more apparent, however, when she begins discussing her experiences with her own name: the jokes about her "gnat" ancestors, Terry Nut, and Terry National, then the experiences with her married name. Her humor seems to be based mainly on her surprising recollection of details concerning her name, her clever invention of absurd name combinations, and a finely tuned mixture of surprising the audience and meeting its expectations. In paragraph 5, even though she has led you to expect that something unusual would be coming ("Even the bank screwed up"), she probably surprised you when she said that the title card for her car identified her as Terry National.

As for exaggeration, Splett may not be stretching the facts. Even if she is, you are likely to accept them because she has established a contract of humor with you, and readers of humor expect a certain amount of exaggeration. Most of her details are probably factual, though you can suspect that she has invented the names her mother didn't use and the ones she dismissed as possibilities for her own children. She can also be suspected of exaggeration when she envisions her daughter's choice of a married name.

Purpose

The point of Splett's essay is that parents ought to be careful in naming their children. She expresses this point a number of times by repeating the phrase about parents being provoked to certain actions. A secondary purpose then might be *persuasion*. Information is not important in this essay except for its humorous and persuasive effects. It's not important for you to remember Splett's experiences with her names; what is important is that, first, you enjoy the essay, and, second, you think carefully about naming your children when the time comes.

EXERCISE

Part of the humor of Splett's essay is the invention of names her mother did not use and names she herself would never give her child. Do a similar invention yourself. Write your name at the top of a piece of paper and then brainstorm (see Chapter 3) a list of first names you are glad you do not *have. If your list seems productive of a humorous piece of writing, use it as the basis for freewriting.*

Reading

This essay is by a professional writer. A noted physician and scientist, Lewis Thomas is best known for his widely read collections of essays. This one deals with an unlikely subject for a humorous essay, punctuation, and you may find that its humor needs to be extracted with an attentive mind. As you read, remember that Thomas is not writing in an English handbook about how to punctuate. What does his purpose seem to be?

Notes on Punctuation
Lewis Thomas

There are no precise rules about punctuation (Fowler lays out some   1
general advice (as best he can under the complex circumstances of English prose (he points out, for example, that we possess only four stops (the comma, the semicolon, the colon, and the period (the question mark and exclamation point are not, strictly speaking, stops; they are indicators of tone (oddly enough, the Greeks employed the semicolon for their question mark (it produces a strange sensation to read a Greek sentence which is a straightforward question: Why weepest thou; (instead of Why weepest thou? (and, of course, there are parentheses (which are surely a kind of punctuation making this whole matter much more complicated by having to count up the left-handed parentheses in order to be sure of closing with the right number (but if the parentheses were left out, with nothing to work with but the stops, we would have considerably more flexibility in the deploying of layers of meaning than if we tried to separate all the clauses by physical barriers (and in the latter case, while we might have more precision

and exactitude for our meaning, we would lose the essential flavor of language, which is its wonderful ambiguity)))))))))))).

The commas are the most useful and usable of all the stops. It is highly important to put them in place as you go along. If you try to come back after doing a paragraph and stick them in the various spots that tempt you you will discover that they tend to swarm like minnows into all sorts of crevices whose existence you hadn't realized and before you know it the whole long sentence becomes immobilized and lashed up squirming in commas. Better to use them sparingly, and with affection, precisely when the need for each one arises, nicely, by itself.

I have grown fond of semicolons in recent years. The semicolon tells you that there is still some question about the preceding full sentence; something needs to be added; it reminds you sometimes of the Greek usage. It is almost always a greater pleasure to come across a semicolon than a period. The period tells you that that is that; if you didn't get all the meaning you wanted or expected, anyway you got all the writer intended to parcel out and now you have to move along. But with a semicolon there you get a pleasant little feeling of expectancy; there is more to come; read on; it will get clearer.

Colons are a lot less attractive for several reasons: firstly, they give you the feeling of being rather ordered around, or at least having your nose pointed in a direction you might not be inclined to take if left to yourself, and, secondly, you suspect you're in for one of those sentences that will be labeling the points to be made; firstly, secondly, and so forth, with the implication that you haven't sense enough to keep track of a sequence of notions without having them numbered. Also, many writers use this system loosely and incompletely, starting out with number one and number two as though counting off on their fingers but then going on and on without the succession of labels you've been led to expect, leaving you floundering about searching for the ninethly or seventeenthly that ought to be there but isn't.

Exclamation points are the most irritating of all. Look! they say, look at what I just said! How amazing is my thought! It is like being forced to watch someone else's small child jumping up and down crazily in the center of the living room shouting to attract attention. If a sentence really has something of importance to say, something quite remarkable, it doesn't need a mark to point it out. And if it is really, after all, a banal sentence needing more zing, the exclamation point simply emphasizes its banality!

Quotation marks should be used honestly and sparingly, when there is a genuine quotation at hand, and it is necessary to be very rigorous about the words enclosed by the marks. If something is to be quoted, the *exact* words must be used. If part of it must be left out because of space limitations, it is good manners to insert three dots to indicate the omission, but it is unethical to do this if it means connecting two thoughts which the original author did not intend to have tied together. Above all, quotations marks should not be used for ideas that you'd like to disown, things in the air so to speak. Nor should they be put in place around clichés; if you want to use a cliché you must take full responsibility for it yourself and not try to fob it off on anon., or on society. The most objectionable misuse of quotation marks, but one which illustrates the dangers of misuse in ordinary prose, is seen in advertising, especially in advertisements for small restaurants, for example "just around the corner," or "a good place to eat." No single, identifiable, citable person ever really said, for the record, "just around the corner," much less "a good place to eat," least likely of all for restaurants of the type that use this type of prose.

The dash is a handy device, informal and essentially playful, telling you   7
that you're about to take off on a different tack but still in some way connected with the present course—only you have to remember that the dash is there, and either put a second dash at the end of the notion to let the reader know that he's back on course, or else end the sentence, as here, with a period.

The greatest danger in punctuation is for poetry. Here it is necessary to   8
be as economical and parsimonious with commas and periods as with the words themselves, and any marks that seem to carry their own subtle meanings, like dashes and little rows of periods, even semicolons and question marks, should be left out altogether rather than inserted to clog up the thing with ambiguity. A single exclamation point in a poem, no matter what else the poem has to say, is enough to destroy the whole work.

The things I like best in T. S. Eliot's poetry, especially in the *Four*   9
Quartets, are the semicolons. You cannot hear them, but they are there, laying out the connections between the images and the ideas. Sometimes you get a glimpse of a semicolon coming, a few lines farther on, and it is like climbing a steep path through woods and seeing a wooden bench just at a bend in the road ahead, a place where you can expect to sit for a moment, catching your breath.

Commas can't do this sort of thing; they can only tell you how the   10
different parts of a complicated thought are to be fitted together, but you can't sit, not even take a breath, just because of a comma,

Questions

1. What assumptions of common knowledge does Thomas make concerning his audience?
2. In what ways does his discussion of punctuation differ from one in an English handbook?
3. What does Thomas tell you about himself in this essay?
4. Thomas begins stating his thesis in his first sentence but is interrupted by the numerous parenthetical details and never returns to it. Complete the sentence: "There are no precise rules about punctuation, but. . . ."
5. Which paragraph did you find the most entertaining? Why?

6. What purpose other than entertainment might Thomas have had for writing this essay?

7. Find examples here of some of the devices of humor: exaggeration, repetition, and surprise.

Discussion

Thomas writes about punctuation as one writer to another. He assumes that other writers, his readers, will enjoy his play with the marks that are the materials all writers work with. In contrast to Terry Splett's essay, which initiates its humor in the title, Thomas's has a title that seems to indicate a serious purpose. But his first paragraph sets the humorous tone, by exaggeration. As you began reading, you may not have known what Thomas was doing in this paragraph; you may have thought that this is a terribly difficult to read piece of writing; however, the backwash of parentheses at the end of the paragraph would have told you that something unexpected was going on.

Thomas's essay seems meant more to be entertaining than to be funny. Yet he uses the same devices of humor Splett does. Exaggeration seems to be his major device: twelve parenthetical phrases in one sentence, for example, and six semicolons in a paragraph. He illustrates exclamation points with an exaggerated use of them and commas with exaggerated omission and then use. Each mark of punctuation is illustrated with extreme examples. Like Splett, Thomas also balances surprise with fulfilled expectations. In the first paragraph, you can expect to see each mark of parenthesis paired with another, so the delay of their appearance until the end of the paragraph comes as a surprise. Having caught on to what he is doing, in each subsequent paragraph you expect to see the marks illustrated; even so, you are probably a little surprised to discover how Thomas has treated each one. His use of repetition is associated mainly with his exaggeration.

Development and Purpose

Thomas's method of development is *classification*. However, Thomas seems to select the marks of punctuation in no particular order: first parentheses, then commas, semicolons, colons, exclamation points, quotation marks, and the dash. He doesn't even discuss periods or apostrophes. Except for beginning with parentheses and his omissions, he does seem to follow H.W. Fowler's order in *Modern English Usage*, which he refers to in his first paragraph. Thomas uses Fowler's terminology too, calling the marks "stops." In fact, Thomas may have set out to parody the entry on stops in Fowler's standard reference work. But why begin with parentheses? Probably because doing so sets the tone for the essay better than any other portion of it would.

Thomas's primary purpose in writing undoubtedly was to *entertain*. However, he also seems to have a secondary purpose—to show that even though punctuation marks have "no precise rules," they do perform particular functions and follow certain conventions. Semicolons, for example, give "a pleasant little feeling of expectancy," colons "give you the feeling of being rather ordered around," and exclamation points seem to be "shouting to attract attention." And Thomas does clearly have a preference for the semicolon, returning to it in paragraph 9, praising it as "a place where you can expect to sit for a moment, catching your breath." In Chapter 13, in another essay on punctuation, Roger Garrison declares the semicolon his "personal favorite" too, having "scatter[ed] semicolons with wild abandon" in a first draft and now recommending that his readers "be careful not to overuse" them.

EXERCISE

Do you have a "personal favorite" mark of punctuation? Select a mark that interests you from the following list and write a paragraph that, like Thomas's essay, discusses the mark and illustrates it as well. Exaggerate to excess in using the mark.

.	Period
( )	Parentheses
;	Semicolon
—	Dash
:	Colon
-	Hyphen
,	Comma
'	Apostrophe
?	Question mark
" "	Quotation marks
!	Exclamation point

Writing

Write an essay that entertains by means of exaggeration, repetition, surprise, and fulfilled expectations. Choose a familiar subject, something that you are well acquainted with and that your readers will be familiar with too. Like Thomas, you might select an aspect of writing, such as spelling or capitalization, or, like Splett, you might select an aspect of your life. Jokes at the writer's own expense are generally more acceptable to readers than those that seem to belittle other people. Splett's essay on names might have inspired some thoughts about names that you would like to write about. Here are a few other possible topics:

- Books
- Pencils or pens
- Coffee mugs
- Road signs
- Birthdays
- Holidays

Remember Thurber's advice not to be too amused by your own humor, and remember to control your exaggeration, to spread the humor out rather than have punch lines one on top of another, and to balance surprise with fulfilled expectations.

Moving an Audience to Serious Thought

A common purpose for writing is to stir the minds of readers to serious thinking about serious issues. Such essays may in part have a persuasive purpose, and they usually derive from the writers' own reflections about the issues; however, mainly they are meant to touch readers, to move them to new thoughts. A writer may write about the sterility of life for residents in a nursing home. Another may consider the relationship between pain and dying, the difficulty of watching a child die, or the pleasure of listening to an elderly man play "O Tannenbaum" on a pan flute. By using techniques of emotional appeal, these writers could stir their readers to think new thoughts.

These techniques are similar to those employed in entertaining: sharing the backgrounds and experiences of the audience, balancing the expected with the unexpected, and repeating emotionally laden terms. To move an audience, a writer must understand what is important to that audience and must touch familiar chords. Most people have known someone in a nursing home, and describing life there makes an appeal to familial ties and memories. Along with the expected, however, the writer keeps audience interest with the unexpected: a father and son playing cribbage in the visitors' lounge of the nursing home, the similarity between a great-grandmother being left in a nursing home and a son or daughter being left at college. A writer appeals also with the repetition of words that carry emotional weight, like *old* or *growing old, loneliness,* and *happiness.*

Essays that are meant to move an audience can appeal to all the emotions people experience—anger, fear, love, pity, hatred, and so on. Emotions are powerful forces, capable of great good and great harm. Writers who appeal to them should therefore do so ethically and responsibly. Appealing to fear or hatred of a group of people can result in dire consequences, though appealing to fear of our own reckless acts can bring about heedful behavior. Writing that sets out to have readers pity themselves has negative effects, whereas writing that appeals to pity for others can bring about social good.

In the two essays that follow, professional writers appeal to the emotions of their readers for the purpose of encouraging serious thought about serious subjects.

Reading

In this excerpt from the essay "The Winter of Man," scientist-essayist Loren Eiseley writes about fear. Observe how he uses repetition and other emotional appeals to identify those things that deserve to be feared and considered.

The Winter of Man

Loren Eiseley

Has the earth's glacial winter, for all our mastery of science, surely   1
subsided? No, the geologist would answer. We merely stand in a transitory spot of sunshine that takes on the illusion of permanence only because the human generations are short.

Has the wintry bleakness in the troubled heart of humanity at least   2
equally retreated?—that aspect of man referred to when the Eskimo, adorned with amulets to ward off evil, reiterated: "Most of all we fear the secret misdoings of the heedless ones among ourselves."

No, the social scientist would have to answer, the winter of man has not   3
departed. The Eskimo standing in the snow, when questioned about his beliefs, said: "We do not believe. We only fear. We fear those things which are about us and of which we have no sure knowledge. . . ."

But surely we can counter that this old man was an ignorant remnant of   4
the Ice Age, fearful of a nature he did not understand. Today we have science; we do not fear the Eskimo's malevolent ghosts. We do not wear amulets to ward off evil spirits. We have pierced to the far rim of the universe. We roam mentally through light-years of time.

Yes, this could be admitted, but we also fear. We fear more deeply than   5
the old man in the snow. It comes to us, if we are honest, that perhaps nothing has changed the grip of winter in our hearts, that winter before which we cringed amidst the ice long ages ago.

For what is it that we do? We fear. We do not fear ghosts but we fear the   6
ghost of ourselves. We have come now, in this time, to fear the water we drink, the air we breathe, the insecticides that are dusted over our giant fruits. Because of the substances we have poured into our contaminated rivers, we fear the food that comes to us from the sea. There are also those who tell us that by our own heedless acts the sea is dying.

We fear the awesome powers we have lifted out of nature and cannot   7
return to her. We fear the weapons we have made, the hatreds we have engendered. We fear the crush of fanatic people to whom we readily sell

these weapons. We fear for the value of the money in our pockets that stands symbolically for food and shelter. We fear the growing power of the state to take all these things from us. We fear to walk in our streets at evening. We have come to fear even our scientists and their gifts.

We fear, in short, as that self-sufficient Eskimo of the long night had   8
never feared. Our minds, if not our clothes, are hung with invisible amulets: nostrums changed each year for our bodies whether it be chlorophyll toothpaste, the signs of astrology, or cold cures that do not cure: witchcraft nostrums for our society as it fractures into contending multitudes all crying for liberation without responsibility.

We fear, and never in this century will we cease to fear. We fear the end   9
of man as that old shaman in the snow has never had cause to fear it. There is a winter still about us—the winter of man that has followed him relentlessly from the caverns and the ice. The old Eskimo spoke well. It is the winter of the heedless ones. We are in the winter. We have never left its breath.

Questions

1. What does Eiseley mean by "The Winter of Man"?
2. Eiseley uses several terms to refer to magic: *shaman* for the Eskimo, *amulets* and *nostrums* for the paraphernalia of magic, *witchcraft, ghosts,* and *evil spirits.* How do these words represent fears of people in our world today?
3. Who are "the heedless ones among ourselves" whom Eiseley says we should fear?
4. In addition to repeated references to magic, how does Eiseley use repetition to appeal to the emotions of the audience?
5. What purpose do you think Eiseley hopes to achieve?

Discussion

Most people don't have much fear of winter. We may not like the cold, and we may acknowledge that snow and ice on the streets and highways are dangerous, but we don't really *fear* winter. Those of us who live in warm climates don't even give it much thought, and those who live in northern regions just put on a warmer coat and heavier boots, try to adjust their driving to the road conditions, and at the end of the day return to a home that is insulated and heated. But Eiseley challenges us to think about a glacial winter that cannot be closed out and protected against, one that any sensible person would fear.

That glacial winter is an analogy for something within ourselves that we should fear: the heedlessness with which we commit actions endangering our very lives. And like the Eskimo with amulets to ward off evil, we have our little nostrums that provide us with a feeling of safety from the results of our communal heedless actions. Eiseley thus blends the analogies of winter and magic to show what dangers humanity has placed itself in and what powerless measures we are taking to combat those dangers.

Thesis

In addition to his *repetition* of words related to his two analogies, Eiseley repeats the key word *fear*. Its first incidence is in paragraph 2, where he quotes the Eskimo: "Most of all we fear the secret misdoings of the heedless ones among ourselves." This quotation serves as Eiseley's *thesis* sentence, and the major part of his essay tells what heedless acts we fear. Even though the essay was first published in 1972, the list is timely. We still fear for our water and air and food. We still fear one another. We still fear illness. This, said Eiseley, returning to his analogy, is winter, this fear that we bring upon ourselves.

EXERCISE

Explore a metaphor that contrasts with Eiseley's metaphor of winter. Instead of representing fears for the environmental evils people have created, use the analogy of summer to describe an emergence from the winter and its fears. Make a list of changes that would have to happen, and then compare lists with a group of classmates. What must be done to enable an analogous change of seasons?

Reading

The following essay begins "This isn't going to be easy. Nor is it going to be funny." It is neither easy nor funny because it is a father's account of his son's funeral. Al Sicherman, a columnist for the Minneapolis *Star Tribune*, usually writes humorous columns, but this time he writes only of sadness. His purpose for writing such a difficult and painful piece is to move his readers to think about the consequences of using drugs. As a parent he writes to other parents, but his message is just as vital to contemporaries of his son.

Sicherman is writing from Minneapolis, Minnesota, about a son who died while at school at the University of Wisconsin at Madison. As you read this essay, notice what techniques Sicherman uses to appeal to the audience.

Be Scared for Your Kids

Al Sicherman

Dear, dear friends: This isn't going to be easy. 1

Nor is it going to be funny. 2

My older son, Joe, of whom I was very, very proud, and whose growing- 3
up I've been privileged to chronicle occasionally in the newspaper, died last

month in a fall from the window of his seventh-floor dorm room in Madison, Wisconsin. He had taken LSD. He was eighteen years old.

To say he had his whole life ahead of him is unforgivably trite—and unbearably sad.   4

I saw him a week before he died. It was my birthday, and he spent the weekend with his stepmother and me. He was upbeat, funny, and full of his new activities, including fencing. He did a whole bunch of very impressive lunges and parries for us.   5

The next time I was with him, he was in a coffin.   6

He must not have known how treacherous LSD can be. I never warned him, because, like most adults, I had no idea it was popular again. I thought it had stopped killing kids twenty years ago. Besides, Joe was bright and responsible; he wouldn't "do" drugs. It didn't occur to me that he might dabble in them.   7

His mother had warned him about LSD, though; she knew it was back because Joe had told her about a friend who had taken it. Obviously he didn't listen to her advice. At eighteen, kids think they're invulnerable. They're wrong.   8

Joey was a very sweet, very funny kid. And even before he had anything particularly funny to say, he had great timing. When he was about six, I asked him what he wanted to be when he grew up. He paused, just long enough, and said, "A stand-up physicist."   9

I went to the mortuary in Milwaukee several hours before the funeral to have a chance to be with him. I spent most of the time crying and saying dumb things like "I would have caught you" and "I would have traded with you." I wish I could say that I sang him a lullaby, but I didn't think of it until several days later. I went ahead and did it then, but it was too late. It would have been too late in any case.   10

Joe was not a reckless kid: Last summer he turned down my wife's suggestion that the family go on a rafting trip through the Grand Canyon; although he loved amusement-park rides, he thought that sounded too risky. So we went sailing and miniature golfing instead. But he took LSD. Apparently he figured that wasn't as dangerous.   11

When he was about seven or eight, Joey attended a camp for asthma sufferers. When asked "What do you do at asthma camp?" he responded, cheerfully, "Wheeze!"   12

The coffin is always closed in traditional Jewish funerals, and as I sat with him that morning before the funeral, I minded that. I felt so far from him. I finally decided that I had the right to open it briefly, even if it was against some rule. In fact, I rationalized, Joe probably would like my breaking the rule. So I raised the lid.   13

He was in a body bag.   14

I'm not surprised that kids don't listen to their parents about drugs. Adults' standards of risk are different from theirs, and they know it; and they discount what we tell them. But we must tell them anyway.   15

Joe's aunt, a teacher, says that when you warn kids about something dangerous—something that kills people—they always say "Name one." OK, I will. Joe Sicherman. You may name him, too. Please.   16

Joe's first job was in Manchester, New Hampshire, where his mother had moved 17
with him and his younger brother nine years ago. He was a carry-out boy in a
supermarket. One day he came to the rescue of a clerk faced with a customer who spoke
only French and who wanted to use Canadian money. Armed with his two years of
high-school French, Joe stepped forward and explained "Madame, non!" She seemed
not to understand. That, he said, was when he rose to the very pinnacle of linguistic
and supermarket expertise: "Madame," he said, with a Gallic shrug of his shoulders,
"augghhhhh!" The woman nodded and left.

Because the coffin is always closed, nobody expected anyone to look 18
inside. There were blood spatters on the body bag.

It's entirely possible that warning your kids won't scare them away from 19
LSD. But maybe it will. I wish I could tell you how to warn them so it would
work, but I can't.

This is the generation gap reduced to its most basic: It is parents' worst 20
fear that something terrible will happen to their kids; it is kids' constant
struggle to be free of the protection of their parents.

Joe's next job was in Shorewood, Wisconsin, a Milwaukee suburb, where his 21
family moved just before his junior year in high school. It was a summer job as a soda
jerk. He confided to me that he worked alongside a "soda idiot" and that his boss was
"a soda &#%@." Actually, I think he enjoyed it. He told me one day that he was
"acquiring meaningful insights into the Sundae Industry." Like: If you say "yes" to
"Do you want a lid on that?" you're going to get less whipped topping.

Traditional Jewish funerals leave no room for the stage of grief that 22
psychologists call "denial." When you leave the cemetery, you can have no
doubt that the person is dead. In fact, you might say that these funerals are
brutal. I could avoid telling you about it, and spare us both some pain, but I
think I owe it to Joe—and to every parent—to let this be as forceful as possible.

When the graveside prayers were over, workmen lowered Joe's coffin 23
into the ground and then eased a concrete cover down into the hole until it
covered the metal burial vault. The cover had Joe's name on it. They pulled
the green fake-grass cloth off the pile of dirt next to the grave, and the rabbi
and the cantor each threw a shovelful of earth onto the vault lid.

Then they handed the shovel to Joe's fifteen-year-old brother, David. 24

It occurs to me now that what I might have done is ask Joe what kind of 25
drugs were around. Maybe my genuine alarm at the reemergence of LSD
would have registered with him. I'm certainly going to be less self-assured
about how I deal with this subject with David. He's a wonderful kid, too, and
while I don't want to smother him, I don't want to assume anything, either.

I didn't take Joe for granted; I think I encouraged him and delighted in 26
him and celebrated with him. But I certainly took his *life* for granted.
Parents must not do that. We must be scared for them. They don't know
when to be scared for themselves.

Although his humor had become somewhat acerbic recently, Joe remained a sweet, 27
thoughtful kid. When, as I often did, I wound up apologizing to him because a
weekend or a vacation hadn't worked out the way I'd hoped, he always patted my
hand—literally or figuratively—and let me know he loved me anyway.

He took good care of others, too. He spent most of his grandfather's ninetieth birthday 28
party making sure that his stepmother had somebody to talk to besides my ex-wife's family.

And on that last birthday visit with me in early October, he talked a little about his 29
concerns and hopes for his brother. One of those concerns was drugs.

Then they handed the shovel to me. 30

Later I overheard my wife say that the expression on my face when I 31
turned away, having shoveled dirt onto my son's coffin, was the most awful
thing she'd ever seen.

Whenever I thought about Joe recently, it was about college and inde- 32
pendence and adulthood, and his latest involvements: His attempt to produce an English paper that was more interesting than what the instructor
had asked for, the raucous rock band he and his friend put together over
the summer, his plans to rent a cabin with a bunch of kids at winter break.

Now, suddenly, I'm no longer looking at the moment, but instead at the 33
whole life. And in some automatic averaging-out, in my mind I'm sometimes calling him "Joey," his little-boy name.

He told his mother a year ago that he wanted his senior year in high school to be 34
the best year he'd ever had, and on the drive to Madison to start college this fall, he told
her that, despite lots of typical teenage domestic tension, it had been. He said he'd
accomplished everything he'd set out to do—except to have a mad, passionate affair
with a woman he didn't even know.

She refrained from asking the obvious question. 35

Then they handed the shovel to his mother. 36

Even though it is only three weeks since his death, I find that the reality 37
of Joey is beginning to turn sepia. He will be forever eighteen. And his life
will forever stop in 1989. That saddens me so much. It's not just that he
won't have a career, maybe get married, have kids, all those things we hope
might happen for a promising young person. He won't go out for pizza
anymore either, or come into a warm house on a cold night, or imitate
Martin Short imitating Katharine Hepburn, or scuff through piles of leaves.

And I won't ever see him again. 38

Joe had been very involved in high-school journalism. He won a statewide award 39
for feature writing in New Hampshire, and he was news editor of the school paper in
Shorewood. He contributed a great deal of that paper's humor edition in May,
including a large advertisement that read, in part:

"Attention! All available slightly twisted females: Marry Me! I am a nice guy, a 40
National Merit semifinalist, devastatingly handsome, relatively inexpensive, house-
broken, handy with tools, easily entertained, a gentleman in the truest sense of the
word, and I think I am extremely funny. In fact, I think I am the funniest guy on
earth! . . . Please call immediately. Operators are standing by. (I am in great de-
mand.) . . . Kids—Please get permission from your parents before calling."

Then they handed the shovel to his stepmother. 41

In his sermon at David's bar mitzvah last year, the rabbi used a phrase 42
I'd never heard before. It caused me to weep at the time; I wasn't sure why. It's
come back to me again and again recently. It isn't consoling, nor even helpful.
But it is pretty, and in an odd way it puts events into a much larger perspective.

"All things pass into mystery."   43

At one point during that last visit, we went to a craft fair where Joe noticed   44
someone selling hammered dulcimers. He had never played one, but he'd played the
guitar for quite a few years, which must have helped. He picked up the hammers and
began to fool around, and soon he drew a small crowd with something that sounded
like sitar music. He asked about the price; they were expensive. I keep finding myself
thinking that it would be neat to get him one. I should have done it then.

Then they handed the shovel to his only living grandmother; it took   45
her two tries to get enough dirt on the shovel. Neither of his grandfathers
could bring himself to do it. But many of Joe's friends, weeping, took a turn.

I hope someday to be able to write about Joe again; I probably won't be   46
writing a humor column for a while. In the meantime, I want folks to know how
I think he would have turned out. He would have been a *mensch*—a decent,
sincere man, the kind you're proud to know. He already was. Damn drugs.

A year or so ago, the four of us played charades, a vacation tradition. Joe drew   47
"The Sun Also Rises," which he did in one clue. He stretched an imaginary horizon
line between his hands then slowly brought his head above it at one end and traversed
an arc, grinning from ear to ear. It took us about five seconds to get it. Body bag or no,
that's how I want to remember him.

The last thing I wrote about him appeared in the newspaper the   48
morning he died. He told me that he and a friend decided one Saturday
afternoon to hitchhike to a rock concert near Milwaukee. He realized, he
said, that now that he was away from home, he didn't have to ask anybody if he
could go or tell anybody that he was going. He just decided to do it, and he did
it. I wrote about what a heady experience that was, to be independent at last.

There's a fair measure of irony in that column. We're told that the rock   49
concert is where he got the LSD, and where he took his first trip.

That trip, I understand, went OK. This one killed him.   50

Although Joe apparently was with friends most of the evening, the   51
police said he was alone when he went out the window. We'll probably never
know exactly what happened in those last minutes, but judging by our own
reading of him and by what lots of others have told us, we're sure he wasn't
despondent. Many of his friends, including one who spoke at his funeral,
said that he was very happy and enjoying his life in Madison.

The likeliest explanation we've heard is that he had the LSD hallucina-   52
tion that makes a person think he can fly. In any case, a little after one o'clock
Sunday morning, October 15, somebody studying across the courtyard saw
a curtain open and then a body fall. Joe didn't cry out.

I have since, many times.   53

Questions

1. Characterize the tone of the essay. How does Sicherman establish it?
2. How does he establish his credibility?
3. What facts does Sicherman tell you about his son's use of drugs? What does he
   tell you about the effects of LSD?

4. Does Sicherman blame himself for his son's use of LSD?

5. How does Sicherman use repetition to achieve his intent of moving an audience?

6. What portions of the essay do you find particularly effective?

7. This essay appeared three weeks after Joe Sicherman's death. Do you think his father would have changed anything had he written it after more time had elapsed, say several months?

Discussion

People expect to attend the funerals of grandparents, parents, and aged aunts and uncles; they do not expect to attend the funerals of their children. Nor did Al Sicherman expect to attend the funeral of his son Joe, and he is obviously grief-stricken. When people try to adjust to the death of someone they care about, they run a gamut of emotions—shock, denial, anger, guilt, and resignation. Rather than avoiding the issue of his son's death and writing a column about some innocuous subject, Sicherman uses this emotional time to move his readers to an awareness of how serious even a limited use of drugs can be. In his essay you may have found evidence of many emotions related to his grief.

Thesis and Development

To make his point that drugs are deadly, Sicherman recounts the experience of his son's funeral and his thoughts at the mortuary and the graveside. The development of the essay has a sequential, or *chronological*, framework enclosing his ruminations on the life of his son. With each passing of the shovel, he adds more thoughts. He does not explicitly state his *thesis;* however, throughout the essay he supports the controlling idea that drugs are deadly. Parents should warn their kids, he implies, and kids should stay off drugs.

The *Star Tribune* printed Sicherman's column on the front page of the Sunday edition, and it was read by thousands. One reader's response, "Fatal Trip," is included in Chapter 15. You might want to read it now and compare your response with it.

EXERCISE

Freewrite (see Chapter 3) for fifteen minutes about a subject that affects you emotionally and that you want other people to think about, perhaps the death or illness of someone you care for. Consider beginning with a controlling analogy as Eiseley does in "The Winter of Man," or a sequential structural framework, as Sicherman does.

Writing

Use your freewriting as the basis for an essay with the purpose of moving an audience to new thoughts. You might want to engender an awareness of threats to our global environment, the dangers of using drugs, or the growing problem of AIDS. Or you might concentrate on something positive, like the emotional lift gained from cheering nursing home residents, collecting donations for the Salvation Army, cleaning up a beach, and so on. Persuasion and reflection may be secondary aims, but try to focus on moving an audience to feel the way you do.

ADDITIONAL READINGS FOR DISCUSSION

Reading

Student writer Jeff Hedin writes about getting old. His essay is partly reflection but mostly an appeal to the reader to feel as he does about growing old and living in a nursing home. What do you think is Hedin's purpose for writing?

Nursing Homes and Growing Old
Jeff Hedin

Some days time flies. Other days time drags. But still we get older. 1 Eventually, we'll all be old people struggling to carry out our lives. It worries me to be old. I fear how my life will be. Will I be able to care for myself? Will my wife be alive to share my days? Will I end up living in a nursing home? I'm still a 24-year-old college student whose other worries involve graduation, finding a job, and getting married someday.

It may not have crossed your mind about getting old. We're all still 2 young and active. We lead busy lives and have many goals to attain. Who has time to think about growing old? We are living for now. I want to be happy in my old age. The one place I don't want to end up in is a nursing home.

In the past year or so I had my first experience with a nursing home. My 3 grandmother was unable to take care of my great-grandmother and was forced to place her in a nursing home. It was a shock for me to find this out. My great-grandma was a strong, sharp-minded woman. She was always in control of herself and was very active. But physically she was no longer strong. She needed more care than my grandma could give her.

I first visited the home two summers ago. The grounds were tidy and 4 the surroundings were quiet. Entering the shiny steel-framed door, I noticed a group of residents sitting on either side of the doorway. They were quiet and passive. Their frail bodies sat tilted, as if propped up by some invisible support. Their eyes stared in all directions but saw nothing. Some had mouths hung open. Others had trembling lips and teetering heads.

I walked down the long hallway. The floor tile was bone white. Fluorescent lights bleached the shadows on the wall. It was so clean and so sterile. A man in a wheelchair slowly pulled himself along the railing mounted to the wall. He had no legs. Another woman in a wheelchair sat in her doorway. Was she waiting for someone? Or had somebody just put her there to get her out of the way?   5

I scanned the small nameplates that marked each room until I found my great-grandma's room. I peered inside her room and she smiled when she saw me. Her hands sat folded on her lap. A small wool blanket covered her knees. She looked good but not as good as she did when she lived at home. It was so strange to see her in this foreign place. She didn't belong here.   6

We talked for a while. I tried to say things that would cheer her up, to make her feel less lonely. I could see she wasn't happy here and that she wanted to go home. But she wouldn't put up a fuss. She didn't want to upset anyone. I was upset, but not from her. My first visit to a nursing home was a depressing and sobering event. I now knew what this place was like, and I felt bad that my great-grandma didn't like being here. I knew I never wanted to live there.   7

Once on a weekend, I visited her with the rest of my family. My dad came in and said "Hello" and gave her a hug. We visited for a few minutes, and then my dad asked me if I wanted to go to the visitors' lounge for a game of cribbage. He wanted to smoke a cigarette but he also didn't like the feeling of this place. Playing a game of cards was the only way he could forget he was visiting here and that his grandmother had to stay.   8

I often picked up my grandma and went with her to visit the home. She tried to go every day. But sometimes the weather was too bad or there was no one to drive her down. Great-grandma would sit in her chair and wait for someone to come. What else could she do? When we did visit it was the same scene over and over. I tried cheering her up and making her laugh. Yet she still seemed lonely and homesick.   9

On last Thanksgiving Day, Grandma and I drove to Melrose for another visit. We were surprised to see Grandma's sister and family already there. We all sat in the lounge, playing cards and drinking coffee. Great-grandma was having a good time. It was the happiest I'd seen her there. As the afternoon wore on we knew we had to get going. What a terrible feeling to have friends and family around and at the end of the day they leave but you have to stay. It reminded me of when my parents moved me to college for the first time. We unloaded my belongings and then went out to dinner. Afterwards, they brought me back to my apartment and left. I didn't want them to leave. I was afraid of being alone. Did Great-grandma feel the same way?   10

Two days after Thanksgiving I was sleeping on my parents' couch. It was early morning and the telephone rang. Dad answered it and after a few seconds of conversation I could tell that Great-grandma had died.   11

Growing old is a sure thing. One morning I'll wake up gray and 12
wrinkled. But I want to wake up at home, not in some hospital-like environment. A nursing home is not a home. It's an institution. It reminds me
of the hospital "dying rooms" of World War I that I learned about in my
European history class. These were places where dying soldiers were put so
they wouldn't disturb others and so there would be more bed space for
others. It's just a final stop before your train comes to an end.

What can we do to prevent staying in a nursing home? Do we live with 13
our sons and daughters and grandchildren? They don't want us getting in
the way of their young lives. It's too hard for them. Do we try to live on our
own? We might be too frail to climb out of bed. Can our spouses take care of
us? Sure, if they are even well enough to take care of themselves.

It looks to me as if a nursing home is the only alternative. I don't think 14
anyone will discover a drug that stops the aging process by the time I get
old. I better reserve a wheelchair.

Questions

1. What is Hedin's purpose for writing this essay? Who might his intended audience be?
2. Do you agree with Hedin about growing old? How do your feelings differ from
   his? How might your feelings differ if you were older, say fifty?
3. What does Hedin dislike about nursing homes?
4. Hedin compares the way his great-grandmother must have felt when the family
   left her with the way he felt when his parents left him at college. In what other
   ways can you compare nursing home life with college life?
5. What techniques does Hedin use to appeal to your emotions?

Reading

Black civil rights leader Martin Luther King, Jr., led sit-ins, boycotts, and
marches as nonviolent resistance to segregation and unfair practices against
African-Americans. On August 28, 1963, he stood on the steps of the Lincoln
Memorial and addressed 200,000 people assembled in the nation's capital
for the cause of civil rights. "I Have a Dream" is that speech.

I Have a Dream

Martin Luther King, Jr.

Five score years ago, a great American, in whose symbolic shadow we 1
stand, signed the Emancipation Proclamation. This momentous decree
came as a great beacon light of hope to millions of Negro slaves who had

been seared in the flames of withering injustice. It came as a joyous day-break to end the long night of captivity.

But one hundred years later, we must face the tragic fact that the Negro 2
is still not free. One hundred years later, the life of the Negro is still sadly crippled by the manacles of segregation and the chains of discrimination. One hundred years later, the Negro lives on a lonely island of poverty in the midst of a vast ocean of material prosperity. One hundred years later, the Negro is still languishing in the corners of American society and finds himself an exile in his own land. So we have come here today to dramatize an appalling condition.

In a sense we have come to our nation's capital to cash a check. When 3
the architects of our republic wrote the magnificent words of the Constitution and the Declaration of Independence, they were signing a promissory note to which every American was to fall heir. This note was a promise that all men—yes, black men as well as white men—would be guaranteed the unalienable rights of life, liberty, and the pursuit of happiness.

It is obvious today that America has defaulted on this promissory note 4
insofar as her citizens of color are concerned. Instead of honoring this sacred obligation, America has given the Negro people a bad check, a check which has come back marked "insufficient funds." But we refuse to believe that there are insufficient funds in the great vaults of opportunity of this nation. So we have come to cash this check—a check that will give us upon demand the riches of freedom and the security of justice. We have also come to this hallowed spot to remind America of the fierce urgency of *now*. This is no time to engage in the luxury of cooling off or to take the tranquilizing drugs of gradualism. *Now* is the time to make real the promises of Democracy. *Now* is the time to rise from the dark and desolate valley of segregation to the sunlit path of racial justice. *Now* is the time to open the doors of opportunity to all of God's children. *Now* is the time to lift our nation from the quicksands of racial injustice to the solid rock of brotherhood.

It would be fatal for the nation to overlook the urgency of the moment 5
and to underestimate the determination of the Negro. This sweltering summer of the Negro's legitimate discontent will not pass until there is an invigorating autumn of freedom and equality; 1963 is not an end, but a beginning. Those who hope that the Negro needed to blow off steam and will now be content will have a rude awakening if the nation returns to business as usual. There will be neither rest nor tranquility in America until the Negro is granted his citizenship rights. The whirlwinds of revolt will continue to shake the foundations of our nation until the bright day of justice emerges.

But there is something that I must say to my people who stand on the 6
warm threshold which leads into the palace of justice. In the process of gaining our rightful place we must not be guilty of wrongful deeds. Let us not seek to satisfy our thirst for freedom by drinking from the cup of bitterness and hatred. We must forever conduct our struggle on the high plane of dignity and discipline. We must not allow our creative protest to degenerate into physical violence. Again and again we must rise to the

majestic heights of meeting physical force with soul force. The marvelous new militancy which has engulfed the Negro community must not lead us to a distrust of all white people, for many of our white brothers, as evidenced by their presence here today, have come to realize that their destiny is tied up with our destiny and their freedom is inextricably bound to our freedom. We cannot walk alone.

And as we walk, we must make the pledge that we shall march ahead. 7 We cannot turn back. There are those who are asking the devotees of civil rights, "When will you be satisfied?" We can never be satisfied as long as the Negro is the victim of the unspeakable horrors of police brutality. We can never be satisfied as long as our bodies, heavy with the fatigue of travel, cannot gain lodging in the motels of the highways and the hotels of the cities. We cannot be satisfied as long as the Negro's basic mobility is from a smaller ghetto to a larger one. We can never be satisfied as long as a Negro in Mississippi cannot vote and a Negro in New York believes he has nothing for which to vote. No, no, we are not satisfied, and we will not be satisfied until justice rolls down like waters and righteousness like a mighty stream.

I am not unmindful that some of you have come here out of great trials 8 and tribulations. Some of you have come fresh from narrow jail cells. Some of you have come from areas where your quest for freedom left you battered by the storms of persecution and staggered by the winds of police brutality. You have been the veterans of creative suffering. Continue to work with the faith that unearned suffering is redemptive.

Go back to Mississippi, go back to Alabama, go back to South Carolina, 9 go back to Georgia, go back to Louisiana, go back to the slums and ghettos of our northern cities, knowing that somehow this situation can and will be changed. Let us not wallow in the valley of despair.

I say to you today, my friends, that in spite of the difficulties and 10 frustrations of the moment I still have a dream. It is a dream deeply rooted in the American dream.

I have a dream that one day this nation will rise up and live out the true 11 meaning of its creed: "We hold these truths to be self-evident, that all men are created equal."

I have a dream that one day on the red hills of Georgia the sons of 12 former slaves and the sons of former slaveowners will be able to sit down together at the table of brotherhood.

I have a dream that one day even the state of Mississippi, a desert state 13 sweltering with the heat of injustice and oppression, will be transformed into an oasis of freedom and justice.

I have a dream that my four little children will one day live in a nation 14 where they will not be judged by the color of their skin but by the content of their character.

I have a dream today. 15

I have a dream that one day the state of Alabama, whose governor's lips 16 are presently dripping with the words of interposition and nullification, will be transformed into a situation where little black boys and black girls will be able to join hands with little white boys and white girls and walk together as sisters and brothers.

I have a dream today. 17

I have a dream that one day every valley shall be exalted, every hill and 18 mountain shall be made low, the rough places will be made plain, and the crooked places will be made straight, and the glory of the Lord shall be revealed, and all flesh shall see it together.*

This is our hope. This is the faith with which I return to the South. With 19 this faith we will be able to hew out of the mountain of despair a stone of hope. With this faith we will be able to transform the jangling discords of our nation into a beautiful symphony of brotherhood. With this faith we will be able to work together, to pray together, to struggle together, to go to jail together, to stand up for freedom together, knowing that we will be free one day.

This will be the day when all of God's children will be able to sing with 20 new meaning

My country, 'tis of thee,
Sweet land of liberty,
   Of thee I sing:
Land where my fathers died,
Land of the pilgrims' pride,
From every mountainside,
   Let freedom ring.

So let freedom ring from the prodigious hilltops of New Hampshire. 21 Let freedom ring from the mighty mountains of New York. Let freedom ring from the heightening Alleghenies of Pennsylvania. Let freedom ring from the snowcapped Rockies of Colorado. Let freedom ring from the curvaceous peaks of California.

But not only that. Let freedom ring from Stone Mountain of Georgia. 22 Let freedom ring from Lookout Mountain of Tennessee. Let freedom ring from every hill and molehill of Mississippi. From every mountainside, let freedom ring.

When we let freedom ring, when we let it ring from every village and 23 every hamlet, from every state and every city, we will be able to speed up that day when all of God's children, black men and white men, Jews and Gentiles, Protestants and Catholics, will be able to join hands and sing in the words of the old Negro spiritual, "Free at last! Free at last! Thank God almighty, we are free at last!"

Questions

1. What is the effect of King's abundant use of repetition? Consider paragraphs 7, 9, 11–18, and 21–23.

---

*Isaiah 40:4–5.

2. What three political documents does King refer to in the first three paragraphs? What other familiar documents does he quote?

3. King uses several analogies in this appeal. In paragraph 3 he describes the civil rights movement as cashing a check. What other analogies does he use, and what does he mean by them?

4. Why does King not support violence for achieving civil rights?

Reading

Louis J. Camuti was a cat doctor in New York City—a cat doctor in great demand, who was allergic to cats, had CATS on his license plates, and was still practicing veterinary medicine well into his eighties (he died in 1981). The essay that follows is a portion of one of the chapters in his book *All My Patients Are under the Bed,* which he wrote with Marilyn and Haskel Frankel. Contrary to most of his stories, this one is about a dog. Read the essay for fun—for entertainment—because that's why it was written.

Putting Tiny to Sleep

Louis J. Camuti

While I can't remember how my first client ever found me—I was in the Bronx and she was in Brooklyn—I remember everything else about the case. And if the lady is still alive, I'll bet she remembers me, too.   1

It was a weekday morning and I was looking through the newspaper, trying to figure out this new world we were entering now that the war was over.   2

Everything was changing in postwar America, and the changes affected everything, even the practice of animal medicine. Horses had once been the bulk of any veterinarian's practice—and certainly, they constituted the bulk of my experience—but now, suddenly, they were a disappearing breed. The newly popular automobile was removing them from the streets of the city. The carriage horse, fire horses, wagon horses, trolley horses—they were all going. Veterinarians who once looked down their noses at treating household pets were now more than interested in treating them. My problem, of course, was not one of switching from the treatment of horses to cats and dogs, but of finding any patients.   3

And then the telephone rang. The lady's voice was warm and sad. "Dr. Camuti, can you come to Brooklyn? My dog, Tiny, has to be put to sleep."   4

I didn't even stop to ask what the matter was with the dog. I said I was on my way.   5

I had just enough money for carfare both ways and to buy a bottle of chloroform at the neighborhood pharmacy. It wasn't until I was seated in the subway train that I began to wonder about what was wrong with Tiny—I pictured a small dog about the size of a cocker spaniel—to warrant his being put away.   6

Today, of course, I would refuse to accept such a request until I had   7
checked the animal out thoroughly and was convinced that it couldn't be
saved. But then I was young and desperate to prove to myself and the world
that I was indeed a veterinarian. And you had to have at least one client for
that—this one was mine.

It took almost two hours to get to the address I had been given, an   8
apartment on the third floor of a brownstone. The woman who opened the
door was middle-aged, a thin lady with a worried face. Behind her, I could
hear a dog barking very healthily.

Tiny turned out to be a St. Bernard who seemed surprisingly frisky. I   9
was startled by the animal's size and by its seeming state of good health. But
I assumed it was a sick dog or the woman wouldn't have wanted it put to
sleep. Back then, I automatically believed that everyone was in his or her
right mind, and that people who had pets loved them.

Today I know better. As I said, "All of my clients are normal, but some   10
are more normal than others."

I told the woman to bring her dog into the bathroom. I followed her in.   11
She said, "I know you'll understand, but I just can't be in the apartment
while you do it, Doctor. I'm going out for a walk. I'll come back after.

I nodded, and she left, closing the door behind her. I sat down on the   12
closed toilet and fished the bottle of chloroform out of my jacket pocket. I
took a towel off the bar by the sink and began to open the bottle. That was
when I made my big mistake—I didn't realize that the bathroom was so
small and that there was no ventilation. But between my own nervousness
at what I was about to do and trying not to look at Tiny, who was licking at
my hand, I don't think I knew where I was.

The last thing I remember was pouring chloroform into the towel.   13

I came to on the floor of the bathroom staring up at the ceiling. Tiny   14
was licking my face, and the woman was glaring down at me.

I pulled myself to my feet. I had to hold on to the sink because the room   15
seemed to be swaying and my knees felt as if they had turned to Jell-O. The
woman opened her mouth to say something, but I cut her off. "No charge,"
I said, and lurched from the apartment.

It wasn't a great start at being a veterinarian.   16

Questions

1. This is a narrative essay, developed in chronological order. Make a rough
   outline of the events, beginning with "Camuti gets a telephone call."

2. This is a true story, dependent only on the writer's memory thirty-five years
   later. How does Camuti handle the fact that he doesn't remember all the
   details?

3. Name four things that Camuti learned from this incident.

4. How does Camuti balance audience expectations with surprise in telling this
   story?

Reading

Ron Heck is a student writer who likes to write but sometimes has trouble deciding on a subject. This essay "just happened" one afternoon in a shorter, rougher form than it appears here. Using feedback from his classmates and teacher and his own good sense of language, he made two or three more drafts and ended with this one. It's an essay purely for entertainment.

Decisions on a Saturday

Ron Heck

Another day was nearing an end. It was Saturday, and I had spent the day trying to decide on the direction my life should go while comparing it to the way it was going. I didn't have much to compare it to, judging by the hours I spent that afternoon flipping channels to various uninteresting shows. Aside from TV fossils like Gilligan and the Brady Bunch, a televised dog show seemed the most enlightening.   1

A poodle was walking on its hind legs when I turned the channel again. There were many shows which were equally dull, and I could not decide on one. Maybe the shows are genuinely stimulating, and it is I who am dull and two-dimensional, I thought, intrigued by the queer possibility.   2

I slumped down in the chair, pressing the side of my face into the plump, green cushion. My back lay flat against the bottom cushion and my legs were sprawled out haphazardly on the floor ending in bare feet. My feet were cold, and the dust from many posteriors upon the cushion made me sneeze. This is life, I thought. What a dismal thought.   3

It must have been my eighteenth round of scanning the entire thirty-one channels when I got the urge to go for a walk. I turned off a shopping program and set down the remote control. It left an imprint in my hand, and my body was reluctant to move, but I managed to sit up. Gradually flexing the hand that had held the remote, I managed to put on my brown loafers, not bothering with socks, and left the house.   4

North of the house was a park. It was near a small river and used to be an airport but was now a field declared by the city to be a park. Runways still criss-crossed the field, but they were cracked and overrun by weeds from not being used. A wooden bridge connected the field with some woods across the river. There were numerous footpaths among the trees.   5

I strode out of the yard and onto the sidewalk, strangely conscious of each step I made. I became amazed and somewhat delighted at all the decisions involved in walking. The grade school rhyme, "Step on a crack, break your mother's back," came to mind as I eyed the concrete squares passing beneath me. My mother's back had never broken before, and I began deliberately stepping on the cracks as they came. This one's for Aunt Sarah, I pronounced as I pounced on an especially ragged one.   6

Two elderly women who probably knew my Aunt Sarah surprised me.   7
I had been so engrossed in watching the sidewalk that I didn't notice their
approach and had to decide quickly to say hi or pretend not to see them.
They spoke first.

"Hello," they said.   8

"Hi," I said. It was the first word I had said all afternoon.   9

After looking back to see that the two grandmothers' backs were intact,   10
I found myself making countless more decisions along the way to the
bridge: to walk through a sprinkler or not; to pass between the blue and red
cars or to cut between the blue and yellow ones; or to take the long path
around the field or to venture across it.

And so, wet from the sprinkler, edging between the blue and yellow   11
cars, and making a short cut, I reached the bridge. The scrape-plop of my
shoes on the bridge boards sounded important and purposeful, the way a
woman lawyer's heels might sound in the granite halls of a courthouse. Or a
cowboy's boots in their slow stride across worn boards in a saloon of the 1800s.

I decided to check out the river and leaned over the rail. It hadn't   12
changed much. It seemed a little lower and slower. Green stuff had grown
to a thick layer in the water, hiding most of the bottom from view. A turtle
lazily floated with the current and then hid under some of the green stuff.
Algae, I suppose.

A teenage couple was further down on the bridge loudly discussing   13
something or other, which disrupted my thoughts, and I began to flex my
hand. The stiffness had gone, and I noticed my jeans were nearly dry.
Metallica was better, insisted the girl. Uh-uh, Ozzy Osbourne was better,
replied the boy.

I withheld stating my preference and decided to go back home.   14

Questions

1. Have you ever spent a Saturday afternoon like Heck's, when you were so
   wrapped up in boredom that the biggest decision you could make was whether
   to watch the dog show or "Gilligan's Island," to step on a crack or not? Does
   Heck learn anything by taking his walk?

2. Heck treats decision making ironically. Unable to make a big decision on the
   direction of his life, he concentrates on many little decisions. What do these
   decisions say about his state of mind?

3. How does Heck balance reader expectations with surprise? What details did
   you expect? Which ones were unexpected?

4. What does Heck tell you about himself in this essay?

CHAPTER 9

To Record: Writing with Emphasis on the Subject

A writer may attempt to record what is immediately present in his environment, the events, the appearance of things. He is saying what his world is like at that moment.

—James Britton

Recording may be one of the oldest purposes for writing. As long ago as 4000 to 3000 B.C., people in the ancient civilizations of Mesopotamia, China, Egypt, and Mexico were using writing to record financial transactions, laws, and important events. Their records were meant to be permanent, and, being inscribed on stone or sun-dried bricks, some have endured to the present day. Today, the most permanent kind of record we keep is what we put on gravestones.

Most of our records are meant to be only semipermanent or even short-term. We keep records of conversations, correspondence, interviews, activities, events, impressions, finances, purchases, concerts, dramas, games, and so on. These records may be in the form of minutes, news articles, letters, notes, journal entries, and they may be recorded on paper, film, tape, disk—by means of pen or pencil, typewriter, computer, tape recorder, camera, and so on.

In academic work, you use note taking as a means of recording lectures, group discussions, readings, laboratory experiments, assignments. When you research a subject, you may interview knowledgeable people and record their responses both on paper and on tape. In both your academic work and your personal life, you may keep records of your activities, feelings, and impressions in a journal or in letters to parents or friends. Undoubtedly your purpose in recording is not to make as permanent a record as the Mesopotamians did with cuneiform on bricks, but you do intend to keep information in a form that you can refer to later or that someone else can read and understand. Records sometimes remain in their rough form, as class notes might, but they also are revised as reports, such as reports of laboratory experiments, of reading and research, interviews, and so on.

Journals

In Chapter 6, journals are presented as a way of recording reflections, personal activities, observed events, and impressions. This chapter reiterates the value of journals as records that may later serve as sources of ideas for writing. If you want to begin keeping a journal, read "The Journal" and "Journals Made Public" in Chapter 6 about how to get started. Then begin recording what is going on around you—what you see, what you think, what you question, what you experience. Once you have set aside a time for writing in your journal, vow to yourself that you will persist. When you occasionally read back over what you've written, you will discover that you have indeed kept a record of your life. You will find details about events you otherwise would remember only vaguely, you may see changes in your attitudes toward particular issues or people, and you might decide that some of this is good writing that could serve as the kernel for more formal writing.

When you write in your journal, you are ordinarily the only audience. Your personal journal is your writing to yourself about the world as you see it. You don't have to worry about how long to make your entries, how to punctuate your sentences and spell your words, or whether you can use language that might offend someone else. It's only when you decide to revise these records as a type of public writing that you need to consider such matters.

Letters

You may sometimes keep personal records in the form of letters to people you care about. Usually the primary purpose of such letters is to maintain that relationship while you are separated by distance and social environment. You record your daily activities, your frustrations, your joys, and so on, hoping that through continuing contact about ordinary things you will keep your relationship close. While you may also be able to achieve this purpose through telephone calls, the advantage of the letter is that it can be read again and again as a reminder of your presence.

Letters are sometimes saved and thus become semipermanent records somewhat like journals. Biographies and histories are often written on the basis of old letters found in attics or shoeboxes. Because of George Washington's letters to Sally Fairfax, we know of his extramarital passion for this wife of his close friend. Lovers and mothers and grandmothers save letters that years later, like photographs, record informally what the world was like at the moment they were written. Letters from people serving in war zones become records of life under combat; two such letters are included in this chapter.

Notes

How many notebooks do you estimate you've gone through since you started school? In your lifetime you have undoubtedly taken innumerable pages of notes, and you can be certain that you have many more to go. Students take notes as records of their learning. Like journal entries, notes are mainly for the writer's eyes, but notes are often more systematic than journal entries in recording subject matter that must be remembered and understood. You take notes on lectures, reading, and group activities because you need those records for reviewing, studying, writing into reports, and so on.

To take efficient notes on a *lecture*, you must first be an active listener, looking for main ideas, key words, definitions, repetitions for emphasis, cues for relative importance of details. You can't allow yourself to be distracted by the speaker's appearance, vocal intonations, or the discomfort of the surroundings. You take your notes in a way that makes them accessible to you. For most people and most lectures, formal outlines are not the most efficient kind of note taking. However, indention of subordinate material does give a cue about its relative significance. Some people prefer taking notes on paper marked with a wide left margin, as much as 2 or 3 inches, so that on the right they can record information from the lecture and on the left their insights, summaries, reviews, and special notes to remember. In the left margin they might also record special notes of related textbook material, which might look like those in Figure 9-1.

Students experienced in note taking say they have altered and improved their recording habits over time. Here are a few tips they share:

Tips for Taking Notes on Lectures

1. Watch the professor. If he or she conspicuously reads from notes, you know that what is said next is worth taking notes on. It invariably turns up on the exam.
2. Take notes on everything the professor writes on the blackboard.
3. Make a note that applies the concepts of the lecture to something you know. It's easier to remember a personal application.

Lecture notes from political science	11/23

govt. task	One could consider the most important task of any govt to be:
	Provide for security of people & territorial integrity of the state. Lacking ability to do so would prevent govt from performing other basic functions of a govt.

threats to security	Why external threat remained persistent
	    1. nature of intl. system--anarchic in nature
	    2. " " nation/state
	    3. " " of individuals

reaction to threats to security	First experiment: concert of Europe 1815-1854 --a reaction to Napoleonic threat --maintained peace because supportive connections such as language, religion, marriage, customs --no public opinion

Concert of Europe	2 Principles
	1. All had common responsibility to maintain
	    territorial status quo treaties of 1815
	2. Changes should be made with all of Concert's
	    formal and common consent

	--elaborated rules of conduct
end	--system broke down with introduction of nationalism and rise of Bismarck

Figure 9-1.   Lecture Notes.

Tips (continued)

4. At the end of the day, review and summarize your lecture notes, phrasing them in your own words. Likewise, review and summarize your highlighted readings. Then at test time you won't have pages of highlights to review, and your own rephrasings will make it easier to recall information.
5. When you review and rephrase, take time to classify, grouping information into categories that make sense to you.
6. Look for concepts, not individual pieces of information. However, if you don't know what to expect from the teacher, you will probably have to note just about everything.

To take notes on *reading assignments,* plan on going over your assignments more than once. Be an active reader by first skimming the assigned material; get an overall view by reading headings, noting italicized or boldfaced type words, scanning diagrams, and reading the first sentences in paragraphs. If there are questions at the end of the reading, study them; then as you read look for answers. When you take notes, you may want to summarize each chapter or section for later review.

The most efficient primary method of taking notes on reading is probably making notes in the text itself—assuming that the book is yours or, in the case of library materials, you have made your own copies. You probably already have some system of making notes as you read: highlighting important lines, perhaps, or making checks in the margin. Both systems can be more effective, however, if you refine and elaborate on them. Here are some techniques used by experienced student note takers:

Tips for Taking Notes on Reading

1. Use underlines to further accent highlighted material.
2. Use asterisks to point out information to be memorized.
3. Use circles to call attention to important words.
4. Use question marks to indicate material you want to ask the teacher about.
5. Make page summaries, brief notations on the content of each page.
6. Combine lecture and reading notes on a single summary page.

Figure 9-2 shows a sample annotated page from a textbook.

274   **Energy Conservation**

Table 9-7
Distribution of Energy Use in the Transportation Sector

Mode	Percentage
Automobiles	50
Trucks	24
Air, passenger and freight	7
Military	5
Rail, freight	3
Water	4
Pipeline	4
Miscellaneous passenger, including bus and rail	3

Transportation

The ways energy is used in the transportation sector are shown in Table 9-7. As could have been assumed, trucks and cars dominate the use of energy, and these vehicles largely employ internal combustion engines fueled by gasoline or diesel oil. The dynamics of automobile motion and fuel consumption will be discussed in some detail in Chapter 12 so that only the general aspects of the problem will be brought up here.

Americans have been infatuated with the automobile for 60 or 70 years. We have more cars per capita, and we drive more miles per capita, than the citizens of any other country. In 1972, some 10,400 passenger miles were driven per capita in the United States compared to 5800 in the second leading country, Canada. Western European countries averaged about 4000 passenger miles per capita. In the same year, 349 gallons of gasoline for auto transportation were used per capita in the United States compared to 90 in Europe. The potential for energy conservation in automobile transportation in the United States is clearly tremendous.

The solution to the problem lies in two different areas: the greater use of more efficient modes of transportation and increased efficiency of the automobile. Because of the convenience of the auto, the U.S. public transportation system has deteriorated very badly in the last 50 years or so. The efficiency of various modes of transportation is shown in Table 12-2; it is clear that we have opted for an inefficient mode, because most travel is by little more than one occupant in an auto. Since 1973, there has been effort by federal and local governments to improve public transportation in the cities, but this has not as yet made a major difference in the use of the automobile. Car or van pooling, sharing the ride, and so forth are more widely used for commuting to work where an inadequate bus or train system exists. We are also finally giving thought to urban design so that the distances the average person must travel for employment or for shopping are reduced from those with the present unplanned sprawl.

It appears, however, that the major energy conservation gains that will be made in

Handwritten annotations: 10,400 miles U.S · 5,500 next country · 2 solutions · The U.S is major Consumer of energy, for tranp, esp. autos. We are making little progress in energy efficiency

Figure 9-2.   Annotated Page from a Textbook. (Source: Jack J. Kraushaar and Robert A. Ristinen, *Energy and Problems of a Technical Society*, rev. ed. New York: Wiley, 1988.)

Although the most common note taking in school is in response to lectures and reading, you may sometimes need to fill another recording role—in *group activities*. Being recorder may mean (1) that you will later report to the class as a whole, and (2) that you must keep a record for later reference by the group. Whatever the purpose, your notes must be accurate and thorough. Here are some tips for taking such notes:

Tips for Taking Notes on Group Activities

1. Be an attentive and active listener.
2. Record discussions completely yet briefly.
3. Be objective. Don't be biased in favor of a single view.
4. Ask for clarification when you don't understand.
5. Record differences of opinion.
6. Be especially thorough in noting conclusions.
7. Keep an accurate record of dates and names.

Being recorder for a group is similar to being recording secretary for a committee or an organization; your report is like minutes of a meeting. While the role of recorder is important to successful group work, you may find that the demands of recording limit your ability to participate in discussions, something to consider when you agree to keep the records.

Records are often singular in purpose, merely to keep an account for later reference or review. Note taking on lectures and reading is like that. But, as we have seen, records also communicate ideas and maintain continuity. Frequently, too, records also are revised for another purpose, such as to report, like most of the documents in Chapter 10. The essays and writing assignments in this chapter represent a few of the many kinds of writing done for the purpose of recording: letters, records of how the weather or some other natural phenomenon affects people, records of group actions, and interviews.

Recording in Personal Letters

One of the most common purposes for writing is to contact friends and relatives we know and care about—to tell them what we're doing, what we're thinking, and what matters to us at the moment. The letter serves as a record of our thoughts and experiences. If the recipient of a personal letter has a question about the details of your story or precisely where you will meet her next week, she only needs to get out the letter and refresh her memory.

As Garrison Keillor points out in "How to Write a Personal Letter" in Chapter 13, people like to receive letters; your letter is a part of you, sealed up in an envelope and waiting in the mailbox.

Reading

Here are two personal letters by Lynda Van Devanter, an army nurse in Vietnam. The letters, sent to her parents five months apart, told them what her life was like in the war zone and maintained the continuity of her relationship with them. Published in her book *Home before Morning,* the letters serve now as a record of that period in her life. Van Devanter's letters were recorded on paper; between the two letters is a communication from her father recorded on tape. As you read the letters, observe how they record not only events but Van Devanter's changing attitudes also. When you read the transcript of the taped "letter," determine what her father's purposes might have been for saying what he does.

Dear Mom and Dad

Lynda Van Devanter

Dear Mom and Dad,

Things go fairly well here. Monsoon is very heavy right now—have   1
barely seen the sun in a couple of weeks. But this makes the sky that much prettier at night when flares go off. There's a continual mist in the air which makes the flares hazy. At times they look like falling stars; then sometimes they seem to shine like crosses.

At 4:16 A.M. our time the other day, two of our fellow Americans landed   2
on the moon. At that precise moment, Pleiku Air Force Base, in the sheer joy and wonder of it, sent up a whole skyful of flares—white, red, and green. It was as if they were daring the surrounding North Vietnamese Army to try and tackle such a great nation. As we watched it, we couldn't speak at all. The pride in our country filled us to the point that many had tears in their eyes.

It hurts so much sometimes to see the paper full of demonstrators,   3
especially people burning the flag. Fight fire with fire, we ask here. Display the flag, Mom and Dad, please, everyday. And tell your friends to do the same. It means so much to us to know we're supported, to know not everyone feels we're making a mistake being here.

Every day we see more and more why we're here. When a whole   4
Montagnard village comes in after being bombed and terrorized by Charlie, you know. There are helpless people dying everyday. The worst of it is the children. Little baby-sans being brutally maimed and killed. They've never hurt anyone. Papa-san comes in with his three babies—one dead and two covered with frag wounds. You try to tell him the boy is dead but he keeps

talking to the baby as if that will make him live again. It's enough to break your heart. And through it all, you feel something's missing. There! You put your finger on it. There's not a sound from them. The children don't cry from pain; the parents don't cry from sorrow; they're stoic.

You have to grin sometimes at the primitiveness of these Montagnards.   5 Here in the emergency room, doctors and nurses hustle about fixing up a little girl. There stands her shy little (and I mean little—like four feet tall) Papa-san, face looking down at the floor, in his loin cloth, smoking his long marijuana pipe. He has probably never seen an electric light before, and the ride here in that great noisy bird (helicopter) was too much for him to comprehend. They're such characters. One comes to the hospital and the whole family camps out in the hall or on the ramp and watches over the patient. No, nobody can tell me we don't belong here.

Love,
Lynda

Hi, Lynda, this is your father. Right now, I'm home by myself. After you   1 suggested it, we scooted out to Gem and found ourselves a nice little old cassette recorder and player so we could start sending you tapes. I hope everybody here doesn't suffer from mike fright.

One of the things the moon landing made me realize is how common-   2 place everything seems once it's happened. We've all picked up a feeling of ennui. Gee, these guys were up on the moon, they were wandering around on its surface, they shot the thing up there and shot it back down, and an awful lot of people are terribly unimpressed. It sort of reminds me of an old joke: This young boy takes his uncle to a circus where a guy climbs a 150-foot pole and stands on his head. On his right foot he hangs two or three circular horseshoes and twirls them. He does the same thing on his left foot. With his left hand, he juggles three balls, and with the right hand, he plays a clarinet solo. The young boy says to his uncle, "Ain't he the greatest?" The old guy looks at him and says, "A Benny Goodman he ain't."

So many of us look at everything that happens with that attitude. We   3 forget that there are so many wonderful things that people are doing. Regardless of whether these guys had been the first or the twenty-first guys on the moon, we should be proud of them and never take them for granted. It's a great, great achievement for these good old United States.

I guess there were a lot of things that I never did tell you before you left   4 home. One is that I'm proud that you're doing what you're doing. Even before the Japanese bombed Pearl Harbor, I was trying to get into the service. At the time, I thought I had it made in the Marine Corps. They were taking young college graduates as possible officer candidates, so I went down and saw old Colonel Miller at the Marine Corps Reserve in Washington. When he saw my glasses, he suggested that I take them off when I came back for the eye exam. I had already memorized the chart so I'd have no problem.

When I went for my physical, the doctor started asking me a lot of usual   5 questions. Pretty soon in the game, I suggested taking the eye examination because I was afraid of forgetting the chart. But this guy was a pretty sharp operator. He said, "I know damned well you wear glasses." So I had to show him my glasses. He looked through them and said, "That refraction's too big for the Marines, buddy boy. You go home."

Later, I took the physical for the Army a couple of times but my blood pressure was too high for them. That was about the time that Nancy came along. I went back and appealed my case with the surgeon general. He ordered the Army to give me another physical, but they weren't buying. They wouldn't take me. It wasn't that I was anxious to be there, but I felt like I owed a little something to my country. I guess this is why I'm so pleased that you're in the Army. I'm living vicariously now. You are me and I'm in. As I said before, I'm very proud.

Dear Mom and Dad,

I don't know where to start except to say I'm tired. It seems that's all I ever say anymore. Thank you both for your tapes and all the little goodies in the Christmas packages. Christmas came and went marked only by tragedy. I've been working nights for a couple of weeks and have been spending a great deal of time in post-op. They've been unbelievably busy. I got wrapped up in several patients, one of whom I scrubbed on when we repaired an artery in his leg. It eventually clotted and we did another procedure on him to clear out the artery—all this to save his leg. His name is Clarence Washington.* I came in for duty Christmas Eve and was handed an OR slip for Clarence—above-knee amputation. He had developed gas gangrene. The sad thing was that the artery was pumping away beautifully. Merry Christmas, kid, we have to cut your leg off to save your life. We also had three other GIs die that night. Kids, every one. The war disgusts me. I hate it! I'm beginning to feel like it's all a mistake.

Christmas morning I got off duty and opened all my packages alone. I missed you all so much. I cried myself to sleep. I'm starting to cry again. It's ridiculous. I seem to be crying all the time lately. I hate this place. This is now the seventh month of death, destruction, and misery. I'm tired of going to sleep listening to outgoing and incoming rockets, mortars, and artillery. I'm sick of facing, every day, a new bunch of children ripped to pieces. They're just kids—eighteen, nineteen years old! It stinks! Whole lives ahead of them—cut off. I'm sick to death of it. I've got to get out of here.

I'm so glad that Steve finally got out. He was lucky to have made it through a year in this hellhole without getting seriously wounded. I never got to talk to him, but I understand the bitterness in his letters home, now, in a way I couldn't when I first got here. When I finally got someone in his unit on the phone the other day, they said he'd just left for Saigon to catch his Freedom Bird. With any luck, he's somewhere over Japan about now, and free from this green suck. I envy him.

6

1

2

3

---

*Names have been changed to protect individual privacy.

I found out a couple of weeks ago that Barbara has been transferred to   4
a unit near where Steve was. I've written her a few times but gotten no
answer, and the phone lines in her area are utterly awful, so I haven't been
able to reach her. I hope she's okay.

I just heard another chopper come in. I better go. They need me in   5
the OR.

Peace,
Lynda

Questions

1. Compare Van Devanter's attitude toward her work in her first letter, recorded near the beginning of her tour of duty, with her attitude in the second letter, written five months later. What evidence of change do you see?

2. In the first letter, what does Van Devanter tell you about the nature of the work she does as a nurse in Vietnam? What does she tell you in the second letter?

3. The first paragraph of the intervening message introduces Van Devanter's father on the tape recording. What other recording purposes can you discover in the remainder of the message? What purposes other than recording might he have?

4. In her first letter Van Devanter directs her parents to "display the flag," but in a note preceding her second letter she says, "I threw away the rhinestone flag I had previously worn on my uniform." How does this change apply to the change in attitude you discussed in question 1? Relate these attitudes to today's attitudes about flag burning and flag waving.

5. Van Devanter's father responds to her flag-waving letter by saying, "I'm proud that you're doing what you're doing." If you were her father, how would you respond to Lynda's second letter?

6. What revisions might Van Devanter have made in her letters before including them in her book?

Discussion

As her personal record, Van Devanter's letters tell what her world was like at the moment of writing:

> Things *go* fairly well here.
> Monsoon *is* very heavy right now.
> It *hurts* so much sometimes to see the paper full of demonstrators.
> I'*m* tired.
> The war *disgusts* me.
> They *need* me in the OR.

Her verbs are present tense, indicating attitudes and actions at the time of the writing. When she uses past tense verbs ("I *missed* you all so much," "Steve finally *got* out"), it is to support present attitudes with past actions.

As letters to her parents, these pieces of writing are personal, but they allow you, an outside viewer, to witness some personal expressions: "I cried myself to sleep," "I missed you all so much." In preparing her book, Van Devanter intentionally included these and other letters to record for a broader audience what service in Vietnam was like. You are therefore able to perceive the daily personal experience of living through a war, to see how initial idealism deteriorates into weariness and anger, and to know the toll that death and dying have on the living as well as the dead.

Do you have occasion to write regularly to your parents or someone else close to you? Perhaps such a record of your college life will be interesting to you a few years from now. Can you imagine your children twenty or thirty years from now reading about what college life was like for you in the 1990s?

EXERCISE

Work in a group of three to five people in class, with one of you designated recorder, and try to recall your first impressions of your college campus—its buildings, the older students, the bookstore, whatever you remember. Then compare your current percep-tions of the campus. How have your attitudes changed? How do you account for the changes? Do these changes have any parallels to Van Devanter's?

Writing

Write a personal letter to your parents or someone else you care about. Record what your world is like at this moment—what is happening, what you are thinking, what your attitude toward school is. Write about the things you would talk about if the recipient were with you. The letter may be very personal. Before you send it, revise the letter for a public audience; then send the personal letter to the intended recipient and use the revision for your class assignment.

Recording Reactions to Nature

People react to their environment. Suicides are more common in win-ter, riots in summer. Depression responds favorably to light—the more light, the less depression. On cloudy days, people are often as gloomy as the weather; on sunny days, their outlook is brighter. These are just generali-zations, of course. Some people like rainy days, and some like winter, but these people too are responding to their environment.

People like to record their reactions to nature. If you talk to a distant relative or friend on the telephone, the conversation is likely to include a discussion of the comparative weather. If you receive a letter from that person, you may get a report of the weather and the writer's reaction to it. People wish it wouldn't rain—or wish it would. They wish the temperature were higher—or lower. They wish the wind would blow—or not blow.

Most of the time our reactions to nature are rather mild, just something to talk or write about when we can't think of anything else to say. Sometimes, however, nature behaves in unexpected ways, and then our reactions are more pointed. Earthquakes, for example, have devastating effects, and the more affected we are by them the stronger our reactions. If you lose your home, you react strongly. If someone you know loses a home, you are still affected. If you see people on television who have lost their homes, you are sympathetic but mostly glad that you haven't experienced the devastation. We have similar reactions to floods, hurricanes, tornadoes, and other extraordinary natural events. Following one of these events, we encounter numerous records of personal and public reactions. We see homeless people interviewed on television, and we read about them in newsmagazines.

Still, not all unexpected natural events are catastrophic. Some just affect the way we feel. An unexpected cool breeze in the middle of the summer refreshes us, and a warm one in the spring lifts our spirits.

Reading

This essay is excerpted from the chapter "Los Angeles Notebook" in Joan Didion's reflective book *Slouching towards Bethlehem*. In these paragraphs, Didion records what the Santa Ana wind is like and how people in Los Angeles react to it. As you read, notice how much of the record is from Didion's own experience and how much from other sources. Find out what is bad about this wind and what its effects are.

The Santa Ana
Joan Didion

There is something uneasy in the Los Angeles air this afternoon, some   1
unnatural stillness, some tension. What it means is that tonight a Santa Ana will begin to blow, a hot wind from the northeast whining down through the Cajon and San Gorgonio Passes, blowing up sandstorms out along Route 66, drying the hills and the nerves to the flash point. For a few days now we will see smoke back in the canyons, and hear sirens in the night. I have neither heard nor read that a Santa Ana is due, but I know it, and almost everyone I have seen today knows it too. We know it because we feel it. The

baby frets. The maid sulks. I rekindle a waning argument with the telephone company, then cut my losses and lie down, given over to whatever it is in the air. To live with the Santa Ana is to accept, consciously or unconsciously, a deeply mechanistic view of human behavior.

I recall being told, when I first moved to Los Angeles and was living on   2
an isolated beach, that the Indians would throw themselves into the sea when the bad wind blew. I could see why. The Pacific turned ominously glossy during a Santa Ana period, and one woke in the night troubled not only by the peacocks screaming in the olive trees but by the eerie absence of surf. The heat was surreal. The sky had a yellow cast, the kind of light sometimes called "earthquake weather." My only neighbor would not come out of her house for days, and there were no lights at night, and her husband roamed the place with a machete. One day he would tell me that he had heard a trespasser, the next a rattlesnake.

"On nights like that," Raymond Chandler once wrote about the Santa   3
Ana, "every booze party ends in a fight. Meek little wives feel the edge of the carving knife and study their husbands' necks. Anything can happen." That was the kind of wind it was. I did not know then that there was any basis for the effect it had on all of us, but it turns out to be another of those cases in which science bears out folk wisdom. The Santa Ana, which is named for one of the canyons it rushes through, is a *foehn* wind, like the *foehn* of Austria and Switzerland and the *hamsin* of Israel. There are a number of persistent malevolent winds, perhaps the best known of which are the mistral of France and the Mediterranean sirocco, but a *foehn* wind has distinct characteristics: it occurs on the leeward slope of a mountain range and, although the air begins as a cold mass, it is warmed as it comes down the mountain and appears finally as a hot dry wind. Whenever and wherever a *foehn* blows, doctors hear about headaches and nausea and allergies, about "nervousness," about "depression." In Los Angeles some teachers do not attempt to conduct formal classes during a Santa Ana, because the children become unmanageable. In Switzerland the suicide rate goes up during the *foehn,* and in the courts of some Swiss cantons the wind is considered a mitigating circumstance for crime. Surgeons are said to watch the wind, because blood does not clot normally during a *foehn.* A few years ago an Israeli physicist discovered that not only during such winds, but for the ten or twelve hours which precede them, the air carries an unusually high ratio of positive to negative ions. No one seems to know exactly why that should be; some talk about friction and others suggest solar disturbances. In any case the positive ions are there, and what an excess of positive ions does, in the simplest terms, is make people unhappy. One cannot get much more mechanistic than that.

Easterners commonly complain that there is no "weather" at all in   4
Southern California, that the days and the seasons slip by relentlessly, numbingly bland. That is quite misleading. In fact the climate is characterized by infrequent but violent extremes: two periods of torrential subtropical

rains which continue for weeks and wash out the hills and send subdivisions sliding toward the sea; about twenty scattered days a year of the Santa Ana, which, with its incendiary dryness, invariably means fire. At the first prediction of a Santa Ana, the Forest Service flies men and equipment from northern California into the southern forests, and the Los Angeles Fire Department cancels its ordinary non-firefighting routines. The Santa Ana caused Malibu to burn the way it did in 1956, and Bel Air in 1961, and Santa Barbara in 1964. In the winter of 1966–67 eleven men were killed fighting a Santa Ana fire that spread through the San Gabriel Mountains.

Just to watch the front-page news out of Los Angeles during a Santa Ana   5
is to get very close to what it is about the place. The longest single Santa Ana period in recent years was in 1957, and it lasted not the usual three or four days but fourteen days, from November 21 until December 4. On the first day 25,000 acres of the San Gabriel Mountains were burning, with gusts reaching 100 miles an hour. In town, the wind reached Force 12, or hurricane force, on the Beaufort Scale; oil derricks were toppled and people ordered off the downtown streets to avoid injury from flying objects. On November 22 the fire in the San Gabriels was out of control. On November 24 six people were killed in automobile accidents, and by the end of the week the Los Angeles *Times* was keeping a box score of traffic deaths. On November 26 a prominent Pasadena attorney, depressed about money, shot and killed his wife, their two sons, and himself. On November 27 a South Gate divorcée, twenty-two, was murdered and thrown from a moving car. On November 30 the San Gabriel fire was still out of control, and the wind in town was blowing eighty miles an hour. On the first day of December four people died violently, and on the third the wind began to break.

It is hard for people who have not lived in Los Angeles to realize how   6
radically the Santa Ana figures in the local imagination. The city burning is Los Angeles's deepest image of itself: Nathaniel West perceived that, in *The Day of the Locust;* and at the time of the 1965 Watts riots what struck the imagination most indelibly were the fires. For days one could drive the Harbor Freeway and see the city on fire, just as we had always known it would be in the end. Los Angeles weather is the weather of catastrophe, of apocalypse, and, just as the reliably long and bitter winters of New England determine the way life is lived there, so the violence and the unpredictability of the Santa Ana affect the entire quality of life in Los Angeles, accentuate its impermanence, its unreliability. The wind shows us how close to the edge we are.

Questions

1. From Didion's essay, make a list of features describing the Santa Ana wind; then make a list of features describing human reactions to the wind. Relate the two lists and try to draw some inferences, or conclusions, on what features of the wind cause the observed reactions.

2. Didion describes the Santa Ana as a *foehn* wind. What is a *foehn* wind, and what effects is it said to have on people? Which of these effects have scientific support and which are anecdotal? Do you know of other "malevolent" winds?

3. What does Didion tell you about herself in this essay?

4. What does Didion say about how the city of Los Angeles feels about fire?

5. This essay was published in the 1960s. Can you update it with more recent accounts of the effects of the Santa Ana or other *foehn* winds?

Discussion

Like Van Devanter's letters recording life in Vietnam, Didion's essay records the present:

> There *is* something uneasy in the Los Angeles air this afternoon.
> The baby *frets*.
> I *recall* being told.
> The children *become* unmanageable.

Didion records what Los Angeles is like with the coming of the Santa Ana wind. And, again like Van Devanter, she uses past tense verbs to recall events that support her record of the present:

> The Pacific *turned* ominously glossy.
> The heat *was* surreal.
> The Santa Ana *caused* Malibu to burn the way it did in 1956.

Records of occurring events often draw on past events for support and interest.

Development

Didion's essay is developed mainly by *cause and effect*. It introduces a single cause—the Santa Ana wind—and describes various effects on people and the environment. In describing these effects, Didion records her own feelings, the actions of others, and testimony from other people, in both the present and the past. Concerning the effects on herself, she says:

> I rekindle a waning argument with the telephone company, then cut my losses and lie down, given over to whatever it is in the air.
> I could see why [the Indians would throw themselves into the sea]. The Pacific turned ominously glossy during a Santa Ana period, and one woke in the night troubled not only by the peacocks screaming in the olive trees but by the eerie absence of surf. The heat was surreal.

About the effects on others, here are some examples:

The baby frets. The maid sulks.

On November 26 a prominent Pasadena attorney, depressed about money, shot and killed his wife, their two sons, and himself. On November 27 a South Gate divorcée, twenty-two, was murdered and thrown from a moving car.

Didion records the testimony of others, referring to the work of an Israeli physicist and other scientists and quoting detective-story writer Raymond Chandler: "On nights like that . . . every booze party ends in a fight. . . . Anything can happen." She also observes the effects on the environment: the "unnatural stillness," the "ominously glossy" sea, the "incendiary dryness" of the forests.

She includes statistics, "front page" history, definition (of the *foehn* wind), and her own inferences. Her final statement may be read as Didion's thesis: "The wind shows us how close to the edge we are." It draws together all her details and makes an inference about them.

EXERCISE

In your journal or on a separate sheet of paper, write a paragraph that, like Didion's first paragraph, begins "There is something _____ *in the air" to describe something that is going on around you—perhaps related to the weather, perhaps anticipating an event (such as exams, a holiday, the end of the term). Describe how you feel and what you observe.*

Writing

Keep a daily record for a week, noting the weather and the reactions to it in yourself, the people around you, and your environment. Note what people say about the weather and whatever changes you observe in their behavior that may be weather related. Some people, for example, get sinus headaches when the weather is about to change; some respond favorably to sunshine and gloomily to clouds and rain; some lose their tempers easily in hot and muggy conditions. Record their weather-related stories and your reflections on the kind of weather you are experiencing. Be a close observer, and make your notes as complete as necessary for you to carry out the second part of this project.

After keeping your record for a week, select *one* weather condition you have described and use it to write a *public* record. Describe the weather conditions and record the reactions you have observed. Add weather-related stories you may have heard; any statistics you may have gleaned from radio, television, or newspapers; any inferences you have made from your observations. If you have experienced similar or contrasting weather in other locales, you may be able to make some comparative observations. To give your record immediacy, use present tense verbs, as Didion does, to describe the weather as it is happening, but use past tense as appropriate when relating stories or past weather occurrences.

In revision, see that your essay is now a *public* record rather than the collection of private notes it began with. While your notes may have been cryptic or truncated—for example, "Rain again, gloom again"—in your public record you need to fill out your sentences and explain your statements. Also, you may have to identify your locale, the dates you are covering, and something about yourself, such as your age or length of time at this locale and your usual attitude toward weather. Think of your readers; they probably have weather-related stories they could tell too, so make yours one they can relate to.

Recording Interviews

An important source of information for essays and reports is interviews of experts. When acquiring information, you can learn from many sources: textbooks, encyclopedias, almanacs, newspapers, professional journals, popular magazines, and so on. But in an interview you may be able to get firsthand information that is not available any other way. If you want to write a persuasive essay about the need for adequate parking space on your campus, you can greatly strengthen your case by knowing what the university is planning to do to make adequate parking space available, information that can be gained from your buildings and grounds supervisor. In writing about the need for more street lighting, you can find out from the city engineer what the plans, problems, and possibilities are for improvements. If you want information about the use of DNA "fingerprinting" in your local court system, you might talk to a judge or a criminal lawyer.

When you need information, consider interviews as a source. Then decide who would be the best available expert for you to interview. You might refer to the yellow pages of your telephone directory or the city directory in your library; you might ask if one of your teachers could recommend someone, or go to the chair of the department that teaches the subject you are investigating. Local firms and nonprofit organizations with interests in your subject are other sources. Once you have decided on someone who could help you, telephone or write that person requesting an interview. Introduce yourself and your interest in the subject, tell why you are contacting this person, and request the interview, suggesting a time you think will be agreeable to both of you.

Once the interview is arranged, prepare your questions carefully. For the most part, ask specific questions. A question like "What are the city's plans for improving street lighting?" may not give you the information you are seeking. If you want to know about the possibilities of improved lighting in a specific area, ask the specific question: "The sidewalks along Fifth Street are a major pedestrian traffic area, yet the street has several poorly lighted spots. Does the city have any plans to improve lighting in those places?" Whenever you ask a question calling for a yes or no answer, plan to follow up with another question if the information is not forthcoming: "What are those plans?" or "What can be done to change those plans?"

Arrive at the interview on time. Follow your plan, but be open to new, unexpected directions. If your interviewee wanders off the subject, however, get the interview back on track with one of your prepared questions. Let your interviewee do the talking. Listen carefully, taking only as many notes as necessary to help your memory later. If your interviewee doesn't object to a tape recorder and you can use one without distractions, consider taking one along. End the interview with a concluding question such as "Is there anything else you would like to tell me?" Depending on your purpose for the information you have collected, you may need to find out if your interviewee wants a copy of your report of the interview.

Immediately following the interview, make a complete record of it based on your notes. This is not your finished report or summary; it's your record made while the interview is fresh in your mind. You will probably write the report later, after you have thought more about the information or done more information gathering.

Two records of interviews follow. The first is a revised transcription, and the second is written in essay form using quotations and paraphrases of the interviewee's statements.

Reading

Here's a transcript of an interview between a reporter from *New Perspectives Quarterly* and the Reverend Jesse Jackson—a political, social, as well as religious spokesperson on drug use. As you read, observe how the interviewer directs the interview, seeks out specific answers, and leads into new directions.

Drug Use Is a Sin

New Perspectives Quarterly Interview with the Reverend Jesse Jackson

NPQ: By waging the first drug war battle in Washington, DC, Federal   1
Narcotics Director William Bennett targeted the black population of the inner city. Is the focus in the right place?

Jesse Jackson: One hundred fifty billion dollars in illegal drugs flow   2
into this country every year. Americans, which represent six percent of the

world's population, consume half the world's drugs. The African-American population of the inner city does not have enough cash resources to buy up all those drugs.

Drug use and criminality are not solely the domain of the urban "underclass." To give the drug runner and the drug user a dark face merely offers false comfort, since the problem is truly elsewhere.   3

Furthermore, this drug epidemic is not just a problem of despairing youth from families broken over time by slavery and poverty. There is a crisis of values in the family structure of all Americans, not just the "underclass." And this crisis is reinforced by the culture: The betrayals, casual infidelities, and materialism promoted by TV programs like "Dallas" often have more access to the minds and impressions of our children than church, schools, or parents.   4

Drug lords are the masters and drug users are slaves. And the slaves come in all colors, sizes, races, and sexes. It is simply misguided to ignore the universal character of drug use—among pilots and train engineers, public officials, ministers, doctors, stockbrokers, lawyers, college professors—and only focus on the black or the brown dimension of it.   5

New York Senator Alfonse D'Amato once went to the Bronx wearing casual clothes to prove he could buy crack openly on any street corner. Yet, he could just as easily have walked down to the bathroom in the federal building in his usual suit. He could have gone to Battery Park, overlooking the Statue of Liberty, and gotten any quantity or quality of drug he wanted. Or, he could have gone to any suburban school.   6

This said, in one respect William Bennett is right to focus on Washington, DC. When gangs bring their drug supply and weapons right into the heart of our democracy they are displaying open contempt for the government and the American people. To set up shop right in the face of the president, in the very city where the justices of the Supreme Court live and work, and where Congress presides, is a bold sign of contempt for the whole American system.   7

This drug trade must be crushed and the drug lords must be busted. If Communists were infiltrating us this way, causing the death of Americans in our capital, we would have a very different attitude. We still have too much tolerance for drug-related death.   8

NPQ: While drug use is very widespread in America, it is also quite dispersed. However, the focus seems to have fallen on the inner city and the underclass because of the concentration and escalation of drug-related crime and violence.   9

Jackson: There is no question that the combination of drug sickness, greed, the availability of Uzi machine guns, and AK-47's is a formula for disaster.   10

NPQ: After all, the violence isn't with the airline pilot or the. . . .   11

Jackson: The hell it isn't. When there is a train wreck, that's violence. When a plane crashes, that's violence. When workers are mauled on the   12 assembly line, that's violence, or when their relatives are in jail or dead because of drugs, that's violence.

It is a cop-out to focus only on gang violence and not on the extent of drug-related violence around the country. 13

NPQ: To continue your analogy between the drug invasion and Communist aggression, are you saying that the Bush Administration is soft on drugs? 14

Jackson: No, I wouldn't say that they are soft. They are hard on what they know, but their knowledge is soft and their resources are limited. 15

Bennett needs to have cabinet status and a real budget. He has neither the authority nor the budget to fight a drug war. And, so far, neither does he have the vision. 16

NPQ: What about Jack Kemp's proposals to evict drug users and their families from public housing and to require ID cards for public housing residents? 17

Jackson: Does that include those who have government subsidized FHA and VA loans who get caught with drugs? Does that include those who pay their rent with government salaries who get caught using drugs? Does that include the middle class who, as beneficiaries of a government subsidy, deduct their home mortgage payment from their taxes? 18

There is obviously a racial premise in this narrow and inadequate solution. 19

NPQ: What is your program for stopping drug use? 20

Jackson: Cut the supply at the source, strengthen interdiction, educate the innocent, rehabilitate the sick, and enforce swift and tough punishment for the purveyors of death—the drug lords who are nothing more than terrorists. 21

Since the flow of drugs into the United States is an act of terrorism, anti-terrorist policies must be applied. If someone is caught bringing drugs into this country and selling them here, if someone is caught transmitting the death-agent to Americans, that person should face war-time consequences. The line must be drawn. 22

NPQ: How do you propose to cut the supply and strengthen interdiction? 23

Jackson: Drug interdiction should be elevated to a central position in our foreign policy. The Secretary of State should convene all the heads of state from those nations where the drugs are grown, especially from south of our border: Mexico, Colombia, Peru, and Bolivia. A multilateral plan must be worked out that includes debt forgiveness and economic development assistance, including programs for the development of alternative crops. 24

And the United States must supply military support, where needed, because in countries like Colombia the drug lords have private armies stronger than the standing armies. 25

We must also be more effective in stopping the flow of drugs. I have   26
been in Florida with Coast Guard officials. They know how 90 percent of
the drugs come into this country: In recent times, five of the six Coast Guard
cutters assigned to stop the flow of drugs have been deployed to turn back
Haitian boat people, not drugs. Five-sixths of the anti-drug fleet that should
have been devoted to chasing drug peddlers was, instead, chasing Haitians.

Finally, the $150 billion drug trade is being laundered in somebody's   27
banks. There is not an adequate challenge to the people who launder
money. Political authorities in the border areas, by and large, turn their
heads to these accomplices to murder.

NPQ: What about punishment?   28

Jackson: Swift punishment for pushers because they are terrorists.   29

NPQ: Meaning heavy sentences without the possibility of parole?   30

Jackson: Yes. Stiffer prison sentences and better nets.   31

NPQ: But isn't there a limit? Dr. Alim Muhammed, who runs the   32
Nation of Islam's "dopebuster" program in Washington's northeast section,
told us that of the 200,000 black males who live in Washington, 10,000 of
them are incarcerated.

Jackson: If prison is warranted, we have to use it.   33

NPQ: If pushers should be treated as terrorist purveyors of death,   34
does that mean they deserve the death penalty?

Jackson: I am not inclined to say pushers deserve the death penalty. I   35
am not sure that the state has the moral authority to kill.

NPQ: More than anything you have seen in your long career working   36
for social change, does this drug scourge make you come the closest to
favorably considering the death penalty?

Jackson: Yes. This drug scourge makes me think that real punishment   37
is necessary. When people are openly unemployed but can flash their
expensive wares in the face of circumstantial evidence that they are drug
lords, it makes me think that there must be a drastic way to stop them from
manipulating our system.

The drug lords laugh at the system, which is not designed for people   38
who believe crime is something that pays.

NPQ: Beyond stiffer sentences and better nets, how can demand for   39
drugs be dampened?

Jackson: The whole environment that leads to drug use must be   40
changed. There is a need for pre-natal care, day care, Headstart, job training,
affordable housing, jobs with some purpose, and the minimum wage must
be raised.

And there must be education against drugs to bolster moral resistance.   41

NPQ: Where will that education come from? In our system, doesn't   42
moral resistance spring from the community and civil society—the churches,

family and parental authority, and so on? Government, after all, is not a religious institution; the Constitution is not a moral code for individual behavior, but a framework for protecting the chosen behavior of individuals.

Jackson: The main responsibility for cutting supply falls on the gov-   43
ernment. Cutting demand, I agree, must come more from the community.

NPQ: Okay. But who? How? For years you have been stumping the   44
country, preaching "down with dope, up with hope." Nancy Reagan has been pushing *Just Say No.* Nevertheless, drug use has risen in many areas.

Jackson: Well, there wasn't enough real work going on at enough   45
levels. I was crying out in the wilderness.

For too long, drugs were not seen as a national threat. Now, many   46
officials have gone from the extreme of ignoring the drug scourge to putting a racial label on it. So, the ready answer has been to kick suspected drug dealers and users out of their homes and lock them up.

NPQ: Some groups, including the Nation of Islam, seem to have an   47
effective approach to moral education and rehabilitation. Their objective is to restore cultural integrity to the community and the family, and to provide structure and discipline without government interference. They don't look to a white, Republican administration to solve the problems of their community.

Do you agree with their approach?   48

Jackson: Some people need cultural affirmation; discipline is also im-   49
portant. This is one dimension.

I know that the Muslims have been effective in routing drug pushers by   50
patrolling the housing projects. As long as this type of solution is within the law, it should be encouraged. Parents, in their off-time, should patrol the school areas so that drug pushers will determine that the area is too hot to sell drugs. Neighborhood patrols are also important.

NPQ: Where do you depart and where do you share common   51
ground with Drug Czar William Bennett's approach?

Jackson: This administration thinks it can get people off drugs by   52
threatening to evict them from their homes. People who crave drugs do not stop to consider where they live. They are already walking on air. The first thing the drug czar should know is the nature of drug addiction: Drug addicts are sick and sick people need medical care. Yet, where is the budget for care and rehabilitation?

Is the Bush Administration going to put them all in jail? Jail is also   53
public housing. What is the point of shifting people from one form of public housing to another form of public housing? In fact, jail is more expensive to the taxpayer.

Administration officials have jumped up with instant solutions before   54
they have an analysis. Why don't they convene a summit with leaders not only of drug-producing countries, but with mayors, police chiefs, health officials, and former users who have been wrestling with the drug problem

long before it was on Bennett's mind? That would at least enable Bennett to get a grip on the nature and depth of the crisis. The approach should not be confrontational or racial. It should not focus on Washington, DC, and it should be bipartisan.

NPQ: Drug use seems such an intractable vice to some that they are   55 proposing decriminalization to remove the violence and the high illicit profits.

Might that be part of a solution, especially since so much drug use is   56 casual, not destructively addictive?

Jackson: I don't believe that. You may take away the profits but you   57 won't take away the poison. Drugs are poison. Taking drugs is a sin. Drug use is morally debased and sick . . .

NPQ: . . . Which means those Americans who use drugs—25 percent   58 of the population—are morally debased . . . ?

Jackson: It is true that Americans are witting allies to the drug flow.   59 Many of them are both enjoying and profiting from drugs. These same Americans wouldn't enjoy communism or fascism in the same way; they wouldn't enjoy an invasion and occupation by the Russians. But they seem to enjoy the occupation of drugs. Popping pills is pleasure. Taking drugs creates euphoria, happiness, good feelings, gratification.

With all the war-room strategies this nation has had for fighting foreign   60 enemies, we have never had an enemy this syrupy and slick. We have never had a time in which our own army wanted to engage the enemy for purposes of gratification. This enemy is more devastating than the enemy in the other uniform with the other ideology. This time the enemy is us. People are not being force-fed drugs. They are volunteering for this slow suicide.

NPQ: You are a religious man. Where does the moral resistance to the   61 short-term gratification of drugs come from?

Jackson: Values. They are taught by family, synagogue, temple, church.   62 There must be something ingrained that makes one resist the consumption of drugs; the same thing that makes one want to resist hating people and exploiting people. Drug abuse is a form of self-hatred and self-exploitation.

A commitment to life means a commitment to avoid the short-term   63 pleasure and long-term pain of drugs.

NPQ: But isn't the very ethos of this culture, in 1989, short-term   64 gratification . . . ?

Jackson: . . . Short-term pleasure, long-term pain, which means the   65 drug crisis, in the last analysis, is a cultural crisis.

Questions

1. Does the interviewer get the expected answer from the first question?
2. Some of the questions seem to have been planned in advance and others developed in the process of the interview. Find examples of each kind of question.

3. What kind of information do the planned questions imply that *New Perspectives Quarterly* was seeking from Jackson?

4. Find an instance where the interviewer expresses an opinion, and consider what the purpose was. Does the interviewer achieve the purpose?

5. Jackson responds to the *NPQ* interviewer as a politician, a social activist, and a clergyman. Find examples of responses in each of these roles.

Discussion

The *New Perspectives Quarterly (NPQ)* interviewer clearly had planned some questions to ask. You can see them at places where the questioning takes a new direction rather than derives from Jackson's previous statement. One such question is paragraph 20: "What is your program for stopping drug use?" This question seems only loosely related to Jackson's statement in paragraphs 18 and 19 regarding the racial nature of Jack Kemp's proposals. Jackson's answer, however, seems to lead directly to the next question: "How do you propose to cut the supply and strengthen interdiction?" So, the interviewer's questions can be seen as originating in two ways: from advance preparation and from Jackson's statements.

The questions also seem to open up the possibility for Jackson to respond from his three public roles: politician, social activist, and clergyman. When the interviewer asks "Are you saying that the Bush Administration is soft on drugs?" (paragraph 14), a political response is solicited. Asking "How can demand for drugs be dampened?" (paragraph 39), the interviewer invites a social response. "Where does the moral resistance to the short-term gratification of drugs come from?" (paragraph 61) elicits a religious response. Such questions aid the interviewer in controlling the focus of the interview and even the role of the interviewee.

Paragraphs

Readers have certain expectations of *paragraphs:* that they won't be excessively long, that the first sentence or two will somehow orient them to the paragraph's content, that the sentences in the paragraph will be connected, and that the paragraph won't shift to a new subject without warning. Paragraph indentions are a graphic feature of written expression, usually with no correspondence in speech, and they are often a feature of revision, added where the text makes a slight shift in subject. Interviews are oral; the transcriber, in addition to adding punctuation and spelling, must therefore make a decision about paragraphing.

Jackson's reply to the first question is long—roughly 400 words, much too long for a single paragraph. Paragraphing, then, had to be added in the written transcription. What prompted the transcriber to indent? Each of the seven paragraphs can give us some inkling. The first paragraph concentrates on dollars spent on drugs, whereas the second amplifies the racial issue. The third paragraph shifts to a broader moral issue, and the fourth shows the spectrum of drug use. The fifth is devoted to Senator D'Amato. In the sixth Jackson returns to the question by addressing the drug war in Washington, DC, and in the final paragraph he eloquently calls for stepping up the drug war. Each paragraph is connected to the one before it, but each addresses a slightly different aspect of the answer.

Style

This record of an interview probably had some editing before it appeared in *New Perspectives Quarterly;* at the same time, it's probably also an accurate record of the dialogue between the *NPQ* interviewer and Jesse Jackson. As a record, the transcript uses present tense verbs:

Is the focus in the right place?
Drug lords *are* the masters and drug users are slaves.
Do you *agree* with their approach?
The drug lords *laugh* at the system.

If this record were used in a report, many of the statements would be changed to past tense:

NPQ asked if Jackson thought the focus *was* in the right place.
Jackson *asserted,* "Drug lords are the masters and drug users are slaves."
NPQ questioned whether Jackson *agreed* with the Muslims' approach.

Exceptions to this kind of change are direct quotations and statements of general truths or recurring actions:

Jackson replied that the drug lords only *laugh* at the government's actions.
Jackson answered, "This administration *thinks* it *can get* people off drugs
 by threatening to evict them from their homes."

EXERCISE

Select a portion of the New Perspectives Quarterly *interview with Jackson (three or four questions and answers) and rewrite it as a report, making changes as necessary to move the interview from recording to reporting.*

Reading

In contrast to the preceding interview, which is a transcription of a dialogue, the following record is written in essay form. In it, John E. Cooney, having interviewed Robert Donnell for a feature in the *Wall Street Journal* (1974), describes Donnell's idiosyncratic work. As you read, observe how Cooney uses direct quotations and paraphrases to record the interview.

By Whom the Bells Toll

John E. Cooney

At 1:00 P.M. each weekday, Robert Donnell rushes to a small room high in   1
Parliament Hill's Peace Tower in Ottawa where he erupts in a frenzy of activity:

Arms and legs flailing, he slides jerkily back and forth across a long oak   2
bench. Like a masseur gone mad, he mercilessly punches, pounds, and slaps rows of short, broomhandle-like sticks jutting from a wooden panel in front of him. He furiously kicks and stomps wooden slats on the floor.

"I try . . . to put as much . . . of myself . . . into this . . . as I can," says a   3
huffing Mr. Donnell, his face perspiring and nearly crimson after an uninterrupted fifteen minutes of such feverish activity.

That grueling routine is Mr. Donnell's way of giving a recital. He's   4
Canada's official Dominion Carillonneur, the man who plays the Peace Tower bells that delight residents as well as foreign dignitaries and tourists who visit the nation's capital. He's the only full-time carillonneur in the country. But while most musicians enjoy audience acclaim, the carillonneur is hidden in the belfry so few folks know of his mighty exertion. In fact, most people who hear his performances don't even know he's playing.

"A lot of people think the bells are playing electrically," complains Mr.   5
Donnell, a trim, dapper bachelor in his late fifties. "Whenever I overhear someone saying that I tell them 'No . . . It's me up in there doing that.'"

Indeed, it has been Mr. Donnell up in the Peace Tower doing that since   6
1939, when he became only the second carillonneur ever appointed to the civil service post that now pays $21,000 a year. (He's listed in the federal phone book's yellow pages under "Branches & Services" of the House of Commons.) And in the past thirty-four years, he has never missed one of the fifteen-minute or hour-long recitals he schedules nearly each week that he's in town.

"Fortunately, I'm very healthy," he says. "Anyway, there's nobody to fill   7
in for me if I get sick."

His good health may have something to do with the rigorous exercise   8
he gets on the job. A carillon—an outgrowth of small bells that struck time in fifteenth-century clock towers in Belgium and the Netherlands—must have at least twenty-three bells. The Peace Tower's has fifty-three, weighing from 10 to 22,400 pounds. The carillonneur's strength goes into banging away at the foot pedals and wooden keyboard—the instrument is modeled after a three hundred-year-old Flemish design—that move bell clappers. The heaviest clapper is 504 pounds, and only the strongest blows get it to gong.

"Playing can really prove exhausting," acknowledges Mr. Donnell,   9
exhibiting calluses like a karate expert's along the edges of his fast hands.

Besides the calluses, Mr. Donnell puts up with another drawback most   10
musicians don't have. He can't practice, at least not on the bells, because
he'd disturb Parliament—and much of the rest of the city as well. To
compensate, he has a keyboard not connected to the bells in a practice room
where he knocks out muted tunes. "It isn't exactly like practicing on the real
thing," he admits.

Playing, writing, and arranging music absorb most of his time. Even his   11
vacations are sort of a busman's holiday since he frequently spends them in
Europe searching for rare music that was composed just for carillons. In
addition, he keeps in touch with fellow carillonneurs through the North
American Guild of Carillonneurs, an organization that—with the exception of
Mr. Donnell and a handful of full-time bellmen in the United States—
consists of about two hundred part-time carillonneurs. And since Mr. Donnell is recognized within his limited circle as one of the best, he occasionally
goes on concert tours that have taken him as far away as Australia.

Although carillonneurs are relatively obscure today, from the sixteenth   12
through the eighteenth centuries carillons and the men who played them
were famous in many a Flemish town. There are accounts of rival carillonneurs competing for honors. And one of the treasures of war was to seize a
city's carillon to be later ransomed back as the town's most precious possession. When France's King Louis XIV captured the city of Mons in 1691, for
example, the formal treaty between the conqueror and the city calls for the
ransom of the bells.

Today, "one thing that may deter people from studying the carillon is   13
that many bell towers have only stairs leading to the keyboard. By the time
you get there, you're already tired," says Mr. Donnell, recalling the five
hundred-step hike he had to the Michelin, Belgium, belfry where he
studied. Now, he rides an elevator to work.

Since taking over the carillonneur post at Parliament, Mr. Donnell has   14
arranged and played literally hundreds of different works, including Bach's
"Toccata in D Minor," Gershwin's "Porgy and Bess," and his own work,
"Canadian Folksong Medley"—and, for Franklin Roosevelt, "Home on the
Range."

He regularly performs when statesmen visit Parliament, but "I never   15
get to see the statesmen I play for," he says. "Their schedules are too tight to
allow them time to come up for a visit."

Questions

1. What makes the work of a carillonneur "grueling"?
2. From this record, reconstruct the questions that Cooney might have taken with
   him to the interview.
3. If carillons can be played electrically, as most are today, what would be the
   advantage of having a carillonneur?
4. What kind of activity did you think Cooney was describing as you read the first
   three paragraphs?

5. What do you think were the determining factors for Cooney to sometimes use direct quotations and other times use paraphrases of Donnell's statements?

Discussion

"Interesting people with intriguing stories"—this is why *Wall Street Journal* interviews people like Robert Donnell with unfamiliar names but with stories that are evidence of the variety of life. This reading could just as easily fit in Chapter 14, To Praise or Censure, for it praises the carillonneur in a way similar to how student writer Beth Zamzow praises the "Pumpkin King," in another essay that evolved from an interview.

Unlike the Jesse Jackson interview, this record of an interview is written as an essay. In such a record, much of the dialogue is probably lost in the writer's selection process; however, the reader also gains information that is not available in a transcription. Here Cooney uses not only direct quotation, as in a transcription, but description as well: he describes the exertion required for playing the bells, and he tells you a little about Donnell's appearance. Also, he paraphrases and summarizes a large part of the discussion, making a piece of writing briefer than a complete transcription of the interview would be.

Style

Cooney writes as if the interview is taking place in the present. He is in the bell tower with Donnell, watching him play and then talking with him. Notice, however, that Cooney's presence is only implied. (By contrast, in the Jackson interview the *NPQ* interviewer is identified with each question.) Nowhere does Cooney refer to himself.

Most of Cooney's verbs are in the present tense:

He *slides* jerkily back and forth.
Mr. Donnell *puts* up with another drawback most musicians *don't have*.

Cooney uses the past tense only to relate past experiences: "He *became* only the second carillonneur ever appointed to the civil service post." Quotations are set off in paragraphs, separating Donnell's words from Cooney's writing about the interview.

EXERCISE

Cooney doesn't really end his essay with a conclusion; it just closes with his last quotation from Donnell. Write an additional paragraph that makes an overall concluding statement about Robert Donnell as you perceive him from reading this essay.

Writing

Use interviewing as a method of getting information about a subject that interests you or one you need to report on for another class. Select your interviewee on the basis of qualifications to provide accurate information. After arranging the interview, write out the questions that will give you the information you need. During the interview, take enough notes to aid your memory; use a tape recorder if you have one and if your interviewee doesn't object. Immediately after the interview, fill out your notes.

If you were able to use a tape recorder, write a transcription like that of the Jackson interview. If you are writing your record from notes, you will need to paraphrase and summarize much of the interview, as Cooney does, quoting only when you were able to write down the exact words. Let your interviewee read your rough draft for accuracy and perhaps the addition of something you've omitted.

Recording Group Actions

In school, most of your note taking is probably for the purpose of recording lectures, assignments, and reading, as discussed in the introduction to this chapter. Sometimes, however, you may find yourself in the role of recording secretary, taking notes on the actions and discussions of a committee, an organization, or a collaborative group for one of your classes. Taking notes of this kind is like taking minutes of a meeting and then putting them in a form that others can read and that will be suitable for an official record.

If you are the recorder at a meeting, you will probably do more listening than speaking. You may want to use a tape recorder as a backup for your notes. Minutes must be accurate, complete, and objective. When recording discussions, you can summarize or paraphrase what members of your group say. At other times, such as for motions or specific decisions, you need a word-for-word record, including the names of the people who make and second the motions or suggest the decisions. When actions are to be taken, tell specifically what those actions are, who is to act, and when and where the action is to take place; for example, "Mary Carlin will report at the October meeting on the results of her telephone survey regarding new members."

Be objective in your recording, avoiding wording such as "Mary Carlin *generously* volunteered to conduct the telephone survey." And be consistent in your references to people. You can refer to them in one of several ways: by last name only (Carlin), by first name and last name (Mary Carlin), by first initial and last name (M. Carlin), by first name (Mary), or by a name preceded by title (Ms. Carlin). If you begin using first and last names, follow this form throughout the record.

As for the content of minutes, *Robert's Rules of Order* recommends the following:

1. The name of the group
2. The date, time, and place of the meeting
3. The names of the presider and the secretary
4. The fact that the previous minutes were approved or corrected
5. A separate paragraph for each subject
6. The exact wording of all motions and whether they were passed defeated, or tabled
7. The hour of adjournment
8. The signature of the recording secretary (and possibly of the chairperson)

Minutes may also show the names or the number of people present, a list of summary of reports read and approved, and the date and place of the next meeting.

A record of an informal meeting or of a collaborative group discussion in class would be less formal than the minutes just described, but it would contain some of the same elements: names, date, summary of the discussion, specific actions and decisions taken, work to be completed with the names of people assigned to carry out specific assignments, and whatever else is appropriate for the session.

Reading

What follows is the record of an informal organizational meeting for a new English club. In the form of minutes, the record shows who was present, what discussions and actions took place, and what was decided.

**Minutes of the Organizational Meeting
for a New English Club
October 16, 19——**

**Present: C. Burns, H. Dahlquist, M. Hagemeister, L. Juarez,
M. Ledoux (Chair), E. Lee, J. Stang, H. Theis, R. White**

M. Ledoux as convenor called the meeting to order at 1:05 P.M.

1. *Election.* By voice ballot, M. Ledoux was elected chair and H. Theis secretary.
2. *Purpose of club.* After an extended discussion concerning the purpose of the club and the fact that no English club on campus currently encourages writing and publication by its members, the following motion was made and passed:

    The purpose of this new English club will be to promote writing by its members, to encourage publication in campus newspapers and magazines, to attend plays as a group, and to report on new and interesting books. (H. Dahlquist, J. Stang)

3. *Name of the club.* Several possible names were suggested. Approved by voice ballot, The Writers' Circle will be the name of the new club.
4. *Meetings.* Following a discussion of the desirability and disadvantages of various times, the group agreed by consensus on the third Thursday of each month at 7:00 P.M. The chair will see if the English Department's conference room will be available as a meeting place.
5. *Sponsor.* For the purposes of advising and visibility in the English Department, the club agreed by consensus to have a faculty sponsor. The chair will ask Professor Janet Johnson if she will consent to be the sponsor.
6. *Promotion of the club.* Several means of promotion of the club were proposed, among them speaking briefly at the next English Department meeting to ask faculty to promote the club, putting up posters in the English building to advertise the next meeting, se ding postcards to English majors and minors, announcing the meetings on classroom blackboards, and asking faculty to read announcements of meetings. The following motion passed:

> That the chair speak briefly at the next English Department meeting to encourage faculty promotion of the club, that two volunteers make posters for the English building announcing the next meeting, and that two volunteers write announcements of the next meeting on classroom blackboards. (E. Lee, R. White)

E. Lee and H. Theis volunteered to make and put up the posters, and R. White and H. Dahlquist will write notices on the blackboards.

The meeting adjourned at 1:55 P.M. The next meeting will be held November 19 at 7:00 P.M.—in the English Department conference room if approved. Agenda: how to get published on campus.

—Harold Theis, secretary

Questions

1. Some aspects of these minutes conform to the recommendations in *Robert's Rules of Order*, such as the time of the meeting. Name others.
2. Some aspects of these minutes are a result of the secretary's (or organization's) choice, such as listing the names of everyone present. What are some choices not covered in the *Rules*?
3. Even though *Robert's Rules of Order* doesn't require the names of the people attending a meeting, Theis included them. What do you see as the advantages of doing so in the minutes of this meeting?

Discussion

Minutes of a meeting and notes of collaborative group discussions record actions. Both are evidence that speaking does things. Language is more than sounds formed by air passing over vocal cords and through the mouth. It's more than black marks on a page. When people use language, they are creating a relationship in which their words cause an effect.

To create the desired effect, speakers and writers must first use the appropriate words. If they say "Pugga woc" when they mean "Please pass me the popcorn," the effect will be bewildered glances. But if they say "Please pass me the popcorn," they will probably get the popcorn. Of course, they can also say something like "Would you mind closing the door?" in which case they would expect not the answer "Yes, I would mind closing the door" but the result of the door getting closed. "Would you mind closing the door?" is an accepted way of asking politely for someone to close the door.

Minutes and notes of group meetings record words as actions. In the English club minutes, the words spoken and recorded had the action of creating a new organization of people with mutual interests. The notes of a classroom group discussion may record contributions toward a paper you are writing together—the effect being a document. Even if there is no discernable product, the effect of the discussion on group members still exists. If, for example, your group has been asked to discuss ways of combating racial discrimination on campus, the words of each of you will affect the others in the group, and there will be a joint effect of greater awareness of discrimination, which the record will show.

EXERCISE

The minutes for the new English club are written rather formally to serve as an official record. Suppose that you and a group of classmates are working together on an assignment to propose a new English club. You discuss the same matters recorded in these minutes, but the report is informal. As recorder, write that informal record, being as specific as necessary so that the chair of your group can report your decisions to the class as a whole.

Writing

Assume the role of recording secretary for an organization whose meetings you attend, and write minutes for one of the meetings. Include the information that *Robert's Rules of Order* recommends, summarizing discussions and recording motions word for word. Use a consistent format, either the one shown in the reading or another appropriate one.

ADDITIONAL READINGS FOR DISCUSSION

Reading

This student essay is the record of an interview. Like John E. Cooney's essay on the carillonneur Robert Donnell, this essay quotes some of the interviewee's words directly and records others indirectly; it also includes description and background. As you read, try to reconstruct Dulgar's interview questions.

Playin' Bones

Peter E. Dulgar

When fall comes to central Minnesota, so does fall festival; and when fall festival comes to St. Patrick's Church, so does Richard Bettendorf. Richard is a very special man, but it's hard to tell just by looking at him. A natural, sunny smile lights his face, the kind they used to grow a lot of on the plains. He wears dark baggy pants, one of those cardigan-things that all old men seem to wear sooner or later, and a speckled tweed hat. A hearing aid perches rather noticeably on his left ear, but anyone studying him that close will also notice his eyes and the way they gleam. His face is warm and brown, like old deerskin. On the surface nothing about him is extraordinary; he's just a wrinkled old country man, a lot like all old men. What Richard does with four small pieces of wood, however, is truly unique.

He plays them. The pieces of wood are called "bones," and Richard plays music with them—like music heard nowhere else. He does it by holding them between his second and third fingers, two in each hand, and rolling his wrists until the bones vibrate together. The sound produced is somewhere between a clack and a chirp, and Richard plays like the fields are full of crickets wearing wooden shoes. "Playin' bones is easy," he says, "but ya gotta have it in ya ta get it out!"

His bones are old and worn and slightly curved, like the bones of his body. They were made from a block of ebony wood, imported from Africa over fifty years ago. It cost him fifty dollars at the time, and that was enough to break his young bank account, but it was worth it for real ebony bones. "Ebony is the hardest wood in the world, ya know," he explains, and no one cares if he's right or not. Years of sweat and good times have flowed from his fingers into these pieces of wood, and today they reflect a soft, warm happiness from the hard, black wood.

Richard taught himself to play when he was a young man in his twenties, and he's been playing ever since, wherever people will listen. He's even been on the radio in Chicago. "I'd like to play 'Sweet Georgia Brown' over the loudspeaker at a Harlem Globetrotters game," he says, "but I just haven't been able to make it to Minneapolis yet."

This year he's accompanying Virg and the Eldoradoes, a Johnny Cash 5
style band hired to entertain at the festival. It doesn't matter what kind of
band he plays with, though; the sound of bones goes good with anything.

Richard lives in Foley. He used to own the movie theatre with his 6
brother, but now he's retired and he gives his full attention to the bones.
When the festival band takes a break, he strolls over to a group of old-timers
under an oak tree. They all know him, for these are friends he's made over
the last seventy years or so, and the conversation is rich with memories and
old stories. One of his friends brought a banjo and he's playing with the band
too. Richard teases him, switching his own tweed hat for his friend's baseball
cap, as they improvise a little tune while waiting for the band to return.

Richard is seventy-seven years old, but you can't tell it when he plays, 7
kicking his heels up forwards and backwards and gyrating his shoulders in
an effort to lift himself off the ground. He smiles when he plays, so widely
the corners of his mouth endanger his ears, and it seems as if the combination of happiness and motion is enough to lift him above the ground, just
a little bit. People stop to watch him play, some dance, others just smile and
clap their hands, but nobody passes by.

Questions

1. Reconstruct the questions Dulgar might have asked Bettendorf when he interviewed him.

2. Where would you guess the interview took place?

3. This essay might appropriately be placed in Chapter 14, To Praise or Censure.
What words and phrases show that Dulgar admires his interviewee?

4. Does this record of an interview work well as an essay, or would it be more effective
in question and answer form like the Jesse Jackson interview? Explain your answer.

CHAPTER 10

To Report: Writing with Emphasis on the Subject

> *If in speaking to my friend I treat the events . . . as* what
> happened, *the subject will necessarily partake a little more of
> my mind and a little less of the original matter. Although the
> order of events will still be chronological, it is now my memory
> and not my perceptual apparatus that is doing the selecting.*
> —*James Moffett*

Reporting is a kind of writing you've no doubt had experience with. In school, you've probably written book reports, telling what books you've read and what they are about. In science classes you may have written lab reports after completing certain experimental procedures. For other classes, you may have written research papers—reports of reading you did on specific topics with your analyses of that reading and your conclusions. **Reports** are accounts of something done, read, observed, discussed, thought, or experienced.

Unlike recording, in which an observer describes events while they are still happening, reporting usually tells *what happened:* where you went and what you saw on a trip to Mexico, for example; what book or story you read and how you responded to it; what chemicals you combined and what reactions you observed; how the play-off game was played and who was voted most valuable player; what happened when you auditioned for your first part in a play; what happened and how you felt at your first concert; and so on. All these events have already happened when you report them. What you write therefore depends not only on the accuracy of your observation but on your ability to remember the events as well.

Reports of past events, logically, are usually written in the past tense:

At first I *did* not *understand* J. M. Coetzee's *Foe,* but as I *continued* to read I *found* the events to be making more sense.

We *stayed* in a little village near the Pacific Ocean.

As I *stepped* onto the stage, I *didn't know* where to look: at the casting director, at the empty seats, or at the other people on stage.

Some reports, though, tell what something is like, and they are handled differently. When you return from your trip to Mexico, for example, you may report to your friends not only what you did but what Mexico is like as you observed it: "The villages *are* dusty but *have* a lot more character than you *see* in the packaged tours of the cities." Such descriptions are signaled by present tense verbs because, even though your observations took place in the past, you assume that what you observed is still true. If other travelers visit the parts of Mexico you visited, they may be able to view the same things you observed. Book reports similarly use present tense to tell what the book is about, because what you describe is still true: "The narrator of *Foe is* a woman castaway who *shares* Robinson Crusoe's island with Crusoe and Friday." If another reader picks up *Foe* and reads it, the narrator will still be a woman castaway.

Accuracy of Reports

As a reader and a writer of reports, you should be aware that a report filters information through the writer's mind and is only as accurate as the writer makes it. The account is influenced by three factors:

1. The writer's perceptions of the event,
2. The writer's memory of the event,
3. The decisions the writer makes about which details to include.

You may have observed how two people can report the same event in widely divergent ways, despite the fact that they both have attempted to report the facts accurately as they perceived, remembered, and selected them.

As people observe events, their perceptions are influenced by their past experiences. A carpenter, for example, notices how a wooden structure disintegrates in an earthquake, whereas the owner of the building sees a distressingly expensive pile of rubble. An auto mechanic driving his car down the highway hears a hole in an exhaust pipe that would be just noise to someone with an untrained ear. Perceptions are also influenced by the observer's emotional state; what a person sees is in part determined by whether that person is happy, depressed, angry, and so on. The owner of the damaged building, for example, has a great deal more emotional involvement than does the carpenter, a bystander. And observations are influenced by a host of other factors, including seeing only what we want to see or expect to see, as well as being distracted by interruptions.

What you remember and select for reporting is determined by various factors too: your physical and psychological state while remembering (as well as when the event occurred), your reasons for remembering, your ability to recall details, the degree of your interest in the event, and so on. Because memory is sometimes incomplete and inaccurate, written records are important aids for preparing reports. If you take notes of your impressions while reading a book, for example, you have more than your memory to work with when you write your report. A prominent influence on what you remember and select for reporting is possible secondary purposes for reporting. Do you want to *persuade* someone to travel to Mexico (or not to travel to Mexico), to read a book (or not to read it)? Or do you want to *inform* readers about a good place to go in Mexico or a good book to read? Do you want to *entertain* readers about the humorous aspects of your trip? The details you remember and select are determined in part by your reasons for reporting.

Development

Events are often reported in *chronological* order. In narrating your report of a trip or an audition or an accident, you usually start at the beginning and proceed in time sequence to the end. In reporting what something is like, however, you may use some other means of development—*spatial,* for instance, in reporting what a certain Mexican village is like, or most important to least important for telling what a book is about. At times your report may be developed *causally,* showing how certain events brought about other events, or by *comparison,* showing how two events are similar. Reports are often developed in more than one way; a research report, for instance, is likely to use *definition, cause and effect, narration,* and other methods of development.

Reports frequently include direct quotations and other references attributable to other people. If you are reporting dialogue, for instance, you try to reconstruct the actual words of the people you are quoting; quote accurately, in other words, and enclose the statements in quotation marks. In other cases, you may want to report people's reactions to the events you are recounting. Any time you report the words or opinions of others, be careful to name those people so your reader understands that these are not your thoughts.

The readings and writing assignments in this chapter highlight several kinds of reports that you may have occasion to write: a narration of a personal experience, a description and narration of an observed incident, a description of a natural phenomenon, and a book report. The additional readings include a report on a product development, excerpts from a report on the resolution of the Cuban missile crisis, and a report on racism in the 1940s.

Narrating a Personal Experience

One of the most common kinds of reports is the **narration** of a personal experience. Most people do a little of this nearly every day. Families, roommates, or friends get together and report on the interesting events of the day. We enjoy telling our stories and hearing someone else's. These stories are generally assumed to be true, so if we want to repeat someone else's story we can do so trusting its accuracy. But most of us know people who tend to exaggerate, and we're less likely either to believe their stories, no matter how interesting, or to repeat them.

Written reports of personal experiences are assumed to be true too. While readers acknowledge that the writer's account may omit some irrelevant details and may depend on how well the writer remembers the event, readers don't expect exaggeration and fabrication. If the experience is interesting enough to report, it doesn't require elaboration beyond what actually happened.

At the same time, reporters of personal experiences are free to express their own reactions to their experiences: "I was afraid I wouldn't get out of the bus alive." "There was once a time when I wondered what it would be like to float above the earth in a hot-air balloon." "Being a participant in the rally was one of the most significant things I have done." Readers welcome such expressions, because through them they are able to understand the significance of the narrated events.

Reports of personal experiences are usually developed in *chronological* order, from the beginning of the experience to its conclusion. Sometimes the *thesis* is not expressed but is implicit in the selection of details and the writer's expressed reactions. When the thesis is stated, it is just as likely to occur at the end of the report as at the beginning.

Reading

The following essay is an example of a personal experience narration by a college student. Janice Anderson wanted to report an incident that causes her some chagrin when she looks back on it yet some pleasure at having participated in it. As your read, note how she develops her report and how she reacts to the incidents.

Ever Green

Janice Anderson

I had been wanting to do it for a long time. The first time I thought to   1
do it was at Valley Fair three years ago. I don't know why I didn't do it then. Maybe I thought it was silly or vain. Maybe I was just too cheap. But there I

was at the State Fair, standing outside the "Superstar" booth handing over my ten dollars so I could record myself singing on professional sound equipment. Maybe someone important would hear my recording and offer me a fabulous contract! Surely at least the concession owners would want to use it to advertise.

My heart was racing just like when I had been a green soloist in my 2 junior high school choir. I couldn't believe my reaction. I'd had years of vocal training, had sung solos often, and had sung eight seasons with the finest civic choir in the city. I was a real musician! Why was I experiencing major stress over a simple two-minute recording? But maybe a little tension would get my adrenaline flowing, and that would help me. So, did I want to be Barbra Streisand or "The Jets"?

"What song d'ya wanna sing?" the matter-of-fact, gum-chewing blonde 3 behind the counter asked.

"Evergreen." I had decided to be Barbra. "Will I have sheet music?" 4

"No, ya'll have a word sheet. We've found sheet music just confuses most 5 people. They don't know how to read it. What's yer name?"

"Janice Anderson. I'd prefer sheet music, if you have it." 6

She typed my name on a label. How could anyone with such long 7 purple fingernails (obviously fake) type so quickly, flick the label off its paper backing so easily, and stick it on the cassette so accurately?

"Will I be able to hear the tape before I take it? My daughter had a bad 8 experience at a recording booth once. There was something wrong with the tape. The sound was distorted somehow, or not mixed well."

"Sure. If ya' wanna, Janice. We'll play it over the loudspeakers after. 9 Okay, Janice, just wait a minute and someone will call ya' when it's yer turn."

My heart picked up its pace. It seemed an eternity before I was called. 10

"Janice? Come with me." I can't remember what the young woman who 11 took me into the booth looked like. I think her name was Sheena. She was very efficient. She had the instructions memorized and recited them as she led me down the miniature hallway, opened the door, and shooshed me into a carpeted upright coffin.

The shag wall was looped with electric cords that came together at the 12 base of the microphone stand. They snaked up to a black bulbous micro-phone which took up most of the available space. The mesh covering made it look like the eye of a giant fly. A naked hook stared down at me from amongst carpet fibers, and a narrow vertical window exposed my blue-jeaned rear to the world.

"You'll hear a singer through the headphones along with the music, but 13 you'll hear only your own voice on your tape. Bill will play it once through for you to practice. Then you'll be recorded. Stand close to the mike. Sing loud and don't touch the microphone. Okay, Janice? Any questions?" She didn't wait for a response. "Good. Have fun. Remember, Janice, sing loud and don't touch the microphone!" She spoke to me as if I were a child or a nursing home resident with senile dementa.

"Okay," I guessed. It was strange how many questions I had before I   14
entered, and how blank my mind had become in those few short steps from
the outside world.

Sheena hung the plastic-coated word sheet on the wall hook. When I   15
started to look at the words, she adjusted the microphone height and
clapped the headphones over my ears. The almost soundless static coming
through the headphones opened all eight of my sinuses and expanded my
mind as well. My body was entombed, but my head was larger and lighter
than a hot-air balloon.

"Sing loud and don't touch the microphone" kept repeating in my mind.   16

"Hi there, Janice," came a smoothly modulated, calm masculine voice.   17
Must be Bill, I thought. I remember seeing a faceless back on a swivel chair
with what seemed like at least four arms reaching about on a wide, tall
control panel. He reminded me of the "Phantom of the Opera." I never saw
his face, but I knew that, had he ever swiveled around, girls on the street
would have screamed in horror. But he was very kind sounding, in spite of
his obvious hurry. Bill repeated, word for word, what Sheena had said and
asked if I was ready for the practice run.

"Okay, Janice. Remember, sing loud and don't touch the microphone!"   18

An introduction began. In order to get my mouth near the microphone   19
and still see the word sheet, I had to crane my neck back, making my Adam's
apple stick out like an elbow joint. I felt like a pelican trying to swallow a fish.
The music filled the airy space inside my head. So, with fists clenched at my
sides and muscles clenched in my throat, I sang loud and *didn't touch the
microphone*!

I could tell that the sounds coming from my mouth were horrible. I did   20
indeed sound like I had a fish stuck in my throat. As my heart beat even
faster in panic, I forgot every bit of vocal technique I had ever learned. I
sometimes hung under the pitch. Then other times I would overcorrect
and add too much vibrato. Sometimes my voice would patch out, giving
momentary interruptions of silence into a sustained note. "You and I will
make each night a first, every day a beginning" was the only line that
sounded okay. But one gorgeous line does not make a good recording! I
hadn't sounded so green since my first solos in junior high.

"Well, Janice. How did it go? Are you ready to record?" Bill asked with   21
his best disc jockey voice.

"Could you turn the volume down on the singer, please? It's kind of   22
distracting." I was sure that would help.

"Okay. Here we go. Remember, sing loud and don't touch the micro-   23
phone!"

Nausea accompanied my ever-quickening heart rate. I was afraid that if   24
it beat any faster, I'd pass out and throw up at the same time. I took a deep
breath, closed my eyes briefly in meditation, and told myself I could handle
it. I couldn't afford to make mistakes *this* time.

The recording was a little better than the practice in that I was closer to   25
the pitch more often. When I missed one of the entrances, I made up for it

by slipping in smoothly, as if I had wanted to come in late for a dramatic effect. As before, "You and I will make each night a first, every day a beginning" was great. However, the patching out continued and got even worse, and my breath control left me. I was breathing in unnatural places, like "Love, soft as (breath) an easy (breath) chair," and running out of air at the end of phrases. In order to sustain the last note, I took a big gulp in the middle of the final "evergreen."

I don't remember walking out. I only remember standing and waiting   26
on the sidewalk outside the booth. Everyone else's tapes sounded so good as they were played over the loudspeakers. Maybe I'd been too critical of myself, what with my trained ear and all. Maybe I'd sound just as good—or even better!

I watched the gum-chewing blonde with the purple fingernails hand a   27
young woman her recording of "The Rose."

"Ya' sounded real great!" She flashed a smile as she thanked her for her   28
business.

I suppose she says that to everyone, just as she is trained to call all   29
customers by their first names, I thought. It *was* a pleasant rendition of "The Rose," but far from "great."

The introduction to "Evergreen" started up. And so did my heart.   30
Then my heart sank when I heard what must have been my voice. It sounded like a nervous junior high school soloist.

As I sheepishly stepped to the counter to claim my tape, I avoided   31
making eye contact with Ms. Purple-Nails. I just wanted to take the tape and disappear. But she seemed to feel that saying a final word was part of her job.

"Ya were, ah . . . pretty good, Janice," she said as she finally handed me   32
my tape.

The label read, "Janice Anderson. Evergreen." It should have said,   33
"Janice Anderson. Ever green."

When I go back next year, I'll try a different song. I plan to hold the   34
word sheet in my hand. And I might even touch the microphone.

Questions

1. Anderson does not state her thesis explicitly. In your own words, state the controlling idea of her essay, write it in a sentence, and then compare your sentence with those of others in your class. How do you account for any differences you find?

2. Anderson recalls experiencing several emotions during the incident she reports. What are those emotions, and to what is she reacting with each new emotion?

3. Describe each of the three people other than the writer participating in this incident. Which one does Anderson characterize most vividly?

4. Does Anderson digress at all from her chronological development of her story?

5. Explain the meaning of the title, "Ever Green."

Discussion

Anderson takes a simple event and makes a story of it that would interest a wide audience. To the basic report "I made a tape recording of myself singing 'Evergreen' at the state fair, and it was horrible" you would probably respond "So what?" But Anderson goes beyond the basic report by adding details and personal reactions. The story is still true and accurate—but more so. The expanded report gives readers a description of the recording studio and the people employed there, it recounts the conversations as Anderson remembers them, and it tells how Anderson felt from beginning to end. She had to remember and recount the details of the incident.

Whenever you narrate a personal experience, you have more details in your head than you put on paper. They may not readily come to the surface, but they're there. Most times writers don't prod their memories enough to take full advantage of what they know. Perhaps they're accustomed to telling their stories orally, with an audience beside them to coax out the details: "Then what did you say?" or "But what did she look like?" or "How did you feel about that?" When you write, you need to put yourself in the role of audience as well as that of writer so you can see what details you should include—details that help your readers see the event as you do, or as you want them to. To assist your memory, try using some of the prewriting suggestions in Chapter 3: the journalist's questions, for example, or free-writing or brainstorming.

Thesis

Even after including as many descriptive and personal details as she did in this essay, Anderson still knows more about the incident than you do. She didn't say everything she could have. You don't know, for example, what all the choices of songs were, but Anderson does, or did. How did she decide what to include and what to omit? In revising narratives, writers often have to perform two actions. The first one (adding details) we've already discussed; the second one (deleting details) is just as important. Rough drafts of narratives often go on and on, off on tangents, touching on irrelevant information. In deciding what to add and what to omit, Anderson needed to think in terms of *thesis*—the overall controlling idea that will hold the essay together and make the impression on her audience that she is striving for.

In this essay, as often in narratives, the thesis sentence is unexpressed. Of course, not expressing a thesis is not the same as not having one. A writer must have a controlling idea to complete an essay—perhaps not when beginning to write but certainly during revision, when deciding what to add and what to delete. Often when a thesis is implied, the title expresses it. Anderson plays on words in using her title "Ever Green," to imply her thesis. Is she saying that she knows she showed herself to be an amateur yet that she enjoyed the experience anyway and knows she can do better? Such a thesis requires her to give a background of her singing experience, to make herself look a little foolish in her self-pride, to show how routine the recording is for employees of the makeshift studio, and to report her reactions throughout the experience.

Paragraphs

Another matter that frequently requires attention in revising narratives is paragraphing. When drafting a report of an event, you, like many writers, may compose one long *paragraph*. But long paragraphs are a problem for readers, who like to encounter white space now and then as a rest. Paragraphs have a more important function, though, something like that of punctuation: they are a signal to the reader that here is a shift, that one part of the topic is completed and the writer is about to embark on another. This is why paragraphing in personal narratives is so difficult—the shifts are often minuscule.

In revising long narrative paragraphs, you need to look for these subtle changes. They may be shifts in time or location, as when Anderson shifts for paragraph 19, "An introduction began," and for paragraph 26, "I don't remember walking out." Another reason for beginning paragraphs accounts for most of Anderson's shifts. "Ever Green" consists of a great deal of quoted conversation, and writers conventionally begin a new paragraph for each new speech. So Anderson has separate paragraphs, for example, for the speeches of the receptionist and for her own responses.

EXERCISE

Report a conversation you have had recently, using direct quotations and making an effort to put down the exact words of both the other speaker and yourself. Begin a new paragraph each time the speaker changes. Note that commas and periods are usually written inside the closing quotation marks.

Writing

Report a personal experience. It may be something quite simple, like Janice Anderson's report of making a tape recording, but in recounting the details of the incident and your reactions to it you can make it interesting to others. Prod your memory for details, asking the journalist's questions (see Chapter 3). Or brainstorm, or freewrite.

As you compose, report the experience chronologically, from beginning to end. Describe the setting for your readers, telling where the incident took place and what the circumstances were. Describe the other participants.

Report conversations as direct quotations. Tell how you felt throughout the occurrence.

Select an expressive title, one that reflects your controlling idea whether or not you express that idea in a thesis sentence. Revise for paragraphing, so that you begin new paragraphs at shifts of time and place, as well as at shifts of speakers in conversation. Delete irrelevant details and add details where your readers might have questions.

Reporting an Observed Incident

If you were to think of all the reporting you do, next in frequency to personal experiences might be incidents you have observed. You witness an accident, or a fight, or a wedding, or a building being razed, and all these are worth reporting to another person. If you're like most people, you like to tell stories. And factual stories are usually easier to tell, because you don't have to invent details; you just remember them.

Sometimes your reports may be based on notes you've taken—on records, that is. In biology class, you record your experiments or observations and then write up your notes as a report. On your vacation trip, you may keep a journal, a daily account of your observations, and later report your experiences to a friend or relative. You may take notes on a painting or a play you've seen and then write a report about it.

How good are you at observing? Do you pay attention to details around you? If you witness a hit-and-run collision, for example, do you notice the model, make, and color of the car that fled? Or take another example, something less startling: the person who sits in front of you in English class has just had her hair cut and styled. Do you notice? Can you remember what her hair looked like before?

Reports of observations usually attend closely to details. They tend to be *descriptive* rather than narrative. Since they report what a person has seen, they may be developed *spatially* rather than chronologically.

Reading

The following essay reports close observations by a student of nature. Franklin Russell was a free-lance writer, born in New Zealand but commissioned by a Toronto magazine to observe life at a pond in Ontario, Canada. Before staking out his pond, he was no more experienced at pond watching than you probably are, but he learned to apply the objectivity of the scientist and the imagination of the artist. This essay, taken from his book *Watchers at the Pond*, reports his observations. As you read, watch for signs of the author's attitude toward his subject and of his presence in the report.

The Hunt

Franklin Russell

The pond swarmed with creatures whose lives depended on guile, dissimulation, stealth, on strength and speed. The hunters ranged the pond from the high upper air, where the red-tailed hawk hovered, to the mud bottom, where dragonfly larvae lurked in endless ambush.   1

The death of the towhees in the southern forest was an insignificant incident in one hunting day. Before dusk the sharp-shinned hawk had killed again several times. But the towhees' death exemplified the perfection attained by some hunters in securing their prey.   2

Among these creatures were hawks, owls, wasps, robber flies, minks, weasels, mantises, and crows. Perhaps the most imposing was the red-tailed hawk. His scream in the hot sky gripped the senses, and the vertical fall of his body terrified the forest. Another was the great horned owl whose booming night call jerked sleeping crows out of their sleep. If crows dreamed, they would have visions of great horned owls.   3

But size was no criterion of the hunter's skill and power. Few creatures better personified the hunt than the robber fly. One had appeared now, and his arrival had been so fleet that he was still unseen at the pond. He was black, slender-bodied, hunch-shouldered, with enormous multifaceted eyes and long hooked legs. He stayed unmoving on a cattail stem, his eyes glistening and watching. The pond sparkled. The trees murmured in the wind of a new season. The frogs were silent at midday.   4

The fly was motionless one moment and gone the next. Only the acutest eye could follow him low across the water on a course of interception that ended at a droning bumblebee. The impact flung the bee into the grass. He squirmed to sting the fly, but the powerful grip of hooked legs held him tightly till a sting jabbed into his back. He was still struggling feebly when the fly inserted a sucking beak and began withdrawing his body fluids.   5

Meanwhile, another robber fly arrived, flashed over the feeding fly at pondside, and disappeared toward the northern trees. She saw a large beetle scuttling over some bare ground and dropped and straddled him before he even saw her. The beetle ran while the fly pushed her sting at his heavy armor, seeking to find the chink that made him fatally vulnerable. She found it, and as the beetle slowed his scuttling run she unsheathed a cutter from her mouth and sawed a hole in his back. Through this she inserted her beak and sucked. The beetle quivered and died.   6

It was a time of hunters lurking behind the peaceful façade of the pond. A yellowthroat jerked out his song in a thicket. A volley of crow calls rose from the marsh. A big green darner dragonfly hovered over the feeding robber fly for a moment, then flicked over some blossoming chokeberries to the pond. He lowered a scoop formed by his hair-fringed front legs and drove through a swarm of gnats flying close to the surface of the water. A   7 dozen of them were imprisoned in the scoop, and while still flying, the dragonfly chewed them dry and dropped their bodies in the water.

As long as a dragonfly patrolled the pond, no insect was safe. Some of the hundreds of dragonflies there were as big as small birds, and all had double wings outstretched flatly from their bodies. All had great compound eyes that were almost omnipercipient, so widely and minutely did they see. The big green darner saw a wolf spider running through grass on the pond bank. At the same time and in the opposite direction, he was watching a monarch butterfly resting on a twig. The dragonfly's head was flexibly joined to his body so he could drop his head and look underneath and behind, and fly, as a result, with exceptional precision. He might be halfway across the pond and flick himself one hundred wingspans into the path of a butterfly. He would be eating before landing with his struggling victim. 8

The dragonflies were catholic hunters and cannibals. The green darner paused over a leaf, then struck at a smaller, bright red dragonfly nearby. But his prey eluded him. He flew backwards, then whisked off sharply and hit a low-flying wasp. The two creatures tumbled into a mass of aquatic plants, the stingless dragonfly trying to kill the wasp before she could drive in her sting. The insects disappeared into the greenery, and the bright sun glittered on the tranquil pond. 9

The wasps greatly outnumbered the dragonflies at the pond and were their antithesis. They were members of a great family of earth insects who had evolved lives of refinement and ingenuity, in contrast to the dragonflies' simple attributes of speed, power, and rapacity, which were virtually unchanged since primeval times. Some wasps, not seen at the pond, used small pieces of wood as tools to dig their burrows. Others, at the pond, were knowing enough to wrestle armor-sheathed victims till their bodies bent and a small crack appeared. The wasps would then sting through it. All the wasps were shelter builders, and they were both solitary and communal. 10

The silent struggle between wasp and dragonfly continued in the greenery; nearby, six different wasps lingered on a cluster of lily pads. All had come to drink. A solitary wasp, black and skinny, his body longer than his wings and his head joined to his body by a short, exceptionally thin neck, rested on one leaf. He looked light and fragile, and a puff of wind moved him fractionally. Near him was a cicada killer three or four times his size, with massive abdomen, thorax, head, eyes, and wings. As a hunter of creatures equaling or exceeding her size and weight, she needed vigorous strength. Her shiny black body was half-circled by yellow bands, and she seemed remote, in the evolutionary process, from the fragile solitary wasp. 11

Elsewhere, communal wasps were working. The sun flickered over the iridescent coat colors of the purple mud daubers, making them blue one instant, then green or purple. Potter wasps—shiny black and yellow, delicate and industrious—gathered clay to make small spherical nests. Paper wasps, with yellow stripes over green abdomens and red spots decorating their sides, were masticating wood fiber to make a nest. The puzzle of the 12 wasps was why some collected into communities and fed their youngsters on nectar while others were solitary and fed their larvae on red meat.

The robber fly was still feeding on the beetle when a hunting wasp 13 hummed through the whispering green of oak and hickory. She had seen the shiny brown face mask of a large caterpillar bobbing up and down as he chewed on a leaf, his body invisible against it. The wasp alighted on the leaf, and the caterpillar tautened into a ball and dropped. Down he fell, glancing from leaf to leaf and then hitting a branch and ricochetting into the apparent safety of thick grass.

The wasp sank slowly after him. She found his rolled-up body wedged 14 between two grass stems, and with deliberation, she stung him twice. The stings might kill him or they might merely paralyze; it did not matter. His meat would still be edible when the wasp's egg hatched inside his body later. She gripped him now and pulled him free from the grass. In a moment she was in the air with him, headed for her subterranean burrow and the laying of one egg.

A yellow-banded wasp rose slowly and awkwardly from the pond green- 15 ery. She had been severely bitten and partially blinded by the dragonfly, but she had killed him at last, driving her sting through a chink in the cluster of his six legs. The poison paralyzed the dragonfly's simple organs and stopped his long tubular heart. The wasp resumed her interrupted journey.

Questions

1. What kind of hunt does Russell describe? Who are the participants? Who are the hunters and who are the hunted?

2. At what point in this description does the actual report of events begin?

3. What do you learn about the author and his attitudes toward his subject? What is the tone of this essay? What does the tone tell you about Russell's purpose?

4. The hunt Russell describes often ends in death. What does his attitude toward these deaths seem to be? How do you account for statements like "As long as a dragonfly patrolled the pond, no insect was safe" (paragraph 8) and "The death of the towhees in the southern forest was an insignificant incident in one hunting day" (paragraph 2)?

5. What does Russell's report tell you about the "peaceful façade" of the pond?

6. In writing this report, Russell probably did not rely totally on his memory. If you were assigned the task of reporting a pond observation, what kind of record might you keep?

Discussion

Try to imagine how Russell's notes might have looked. Like many reports, "The Hunt" probably began as notes recording the author's observations. He would have had jottings on the activities of the robber fly, the dragonflies, and the wasps. Probably watching with binoculars, he would even have observed in close detail the insects' appearances. Though he relies mostly on his vision, he paid attention to sounds too, such as the song of the yellowthroat and the calls of the crows. Notes are often not recorded in the same order as the report that utilizes them, and Russell's notes may not have been in the order of events reported here; he probably saw the dragonflies overhead while watching the robber flies and heard the yellowthroat and the crows throughout his observation.

You probably find, too, that after you have made notes you order them. After you do some reading for a report, you probably shuffle your notes into an order that seems appropriate for your report. Because of this need to rearrange notes, note takers often use note cards or small notepads for recording specific observations, descriptions, insights, summaries, and so on.

Thesis and Development

In writing his report, Russell may have rearranged some of the details in his notes, selected some details and omitted others, and added information that would connect this description with the previous chapter of his book and give significance to his observations. Was the robber fly the first hunter he observed? It seems so, although he may have been observing all three hunter groups—robber flies, dragonflies, and wasps—at once. Since he can't report them all at once, he needs to begin somewhere. Connecting the dragonflies and the wasps is easy, because they hunt and attack each other. Beginning with the robber fly, Russell gives the impression of simultaneity by noting the dragonfly hovering over the feeding robber fly, then (paragraph 13) reporting that the robber fly is "still feeding on the beetle."

The first three paragraphs of "The Hunt" have a purpose other than to report and are probably not drawn from Russell's record, at least not in the form that is here. Paragraph 1 provides an overview of the essay, something that can't easily be accomplished while note taking is in progress. In this paragraph Russell also states his *thesis,* that life on the pond depends on cunning and vigor. This is his insight into the events he observed; it may have occurred to him only after he had completed his observations or perhaps at some time while he was observing. But it would not have been at the beginning of his notes. The second sentence of this paragraph amplifies the first by defining the scope of the hunt, from the upper air to the bottom of the pond.

Paragraph 3 also defines the scope and setting, before the writer narrows down to the insect hunters. Paragraph 2 serves a double purpose: to link this chapter to the previous one, in which Russell reports that the towhees had been killed, and to emphasize again that success in the hunt depends on a highly developed skill.

Paragraph 4 begins the *chronological* report of what actually happens at the pond. Robber flies catch a bumblebee and a beetle, dragonflies "as big as small birds" catch any insect that strikes their fancy, including other dragonflies, and a wasp stings a caterpillar while another finally overcomes an attacking dragonfly. The report ends when the victorious wasp resumes "her interrupted journey." The entire report covers only minutes of an observation.

EXERCISE

Be a close observer. Place yourself where you can record observations of people, animals, insects, or something else that has actions you can record, such as airplanes, taxis, and bicycles. Watch and listen, noting what happens. Record only your observations; don't interpret actions or impute motives.

Writing

Using your notes from the preceding exercise, revise them as a report. Read over your record and decide on an overall controlling idea that can serve as your thesis sentence. Like Russell, you may need to define the scope of your report. You may find it necessary to rearrange the details of your record, to delete some that seem irrelevant to your thesis, and to add some from your memory so that the connections between the details you report are clear to readers. You will probably find that a chronological or spatial arrangement works best.

Use coherence devices to help your reader fit events together. Note how Russell in paragraph 6 leads into his description of the actions of the second robber fly: "Meanwhile, another robber fly arrived." To introduce his report of the dragonflies, he shifts from the pondside to the sounds of the birds, then notes the hovering dragonfly. Later he links his report on the wasps back to his beginning by observing the wasp humming over the feeding robber fly.

Be descriptive. Use sight imagery so that your readers can see what you have seen. And use your other senses as appropriate: hearing, touch, smell, and taste. Use adjectives that evoke images and actions; Russell, for example, uses *"feeding* fly," *"stingless* dragonfly," *"shiny black* body," *"armor-sheathed* victims," *"spherical* nests." Like Russell, use verbs that denote specific actions: "the impact *flung* the bee," "a sting *jabbed* into his back," "a yellowthroat *jerked out* his song," "the two creatures *tumbled*," "the sun *flickered*." Use concrete nouns, too: "unsheathed a *cutter* from her *mouth*," "blossoming *chokecherries*," "whispering *green* of *oak* and *hickory*," "pond *greenery*."

Describing a Natural Phenomenon

People often describe phenomena of nature. Whether you live in Minnesota or Florida, you like to hear how deep the snow was in International

Falls—or how cold it was in January. Hurricanes in Florida or elsewhere are reported throughout the country. Earthquakes and mudslides in California make national news, along with fires in Wyoming, unremitting heat and humidity in the nation's midsection, floods on the Mississippi and other rivers, predicted melting of the polar ice caps and flooding of coastal cities, threats to the ultraviolet-screening capacity of ozone, and so on. Wherever we live, nature is part of us, part of our world; we want to read about it, and we often write about it.

An example of this kind of writing follows, in which Rachel L. Carson describes the legendary Sargasso Sea, a nearly stagnant part of the Atlantic Ocean. Reports like this one tell *what something is like,* as opposed to *what happened.* In reporting what something is like you generally use a *spatial* arrangement. This arrangement may be ordered, such as vertical or horizontal movement, or it may seem random—each part described as the writer encounters it. *Ordered* spatial arrangement might be exemplified by describing a person from head to toe or a garden from where you enter it to where you leave it. You might use a *random* spatial arrangement for describing a woods or a beach as each part registers in your consciousness.

Reports of what something is like are usually written with present tense verbs, as in the following sentences:

> The beach only *seems* barren in the winter.
> The river *rises* each year in proportion to the rains in the basin it drains.
> Even though a hurricane *gives* plenty of warning of its arrival, it always *seems* to strike with an unexpected force.

These examples also demonstrate that when you describe what something is like, you do not report a specific incident; rather, you report the way something usually happens or acts or is.

Reading

In "The Sargasso Sea," noted nature writer Rachel L. Carson reports what the Sargasso is like: why it is such a weedy jungle in the middle of the Atlantic Ocean, what kinds of sea creatures live there, what it is, and what it is not. As you read, note how she arranges her description and how she writes in the present: what was true in 1951, when she wrote, is true today; the Sargasso Sea is still there, along with its weeds and their inhabitants.

The Sargasso Sea
Rachel L. Carson

The central oceanic regions, bounded by the currents that sweep   1
around the ocean basins, are in general the deserts of the sea. There are few

birds and few surface-feeding fishes, and indeed there is little surface plankton to attract them. The life of these regions is largely confined to deep water. The Sargasso Sea is an exception, not matched in the anti-cyclonic centers of other ocean basins. It is so different from any other place on earth that it may well be considered a definite geographic region. A line drawn from the mouth of Chesapeake Bay to Gibraltar would skirt its northern border; another from Haiti to Dakar would mark its southern boundary. It lies all about Bermuda and extends more than halfway across the Atlantic, its entire area being roughly as large as the United States. The Sargasso, with all its legendary terrors for sailing ships, is a creation of the great currents of the North Atlantic that encircle it and bring into it the millions of tons of floating sargassum weed from which the place derives its name, and all the weird assemblage of animals that live in the weed.

The Sargasso is a place forgotten by the winds, deserted by the strong flow of waters that girdle it as with a river. Under the seldom-clouded skies, its waters grow warm and heavy with salt. Separated widely from coastal rivers and from polar ice, there is no inflow of fresh water to dilute its saltiness; the only influx is of saline water from the adjacent currents, especially from the Gulf Stream or North Atlantic Current as it crosses from America to Europe. And with the little, inflowing streams of surface water come the plants and animals that for months or years have drifted in the Gulf Stream.   2

The sargassum weed is a brown alga that lives attached to rocks along the coasts of the West Indies and Florida. Many of the plants are torn away by storms, especially during the hurricane season. They are picked up by the Gulf Stream and are drifted northward. With the weeds go, as involuntary passengers, many small fishes, crabs, shrimps, and innumerable larvae of assorted species of marine creatures, whose home had been the coastal banks of sargassum weed.   3

Curious things happen to the animals that have ridden on the sargassum weed into a new home. Once they lived on a rocky shore, a few feet or a few fathoms below the surface, but never far above a rocky bottom. They knew the rhythmic movements of waves and tides. They could leave the shelter of the weeds at will and creep or swim about over the bottom in search of food. Now, in the middle of the ocean, they are in a new world. The bottom lies two or three miles below them. Those who are poor swimmers must cling to the weed, which now represents a life raft, supporting them above the abyss. Over the ages since their ancestors came here, some species have developed special organs of attachment, either for themselves or for their eggs, so that they may not sink into the cold, dark water far below. The flying fish make nests of the weed to contain their eggs, which bear an amazing resemblance to the sargassum floats or "berries."   4

Indeed, many of the little marine beasts of the weedy jungle seem to be playing an elaborate game of disguise in which each is camouflaged to hide   5 it from the others. The Sargasso sea slug—a snail without a shell—has a soft, shapeless brown body spotted with dark-edged circles and fringed with flaps and folds of skin, so that as it creeps over the weed in search of prey it can scarcely be distinguished from the vegetation. One of the fiercest carnivores of the place, the sargassum fish Pterophryne, has copied with utmost fidelity the branching fronds of the weed, its golden berries, its rich brown color, and even the white dots of encrusting worm tubes. All these elaborate bits of mimicry are indications of the fierce internecine wars of the Sargasso jungles, which go on without quarter and without mercy for the weak or the unwary.

In the science of the sea there has been a long-standing controversy　6 about the origin of the drifting weeds of the Sargasso Sea. Some have held that the supply is maintained by weeds recently torn away from coastal beds; others say that rather limited sargassum fields of the West Indies and Florida cannot possibly supply the immense area of the Sargasso. They believe that we find here a self-perpetuating community of plants that have become adapted to life in the open sea, needing no roots or hold-fasts for attachment, and able to propagate vegetatively. Probably there is truth in both ideas. New plants do come in each year in small numbers, and now cover an immense area because of their very long life once they have reached this quiet central region of the Atlantic.

It takes about half a year for the plants torn from West Indian shores to　7 reach the northern border of the Sargasso, perhaps several years for them to be carried into the inner parts of this area. Meanwhile, some have been swept onto the shores of North America by storms, others have been killed by cold during the passage from offshore New England across the Atlantic, where the Gulf Stream comes into contact with waters from the Arctic. For the plants that reach the calm of the Sargasso, there is virtual immortality. A. E. Parr of the American Museum [of Natural History] has recently suggested that the individual plants may live, some for decades, others for centuries, according to their species. It might well be that some of the very weeds you would see if you visited the place today were seen by Columbus and his men. Here, in the heart of the Atlantic, the weed drifts endlessly, growing, reproducing vegetatively by a process of fragmentation. Apparently almost the only plants that die are the ones that drift into unfavorable conditions around the edges of the Sargasso or are picked up by outward-moving currents.

Such losses are balanced, or possibly a little more than balanced, by the　8 annual addition of weeds from distant coasts. It must have taken eons of time to accumulate the present enormous quantities of weed, which Parr estimates as about 10 million tons. But this, of course, is distributed over so large an area that most of the Sargasso is open water. The dense fields of weeds waiting to entrap a vessel never existed except in the imaginations of sailors, and the gloomy hulks of vessels doomed to endless drifting in the clinging weed are only the ghosts of things that never were.

Questions

1. What does Carson say the legendary Sargasso Sea is like? How does she compare the real sea to the legendary one?

2. What are the causes of this weedy sea?

3. Name some of the "curious things" that happen to the sea creatures inhabiting the sargassum weeds.

4. Carson attributes the natural adaptations of the Sargasso's inhabitants to the "fierce internecine wars" that take place in the weedy jungle. Compare these adaptations of hunters and hunted with those of the creatures Russell describes in "The Hunt."

5. In describing the Sargasso, Carson uses several methods of development. Find instances, perhaps more than one of each, of these methods: classification, contrast, cause and effect, definition, and process analysis. If necessary, refer to "Methods of Developing and Arranging Paragraphs and Essays" in Chapter 4.

6. Does Carson state her thesis? Phrase her controlling idea in your own words.

7. How would the effects of Carson's essay be changed if she had used past tense verbs to describe the Sargasso: *were* instead of *are, lay* instead of *lie,* and so on?

Discussion

Carson arranges her descriptive report spatially. In paragraph 1 she places the Sargasso Sea in the broader expanse of the Atlantic Ocean, moving inward to the Sargasso itself. Still progressing from larger to smaller, in paragraph 3 she describes the sargassum weed and then in paragraphs 4 and 5 the inhabitants of the weed. In the final paragraphs she moves back to the weeds, broadening out to account for them as part of the whole Atlantic. If you were not conscious of this orderly progression, you can credit Carson's skill in essay development and coherence.

Coherence

Carson clarifies the scope of her essay in the final sentence of paragraph 1: It's the Sargasso Sea, the sargassum weed, and "the weird assemblage of animals that live in the weed." Is this the sentence you identified as her *thesis*? It may well be so regarded, since the purpose of this essay is to report what this natural phenomenon is like. Because Carson has clearly announced the scope of her essay, it is no surprise when in the next paragraph she launches into a description of the sea and its origins, nor when she progresses to discussing the weeds and then the animals. But her *coherence* doesn't rely only on her announcement of scope; she also links each new development to that announcement by *repetition of key words,* together with their synonyms, related words, and pronouns referring to them.

Notice the opening sentences of paragraphs 2, 3, and 4. Each one names the subject of its paragraph—"The Sargasso," "The sargassum weed," and "the animals" that inhabit the weed. Each mention of these key words links new paragraphs to the scope, or thesis, sentence and therefore to the essay as a whole. The opening sentences of other paragraphs also relate to the essay as a whole by means of this kind of repetition. Paragraph 5 refers to "the little marine beasts," paragraph 6 to "the drifting weeds," paragraph 7 to "the plants," and the final paragraph to "weeds."

Repetition achieves coherence within paragraphs as well. To see how the repetition of key words and related words connects sentences within a paragraph, take a closer look at paragraph 3. The key term here is *sargassum weed*. After mention of this term in the first sentence, thus linking the paragraph to the thesis, a synonym, *alga* (a Latin word meaning "seaweed," its plural being the more familiar *algae*), is introduced. Sentence 2 uses a second synonym, *plants;* sentence 3 a pronoun, *they;* and sentence 4 a part of the original term, *weeds*. Study other paragraphs for similar uses of key word repetition to achieve coherence.

EXERCISE

Write a paragraph that patterns the style of paragraph 2 in "The Sargasso Sea."
Begin "The _____ is a place _____ ," writing about a place you know in
sentences similar to those Carson uses. When you have finished, compare your
paragraph with those of your classmates and discuss the thinking you did while
composing—how much you concentrated on your subject and how much on Carson's
sentence patterns.

Writing

Write an essay that describes a place, perhaps the same one you described in the preceding exercise, for the purpose of reporting to readers what this place is like. In prewriting, try using the classical probes (see Chapter 3). Because they are related to methods of development, the probes may help you think of ways of classifying components of your subject, analyzing causes and effects, defining or identifying your subject, contrasting different aspects of it, or showing how the subject has developed into what it is now. Decide on the most appropriate manner of arranging your description—probably some spatial way. After drafting, check your methods of arrangement and development and the tense of your verbs. See whether your paragraphs are coherent: are they all connected to a sentence that states the scope of your essay, and are the sentences within paragraphs related to one another?

Writing a Book Report

You have probably written book reports before, and you will probably write them again. They're a common kind of school report because assigning them achieves several purposes; gets you to read the book (or enough of it to report on), gets you to think about the subject of the book, and gets you to write an essay. Under the best of circumstances, book reports also inform readers about the content of the book and interest them in reading the book carefully.

Book reports, or reviews as they are sometimes called, do mainly two things: (1) *report* on the content and/or style of the book, and (2) *respond* to the content and/or style. Doing either requires that you read the book.

The main purpose of a book report is to report on the content and/or style of the book. You don't need to give a plot summary of the book or try to cover every chapter. However, you do need to show an understanding of the entire book. You might give background on the occasion for the book, such as new discoveries in its subject area. You might tell something about the author's credentials for writing on the subject. You need to give an overall view of the book, including the author's main point and emphasis. You ought to tell readers what interested you most in the book.

Responding to the reading may be more difficult. To aid you in thinking about what you have read, use the Questions for Active Reading (page 6) and the Questions about Audience for Reading (page 25). When you ask questions such as "What is the writer's purpose in writing?" and "What does the writer do to stimulate my interest?" you will generate thoughts about the book. Continued use of questions like these is likely to produce the beginnings of a response, which will probably continue to develop as you write. (Summary and response are discussed in greater detail in Chapter 15.)

Reading

The book report that follows was written by a student in response to a book he read for his own enjoyment. The report consists mainly of information that interested him and that he thought might be of interest to other readers. Does Witzman give reasons for his favorable response?

Science Fact More Exciting Than Science Fiction

Paul Witzman

In 1985, Bob Ballard of Woods Hole Oceanographic Institute amazed   1
the world with his announcement that he'd found the *RMS Titanic*, lost for more than seventy-three years. He substantiated his claim by showing pictures taken by an underwater robot. The wrecked ship was seen resting

on the side of a mountain two and a half miles below the surface of the Atlantic Ocean. The next year Ballard, working with a group of French and American scientists, visited the *Titanic's* grave in a special deep sea diving submarine. *Her Name, Titanic* (New York: McGraw, 1988) is an exciting book written by Charles Pellegrino, one of the scientists who worked on the *Titanic* project. This book skillfully helps the reader understand why the *Titanic's* sinking in 1912 was so tragic, why the event is still significant today, and the incredible technology and effort it took to find and visit her.

Pellegrino provides his readers with a wealth of background information including a short biography of Bob Ballard, the expedition's leader, and how Pellegrino himself became involved in and affected by this project. Pellegrino is a scientist with many interests, the most compelling of which is space exploration and the search for alien life forms. It is his theory that there are oceans inside certain icy moons, especially Jupiter's moon Europa, and that life exists there. To develop a vehicle that could explore such an ocean he enlisted the help of Ballard, who had successfully designed machines that are able to probe the farthest depths of the Earth's oceans. That is when Ballard infected Pellegrino with his desire to find the *Titanic*. 2

The book transports the reader to April 15, 1912, and gives a feeling of what it must have been like to be aboard the sinking ship—that feeling of total helplessness and regret that those who were aware of the ship's plight experienced. The *Titanic* had been warned by other ships at least six times that an ice field lurked in her path, yet she still proceeded at full speed. Her lookouts on the top deck were not provided with binoculars, making it impossible for them to spot hazards with enough warning to alter the huge liner's course. Once the iceberg, a glowing mountain of ice, was discovered to be directly in the *Titanic's* path, the captain steered the ship as far to the left as possible. The captain's reaction seemed wise at the time, but the 950-foot-long liner could only turn enough to prevent a direct impact, allowing the starboard side of the ship to scrape the iceberg. 3

The impact was hardly felt by most of the passengers. It wasn't known that the ship had even suffered any damage until Thomas Andrews, the ship's designer, and the captain toured the lower decks a half hour later. There they found a 300-foot-long series of leaks in the *Titanic's* inch-thick steel-plated hull through which hundreds of gallons of water leaked each minute. As soon as Andrews surveyed the damage he knew that his unsinkable liner was going to sink and that, because the ship hadn't been fitted with enough lifeboats to save even half of her passengers and crew, there was going to be a great loss of life. What Andrews never knew is that a ship capable of rescuing everyone aboard the *Titanic* was only a few miles from her side and for some reason, believed by many to be fear of striking the same iceberg that doomed the *Titanic*, the *California* never responded to the distress flares and wireless SOS's that lasted almost two hours. 4

Most of the people aboard the sinking ship did not realize or believe that the *Titanic* was sinking. They had so much faith in the claims that the 5 ship was unsinkable that they refused to board the few available lifeboats. One survivor recalled that as the bow of the ship sank deeper and deeper in the dark water many of the cabins dipped below the water level long before they became flooded. She remembers looking over the side of her lifeboat and seeing a man peering out of a porthole that was five feet below the water level and that the light from his cabin cast an eerie greenish glow in the water.

Probably one of the least known and most troubling facts about this   6
disaster is that the third-class passengers, most of whom were Irish immigrants bound for a new life in America, and the entire Italian kitchen staff were locked in their cabins on the lower decks and were never allowed to go up to the boat decks where there was some hope of survival. Consequently, most of these people had drowned in their cabins up to an hour before the first-class passengers were aware that the *Titanic* was sinking. Within two hours of striking the iceberg, she sank to the ocean floor, where she would rest in total darkness undisturbed until 1985.

Pellegrino tells about the space-age equipment employed in the search   7
for the ship, which lasted from the beginning of June until September 1, when at one o'clock in the morning the *Titanic* was found. The underwater robot Argo, equipped with several 200,000 ASA cameras, virtually able to "see" in total darkness, sent the first pictures of the ship resting on the ocean floor. The first reaction of the ecstatic scientists was uncontrollable excitement and amazement at the photographs. This feeling, however, was soon replaced with a sense of mourning that affected the entire French and American crew aboard the *Knorr*. It was an emotion that no one had expected while on this adventure of a lifetime. Seeing the empty lifeboat davits that had last been seen the night fifteen hundred people perished in the cold and lonely Atlantic made time come unstuck for the explorers. For several days after their discovery many of the scientists couldn't eat or sleep as they pondered the terrible tragedy that had occurred in that place seventy-three years earlier. Ballard likened the mourning, which for him lasted nearly a year, to a nervous breakdown.

As a reader, one is able to experience somewhat the same mourning the   8
scientists did in 1985. Pellegrino tells of the *Titanic*'s sinking, using dramatic accounts given by survivors who are still alive today; of the exploration in 1985 and 1986; and of the wealth of technical information recently compiled that explains how the *Titanic* actually sank. These three different stories are perfectly fused into one, allowing the reader to know what the scientists knew and to experience what they experienced.

Questions

1. Book reports are sometimes written to persuade people to read the book. Does Witzman tell you enough about *Her Name, Titanic* to interest you in reading it? Explain your answer, telling what interests you or why you are not interested.

2. This book report is more *report* than *response*. What is Witzman's response to the book?

Discussion

Witzman reports here on a book he enjoyed reading. This is the type of report you might make orally, in conversation with a friend: "I just read a good book; it's all about the sinking and rediscovery of the *Titanic*." Then if you're lucky your friend will say, "Oh? Tell me about it." And you can relate what really interested you about the book.

Your written report, of course, is more formal. First, it attracts an interested reader with an attention-getting title. Then an introduction gives enough details to keep the reader going. It names the book and its author and includes, in parentheses, other publishing information that may be necessary for the reader to locate the book in a bookstore. The introduction also gives a brief overview of the book, perhaps a little background on the author, and an assessment of the book. Then the body of the report recounts the aspects of the book that interested you the most and supports your assessment of the book.

In concluding, your written book report makes sure the reader knows how you feel about the book. In conversation you might say, "It was a really great book. You ought to read it." In writing, however, you would be more formal, as Witzman is: "These three different stories are perfectly fused into one, allowing the reader to know what the scientists knew and to experience what they experienced."

EXERCISE

Select a book that you might be able to report on and explore your reactions to it by asking the Questions for Active Reading on page 6 and the Questions about Audience for Reading on page 25.

Writing

Write a report on a book you have read recently—one you've read either for school or for pleasure, possibly the one you explored in the preceding exercise. Report on what interests you about the book, assuming that a reader will be interested too. Include enough details so that a reader will get the flavor of the book and a sense of its treatment of the subject matter.

Somewhere in your first paragraph, name the author and the title of the book and, in parentheses, its city of publication, the name of the publisher, and the date of the publication.

ADDITIONAL READINGS FOR DISCUSSION

Reading

"The Patagonian Wind" is excerpted from George Gaylord Simpson's book *Attending Marvels,* published in 1934 as a report of Simpson's first scientific expedition to the Argentine territory of Patagonia. A paleontologist of note, Simpson went to South America looking for fossils but also found a largely undeveloped land and a revolution in progress. He writes here about the famous Patagonian wind—chillingly cold and so strong it carries rocks large enough to break plate-glass windows on impact. What details convince you that Simpson's description is accurate?

The Patagonian Wind

George Gaylord Simpson

Established in this home from home, I went out into the wind to   1
explore the town. The terrible Patagonian wind! It is the constant background of any Patagonian memories. It is the most fundamental fact of life there. Only the day before I arrived, it had shown its teeth in a particularly impressive way.

An airline had been established, running almost the whole length of   2
Patagonia and linking it with the northern Argentine. Savage places are now almost everywhere marked by such incongruities, the impingement of some modern invention on a background still primitive. In such places civilization no longer develops sanely and harmoniously. It breaks out in spots like a disease. People who never saw a book and whose ideas of sanitation would offend a chimpanzee may possess phonographs and sewing machines. Places inaccessible by any road may be quickly reached by plane. The heart of Patagonia is within one day of high civilization by the airline, when it runs.

The day before I landed, the plane had taken off for Deseado, the next   3
town of importance to the south. Hoping to beat the wind, which usually gains vigor with the sun, the plane took off before dawn, but on this day the wind had anticipated and early reached its full force. The pilot was hardly well in the air before he realized that he could never make his destination. He worked back to the landing field, but the gale had now reached such force that attempting to land meant almost certain death or injury for himself and his passengers. He had no choice but to try for Deseado, trusting to luck to find some lull in the wind there, but as he headed the plane into the wind again he found with horror that he could make no headway against it.

Then began a duel which lasted for nearly four hours. The powerful 4
motor and the wind were almost evenly matched. Sometimes the plane
would gain a few hundred yards, then the savage wind from the distant
cordillera would retaliate and drive the plane out over the open sea. For
most of the time the two were so evenly balanced that the plane simply hung
as if suspended in space. All this time it was never quite out of sight from the
field from which it had risen.

When a plane lands at these Patagonian fields, a detachment of soldiers 5
hooks ropes to metal rings in the wings the instant it touches ground and
hangs on to these to keep the plane from blowing away. While the plane was
fighting to get back over the field, watchers from the ground had sent
hurriedly for men to try to hold it, if it could land at all. His gasoline supply
nearly exhausted, the pilot made a landing with superb skill, the ropes were
hooked on, and the passengers safely removed. Hardly were they out of the
plane, when a strong gust whipped it over and the propeller, left whirling
to help hold the ship, killed one soldier and horribly mangled another.

That was not a very unusual gale, or a brief storm. The wind frequently 6
blows so for days at a time. Its brutal force and nerve-destroying continuity
almost pass belief. They have given rise to many tall tales and popular
legends which gild the lily and exaggerate the immense. It is probably not
true that a man once inadvertently fired a rifle straight into the wind and
was killed by his own bullet as it was blown back. It is somewhat more
plausible, but still not well authenticated, that a Patagonian chicken was
accidentally taken by the breeze from the rear and completely plucked so
that its owner had to knit it a sweater. But it is true, by the witness of my own
eyes, that the wind blows stones large enough to break plate glass, that wild
geese trying to fly into it are often rapidly carried backward, and that it is
sometimes impossible for a man to progress against it except on his hands
and knees, clutching bushes for anchorage.

So on my first afternoon in this unpromising land I fought my way 7
miserably through the dust-colored streets. . . .

My lads assure me that I have not yet seen it at its worst, but already I 8
can see that the Patagonian wind deserves its reputation.

Questions

1. Considering that this essay was written almost sixty years ago and what Simpson
   says about the airplanes in use then, what kind of craft do you think he is
   describing? How might a plane today react to the Patagonian wind?

2. Simpson's report of the Patagonian wind is similar to Rachel L. Carson's essay
   on the Sargasso Sea in that they both describe a natural phenomenon. But the
   essays are different too. Simpson, for example, writes from his own experience
   and the experience of people he has talked to, whereas Carson writes as an
   objective third-person observer. Read Carson's essay and note other differences
   between it and Simpson's.

3. Aside from its combat with airplanes, what do you learn about the Patagonian wind from reading Simpson's essay? List some details.

4. In Chapter 9, Joan Didion describes the Santa Ana wind in California. Read her essay (page 231) and compare it with Simpson's. What similarities and differences do you see in the winds and in the ways the two writers describe them?

5. Simpson's story seems fantastic, yet it is a true account of the struggle between wind and aircraft. Using his story as inspiration, write a paragraph that is fantastic but *not* true, an exaggeration. Begin "The wind was so strong that. . . ."

Reading

In *Revolution in Time*, David S. Landes discusses the relationship between clocks and the making of the world. In this excerpt, he reports on the competition between expensive Swiss-made jeweled watches and the "cheap time" Timex watches, as well as the effects this "revolution in time" had on attitudes toward timepieces. What influence might the development of Timex watches have had on your attitudes?

The Timex Watch
David S. Landes

Remember the law of nemesis? Success invites emulation and challenge. The extraordinary Swiss domination of the watch manufacture had been a provocation to potential competitors from the eighteenth century on. These now mounted a new assault, more serious than any before. . . .   1

The answer was the Timex, a superior *clock-watch*—that is, an unjeweled, clock-type watch with pin-lever escapement. Instead of ordinary steel, Lehmkuhl's engineers used armalloy, a new hard metal developed during the war that gave service as good as that of many stone pallets and bearings; and its designers packaged these movements in plain, clean cases that contrasted sharply with the chunky, manifestly economical lines of the old Ingersolls. The first, simple models sold at $6.95 to $7.95—a lot more than a dollar; but then, the dollar was not what it had been, and the Timex looked the money and more. With success, the company added complications: sweep seconds, shockproofing, waterproofing, calendar indications, self-winding—all the special features that made Swiss watches so attractive to a wide range of clienteles. Rebuffed by the traditional trade channels (jewelers, watchmakers), United States Time sold these watches in every available retail outlet: drugstores, supermarkets, variety stores, airport shops, hardware stores, tobacconists—a quarter of a million points of sale at the peak. They were selling not elegance or prestige but cheap time, and at those prices, people could afford not one watch but two or three or more, with faces and straps to match a variety of outfits.   2

The Timex was not the world's most accurate watch. It kept time within   3
a minute or two a day. But this was accurate enough in a world of radio time
announcements and telephone time. All one had to do was adjust the watch
each morning, and it would give close enough readings for just about any
activity. And Timexes were made for just about any activity. Timex salesmen
convinced retailers of their solidity by slamming them against counters and
dunking them in pails of water. Television advertising featured Timexes
undergoing "torture tests": watches fastened to the hooves of galloping
horses, to a spinning ship's propellor, to a high diver at Acapulco, to the
pontoons of amphibian airplanes. There is even the story of the Timex that
was still going after five months in a man's stomach. The man, a New
Yorker, had swallowed it when confronted by a mugger. Greater love . . .
When the watch was removed, of course, the time was no longer correct, but
the surgeon generously allowed that the watch may have been wrong at the
time it was swallowed.[1]

The makers of conventional jeweled watches were horrified. Was that   4
any way to treat a watch? Neither their egos nor their products could stand
up to that kind of abuse. Timex couldn't have cared less.

Here was value for money. The whole success story rested, in the last   5
analysis, on the productivity of Timex's workers, who were equipped with
the most efficient machines that money could buy and five hundred tool-
makers could design. In this area, Timex represented the culmination of
two centuries of striving: parts were standardized and made interchangeable not only within plants but among plants; and machines were auto-
mated as much as possible so as to reduce the human element to a minimum. As one of the managers put it: "When we put a watch together with
relatively unskilled labor, it must be able to run accurately the minute the
last wheel is put in place. We can't afford the petty troublesome adjustments
that are found in the handmade watch industry."[2]

To achieve this end, Timex simplified its designs to the extreme. Carp-   6
ing watchmakers noted that Timex cases were riveted, and hence could not
be opened for repair. But Timex made no pretense at maintenance or
repair. When a Timex stopped running, the owner simply threw it away
and bought another—if he did not already own a spare or two.

In 1960, eleven years after United States Time brought out the first   7
Timex, it made eight million of them. That was more than the total
output of the Japanese watch industry and more than three times the
entire United State production of jeweled watches. In 1962, one out of
every three watches sold in the United States bore the name Timex. By
that time the company was bringing out higher-priced lines of jeweled
watches, which it sold like the others in such outlets as drugstores and
airport shops, but which it also used to penetrate the jewelry trade.
These watches were cheaper than comparable Swiss pieces; yet they gave
equivalent service, were repairable at the plant, and were sold at conventional markups. Another ten years (1973), and Timex had 45 percent

of the American market, 86 percent of domestic watch production.³ An astonishing performance.

Appetite grows with the eating. All this success led Timex to look around for new worlds to conquer. It moved first into Canada and Britain, then into South Africa, perhaps because its marketing techniques were easier to introduce into English-speaking societies. By the mid-[1960s] it was ready to move into France, setting up a plant at Besançon in the heart of French watch country to produce watches under the brand name "Kelton." Then it was Germany's turn: "They [German watch producers] were trying to sell West German customers on the idea that expensive wristwatches added to the owner's prestige. We set out to fill the vacuum in the lower price watch market and convince buyers that good watches don't have to be expensive."⁴   8

In each of these invasions of "hostile" territory, Timex adjusted its marketing to the special circumstances of local tastes and trade. In Germany, for example, it was crucial to gain the cooperation of jewelers and specialty watch stores, which accounted for more than three quarters of all watch sales in the country. Timex systematically wooed these outlets, offered an array of special inducements, including markups comparable to those on other watch lines and handling commissions on all repair jobs. It also spent millions of marks to test-market its line and prepare the ground for its usual publicity blitz. Within two or three years (1967–68) it was selling over half a million units, and the Swiss were complaining that Timex was compelling them to sell cheaper in the German market in order to hold their place. (A few years later, they were lamenting similar pressures in the East Asian market, where the surging Japanese industry was already pressing them on jeweled watches.) At that point (1972–73), the former United States Time Corporation, renamed in 1969 the Timex Corporation, was making 30 million pieces around the world, had sales of $200 million, and employed some 17,000 people in twenty plants. So potent had been its impact that the Fédération Horogère made a point of studying its operations in minute detail and reported its findings to the Swiss industry in a monograph, "The Timex Formula."   9

This was the good old Swiss response to challenge: study it and learn from it. Nothing that Timex did was radically different from what had gone before; it was just that Timex had pushed modern techniques of production and marketing to their logical conclusion. Timex, in other words, was the extreme expression of older developments. The Swiss felt there was no reason why they should not or could not follow suit.   10

Just about this time, however, the Swiss watch industry found itself confronted by a very different kind of challenge, one that rested on a radical transformation of the technology of time measurement and resulted in the creation of what still looked like a watch but was in reality a new product. This was the quartz revolution, and the Swiss watch industry had far more difficulty coping with it than with the Timex formula.   11

[1]*Boston Globe* May 1, 1981, p. 1.
[2]"A Time Bomb for Watchmakers," *Business Week* Nov. 16, 1963, p. 6.
[3]Wilhelm Hill, "Die Wettbewerbsstellung der schweizerischen Uhrenindustrie," typescript, pp. 5, 92–93.
[4]"How Timex Hit German Markets with Top Quality, Durability—and the Hard Sell," *Business Abroad* Feb. 5, 1968, p. 9.

Questions

1. Reconstruct from Landes's essay the chronology of the marketing of Timex watches, beginning with the year the first one was sold and ending with the "Timex Formula" report. List dates and significant events. What other historic events were occurring at the same time?

2. Why was the Timex watch successful in its marketing? Give several reasons.

3. What changes in attitudes toward timepieces did the Timex bring about? Do you regard these changes as beneficial?

4. This essay reports the development of a product. What other products have changed attitudes and life-styles as a result of their development?

5. Landes opens with a question: "Remember the law of nemesis?" Most people probably don't. The word *nemesis* as it is used today often means "an unbeatable rival" or "an avenger," deriving from the name of the Greek goddess of divine retribution (it was Nemesis who caused the unloving Narcissus to fall in love with himself). The "law" says that our actions come back to haunt us. Explain how one or more of these definitions apply to the Swiss watchmakers.

Reading

Robert F. Kennedy, U.S. attorney general while his brother John F. Kennedy was in the White House, was in an advantageous position for lending advice, as this report of a critical period in American history shows. In October 1962, the United States and the Soviet Union were on the brink of war as a result of the Soviet Union deploying missiles and atomic weapons in Cuba and the United States's response of blockading all shipping to Cuba. In the excerpt here, Robert Kennedy reports the resolution of that confrontation. Do you regard it as an objective report?

Resolving the Cuban Missile Crisis

Robert F. Kennedy

On Tuesday morning, October 16, 1962, shortly after 9 o'clock, President Kennedy called and asked me to come to the White House. He said that we were facing great trouble. Shortly afterward, in his office, he told me that a U-2 [spy plane] had just finished a photographic mission and that the intelligence community had become convinced that Russia was placing missiles and atomic weapons in Cuba.

That was the beginning of the Cuban missile crisis—a confrontation between the two giant atomic nations, the U.S. and the U.S.S.R., which brought the world to the abyss of nuclear destruction and the end of mankind. From that moment in President Kennedy's office until Sunday morning, October 28, that was my life—and for Americans and Russians, for the whole world, it was their life, as well. . . .

At 6 o'clock [on Friday, October 26] the message [from Nikita Khrushchev] came. There was no question that the letter had been written by him personally. It was very long and emotional. But it was not incoherent, and the emotion was directed at the death, destruction, and anarchy that nuclear war would bring to his people and all mankind.

We must not succumb to "petty passions" or to "transient things," he wrote, but should realize that "if indeed war should break out, then it would not be in our power to stop it, for such is the logic of war. I have participated in two wars and know that war ends when it has rolled through cities and villages, everywhere sowing death and destruction." The United States, he went on to say, should not be concerned about the missiles in Cuba; they would never be used to attack the United States and were there for defensive purposes only. "You can be calm in this regard, that we are of sound mind and understand perfectly well that if we attack you, you will respond the same way. But you too will receive the same that you hurl against us. And I think that you also understand this. . . . This indicates that we are normal people, that we correctly understand and correctly evaluate the situation. Consequently, how can we permit the incorrect actions which you ascribe to us? Only lunatics or suicides, who themselves want to perish and to destroy the whole world before they die, could do this."

But he went on: "We want something quite different . . . not to destroy your country . . . but despite our ideological differences, to compete peacefully, not by military means."

There was no purpose, he said, for us to interfere with any of his ships now bound for Cuba, for they contained no weapons. He then explained why they carried no missiles: all the shipments of weapons were already within Cuba. This was the first time he had acknowledged the presence of missiles in Cuba. He made reference to the landing at the Bay of Pigs and the fact that President Kennedy had told him in Vienna that this was a mistake. He valued such frankness, wrote Khrushchev, and he, too, had similar courage, for he had acknowledged "those mistakes which had been committed during the history of our state and I not only acknowledged but sharply condemned them."

The reason he had sent these weapons to Cuba was because the U.S. was interested in overthrowing the Cuban Government, as the U.S. had actively attempted to overthrow the Communist government in the Soviet Union after their revolution. But then he went on: "If assurances were given that the President of the United States would not participate in an attack on Cuba and the blockade lifted, then the question of the removal or the destruction of the missile sites in Cuba would then be an entirely different question. Armaments bring only disasters. When one accumulates them, this damages the economy, and if one puts them to use, then they destroy people on both sides. Consequently, only a madman can believe that armaments are the principal means in the life of society. No, they are an enforced loss of human energy, and what is more are for the destruction of man himself. If people do not show wisdom, then in the final analysis they will come to a clash, like blind moles, and then reciprocal extermination will begin."

I had a slight feeling of optimism as I drove home from the State   8 Department that night. The letter, with all its rhetoric, had the beginnings perhaps of some accommodation, some agreement. The feeling was strengthened by the fact that John Scali, a very able and experienced reporter for ABC, had been approached by an important official of the Soviet Embassy with a proposal that the Soviet Union would remove the missiles under United Nations supervision and inspection, and the U.S. would lift the blockade and give a pledge not to invade Cuba as its part of the understanding.

On Saturday morning, October 27, I received a memorandum from   9 J. Edgar Hoover of the FBI that gave me a feeling of considerable disquiet. He had received information the night before that instructions from Moscow had been received by certain Soviet personnel in New York, ordering them to prepare to destroy all sensitive documents on the basis that the U.S. would probably be taking military action against Cuba or Soviet ships, and this would mean war. I asked myself as I drove to the White House: If the Soviets were anxious to find an answer to the crisis, why were they giving these instructions to Soviet personnel? Did the Khrushchev letter really indicate a solution could be found?

It was therefore with some sense of foreboding that I went to the   10 meeting of our Ex-Comm committee [Executive Committee of the National Security Council]. My concern was justified. A new, this time very formal, letter had arrived from Khrushchev to President Kennedy. It was obviously no longer Mr. Khrushchev personally who was writing, but the Foreign Office of the Kremlin. The letter was quite different from the letter received twelve hours before. "We will remove our missiles from Cuba, you will remove yours from Turkey. . . . The Soviet Union will pledge not to invade or interfere with the internal affairs of Turkey; the U.S. to make the same pledge regarding Cuba."

The Joint Chiefs of Staff joined the meeting and recommended their   11 solution. It had the attraction of being a very simple next step—an air strike on Monday, followed shortly afterward by an invasion. They were not at all surprised that nothing had been achieved by limited force, for this is exactly what they had predicted.

The State Department submitted a draft of a letter for response from   12 President Kennedy to Khrushchev. It answered the arguments made in

Khrushchev's latest letter, maintaining that we could not remove the missiles from Turkey and that no trade could be made.

I disagreed with the content and tenor of the letter. I suggested, and   13
was supported by Ted Sorensen and others, that we ignore the latest Khrushchev letter and respond to his earlier letter's proposal, as refined in the offer made to John Scali. There were arguments back and forth. Everyone was tense; some were already near exhaustion; all were weighted down with concern and worry. President Kennedy was by far the calmest. Finally, when we almost seemed unable to communicate with one another, he suggested with a note of some exasperation that—inasmuch as I felt so strongly that the State Department's various efforts to respond were not satisfactory—Ted Sorensen and I should leave the meeting and go into his office and compose an alternative response, so he could then decide between the two. Forty-five minutes later, we took it to him and to the whole group. He worked on it, refined it, had it typed, and signed it. It accepted Khrushchev's "offer."

I had promised my daughters for a long time that I would take them to   14
the horse show, and early Sunday morning I went to the Washington Armory to watch the horses jump. In any case, there was nothing I could do but wait. Around 10 o'clock, I received a call at the horse show. It was Secretary [of State Dean] Rusk. He said he had just received word from the Russians that they had agreed to withdraw the missiles from Cuba. . . .

President Kennedy understood that the Soviet Union did not want war,   15
and they understood that we wished to avoid armed conflict. During our crisis talks, he kept stressing the fact that we would indeed have war if we placed the Soviet Union in a position she believed would adversely affect her national security, or such public humiliation that she lost the respect of her own people and countries around the globe. The missiles in Cuba, we felt, vitally concerned our national security, but not that of the U.S.S.R.

Even after it was all over, he permitted no crowing that would cause the   16
Soviets to eat crow. He made no statement attempting to take credit for himself or his Administration for what had occurred. He instructed all members of the Ex-Comm and Government that no interview should be given, no statement made, which would claim any kind of victory. He respected Khrushchev for properly determining what was in his own country's interest and what was in the interest of mankind. If it was a triumph, it was a triumph for the next generation and not for any particular government or people.

Questions

1. List Robert Kennedy's activities regarding the Cuban missile crisis, from his call to the White House to the end of the confrontation.

2. In this excerpt from Kennedy's report, we have two letters from Nikita Khrushchev proposing resolutions of the crisis. Characterize the tone and summarize the message of each letter.

3. In resolving the missile crisis, President Kennedy was faced with responding to two radically different letters from Khrushchev and deciding among three very different kinds of advice: (1) attack Cuba (Joint Chiefs of Staff), (2) answer Khrushchev's second letter refusing the conditions (State Department), and (3) ignore the second letter and respond to the first letter, accepting the offer (Robert Kennedy). Project possible outcomes of the crisis for each of the first two suggestions.

4. Kennedy reports events objectively—as both observer and participant. Find instances that strike you as especially objective when you might expect some expression of emotion. Then find instances where he is less than objective— expressing his own opinions or feelings.

5. The Cuban missile crisis occurred in 1962. President Kennedy was assassinated in 1963. Robert Kennedy was killed in 1968 while campaigning for the presidential nomination, and Martin Luther King, Jr., was murdered that year in the midst of his nonviolent civil rights campaign. Compare events of the 1960s with events in the 1980s and 1990s. How might our world be different today if the Kennedys and King had not been killed during their politically active lives?

Reading

Here's a report of a childhood incident experienced by Todd Cota, a student writer. The confrontation is a minor one by global standards, yet it was a critical point in one little boy's growing up. What makes a story like this interesting for a reader?

"Little" Jimmy
Todd Cota

From the early years of my life came many learning experiences that   1
have kept me in line when temptations arose from the depths of trouble.
Trouble is something all children battle, some of it self-inflicted, some not.
Around the age of eight I fell prey to one of those predicaments. Definitely
not one I enjoyed, but one most surely I learned from.

My father, a young man only in his late twenties at the time, tried to   2
teach me to be a good person and under all circumstances to stand up for
myself. There came a time when I felt that was what I was doing, although
my punishment showed otherwise.

"Little" Jimmy, as the grown-ups called him, constantly terrorized all   3
the other kids in the neighborhood. We knew him as "Lard Butt" and
thought that this name described him more appropriately. Maybe to the
adults he was little, but to us he was huge. One day while I was innocently
playing with the other children, Jimmy showed up. We all knew it wasn't to
join in, at least not to play.

What made this day different from the other times he interrupted us   4
was that this day of terrorism was centered on me. He started intimidating
me with name calling and pushing, terrifying me enough that I wet my
pants. All of the other kids broke out in laughter at this, which only made me
feel more insecure. I allowed this abuse to continue until he called me that
one name I think all little boys hate, "Wuss." With all my might I wound up
a punch and gave it to Jimmy right in the gut. It seemed to cause little
damage, though, for he punched me hard enough in the face to knock me
flat on my butt. I think my hitting him was something new, because Jimmy
lost control and continued to kick and hit me until I was huddled on the
ground, crying in complete defeat.

I ran into the house bawling, trying to explain to my father through   5
sobs and short breaths how I was so violently beat up. He remarked, "Don't
you take that from anybody. You go right back out there and give him all
you've got!" Knowing that my skinny figure was no match for Jimmy's bulky
one, I grabbed my bat on my way out. With this new weapon in my hand I
was feeling pretty tough.

I walked right up to Jimmy and threatened to kill him for what he had   6
done. He looked down at me and acted as if he was scared, shaking and
pleading with me not to hurt him. Then he broke out in the sickening fit of
laughter that he always used to ridicule others. His laughter was silenced by
the hollow sound of my wooden bat hitting his skull. Everything went quiet.
All the kids just stared at me in awe and then down at Jimmy, who was lying
on the ground, not moving or making a sound.

Jimmy's father must have been watching the whole conflict, for he was   7
out of his house and running straight at us as quick as his short, fat legs
would carry him. He rushed to the side of his defeated son, who miracu-
lously came to as soon as his father arrived. After tending to Jimmy, he
turned on me with a look of hatred in his eyes. I finally knew where Jimmy
had received his mean streak. That revelation came to me while his father
was shaking me back and forth. At about the moment I thought I was going
to lose what few teeth I had, my dad tore Mr. Swittock off me and punched
him in the mouth. After facing him off and threatening to put him in the
hospital if he ever laid another hand on me, Dad brought me home,
hugging me the whole way.

As soon as the front door closed behind us his attitude changed. When   8
he began that famous sentence all parents use, "This is going to hurt me
more than it's going to hurt you," I knew I was in trouble. He turned me
over his knee and gave me a spanking that felt like one my mother would
give—nothing compared to the beating I had just received from Jimmy. My
father's reason for the punishment was that I had used inappropriate
behavior while defending myself. Before leaving my room, he told me to
think about what I had done. I followed his advice and thought about what
had happened. I smiled then and still smile now whenever I remember the
incident I had with little Jimmy.

Questions

1. Does Cota's confrontation with "Little" Jimmy recall similar incidents in your childhood—either experienced or observed? What do children learn from such experiences?

2. Were you surprised that Cota picked up the baseball bat on his way back out? How might the story have ended if he had not taken the bat with him? With classmates, discuss alternative outcomes.

3. Like Janice Anderson's "Ever Green," " 'Little' Jimmy" presents a selection of details. Cota remembers more about this incident than he reports—what the children were playing when Jimmy came out, for example, or what time of year or day of the week it was. Does his report leave in your mind any questions that might have been answered with additional details?

4. As is common with narratives, paragraph breaks occur here at shifts in the action, time, or place. What shifts in action occur at each break?

Reading

This excerpt from Maya Angelou's *Gather Together in My Name* (1974) reports an experience of racism in the American South in the 1940s, shortly after World War II. Even though what she reports is a specific incident that she experienced, in recounting it Angelou reports much more. What does this story tell you about racism today?

The Principle

Maya Angelou

The days eased themselves around our lives like visitors in a sickroom. 1
I hardly noticed their coming and going. Momma* was as engrossed as she'd allow herself in the wonder of my son. Patting, stroking, she talked to him and never introduced in her deep voice the false humor adults tend to offer babies. He, in turn, surrendered to her. Following her from kitchen to porch to store to the backyard.

Their togetherness came to be expected. The tall and large dark-brown 2
woman (whose movement never seemed to start or stop) was trailed one step by the pudgy little butter-yellow baby lurching, falling, now getting himself up, at moments rocking on bowed legs, then off again in the wave of Momma. I never saw her turn to stop to right him, but she would slow her march and resume when he was steady again.

My pattern had arrived from old exotic Texarkana. And I dressed for 3
the trek downtown, and checked my hair, which was straightened to within

---

*"Momma" was Angelou's grandmother.

an inch of its life and greased to desperation. From within the Store, I felt the threat of the sun but walked out into the road impelled by the missionary zeal.

By the time I reached the pond and Mr. Willie Williams' Dew Drop In, the plastic seemed to have melted to the exact shape of my feet, and sweat had popped through the quarter inch of Arrid in my armpits.   4

Mr. Williams served me a cold drink. "What you trying to do? Fry your brains?"   5

"I'm on my way to the General Merchandise Store. To pick up an order."   6

His smile was a two-line checkerboard of white and gold. "Be careful they don't pick you up. This sun ain't playing."   7

Arrogance and stupidity nudged me out of the little café and back on the white hot clay. I drifted under the shade trees, my face a mask of indifference. The skin of my thighs scudded like wet rubber as I walked deliberately by the alien white houses and on to my destination.   8

In the store the air lay heavily on the blades of two sluggish overhead fans, and a sweet, thick odor enveloped me at the cosmetic counter. Still, I was prepared to wander the aisles until the sun forgave our sins and withdrew its vengeance.   9

A tall saleswoman wearing a clerk's smock confronted me. I tried to make room for her in the narrow corridor. I moved to my left, she moved to her right. I right, she left, we jockeyed a moment's embarrassment and I smiled. Her long face answered with a smile. "You stand still and I'll pass you." It was not a request for cooperation. The hard mountain voice gave me an order.   10

To whom did she think she was speaking? Couldn't she see from my still-white though dusty gloves, my starched clothes, that I wasn't a servant to be ordered around? I had walked nearly three miles under a sun on fire and was neither gasping nor panting, but standing with the cool decorum of a great lady in the tacky, putrid store. She should have considered that.   11

"No, you stand still and I'll pass around you," I commanded.   12

The amazement which leaped upon her face was quickly pushed aside by anger. "What's your name? Where you from?"   13

A repetition of "You stand still and I'll pass around you" was ready on my tongue, when the pale woman who had taken my order slack-butted down the aisle toward us. The familiar face brought back the sympathy I had felt for her and I explained the tall woman into limbo with "Excuse me, here comes my salesgirl."   14

The dark-haired woman turned quickly and saw her colleague approach. She put herself between us, and her voice rasped out in the quiet store: "Who is this?"   15

Her head jerked back to indicate me. "Is this that sassy Ruby Lee you was telling me about?"   16

The clerk lifted her chin and glanced at me, then swirled to the older   17 woman, "Naw, this ain't her." She flipped the pages of a pad in her hand and continued, "This one's Margaret or Marjorie or something like that."

Her head eased up again and she looked across centuries at me. "How do you pronounce your name, gal? Speak up." 18

In that moment I became rootless, nameless, pastless. The two white blurs buoyed before me. 19

"Speak up," she said. "What's your name?" 20

I clenched my reason and forced their faces into focus. "My name"— here I drew myself up through the unrevenged slavery—"Is Miss Johnson. If you have occasion to use my name, which I seriously doubt, I advise you to address me as Miss Johnson. For if I need to allude to your pitiful selves, I shall call you Miss Idiot, Miss Stupid, Miss Fool, or whatever name a luckless fate has dumped upon you." 21

The women became remote even as I watched them. They seemed actually to float away from me down the aisle; and from watching their distant faces, I knew they were having trouble believing in the fact of me. 22

"And where I'm from is no concern of yours, but rather where you're going. I'll slap you into the middle of next week if you even dare to open your mouths again. Now, take that filthy pattern and stick it you-know-where." 23

As I strode between the two women I was sheathed in satisfaction. There had been so few critical times when my actions met my approval that now I congratulated myself. I had got them told and told correctly. I pictured the two women's mouths still open in amazement. The road was less rocky and the sun's strength was weakened by my pleasure. Congratulations were in order. 24

There was no need to stop at Mr. Williams' for a refreshing drink. I was as cool as a fountain inside as I headed home. 25

Momma stood on the porch facing the road. Her arms hung at her sides and she made no motions with her head. Yet something was wrong. Tension had distorted the statue straightness and caused her to lean leftward. I stopped patting myself on the back and ran to the Store. 26

When I reached the one-step porch, I looked up in her face. "Momma, what's the matter?" 27

Worry had forced a deep line down either side of her nostrils past her stiffly held lips. 28

"What's wrong?" 29

"Mr. Coleman's granddaughter, Miss June, just called from the General Merchandise Store." Her voice quaked a little. "She said you was downtown showing out." 30

So that's how they described my triumph to her. I decided to explain and let her share in the glory. I began, "It was the principle of the thing, Momma—" 31

I didn't even see the hand rising, and suddenly it had swung down hard against my cheek. 32

"Here's your principle, young miss." 33

I felt the sting on my skin and the deep ache in my head. The greatest 34
hurt was that she didn't ask to hear my side.

"Momma, it was a principle." My left ear was clogged, but I heard my 35
own voice fuzzily.

The hand didn't surprise me the second time, but the same logic which 36
told me I was right at the white store told me I was no less right in front of
Momma. I couldn't allow myself to duck the blow. The backhand swing
came down on my right cheek.

"Here's your principle." Her voice had a far-away-tunnel sound. 37

"It was a principle, Momma." Tears poured down my burning face, and 38
ache backed up in my throat.

The hand came again and again each time I mumbled "principle," and 39
I found myself in the soft dust in front of the porch. I didn't want to move.
I never wanted to get up again.

She stepped off the porch and caught my arms. "Get up. Stand up, I say." 40

Her voice never allowed disobedience. I stood, and looked at her face. 41
It glistened as if she had just dashed a pan of water over her head.

"You think 'cause you been to California these crazy people won't kill 42
you? You think them lunatic cracker boys won't try to catch you in the road
and violate you? You think because of your all-fired principle some of the
men won't feel like putting their white sheets on and riding over here to stir
up trouble? You do, you're wrong. Ain't nothing to protect you and us
except the good Lord and some miles. I packed you and the baby's things,
and Brother Wilson is coming to drive you to Louisville."

That afternoon I climbed into a horse-drawn wagon, and took my baby 43
from Momma's arms. The baby cried as we pulled away, and Momma and
Uncle Willie stood waving and crying good-bye.

Questions

1. What "principle" was Angelou standing up for? Think of some corresponding
   modern-day principles. What principle motivated Angelou's grandmother to
   send her to Louisville?

2. What were your reactions as you read this narrative? What did you think when
   the narrator defied the woman at the General Merchandise Store? How did you
   feel when her grandmother struck and scolded her?

3. In his "I Have a Dream" speech (page 211), Martin Luther King, Jr., refers to
   a "bad check" to describe the rights of the people once enslaved in the American
   South. What does Angelou's story tell you about residual effects of slavery?

4. What do you learn about the narrator? What does she tell you about herself at
   the time of the incident? Does she tell you how she feels about the incident at the
   time of writing about it, about thirty years later?

5. The underlying theme of this narrative is Angelou's thesis. State it in your own
   words.

CHAPTER 11

To Inform: Writing with Emphasis on the Subject

> *One of the best habits you can develop is that of studying the essays you find both enjoyable and informative.*
> —*Richard Marius*

Information surrounds us. From the bite-sized chunks of television news to the billboards we pass along the road, from public addresses to textbooks, we are bombarded every day with information. Can you think of any writing or speaking situation in which information of some kind is not passed on? You write your parents what your grades are this term, you read in your history textbook about the causes of the Civil War, you hear on television what the issues are in the senatorial elections, you read in the daily newspaper what's happening in Israel or South Africa or Atlanta, Georgia. Even when you just say "Hi, how are you?" you imply information: that you recognize the other person, that you acknowledge a social convention, and that you are inclined to be friendly. Much of what we read is written with informing as at least one of its purposes—on what's happening in politics, on what the newest trends in fashions or automobiles are, on how to judge the relative merits of blenders or television sets, and so on.

As shown in Chapter 10, much informational writing takes the form of *reporting,* relating what *has happened* or what has been done in specific circumstances. And as shown in Chapter 9, it also takes the form of *recording,* telling what *is happening.* The present chapter concentrates on communicating information in a more generalized sense—necessarily including what is happening or has happened but concentrating on what happens in given circumstances, implying that an audience needs to know or would want to know.

You inform when you take on a situation that needs to be changed—for example, inadequate day care for children of working mothers. You inform when you share something that you think others might profit from knowing, such as the effects of anorexia or bulimia on a person's social life, or the academic consequences of sports involvement, or the advantages of air bags in automobiles. You inform also when you define terms that may be unfamiliar to other people, such as *perestroika, endometriosis,* and *Judaism.* In short, you **inform** when your purpose is to communicate knowledge about situations that other people ought (in your opinion) to know about or might want to know about.

Information tells you something *new* and maybe even surprising. Or it gives you a different perspective on something familiar. Most of what you read in this and other textbooks is meant to broaden your knowledge. Newspapers inform by keeping you current with world events, and magazine articles inform you about topics as wide-ranging as the magazines themselves.

If what you read is not new to you, either in the information it conveys or in its perspective, you are likely to lose interest. If, as sometimes happens with student readers, you are required to read or review writing that is not fresh and lively, you need to find ways of overcoming your lack of interest, forcing yourself to read actively, as Chapter 1 advises. It also often happens that writers build new information on old information, and if you give up too soon on the old information you will miss the new.

Whenever your purpose for writing is to inform, you probably have other purposes as well—to persuade, to instruct, to entertain, to praise, or to do something else. If you write, for example, to inform teenage girls about the dangers of anorexia nervosa, you undoubtedly also want to persuade them to get help if they find themselves with the symptoms. If you write to inform fellow college students about the stress that can result from working and attending college at the same time, you may also want to instruct them on ways to relieve that stress. If you write a mainly informative essay on shopping for a good used car, you may adopt a tone that makes the essay entertaining as well.

Sometimes writing that *seems* to be mainly informative is really something else. When you read about the election issues, for example, the writer may be trying to persuade you to vote for a particular candidate, and awareness of that purpose will prompt you to search for bias in the selection of details and choice of words. Critical readers learn to look for underlying purposes in pieces of writing that seem to be informative, asking questions such as these:

- Why does the writer want to inform me about this subject?
- Does informing outweigh other purposes in amount of coverage?
- Do I find any exaggeration or discrepancies in the facts?

Having underlying purposes is not a bad thing; it's a common, often necessary, aspect of writing. When you write to your parents about your grades, your purpose may be in part to inform, but primarily you want to persuade them that you're doing as well in school as they should expect. These are dual purposes that both you and your parents are aware of. From the writer's perspective, you select details and choose words that may not give all the facts but will support your persuasive purpose. From the reader's perspective, your parents recognize that you have another, justifiable reason for wanting to impart the information you choose to include.

Informing is certainly a dominant purpose in writing. You will encounter it in almost all the essays in this book, as well as in most of the reading you do elsewhere. In this chapter you will see essays that inform about serious situations and common experiences, that seek to persuade as well as to inform, and that inform by definition.

Informing about a Serious Situation

One of the most compelling reasons for writing is to inform other people about something the writer regards as a serious situation, with the understanding that informed people act responsibly. Much has been written about AIDS, or acquired immunodeficiency syndrome, for example, and about alcohol and drug abuse. You read something more about the dangers to the earth's environment almost every day. You hear about increasing numbers of homeless people living on the cities' streets, about crime out of control, about growing numbers of teenage pregnancies. There is no lack of serious situations that some people know about and want to inform others about. In your own neighborhood or on your own campus, all you need to do is look around you to see serious situations: conflict over restrictions for drinking alcoholic beverages, inefficient registration procedures, deterioration of city neighborhoods or small-town shopping districts, depression among college students, and so on.

When you write about situations that you regard as serious enough to tell others about, you hope that by informing you can bring about change. Whether you specifically state that position or not, it is very likely an underlying purpose.

Reading

Try to imagine yourself not being able to read. You can't read the words on this page. You can't read the menu in a restaurant. You can't read the newspaper. You can't read the instructions on how to install your new stereo. In fact, when you go to buy your stereo, you can't read the list of comparative features of various stereo systems. Because you can't read, you also can't write. You can't get a college degree, and your job possibilities are limited. Illiteracy is a very serious situation; this is what Jonathan Kozol wants you to understand from reading this opening chapter from his book *Illiterate*

America. In this chapter, he shares his concern about the problem and the need to do something to alleviate it. First read the essay to see what he says. Then be prepared to discuss the devices he uses for getting you involved.

A Third of the Nation Cannot Read These Words

Jonathan Kozol

He is meticulous and well-defended.   1

He gets up in the morning, showers, shaves, and dresses in a dark gray   2
business suit, then goes downstairs and buys a New York *Times* from the
small newsstand on the corner of his street. Folding it neatly, he goes into
the subway and arrives at work at 9:00 A.M.

He places the folded New York *Times* next to the briefcase on his desk   3
and sets to work on graphic illustrations for the advertising copy that is
handed to him by the editor who is his boss.

"Run over this with me. Just make sure I get the gist of what you really   4
want."

The editor, unsuspecting, takes this as a reasonable request. In the   5
process of expanding on his copy, he recites the language of the text: a
language that is instantly imprinted on the illustrator's mind.

At lunch he grabs the folded copy of the New York *Times,* carries it with   6
him to a coffee shop, places it beside his plate, eats a sandwich, drinks a beer,
and soon heads back to work.

At 5:00 P.M., he takes his briefcase and his New York *Times,* waits for the   7
elevator, walks two blocks to catch an uptown bus, stops at a corner store to
buy some groceries, then goes upstairs. He carefully unfolds his New York
Times. He places it with mechanical precision on a pile of several other recent
copies of the New York *Times.* There they will remain until, when two or
three more copies have been added, he will take all but the one most recent
and consign them to the trash that goes into a plastic bag that will be left for
pickup by the truck that comes around during the night and, with a
groaning roar, collects and crushes and compresses all the garbage of the
occupants of this and other residential buildings of New York.

Then he returns upstairs. He opens the refrigerator, snaps the top from   8
a cold can of Miller's beer, and turns on the TV.

Next day, trimly dressed and cleanly shaven, he will buy another New   9
York *Times,* fold it neatly, and proceed to work. He is a rather solitary man.
People in his office view him with respect as someone who is self-contained
and does not choose to join in casual conversation. If somebody should
mention something that is in the news, he will give a dry, sardonic answer
based upon the information he has garnered from TV.

He is protected against the outside world. Someday he will probably be   10
trapped. It has happened before; so he can guess that it will happen again.
Defended for now against humiliation, he is not defended against fear. He
tells me that he has recurrent dreams.

"Somebody says: WHAT DOES THIS MEAN? I stare at the page. A thousand copies of the New York *Times* run past me on a giant screen. Even before I am awake, I start to scream." 11

If it is of any comfort to this man, he should know that he is not alone. Twenty-five million American adults cannot read the poison warnings on a can of pesticide, a letter from their child's teacher, or the front page of a daily paper. An additional 35 million read only at a level which is less than equal to the full survival needs of our society. 12

Together, these 60 million people represent more than one third of the entire adult population. 13

The largest numbers of illiterate adults are white, native-born Americans. In proportion to population, however, the figures are higher for blacks and Hispanics than for whites. Sixteen percent of white adults, 44 percent of blacks, and 56 percent of Hispanic citizens are functional or marginal illiterates. Figures for the younger generation of black adults are increasing. Forty-seven percent of all black seventeen-year-olds are functionally illiterate. That figure is expected to climb to 50 percent by 1990. 14

Fifteen percent of recent graduates of urban high schools read at less than sixth grade level. One million teenage children between twelve and seventeen cannot read above the third grade level. Eighty-five percent of juveniles who come before the courts are functionally illiterate. Half the heads of households classified below the poverty line by federal standards cannot read an eighth grade book. Over one third of mothers who receive support from welfare are functionally illiterate. Of 8 million unemployed adults, 4 to 6 million lack the skills to be retrained for hi-tech jobs. 15

The United States ranks forty-ninth among 158 member nations of the U.N. in its literacy levels. 16

In Prince George's County, Maryland, 30,000 adults cannot read above a fourth grade level. The largest literacy program in this county reaches one hundred people yearly. 17

In Boston, Massachusetts, 40 percent of the adult population is illiterate. The largest organization that provides funds to the literacy programs of the city reaches 700 to 1,000 people. 18

In San Antonio, Texas, 152,000 adults have been documented as illiterate. In a single municipal district of San Antonio, over half the adult population is illiterate in English. Sixty percent of the same population sample is illiterate in Spanish. Three percent of adults in this district are at present being served. 19

In the State of Utah, which ranks number one in the United States in the percent of total budget allocated to the education sector, 200,000 adults lack the basic skills for employment. Less than 5 percent of Utah's population is black or Hispanic. 20

Together, all federal, state, municipal, and private literacy programs in the nation reach a maximum of 4 percent of the illiterate population. The federal government spends $100 million yearly to address the needs of 60 21 million people. The President has asked that this sum be reduced to $50 million. Even at the present level, direct federal allocations represent about $1.65 per year for each illiterate.

In 1982 the Executive Director of the National Advisory Council on   22
Adult Education estimated that the government would need to spend about $5 billion to eradicate or seriously reduce the problem. The commission he served was subsequently dismissed by presidential order.

Fourteen years ago, in his inaugural address as governor of Georgia, a   23
future President of the United States proclaimed his dedication to the crisis of Illiterate America. "Our people are our most precious possession . . . Every adult illiterate . . . is an indictment of us all . . . If Switzerland and Israel and other people can end illiteracy, then so can we. The responsibility is our own and our government's. I will not shirk this responsibility."

Today the number of identified nonreaders is three times greater than   24
the number Jimmy Carter had in mind when he described this challenge and defined it as an obligation that he would not shirk.

On April 26, 1983, pointing to the literacy crisis and to a collapse in   25
standards at the secondary and the college levels, the National Commission on Excellence in Education warned: "Our Nation is at risk."

Questions

1. What does Kozol do to interest you in illiteracy? Does he make you want to do something about illiteracy? Does he convince you that illiteracy is a serious situation?

2. What reason might Kozol have for writing a book about illiteracy and for writing a chapter packed with as many details as the one you just read?

3. What are the implications of the statement that "one million teenage children between twelve and seventeen cannot read above the third grade level" (paragraph 15)?

4. What does it mean to taxpayers that the cost of eradicating illiteracy in this nation could be billions of dollars? Considering the cost and the unlikelihood of those billions being allocated, how might the situation be relieved by other means?

5. Kozol's book was published in 1985. Do you think the problem has improved since then or worsened?

6. What methods of development does Kozol use in this essay?

7. In your own words, state Kozol's thesis.

Discussion

Illiteracy is a serious situation. The facts that Kozol presents are disturbing: One-third of adult Americans do not have survival literacy skills, one million teenagers read below the fourth-grade level, the number of illiterate people in the United States tripled from 1971 to 1985. Perhaps because readers' interests vary, Kozol has filled this first chapter of his book with facts to make certain he touches every one of its readers. Even before he gets to recounting the facts, he attracts reader interest with his short narrative of a day in the life of an unnamed illiterate graphic artist, a man who looks like any other New York office worker and commuter but lives in daily fear that someone will ask him about the words in the newspaper he carries.

Do you know someone who can't read? Try to imagine what it's like to be illiterate. How disabling would this inability be? What would you have to give up if you couldn't read? What would you not know? How would your life be changed? Inability to read can be a serious handicap. Still, if you are like many people, you will admit that you don't do much reading other than what you have to do.

How much *do* you read—beyond your class assignments, that is? Do you read a daily newspaper, subscribe to and read magazines? How often do you read a novel or other book? Perhaps you have never thought that this type of nonreading might be a disability too. Would your life be changed in any way if you did more reading? The answers to these questions are outside the scope of Kozol's essay, yet their implications are nearly as great as those of the issues he addresses. Nonreading is a serious situation.

Implied Thesis

Kozol does not state his *thesis.* He begins with a *narrative,* then devotes the remainder of the essay to relating *facts.* Yet the narrative and all his facts point to the unstated ideas that the rate of illiteracy in the United States is excessive and that something must be done to reduce it. The closest he comes to stating a thesis is in his last paragraph, where as a final warning he quotes from the National Commission on Excellence in Education: "Our Nation is at risk." This statement might be read as *informative,* meaning, "The rate of illiteracy in the United States is excessive" or as *persuasive,* meaning, "As a nation, we must act to correct the alarming rate of illiteracy." An informative thesis stresses information, whereas a persuasive thesis tries to move an audience to new thoughts or actions.

Even though Kozol's essay is openly informative, implying that readers want to know these facts, he clearly has another purpose. Even though he doesn't ever say that readers ought to attack the alarming problem of illiteracy, he clearly implies throughout the essay that this is what he intends.

EXERCISE

Freewrite (see Chapter 3) for ten minutes on one of these topics:

- How your life would be different if you couldn't read and how you would feel about the disability
- A serious situation that demands public attention

Writing

Write about a problem that you regard as serious. Bear in mind that your primary purpose is to inform your readers, even though, like Kozol, you may well have persuasion as a second purpose. Use facts and narrative to make your point; do not tell your audience what to think or what action to take. Your informative thesis sentence, like Kozol's, may be implied, or you may state it explicitly. If you have a persuasive thesis as well, imply it.

The volume of information you have to communicate on your topic may not be as great as Kozol's; however, if you choose a topic that interests you, the chances are good that you can tell your readers something that is new to them. Here are some ideas for topics, but what you choose to write about may not be included:

- An AIDS epidemic
- Television news "shows"
- Drunk driving
- Drug addiction
- Effects of daytime "soaps" on children

These are all broad topics, as is Kozol's, but like Kozol you can select facts that are likely to achieve your purpose of informing your audience.

Informing Based on Common Experience

People have many experiences in common. Worldwide, people know the feel and taste of water. Throughout the ages, sunlight has felt the same as it does today, the moon has looked the same, people have known the same kind of anger, love, and hate that we today know. Because we're human, we have common experiences. Yet how much do we actually know about those experiences—about water and the sun and the moon, even about our own emotions? We could probably learn something about all of them.

While much informative writing is intended to tell readers something outside their experience—something they don't know—a great deal of information tells readers something new about a subject they are already familiar with. You know the stars, for example; they're a familiar part of your world. Yet an essay on their components, relative ages, and so on would likely tell you something new. Pizza may be one of your favorite foods, but do you know its origins? Again, familiar subject, new information.

Sometimes, to write about new information on familiar subjects some special reading is necessary. For instance, if you were interested in the history of pizza, you would probably have to do a little research. But there are many subjects that each of us knows a little better than most other people do. Those are subjects of informing based on *common experience*. You might know the characteristics of a good surfboard or good skis. You might know what baseball cards are most prized by collectors. You might know the components of good clean water for drinking, swimming, and other purposes. You might know the various kinds of hair that grow on people's heads. You might even know the history of pizza.

This section has two readings that explore things most people have in common. The first is on the physical senses and the second on the burning of firewood.

Reading

Unless one or another of your physical senses is impaired, you probably give little thought to the fact that you can see, hear, touch, taste, and smell. You're accustomed to seeing trees and grass turn green in the spring, water sparkle in the sunshine, traffic signals change from red to green. Neither is it remarkable that you hear the airplane flying over your head, the rush-hour traffic passing while you stand at the corner, the grackles settling into the trees for the night. You take your senses for granted.

In the essay that follows, George R. Harrison, a distinguished physicist specializing in optics, looks at our physical senses. Harrison concentrates mainly on vision to make his point about all the senses and to instill in his readers a fresh admiration for the capabilities of our ordinary physical senses. As you read the essay and encounter what may be new information about a familiar subject, notice the words and phrases that might be intended to persuade you to admire what your senses can do.

Senses

George R. Harrison

Now, what is a man? His body, "in form and moving" so "express and admirable," is made of protons, neutrons, and electrons; and he thinks with a brain composed of these and operating with the three fundamental forces of the physical world. To say this is not materialism, for if "God works in most mysterious ways His wonders to perform," not the least of His works, as we can see, involve protons, neutrons, and electrons. The study of their combinations helps us to understand our five senses, five paths of awareness to the brain, five "windows of the soul," by which we have our only contact with the external world.

Calling our senses five is an oversimplification, for we have more than five senses; we have at least three types of touch sensation: heat, pressure, and pain; and four types of taste, so that every flavor is a combination of sweet, salty, sour, and bitter. (The child who doesn't mind cod-liver oil and hates spinach is not being ornery; his taste buds merely respond differently from those of his mother.) We also have four types of vision, which all happen to involve the same pairs of eyes. The first type, night-vision, records no color, but paints its images in black and white on the retina; it operates best in faint light and is nearly 500 times as sensitive as the other three types of vision. These combine to give us more than 100,000 different sensations of color.

So sensitive are our retinas to green light—that is, to light whose waves are about one 50 thousandth of an inch long—that they can pick up as little as one 500 thousandth of a millionth of a millionth of a watt of power, and we can see a candle many miles away.

How was this sensitive detecting device developed, which is more elegant than any television camera? It contains a sharply focusing lens, surrounded by light-sensitive molecules which adjust it automatically to give the clearest image; self-regulating diaphragm, the pupil, and a shutter, the eyelid; and uses two projectors with which it introduced 3-D into vision some millions of years before the movies got around to this in 1953.

The marvelous twin cameras which send sensations to our brain from every object illuminated by even a millionth of the brightness of full sunlight sort out light rays so carefully that we get the fullest impact of reality through seeing. If necessary we can in addition verify the existence of an object by touching it, hearing it, smelling it, or tasting it. Beyond this, nature does not take us in contacting physical reality. And she has developed many forms of energy, such as cosmic rays and magnetic fields, which we cannot sense at all, yet which are no less real than those we sense directly.

So our senses are by no means perfect, and after exclaiming about the wonders of the eye, we must now examine its limitations. First, it is blind to more wave lengths of light than it can see. While insects can see somewhat with short-wave ultra-violet rays, humans cannot. (These insects, incidentally, have eyes consisting of multiple cones especially fixed for judging the direction of the sun for navigational purposes, and sometimes have polarizing filters to help steer by scattered light when the sky is overcast.) Also the sharpness of our vision is limited, and our lenses tend to deform and become cloudy. But now that nature has developed in man the brain needed to think scientifically, he can use this to extend his senses much beyond what nature has done.

Scientists have learned to supplement the sense of sight in numerous ways. In the front of the tiny pupil of the eye they put, on Mount Palomar, a great monocle 200 inches in diameter, and with it see 2000 times farther into the depths of space. Or they look through a small pair of lenses arranged as a microscope into a drop of water or blood, and magnify by as much as 2000 diameters the living creatures there, many of which are among man's most dangerous enemies. Or, if we want to see distant happenings on earth, they use some of the previously wasted electromagnetic waves to carry television images which they re-create as light by whipping tiny crystals on a screen with electrons in a vacuum. Or they can bring happenings of long ago and far away as colored motion pictures, by arranging silver atoms and color-absorbing molecules to force light waves into the patterns of the original reality. Or if we want to see into the center of a steel casting or the chest of an injured child, they send the information on a beam of penetrating short-wave X rays, and then convert it back into images we can see on a screen or photograph. Thus almost every type of electromagnetic radiation yet discovered has been used to extend our sense of sight in some way.

The evolution of the other senses is as interesting as that of vision, which nature has developed to nearly the maximum sensitivity permitted by the structure of light itself. Our ability to hear the commonest sound waves has reached its maximum possible sensitivity also. Some persons even are bothered by noises which arise from the random motions of molecules in the nerve endings of their ears. The threshold of sound awareness is said to be about the same in a human being, a catfish, or a bird, and the long-vaunted greater sensitivity of hearings of dogs and other animals probably arises from their ability to hear higher tones than we, and because they have less to distract them. 8

In many directions of evolution nature is stopped by limitations in her own materials. There are some things that just take too long to work out with protons and electrons by repeated trial and error, as, for example, to develop a wheel on a living creature. But often man can get around such blocks by taking thought. We fasten wheels to ourselves with automobiles, and our sense of hearing has been extended on radio waves so that we can hear the sound of a dropped pin around the world. 9

Thus, though we sense directly only a few of the energy manifestations in the external world, science has taught us how to transform many others so as not only to bring them into our ken, but to bend them to our service. And science reveals man's physical body as a fascinating assemblage of the same protons, electrons, and neutrons that constitute a stone, functioning in an even more remarkable cooperative effort. But not yet is this the whole of Man. 10

Questions

1. What new information about vision did you encounter in Harrison's essay?
2. Among the many facts that Harrison presents, what would you most like to remember?
3. What words and phrases express Harrison's admiration for the physical senses?
4. Of Harrison's several methods of development, which made his subject most interesting to you?
5. Locate several key words in "Senses" and show how their repetition links parts of the essay.

Discussion

Harrison clearly can speak with authority on optics. Writing on a subject with which he has had much experience, he informs readers about aspects of it they had not previously considered. He has this subject in common with his readers; however, he is more informed about it than we are.

Thesis

Harrison states a preliminary *thesis* in his first paragraph: that science can help people understand their five senses. Then, after eight paragraphs using science to explain the senses, in particular vision, he concludes by stating his thesis more fully: Science not only helps us to understand the senses but allows us to transform our perceptions for our benefit.

Consider Harrison's attitude toward vision and the other physical senses. Beginning in his introduction, he uses words and phrases that express his admiration. Amid references to the Bible, he states that science can uncover some of the mysterious ways of God. He sees the five senses as "windows of the soul," through which an individual perceives the external world. Knowledge depends on them. Elsewhere in the essay, Harrison uses words like *marvelous* (paragraph 5) to refer to the eyes.

Development

Harrison develops his essay by several methods. In paragraphs 4 and 5 he uses the *analogy* of a camera, employing photographic terms to describe the parts of the eye. Writers often use analogy for describing something unfamiliar or difficult by means of something more familiar. Perceptions of the senses are particularly hard to describe. Analogy says, "Subject A (the function of parts of the eye) is like Subject B (the function of parts of a camera)," when Subject A is unknown and Subject B is known. If you want to tell someone what something smells like, you might say, "The flower smells like root beer." Analogous things are alike in enough ways to be useful in explaining, but they are never alike in all ways. Eyes and cameras, for example, have obvious differences, as do flowers and root beer.

In developing his essay, Harrison also uses a type of *comparison*. After extolling what he calls the "wonders of the eye," in paragraphs 6 and 7 he examines the eye's shortcomings: its blindness to certain wavelengths and its limited sharpness. Comparisons of this type look at pros and cons, pluses and minuses, advantages and disadvantages. Harrison devotes little space to the limitations of natural vision, using them instead as a transition to his next point, which examines what scientists have done to overcome these limits.

He develops the next paragraph, the seventh, by *exemplification*, suggesting several ways by which scientists extend the sense of sight. The paragraph begins with a topic sentence—"Scientists have learned to supplement the sense of sight in numerous ways"—indicating its direction, and it concludes with a reiteration of the topic—"Thus almost every type of electromagnetic radiation yet discovered has been used to extend our sense of sight in some way."

In paragraph 8 Harrison broadens his subject from vision to all the senses; then in paragraph 9 he again brings up limitations, this time regarding nature. He cites the example that nature has not been able to put wheels on living creatures but adds that nature has enabled the human brain to get around that limitation. In the final paragraph of this passage, Harrison summarizes his position on the physical senses before getting on to his next subject, the mind.

Coherence

New information builds on old information. This principle accounts for how you learn and remember. When you hear or read something new, you relate it to what you already know—comparing it, classifying it, chunking it in your memory with something similar. When Harrison tells you about the eye's sensitivity to green light, you probably try to remember any experiences you might have had seeing green light at a distance. Then you may consider the implications of this characteristic of vision. You put it away in your mind with something that is already there.

You can take advantage of this feature of learning by using it to make your sentences *coherent*. When you write a sentence, put the *old information*, a reference to what you've already said, at the beginning; then set down the *new information*. As an example of how this principle works, examine the sentences of the preceding paragraph. The first words of the first sentence, "New information," refer to an earlier discussion, and the remainder of the sentence, "builds on old information," makes a new assertion. The beginning of the second sentence, "This principle," encapsulates the first sentence, and the remainder makes a new assertion. Then the first part of the third sentence more or less rephrases what has already been stated and expands on it with new information. The final two sentences carry on with the new information begun in the third sentence. This paragraph illustrates one way to relate sentences to one another—through the "old information" connection. As you have seen, though, not all sentences work this way; they would be tiresome if they did.

Another method of gaining coherence is the use of *key words*. Notice how Harrison indicates relationships. Paragraph 2 begins, "Calling our senses five is an oversimplification," relating directly to his thesis reference to "our five senses," stated in paragraph 1. Paragraph 3 relates to paragraph 2 by repeated reference to retinas, a word introduced in paragraph 2. Harrison achieves overall coherence with every mention of the senses, because by so doing he connects new information to the key thesis word *senses*. Finally, his conclusion amplifies the simpler thesis stated in the introduction, completing the discussion of the senses and leading into the next section of the longer essay from which this portion was excerpted.

When you study how other writers achieve coherence, remember that you are examining *finished* essays, final drafts that, as a result of revision, are logically organized, adequately developed, clearly stated, and smoothly coherent. Harrison's essay, like those you write, was once a rough draft. Rough drafts usually are *not* logically organized, adequately developed, clearly stated, and smoothly coherent. When writers begin writing, they don't always know precisely where they are going, so all the parts of their essays or other writings don't relate to one another. In fact, writers often have to add parts and discard others before they're finished.

The coherence of a final draft is achieved with repeated revision and editing. In your composing and revising, you likely find the same to be true: Your rough drafts are *rough.* But one task to accomplish in revision is to make your connections clear, to show how sentences and paragraphs relate to one another, in other words, to make your writing coherent.

EXERCISES

1. Begin with the key word *senses* and examine Harrison's essay for all repetitions of it in this and related forms (for example, *sensations*), including pronouns referring to it. How does repetition of this single word connect parts of the essay?

2. Practice using *analogy* for description. Choose one of the topics listed at the end of this exercise and write a short analogy using Harrison's fourth paragraph as a guide. To write an analogy, you need to use the terminology of the second, the known, subject to describe the first, the subject you want to clarify. The second subject is something familiar to most people; the first is something that is difficult to describe. Harrison, for example, describes the eye (first subject) as having parts like a camera (second subject): an automatically adjusting lens, a self-regulating diaphragm, a shutter, and two 3-D projectors.

   If you want, think of your own topic, something difficult to explain that you can describe in terms of something that most people know. Or here are some topics for you to choose from:

   - Hope is like . . .
   - A computer disk is like a . . .
   - Reading is like . . .
   - Sunlight is like . . .
   - Sight (hearing, taste, smell, touch) is like . . .

Reading

We've all seen fires. We admire the flames even while we are fearful of their consequences. But do we really know what a fire is? Have you ever thought about what makes the flames? Or where the flames come from? What happens when something burns? In the paragraph that follows, an excerpt from a longer piece by the same name, John McPhee describes firewood burning in a fireplace: not how to make a fire but what happens to a log when it burns. Read it as an example of a familiar kind of writing, one that informs readers for greater understanding of common experiences.

Firewood

John McPhee

Science was once certain that firewood was full of something called   1
phlogiston, a mysterious inhabitant that emerged after kindling and danced around in the form of light and heat and crackling sound—phlogiston, the substance of fire. Science, toward the end of the eighteenth century, erased that beautiful theory, replacing it with certain still current beliefs, which are related to the evident fact that green wood is half water. Seasoning, it dries down until, typically, the water content is twenty per cent. Most hardwoods—oak, maple, cherry, hickory—will season in six months. Ash, the firewood of kings, will season in half the time. When firewood burns, it makes vapor of the water. The rest of the log is (almost wholly) carbon, hydrogen, and oxygen—the three components of cellulose, also of starch and sugar. When a log is thrown on the fire, the molecules on the surface become agitated and begin to move vigorously. Some vibrate. Some rotate. Some travel swiftly from one place to another. The cellulose molecule is long, complicated, convoluted—thousands of atoms like many balls on a few long strings. The strings have a breaking point. The molecule, tumbling, whipping, vibrating, breaks apart. Hydrogen atoms, stripping away, snap onto oxygen atoms that are passing by in the uprushing stream of air, forming even more water, which goes up the chimney as vapor. Incandescent carbon particles, by the tens of millions, leap free of the log and wave like banners, as flame. Several hundred significantly different chemical reactions are now going on. For example, a carbon atom and four hydrogen atoms, coming out of the breaking cellulose, may lock together and form methane, natural gas. The methane, burning (combining with oxygen), turns into carbon dioxide and water, which also go up the flue. If two carbon atoms happen to come out of the wood with six hydrogen atoms, they are, agglomerately, ethane, which burns to become, also, carbon dioxide and water. Three carbons and eight hydrogens form propane,

and propane is there, too, in the fire. Four carbons and ten hydrogens— butane. Five carbons . . . pentane. Six . . . hexane. Seven . . . heptane. Eight carbons and eighteen hydrogens—octane. All these compounds come away in the breaking of the cellulose molecule, and burn, and go up the chimney as carbon dioxide and water. Pentane, hexane, heptane, and octane have a collective name. Logs burning in a fireplace are making and burning gasoline.

Questions

1. In what ways has "Firewood" added to your understanding of fire?
2. What old information does McPhee build on?
3. What does McPhee say happens when a log burns? What makes the flames? What goes up the chimney?
4. In what ways is the modern understanding of what happens when a fire burns different from the old one? In what ways are the two understandings similar?
5. How would McPhee's emphasis change if his last sentence, "Logs burning in a fireplace are making and burning gasoline," were instead at the start of his paragraph, following his opening statement that science has erased the phlogiston theory with a new one?
6. Does McPhee, in addition to his purpose of informing, have a secondary purpose similar to Harrison's—to evoke admiration and a new understanding of his subject matter? Support your answer with details from the paragraph.

Discussion

Like Harrison's "Senses," "Firewood" relates scientific discoveries about a familiar subject. Science can tell us what the substance of fire is. Take a closer look at "Firewood." McPhee first brings up an old term, *phlogiston,* then concludes with a new one, *gasoline,* for collectively describing the compounds that emerge in flames. Some people might say that the two terms are actually referring to the same thing and that science hasn't progressed much over the centuries. Others would argue that the term *gasoline* encompasses a much greater understanding of the substance of fire.

Development

McPhee's method of developing his paragraph is *chronological,* to describe what happens when fire burns. After introductory facts about the characteristics of firewood, he begins the process: "When a log is thrown on the fire." Note the steps: agitation of molecules, breakup of molecules, formation of new molecules. At this point, McPhee says, "Several hundred significantly different chemical reactions are now going on"; the remainder of the paragraph describes some of these reactions.

The paragraph now moves from the *less emphatic* to the *more emphatic*. Note how McPhee begins with the production of methane out of one carbon atom and four hydrogen atoms, then gradually increases the numbers of carbon and hydrogen atoms as he names the compounds they produce. At the end it seems that he tries to surprise his readers a little with his identification of the burning compounds—pentane, hexane, heptane, and octane—as gasoline.

Secondary purpose

The next time you watch a log burning in a fireplace, or some other kind of fire, give a little thought to the chemistry of burning, to the water vapor escaping up the chimney, and to the fact that that log is making and burning complex chemicals. Then ask yourself if McPhee might have a secondary purpose similar to Harrison's: to inspire admiration for the wonders of nature.

EXERCISE

Writers influence audience response not only by their choice of words but by their sentence style as well. In the following series, McPhee uses two sentences only two words long to convey part of the intensity and the variety of molecular actions:

When a log is thrown on a fire, the molecules on the surface become agitated and begin to move vigorously. Some vibrate. Some rotate. Some travel swiftly from one place to another.

The two sentences "Some vibrate" and "Some rotate" may look like sentence fragments since they are so short, but because each has a subject, "Some," and a verb, they are truly sentences. Read the whole series of four sentences again, think about them, and then write four sentences of your own that follow this pattern. Write about something that also has a variety of actions, for example, a fish tugging on a line, people waiting in lines, or drivers stopped for a traffic signal. After these four sentences, write a few more to extend your description.

Writing

Write an essay about something that most people have in common but that you may be able to explain better than most. There are probably many familiar aspects of everyday life that you can say something about that not everyone knows. Your purpose, in addition to informing, could be to instill in your audience an appreciation for your subject. Here are some ideas for you to use as starters:

- Fast-food hamburgers—what's behind the wrapper
- Fingernails—what they are, how they grow, and so on
- Water—its components, its sources, and so on
- Ears—their parts, how they hear

After selecting a topic, explore it with one of the prewriting strategies discussed in Chapter 3—perhaps clustering. As your ideas begin to take direction, strike out those that no longer fit. Eventually you should be able to step back and ask yourself what idea holds all your thoughts on the subject together. At this point you may want to rearrange some of your connecting lines. State your central idea as a sentence, and you have a working thesis. Then you can arrange your ideas into what seems to be a workable order.

If you have trouble getting started, look again at how Harrison and McPhee begin. Both authors generate audience interest by first referring to something related to their subject, Harrison somewhat philosophically with his biblical references, McPhee bringing up the old word for fire. Harrison clearly states his subject and thesis in his introductory paragraph and again at the end, while McPhee ties his paragraph together at the end by naming the modern word for the substance of fire.

As you write, assume that your audience is familiar with your subject (just as they know what the senses and fire are) but will be interested in the new information you are sharing. In revision, give special attention to coherence, connecting related sentences and paragraphs with repetition of key words and application of the old information/new information principle.

Informing with a Persuasive Purpose

How often do you read articles that have an ostensible purpose of informing but in fact, by means of absorbing you in the information, are meant to persuade you? This is a common type of discourse. Most advertisements and commercials, for example, *look* as if they are informing you—about the best sunscreen or the tastiest yogurt or the latest in blue jeans fashions—but in fact their purpose is to persuade you to buy the product. Commentaries and editorials in newspapers appear to reveal the latest facts about the most current issues—and indeed they do—but the commentators are also trying to convince you to agree with their opinions. For example, when you read an informative column about religious and satanic cults, the writer may be trying to persuade you to avoid organizations of this type. Editorials that inform you about dangers to the environment have a persuasive purpose also—to convince you to get involved in conservation.

Sometimes informing with an underlying persuasive purpose is deceptive, as in this paragraph from a sales letter:

> Whether you're contemplating the purchase of additional life insurance now or at some future date, I have some interesting ideas to share with you that will be useful in your planning. In exchange for the opportunity to share these ideas, I will make and keep the following promises as a condition of our visit: (1) I will make no attempt to sell you anything in this visit, and (2) unless you specifically request it, no return call will be made. That's fair, isn't it, Mr. Brown?

The writer of this letter is surely not offering, only out of the goodness of his heart, to help Mr. Brown in his insurance planning. Such deception undercuts the writer's credibility and puts the reader on the defensive. If you were its recipient, you would likely file this letter in the wastebasket.

Usually, however, there is no deception in having dual purposes. Both writer and reader understand that the intention is to persuade with facts. Deception occurs when the writer pretends to be only conveying information, as in the example paragraph, and when the reader does not read actively enough to realize the writer's intention. (Persuasion as a primary purpose for writing is discussed in Chapter 7.)

Facts (Forms of Evidence)

Informative essays consist largely of facts, or evidence that can support statements of opinion. (See also the discussion in Chapter 7.) Facts are information that can be verified, such as examples, testimony, statistics, and historical evidence.

An *example* is a specific, concrete instance of the general principle or issue. It does not restate the issue; it illustrates it. In the following paragraph from an essay advising an informed use of euphemisms, the student writer's first sentence makes an assertion, and the remaining sentences illustrate it by examples:

> Workers view their jobs as being more respectable when certain euphemisms are used. "Sanitation men" collect the garbage, "animal welfare officers" catch stray dogs, and those who seek "counsel" need a lawyer. An "administrative aide" would probably type the boss's letters, while a "domestic engineer" would plan and prepare the family's evening meal.

A reader could corroborate these examples by listening to language use and by questioning other people about what the terms mean to them.

Testimony is a statement about the issue by an expert, either paraphrased or quoted. Television commercials have rugged-looking men selling auto mufflers, women using laundry products, kids eating lunchbox-sized packages of pudding and applesauce. And though we may disagree with such stereotyping, the advertisers' research shows that such testimony sells products. Writers often use testimony to bolster their credibility by reporting what people more knowledgeable than they have said on the subject. Testimony may come from interviews, letters, conversations, reading, and a variety of other sources. The authority of the expert is often cited; for example, the phrase "George R. Harrison, a distinguished physicist specializing in optics" tells you in what way the writer is qualified to write on the subject. The source of the information is usually named also, for example:

> In *A Brief History of Time* (Toronto: Bantam, 1988), noted British physicist Stephen W. Hawking maintains that scientists have not yet answered the essential question, "How or why were the laws and the initial state of the universe chosen?" (173).

In addition to identifying the author and title of the source, the writer gives publishing information and the page number from which this information was drawn.

Statistics are numbers compiled competently and applied appropriately to the issue. Readers often expect statistics to be a part of the information conveyed in a piece of writing. Here is an example of how a student writer uses statistics in an essay urging people to wear seat belts:

> Over 22,576 people die in car accidents each year. According to the National Highway Traffic Administration, 9,900 of those lives could have been saved if the occupants of the vehicles had been wearing seat belts.

Jonathan Kozol's essay on illiteracy in America shows how a writer uses statistics to inform and persuade.

Historical evidence is verifiable information concerning actual occurrences. It may come from our experience, observations, or reading. Like statistics, testimony, and examples, historical evidence must be true. Unlike fiction, where writers can invent, elaborate on, and exaggerate details, informative writing is based on an implied contract between writer and reader ensuring the truth of the facts it reports. Violations of this contract destroy a writer's credibility. Writers therefore try to be sure of the truth of their information, while readers question any facts that appear to be inaccurate.

Facts—whether in the form of examples, testimony, statistics, or historical evidence—are persuasive in addition to their primary purpose of informing. Essays with a main purpose of persuading often use facts to support opinions; essays with an informative purpose use them less to back up opinions than to lead readers to form their own opinions.

Reading

The following short article from *Audubon* magazine informs readers about the effects of people releasing balloons to celebrate special events. It presents facts throughout and does not express the opinions of the writer or a position of the magazine. However, as you read, look for an underlying persuasive purpose.

Halftime Balloons a Pretty Problem
from *Audubon* magazine

Thousands of balloons released at sporting events may be a deceptive threat to wildlife. The problem is hard to measure, says Peter Hibbard of the Balloon Alert Project, an organization he runs with his wife, Susan, out of their Toms River, New Jersey, home. A schoolteacher and part-time naturalist at Island Beach State Park, Hibbard says a sperm whale that washed ashore three years ago died because a balloon it ate clogged its digestive tract. Balloons also have been implicated in the deaths of both leatherback and hawksbill sea turtles, which apparently mistake them for food.   1

Some measure of the amount of plastic waste added to the environment by balloon releases can be inferred from the numbers of balloons launched: 20,000 at halftime festivities at Hawaii's Hula Bowl, a quarter-million by the U.S. Bicentennial Committee on the nation's 200th birthday, 1.1 million by Disneyland, and 1.5 million by the city of Cleveland.   2

Released balloons travel fast and far, says Hibbard. He found a balloon on the New Jersey shore that had traveled 150 miles in only three and a half hours after escaping a realty company in Fairfax, Virginia. What Hibbard finds particularly disturbing is that the releases are a form of deliberate pollution that suggests to children that "it is okay to pollute." The Balloon Action Project, he says, is supporting a bill in the New Jersey Legislature that would ban promotional releases.   3

Questions

1. Point to facts in "Halftime Balloons" that are *example, testimony, statistic,* and *historical evidence.*
2. Are the facts adequate? How could you verify them?
3. What does the writer of the article tell you about Peter Hibbard's authority to testify on the subject?
4. Compare the facts in paragraph 1 with those in paragraph 2. Which paragraph provides stronger evidence?
5. What do these facts tell you about balloon releases?
6. Given these facts, what do you think *Audubon* wants to persuade its readers to do?

Discussion

"Halftime Balloons" is not openly persuasive. The first sentence expresses an *informative* thesis: "Thousands of balloons released at sporting events may be a deceptive threat to wildlife." Below the surface, however, you may have detected another, a *persuasive*, thesis, something like "Balloons should not be released to promote special events." Or, stated more forcefully, "Try to get promotional releases of balloons banned in your state." The informative thesis is expressed; the persuasive thesis is implied.

Examine how the facts of the article support the contention about the dangers of balloon releases. There seems little doubt that the wildlife died as a result of balloon ingestion, as paragraph 1 states; autopsy could establish this as fact. There is also little disputing the numbers of balloons lofted, detailed in paragraph 2; verification could be achieved in a number of ways. The argument weakens, however, in establishing that the facts in paragraph 1 are caused by the facts in paragraph 2. That is, to the question of why the wildlife died after swallowing balloons, the answer is that large numbers of balloons were released at sporting and other events. Releases like these may well be the actual cause of the deaths, but skeptical readers would question the strength of the inferential link between both sets of facts.

The facts in "Halftime Balloons" are probably all true—verifiable, that is. But the causal link between them is weak. To show that balloon releases at sporting events are responsible for the deaths of wildlife, the article could connect the two incidents—perhaps with an additional fact, such as that the balloons removed from the digestive tracts of the dead animals were imprinted "Hula Bowl" or "U.S. Bicentennial" or something else that identified the lethal balloons with a particular large balloon release.

Development

This article deals with *causes and effects*. It names a single cause—the releasing of large numbers of balloons—and several effects. Cause and effect is a common method of developing ideas, because it seems that people like to ask Why: Why did the Chernobyl nuclear reactor melt down? Why did my holiday photographs turn out so dark? Why is my car making that odd noise? Why did the sperm whale die, and why was it able to ingest a balloon? Or people want to know what the effects of an action will be: How will this tuition increase affect me? How will the new recycling law change my life-style? How would the proposed New Jersey bill on balloon releases affect unnecessary deaths of wildlife?

This article asks why the sperm whale and other wildlife died with balloons in their digestive tracts. The first sentence states the answer: "Thousands of balloons released at sporting events may be a deceptive threat to wildlife." This sentence implies cause and serves as the thesis for the article. The remainder of the first paragraph alleges effects of that cause, giving examples of wildlife deaths because of balloon ingestion, and the second paragraph again alleges causes by citing large balloon launchings. The final paragraph deals with causes and suggests a legal solution to the problem.

EXERCISES

1. Rewrite "Halftime Balloons" for an audience other than *Audubon* readers—perhaps readers of *Sports Illustrated, Money,* or your campus newspaper. Your facts may remain the same, but with a different audience you will probably use them differently to support a different underlying persuasive thesis.

2. You have examined the facts in "Halftime Balloons" for their type and verifiability. Now examine the facts in Jonathan Kozol's "A Third of the Nation Cannot Read These Words" on page 296, looking for examples, testimonies, statistics, and historical evidence and asking whether the facts seem verifiable to you.

Writing

Write a short essay that has the purpose of informing with a secondary purpose of persuading. Select a problem and ask Why? What is its cause? Then provide facts about both causes and effects. Make sure your connections are tight. If you like, begin with your informative thesis as "Halftime Balloons" does, and imply your persuasive thesis (whatever you want your audience to do). Here are a few problems to consider:

- Throwing away aluminum cans rather than recycling them
- Walking across grass rather than using sidewalks
- Arriving late for class (meetings, appointments, and so on)

Informing by Definition

Information sometimes comes in the form of definitions (see Chapter 5). You have seen this type of information in textbooks, magazines, newspapers—in any publication where informing is a purpose. You read about "good cholesterol" and "bad cholesterol," about illiteracy, about freedom versus responsibility, and so on.

Definitions identify. They tell what something is and how a writer is using a particular term. When you read about DNA, it's not enough to be told that the letters stand for deoxyribonucleic acid. You want to know what deoxyribonucleic acid is. Neither is it satisfactory to have only a dictionary definition telling you that deoxyribonucleic acid is some kind of "polymeric chromosomal constituent of living cell nuclei." In fact, by this time you might be more confused than ever. What you need is a description of DNA, an explanation of what it does, an example of how it works, a discussion of its variations and its effects, and so on. That might be an entire essay.

You frequently find definitions in textbooks. In a textbook on energy and society, for example, you would be likely to find definitions of kinetic energy, potential energy, nuclear energy, chemical energy, and so on. In a guide to the study of poetry, you would find definitions of imagery, figurative language, rhyme, meter, and other terms necessary to your understanding of the components of poems. As a reader of textbooks, you expect definitions of terms you don't know.

Writers often use definitions as only a portion of their books and essays, defining new terms or their specialized use of familiar terms. The textbook on energy does more than define terms, and the book on poetry is mainly a collection of poems. An essay on religious cults would define how the writer is using the term *cult* before discussing recruiting and indoctrination. An essay explaining how a friend died of hypothermia would first define *hypothermia*.

Reading

William Zinsser in his book *On Writing Well* defines *taste*—not the physical sense that detects sweet, salty, sour, and bitter, but an intuitive sense that enables people to do something right. Zinsser, after declaring that taste can't be defined, attempts to define it and to relate it specifically to writing. As you read, ask yourself: what is taste, as Zinsser defines it? At what point in his essay do you understand what he means by taste?

Taste

William Zinsser

What finally separates the good writer from the breezy writer is a quality so intangible that nobody even knows what it is: taste. It can't be defined, but we know it when we see it. A woman with taste in clothes delights us with her ability to turn herself out every day in a combination that's not only stylish and surprising; it's also exactly right. Taste is the instinct to know what works and to avoid what doesn't.   1

In the arts, knowing what not to do is a major component of taste. Two jazz pianists may be equally proficient at the keyboard. The one with taste will put every note to useful work in telling his story; the one without taste will drench us in ripples and other unnecessary ornaments. A painter with taste will trust his eye to tell him what needs to be on his canvas and what doesn't; the one without taste will give us a landscape that's too pretty, or too cluttered, or too gaudy in its colors—anyway, too something.   2

I realize that I'm trying to pin down a matter that's highly subjective 3
and that has no firm rules. One man's beautiful painting is another man's
kitsch. It's also true that taste changes with the decades—yesterday's charm
is rejected today as junk, but tomorrow it will be back in vogue, certified
once again as charming. So why do I even bring the problem up? Mainly to
remind you that it exists. Taste is an invisible current that runs through all
writing, and you should be aware of it.

Sometimes, in fact, it's not invisible. Every art form has a hard core of 4
verities that survive the fickleness of time. There must be something in-
nately pleasing, for instance, in the proportions of the Parthenon; Western
man continues to let the Greeks of two thousand years ago design his major
public buildings. In music, the fugues of Bach have a timeless elegance that's
rooted in the timeless laws of mathematics.

Does writing have any such guideposts for us? Not many—writing is the 5
expression of every person's individuality, and in general we can only say
that we know what we like when it comes along. Still, as in the other arts,
taste is partly a question of knowing what to omit. Clichés, for example. If a
writer litters his prose with platitudes—if every idea is first and foremost
and in the last analysis one that hits the nail on the head—we can safely infer
that the writer lacks an instinct for what gives language its freshness.
Faced with a choice between the novel and the banal, he goes unerringly
for the banal.

Extend the point beyond clichés to include a writer's larger use of 6
words. Again, freshness is a critical factor. Taste chooses words that have
originality, strength, and precision; non-taste veers into the breezy vernac-
ular of the alumni magazine's class notes—a world where people in authority are the top brass or the powers-that-be. What exactly is wrong with "the
top brass"? Nothing—and everything. Taste is knowing that it's better to call
people in authority what they are: officials, or executives, or the president of
the company. Non-taste reaches for the cute synonym.

But finally taste is a mixture of qualities that are beyond defining: an 7
ear, for instance, that can hear the difference between a sentence that limps
and a sentence that lilts, or an intuition that knows when a casual phrase
dropped into a formal sentence will not only feel right but will seem to be
the inevitable choice. Does this mean that taste can't be learned? Yes and no.
Perfect taste, like perfect pitch, is a gift from God. But a certain amount can
be acquired. The trick is to study those who have it.

Questions

1. In your own words, define *taste* as Zinsser uses it.
2. If you were to decide to produce writing that fits Zinsser's definition, how would
   you proceed?
3. With few guideposts (paragraph 5), how would you know if you had succeeded
   in producing tasteful writing?

4. How can you tell when something is strikingly new instead of overused and worn-out?

5. Which of Zinsser's definitions of taste is clearest for you?

Discussion

Zinsser applies his definition of taste specifically to writing. Unfortunately, he asserts, there are very few guideposts to tasteful writing. And those guideposts depend on the writer's ability to tell the difference between the "novel" and the "banal," between a "sentence that lilts" and a "sentence that limps." It would seem that experienced writers have the advantage. Zinsser says further that perfect taste is "a gift from God."

However, all is not lost, for Zinsser adds, "a certain amount [of taste] can be acquired." You can acquire taste in writing from those who already have it, by studying how they write and learning from their style and usage. Like acquiring taste in clothes by observing how other people dress, in particular those you admire, you can acquire taste in writing by observing how writers you admire select and combine words and phrases. By "reading as a writer," as discussed in Chapter 1, you learn from those who already have acquired a certain taste in writing.

Development

Notice how Zinsser uses *exemplification* to develop his definition. In paragraph 1 he has an example of people with taste in clothing. In paragraph 2 he uses examples of taste in the arts—music and painting—and, in paragraph 4, examples of timeless taste. In each paragraph he makes a general statement and then illustrates it with examples. You'll find this pattern also in paragraphs 5 and 6. Paragraph 3 is a departure in which he focuses his discussion, and his concluding paragraph sums up his nebulous subject.

EXERCISE

Practice Zinsser's style. Rewrite his second paragraph by substituting something else for "the arts." You might begin with this first sentence: "In baseball, knowing what not to do is a major component of taste." Or you might begin with "In dressing . . ." or with "In telling jokes . . ." or with some other topic. Follow Zinsser's sentence patterns throughout the paragraph, making changes where needed so the paragraph will fit your topic.

Writing

Define something not easily defined. Write a definition that comes out of your experience, one that you work out as you write. One effect of defining is that in telling someone else your understanding of a particular term, you clarify for yourself what that understanding is. By making tentative definitions in areas not yet fully explored, you may be constructing new knowledge. So, in carrying out this assignment, don't select a subject that is too easy for you. If you write on *perfection,* for example, you will probably develop your own understanding of what you think perfection is. Like Zinsser, you might want to admit to your reader that you are only experimenting with a definition.

Here are a few topics inspired by Zinsser's essay:

Taste	Armament
Perfection	Junk
Hope	Guidepost
Shoddy	Current
Typical	Gift
Novel (as an adjective meaning "new")	Kitsch

To assist in narrowing your topic and deciding what you can say, you may want to begin by brainstorming (see Chapter 3). Select an aspect of the topic that interests you the most, and continue brainstorming on the narrower topic, trying to think of examples that will illustrate it. Group the items on your list and formulate a tentative thesis. As you compose, you may find that exemplification is a particularly useful method of development, as it is in "Taste." Try developing your definition with examples rather than relying on your dictionary.

If in your writing you name a word as a word, instead of the thing it represents, underline (or italicize) the word. Here's an example: "The word *taste* is used in many ways other than to represent quality." But compare "Taste is the instinct to know what works and to avoid what doesn't." The first sentence refers to the word, the second to the thing the word represents, taste itself.

ADDITIONAL READINGS FOR DISCUSSION

Reading

This informative essay, published in January 1989, has a secondary purpose of persuasion. Notice how, like "Halftime Balloons a Pretty Problem," it has an underlying persuasive thesis and is developed by analyzing causes and effects.

Deadly Danger in a Spray Can

Michael D. Lemonick

When they were first synthesized in the late 1920s, chlorofluorocarbons (CFCs for short) seemed too good to be true. These remarkable chemicals, consisting of chlorine, fluorine, and carbon atoms, are nontoxic and inert, meaning they do not combine easily with other substances. Because they vaporize at low temperatures, CFCs are perfect as coolants in refrigerators and propellant gases for spray cans. Since CFCs are good insulators, they are standard ingredients in plastic-foam materials like Styrofoam. Best of all, the most commonly used CFCs are simple, and therefore cheap, to manufacture.   1

There is only one problem. When they escape into the atmosphere, most CFCs are murder on the environment. Each CFC molecule is 20,000 times as efficient at trapping heat as is a molecule of CO_2. So CFCs increase the greenhouse effect far out of proportion to their concentration in the air.   2

A more immediate concern is that the chlorine released when CFC molecules break up destroys ozone molecules. The ozone layer, located in the stratosphere, between 10 and 30 miles up, is vital to the well-being of plants and animals. Ozone molecules, which consist of three oxygen atoms, absorb most of the ultraviolet radiation that comes from the sun. And ultraviolet is extremely dangerous to life on earth.   3

The small amount that does get through to the earth's surface inflicts plenty of damage: besides causing sunburn, the rays have been linked to cataracts and weakened immune systems in humans and other animals. Ultraviolet light carries enough energy to damage DNA and thus disrupt the workings of cells, which is why excessive exposure to sunlight is thought to be the primary cause of some skin cancers.   4

When scientists first warned in the 1970s that CFCs could attack ozone, the United States responded by banning their use in spray cans. (Manufacturers switched to such environmentally benign substitutes as butane, the chemical burned in cigarette lighters.) But the rest of the world continued to use CFC-based aerosol cans, and overall CFC production kept growing. The threat became far clearer in 1985, when researchers reported a "hole" in the ozone layer over Antarctica. Although the size of the hole varies with the seasons and weather patterns, at times Antarctic ozone has been depleted by as much as 50 percent in some spots. As a result of this disturbing development, twenty-four nations, including the United States and the Soviet Union, met in Montreal two summers ago and agreed to cut back on CFCs. The so-called Montreal Protocol is designed to achieve a 35 percent net reduction in worldwide CFC production by 1999.   5

That is not good enough, however. The same stability that makes CFCs   6
so safe in industrial use makes them extremely long-lived: some of the CFCs
released today will still be in the atmosphere a century from now. Moreover,
each atom of chlorine liberated from a CFC can break up as many as
100,000 molecules of ozone.

For that reason, governments should ensure the careful handling and   7
recycling of the CFCs now in use. Said Senator Albert Gore of Tennessee:
"Much of what reaches the atmosphere is not coming from industrial
sources. It's things like sloppy handling of hamburger containers." When
plastic-foam burger holders are broken, the CFCs trapped inside escape.
Discarded refrigerators release CFCs as well, and, noted Gore, a significant
part of the U.S. contribution to CFC emissions comes from "draining
automobile air conditioners and leaving the stuff in pans where it boils off."
Such release of CFCs could be prevented if consumers and businesses were
offered cash incentives to return broken-down air conditioners and refrigerators to auto and appliance dealers. Then the units could be sent back to
the manufacturers so that the CFCs could be reused.

While recycling will help, the only sure way to save the ozone is a   8
complete ban on CFC manufacture, which should be phased out over the
next five years. Fortunately, as the Montreal Protocol demonstrates, banning CFCs will be far simpler than reducing other dangerous gases. "The
CFC producers are a small club of countries," said Brice Lalonde, France's
Environment Secretary. But a ban could admittedly be economically dis-
ruptive to the entire world: the annual market for CFCs is some $2.2 billion.
The Soviet Union, which is a heavy user of CFCs, will have a particularly
tough time phasing out the chemicals. "I agree with the ban in principle,"
said Vladimir Sakharov, a member of the Soviet State Committee for Environmental Protection, "but in practice it will be extremely difficult. Our
economy is not as flexible as others."

To make the transition easier, chemical companies are working hard to   9
find practical substitutes for CFCs. The most promising approach so far is to
use CFC family members that are chemically altered to make them less
dangerous to the environment. The chlorine-free substance HFC-134a, for
example, is most likely to be used in refrigeration devices.

The major drawback to CFC substitutes is the high cost of making   10
them. It may be that until better manufacturing techniques are developed,
consumers will have to pay more for affected products. The prospect is not
a pleasant one, but it is a small price to pay for curbing the greenhouse effect
and saving the life-preserving ozone layer.

Questions

1. What is the problem with chlorofluorocarbons (CFCs)?
2. What are the most common sources of CFCs?
3. What is the essay's informative thesis?

4. State in your own words the implied persuasive thesis of this essay.

5. What does Lemonick's selection of details tell you about his intended audience?

6. Name some of the implications, both direct and indirect, of people acting worldwide to significantly reduce CFCs.

7. Study the cause and effect development of this essay. Does the essay begin with cause or effect? What is the primary cause? the primary effect? What facts does Lemonick use to establish the link between cause and effect? Are these connections weak at any point?

8. What solutions to the problem does the author propose?

Reading

Like Zinsser's "Taste," the following essay informs by definition. Most people have heard about lichens (pronounced "lie-kens") but cannot really say what they are. In developing her definition, Kathleen Almy uses exemplification, classification, cause and effect analysis, and comparison.

Lichens: Nature's Paintbox
Kathleen Almy

Appearing at times as if an artist has splashed paint on tree trunks and across the faces of rocks, lichens present a display as vibrant as wildflowers. Yet most people know very little about these exotic plants. Striking in variety as well as in color, lichens are useful to humans and serve as excellent reminders of both nature's fragility and its resilience.   1

Lichens make up just one group of the world's nonflowering plants; others include bacteria, algae, fungi (such as mushrooms), ferns, and coniferous trees (such as pines). About one third, or 100,000, of the world's plant species don't produce flowers; roughly 20,000 of them are lichens.   2

Like most plants that don't flower, lichens can survive extremes in temperature and moisture. They can thrive in lush tropical rainforests—and in dry desert valleys unfit for most living things. They can be found buried under Arctic ice and snow, on a windswept alpine peak, in the branches of an evergreen, on an old fence post or rusting car, or even on the backs of certain beetles in New Guinea.   3

In the Arctic and the Antarctic, where temperatures plunge well below freezing, lichens easily outnumber other plant species in both number and variety. Experiments have also shown that some lichens survive temperatures above 400 degrees Fahrenheit, and that some can live without water for more than a year. A lichen's response to dryness is simple: When there isn't enough moisture, it enters a period of "suspended animation" in which it barely grows. When the rains come again, the plant absorbs moisture like blotting paper. Some species can hold as much as thirty times their weight in water.   4

Lichens grow at different rates, depending on the species and the 5
surrounding environment. During the course of a year, some grow less
than a millimeter while others increase by 10 millimeters. Lichens compensate for their slow growth by being long-lived: Some colonies in Greenland
are thought to be more than 4,000 years old.

Although they endure extreme conditions, most lichens are easily 6
damaged by air pollution. Some will survive only if the air is pollution-free.
Because lichens accumulate minerals (mainly from the air and rainfall),
they are sensitive to contamination. Scientists can determine the spread of
pollution from an industrial source by analyzing the lichens in the surrounding area.

Pollution doesn't harm just the lichens. Reindeer, which feed on a type 7
of lichen called reindeer moss, are easily contaminated by radiation. The
animal passes the radioactive substances on to humans and other animals
that consume its meat, milk, or cheese. After the 1986 Chernobyl nuclear
accident in the Soviet Union, entire herds of reindeer in Sweden, Norway,
and Finland were put to death to reduce the threat to humans.

Each lichen is made up of two plant types—fungi and blue-green or 8
green algae—living together. A look through the microscope at a lichen's
body, or thallus, reveals a network of fungal threads, called hyphae, surrounding an individual alga cell. The alga is capable of photosynthesis—it
uses sunlight to combine carbon dioxide and water to make carbohydrates,
the lichen's food. The fungus depends on this food from the alga. Botanists
aren't sure what the fungus contributes in return, although researchers
have proposed several theories to explain the partnership. Some believe
that the fungus is a parasite, freeloading from the alga. Others argue that
the relationship is mutual: The fungus pulls its weight by providing water
and minerals for photosynthesis and by protecting the alga.

Lichens fit into three groups: crustose (crusty), foliose (leafy), and fruticose (shrubby). All three types live in the soil and on rocks and trees. 9
Crustose lichens are generally flat. Foliose lichens are anchored only in
spots and usually have lobed edges, like leaves. The fruticose varieties have
many branches and grow upright on land or hang from trees.

Lichens are called pioneer plants because they can take hold on bare 10
rock, in sand, or in soil where other plants cannot grow and begin to form
a soil suitable for mosses, ferns, and larger plants. The decaying action of
lichen acids combines with weathering (the natural action of wind and water
on the land) to wear away a rock's surface, converting the minerals there to
new compounds. These join the developing soil, where other organisms
can use them.

Lichens are important to most ecosystems. All life forms need nitrogen, 11
but few can use it as it occurs naturally in the air. Lichens that contain
"nitrogen-fixing" blue-green algae can convert nitrogen in the atmosphere
to compounds that other organisms can use. In the tundra, lichens may
cover miles of open ground, providing food for reindeer and caribou; the
plants make up as much as 60 to 90 percent of the diet of these grazing

animals. Warblers in the Arctic build their nests from lichens, while snails, slugs, and some moth larvae use the plants for both food and shelter. One small insect camouflages itself by covering its body with bits of lichen; the common name, "trash carrier," aptly fits this moving pile of debris.

Humans have also found uses for lichens—as cosmetic ingredients, leather-tanning agents, fibers for clothing and shoes, and medicines. In fact, the word *lichen,* from the Greek word meaning "leprous," refers to the plant's scaly growth on tree bark and its use in treating leprosy.   12

Although many lichens have relatively high food value, they contain chemicals that make them taste bitter. Even so, they have been a source of starches, vitamins, and minerals for people in some parts of the world. The "manna from heaven" described in the Bible was probably a lichen blown down from high mountain slopes to the desert. Rock tripe, a leathery lichen that grows on rocks, was a common meal for Pacific Coast Indians and also nourished French explorers in the area. Early Arctic explorers survived almost entirely on rock tripe for weeks.   13

The chemicals that give lichens their coloring are also useful to humans as dyes, producing earthy shades of yellow, red, and blue. The colors of Scottish wool tweeds were once made from lichen dyes. The cudbear lichen is a source of dye for litmus paper, used to measure chemical acidity. The perfume industry also uses lichens as stabilizers, and large quantities of oakmoss are harvested for soaps and perfumes.   14

Lichens aren't as obviously beautiful as many plants because they don't produce attention-grabbing flowers. But a close look reveals a complex and colorful plant that is important to animals, humans, and other plants.   15

Questions

1. What are lichens? How are they "nature's paintbox"?
2. Name several uses for lichens.
3. Pollution causes problems both directly and indirectly. In paragraph 7 Almy mentions a problem with reindeer. Can you think of other problems, either direct or indirect, brought about by air pollution on lichens?
4. Almy expresses her thesis in paragraph 1: "Lichens are useful to humans and serve as excellent reminders of both nature's fragility and its resilience." How does she support this two-part thesis?

Reading

Here is another example of informing by definition. Student writer Patricia M. Mahon defines a term that is probably unfamiliar to most people; however, she has reason to believe that her readers ought to have a basic understanding of it. Do you feel that you are among her intended readers?

Understanding Endometriosis

Patricia M. Mahon

Endometriosis—the presence of endometrial tissue outside its normal location lining the uterus—remains a word unfamiliar to many, but its symptoms and complications have baffled doctors for more than a century. Although endometriosis has been wrongly nicknamed "the career women's disease" because it often affects women in their twenties and thirties who postponed having children, experts now know that this disease strikes women of every lifestyle and occupation, from their teens until menopause.

The term was coined in 1922 from the word *endometrium,* the tissue lining the uterus which builds up and then sheds each month during a woman's menstrual cycle. *Endo* is a Greek word meaning "within," and *metri* refers to the Greek *metra,* or uterus. *Osis* is a suffix that means an abnormal or diseased condition. Together you have "an abnormal condition within the uterus." Like the lining of the uterus, endometrial growths usually respond to the woman's hormones—they build up tissue, break down, and cause bleeding. However, unlike the lining of the uterus, endometrial tissue outside the uterus has no way of leaving the body. The result is internal bleeding, inflammation of the surrounding areas, and formation of scar tissue.

Endometriosis is commonly found in the abdomen—on the ovaries, fallopian tubes, ligaments supporting the uterus, outer surface of the uterus, and lining of the pelvic cavity. Occasionally, the growths are found in abdominal surgery scars, but there have been rare instances of growths outside the abdomen—in the lung, arm, and thigh.

The most common symptoms of endometriosis are pain, infertility, and heavy or irregular bleeding. Other symptoms may include fatigue and intestinal upset. Yet, curiously, nearly one-half of the women with endometriosis have no symptoms at all. Medical research shows that the amount of pain is not always related to the extent of visible growths. Some women with extensive visible endometrial growths have no pain; others with a few small growths have incapacitating pain. This is one of the many puzzles of endometriosis and an indication of the lack of understanding of the actual disease process. Not all women with endometriosis are infertile, though infertility is a common result with the progression of the condition.

Treatment for endometriosis has varied over the years, but no cure other than hysterectomy and removal of ovaries has yet been found, and even that treatment may be in question. Recent research has shown that even after such drastic measures, women may see a continuation or recurrence of the disease.

Although painkillers are usually prescribed for the pain of endometriosis, hormonal treatments attempt to stop ovulation and put the disease into remission. Because pregnancy often causes a temporary remission of symptoms and because it is believed that infertility is more likely the longer the disease is present, women with endometriosis are often advised not to postpone pregnancy. Conservative surgery, involving removal and cauterization of the growths, is also done and can relieve symptoms and allow pregnancy to occur in some cases.

Early information and knowledge will help women to recognize endometriosis. For the first time in 150 years, the facts about the disease have become available. Endometriosis is open for discussion, questioning, and exploration, not only by the medical profession but by all women.

7

Source of information: Endometriosis Association, Milwaukee, Wisconsin

Questions

1. Who do you think Mahon's primary audience is? Support your answer with evidence from the essay.
2. Sketch a rough outline of the essay, writing a phrase for each paragraph. Does the sequence of development seem logical to you? Is there anything you would add—or omit? How do you feel about her dictionary type beginning?
3. Study Mahon's essay for coherence, noting especially repetition of key words (page 273) and use of the old information/new information principle (page 305).
4. William Zinsser also defined a term for the purpose of information. Compare Mahon's essay with Zinsser's "Taste" on the basis of development and treatment of the word itself.

Reading

Most people can tell what life was like at another time, comparing "then" with "now." The following essay by Frederick Lewis Allen begins with telling "the way it was" in 1900, then generalizes about how everyday life has changed since the time when horses were the primary mode of transportation. Using Allen's descriptions, see if you can envision how your neighborhood might have looked in 1900.

The Way It Was
Frederick Lewis Allen

If a neatly adjusted time machine could take you back to the Main Street of an American town in 1900, to look about you with your present-day eyes, your first exclamation would probably be, "But look at all those horses!"

1

For in that year 1900 there were registered in the whole United States only 13,824 automobiles (as compared with over 44 million in 1950). And they were really few and far between except in the larger cities and the

2

well-to-do resorts. For in 1900 everybody thought of automobiles asplay-things of the rich—and not merely of the rich, but of the somewhat adventurous and sporting rich: people who enjoyed taking their chances with an unpredictable machine that might at any moment wreck them. There were almost no paved highways outside the cities, and of course there were no roadside garages or filling stations; every automobilist must be his own desperate mechanic. Probably half the men and women of America had never seen a car. When William Allen White organized a street fair in Emporia, Kansas, in 1899, the automobile which was brought there for the occasion—and proved to be the most exciting exhibit of the fair—came from Chicago by rail; it was the first automobile ever to have crossed the Missouri River.

But horses were everywhere, pulling surreys, democrats, buggies, cabs, delivery wagons of every sort on Main Street, and pulling harvesters on the tractorless farms out in the countryside. ₃

The sights and sounds and sensations of horse-and-carriage life were part of the universal American experience: the clop-clop of horses' hoofs; the stiff jolting of an iron-tired carriage on a stony road; the grinding noise of the brake being applied to ease the horse on a downhill stretch; the necessity of holding one's breath when the horse sneezed; the sight of sand, carried up on the tires and wooden spokes of a carriage wheel, spilling off in little cascades as the wheel revolved; the look of a country road overgrown by grass, with three tracks in it instead of two, the middle one made by horses' hoofs; the special male ordeal of getting out of the carriage and walking up the steeper hills to lighten the load; and the more severe ordeal, for the unpracticed, of harnessing a horse which could recognize inexperience at one scornful glance. During a Northern winter the jingle of sleigh bells was everywhere. On summer evenings, along the tree-lined streets of innumerable American towns, families sitting on their front porches would watch the fine carriages of the town as they drove past for a proud evening's jaunt, and the cognoscenti would wait eagerly for a glimpse of the banker's trotting pair or the sporting lawyer's 2:40 pacer. And one of the magnificent sights of urban life was that of a fire engine, pulled by three galloping horses, careening down a city street with its bell clanging. ₄

It is hard for us today to realize how very widely communities were separated from one another when they depended for transportation wholly on the railroad and the horse and wagon—and when telephones were still scarce, and radios non-existent. A town which was not situated on a railroad was really remote. A farmer who lived 5 miles outside the county seat made something of an event of hitching up and taking the family to town for a Saturday afternoon's shopping. (His grandchildren make the run in a casual ten minutes, and think nothing of it.) A trip to see friends 10 miles away was likely to be an all-day expedition, for the horse had to be given a chance to rest and be fed. No wonder that each region, each town, each farm was far more dependent upon its own resources—its ₅

own produce, social contacts, amusements—than in later years. For in terms of travel and communication the United States was a very big country indeed.

No wonder, furthermore, that the majority of Americans were less   6 likely than their descendants to be dogged by that frightening sense of insecurity which comes from being jostled by forces—economic, political, international—beyond one's personal ken. Their horizons were close to them. They lived among familiar people and familiar things—individuals and families and fellow townsmen much of their own sort, with ideas intelligible to them. A man's success or failure seemed more likely than in later years to depend upon forces and events within his own range of vision. Less often than his sons and grandsons did he feel that his fortune, indeed his life, might hang upon some decision made in Washington or Berlin or Moscow, for reasons utterly strange to his experience. The world at which he looked over the dashboard of the family carriage might not be friendly, but at least most of it looked understandable.

Questions

1. Using a dictionary, try to find out what kinds of vehicles surreys, democrats, buggies, cabs, delivery wagons, and harvesters were.

2. The word *careen* has two rather different meanings. Its older meaning is "to lean to one side, as a ship does"; a more contemporary meaning is "to move rapidly and in an uncontrolled manner." Which meaning do you think Allen intended when he used the word in paragraph 4?

3. How does Allen appeal to the senses—sight, hearing, and others—in his descriptions?

4. In comparing present-day life with that of 1900, what aspects of life does Allen consider?

5. What does Allen say are the effects of the changes he writes about? Can you think of other effects?

6. Is Allen judgmental about the changes that have occurred since 1900? What is his attitude toward them?

7. Where do you find the thesis of the essay? State it in your own words.

Reading

Like Harrison's "Senses" and McPhee's "Firewood," this essay is about something common to most people: in this case, beer. Your experience is probably limited to drinking it, however. Here are the facts: defined, classified, analyzed. In what ways is the essay informative?

Beer Facts

from *Minnesota Monthly*

The term *beer connoisseur* at first seems an oxymoron. Refinement is not [1] among the attributes of the stereotypical American beer lover—a hairy-knuckled lout who swills down can after can of suds while watching professional bowling on TV. Beer is widely regarded as wine's poor cousin, and most restaurants would never dream of compiling a "beer list" for finicky patrons.

These are facts: (1) Beer is more ancient a libation than wine, with the [2] capability of subtle textures and flavors of indescribable variety; and (2) brewing is more complicated than winemaking.

"Brewing is a very ancient art, but it's a very new science," says Mark [3] Stutrud, president of Summit Brewing Company in St. Paul. By which he means: Beer has been brewed in the same basic way for centuries, but only recently have brewers begun to understand brewing's complex biochemical processes.

On paper, at least, brewing sounds simple. Theoretically, only four [4] ingredients are needed: malted barley, water, hops, and yeast (the latter two being agents of fermentation, flavoring, and preservation rather than ingredients *per se*). The *Reinheitsgebot*, the Bavarian purity law of 1516, dictated that only malted barley, water, hops, and yeast could be used to make beer. Nowadays, however, the major brewers use "adjuncts"—grains other than barley, usually corn and rice—to achieve a thinner, lighter, uniform beverage. It's left to the "craft brewers"—microbrewers, brewpubs, and small regional breweries—to boast about adhering to the *Reinheitsgebot*. And boasting is justified, because an all-malt beer tastes smoother and more flavorful than a beer whose barley grains have been diluted by an adjunct. Even a novice drinker will note a pronounced taste difference between, say, Budweiser, whose formula is probably around 60 percent malt and 40 percent rice, and an all-malt concoction like Summit Extra Pale Ale or Ulmer Lager.

Beer is basically a fermented beverage made from grain. Barley is the [5] best beer-base grain, though it is equally possible to brew beer from wheat, corn, rice, oats, or rye. (The *Reinheitsgebot* was later amended to allow wheat beers.) In order for barley grains to ferment, they must first undergo malting—a difficult process that involves steeping the barley in water and then drying it (and, finally, roasting it, if dark beer is desired). Many small brewers, even the perfectionist craft brewers, sidestep the malting chore by buying their barley already malted.

Minnesota is in the heart of six-row-barley country, but the state's craft [6] brewers generally prefer the two-row Klages malt grown in the Pacific Northwest and Canada. Both Summit and James Page Brewing of Minneapolis use two-row malt, which is said to impart a smoother taste to an all-malt beer. Just about all of the large brewers, however, come to Minnesota and the Dakotas for their malt. (One exception: Anheuser-Busch's Michelob brand uses two-row malt.)

After malting, the barley is fed into a giant vat called a mash tun and   7
mixed with hot water. It is here that the malt's starches are converted to
fermentable sugars. The resulting porridgelike mash is usually filtered (or
"clarified") in a separate kettle, the lauter tun. The strained liquid, called
wort, is essentially unfermented beer. The wort then goes into the brew
kettle, where hops are added and the mixture is boiled.

The common hop, *Humulus lupulus,* is the crucial vine flower that gives   8
beer its bitterness and aromatics. It is also a natural preservative, with
medicinal qualities. Without hops, beer would taste thick and bland. The
Flemish, in the fifteenth century, were the first to use hops in their beer.
Before entering the fermentation tank, the wort is cooled and the spent
hops are removed.

The all-important yeast, the single-celled fungus organism, is added   9
("pitched") in the fermentation tank. An old saw says: "Malt is the soul of
beer, but yeast gives the beer its character." Yeast converts the sugars in
barley to alcohol and carbon dioxide. Because it's an active, living organism,
yeast can behave erratically and cause countless headaches for brewers.

The two basic yeast strains are *Saccharomyces cerevisiae,* for ales, and   10
Saccharomyces carlsbergensis, for lagers. The former usually rises to the top
when it has finished fermenting, while the latter settles at the bottom. The
vast majority of beer consumed in this country, well over 90 percent, is
lager. Pilsner-style lager, named after the Bohemian brewery where it
originated in 1842, is the most common beer style. Pilsners are distinguished by their dry taste and clear, pale-gold color, though there are many
local variations around the world.

Fermentation can take anywhere from several days to several months,   11
depending on the style of beer desired. Most brewers opt to pasteurize their
beer, to kill off potentially harmful bacteria, before the bottling process is
completed. Unfortunately, pasteurization also kills off some of the beer's
natural taste and bouquet, which is why connoisseurs prefer to drink draft
beer (usually unpasteurized) whenever they can.

Questions

1. Do you agree with the writer that beer is a more respectable beverage than
   people commonly think?
2. What is the *Reinheitsgebot,* and what effect does it have on brewing today?
3. What details in this essay tell you it was written for a Minnesota audience? What
   does the essay say about brewing for people who live elsewhere?
4. By what methods is this essay developed?
5. Examine the facts in the essay for examples, testimonies, and statistics. Do you
   find other types of facts?
6. By what methods of coherence does the writer of this essay connect thoughts
   within paragraphs? Concentrate on paragraphs 4 and 5.

CHAPTER 12

To Explain: Writing with Emphasis on the Subject

Much of the writing we are asked to do in school or work involves explaining someone else's thinking. To do this well we must get inside that other person's idea.

—Peter Elbow

Explaining as a purpose for writing has aspects of both informing and instructing. **Explaining** tells *why* something is the way it is or *why* something works the way it does. Sometimes it analyzes *how* something works. If someone asks you how an accident happened, that person wants not just information about the accident but an explanation as well. *Information* gives answers to questions about *what,* instruction to questions about *how; explanation* gives answers to questions about *why* as well as *what* or *how.* Even when an explanation answers *what* or *how,* it implies *why.*

Television weather forecasts are an example of explanation. They tell you not only *what,* "it will rain tomorrow," but *why,* "a warm front is approaching and drawing moisture from the gulf." Elaborate maps and computer-enhanced satellite pictures assist the explanation. As another example, consider a magazine article that not only tells you about over-the-counter pain pills being a potential cause for damage in liver and kidneys but also explains why and how these effects occur. Or, a newsmagazine explains why employees' company loyalty is dying, and another tells why community activists take the drug war into their own hands. Explaining gives reasons, or causes.

Sometimes explanation takes the form of definition. Someone asks you, "What do you mean by *computer literate?*" and you explain what you mean when you use the term. Or an exam question asks you to define *metonymy,* so you explain its meaning as you understand it, giving some examples.

Like information, explanations are often an aspect of persuasive writing. A writer explaining the dangers of a combined dosage of aspirin and acetaminophen probably wants to persuade readers to be more aware of how they use over-the-counter pain pills. A writer explaining the latest oil spill urges greater government control, and one explaining the effects of cigarette smoking on health wants readers to quit smoking or not to start.

Explanations are a common part of schoolwork. First you learn, and then you explain. In quizzes and exams, explanation is often required as an accompaniment to *yes* or *no* answers: "Do you agree with the author? Explain your answer"; "Has the author convinced you of her position? Explain why or why not." Sometimes the exam question simply asks you to explain: "Explain the scientific method"; "Explain how the American ideal of self-help influenced the literature of the late nineteenth century." Sometimes in school the *student* asks for explanations. If an instructor's lecture or your textbook reading is unclear, you may ask for an explanation. Or you may ask the university administration for an explanation of a new policy, say on the repeating of courses.

An explanation presents the writer's understanding of the facts. Explanations therefore require information, or facts, *plus* a discussion of how or why the facts occurred. Explanations include a step of filtering the facts through the writer's mind that purely informative writing does not. Information states the facts as the writer perceives them, so it is influenced by the writer's mind. But explanation, in requiring the writer to account for the facts, requires not only the writer's perceptions and screening of the facts but even more the ability to analyze them and draw inferences from them.

For example, if you were writing an explanation of fatalities in automobile collisions, you would first collect information—possibly by finding statistics in almanacs, reading articles on causes of fatalities, and consulting with a traffic engineer on ways to prevent fatalities. While collecting your information, you would screen out some as irrelevant and, for various reasons, you might simply fail to notice other information that could have been useful to you. You would perceive on the basis of what interested you and what you expected to need in writing your explanation. After you had collected information on traffic fatalities, you would analyze it for causes and types of collisions, immediate causes of death in collisions, the process of impact, and so on, again according to your interests and needs. What inferences you would then draw from your information would be individual, as a result of your thinking processes.

Think of every member of your class starting out with the same statistics, articles, and so on, then each of you writing an explanation of the causes of traffic fatalities. You would each draw different inferences, and all your explanations would be unique. Explanations, then, demand careful, critical reading, with the reader asking pointed questions—such as these:

- Is the writer truly informed?
- Do the conclusions follow logically from the facts?

- Is the writer overlooking important information?
- What are some other possible conclusions?

Writers must be careful about the accuracy and relevance of the information they gather and the care with which they analyze that information and draw inferences from it.

Explanations utilize a variety of methods of development. Cause and effect analysis is common, as in explaining how pain pills affect the health of kidneys and liver or in discussing the reasons for the decline of employees' loyalty to their companies. Other methods are useful too. If you were explaining geothermal energy, you might use a combination of methods: *cause and effect analysis* to discuss the source of the heat energy; *exemplification* to show what geothermal energy is (geysers, volcanic eruptions, and hot springs); *classification* to explain the kinds of geothermal energy (hot water reservoirs, natural steam reservoirs, geopressured reservoirs, the normal geothermal gradient, hot dry rock, and molten magma); *comparison* with other types of energy; *process analysis* to show how geothermal energy has developed and how it is mined; and *analogy* to explain how geothermal energy is like energy from other sources.

If you were explaining hyperactivity in children, you might begin by *defining* what hyperactivity is as you perceive it, conjecturing *causes,* delineating *effects,* and providing *examples.* You might consider the effects and side effects of drug therapy, you might quote the opinions of medical experts, and you might refer to teachers' experiences with hyperactive children. Thus, in explaining hyperactivity, you tell *what* it is, *how* it affects children, and *why* it is an elusive problem.

The essays in this chapter illustrate the broad range of explanation. Almost anything can be the subject of explanation—effects of an exploded hydrogen bomb, reasons for relinquishing custody of one's children, how one views one's friends. These essays also illustrate how broad-ranging the means of developing explanations can be—for example, cause and effect analysis, classification, narration of personal experience, exemplification, and definition.

Explaining by Analogy and Exemplification

Probably from time immemorial people have been explaining what it is like to be human. Early Christians tried to explain what true love, or *agape,* was like. Hebrews explained original sin. Plato, in his "Allegory of the Cave," explained the difficulty of perceiving truth. Every now and then, someone comes up with a new explanation of intuition or cognition or pain—or desire, fear, anger, or any of the other emotions that human beings share. These characteristics have one thing in common: They are difficult to describe. If they were easy to explain, the explanations would now be common knowledge. Each time someone attempts to explain one of these human characteristics, he or she must analyze available data and then make an inferential leap, acquire an insight to say something new about a familiar yet enigmatic subject. Then, to make that insight clear to readers, the writer might use *analogy*, showing how the characteristic is like something already understood, or *exemplification*, giving specific instances of the characteristic as the writer views it. (See Chapter 4.)

Reading

In the essay that follows, philosopher-physician-scientist Lewis Thomas attempts to explain the human ability to discern by intuition—sidelong glances that put two and two together without resort to calculation, that provide insights based on unconscious knowledge, that deal with ambiguity as no computer can. As you read, note how Thomas uses this idea to explain what human beings know and how they could use their knowledge to meet new challenges to understanding the earth.

The Corner of the Eye

Lewis Thomas

There are some things that human beings can see only out of the corner   1
of the eye. The niftiest examples of this gift, familiar to all children, are small, faint stars. When you look straight at one such star, it vanishes; when you move your eyes to stare into the space nearby, it reappears. If you pick two faint stars, side by side, and focus on one of the pair, it disappears and now you can see the other in the corner of your eye, and you can move your eyes back and forth, turning off the star in the center of your retina and switching the other one on. There is a physiological explanation for the phenomenon: we have more rods, the cells we use for light perception, at the periphery of our retinas, more cones, for perceiving color, at the center.

Something like this happens in music. You cannot really hear certain   2
sequences of notes in a Bach fugue unless at the same time there are other notes being sounded, dominating the field. The real meaning in music comes from tones only audible in the corner of the mind.

I used to worry that computers would become so powerful and sophis-   3
ticated as to take the place of human minds. The notion of Artificial Intelligence used to scare me half to death. Already, a large enough machine can do all sorts of intelligent things beyond our capacities: calculate in a split second the answers to mathematical problems requiring years for a human brain, draw accurate pictures from memory, even manufacture successions of sounds with a disarming resemblance to real music. Computers can translate textbooks, write dissertations of their own for doctorates, even speak in machine-tooled, inhuman phonemes any words read off from a

printed page. They can communicate with one another, holding consultations and committee meetings of their own in networks around the earth.

Computers can make errors, of course, and do so all the time in small, irritating ways, but the mistakes can be fixed and nearly always are. In this respect they are fundamentally inhuman, and here is the relaxing thought: computers will not take over the world, they cannot replace us, because they are not designed, as we are, for ambiguity.   4

Imagine the predicament faced by a computer programmed to make language, not the interesting communication in sounds made by vervets or in symbols by brilliant chimpanzee prodigies, but real human talk. The grammar would not be too difficult, and there would be no problem in constructing a vocabulary of etymons, the original, pure, unambiguous words used to name real things. The impossibility would come in making the necessary mistakes we humans make with words instinctively, intuitively, as we build our kinds of language, changing the meanings to imply quite different things, constructing and elaborating the varieties of ambiguity without which speech can never become human speech.   5

Look at the record of language if you want to glimpse the special qualities of the human mind that lie beyond the reach of any machine. Take, for example, the metaphors we use in everyday speech to tell ourselves who we are, where we live, and where we come from.   6

The earth is a good place to begin. The word *earth* is used to name the ground we walk on, the soil in which we grow plants or dig clams, and the planet itself; we also use it to describe all of humanity ("the whole earth responds to the beauty of a child," we say to each other).   7

The earliest word for earth in our language was the Indo-European root *dhghem,* and look what we did with it. We turned it, by adding suffixes, into *humus* in Latin; today we call the complex polymers that hold fertile soil together *humic* acids, and somehow or other the same root became *humility.* With another suffix the word became *human.* Did the earth become human, or did the human emerge from the earth? One answer may lie in that nice cognate word *humble. Humane* was built on, extending the meaning of both the earth and ourselves. In ancient Hebrew, *adamha* was the word for earth, *adam* for man. What computer could run itself through such manipulations as those?   8

We came at the same system of defining ourselves from the other direction. The word *wiros* was the first root for man; it took us in our vanity on to *virile* and *virtue,* but also turned itself into the Germanic word *weraldh,* meaning the life of man, and thence in English to our word *world.*   9

There is a deep hunch in this kind of etymology. The world of man derives from this planet, shares origin with the life of the soil, lives in humility with all the rest of life. I cannot imagine programming a computer to think up an idea like that, not a twentieth-century computer, anyway.   10

The world began with what it is now the fashion to call the "Big Bang." Characteristically, we have assigned the wrong words for the very beginning of the earth and ourselves, in order to evade another term that would cause   11 this century embarrassment. It could not, of course, have been a bang of any sort, with no atmosphere to conduct the waves of sound, and no ears. It was something else, occurring in the most absolute silence we can imagine. It was the Great Light.

We say it had been chaos before, but it was not the kind of place we use the word *chaos* for today, things tumbling over each other and bumping around. Chaos did not have that meaning in Greek; it simply meant empty.   12

We took it, in our words, from chaos to cosmos, a word that simply meant order, cosmetic. We perceived the order in surprise, and our cosmologists and physicists continue to find new and astonishing aspects of the order. We made up the word *universe* from the whole affair, meaning literally turning everything into one thing. We used to say it was a miracle, and we still permit ourselves to refer to the whole universe as a marvel, holding in our unconscious minds the original root meaning of these two words, miracle and marvel—from the ancient root word *smei*, signifying a smile. It immensely pleases a human being to see something never seen before, even more to learn something never known before, most of all to think something never thought before. The rings of Saturn are the latest surprise. All my physicist friends are enchanted by this phenomenon, marveling at the small violations of the laws of planetary mechanics, shocked by the unaccountable braids and spokes stuck there among the rings like graffiti. It is nice for physicists to see something new and inexplicable; it means that the laws of nature are once again about to be amended by a new footnote.   13

The greatest surprise of all lies within our own local, suburban solar system. It is not Mars; Mars was surprising in its way but not flabbergasting; it was a disappointment not to find evidences of life, and there was some sadness in the pictures sent back to earth from the Mars Lander, that lonely long-legged apparatus poking about with its jointed arm, picking up sample after sample of the barren Mars soil, looking for any flicker of life and finding none; the only sign of life on Mars was the Lander itself, an extension of the human mind all the way from earth to Mars, totally alone.   14

Nor is Saturn the great surprise, nor Jupiter, nor Venus, nor Mercury, nor any of the glimpses of the others.   15

The overwhelming astonishment, the queerest structure we know about so far in the whole universe, the greatest of all cosmological scientific puzzles, confounding all our efforts to comprehend it, is the earth. We are only now beginning to appreciate how strange and splendid it is, how it catches the breath, the loveliest object afloat around the sun, enclosed in its own blue bubble of atmosphere, manufacturing and breathing its own oxygen, fixing its own nitrogen from the air into its own soil, generating its own weather at the surface of its rain forests, constructing its own carapace from living parts: chalk cliffs, coral reefs, old fossils from earlier forms of life now covered by layers of new life meshed together around the globe, Troy upon Troy.   16

Seen from the right distance, from the corner of the eye of an extrater- 17
restrial visitor, it must surely seem a single creature, clinging to the round
warm stone, turning in the sun.

Questions

1. How does Thomas explain looking "out of the corner of the eye"? What
   examples does he give? Have you ever noticed this phenomenon before? Can
   you think of other examples?
2. Why is Thomas not worried about computers taking the place of human minds?
3. How does Thomas use language for relating earth and humanity? Which of
   these explanations of our language is most helpful to you in understanding his
   point about the human mind?
4. What is the "deep hunch" that separates computers and human minds?
5. Thomas says that the greatest puzzle yet to be comprehended is the earth itself.
   How can we perceive this familiar world out of the corner of our eyes in order
   to discover new and surprising things?
6. What do you learn about Thomas from reading this essay? How does he use the
   first-person pronouns *I* and *we?*
7. Explain intuition from your own experience.

Discussion

There is a Persian fairy tale about three princes from an island once
called Serendip (now Sri Lanka). Every time these princes went on a journey,
they discovered something valuable quite by accident. While looking for one
thing, they unexpectedly found another. From the experiences of these
mythical princes derives the word *serendipity* to describe unexpected and
fortunate discoveries. Thomas seems to be describing such discoveries when
he says that by focusing on one object we can see another more clearly. He
uses examples of looking at stars and listening to music. What other examples can you think of?

Computers, Thomas says, can't see out of the corners of their eyes—not
because they don't have eyes but because they don't have intuition, or
hunches, those mysterious flashes of knowledge synthesized from expertise
and experience. With this kind of knowledge, people understand metaphors (for example, "rained cats and dogs") and ambiguities, such as the
many meanings for the word *earth.* They can also be surprised at new
discoveries concerning the rings of Saturn, amazed at the birth of a child,
awed at the splendor of another sunset. For this reason, Thomas is no longer
frightened at the possibilities of computer brains. They can never equal the
capabilities of the human brain.

Development

In developing his explanation of the capability of the human brain to discover new things and to be surprised at its discoveries, Thomas employs several approaches. He uses the *analogy* of seeing "out of the corner of the eye"—that peculiar ability to see stars and listen to music by concentrating on different stars and other components of the music. Insights often come this way: while we're studying one thing, we understand something else. This is a distinctly human capability, he says, in contrast to that of a computer brain, which cannot handle perceptions gained by this means. For several paragraphs Thomas then illustrates by *exemplification* the human capability for comprehending the ambiguities of language and understanding what our words say about our lives. Earth and humanity, he says, are conceptually intertwined by the similar roots of the words we use to describe them. All these illustrations show how we see out of the corners of our eyes: while using the word *humane* we think of a peculiarly *human* feature; when using the word *earth* for any one of its many meanings we are cognizant also of all the related meanings.

In paragraph 13 Thomas moves to considering the capacity of the human brain to discover the universe and to marvel at discoveries, using as an example the discoveries concerning the rings of Saturn. To identify "the greatest surprise" not yet fully explored (paragraph 14), Thomas first contrasts what it is *not*—the great surprise is not Mars, Jupiter, or Venus. In paragraphs 16 and 17 he states the point of his essay, that the earth is more amazing than any other discovery in the entire universe could be and that if we just look at it out of the corners of our eyes we will be able to see how splendid it is.

EXERCISE

Experiment with looking "out of the corner of the eye." Try looking at stars, tree branches, windows or other features of buildings, or a distant geographic feature. Then write a page, in your journal or elsewhere, describing the physical and psychological aspects of the experience.

Writing

Explain a characteristic that human beings share. Like Thomas, you probably have no definitive knowledge on the subject, but you can explain the characteristic as you understand it. Choose something that interests you and that is still largely open to consideration. Here are a few topics that might spark ideas for you:

- Intuition
- Pain
- Fear
- Attitudes toward pets
- Attitudes toward gardening
- Smiles

After selecting a topic, observe the attribute in yourself and others and speculate about how and why it happens. Begin asking questions about it, perhaps using the classical probes (see Chapter 3), because they lead to various methods of developing ideas as well as discovering them. Ask some questions like these:

1. What is *x*?
2. How many varieties of *x* do I know of?
3. What are the components of *x*?
4. How does *x* compare with similar things?
5. How does *x* differ from similar things?
6. How does *x* work?
7. What are some examples of *x*?
8. What are the causes of *x*?
9. What are the effects of *x*?

As ideas emerge, think about a point for your explanation. Thomas's point is that by looking out of the corners of our eyes, we can discover new things about our world. That's an important point, and, once you get going on your topic, you can probably make one that is equally important. You may be able to think of an analogy for explaining your subject, for example "fear is looking over your shoulder all the time." Whether you use analogy or not, try to include enough examples that your readers will understand your point. Consider using more than one method of development to cover your subject as thoroughly as necessary. In your essay, express your point wherever it seems appropriate—near the beginning or, as Thomas does, near the end.

Explaining Causes or Reasons

Do you sometimes feel compelled to explain why you made a particular choice about a personal matter? Not that it's anybody's business, but you still feel the pressure of questions and criticisms from friends, relatives, acquaintances, perhaps even society: Why did you decide to go to this school? Why did you choose to have an abortion? Why did you start smoking cigarettes? Why do you want to live at home? Why? Why? Why?

So you write to explain your choice. You may write your explanation in the form of a letter, an essay, or a journal entry. Sometimes your explanations will influence other people to make similar choices, sometimes absolve you from criticism, and sometimes make you feel better for having written them.

Explanations of personal choices usually give the background for the decision—what your life was like before the choice, what the range of choices was, how you weighed them, how you made your decision. Explanations of this kind may be developed by narrative, giving the chronological history leading to the choice. They may be developed by cause and effect, showing the causes of your choice. And they may use classification in describing the various choices available.

However you choose to develop an explanation and whatever form it takes, what you write comes from your personal experience. You likely don't need to do any background reading, and you probably don't need to consult with anyone on the details. What you do need to do is search your own mind and emotions to try to discover why you made the choice and what your attitudes toward it are. It is very likely that you will need to write several drafts to get an explanation that accurately reflects your reasons for making the choice.

Reading

In the essay that follows, a nontraditional student writer explains why she made a particular choice. Pressured by family, friends, acquaintances, and even strangers to account for what they considered an "unnatural" choice for a mother to make, Coral Watercott thought long and hard about her reasons. In explaining her choice, she wrote several drafts and sought feedback from a variety of readers, among them her classmates and her ex-husband. Here is her final draft. As you read it, consider the difficulty of writing such an essay and observe how she develops her explanation.

Responsible Choices
Coral Watercott

In a society of tradition and accepted ways of doing things, I have   1
chosen in my life to do some things in a very nontraditional way. I am a divorced woman and the noncustodial parent of two daughters and a son. Crystal is ten, Marisa is nine, and Ricky is five. I pay child support and pick up my children every other weekend and alternating holidays. I call them on the phone once a week to connect with them and find out how they are doing at home and in school.

When I relinquished custody of the children to my ex-husband, Rich-   2
ard, I was met with open hostility and indignation from many women. Even those I anticipated getting some support from turned away from me, not able to understand how I, as a mother, could do such a thing. I was verbally

abused by some women and scorned by many. Each woman who learned of my status as a noncustodial parent, those with children and those without, put up an invisible wall and would not hear when I attempted to explain my reasons for the choices I had to make.

Women I respected and thought were my friends openly expressed   3
their anger. I was told by my mother that children belong with their mother, no matter what the situation is. A neighbor came to my place of employment and yelled at me for being so selfish. She couldn't understand how I could do such a thing to my children and still be able to sleep at night knowing the pain I had inflicted on my own flesh and blood. I was pointed at in restaurants and whispered about in the grocery store where I worked.

I spent the first two years of the separation justifying my actions, trying   4
to live with my decision, and struggling to understand why this was such a horrible decision on my part. I was guilt-ridden, ashamed; I began to question my own identity as a woman. I tried to learn why I was different, how I could do this when so many of my own gender were telling me how wrong it was.

I had many reasons for not obtaining custody of my children. Before   5
my separation and divorce, I had to take a long, hard look at my life and what I had to offer the children as their mother and a responsible adult. The only choice I could make was to have the children live with their father.

I grew up in a dysfunctional home. My mother and father were di-   6
vorced when I was twelve years old, and my mother remarried. My father, mother, and stepfather all have serious drinking problems. My parents were all abusive in one form or another, and their abuse had a huge effect on my life, both as a child and as an adult.

When I married Richard, I felt that by moving out of my parents' home   7
and into my own all my problems would disappear. I was going to leave the abuse and the alcohol behind and begin my own life with my own family. I decided then that my life would be very different from that of my parents. My children would never have to suffer the abuse that I had to and I would be the "perfect" parent. I would never abuse my own children the way that I had been abused, and I vowed to myself that I would be just the opposite of my parents.

Six years and three children later, I realized that I was miserable. My life   8
was falling apart and I felt as though I were going crazy. I was drinking heavily and my marriage had disintegrated. One morning, I looked in the mirror and found that I was the one person I never wanted to be—my mother. It was at that moment I realized that I needed help and began to try to put my life back together.

After seeing the damage done to my marriage, I knew there was no   9
way that I could ever save it. I made the decision to separate from my husband. Then the only decision left to make was who the children were going to live with.

I knew in my heart that I had to deal with the issues of abuse in my   10
childhood and that those issues made me an unhealthy parent. Although at

that point I had not physically abused my children, I knew that there had to be some emotional abuse inflicted upon them. I also knew that I was not capable of raising three children alone. I was afraid that there would come a time when I would lose control and hit my children. I had no idea what a good parent was because I had had no role models to learn from. I didn't want my children to grow up as I did. I wanted a better life for them.

Society dictates that mothers obtain custody of their children. Mothers that do not have custody of their children are obviously rotten parents and don't care about their children. Knowing that "good" mothers keep their children, I was in a dilemma. I wanted to be a good mother and give my children a happy life. Yet I knew that I couldn't be a good mother until I worked on the issues of my past. I would be a better mother if I left the children with their father.   11

I did the only thing I could do and still sleep at night. I left the children with their father. He was loving, caring, and sensitive to their needs. I felt secure knowing that the kids would be in his care, that they would be well taken care of and loved.   12

Since that time five years ago, I have dealt with many issues from my childhood and I am now a confident, healthy mother. I have learned how to be a good mother, how to take care of my children and not to make the same mistakes my parents did when they raised me. I have also learned what normal children are like and how they behave. I no longer expect myself to be a perfect parent or expect my children to be perfect kids.   13

I know now that I made the right decision. I still deal with attitudes from women who do not understand my choices and turn away from me. I no longer believe that just because I was born female I make a better parent. I know that men make excellent parents. They have just as much love for their children as women do. I don't feel guilty or ashamed of my decision. In fact, I am proud that I had courage to be honest with myself and loved my children enough to let them go. I am closer now to my children than I ever was. We have a healthy relationship, and they know the reasons they live with their father.   14

If a woman asks me how I could let my children go, I tell her that I did it because I loved them. When I'm asked if I'll obtain custody some day, I reply that it depends on what my children want and how their father feels about it. As long as the kids are happy and healthy, that is all I need to know.   15

I hope that women in today's society faced with issues I have been faced with will look at their situations honestly. Women do have choices and we have the responsibility to make the choices that are best for us, not ones that fit best into the norms of society. Women are not born with innate parenting qualities; these qualities are taught to us by our parents. Women have to learn as much as men about how to be healthy parents. Many of us were raised in dysfunctional homes, and many have yet to deal with the issues of our own childhoods. To raise healthy children for tomorrow's world, we have to work at being healthy parents today.   16

Questions

1. Why does Watercott feel the need to explain her decision to give custody of her children to their father?

2. What is your reaction to Watercott's explanation? Does she adequately explain her reasons for the decision?

3. What are some of the cause and effect relationships in this essay?

4. Whom does Watercott assume as an audience?

5. What is Watercott's purpose for explaining her choice? to persuade? to justify herself? something else?

6. If you had been in Watercott's position, what choice do you think you might have made?

Discussion

The people we associate with have certain ideas of what individuals should do in particular circumstances. Married couples should have children. Couples with children should be married. Mothers should have primary responsibility for child care. When someone goes against the accepted ideas, others in the society exert pressure in the form of disapproval and ostracism. Sometimes the disapproval can be cleared up with an explanation of the reasons for the frowned-upon action. Sometimes the explanation accomplishes no more than to make the explainer feel better.

Watercott seems to have a purpose other than to silence criticism or to make herself feel better. Her repeated references to society and what roles women expect of other women point to a persuasive purpose—perhaps to change attitudes, perhaps to encourage women in similar circumstances to do what they know is right.

Writing an explanation like Watercott's is difficult. In her first draft Watercott didn't face her real reasons for giving up her children. She brought up things like her husband's nice house in the country and his propensity toward fatherhood. She mentioned that she felt the need to return to school. She totally omitted any reference to her childhood, her alcoholism, and her own doubts about her nurturing abilities. The essay was flabby, mainly an attack on society's criticisms. In the revision, however, she was more willing to deal with the issues squarely and was more honest about her shortcomings. The second draft required some editing and a little shuffling of paragraphs, but it was essentially the draft you have read here.

Thesis and Development

Watercott's essay explains reasons for an action. She organizes her explanation from the *specific to the general*, with an overall narrative, *chronological* structure. Throughout most of the essay she writes about her experience; this sentence from paragraph 5 might be considered her thesis: "I had many reasons for not obtaining custody of my children." After explaining her own case, however, she concludes with a much broader, more general statement: "I hope that women in today's society faced with issues I have been faced with will look at their situations honestly." At this point she addresses other women who might be in similar circumstances: "Women are not born with innate parenting qualities; these qualities are taught to us by our parents. " At this point the essay seems to have a purpose other than to justify Watercott's own actions.

Watercott's explanation develops *causally*. She begins with an effect, the relinquishment of custody of her children, and proceeds to discuss causes: her childhood in a dysfunctional and abusive family, her fears that she would become an abusive parent, her alcoholism, her lack of appropriate role models for either parents or children. At paragraph 13 she begins discussing the effects of her decision to give up her children and search for her own identity: she is now a confident, knowledgeable, loving parent, and her children are happy and well cared for.

EXERCISE

Write a journal entry on social pressures, freewriting (see Chapter 3) until you discover a specific instance in which a decision of yours was subject to social pressure. If you do the following writing assignment, this freewriting can open up ideas for you.

Writing

There have probably been times when you have been misunderstood, when a choice you've made was disapproved of by family, friends, or acquaintances. You may have taken a stand on an unpopular issue, befriended a person outside your social group, refused to go along with your friends' activities. At such times, you probably felt that you wanted to explain your position—to tell others why you were convinced that the choice you made was right, and perhaps to encourage others to follow their own conscience and reasoning, not the pressures of the social group.

Write your explanation, either as an essay or as a letter to someone who would be an appropriate audience, someone you want to convince of the merits of your decision. You will probably use cause and effect analysis at least in part. You may also use some narrative as you give background.

Because explaining actions is difficult, you may be dissatisfied with your first draft, so allow plenty of time for heavy revision. If you can, get feedback from two kinds of readers: someone who knows you and the circumstances and someone, like a classmate, who is only an acquaintance. If their advice makes sense, follow it, but rely mostly on your own sense of what needs to be said.

Explaining by Definition

It is often necessary for people to explain their terms when they write. A report on the morphinelike effect of endorphins would explain what these brain chemicals are and how they affect the body's reaction to pain. A discussion of attention-deficit hyperactivity disorder (ADHD) would define this medical term for a particular condition in children. Explanations are often a part of a piece of writing that has another purpose: to report, to persuade, and so on. Like other forms of explanation, explanatory definitions tell *why* and *how* something is the way it is. By telling how endorphins work, a writer defines the word. By telling how hyperactivity affects children and why they may be affected, a writer explains what hyperactivity is.

Reading

Elliott Aronson, a noted behavioral psychologist, wrote a chapter on human aggression in his book *The Human Animal* (1984). He began his chapter by introducing the idea that "we humans have shown ourselves to be an aggressive species. With the exception of certain rodents, no other vertebrates so consistently and wantonly kill members of their own kind." At this point, before going further in his discussion of the psychology of human aggression, he paused to devote three paragraphs to defining *aggression*. What is his explanation of what aggression is?

Aggression Defined
Elliott Aronson

It is difficult to present a clear definition of *aggression* because the term   1
is used in so many different ways in common speech. Clearly, the Boston Strangler, who made a hobby of strangling women in their apartments, was performing acts of aggression. But a football player making a tackle is also considered aggressive. A tennis player who charges the net is called aggressive. So, too, is a successful insurance salesperson who is "a real go-getter." The young girl who staunchly defends her own possessions against the encroachment of other children and the young girl who goes out of her way to clobber her brother are both considered aggressive. On a more subtle level, if a neglected husband sulks in the corner during a party, this may be an act of "passive aggression." Also, a child who wets the bed, a jilted boy

friend who threatens suicide, or a student who doggedly attempts to master a difficult mathematical problem could conceivably be labeled as illustrations of an aggressive tendency in human beings. And what of the violence exerted by the state in its attempt to maintain law and order—and the less direct forms of aggression through which people of one race or religion humiliate and degrade people of different races or religions? If all these behaviors are to come under the blanket term *aggression,* the situation is indeed confused. As a way of increasing our understanding of aggression, we must cut through this morass and separate the "assertive" aspects of the popular definition from the destructive aspects. That is, a distinction can be made between behavior that harms others and behavior that does not harm others. Accordingly, the go-getting salesperson or the student doggedly sticking to the mathematical problem would not be considered aggressive, but the Boston Strangler, the clobbering child, the suicidal boy friend, and even the sulking, neglected husband would all be defined as aggressive.

But this distinction is not altogether satisfactory because, by concentrating on an outcome alone, it ignores the intention of the person perpetrating the act, and this is the crucial aspect of *aggression.* I would define an act of aggression as a behavior aimed at causing harm or pain. Thus, by definition, the football player is *not* considered to be performing an act of aggression if his aim is simply to bring down his opponent as efficiently as possible—but he *is* behaving aggressively if his aim is to cause pain or injury, whether or not he succeeds in doing so. To illustrate, suppose a three-year-old boy slaps at his father in anger. The slap may be totally ineffectual—it may even cause his father to laugh. But it is, nonetheless, an aggressive act. Similarly, the same child may, in total innocence, thrust a sharp elbow into his father's eye, causing severe pain and colorful contusions. Because its painful consequences were unintentional, this would not be defined as an act of aggression.

It might be useful to make one additional distinction regarding intentional aggression, namely, a distinction between aggression that is an end in itself and aggression that is instrumental in achieving some goal. The first we will call *hostile aggression;* the second we will call *instrumental aggression.* Thus, a football player might intentionally inflict an injury on the opposing quarterback in order to put him out of the game and thus increase his own team's probability of winning. This would be instrumental aggression. On the other hand, he might perform this action on the last play of the last game of the season to "pay back" the quarterback for some real or imagined insult or humiliation; this is hostile aggression since the aggressive act is an end in itself. Similarly, dropping a bomb on a ball-bearing factory in Munich in World War II can be considered an act of instrumental aggression, while shooting down defenseless women and children in a Vietnamese village can be considered an act of hostile aggression. The "hit man" working for the Mafia who guns down a designated victim is probably behaving instrumentally; thrill killers, such as members of the Manson family, probably are not.

Questions

1. According to Aronson, what are the problems in trying to define *aggression?*

2. Which of his definitions do you favor—those in the first paragraph, the one in the second, or those in the third?

3. Applying Aronson's definition of *aggression* as behavior aimed at causing harm or pain, decide whether the following acts are aggressive:
   a. A man beating his wife in an alcoholic rage
   b. A twelve-year-old hanging himself
   c. A couple pushing to the front of a line at a movie theater
   d. A teenager stealing an automobile
   e. A two-year-old striking his sister with a stick

4. What effect do the aggressive behaviors described in the first paragraph have on their recipients?

5. What is the tone of Aronson's definition? What does his tone tell you about his purpose?

6. In what ways does Aronson explain the *how* and *why* of aggression?

Discussion

In this essay within a chapter, Aronson begins by showing why he needs to define *aggression:* the term is used so broadly that it could mean almost any assertive act. Given different contexts it could mean a tennis player's manner on the court, a child's wetting the bed, and a student's determination to solve a math problem. With such wide-ranging meanings, definition is necessary, so Aronson defines the word as he uses it. You may not totally agree with Aronson's definition of *aggression,* but in the context of his chapter on the psychological aspects of the behavior, the definition is correct.

Development

Aronson develops his definition from *general to specific,* beginning with a broad definition and gradually narrowing it to one he can work with. From his opening definition of *aggression* as many kinds of assertive acts, he redefines and narrows the term as behavior that harms others, then narrows it still more as behavior *intended* to harm others; finally he divides his definition into two specific kinds of aggressive behavior, hostile and instrumental. From the general, he has developed a very specific definition, one he can use for his extended discussion.

To clarify his definition at each point, Aronson uses another method of development—*exemplification,* explaining each definition with numerous examples. In the final paragraph he uses comparison—contrasting hostile aggression with instrumental aggression.

Thesis

Aronson's definition of *aggression* is found in his second paragraph: "I would define an act of aggression as a behavior aimed at causing harm or pain." This is not his thesis, however. Remember that a thesis is (1) a statement of the subject and (2) an assertion about the subject. The subject of the essay is defining aggression, and this sentence is part of the subject—it defines aggression. It is not an assertion about defining aggression.

A sentence that *does* state the subject and make an assertion about it is the first sentence of the essay: "It is difficult to present a clear definition of *aggression* because the term is used in so many different ways in common speech." Here the subject is defining aggression and the assertion about it is that such definition is difficult. The remainder of the sentence tells how the definition will be developed, by showing the "many different ways" the word is used.

EXERCISE

With classmates, brainstorm (see Chapter 3) a list of aggressive acts and then classify them first as intending to harm others or not, and then as hostile or instrumental. For ease in visualizing your classification, lay out a chart something like this:

Brainstormed list	Intentional harm	Not intentional harm	Hostile aggression	Instrumental aggression

Finally, discuss whether Aronson's definition is adequate for defining aggressive acts as you and your classmates know them.

Writing

Definition is usually part of a larger piece of writing. A writer defines a word because it needs to be clarified in its context. Aronson couldn't discuss the psychological aspects of aggression without first explaining how he was using the term. You're not writing a chapter of a book as Aronson did, but you do have contexts that sometimes require definition. In one of your subjects other than English, select a word that must be precisely defined in order to understand the subject. It may be a word that has multiple meanings, as *aggression* does, or it may be one that is difficult to comprehend without clarification and examples. Here are some idea starters:

- History
- Energy
- Pollution

- Radiation
- Noise

If doing so is appropriate for your context, develop your definition from general to specific, beginning with the broadest use and narrowing to something more particular. However you decide to arrange the development of your essay, you will probably want to use a number of examples to assist you. As you write, remember that this is *your* definition. Other people in other contexts may use the word differently, but in your context you use it the way you define it.

Conventional usage in definitions is that words named as words are underlined or italicized, as you have seen with *aggression*. Words referring to the thing itself, for example the act of aggression, are not underlined or italicized. (See an example on page 346.)

Explaining by Classification

One way people make sense of their world and manage all the information they encounter is to divide and classify. We classify trees as deciduous and coniferous, and we further classify deciduous trees as oaks, maples, elms, and so on, with coniferous trees having other classifications. We could take each item in a class and divide it still further: burr oaks, pin oaks, and so on if we're working with oak trees. We classify much of our world: automobiles, dogs, music, athletics, magazines—most of what we encounter daily. By classifying, we organize information and thus know more about it and make it easier for us to remember. If we classify automobiles as foreign made and American made, each new car that comes along will go into one category or the other. If we classify American-made cars by maker, the distinctions will be even finer, and, as a result of our experience, we may know certain things about items in each class: the durability of parts, for example, the dependability of service, or the likelihood of recalls.

Classification occurs on the basis of shared characteristics, and these characteristics enable us to understand the items of the class. We understand certain things about country music that are not true of jazz. We know things about team athletics that are not true of individual sports. If you were to classify computers, you would look at types of operating systems, kilobyte capacities, the computers' main purposes compared with your purpose, and so on. Knowing that a Zenith is more like an IBM than like an Apple, you would classify the Zenith with the IBM.

Shared characteristics are determined by *principles of classification*, and these principles are dependent on needs. If you were considering buying a computer for word processing, you would classify differently than if you wanted primarily data-processing and spreadsheet capabilities. You would concentrate more on the computers that have features particularly attractive to word processing, making finer distinctions in classifying those features. Your principles for classification might be how functional the keyboard is for word processing, how easy the monitor is on the eyes for long periods, what types of word-processing software can be used with the computer, and whether the software is included in the purchase price. If you were to classify friends, as Judith Viorst does in the essay that follows, your principles of classification might be the locale of the friendships, their intensity, and their function. And because you would be classifying from your own perspective, you would do it according to the kinds of friends you have and how you view friendships.

Reading

In this essay, Judith Viorst explains women's friends by classifying her own. As you read, try to discover the principles of classification that determine Viorst's categories and her perspective on friendships.

Friends, Good Friends—and Such Good Friends

Judith Viorst

Women are friends, I once would have said, when they totally love and support and trust each other, and bare to each other the secrets of their souls, and run—no questions asked—to help each other, and tell harsh truths to each other (no, you can't wear that dress unless you lose ten pounds first) when harsh truths must be told.   1

Women are friends, I once would have said, when they share the same affection for Ingmar Bergman, plus train rides, cats, warm rain, charades, Camus, and hate with equal ardor Newark and Brussels sprouts and Lawrence Welk and camping.   2

In other words, I once would have said that a friend is a friend all the way, but now I believe that's a narrow point of view. For the friendships I have and the friendships I see are conducted at many levels of intensity, serve many different functions, meet different needs and range from those as all-the-way as the friendship of the soul sisters mentioned above to that of the most nonchalant and casual playmates.   3

Consider these varieties of friendship: 4

Convenience friends. These are the women with whom, if our paths weren't crossing all the time, we'd have no particular reason to be friends: a next-door neighbor, a woman in our car pool, the mother of one of our children's closest friends, or maybe some mommy with whom we serve juice and cookies each week at the Glenwood Co-op Nursery.   5

Convenience friends are convenient indeed. They'll lend us their cups and silverware for a party. They'll drive our kids to soccer when we're sick. They'll take us to pick up our car when we need a lift to the garage. They'll even take our cats when we go on vacation. As we will for them.   6

But we don't, with convenience friends, ever come too close or tell too 7
much; we maintain our public face and emotional distance. "Which means,"
says Elaine, "that I'll talk about being overweight but not about being
depressed. Which means I'll admit being mad but not blind with rage.
Which means I might say that we're pinched this month but never that I'm
worried sick over money."

But which doesn't mean that there isn't sufficient value to be found in 8
these friendships of mutual aid, in convenience friends.

Special-interest friends. These friendships aren't intimate, and they 9
needn't involve kids or silverware or cats. Their value lies in some interest
jointly shared. And so we may have an office friend or a yoga friend or a
tennis friend or a friend from the Women's Democratic Club.

"I've got one woman friend," says Joyce, "who likes, as I do, to take 10
psychology courses. Which makes it nice for me—and nice for her. It's fun to go
with someone you know and it's fun to discuss what you've learned, driving
back from the classes." And for the most part, she says, that's all they discuss.

"I'd say that what we're doing is doing together, not being together," 11
Suzanne says of her Tuesday-doubles friends. "It's mainly a tennis relationship, but we play together well. And I guess we all need to have a
couple of playmates."

I agree. 12

My playmate is a shopping friend, a woman of marvelous taste, a 13
woman who knows exactly *where* to buy *what,* and furthermore is a woman
who always knows beyond a doubt what one ought to be buying. I don't
have the time to keep up with what's new in eyeshadow, hemlines, and shoes
and whether the smock look is in or finished already. But since (oh, shame!)
I care a lot about eyeshadow, hemlines, and shoes, and since I don't *want* to wear
smocks if the smock look is finished, I'm very glad to have a shopping friend.

Historical friends. We all have a friend who knew us when . . . maybe 14
way back in Miss Meltzer's second grade, when our family lived in that
three-room flat in Brooklyn, when our dad was out of work for seven
months, when our brother Allie got in that fight where they had to call the
police, when our sister married the endodontist from Yonkers, and when, the
morning after we lost our virginity, she was the first, the only, friend we told.

The years have gone by and we've gone separate ways and we've little in 15
common now, but we're still an intimate part of each other's past. And so
whenever we go to Detroit we always go to visit this friend of our girlhood.
Who knows how we looked before our teeth were straightened. Who knows
how we talked before our voice got unBrooklyned. Who knows what we ate
before we learned about artichokes. And who, by her presence, puts us in touch
with an earlier part of ourself, a part of ourself it's important never to lose.

"What this friend means to me and what I mean to her," says Grace, "is 16
having a sister without sibling rivalry. We know the texture of each other's
lives. She remembers my grandmother's cabbage soup. I remember the way
her uncle played the piano. There's simply no other friend who remembers
those things."

Crossroads friends. Like historical friends, our crossroads friends are 17
important for *what was*—for the friendship we shared at a crucial, now past,
time of life. A time, perhaps, when we roomed in college together; or
worked as eager young singles in the Big City together; or went together, as
my friend Elizabeth and I did through pregnancy, birth, and that scary first
year of new motherhood.

Crossroads friends forge powerful links, links strong enough to endure 18
with not much more contact than once-a-year letters at Christmas. And out
of respect for those crossroads years, for those dramas and dreams we once
shared, we will always be friends.

Cross-generational friends. Historical friends and crossroads seem to 19
maintain a special kind of intimacy—dormant but always ready to be re-
vived—and though we may rarely meet, whenever we do connect, it's
personal and intense. Another kind of intimacy exists in the friendships that
form across generations in what one woman calls her daughter-mother and
her mother-daughter relationships.

Evelyn's friend is her mother's age—"but I share much more than I 20
ever could with my mother"—a woman she talks to of music, of books, and
of life. "What I get from her is the benefit of her experience. What she
gets—and enjoys—from me is a youthful perspective. It's a pleasure for
both of us."

I have in my own life a precious friend, a woman of sixty-five who has 21
lived very hard, who is wise, who listens well; who has been where I am and
can help me understand it; and who represents not only an ultimate ideal
mother to me but also the person I'd like to be when I grow up.

In our daughter role we tend to do more than our share of self- 22
revelation; in our mother role we tend to receive what's revealed. It's
another kind of pleasure—playing wise mother to a questing younger
person. It's another very lovely kind of friendship.

Part-of-a-couple friends. Some of the women we call our friends we 23
never see alone—we see them as part of a couple at couples' parties. And
though we share interests in many things and respect each other's views, we
aren't moved to deepen the relationship. Whatever the reason, a lack of
time or—and this is more likely—a lack of chemistry, our friendship remains in
the context of a group. But the fact that our feeling on seeing each other is
always, "I'm *so* glad she's here" and the fact that we spend half the evening
talking together says that this too, in its own way, counts as a friendship.

(Other part-of-a-couple friends are the friends that came with the 24
marriage, and some of these are friends we could live without. But sometimes, alas, she married our husband's best friend; and sometimes, alas, she
is our husband's best friend. And so we find ourself dealing with her,
somewhat against our will, in a spirit of what I'll call *reluctant* friendship.)

Men who are friends. I wanted to write just of women friends, but the 25
women I've talked to won't let me—they say I must mention man-woman
friendships too. For these friendships can be just as close and as dear as those
that we form with women. Listen to Lucy's description of one such friendship:

"We've found we have things to talk about that are different from what he talks about with my husband and different from what I talk about with his wife. So sometimes we call on the phone or meet for lunch. There are similar intellectual interests—we always pass on to each other the books that we love—but there's also something tender and caring too." 26

In a couple of crises, Lucy says, "He offered himself, for talking and for helping. And when someone died in his family he wanted me there. The sexual, flirty part of our friendship is very small, but *some*—just enough to make it fun and different." She thinks—and I agree—that the sexual part, though small, is always *some*, is always there when a man and a woman are friends. 27

It's only in the past few years that I've made friends with men, in the sense of a friendship that's *mine*, not just part of two couples. And achieving with them the ease and the trust I've found with women friends has value indeed. Under the dryer at home last week, putting on mascara and rouge, I comfortably sat and talked with a fellow named Peter. Peter, I finally decided, could handle the shock of me minus mascara under the dryer. Because we are for each other. Because we're friends. 28

There are medium friends, and pretty good friends, and very good friends indeed, and these friendships are defined by their level of intimacy. And what we'll reveal at each of these levels of intimacy is calibrated with care. We might tell a medium friend, for example, that yesterday we had a fight with our husband. And we might tell a pretty good friend that this fight with our husband made us so mad that we slept on the couch. And we might tell a very good friend that the reason we got so mad in that fight that we slept on the couch had something to do with that girl who works in his office. But it's only to our very best friends that we're willing to tell all, to tell what's going on with that girl in his office. 29

The best of friends, I still believe, totally love and support and trust each other, and bare to each other the secrets of their souls, and run—no questions asked—to help each other, and tell harsh truths to each other when they must be told. 30

But we needn't agree about everything (only twelve-year-old girl friends agree about *everything*) to tolerate each other's point of view. To accept without judgment. To give and take without ever keeping score. And to *be* there, as I am for them and as they are for me, to comfort our sorrows, to celebrate our joys. 31

Questions

1. Viorst classifies friends according to variety and level of intensity. What eight varieties of friends does she discuss? How many levels of intensity does she describe? Would her system of classification work for classifying men's friends?

2. Is Viorst's perspective on friendships the same as yours? Which varieties would you omit if you were classifying friends? What categories would you add?

3. What do you learn about Viorst from what she says about friends?

4. What kind of male friendship does Viorst describe? Do you agree that friendships of this kind are possible for a woman who may be married or may have an intimate relationship with a different man?

5. Can you see any advantage to classifying friends according to variety and intensity? What might have prompted Viorst to write an essay about friends?

6. In what ways does Viorst explain the *how* and *why* of women's friendships?

Discussion

Have you ever told a friend some intimate detail of your life and then discovered that soon everyone you know was talking about it? Have you ever got into trouble by going along with the actions of your friends when your wiser self was telling you not to? These might be some reasons to sit down and examine your friendships. If you talk intimately with a "medium" friend or a "pretty good friend," one who has no close relationship with you, that person may, for a variety of reasons, discuss the details of your life with other people. If your friends are doing things you disapprove of, these friends may not be as close as you thought. To distinguish between friends of this kind and "best of friends" has some advantages. And to classify your friends according to what you do with them might help you to say no when they want you to do things you're not comfortable with.

We don't know what Viorst's reason was for examining her friendships, but with her emphasis on topics of discussion, it might have been betrayal of a confidence. Her introductory paragraphs may support such a view. More to the point for you as a reader, however, is what reason she had for explaining her *classification* of friends in a published essay. She undoubtedly assumed that readers could profit from, or at least be interested in, her explanation. Her purpose for explaining may therefore be to prompt readers to examine their own friendships to see what types they may be.

Thesis and Development

After two background paragraphs on what Viorst "once would have said," the third paragraph and the single-sentence fourth paragraph express the thesis and organization of this essay. Here we have a statement that says there are many varieties of friendship and these varieties are based on such characteristics as levels of intensity, functions, and needs.

Under each category, Viorst then explains its functions and needs. Convenience friends, for example, are people who do little things for us because it is handy to have such mutual aid available from neighbors, but they're people we don't discuss private matters with. With cross-generational friends, by contrast, we may discuss private matters, though it seems from Viorst's description that mainly the younger member of the pair does the discussion, while the older member seems to have the role of adviser.

In keeping with her introductory background about not all women's friends being "soul sisters," Viorst explains the kinds of conversations that might be had with each type of friend. With historical friends, she talks about old times, with special-interest friends she discusses that special interest and rarely anything else, and with part-of-a-couple friends she discusses a variety of subjects but only when they get together as couples. With her men friends she can discuss intellectual interests and enjoy the small flirty part of the relationship.

Viorst's final variety of friendship is the "best of friends." She develops this category within her second principle of classification: intensity of friend-ships, or "levels of intimacy." Only to the best of friends do we "tell all." Only the best of friends can be trusted not to compromise our secrets, can be relied on to comfort us when we need comforting, and can be expected to honestly tell us when we're wrong. These are the friends Viorst once would have said were the only kind of friends. Her essay thus brings the discussion back to the beginning, where she refutes her older idea about friends.

EXERCISE

Combine Viorst's major principles of classification: variety and level of intensity. Make a chart of "medium friends," "pretty good friends," and "very good friends," and then, weighing functions, place each of the eight varieties in one of these levels. Discuss with classmates your decisions and the reasons for your classifications.

Writing

Respond to Viorst's classification of friends with your own perspective on how friends should be classified. Begin with a brainstormed list, jotting down as many kinds of friends as you can think of (see Chapter 3). Push yourself until you have a long list—twelve to fifteen items. Then group your items and eliminate those that don't apply. Compare your list with Viorst's and note differences. Discuss your categories with friends or classmates to get their perspectives. Then begin thinking what you can say about the varieties, functions, or intensities of friendships that may be different from what Viorst has said.

Your introductory paragraphs, like Viorst's, may provide the back-ground for the discussion; in your case, it may be that you disagree with Viorst's categories, that her classification doesn't apply to unmarried college students, that the female perspective isn't relevant to men, that there is no such thing as a "best friend" as Viorst describes her, and so on. Then state your position—how you classify friends.

Determine a specific purpose for writing, such as to show the categories of friendship for college students and to explain why these categories differ from those of mature women. Your purpose might be to explain why no friends can be trusted to keep silent about intimate details of their friends' lives, or why women can't be close friends with men without the relationship becoming sexual. As you consider what to write, decide on a specific audience—such as fellow college students, any men, or any women.

Be specific in your development of each category, explaining how each is different from the others, perhaps quoting friends, giving examples, discussing what you talk about or do with friends in each category. When you have a rough draft, have a classmate read it and tell you if you've omitted something important, if you haven't been clear enough, if you have been unnecessarily wordy, and whatever else you might want to know before completing your revision for a final draft.

ADDITIONAL READINGS FOR DISCUSSION

Reading

The following excerpt from Jonathan Schell's book *The Fate of the Earth* (1982) is an unremitting tale of horror explaining what would happen with the explosion of a hydrogen bomb. First published in *The New Yorker* magazine, the essay is extremely unpleasant reading, and you will want to stop long before you have reached the end. To make matters worse, you will find the paragraphs long, but their very length seems to reflect the weight of the subject matter. If you complete the reading, you will learn more than you ever wanted to know about the consequences of nuclear warfare. (In connection with this reading, you might read Lewis Thomas's reflection "Late Night Thoughts on Listening to Mahler's Ninth Symphony" in Chapter 6 and Holly Sue Anderson's "Nuclear Children" in Chapter 7.)

A Description of the Effects of a One-Megaton Bomb

Jonathan Schell

What happened at Hiroshima was less than a millionth part of a holo-   1
caust at present levels of world nuclear armament. The more than million-fold difference amounts to more than a difference in magnitude; it is also a difference in kind. The authors of *Hiroshima and Nagasaki* observe that "an atomic bomb's massive destruction and indiscriminate slaughter involves the sweeping breakdown of all order and existence—in a word, the collapse of society itself," and that therefore "the essence of atomic destruction lies in the totality of its impact on man and society." This is true also of a holocaust,

of course, except that the totalities in question are now not single cities but nations, ecosystems, and the earth's ecosphere. Yet with the exception of fallout, which was relatively light at Hiroshima and Nagasaki (because both the bombs were air-burst), the immediate devastation caused by today's bombs would be of a sort similar to the devastation in those cities. The immediate effects of a twenty-megaton bomb are not different in kind from those of a twelve-and-a-half-kiloton bomb; they are only more extensive. (The proportions of the effects do change greatly with yield, however. In small bombs, the effects of the initial nuclear radiation are important, because it strikes areas in which people might otherwise have remained alive, but in larger bombs—ones in the megaton range—the consequences of the initial nuclear radiation, whose range does not increase very much with yield, are negligible, because it strikes areas in which everyone will have already been burned or blasted to death.) In bursts of both weapons, for instance, there is a radius within which the thermal pulse can ignite newspapers: for the twelve-and-a-half kiloton weapon, it is a little over two miles; for the twenty-megaton weapon, it is twenty-five miles. (Since there is no inherent limit on the size of a nuclear weapon, these figures can be increased indefinitely, subject only to the limitations imposed by the technical capacities of the bomb builder—and of the earth's capacity to absorb the blast. The Soviet Union, which has shown a liking for sheer size in so many of its undertakings, once detonated a sixty-megaton bomb.) Therefore, while the total effect of a holocaust is qualitatively different from the total effect of a single bomb, the experience of individual people in a holocaust would be, in the short term (and again excepting the presence of lethal fallout wherever the bombs were ground-burst), very much like the experience of individual people in Hiroshima. The Hiroshima people's experience, accordingly, is of much more than historical interest. It is a picture of what our whole world is always poised to become—a backdrop of scarcely imaginable horror lying just behind the surface of our normal life, and capable of breaking through into that normal life at any second. Whether we choose to think about it or not, it is an omnipresent, inescapable truth about our lives today that at every single moment each one of us may suddenly become the deranged mother looking for her burned child; the professor with the ball of rice in his hand whose wife has just told him "Run away, dear!" and died in the fires; Mr. Fukai running back into the firestorm; the naked man standing on the blasted plain that was his city, holding his eyeball in his hand; or, more likely, one of millions of corpses. For whatever our "modest hopes" as human beings may be, every one of them can be nullified by a nuclear holocaust.

One way to begin to grasp the destructive power of present-day nuclear weapons is to describe the consequences of the detonation of a one-megaton bomb, which possesses eighty times the explosive power of the Hiroshima bomb, on a large city, such as New York. Burst some eighty-five hundred feet above the Empire State Building, a one-megaton bomb would gut or flatten almost every building between Battery Park and 125th Street, or

2

within a radius of four and four-tenths miles, or an area of sixty-one square miles, and would heavily damage buildings between the northern tip of Staten Island and the George Washington Bridge, or within a radius of about eight miles, or in an area of about two hundred square miles. A conventional explosive delivers a swift shock, like a slap, to whatever it hits, but the blast wave of a sizable nuclear weapon endures for several seconds and "can surround and destroy whole buildings" [Samuel Glasstone and Philip J. Dolan (eds.), *The Effect of Nuclear Weapons;* Department of Defense and Energy Research and Development Administration, 1977]. People, of course, would be picked up and hurled away from the blast along with the rest of the debris. Within the sixty-one square miles, the walls, roofs, and floors of any buildings that had not been flattened would be collapsed, and the people and furniture inside would be swept down onto the street. (Technically, this zone would be hit by various overpressures of at least five pounds per square inch. Overpressure is defined as the pressure in excess of normal atmospheric pressure.) As far away as ten miles from ground zero, pieces of glass and other sharp objects would be hurled about by the blast wave at lethal velocities. In Hiroshima, where buildings were low and, outside the center of the city, were often constructed of light materials, injuries from falling buildings were often minor. But in New York, where the buildings are tall and are constructed of heavy materials, the physical collapse of the city would certainly kill millions of people. The streets of New York are narrow ravines running between the high walls of the city's build-ings. In a nuclear attack, the walls would fall and the ravines would fill up. The people in the buildings would fall to the street with the debris of the buildings, and the people in the street would be crushed by this avalanche of people and buildings. At a distance of two miles or so from ground zero, winds would reach four hundred miles an hour, and another two miles away they would reach a hundred and eighty miles an hour. Meanwhile, the fireball would be growing, until it was more than a mile wide, and rocketing upward, to a height of over six miles. For ten seconds, it would broil the city below. Anyone caught in the open within nine miles of ground zero would receive third-degree burns and would probably be killed; closer to the explosion, people would be charred and killed instantly. From Greenwich Village up to Central Park, the heat would be great enough to melt metal and glass. Readily inflammable materials, such as newspapers and dry leaves, would ignite in all five boroughs (though in only a small part of Staten Island) and west to the Passaic River, in New Jersey, within a radius of about nine and a half miles from ground zero, thereby creating an area of more than two hundred and eighty square miles in which mass fires were likely to break out.

If it were possible (as it would not be) for someone to stand at Fifth Avenue and Seventy-second Street (about two miles from ground zero) without being instantly killed, he would see the following sequence of events: A dazzling white light from the fireball would illumine the scene, continuing for perhaps thirty seconds. Simultaneously, searing heat would

3

ignite everything flammable and start to melt windows, cars, buses, lamp-posts, and everything else made of metal or glass. People in the street would immediately catch fire, and would shortly be reduced to heavily charred corpses. About five seconds after the light appeared, the blast wave would strike, laden with the debris of a now nonexistent midtown. Some buildings might be crushed, as though a giant fist had squeezed them on all sides, and others might be picked up off their foundations and whirled uptown with the other debris. On the far side of Central Park, the West Side skyline would fall from south to north. The four-hundred-mile-an-hour wind would blow from south to north, die down after a few seconds, and then blow in the reverse direction with diminished intensity. While these things were happening, the fireball would be burning in the sky for the ten seconds of the thermal pulse. Soon huge, thick clouds of dust and smoke would envelop the scene, and as the mushroom cloud rushed overhead (it would have a diameter of about twelve miles) the light from the sun would be blotted out, and day would turn to night. Within minutes, fires, ignited both by the thermal pulse and by broken gas mains, tanks of gas and oil, and the like, would begin to spread in the darkness, and a strong, steady wind would begin to blow in the direction of the blast. As at Hiroshima, a whirlwind might be produced which would sweep through the ruins, and radioactive rain, generated under the meteorological conditions created by the blast, might fall. Before long, the individual fires would coalesce into a mass fire, which, depending largely on the winds, would become either a conflagration or a firestorm. In a conflagration, prevailing winds spread a wall of fire as far as there is any combustible material to sustain it; in a firestorm, a vertical updraft caused by the fire itself sucks the surrounding air in toward a central point, and the fires therefore converge in a single fire of extreme heat. A mass fire of either kind renders shelters useless by burning up all the oxygen in the air and creating toxic gases, so that anyone inside the shelters is asphyxiated, and also by heating the ground to such high temperatures that the shelters turn, in effect, into ovens, cremating the people inside them. In Dresden, several days after the firestorm raised there by Allied conventional bombing, the interiors of some bomb shelters were still so hot that when they were opened the inrushing air caused the contents to burst into flame. Only those who had fled their shelters when the bombing started had any chance of surviving. (It is difficult to predict in a particular situation which form the fires will take. In actual experience, Hiroshima suffered a firestorm and Nagasaki suffered a conflagration.)

In this vast theater of physical effects, all the scenes of agony and death that took place at Hiroshima would again take place, but now involving millions of people rather than hundreds of thousands. Like the people of Hiroshima, the people of New York would be burned, battered, crushed, and irradiated in every conceivable way. The city and its people would be mingled in a smoldering heap. And then, as the fires started, the survivors (most of whom would be on the periphery of the explosion) would be driven to abandon to the flames those family members and other people who were unable to flee, or else to die with them. Before long, while the ruins burned, the processions of injured, mute people would begin their slow progress out of the outskirts of the devastated zone. However, this time a much smaller proportion of the population than at Hiroshima would have a chance of escaping. In general, as the size of the area of devastation increases, the possibilities of escape decrease. When the devastated area is relatively small, as it was at Hiroshima, people who are not incapacitated will have a good chance of escaping to safety before the fires coalesce into a mass fire. But when the devastated area is great, as it would be after the detonation of a megaton bomb, and fires are springing up at a distance of nine and a half miles from ground zero, and when what used to be the streets are piled high with burning rubble, and the day (if the attack occurs in the daytime) has grown impenetrably dark, there is little chance that anyone who is not on the very edge of the devastated area will be able to make his way to safety. In New York, most people would die wherever the blast found them, or not very far from there.

If instead of being burst in the air the bomb were burst on or near the ground in the vicinity of the Empire State Building, the overpressure would be very much greater near the center of the blast area but the range hit by a minimum of five pounds per square inch of overpressure would be less. The range of the thermal pulse would be about the same as that of the air burst. The fireball would be almost two miles across, and would engulf midtown Manhattan from Greenwich Village nearly to Central Park. Very little is known about what would happen to a city that was inside a fireball, but one would expect a good deal of what was there to be first pulverized and then melted or vaporized. Any human beings in the area would be reduced to smoke and ashes; they would simply disappear. A crater roughly three blocks in diameter and two hundred feet deep would open up. In addition, heavy radioactive fallout would be created as dust and debris from the city rose with the mushroom cloud and then fell back to the ground. Fallout would begin to drop almost immediately, contaminating the ground beneath the cloud with levels of radiation many times lethal doses, and quickly killing anyone who might have survived the blast wave and the thermal pulse and might now be attempting an escape; it is difficult to believe that there would be appreciable survival of the people of the city after a megaton ground burst. And for the next twenty-four hours or so more fallout would descend downwind from the blast, in a plume whose direction and length would depend on the speed and the direction of the wind that happened to be blowing at the time of the attack. If the wind was blowing at fifteen miles an hour, fallout of lethal intensity would descend in a plume about a hundred and fifty miles long and as much as fifteen miles wide. Fallout that was sublethal but could still cause serious illness would extend another hundred and fifty miles downwind. Exposure to radioactivity in human beings is measured in units called rems—an acronym for "roentgen equivalent in man." The roentgen is a standard measurement of gamma- and X-ray radiation, and the expression "equivalent in man" indicates that an adjustment has been made to take into account the differences in the degree of biological damage that is caused by radiation of different types. Many of the kinds of harm done to human beings by radiation—for example, the incidence of cancer and of genetic damage—depend on the dose accumulated over many years; but radiation sickness, capable of causing death, results from an "acute" dose, received in a period of anything from a few seconds to several days. Because almost ninety percent of the so-called infinite-time dose of radiation from fallout—that is, the dose from a given quantity of fallout that one would receive if one lived for many thousands of years—is emitted in the first week, the one-week accumulated dose is often used as a convenient measure for calculating the immediate harm from fallout. Doses in the thousands of rems, which could be expected throughout the city, would attack the central nervous system and would bring about death within a few hours. Doses of around a thousand rems, which would be delivered some tens of miles downwind from the blast, would kill within two weeks everyone who was exposed to them. Doses of around five hundred rems, which would be delivered as far as a hundred and fifty miles downwind (given a wind speed of fifteen miles per hour), would kill half of all exposed able-bodied young adults. At this level of exposure, radiation sickness proceeds in the three stages observed at Hiroshima. The plume of lethal fallout could descend, depending on the direction of the wind, on other parts of New York State and parts of New Jersey, Pennsylvania, Delaware, Maryland, Connecticut, Massachusetts, Rhode Island, Vermont, and New Hampshire, killing additional millions of people. The circumstances in heavily contaminated areas, in which millions of people were all declining together, over a period of weeks, toward painful deaths, are ones that, like so many of the consequences of nuclear explosions, have never been experienced.

A description of the effects of a one-megaton bomb on New York City   6
gives some notion of the meaning in human terms of a megaton of nuclear explosive power, but a weapon that is more likely to be used against New York is the twenty-megaton bomb, which has one thousand six hundred times the yield of the Hiroshima bomb. The Soviet Union is estimated to have at least a hundred and thirteen twenty-megaton bombs in its nuclear arsenal, carried by Bear intercontinental bombers. In addition, some of the Soviet SS-18 missiles are capable of carrying bombs of this size, although the actual yields are not known. Since the explosive power of the twenty-megaton bombs greatly exceeds the amount necessary to destroy most military targets, it is reasonable to suppose that they are meant for use against large cities. If a twenty-megaton bomb were air-burst over the Empire State Building at an altitude of thirty thousand feet, the zone gutted or flattened by the blast would have a radius of twelve miles and an area of more than four hundred and fifty square miles, reaching from the middle of Staten Island to the northern edge of the Bronx, the eastern edge of Queens, and well into New Jersey, and the zone of heavy damage from the blast wave (the zone hit by a minimum of two pounds of overpressure per

square inch) would have a radius of twenty-one and a half miles, or, an area of one thousand four hundred and fifty square miles, reaching to the southernmost tip of Staten Island, north as far as southern Rockland County, east into Nassau County, and west to Morris County, New Jersey. The fireball would be about four and a half miles in diameter and would radiate the thermal pulse for some twenty seconds. People caught in the open twenty-three miles away from ground zero, in Long Island, New Jersey, and southern New York State, would be burned to death. People hundreds of miles away who looked at the burst would be temporarily blinded and would risk permanent eye injury. (After the test of a fifteen-megaton bomb on Bikini Atoll, in the South Pacific, in March of 1954, small animals were found to have suffered retinal burns at a distance of three hundred and forty-five miles.) The mushroom cloud would be seventy miles in diameter. New York City and its suburbs would be transformed into a lifeless, flat, scorched desert in a few seconds.

If a twenty-megaton bomb were ground-burst on the Empire State   7
Building, the range of severe blast damage would, as with the one-megaton ground blast, be reduced, but the fireball, which would be almost six miles in diameter, would cover Manhattan from Wall Street to northern Central Park and also parts of New Jersey, Brooklyn, and Queens, and everyone within it would be instantly killed, with most of them physically disappearing. Fallout would again be generated, this time covering thousands of square miles with lethal intensities of radiation. A fair portion of New York City and its incinerated population, now radioactive dust, would have risen into the mushroom cloud and would now be descending on the surrounding territory. On one of the few occasions when local fallout was generated by a test explosion in the multi-megaton range, the fifteen-megaton bomb tested on Bikini Atoll, which was exploded seven feet above the surface of a coral reef, "caused substantial contamination over an area of more than seven thousand square miles," according to Glasstone. If, as seems likely, a twenty-megaton bomb ground-burst on New York would produce at least a comparable amount of fallout, and if the wind carried the fallout onto populated areas, then this one bomb would probably doom upward of twenty million people, or almost ten percent of the population of the United States.

Questions

1. Schell uses the Hiroshima and Nagasaki bombs as reference points because of the tangible evidence of those explosions, saying that the one-megaton bomb is eighty times more powerful than the Hiroshima bomb. What are the effects of comparing the hypothetical explosion with the actual ones?

2. Why does Schell describe the effects of the one-megaton bomb when he says that the twenty-megaton bomb "is more likely to be used against New York"?

3. What is Schell's purpose for explaining the effects of the hydrogen bomb? Does he achieve this purpose with you?

4. Is this essay written for a scientific audience or a popular one? Consider the presence or absence of scientific terminology, the thoroughness and character of the descriptions, and Schell's apparent purpose.

5. Lewis Thomas in "Late Night Thoughts on Listening to Mahler's Ninth Symphony" (Chapter 6) says that information such as this is evidence that "the whole world [is] becoming unhinged." Do you agree that developing the capability to destroy millions of people at one blow is the result of derangement? What is such development evidence of?

Reading

The preceding reading deals with one kind of holocaust, this reading with another. In the essay that follows, translated from the French by Rosette C. Lamont, award-winning author Elie Wiesel explains his need to write about the Holocaust of World War II in which millions of Jews were murdered. Read it as a survivor's search for ways to honor the memory of those who did not survive.

Why I Write: Making No Become Yes

Elie Wiesel

(translated from the French by Rosette C. Lamont)

Why do I write?   1

Perhaps in order not to go mad. Or, on the contrary, to touch the   2
bottom of madness. Like Samuel Beckett, the survivor expresses himself
"en désespoir de cause"—out of desperation.

Speaking of the solitude of the survivor, the great Yiddish and Hebrew   3
poet and thinker Aaron Zeitlin addresses those—his father, his brother, his
friends—who have died and left him: "You have abandoned me," he says to
them. "You are together, without me. I am here. Alone. And I make words."

So do I, just like him. I also say words, write words, reluctantly.   4

There are easier occupations, far more pleasant ones. But for the   5
survivor, writing is not a profession, but an occupation, a duty. Camus calls
it "an honor." As he puts it: "I entered literature through worship." Other
writers have said they did so through anger, through love. Speaking for
myself, I would say—through silence.

It was by seeking, by probing silence that I began to discover the perils   6
and power of the word. I never intended to be a philosopher, or a theolo-
gian. The only role I sought was that of witness. I believed that, having
survived by chance, I was duty-bound to give meaning to my survival, to
justify each moment of my life. I knew the story had to be told. Not to
transmit an experience is to betray it. This is what Jewish tradition teaches
us. But how to do this? "When Israel is in exile, so is the word," says the

Zohar. The word has deserted the meaning it was intended to convey—impossible to make them coincide. The displacement, the shift, is irrevocable.

This was never more true than right after the upheaval. We all knew   7
that we could never, never say what had to be said, that we could never express in words, coherent, intelligible words, our experience of madness on an absolute scale. The walk through flaming night, the silence before and after the selection, the monotonous praying of the condemned, the Kaddish of the dying, the fear and hunger of the sick, the shame and suffering, the haunted eyes, the demented stares. I thought that I would never be able to speak of them. All words seemed inadequate, worn, foolish, lifeless, whereas I wanted them to be searing.

Where was I to discover a fresh vocabulary, a primeval language? The   8
language of night was not human, it was primitive, almost animal—hoarse shouting, screams, muffled moaning, savage howling, the sound of beating. A brute strikes out wildly, a body falls. An officer raises his arm and a whole community walks toward a common grave. A soldier shrugs his shoulders, and a thousand families are torn apart, to be reunited only by death. This was the concentration camp language. It negated all other language and took its place. Rather than a link, it became a wall. Could it be surmounted? Could the reader be brought to the other side? I knew the answer was negative, and yet I knew that "no" had to become "yes." It was the last wish of the dead.

The fear of forgetting remains the main obsession of those who have   9
passed through the universe of the damned. The enemy counted on people's incredulity and forgetfulness. How could one foil this plot? And if memory grew hollow, empty of substance, what would happen to all we had accumulated along the way? Remember, said the father to his son, and the son to his friend. Gather the names, the faces, the tears. We had all taken an oath: "If, by some miracle, I emerge alive, I will devote my life to testifying on behalf of those whose shadow will fall on mine forever and ever."

That is why I write certain things rather than others—to remain faithful.   10

Of course, there are times of doubt for the survivor, times when one   11
gives in to weakness, or longs to shout loudly: "Listen, listen well! I too am capable of victory, do you hear? I too am open to laughter and joy! I want to stride, head high, my face unguarded, without having to point to the ashes over there on the horizon, without having to tamper with facts to hide their tragic ugliness. For a man born blind, God himself is blind, but look, I see, I am not blind." One feels like shouting this, but the shout changes to a murmur. One must make a choice; one must remain faithful. A big word, I know. Nevertheless I use it, it suits me. Having written the things I have written, I feel I can afford no longer to play with words. If I say that the writer in me wants to remain loyal, it is because it is true. This sentiment moves all survivors; they owe nothing to anyone, but everything to the dead.

I owe them my roots and my memory. I am duty-bound to serve as their   12
emissary, transmitting the history of their disappearance, even if it disturbs,

even if it brings pain. Not to do so would be to betray them, and thus myself. And since I am incapable of communicating their cry by shouting, I simply look at them. I see them and I write.

While writing, I question them as I question myself. I believe I have said [13] it before, elsewhere. I write to understand as much as to be understood. Will I succeed one day? Wherever one starts, one reaches darkness. God? He remains the God of the darkness. Man? The source of darkness. The killers' derision, their victims' tears, the onlookers' indifference, their complicity and complacency—the divine role in all that I do not understand. A million children massacred—I shall never understand.

Jewish children—they haunt my writings. I see them again and again. [14] I shall always see them. Hounded, humiliated, bent like the old men who surround them as though to protect them, unable to do so. They are thirsty, the children, and there is no one to give them water. They are hungry, but there is no one to give them a crust of bread. They are afraid, and there is no one to reassure them.

They walk in the middle of the road, like vagabonds. They are on the [15] way to the station, and they will never return. In sealed cars, without air or food, they travel toward another world. They guess where they are going, they know it, and they keep silent. Tense, thoughtful, they listen to the wind, the call of death in the distance.

All these children, these old people, I see them. I never stop seeing [16] them. I belong to them.

But they, to whom do they belong? [17]

People tend to think that a murderer weakens when facing a child. The [18] child reawakens the killer's lost humanity. The killer can no longer kill the child before him, the child inside him.

But with us it happened differently. Our Jewish children had no effect [19] upon the killers. Nor upon the world. Nor upon God.

I think of them, I think of their childhood. Their childhood is a small [20] Jewish town, and this town is no more. They frighten me; they reflect an image of myself, one that I pursue and run from at the same time—the image of a Jewish adolescent who knew no fear, except the fear of God, whose faith was whole, comforting, and not marked by anxiety.

No, I do not understand. And if I write, it is to warn the reader that he [21] will not understand either. "You will not understand, you will never understand," were the words heard everywhere during the reign of night. I can only echo them. You, who never lived under a sky of blood, will never know what it was like. Even if you read all the books ever written, even if you listen to all the testimonies ever given, you will remain on this side of the wall, you will view the agony and death of a people from afar, through the screen of a memory that is not your own.

An admission of impotence and guilt? I do not know. All I know is that [22] Treblinka and Auschwitz cannot be told. And yet I have tried. God knows I have tried.

Have I attempted too much or not enough? Among some twenty-five   23
volumes, only three or four penetrate the phantasmagoric realm of the
dead. In my other books, through my other books, I have tried to follow
other roads. For it is dangerous to linger among the dead, they hold on to
you and you run the risk of speaking only to them. And so I have forced
myself to turn away from them and study other periods, explore other
destinies and teach other tales—the Bible and the Talmud, Hasidism and its
fervor, the shtetl and its songs, Jerusalem and its echoes, the Russian Jews
and their anguish, their awakening, their courage. At times, it has seemed to
me that I was speaking of other things with the sole purpose of keeping the
essential—the personal experience—unspoken. At times I have wondered:
And what if I was wrong? Perhaps I should not have heeded my own advice
and stayed in my own world with the dead.

But then, I have not forgotten the dead. They have their rightful place   24
even in the works about the Hasidic capitals Ruzhany and Korets, and
Jerusalem. Even in my biblical and Midrashic tales, I pursue their presence,
mute and motionless. The presence of the dead then beckons in such
tangible ways that it affects even the most removed characters. Thus they
appear on Mount Moriah, where Abraham is about to sacrifice his son, a
burnt offering to their common God. They appear on Mount Nebo, where
Moses enters solitude and death. They appear in Hasidic and Talmudic legends in which victims forever need defending against forces that would crush
them. Technically, so to speak, they are of course elsewhere, in time and space,
but on a deeper, truer plane, the dead are part of every story, of every scene.

"But what is the connection?" you will ask. Believe me, there is one.   25
After Auschwitz everything brings us back to Auschwitz. When I speak of
Abraham, Isaac, and Jacob, when I invoke Rabbi Yohanan ben Zakkai and
Rabbi Akiba, it is the better to understand them in the light of Auschwitz. As
for the Maggid of Mezeritch and his disciples, it is in order to encounter the
followers of their followers that I reconstruct their spellbound, spellbinding
universe. I like to imagine them alive, exuberant, celebrating life and hope.
Their happiness is as necessary to me as it was once to themselves.

And yet—how did they manage to keep their faith intact? How did they   26
manage to sing as they went to meet the Angel of Death? I know Hasidim who
never vacillated—I respect their strength. I know others who chose rebellion,
protest, rage—I respect their courage. For there comes a time when only those
who do not believe in God will not cry out to him in wrath and anguish.

Do not judge either group. Even the heroes perished as martyrs, even   27
the martyrs died as heroes. Who would dare oppose knives to prayers? The
faith of some matters as much as the strength of others. It is not ours to
judge, it is only ours to tell the tale.

But where is one to begin? Whom is one to include? One meets a Hasid   28
in all my novels. And a child. And an old man. And a beggar. And a
madman. They are all part of my inner landscape. The reason why?
Pursued and persecuted by the killers, I offer them shelter. The enemy
wanted to create a society purged of their presence, and I have brought

some of them back. The world denied them, repudiated them, so I let them live at least within the feverish dreams of my characters.

It is for them that I write, and yet the survivor may experience remorse. 29 He has tried to bear witness; it was all in vain.

After the liberation, we had illusions. We were convinced that a new 30 world would be built upon the ruins of Europe. A new civilization would see the light. No more wars, no more hate, no more intolerance, no fanaticism. And all this because the witnesses would speak. And speak they did, to no avail.

They will continue, for they cannot do otherwise. When man, in his 31 grief, falls silent, Goethe says, then God gives him the strength to sing his sorrows. From that moment on, he may no longer choose not to sing, whether his song is heard or not. What matters is to struggle against silence with words, or through another form of silence. What matters is to gather a smile here and there, a tear here and there, a word here and there, and thus justify the faith placed in you, a long time ago, by so many victims.

Why do I write? To wrench those victims from oblivion. To help the 32 dead vanquish death.

Questions

1. Wiesel says, "You, who never lived under a sky of blood, will never know what it was like. Even if you read all the books ever written, even if you listen to all the testimonies ever given, you will remain on this side of the wall, you will view the agony and death of a people from afar, through the screen of a memory that is not your own." With such a statement, why does Wiesel feel compelled to write about the Holocaust? What does he hope to achieve?

2. The Holocaust illustrates prejudice carried to its ultimate end: genocide, extinction of a race of people considered inferior. Does Wiesel's remembrance of Nazi acts in World War II tell you anything about human tendencies today?

3. Wiesel's essay was published in *The New York Times* Book Review Section and was earlier published by Indiana University Press. Who might his intended audience be?

4. What do you learn about Wiesel from this essay?

5. In "6,000,000" (see Chapter 6), Jidit, an Israeli student, makes an effort to comprehend the magnitude of the Holocaust by trying to count to 6 million, the number of Jews estimated to have been killed in Nazi concentration camps. She is unsuccessful in finding any way of coming close to that number. Does Wiesel have any success in reaching his goals?

Reading

In the following essay, college student Pat Hodge explains why she started using drugs and what the effects of drug use are. How does her title forecast her subject?

Hooked

Pat Hodge

I've always had an extremely active mind. Gifted, they called it in high   1
school; bored, I called it. So I quit after tenth grade to begin college.
However, the fascination with the ability to pass for being much older was
more intense than my fascination with learning. I required a stimulating
environment and found it in drugs and alcohol, so easily available on
campus. This side trip took me away from campus for seven years, and away
from life even longer.

Drug addiction doesn't just deal with the amount of time the user is   2
involved in drugs. It also deals with before the drug use begins and long,
long after it stops. Many things can pave the way for drug use: feelings of low
self-esteem, morality conflicts, and separation from a higher power, or God.
Seldom does some normal, healthy, happy child try drugs once and get
hooked. Normal people don't try even once, much less go back for more.
Unfortunately, it is much easier to see all the warning signals when looking
back, after drug use has begun rather than before.

Drug addiction doesn't just affect the user, it affects society, family,   3
friends, peers, and more. The emotional devastation from drug addiction
can be greater on the family than on the addict. The addict is under the
influence of drugs to keep from feeling pain and emotion, but the family
must feel the full force of their emotions. It is even said that families are
sicker than the addict because they can't identify where their pain is from.
Feeling out of control, crazy, helpless, furious, and a million other uncontrollable emotions that go along with a loved one's use are normal.

These fears are legitimate, because an addict can only do two things,   4
quit or die. There are several ways to die and several ways to quit. Quitting
is harder. The most effective way to quit is by using a twelve-step program
such as AA or NA (Alcoholics Anonymous or Narcotics Anonymous). There
is also God. Really they are both the same except that twelve-step programs
hide the God aspect for a while so they don't scare agnostics away. I've seen
people healed from the compulsion to do drugs, but the twelve-step program helps after that by taking care of behavior problems acquired during
(or before) drug use.

Once an addict becomes "dry" or abstinent, it isn't over; it has just   5
begun. It is also said that an addict stops maturing emotionally when he
or she begins drugs and doesn't start growing again until beginning
recovery. Some people quit using but never change the attitudes, beliefs,
and friends that started them using in the first place. Recovery is actively
trying to improve oneself to better deal with those feelings, situations,
etc., that caused problems in the past. My work is just beginning. At
twenty-five, with husband and children, I am just starting to feel as if I
am growing up.

Questions

1. Hodge says that "normal people" don't try drugs, much less get hooked, and that people use drugs to avoid personal problems. Do you agree? What can you add to her reasons for drug use?

2. In paragraph 4, Hodge makes the chilling statement that there are only two routes open to drug addicts—to quit or to die—and that dying is easier. She then explains an effective way to quit. Do you know of some other ways that are also effective?

3. Hodge speaks of the effects of drug use on others: society, family, friends, and so on. In "Be Scared for Your Kids," in Chapter 8, journalist Al Sicherman vividly mourns the drug-induced death of his son. Can you think of other examples of the effects of drug use on the user's family?

4. Consider the effects of drug use on society. In "Drug Use Is a Sin" in Chapter 9, Jesse Jackson condemns drug use as a blight on society and the flow of drugs into the United States as "an act of terrorism." From the perspective of Hodge's essay, in what ways do users contribute to the terrorism?

5. How does Hodge develop her essay? Analyze each of her paragraphs for evidence of development by cause and effect, comparison, classification, and so on.

Reading

Student writer Terry Splett explains why her family celebrated both Chanukah and Christmas when she was growing up. As an adult remembering what it was like growing up in a Judeo-Christian home, she writes mainly from the child's point of view, trying to understand the differences between being a Christian and being a Jew. As you read, notice how she develops her explanation by comparison.

We Celebrated Chanukah and Christmas
Terry Splett

"Because he's Jewish" was Mom's reply when I asked her why Daddy   1
never went to church with us on Sundays. She explained that he went to a different church with Grandma Nancy and Grandpa Aaron and that when I got older I would understand. So, from the time we were old enough for Sunday School until the time we got confirmed, Mom would pack up the four of us kids and cart us off to church on Sunday mornings. Wishing that he was coming with us and hoping that he wouldn't be lonely while we were gone, we'd all kiss Daddy goodbye as he sat in the easy chair reading the paper. We were used to doing everything together, and somehow leaving him alone on Sunday mornings seemed wrong. But we knew that when we came home Daddy would be in the kitchen putting the final touches

on the breakfast that he had made especially for us, and we would all be together again.

The other kids at church would always ask where my Dad was, and I'd answer proudly that he was Jewish and didn't have to come. Then I'd tell them that he was at home cooking eggs and hash browns for us, knowing how jealous they'd be because they didn't have a Jewish Daddy who had breakfast waiting for them when they got home from Sunday School.   2

I didn't know what Lutheran was, much less Jewish, but I suspected that being Jewish had something to do with the times when we got all dressed up and went to Grandma and Grandpa's house for what Daddy called the High Holidays. We'd all sit down to dinner, but we wouldn't eat right away because Grandpa and Daddy had to say prayers, and we had to be very quiet. Grandpa would sit at the head of the table. He wore a scarf around his neck, which was funny because it wasn't cold in the house, and he always sat on a pillow. Both Grandpa and Daddy wore round, black hats. The hats were so small that I always thought they'd fall off their heads, and I kept warning my dad. My brothers got to wear hats too, but my sister and I couldn't because they were only for boys.   3

Grandma gave each of us a little book, and Grandpa and Dad would take turns reading from the book and taking small sips of wine. Even we kids got to drink wine. We didn't like it but drank it anyway because it made us feel grown up. We couldn't understand what Grandpa and Dad said because they spoke in a different language, but we could follow along in the book that had English underneath the strange letters that I knew they were reading. I remember Daddy had to correct me once when I turned a page because I didn't know that the books were backwards and I was going the wrong way. It always seemed like the prayers took a long time, but finally everyone would say Amen, just like in church, and Grandma would start serving the food.   4

Most of the food was the same kind that we had at home, like chicken, potatoes, and beans. But there were other items that we had only at Grandma's, like gefilte fish and matzo ball soup. We especially liked the round, hollow crackers called mandalah that were meant to be put in the soup but that we ate as snacks.   5

We enjoyed those holidays. It made us feel like we were helping Daddy be Jewish, and I think that made him happy too. There were other holidays that we celebrated as well, Passover and Chanukah. Over the years, Dad would explain the importance of each occasion in a way that we could understand, and that made us enjoy them all the more. Chanukah came around Christmas time each year, and we celebrated both. At home, we had a Christmas tree and Santa always came as we expected, and at Grandma's we had a Chanukah bush, and the Chanukah Man came with presents as well. As children, we loved that time of year. When I grew up, Dad told me that there was no Chanukah Man or Chanukah bush. He said that Grandma had invented them especially for us kids because she knew how much children   6 love Santa Claus and Christmas trees, and she didn't want us to feel left out when we went to her house for the holidays. No one could love us more.

Eventually, I began learning the religious importance of Christmas in   7
Sunday School. I began to learn what Lutheran was, and what Jewish was from the Christian point of view. Somehow, what I was learning seemed to contradict everything that I had learned at home, and I was scared. Mom and Dad had taught us about good and bad, and right and wrong. We knew that it was bad to steal and to swear and to lie. They told us that when good people died they went to heaven, which was a good place. It was where God was. They also told us that when bad people died, they went to a different place, a bad place; Mom called it hell. We didn't want to go to hell. We wanted to go where God was, so we tried very hard to be good.

At church, they talked about good and bad, and heaven and hell as well.   8
They talked about being saved, and that being saved meant going to heaven. They said only Christians would be saved, only good Christians, and all I could think about was my daddy. At home we learned about good people and bad people. At church we learned about good Christians and bad Christians, and I wondered about everyone else, especially my daddy. I didn't understand and wanted to go to my dad's church for answers.

He took me to his church, the synagogue. It reminded me of the   9
Lutheran church in some ways, but in others it was very different. The rabbi wore a long black robe, just like the pastor in church, but he had a long beard and wore one of those hats, a "yarmulke," Dad said. I noticed that all the men wore yarmulkes, and many wore scarfs like Grandpa did. There weren't many children there, and the men sat in a different part of the synagogue from the women. What I remember most was the scrolls. They were beautiful, and the men that held them during different parts of the service handled them with such care that I knew they were very special. I couldn't understand. They never talked about Christians in the synagogue. They talked about the Jewish people. They were the chosen people and were waiting to be saved. The Jewish people would go to heaven. I was relieved because that meant Daddy, but I wondered about Mom and me and the rest of the kids. I was still confused.

After the service, Daddy introduced me to more people than I could   10
remember. He was so excited that I was with him. Everyone was kind and friendly, and I couldn't see any differences between the people here and the people at church. They seemed happy and loving and honest. We were all people, and I was glad that I learned about people the way I did at home. I never learned to separate kinds of people. I wished that churches and synagogues didn't. If they didn't, maybe they'd understand each other better. I knew that I would never completely understand the church or the synagogue. In my own mind I decided that in the end we would all be taken care of because we all believed in God and in Good and in Love.

I told Mom and Dad what I had learned and they were so proud. They   11
both agreed with what I had come to believe, but they warned me that many

people would never understand. That wasn't important to me. What was important was that my family would always be together, and now I knew that we would.

In the following years we continued to celebrate both the Christian 12 holidays and the Jewish holidays, and they were all very special times for my family. One year for Christmas I received a gold cross on a chain to wear around my neck. The following year, for Chanukah, I received a small Star of David. I put it on the gold chain I had received earlier, and for years I never took the chain off. I loved the way the cross and the Star of David hung together from that chain, touching one another. They represented everything that I had learned over the years.

Questions

1. In what ways does Splett compare Chanukah and Christmas? What do the two holidays have in common? In what ways are they different? What was special about the way her family celebrated them? What other holidays does she compare?

2. In what ways does Splett compare Jewish people and Christian people? Why does she have such a hard time seeing the differences?

3. What does the symbolism of the cross and the Star of David on a single chain represent for Splett?

4. What does Splett's experience say about prejudice toward groups of people?

5. What is the tone of this essay?

6. Splett does not explicitly state a thesis. In your own words, tell what her unstated thesis, or controlling idea, is.

CHAPTER 13

To Instruct: Writing with Emphasis on the Subject

To teach is to learn twice.
—Joseph Joubert

As a purpose for writing, **instruction** generally tells a reader *how to do something* or how something is done. This kind of writing might tell you how to make a paper airplane, as the first reading in this chapter does, or how to put your test answers on a computer data sheet, how to assemble a bicycle, or how to use a new stereo system. We are surrounded by instructions—many of them clear and concise, others poorly written and difficult to follow. Have you ever tried to set a digital watch with instructions that were more of a hindrance than a help? Have you ever tried to play a new game on the basis of instructions from your opponent and found new rules cropping up every time you seemed about to win?

Writing to instruct requires careful work. The writer must know the task well, be able to present the steps of the task in sequential order, write them clearly enough so someone who knows nothing about the task can follow them, and omit nothing important. In so doing, the writer will probably learn something new about the task too. Instructions have an obvious pattern of development: They start with the first step and proceed to the last, simple chronological order. They do not include irrelevant details, because such information might be confusing. If materials are required, they are listed.

Writers of instructions must not only know the subject well but must also understand the reader's level of knowledge. If your reader knows nothing about the subject of your instructions, you will need to define your terms and explain each step in detail, whereas if your reader is more knowledgeable, you can feel free to use specialized terminology. At the same time, instructional language must always be exact and correct. This sentence would be

373

difficult to follow because of its inexactness: "Drill a small hole in the support frame." What size is "small"? Where in the support frame should the hole be drilled? Also, for the sake of clarity, avoid using vague words like *this, it,* and *they* to refer to specific actions. The following instructions are unclear because of vague pronouns:

The names of files are kept in directories on a disk. *They* also contain information on the size of the files.

MS-DOS will display a status report and any errors that it has found. An example of *this* can be found in Chapter 5.

To prevent your reader from being confused, sometimes you will want to give your instructions in the form of a list, as the writer of these instructions for beginning a card trick does:

1. Have someone remove any two cards from a shuffled deck.
2. Return the cards to the top of the deck.
3. Shuffle the cards, keeping the two cards on top of the deck.

When you don't list your instructions, use coherence devices to keep your reader with you: *first, next, now that you have completed the first step.* Also give your reader clues for especially critical points: *This is the most important part. Be sure that the thermometer records exactly 238 degrees.* If two operations need to be done at the same time, tell your reader so: *meanwhile, while the sauce is simmering, at the same time.*

Instructions generally speak directly to the reader with the pronoun *you* and imperative voice.

Drill a small hole.
Shuffle the cards.
Hold the control key down while *you* press the F1 key.

Try to avoid using *should,* as in "You should hold the control key down." To consider the needs of your readers and the approach to take in writing your instructions, apply the Questions about Audience for Writing (page 24).

The readings and writing assignments in this chapter all have the purpose of instruction; in a way they are all "how-to" assignments, yet they differ in a number of ways, from having multiple purposes to being only ostensibly instructive.

Following and Writing Instructions

How good are you at following instructions? Have you ever done the exercise that begins by advising you to read all the instructions first, tells you to write your name at the top of the page, then has you do a lot of stupid things like clapping your hands, staring at the ceiling, or yelling out loud, only to tell you at the end to disregard all the instructions except the first two? It may seem as if the only reason for the exercise is to make you look silly, but actually the exercise conveys an important point: it's generally easier to follow instructions if you read them through first so you have some idea of where they're going and what you need to do.

Reading

Here are some instructions by Campbell Morris on making a paper airplane. Take the time to make the "Smooth Flyer" and to fly it. But don't just *make* the plane; also observe *what you do* while you make it: where your problems are, how much you refer to the diagrams, where you have trouble with terminology, where the instructions are easy and where difficult to follow.

Smooth Flyer
Campbell Morris

Your average, everyday kind of dart is unstable and unsuitable to prolonged smooth flying. Here is another glider that is so simple to make but flies incredibly well — even the teacher will be impressed!

1.
Use a sheet of 8½" x 11" paper folded in half lengthwise. Fold the corners in as shown.

2.
Fold the leading edges in as shown.

3.
Fold in half.

4.
Fold wings down, slightly angled as shown. Give the fuselage around 2 cm height. Both height and angle can be experimented with if you wish.

5.
Fold the leading edge of the wing into a long fin. The fin is shown folded upwards. You can fold the fin downwards for an even smoother flight. See which way you think is best. Bring the wings up for the next step.

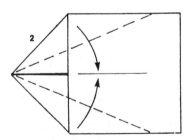

6.
Invert the fold. The dots show
the hidden flaps inside the
fuselage. Where they meet at
the bottom edge of the fuselage
is point C. Fold your inverted fin
from point C to point A. A is the
tail end of the wing crease AB.
Of course you must crease CA
well to invert the fold.

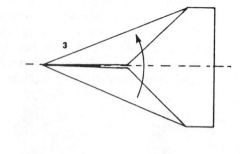

7.
Bring the wings level. The
finished Smooth Flyer should
look like this. (The fin can be
folded downwards as
mentioned in step 5.)

Throwing Instructions
Throw with slight force in a
straight direction. Make sure
the wings are level or slightly
raised.

Questions

1. How did your paper airplane turn out? Does it look like Morris's diagram of the finished Smooth Flyer? Does it fly?

2. Where did you have problems following Morris's instructions?

3. How often did you refer to the diagrams? Where would you make changes in the instructions? Was any terminology a problem for you?

4. Did you read all the instructions before beginning?

5. What have you learned about the way people follow instructions?

Discussion

Instructions are not always easy to follow. Some people have trouble making the Smooth Flyer, while some don't. Reasons for the difficulty vary. Some people seem to be more visually oriented, paying more attention to diagrams than to verbal instructions, while others prefer written guidance. This is why instructions often include both a written guide and diagrams. Diagrams are *not* meant to supplement poorly written instructions.

Unfamiliar terminology is sometimes a problem in following instructions. When you write instructions, make certain that your terms are clear— by explaining them, using synonyms or diagrams, or employing other means. Terms such as "leading edges" and even "the fold" are not transparently clear to all readers. Perhaps some of the terminology in "Smooth Flyer" made carrying out the instructions difficult for you. As a writer of instructions, be patient with your readers. If this is their first time performing the task, everything may be unfamiliar. Give them encouraging words: "You're now halfway finished" or "You've now finished the most difficult part."

Sometimes people have trouble following instructions because they don't read carefully. Readers may skip over words and sentences because they think they already know what the instructions say. They ignore the part, for example, that tells them to attach Wire A to Receptacle C because they've installed enough electronic equipment to know where Wire A should be attached—and proceed to attach it to the wrong receptacle. Writers can forestall this kind of misreading with such directives as "Most important," "Performing this step correctly is critical," or "Make sure you have the section marked 'top' in upper position."

People have many reasons for misreading instructions—some of them the fault of the writer, some the fault of the reader. As a reader, you probably occasionally misread—to your detriment, because you might have to repeat the task. As a writer, you need to take the responsibility of considering how your readers might misread and of trying to prevent any misreading.

EXERCISE

Alone or working with a partner, rewrite the "Smooth Flyer" instructions, revising any parts that you found difficult to follow.

Writing

Write instructions on how to make something. Choose something that can be done in seven to ten steps, something that will have a finished product, something that you know well enough to be absolutely clear about. You might choose another paper-folding activity, like making a box or a different kind of airplane; you might consider how to cut paper dolls or paper snowflakes, how to build a house of cards, or some other activity that involves *making* something. Use diagrams if you wish, but remember if you do that *both* the diagrams and the verbal instructions must be clear. Be careful of terminology, defining any terms your readers may not understand. Keep in mind that not everyone uses even familiar terms in the same way.

Number your steps and use chronological development, presenting the steps in the exact order in which they must be done. Remember that people don't always follow instructions the way we expect them to; try to anticipate what your readers might do—and not do—and what kinds of difficulties they might have. The task you are describing may be easy for you to do, but writing instructions that someone else can follow easily is another matter. Assume an intelligent audience but one that doesn't know what you know about making this thing.

Before making a final copy, read your instructions through, carrying them out in your mind. Try to be an uninformed reader relying on your instructions for performing the task.

Writing Instructions from Experience

Most instructions are written from the writer's own experience. We are able to tell someone else how to make a pizza because of having successfully made pizzas ourselves. If we tell a reader how to change the oil in an automobile, we do so out of our experience in changing oil. It's very difficult to tell someone "do as I say" if you can't also say, or imply, "do as I do."

But it seems that we can always learn something new. Even while writing about something we know well, we learn about it. You may have changed the oil in cars many times and be able to perform the task without thinking much about it, but when you try to tell someone else how to do it, someone who doesn't know what the parts under the car look like, much less what they're called, you will test your own knowledge of this task. It has often been said that if you want to know something really well, you must teach it to someone else.

Reading

In the essay that follows, a professional writer and teacher of writing, Roger Garrison, instructs apprentice writers on how to use punctuation. Because these instructions grew out of his own experience as a writer, and because writers, when writing, punctuate according to practice not rules, Garrison presents guidelines for ways other writers can think of punctuation. He gives only one rule.

Punctuation

Roger Garrison

There are not many precise rules, despite grammar manuals, for com- 1
mas, semicolons, and other typographical marks we use to indicate pauses in written speech. We have only a few stops (places for a reader to pause or take note): period, semicolon, colon, dash, question mark, and parentheses. (An editor once said, "Forget the exclamation point. It should be used only for swearing or direct commands. Otherwise, it reminds me of a kid jumping around the page on a pogo stick. Makes me nervous.")

These few punctuation marks are remarkably easy to understand, if 2
you strip away the finicky rules that have grown up around them.

Punctuation marks are signals to readers. They tell them when to 3
pause, when to stop, when a question has been asked. Except for direct quotations, or quotes within quotes, there are two simple ways to think about these marks.

1. Think of punctuation as breathing or pausing: 4

Comma	,	Half a breath.
Semicolon	;	Three-quarters of a breath.
Period	.	A full breath.
Colon	:	"Stop, a list is coming."
Dash	—	"Emphasis, side comment, definition coming."
Parentheses	()	"I want to tuck a quick fact or comment here."

2. Or think of punctuation as traffic signals: 5

Comma	,	Flashing yellow light: Slow down; look right and left.
Semicolon	;	Flashing red light: Come almost to a stop; then go.

Period	.	Stop sign: Stop full, then go.
Colon	:	Arrow or road sign: "Food, Fuel, Lodging, Next Right."
Dash	—	Detour—be alert.
Parentheses	()	"Caution, alternate route."

If you wonder how to punctuate a sentence, read it aloud. Where are the natural pauses? How long do you want your reader to breathe, to pause? Learn to read your own writing aloud to yourself, slowly, sentence by sentence.   6

One simple rule: You may put a full sentence (independent clause) on either side of a semicolon, a colon, a period, or a dash, or within parentheses—but *not* on either side of a comma, unless you have a compound sentence with a conjunction such as *and* or *but*. The comma splice, or comma fault, places a comma where we need a period (usually) or a semicolon. It "splices" (fastens together) two complete sentences. Example: The car swerved off the road, it went into a ditch.   7

Most Common and Annoying Error

The most persistent mechanical error is a punctuation mistake as in "The elephant lifted *it's* trunk." *STOP!* One of the easiest rules to remember is: *The total number of possessive pronouns that have an apostrophe is one: one's.* So it's always *ours, yours, hers, theirs, its, whose, oneself.*   8

Personal Favorite

I like the semicolon as the most flexible of punctuation marks. (It's a journalist's favorite, too.) It can separate independent clauses (full sentences); it can serve as a longer stop than a comma in a series of phrases where you want separate emphasis; or it can either link or contrast logically connected elements within a sentence—as in this one. But be careful not to overuse it. On an early draft of this book, my editor said, "You scatter semicolons with wild abandon." He was right.   9

Questions

1. What is Garrison's "one simple rule"?

2. Do you think Garrison's guidelines can be more useful to you than rules? Explain your answer.

3. Of Garrison's two ways of thinking about punctuation, which do you prefer: pause marks or traffic signals?

4. What would be the effect of writing the listed information in paragraphs 4 and 5 in normal paragraph form?

5. In paragraph 8 Garrison identifies the error he considers the "most common and annoying." What kind of error disturbs you the most?

Discussion

Garrison makes an important point about punctuation marks: they are *signals* for readers. As such, they are no more interchangeable than road signs and traffic signals are. If a state department of transportation were to put up a red octagonal sign to signal a road curving to the right, drivers would be confused about how to proceed. The same happens with writing. If a writer inserts a period (a stop sign) to signal the end of a phrase (for example, "Picking up the mail."), readers are confused: did they misread? They wonder what the writer means by the period.

Development

After the topic sentence in paragraph 3, "Punctuation marks are signals to readers," Garrison gives two ways of thinking about punctuation marks: as breath marks corresponding to speech (paragraph 4) and as traffic signals (paragraph 5). The appropriate mark gives the necessary signal. In presenting these two ways of thinking about punctuation, Garrison uses a numbered list form, with three columns in each list: one naming the punctuation marks, one illustrating them graphically, and a third interpreting the marks. As seen in Morris's "Smooth Flyer" instructions, writers often rely on lists to draw attention to points in their instructions.

Garrison gives only one rule. When writers follow this rule, they indicate to their readers that they know where their sentences end, and readers then can know where to end them too. Other people writing about punctuation, if they were to reduce their instructions to one rule, would likely name something else: "Use two commas, not one, to set off interrupting modifiers," perhaps, or "Don't use a period until you come to the end of your sentence."

There may be disagreement on the "most common and annoying error" too. For Garrison that error is the faulty *it's*. *It's* and *its* are two entirely different words, the first meaning "it is" or "it has" and the second indicating possession. Using the one with the apostrophe when you need the other gives a faulty signal, something like writing *course* when you mean *coarse*. What Garrison doesn't say is that the apostrophe has two main uses:

1. To indicate something omitted, as in *don't* (do not), *you're* (you are), *who's* (who is or who has), and *class of '91* (1991),
2. To indicate noun (not pronoun) possession, as in "the *paper's* title," "*Dr. Harris's* book," and "the *mail carriers'* car.

It is *not* used to make words plural:

Not: The *Harris's* recently repainted their house. (The correct plural form is *Harrises.*)

And, as Garrison says, the apostrophe is not used in possessive pronouns: neither in *its* or in *his, hers, yours, whose,* and *theirs.*

EXERCISE

Identify your "most common and annoying error" and write a brief explanation of how writers can remember to avoid it. Compare errors and explanations with your classmates.

Writing

Write instructions out of your experience. Everyone can do certain things better than other people can. Garrison wrote as an experienced writer to less experienced writers. You might be quite an expert at repotting a plant or repairing an electrical cord. There is something that you know how to do that other people would like to be able to do too. Write a paper about it, assuming an interested audience.

Begin your paper with a paragraph that, like Garrison's first paragraph, makes an attempt to interest your audience, presenting your subject in a fresh way. In explaining your instructions, consider using numbered lists, but don't attempt to use columns unless they're right for your subject. If headings are appropriate, use them. Like Garrison, use the second-person pronoun, *you,* when addressing your reader, and use the first-person pronoun, *I,* when referring to your own preferences and practices.

Writing Instructions on a Familiar Activity

Most instructive writing tells readers how to do something they don't know how to do. But there is another kind of instructive writing that takes a familiar activity and makes a fresh subject out of it. Examples of such instruction would be "how to clean your room" or "how to make toast." Since most readers don't need to be told how to carry out these activities, such writing has a primary purpose other than instruction, perhaps to entertain, to explain, even to persuade. Even though the essay may convey some new information about how to carry out the activity, its purpose is certainly not simply to instruct.

You might read a humorous essay on how to climb a tree, complete with instructions on taking along plenty of trail mix and letting someone know where you are in case you get stuck for a few hours and can't get down. Or you run across an essay on how to save newspapers, plastic containers, and aluminum cans; it's somewhat instructive but obviously is urging you to begin conserving resources. In having more than one purpose, instructive writing is like most writing.

Reading

Garrison Keillor's "How to Write a Personal Letter" has more than one purpose. Have you ever sat with a blank page in front of you, needing to write something but unable to begin? In the essay that follows, Keillor deals with this problem and others related to the familiar activity of writing a personal letter.

You have probably read or heard something of Garrison Keillor. His old public radio program, "A Prairie Home Companion," became quite a campy classic before he gave it up in 1987. In this and other radio programs and in his books, he has occasionally advised people on how to do something. What better advice could come from a writer than instructions on "How to Write a Personal Letter"? As you read, watch for any purpose other than to instruct.

How to Write a Personal Letter

Garrison Keillor

We shy persons need to write a letter now and then, or else we'll dry up   1
and blow away. It's true. And I speak as one who loves to reach for the phone, dial the number, and talk. I say, "Big Bopper here—what's shakin', babes?" The telephone is to shyness what Hawaii is to February, it's a way out of the woods, *and yet:* a letter is better.

Such a sweet gift—a piece of handmade writing, in an envelope that is   2
not a bill, sitting in our friend's path when she trudges home from a long day spent among wahoos and savages, a day our words will help repair. They don't need to be immortal, just sincere. She can read them twice and again tomorrow: *You're someone I care about, Corinne, and think of often and every time I do you make me smile.*

We need to write, otherwise nobody will know who we are. They will   3
have only a vague impression of us as A Nice Person, because frankly, we don't shine at conversation, we lack the confidence to thrust our faces forward and say, "Hi, I'm Heather Hooten, let me tell you about my week." Mostly we say "Uh-huh" and "Oh really." People smile and look over our shoulder, looking for someone else to talk to.

So a shy person sits down and writes a letter. To be known by another   4
person—to meet and talk freely on the page—to be close despite distance. To escape from anonymity and be our own sweet selves and express the music of our souls.

Same thing that moves a giant rock star to sing his heart out in front of   5
123,000 people moves us to take ballpoint in hand and write a few lines to
our dear Aunt Eleanor. *We want to be known.* We want her to know that we
have fallen in love, that we quit our job, that we're moving to New York, and
we want to say a few things that might not get said in casual conversation:
thank you for what you've meant to me, I am very happy right now.

The first step in writing letters is to get over the guilt of *not* writing. You   6
don't "owe" anybody a letter. Letters are a gift. The burning shame you feel
when you see unanswered mail makes it harder to pick up a pen and makes
for a cheerless letter when you finally do. *I feel bad about not writing, but I've
been so busy,* etc. Skip this. Few letters are obligatory, and they are *Thanks for
the wonderful gift* and *I am terribly sorry to hear about George's death* and *Yes, you're
welcome to stay with us next month* and not many more than that. Write those
promptly if you want to keep your friends. Don't worry about the others,
except love letters, of course. When your true love writes *Dear Light of My
Life, Joy of My Heart, O Lovely Pulsating Core of My Sensate Life,* some response
is called for. Some of the best letters are tossed off in a burst of inspiration,
so keep your writing stuff in one place where you can sit down for a few
minutes and *Dear Roy, I am in the middle of an essay for International Paper but
thought I'd drop you a line. Hi to your sweetie too* dash off a note to a pal.
Envelopes, stamps, address book, everything in a drawer so you can write
fast when the pen is hot.

A blank white 8″ × 11″ sheet can look as big as Montana if the pen's not   7
so hot—try a smaller page and write boldly. Or use a note card with a piece
of fine art on the front; if your letter ain't good, at least they get the Matisse.
Get a pen that makes a sensuous line, get a comfortable typewriter, a
friendly word processor—whichever feels easy to the hand.

Sit for a few minutes with the blank sheet in front of you, and meditate   8
on the person you will write to, let your friend come to mind until you can
almost see her or him in the room with you. Remember the last time you saw
each other and how your friend looked and what you said and what
perhaps was unsaid between you, and when your friend becomes real to
you, start to write.

Write the salutation—*Dear* You—and take a deep breath and plunge in.   9
A simple declarative sentence will do, followed by another and another and
another. Tell us what you're doing and tell it like you were talking to us.
Don't think about grammar, don't think about lit'ry style, don't try to write
dramatically, just give us your news. Where did you go, who did you see,
what did they say, what do you think?

If you don't know where to begin, start with the present moment: *I'm*   10
*sitting at the kitchen table on a rainy Saturday morning. Everyone is gone and the
house is quiet.* Let your simple description of the present moment lead to
something else, let the letter drift gently along.

The toughest letter to crank out is one that is meant to impress, as we all   11
know from writing job applications; if it's hard work to slip off a letter to a
friend, maybe you're trying too hard to be terrific. A letter is only a report

to someone who already likes you for reasons other than your brilliance. Take it easy.

Don't worry about form. It's not a term paper. When you come to the   12
end of one episode, just start a new paragraph. You can go from a few lines about the sad state of rock 'n' roll to the fight with your mother to your fond memories of Mexico to your cat's urinary tract infection to a few thoughts on personal indebtedness to the kitchen sink and what's in it. The more you write, the easier it gets, and when you have a True True Friend to write to, a *compadre*, a soul sibling, then it's like driving a car down a country road, you just get behind the keyboard and press on the gas.

Don't tear up the page and start over when you write a bad line—try to   13
write your way out of it. Make mistakes and plunge on. Let the letter cook along and let yourself be bold. Outrage, confusion, love—whatever is in your mind, let it find a way to the page. Writing is a means of discovery, always, and when you come to the end and write *Yours ever* or *Hugs and Kisses*, you'll know something you didn't when you wrote *Dear Pal*.

Probably your friend will put your letter away, and it'll be read again a   14
few years from now—and it will improve with age.

And forty years from now, your friend's grandkids will dig it out of the   15
attic and read it, a sweet and precious relic of the ancient Eighties that gives them a sudden clear glimpse of you and her and the world we old-timers knew. You will then have created an object of art. Your simple lines about where you went, who you saw, what they said, will speak to those children and they will feel in their hearts the humanity of our times.

You can't pick up a phone and call the future and tell them about our   16
times. You have to pick up a piece of paper.

Questions

1. What makes Keillor an authority on letter writing? Can everyone write such instructions?

2. In what ways does Keillor instruct you on letter writing?

3. In what paragraph does he start telling you how to write a personal letter?

4. What do you see as Keillor's purpose other than instruction?

5. In your own words, summarize what Keillor says about how to write a letter.

Discussion

Keillor may not tell you anything about writing letters that you didn't already know. You probably knew how to begin, and when you write a letter to a friend, you are not likely to "worry about form" or tear up a page when you make a mistake. In fact, you may have decided that telling you and other readers how to write a personal letter is not Keillor's main purpose for writing this essay.

Purpose

Consider what Keillor's purpose might be. In the first five paragraphs, he promotes letter writing as a good thing to do. Only in paragraph 6 does he begin, "The first step in writing letters." Even here he doesn't really tell you the "first step." Instead, he is still persuading you about the value of letter writing. In fact, he never does actually describe any "steps" in writing a letter.

What does he do then? He gives his reasons for why people should write letters (paragraphs 1–5). He addresses attitudes toward letter writing in paragraphs 6 through 8 and 12. Then in paragraphs 9 through 11 he gives some instruction on how to begin, and in paragraphs 13 and 14 he tells you not to worry about form, just to write and discover new things about yourself as you go. The final three paragraphs conclude with more reasons for writing. In five paragraphs he instructs, and in the remainder he promotes letter writing.

If Keillor's purpose was indeed to instruct an audience on how to write a personal letter, he must have had at least one other just as important purpose. Take another look at the essay and consider what other purposes Keillor might have had. What parts of the essay develop those purposes?

EXERCISES

1. Compare Keillor's instructions with those of Morris in "Smooth Flyer," analyzing the two essays on these points: form, tone, content, and purpose.
2. Experiment with focus by rewriting paragraph 9, beginning "Garrison Keillor sat for a few minutes . . ." and making all changes necessary to have the paragraph describe *Keillor* in the act of writing. What is the effect of the change?

Writing

Write an essay about something that, like writing a personal letter, almost everyone knows how to do. Since your audience already knows how to do what you're describing, you will have a secondary purpose: not just to instruct but to convince of something as well. You might also want to try a little humor. Here are some possible topics. Use one of them if you want, but your imagination might discover something more appropriate for you.

- How to wash a car
- How to polish shoes

- How to keep a room clean
- How to listen to music
- How to read a poem

Once you've decided on a topic, write down your purposes. If you were writing about washing a car, for example, your purpose might be

1. To *instruct* someone on how to wash a car;
2. To *persuade* someone that he or she should wash the car.

On the same sheet of paper, write the name of someone you know who would be a good audience for your essay. Now list the steps you'll need to cover for instruction and then some points that might persuade the person you identified as a possible audience. Set this paper aside and write your essay, referring to your notes only when you get stuck or think you might be losing track of your purposes. When you're ready to revise, refer to your notes again; if you missed any important points or details in your essay, add them.

Instructing on New Uses for Familiar Things

Instructions sometimes tell readers about new uses for familiar things. People write articles and books about how to use common household materials for unsuspected purposes. There is an entire book on how to use vinegar, from cleaning water stains to rinsing hair and so on. People occasionally read about how to decorate their homes and rooms with "found" objects, such as rocks, weeds, and driftwood.

Written instructions of this kind often first convince readers that the familiar items are useful for new purposes: forget about the fact that vinegar smells sour; if it rinses your hair clean of soap residue, why not use it? And weeds are not just *weeds;* if you find the right ones they will look quite attractive stuck in a fruit jar. Writers sometimes expose commonly held beliefs so they can instruct their readers on new ways to do things.

Reading

In the essay that follows, Suzette Haden Elgin, retired professor of applied psycholinguistics, tells readers how to detect a lie, and in doing so she promotes a new use for a familiar item—the telephone. First she must refute the commonly held belief that it's easier to lie over the telephone than in face-to-face conversation. In refuting the myth about lies, she instructs readers on how to use the telephone for detecting lies. The author of several books on "verbal self-defense," Elgin calls her writings "first-aid" manuals on what to do when under verbal attack, or how to avoid letting other people get the better of you. As you read this essay from her book entitled

The Last Word on the Gentle Art of Verbal Self-Defense, notice how she establishes her authority: she summarizes "research studies," then goes beyond them to suggest her own explanation.

Telephone Listening

Suzette Haden Elgin

Life is filled with things that are assumed to be true because they are   1
"obvious" or "self-evident." It's always a shock to learn that one of those things is not true at all. It gives you a chance to imagine what it was like to hear from the town crier that the world was round rather than, as was obvious and self-evident, flat.

Among the set of self-evident myths is the idea that if you want to lie   2
you're better off doing it on the phone, where people can't see you and you are therefore more likely to get away with it. That happens to be false; it is in fact easier for people to spot a lie when they hear it on the phone than when they hear it from a person present at the time.

The research studies suggest a number of reasons for this. For example: 3

1. There is less distraction in telephone speech, so the listener can concentrate more easily.
2. There is less emotional involvement in telephone conversation, which eliminates yet another sort of distraction.
3. Pitch changes, which are important to the detection of deceit, are easier to hear when attention is focused entirely on the voice.

I agree with all three of these proposed explanations; they are surely   4
accurate. But I think that the generalization we can draw from them is this: *Without body language feedback, a person who lies cannot obtain the necessary data for the constant fine-tuning required to make lies work.* The auditory (ear) channel of communication alone does not provide enough information for this purpose. The speaker who would like to deceive can't even watch for body syncing or other obvious clues to attention. Which means that on the phone you *can* fake listening!

In person, it's easier for speakers to deceive and very difficult for   5
listeners to do so. On the telephone, this is reversed—it is the listener who can deceive more easily, and the speaker who has difficulty. The ear is a much better judge of lying than the eye is, contrary to what is often assumed—and the very best channel of all for lying is the *face,* which is of course invisible in telephone communication. (It's interesting to consider what this may mean for people who do teleconferencing with video and can see one another as they talk, but we don't yet have enough data on that to come to any firm conclusions about it.)

Knowing this gives you crucial strategic information about the method   6
you choose for carrying on language interactions when you suspect that you

might be dealing with a Phony Leveler.* You are better off having your conversation by telephone. The telephone will keep you from being influenced by the perfect match between the Phony Leveler's speech and body language, which is so convincing when you can see it. And it will keep the Phony Leveler from being able to observe your reactions and make constant linguistic adjustments based on them. That gives you a much better chance in such an interaction than you would have if it were carried on face-to-face.

Used properly, this is a major advantage for the listener. But unless you   7
listen with your full attention, the advantage will be canceled. Half-listening
on the phone, while you read a magazine or watch television or daydream,
will be no more effective than half-listening in person. Listen carefully for
changes in the pitch of the voice; research indicates that when people are
trying to deliberately deceive others the pitch of their voices will rise.

This does not mean that high pitch is a clue to the detection of decep-   8
tion, however. A rise in pitch in the speech of someone who has a naturally
low-pitched voice is just as significant. It is the deviation from the pitch level
established by the speaker as the norm—the *mismatch* between what has
been established as typical and the higher pitch—that warns the listener to
be wary.

Your best strategy as a listener, when you're not certain that you can   9
trust a speaker with whom you plan some sort of interaction, is to have at
least one discussion of the issues by telephone before you have the face-to-
face meeting. That will give you an opportunity to listen for deception in a
situation where the speaker can't use body language and associated feedback skills as tools to influence your perceptions.

Questions

1. What reasons does Elgin say the "research studies" give for its being easier to detect lies over the telephone than face to face? Do these reasons make sense to you? Do they make sense to Elgin?

2. How does Elgin suggest using telephone conversations for detecting lies? Do you agree that liars need body language feedback to make their lies work?

3. Have you ever been told a lie over the telephone? Could you tell that it was a lie? If so, what gave the lie away?

4. Can you think of any other unusual uses for the telephone?

5. What is the tone of this essay? What is Elgin's attitude toward her subject? How does she use the first-person pronoun *I?*

---

* *Phony Leveler* means "liar."

Discussion

To present her method of detecting lies, Elgin must first refute the commonly held belief that it's easier to lie over the telephone. Based on your own experience as a liar or as someone being lied to, can you say that Elgin convinced you that the telephone is better for detecting lies than telling them?

Purpose and Development

What is Elgin's purpose for writing? As the author of a book entitled *The Last Word on the Gentle Art of Verbal Self-Defense*, Elgin is probably not primarily interested in telling you about research on lying or even telling you that it's harder to lie over the telephone than face to face. Her purpose is more likely evidenced in the last four paragraphs: to *instruct* you and other readers on how to avoid being deceived. Her *thesis* is probably something like this: "To tell whether or not someone is lying to you, concentrate on the quality of that person's voice over the telephone." She develops her essay with three main parts:

1. Refuting the commonly held myth "If you want to lie you're better off doing it on the phone" (paragraphs 1 and 2),
2. Presenting new evidence (paragraphs 3 and 4),
3. Instructing the reader on how to use this evidence to handle a difficult problem (paragraphs 5 through 9).

EXERCISE

Make a body language observation. Go to a public place where you can observe two people in conversation but not overhear them. Concentrate on one person, taking notes on how that person uses his or her hands, face, and other body parts in the act of communication—both as speaker and as listener. Without knowing what has been said, write your perceptions about the attitude and purpose of that person in carrying on the conversation.

Writing

Keillor in "How to Write a Personal Letter" argues for writing letters instead of telephoning, and Elgin recommends telephoning in some cases rather than conversing face to face. In this writing, you are invited to take a third stance. Think about the advantages of face-to-face conversation, then write an essay that presents this kind of dialogue in preference to another kind. Like Elgin on using the telephone for exposing liars, select particular circumstances for the conversation you're recommending. First state the advantages as you see them; then write two or three paragraphs that advise readers how to carry on this kind of conversation to achieve their purposes. Use Elgin's essay as a guide. In writing, you will have two aims: to persuade your readers of a special use for face-to-face conversation and to instruct them on the best way to have this conversation.

Using Humor in Instruction

Instructions are usually serious and straightforward; they tell readers how to do something that needs to be done. Sometimes instructions are humorous as well as instructive, like Keillor's essay on letter writing. But, like many other kinds of writing, instructions are often used simply for the sake of humor. Such essays are more common in popular magazines than in academic writing, but sometimes in English classes students have an opportunity to try writing just for fun.

Writing of this kind looks like instructions but usually has an unexpected subject, such as "how to roast a hot dog over an electric range," or takes an exaggerated viewpoint. Readers know from the beginning that this is not serious fare, and they accept it for what it is. (Writing for entertainment is covered in more detail in Chapter 8.)

Reading

Tom Bodett is a humorist who lives in Homer, Alaska. You may have heard his commentaries on public radio's "All Things Considered" or his ads on commercial radio. Whether you live in Alaska or not, you will probably appreciate the humor of "Ditch Diving," because it's more about drivers than about a particular locality. Bodett tells you how to be good at a "sport" not often described. The essay has three parts, plus introduction and conclusion—in other words, it is a variation of the standard five-paragraph essay. Try reading it as a caricature of both winter sports and the essay form.

Ditch Diving
Tom Bodett

The graceful winter sports of skiing, skating, and dog-sledding get a lot   1
of attention around Alaska, but there's another winter activity that nobody seems to appreciate for the art that it actually is—ditch diving. We all become practitioners of this art at one time or another, but none of us seems to hold proper appreciation of what we're doing, perhaps because its aesthetics have never been fully defined for us. Allow me.

To dive you need a road, a ditch, some snow on the ground, and any 2
licensed highway vehicle or its equivalent. Nothing else is required, but a
good freezing rain will speed up the process.

The art of the dive is in the elegance with which you perform three 3
distinct actions. The first one, of course, is that you and your car *leave the
roadway.* Not so fast there, hotshot—remember, this is an art. The manner
and theme of your dive are weighed heavily in this maneuver.

For instance, the "I wasn't looking and drove into the ditch" dive will 4
gain you nothing with the critics. The "He wasn't looking and drove me into
the ditch" dive is slightly better, but lacks character. The "It sucked me into
the ditch" dive shows real imagination, and the "We spun around three
times, hit the ditch going backwards, and thought we were all going to die"
dive will earn you credits for sheer drama. The "I drove in the ditch rather than
slide past the school bus" dive might win the humanitarian award, but only if
you can explain to the police why you were going that fast in the first place.

Okay, so now you've left the road. Your second challenge is to *place the* 5
vehicle. Any dumbbell can put a car in a ditch, but it takes an artist to put one
there with panache. The overall appeal of your installation is gauged by
how much the traffic slows down to gawk at it.

Nosed-in within ten degrees of level won't even turn a head. Burrowed 6
into a snowbank with one door buried shut is better, and if you're actually
caught in the act of climbing out a window, you're really getting somewhere.
Letting your car sit overnight so the snowplows can bury it is a good way of
gaining points with the morning commuter traffic. Any wheel left visibly off
the ground is good for fifty points each, with a hundred-point bonus for all
four. Caution: Only master-class ditch divers should endeavor to achieve
this bonus positioning.

All right, there you are, nicely featured alongside your favorite road- 7
way. The third part of your mission is to *ask for assistance.* Simply walking to
a phone and calling a tow truck will prove you a piker and not an artist at all.
Hit the showers, friend. The grace and creativity you display getting back on
the road must at least equal those you employed while leaving it.

Let's say you were forced into the ditch and are neatly enshrined with 8
one rear wheel off the ground and the hood buried in the berm. Wait until
any truck bigger than your bathroom happens along and start walking in
that direction with a pronounced limp. Look angry but not defeated, as if
you'd walk all night to find the guy who ran you off the road. Look the
driver in the eye like it would have been him if he'd been there sooner. This
is a risky move, but it's been proven effective. If the truck has personalized
license plates and lights mounted all over it, you're in good shape. Those
guys love to show how hard their trucks can pull on things.

I prefer, however, to rely on the softer side of human nature. Addle- 9
brained people hold a special place in our hearts, and I like to play on these
protective instincts. If my car is buried beyond hope, I'll display my tongue
in the corner of my mouth and begin frantically digging at the snow drift

with my hands until someone stops to talk me out of it. If my hands get cold and still nobody's stopped, I'll crawl head-first into the hole I've dug and flail my legs around like I was thrown clear of the wreck. This works every time and has won me many a ditch-diving exhibition over the years.

I certainly hope I've enlarged your appreciation of this undervalued   10 creative medium. I warn against exercising this art to excess, but when the opportunity arises, remember: Hit 'er hard, sink 'er deep, get 'er out, and please, dive carefully.

Questions

1. Outlining a completed essay is sometimes useful for analyzing the essay's structure (see Chapter 5). Analyze Bodett's essay by making an outline that accounts for the subject of each paragraph and shows how each paragraph relates to others.

2. Would you agree that Bodett's primary purpose is *not* to instruct? Explain your answer.

3. At what point did the essay begin to be funny for you?

4. What are Bodett's techniques for achieving humor? Note vocabulary, word combinations (like "buried in the berm," paragraph 8), and selection of details.

5. In what ways does Bodett make fun of sports?

Discussion

Bodett uses instruction as a means of entertainment. He sets the tone in his first paragraph, where he compares ditch diving to other "graceful winter sports" and requests permission to define its "aesthetics" for you. Later he calls you, the reader, "hotshot" and implies that you're about to plunge headlong into the nearest ditch before you read the remainder of the instructions. Bodett achieves humor with vocabulary, selection of details, and a familiar essay form.

Development

"Ditch Diving" is easily recognizable as a variation of the standard five-paragraph essay. In fact, the exaggeration of the form may be considered part of the humor by establishing expectations of what is to follow. Bodett's introduction sets the tone, subject, and circumstance; then a short paragraph, as in any good how-to essay, lists the necessary "equipment." A clear-cut *thesis* is expressed at the beginning of paragraph 3: "The art of the dive is in the elegance with which you perform three distinct actions." This thesis sentence establishes reader expectations by stating the subject ("the art of the dive"), making an assertion about the subject ("is in the elegance with which you perform"), and declaring the method of development ("three distinct actions").

Bodett then discusses the "three distinct actions" that are part of ditch diving:

1. The dive, paragraphs 3 and 4;
2. The style of placement, paragraphs 5 and 6;
3. The call for help, paragraphs 7, 8, and 9.

He concludes in the traditional five-paragraph-essay way—with a summary paragraph.

Coherence

Not only is Bodett's essay tightly structured but it is closely *coherent* as well. Each time Bodett shifts from one aspect of ditch diving to another, he clearly signals the reader:

> Okay, so now you've left the road. Your second challenge is to *place the vehicle.* (paragraph 5)

> All right, there you are, nicely featured alongside your favorite roadway. The third part of your mission is to *ask for assistance.* (paragraph 7)

What he does in these *transitional sentences* is summarize what he just said and then proceed with the next step. This is an obvious way of achieving coherence, but it does ensure that the reader will keep up.

EXERCISE

Brainstorm (see Chapter 3) a list of things people do not *want to do, things like burning toast or getting a sunburn (see topics under the following writing assignment). Then select one topic that interests you and explore some ways of achieving the undesired end. Try clustering (see Chapter 3) to discover some "steps" or "actions" in achieving the end.*

Writing

Write a humorous how-to essay on something that people do *not* want to do, using the topic you explored in the preceding exercise. Adopt a basic essay form with five divisions represented by five or more paragraphs. Introduce your essay in such a way that your reader does *not* take it seriously, list any equipment that is necessary, state your thesis explicitly, and use an obvious means of coherence. Explore your own experience for possible topics, but here are a few ideas to get you started:

- How to burn toast
- How to get a sunburn
- How to spill ketchup on the front of your favorite shirt
- How to lock yourself out of your room, house, or car

As already noted, Bodett's thesis sentence is transparent, being absolutely explicit on how he will develop his essay. While not all thesis sentences have all three parts, for this assignment try including in your thesis all of them—subject, assertion, and method of development.

ADDITIONAL READINGS FOR DISCUSSION

Reading

In the following essay, medical doctor and mental health professional David D. Burns speaks frankly about what doctors know about anger and what people can do to reduce its damaging effects. How does Burns establish his authority?

Ten Things You Should Know about Your Anger
David D. Burns

1. The events of this world don't make you angry. Your "hot thoughts" create your anger. Even when a genuinely negative event occurs, it is the meaning you attach to it that determines your emotional response.

The idea that you are responsible for your anger is ultimately to your advantage because it gives you the opportunity to achieve control and make a free choice about how you want to feel. If it weren't for this, you would be helpless to control your emotions; they would be irreversibly bound up with every external event of this world, most of which are ultimately out of your control.

2. Most of the time your anger will not help you. It will immobilize you, and you will become frozen in your hostility to no productive purpose. You will feel better if you place your emphasis on the active search for creative solutions. What can you do to correct the difficulty or at least reduce the chance that you'll get burned in the same way in the future? This attitude will eliminate to a certain extent the helplessness and frustration that eat you up when you feel you can't deal with a situation effectively.

If no solution is possible because the provocation is totally beyond your   4
control, you will only make yourself miserable with your resentment, so why
not get rid of it? It's difficult if not impossible to feel anger and joy simultaneously. If you think your angry feelings are especially precious and important, then think about one of the happiest moments of your life. Now ask
yourself, How many minutes of that period of peace or jubilation would I be
willing to trade in for feeling frustration and irritation instead?

3. The thoughts that generate anger more often than not will contain   5
distortions. Correcting these distortions will reduce your anger.

4. Ultimately your anger is caused by your belief that someone is acting   6
unfairly or some event is unjust. The intensity of the anger will increase in
proportion to the severity of the maliciousness perceived and if the act is
seen as intentional.

5. If you learn to see the world through other people's eyes, you will   7
often be surprised to realize their actions are *not* unfair from their point of
view. The unfairness in these cases turns out to be an illusion that exists *only
in your mind!* If you are willing to let go of the unrealistic notion that your
concepts of truth, justice, and fairness are shared by everyone, much of
your resentment and frustration will vanish.

6. Other people usually do not feel they deserve your punishment.   8
Therefore, your retaliation is unlikely to help you achieve any positive goals
in your interactions with them. Your rage will often just cause further
deterioration and polarization, and will function as a self-fulfilling proph-
ecy. Even if you temporarily get what you want, any short-term gains from
such hostile manipulation will often be more than counterbalanced by a
long-term resentment and retaliation from the people you are coercing. No
one likes to be controlled or forced. This is why a positive reward system
works better.

7. A great deal of your anger involves your defense against loss of   9
self-esteem when people criticize you, disagree with you, or fail to behave as
you want them to. Such anger is *always* inappropriate because only your
own negative distorted thoughts can cause you to lose self-esteem. When
you blame the other guy for your feelings of worthlessness, you are always
fooling yourself.

8. Frustration results from unmet expectations. Since the event that   10
disappointed you was a part of "reality," it was "realistic." Thus, your
frustration always results from your *unrealistic* expectation. You have the
right to try to influence reality to bring it more in line with your expectations, but this is not always practical, especially when these expectations
represent ideals that don't correspond to everyone else's concept of human
nature. The simplest solution would be to *change* your expectations. For
example, some unrealistic expectations that lead to frustration include:

   a. If I want something (love, happiness, a promotion, etc.), I deserve it.
   b. If I work hard at something, I *should* be successful.
   c. Other people *should* try to measure up to my standards and believe
      in my concept of "fairness."

    d. I *should* be able to solve any problems quickly and easily.

    e. If I'm a good wife, my husband is *bound* to love me.

    f. People *should* think and act the way I do.

    g. If I'm nice to someone, they *should* reciprocate.

    9. It is just childish pouting to insist you have the *right* to be angry. Of   11
course you do! Anger is legally permitted in the United States. The crucial
issue is—is it to your advantage to feel angry? Will you or the world really
benefit from your rage?

    10. You rarely need your anger in order to be human. It is not true that   12
you will be an unfeeling robot without it. In fact, when you rid yourself of
that sour irritability, you will feel greater zest, joy, peace, and productivity.
You will experience liberation and enlightenment.

Questions

1. What does Burns do to get your attention?

2. In what ways does he establish his authority on the subject?

3. Which of his ten points speak to *your* anger? In other words, which ones seem to be useful information?

4. Which of the seven "*unrealistic* expectations" in item 8 describe your frustrations?

5. These "ten things" are simply listed, with no statement of thesis. Why should someone want to know how to deal with anger?

6. What is the tone of the piece?

Reading

    John Irving, author of *The World According to Garp,* The *Hotel New Hampshire,* and other novels, was once a hopelessly bad speller who discovered some tips and tricks to aid in spelling. He shares them in this instructional essay.

How to Spell

John Irving

    Let's begin with the bad news.   1

    If you're a bad speller, you probably think you always will be. There are   2
exceptions to every spelling rule, and the rules themselves are easy to
forget. George Bernard Shaw demonstrated how ridiculous some spelling
rules are. By following the rules, he said, we could spell *fish* this way: *ghoti*.
The "f" as it sounds in enou*gh*, the "i" as it sounds in w*o*men, and the "sh"
as it sounds in fic*ti*on.

    With such rules to follow, no one should feel stupid for being a bad   3
speller. But there are ways to improve. Start by acknowledging the mess
that English spelling is in—but have sympathy: English spelling changed

with foreign influences. Chaucer wrote "gesse," but "guess," imported earlier by the Norman invaders, finally replaced it. Most early printers in England came from Holland; they brought "ghost" and "gherkin" with them.

If you'd like to intimidate yourself—and remain a bad speller forever—just try to remember the thirteen different ways the sound "sh" can be written: 4

*sh*oe	suspi*ci*on
*s*ugar	nau*se*ous
o*ce*an	con*sci*ous
is*s*ue	*ch*aperone
na*ti*on	man*si*on
*sch*ist	fu*ch*sia
*p*shaw	

The good news is that 90 percent of all writing consists of 1,000 basic words. There is, also, a method to most English spelling and a great number of how-to-spell books. Remarkably, all these books propose learning the same rules! Not surprisingly, most of these books are humorless.   5

Just keep this in mind: If you're familiar with the words you use, you'll probably spell them correctly—and you shouldn't be writing words you're unfamiliar with anyway. USE a word—out loud, and more than once—before you try writing it, and make sure (with a new word) that you know what it means before you use it. This means you'll have to look it up in a dictionary, where you'll not only learn what it means, but you'll see how it's spelled. Choose a dictionary you enjoy browsing in, and guard it as you would a diary. You wouldn't lend a diary, would you?   6

Beside every word I look up in my dictionary, I make a mark. Beside every word I look up more than once, I write a note to myself—about WHY I looked it up. I have looked up "strictly" fourteen times since 1964. I prefer to spell it with a *k*—as in "stric*k*tly." I have looked up "ubiquitous" a dozen times. I can't remember what it means.   7

Another good way to use your dictionary: When you have to look up a word, for any reason, learn—and learn to *spell*—a *new* word at the same time. It can be any useful word on the same page as the word you looked up. Put the date beside this new word and see how quickly, or in what way, you forget it. Eventually, you'll learn it.   8

Almost as important as knowing what a word means (in order to spell it) is knowing how it's pronounced. It's gover*n*ment, not goverment. It's Feb-*ru*ary, not Feb*u*ary. And if you know that *anti-* means against, you should know how to spell *anti*dote and *anti*biotic and *anti*freeze. If you know that *ante-* means before, you shouldn't have trouble spelling *ante*chamber or *ante*cedent.   9

I don't have room to touch on *all* the rules here. It would take a book to do that. But I can share a few that help me most: 10

What about *-ary* or *-ery*? When a word has a primary accent on the first syllable and a secondary accent on the next-to-last syllable (sec're-tar'y), it usually ends in *-ary*. Only six important words like this end in *-ery*:   11

cemetery	monastery
millinery	confectionery
distillery	stationery
	(as in pap*er*)

Here's another easy rule. Only four words end in *-efy*. Most people   12
misspell them—with *ify*, which is usually correct. Just memorize these, too,
and use *-ify* for all the rest.

stupefy	putrefy
liquefy	rarefy

As a former bad speller, I have learned a few valuable tricks. Any good   13
how-to-spell book will teach you more than these two, but these two are my
favorites. Of the 800,000 words in the English language, the most frequently
misspelled is *alright;* just remember that *alright* is *all wrong*. You wouldn't
write *alwrong,* would you? That's how you know you should write *all right.*

The other trick is for the truly *worst* spellers. I mean those of you who   14
spell so badly that you can't get close enough to the right way to spell a word
in order to even FIND it in the dictionary. The word you're looking for is
there, of course, buy you won't find it the way you're trying to spell it. What
to do is look up a synonym—another word that means the same thing.
Chances are good that you'll find the word you're looking for under the
definition of the synonym.

Everyone has a few demon words—they never look right, even when   15
they're spelled correctly. Three of my demons are *medieval, ecstasy,* and
rhythm. I have learned to hate these words, but I have not learned to spell
them; I have to look them up every time.

And everyone has a spelling rule that's a bugbear—it's either too diffi-   16
cult to learn or it's impossible to remember. My personal bugbear among
the rules is the one governing whether you add *-able* or *-ible*. I can teach it to
you, but I can't remember it myself.

You add *-able* to a full word: adapt, adaptable; work, workable. You add   17
-able to words that end in *e*—just remember to drop the final *e:* love, lovable.
But if the word ends in two *e*'s, like agree, you keep them both: agreeable.

You add *-ible* if the base is not a full word that can stand on its own: 18
credible, tangible, horrible, terrible. You add *-ible* if the root word ends in
-ns: responsible. You add *-ible* if the root word ends in *-miss:* permissible. You
add *-ible* if the root word ends in a soft *c* (but remember to drop the final *e!*):
force, forcible.

Got that? I don't have it, and I was introduced to that rule in prep   19
school; with that rule, I still learn one word at a time.

You must remember that it is permiss*ible* for spelling to drive you crazy.   20
Spelling had this effect on Andrew Jackson, who once blew his stack while
trying to write a Presidential paper. "It's a damn poor mind that can think
of only one way to spell a word!" the President cried.

When you have trouble, think of poor Andrew Jackson and know that   21
you're not alone.

And remember what's really important about good writing is not good   22
spelling. If you spell badly but write well, you should hold your head up. As
the poet T. S. Eliot recommended, "Write for as large and miscellaneous an
audience as possible"—and don't be overly concerned if you can't spell
"miscellaneous."

Also remember that you can spell correctly and write well and still be   23
misunderstood. Hold your head up about that, too. As good old G. C.
Lichtenberg said, "A book is a mirror: if an ass peers into it, you can't expect
an apostle to look out"—whether you spell "apostle" correctly or not.

Questions

1. What does Irving tell you about his spelling ability?
2. Which of Irving's tips on dictionary use seem the most helpful to you? What tips can you add from your experience?
3. What does Irving say about knowing the rules of spelling and being able to practice them?
4. Irving's instructions are not organized in chronological order. How *does* he organize his points?
5. Who might Irving's intended audience be?
6. What is the most helpful thing Irving says about spelling?
7. Compare Irving's essay with Roger Garrison's on punctuation as two instructional essays about aspects of writing, written by writers out of their experience as writers. In what ways are the essays similar and in what ways different? Which is more useful to you as a writer? Why?

Reading

People often wonder how critics can be so sure that a movie, a play, a
book, or a painting is good or not good. Essayist, novelist, and poet Marya
Mannes encourages people to be their own critics, and in this essay she
provides some guidelines for making judgments on the worth of art.

How Do You Know It's Good?

Marya Mannes

Suppose there were no critics to tell us how to react to a picture, a play,   1
or a new composition of music. Suppose we wandered innocent as the dawn
into an art exhibition of unsigned paintings. By what standards, by what
values would we decide whether they were good or bad, talented or untal-
ented, successes or failures? How can we ever know what we think is right?

For the last fifteen or twenty years the fashion in criticism or appreciation of the arts has been to deny the existence of any valid criteria and to make the words *good* or *bad* irrelevant, immaterial, and inapplicable. There is no such thing, we are told, as a set of standards, first acquired through experience and knowledge and later imposed on the subject under discussion. This has been a popular approach, for it relieves the critic of the responsibility of judgment and the public of the necessity of knowledge. It pleases those resentful of discipline, it flatters the empty-minded by calling them open-minded, it comforts the confused. Under the banner of democracy and the kind of equality which our forefathers did *not* mean, it says, in effect, "Who are you to tell us what is good or bad?" This is the same cry used so long and so effectively by the producers of mass media who insist that it is the public, not they, who decides what it wants to hear and see, and that for a critic to say that *this* program is bad and *this* program is good is purely a reflection of personal taste. Nobody . . . has expressed this philosophy more succinctly than Dr. Frank Stanton. . . . At a hearing before the Federal Communications Commission, this phrase escaped him under questioning: "One man's mediocrity is another man's good program." . . .

But all these, I maintain, are forms of abdication from the responsibility of judgment. In creating, the artist commits himself; in appreciating, you have a commitment of your own. For after all, it is the audience which makes the arts. A climate of appreciation is essential to its flowering, and the higher the expectations of the public, the better the performance of the artist. Conversely, only a public ill-served by its critics could have accepted as art and as literature so much in these last years that has been neither. If anything goes, everything goes; and at the bottom of the junkpile lie the discarded standards too.

But what are these standards? How do you get them? How do you know they're the right ones? How can you make a clear pattern out of so many intangibles, including that greatest one, the very private I?

Well, for one thing, it's fairly obvious that the more you read and see and hear, the more equipped you'll be to practice that art of association which is at the basis of all understanding and judgment. The more you live and the more you look, the more aware you are of a consistent pattern—as universal as the stars, as the tides, as breathing, as night and day—underlying everything. . . .

Can a standard of craftsmanship apply to art of all ages, or does each have its own, and different, definitions? You may have been aware, inadvertently, that craftsmanship has become a dirty word these years because, again, it implies standard—something done well or done badly. The result of this convenient avoidance is a plenitude of actors who can't project their voices, singers who can't phrase their songs, poets who can't communicate emotion, and writers who have no vocabulary—not to speak of painters who can't draw. The dogma now is that craftsmanship gets in the way of expression. You can do better if you don't know *how* you do it, let alone *what* you're doing.

I think it is time you helped reverse this trend by trying to rediscover craft: the command of the chosen instrument, whether it is a brush, a word, or a voice. When you begin to detect the difference between freedom and sloppiness, between serious experimentation and egotherapy, between skill and slickness, between strength and violence, you are on your way to separating the sheep from the goats, a form of segregation denied us for quite a while. All you need to restore it is a small bundle of standards and a Geiger counter that detects fraud. . . .   7

The only salvation for the listener is, again, an instinct born of experience and association which allows him to separate intent from accident, design from experimentation, and pretense from conviction. Much of contemporary music is, like its sister art, merely a reflection of the composer's own fragmentation: an absorption in self and symbols at the expense of communication with others. The artist, in short, says to the public: If you don't understand this it's because you're dumb. I maintain that you are not. You may have to go part way or even halfway to meet the artist, but if you must go the whole way, it's his fault, not yours. Hold fast to that. And remember it too when you read new poetry, that estranged sister of music. . . .   8

Purpose and craftsmanship—end and means—these are the keys to your judgment in all the arts. What is this painter trying to say when he slashes a broad band of black across a white canvas and lets the edges dribble down? Is it a statement of violence? Is it a self-portrait? If it is *one* of these, has he made you believe it? Or is this a gesture of the ego or a form of therapy? If it shocks you, what does it shock you into?   9

And what of this tight little painting of bright flowers in a vase? Is the painter saying anything new about flowers? Is it different from a million other canvases of flowers? Has it any life, any meaning, beyond its statement? Is there any pleasure in its forms or texture? The question is not whether a thing is abstract or representational, whether it is "modern" or conventional. The question, inexorably, is whether it is good. And this is a decision which only you, on the basis of instinct, experience, and association, can make for yourself. It takes independence and courage. It involves, moreover, the risk of wrong decision and humility, after the passage of time, of recognizing it as such. As we grow and change and learn, our attitudes can change too, and what we once thought obscure or "difficult" can later emerge as coherent and illuminating. Entrenched prejudices, obdurate opinions are as sterile as no opinions at all.   10

Yet standards there are, timeless as the universe itself. And when you have committed yourself to them, you have acquired a passport to that elusive but immutable realm of truth. Keep it with you in the forests of bewilderment. And never be afraid to speak up.   11

Questions

1. What is the primary thing a person must do to become an informed critic?

2. Why should people develop standards for judging the arts?

3. In paragraph 9, Mannes names two keys to judgment in all the arts. Do you agree that these are important criteria? Would you name any others?

4. Apply Mannes's principles to a recent piece of art you've observed—or a recent movie or play you've attended, or a recent book you've read. Do her principles for judging work for you?

5. What is the significance of Mannes's statement that we can expect our perceptions of quality to change over time?

CHAPTER 14

To Praise or Censure: Writing with Emphasis on the Subject

What we admire we praise, and when we praise, advance it into notice.

— *William Cowper*

"Out on the ski slopes they look like hand grenades." This statement describing people wearing down-filled coats is not complimentary. Rather, it seems to express disapproval, to censure those people who don't dress and act as Tom Wolfe would have them do, as you will see if you read the remainder of his short piece "The Down-Filled People" later in this chapter. Wolfe's censuring paragraph is paired with one of praise by Gretel Ehrlich. She stands up for cowboys.

Praising and **censuring** are common purposes for writing. Letters of recommendation are a familiar example of praise; in them the writer recounts the positive features of the candidate, downplaying or ignoring the negative. Other examples are obituaries, eulogies, commencement addresses, award ceremonies, "roastings," and book or movie reviews. Censuring comes often in the form of newspaper or television exposés: the governor is charged with spending millions on the official residence, a television evangelist with immoral acts, a senator with accepting illegal gifts. Whatever form this purpose for writing takes, praise or censure, the writer says something about an individual or a group of people—sometimes good things, sometimes bad.

Audience and Writer

When people write to praise or censure, they often have a specific audience in mind, as with commencement addresses, award ceremonies, and "roastings," but at other times the audience is more general, as with obituaries and reviews—which generally appear in newspapers for a wide audience. In some cases, the audience is the subject of the praise or censure. For example, the primary audience of a commencement address is usually the graduating class, and the class is also the subject of that address; at award ceremonies and "roastings," the subject is present and part of the audience but not necessarily the primary audience. With reviews, who the audience is depends on the reviewer's purpose. Reviews usually praise or censure someone's *work*, not the person; reviews of plays, movies, or books concern the work of playwrights, directors, authors, and so on. When you review a classmate's writing, you praise or criticize the work, not the person. (Reviews, or "critiques," are covered in Chapter 15.)

For an audience to willingly accept what a writer says about an individual or an individual's work, the writer must usually establish his or her credentials. If, for example, you as a writer are censuring the makers of a movie, you need to establish at least that you've seen the movie, better yet, that you've seen similar movies—and, even better, that you've written other movie reviews. You may at times have heard speakers or have read writers praising or censuring someone without taking the trouble to learn some basic information—a commencement speaker, for example, who knows nothing about the graduating class, or the reviewer of a concert who doesn't understand the type of music being performed. To be credible in your praise or censure, you must know the subject.

Secondary Purposes

Writing to praise or censure usually has more than one purpose. In a "roasting," the purpose would be not only to praise or censure but to entertain as well; in a eulogy, to inform readers about a death; in a review, possibly to inform, possibly to persuade. In one of the essays in this chapter, British writer W. J. Weatherby's eulogy in praise of Marilyn Monroe, a secondary purpose is to inform readers about the troubled life of this film star. In Wolfe's "The Down-Filled People," a purpose in addition to censure might be to persuade people not to try to dress and act and talk like all the people they associate with.

Descriptive Details

In essays that praise or censure, you'll find a great deal of description, an abundance of specific details. You can't very well praise a classmate's rough draft without some details illustrating how the essay is effectively written. You can't censure a movie or book unless you give some specific details showing how bad it was. Here are some examples of concrete descriptive phrases taken from essays in this chapter:

> No matter what she said, those teeth never parted. I suspected they were dentures because they were too straight and too white.

> If a cow is stuck in a boghole, he [a cowboy] throws a loop around her neck, takes his dally (a half hitch around the saddle horn), and pulls her out with horsepower.

> The woman sat on a straw bale next to the short, thin man and listened to his story.

Since the subject matter of each of these essays is a person or group of people and the purpose to acquaint the reader with those people, the specific details are essential to the essays. There must be enough of them, and they must be clear and vivid.

Praise and censure also make abundant use of the connotations that words acquire—not just their dictionary meanings but the emotional reactions they conjure up as well. Compare "great sensitivity" with "exaggerated frenzy." Don't you react much more favorably to the first phrase? And compare "too straight and too white" with "straight and white." Can teeth be "too straight" and "too white"? Even though straightness and whiteness are to be prized in teeth, perfection in this context is a negative quality.

In addition to the writings by Wolfe, Ehrlich, and Weatherby, this chapter has two student essays—one outright praise, "A Special Kind of King," and the other clearly censure, "The Poetry of Sister Margarete." The additional readings at the end of the chapter are further examples of praise.

Registering Disapproval

Expressions of disapproval are common, especially around election time. Sometimes, in fact, political mudslinging is so dominant that issues are never addressed. On most days, you can pick up the newspaper and find articles that censure someone. Closer to your own experience, you may be able to remember from childhood or your teen years times when you either criticized someone not in your group or received such criticism. When people register disapproval, it is sometimes done in a kindly manner and sometimes not.

Reading

"The Poetry of Sister Margarete" is a student essay in which the writer registers her disapproval of a teacher she once had in school. You have probably wanted to do the same thing at times—and maybe even did, at least orally with your friends and classmates. Susan Wollack criticizes her teacher and tells why she disliked her, filling in with enough details that you can imagine yourself in the classroom.

The Poetry of Sister Margarete

Susan Wollack

I didn't like her. She was pretty enough and petite, but she seemed to lack confidence and overcompensated by trying to make everyone around her feel inadequate. Sometimes I would just stare at her, and my attention would be drawn to her mouth as she talked with her teeth clenched together. No matter what she said, those teeth never parted. I suspected they were dentures because they were too straight and too white. I mused that perhaps she had used Super Poli-Grip in confusion one morning and they were permanently fused together. It was easy to tune her out when she spoke, particularly when her face became a blur except for those teeth.

Her cool green eyes were like ice. They were not unattractive eyes: rather they seemed to hold no intensity, no emotion. I don't recall if she ever really looked at anyone directly; surely there was nothing of recognition in those eyes.

Her face was, I must admit, flawless and perfectly proportioned with her high colorless cheekbones. There was something restrictive about her monotoned voice, which went on and on. Those generous lips would move in exaggerated frenzy to ensure that each word, each syllable and vowel, was pronounced correctly and with emphasis, as if all words held equal importance.

I sat in the front of Sister Margarete's class, so there was no mistaking her presence, no hiding behind anyone so that she could not catch me dozing off in the stuffy classroom of the Old Building, which had been constructed in the 1800s. Did she know that opening a window might tend to refresh us at the last hour of the day's classes? Was she so insecure that she feared that the appearance of an inquisitive fly might distract one of us from her lecture?

I played games with her sometimes. I acquired a manner of napping with my eyes open in a state of semi-comatose whereby I could hear what she was saying as if she were in my dream. I delighted in the knowledge that she would lose control if she caught anyone napping in her class and hoped that she would try to embarrass me by calling on me to repeat what she had said. It happened only once, and the look of surprise at my unabridged recollection of her words was pleasure enough for me to last a lifetime.

"Tell me the three ingredients necessary in writing a short story, Miss Thompson," Sister Margarete hissed, the emphasis on "Miss."

"Beginning, plot, and ending," I recited. "In each short story there should contain a dramatic episode which leads to a crucial moment between two characters or a character and a situation. If the characters have been developed properly and the meaning of the story is clear, the story should be remembered by the reader."

"And how do you make certain that the reader will remember the story, Miss Thompson?" she shot back with the velocity of a returned Ping-Pong ball.   8

"It is important that the story is complete so that the reader doesn't feel cheated at any point and the dramatic portion of the story holds the reader's interest. It is mandatory that the characters are described so that they are understood and the reader may identify with the characters to a certain extent."   9

Sister Margarete's lips tightened in an almost invisible line beneath her nose. I knew she hated me for that instant; I'm sure she had to say many Our Fathers and Hail Marys that night during prayertime in order to reinstate herself in God's grace.   10

Following my glorious triumph, her patterned pace among the desks quickened; I could see her black shrouded figure out of the corner of my eye as she glided to the back of the room to continue her discussion of English.   11

It was difficult for us seniors to concentrate on our studies as thoughts of graduation and illusions about life after graduation consumed our attention. Although it was already May, the heat was still pouring in from the four-foot-high heating vents which stretched along the entire length of the windowed wall. We knew that beyond the confines of the high ornamental ceiling and the surgery-blue walls, a real world was at work. We belonged out there, not in this prison. Sister Margarete's words fell on deaf ears, but still she persisted in her torturous ordeal of teaching.   12

We were studying poetry the day she lost the restricted discipline that she usually controlled our minds with during last period. She stopped in mid-sentence, which had the effect of abruptly shaking me awake for the first time that semester. The unnerving persistence of silence caused shivers to travel up and down my freckled arms, and the last ten minutes of class dragged on. Even the hands of the IBM clock appeared to be stuck. I nearly felt sorry for her as she tried unsuccessfully to recapture her unattentive audience.   13

The next day we reported to a classroom empty of our instructor. On the chalkboard was a hastily scrawled message written in blue chalk. Blue, mind you! We were to report to the hill overlooking the river.   14

"I wonder what is going on?" we discussed in hushed tones as we gathered in front of the chalkboard. With much confusion and some amount of disbelief, we picked up our books and filed out in orderly fashion.   15

There she was, sprawled out on the grass, her black veil billowing in the early May breeze. Her white face betrayed a hint of pinkness as she beckoned us to come closer. Dutifully, we surrounded her and cautiously sat in ladylike fashion on our notebooks.   16

"Tell me what you see and hear and smell and taste," she began. "Look around you and become one with your environment. Now this (and she spread her hands like the Lady of Fatima) is poetry! This is poetry." And she smiled.   17

The days which followed were full of the usual anticipation of the ending of the school year. Yearbooks were signed, party plans were discussed, and caps and gowns were issued. Even though Sister Margarete never again deterred from her lesson plan for the remainder of the year, we all knew that there was more to her than she probably wanted us to be aware of. I still did not like her, but I was pleased that now I felt I knew her. 18

Questions

1. How does Wollack (Miss Thompson) show her disapproval of Sister Margarete's classroom manner?

2. In the "napping" incident, Wollack reveals as much about her own character as about Sister Margarete's. Characterize Sister Margarete; then characterize Miss Thompson. What character features do they share?

3. Why do you suppose the writer disliked Sister Margarete? Do you think it had anything to do with her own character?

4. What does Wollack do to make it possible for you to visualize Sister Margarete? Name some of the specific words and sentences that help you to see her as the writer does?

5. In addition to describing teeth that were "too straight and too white," in what ways does Wollack use connotations of words to influence the reader to see Sister Margarete as she does?

Discussion

Wollack's *thesis* evolves from a simple opening statement, "I didn't like her," to a fuller understanding at the end: "I still did not like her, but I was pleased that now I felt I knew her." The simple statement is enough at the beginning for the reader to know how to approach this essay, but it would not be enough at the end after the reader has experienced two incidents that reveal the complexities of the relationship between the characters. The fuller, evolved thesis at the end complements the simple one at the beginning.

Development

Wollack develops her essay through **exemplification**—specific examples of her relationship with Sister Margarete. In the first example, the napping incident, she describes a demanding, vindictive, authoritarian interrogator, and in the second she seems not quite sure how to present the puzzling contrast of the poetic nun. In both cases, we are seeing Sister Margarete exclusively through the eyes of a student who admittedly didn't like her. We can therefore learn as much about the writer as we can about the subject of the writing. Why would a student "play games" by pretending to be napping and hoping the teacher would pounce on her so she could delight in the thought of the teacher losing control?

Style and Tone

Wollack uses concrete words and phrases to describe Sister Margarete: "cool green eyes were like ice," "high colorless cheekbones," "lips tightened in an almost invisible line beneath her nose," "black veil billowing in the early May breeze." Words like these make it possible for readers to see the subject as the writer does. Words with negative connotations influence the reader too. For example, Wollack describes Sister Margarete's eyes as cool like "ice" rather than comparing them to something admirable like a "refreshing brook" or an "aspen woods in summer." Wollack says that Sister Margarete "controlled our minds"; a more positive statement might have been "kept order in the classroom."

Wollack's *tone* in the essay is objective and impertinent at the same time. She accomplishes this dichotomy by writing from a mature stance while capturing the attitude of the teen. She "recites" in a singsong manner the teacher's definition of a short story. She recalls that the teacher "hissed" her question. She describes the school as a "prison" and a "torturous ordeal." The "triumph" over Sister Margarete was "glorious." From the adult perspective, Wollack looks back on the experience and tries to understand why it was important to her, why she wants to write about it now. She sees the teen "playing games," and she acknowledges that after the poetry incident, even though she still disliked the teacher, she knew the complexities of the nun's personality better. This increased understanding makes it possible for Wollack to conclude by expanding her thesis.

EXERCISE

Think about someone you disliked while growing up. Brainstorm (see Chapter 3) and list as many words as you can think of to describe that person. Force yourself to make a list of at least thirty items.

Writing

Write an essay that describes someone you disliked while growing up. Use your brainstormed list from the preceding exercise to help you get started. Then freewrite (see Chapter 3) one encounter between you and that person that can reveal the antipathy between you. Use direct quotations if they're appropriate. Try to recall a second encounter that reveals another aspect of your relationship, and jot down some notes about what you remember. When you begin to draft, you can organize and pull together the various aspects of your prewriting. Your thesis, like Wollack's, may be a simple statement at the beginning, but as you reveal the complexities of your feelings, your thesis will need to evolve into a statement that reflects those complexities. Coming to this understanding of your own feelings toward the individual you describe may be the most difficult part of this writing. You will need to know why you dislike the person and why that dislike is still important to you.

In your descriptions, use concrete words and phrases—words that name things we can identify with our senses, like "blue chalk," "black veil," and "eyes like ice." As you revise (and this may mean going back over what you've written at any time), ask yourself questions like these:

1. Am I using concrete words and phrases?
2. Is my tone too harshly critical?
3. What am I revealing about myself in this essay?
4. Is my thesis stated clearly?
5. Do my descriptions and my incidents develop my thesis as I have expressed it?
6. Does my evolved thesis reflect those descriptions and incidents?

Praising or Censuring a Group of People

You have no doubt encountered the censure or praise of groups of people. Perhaps a newspaper article praised rescuers after a natural disaster or contributors to a charitable fund. Letters to the editor of your campus newspaper might censure students who participated in a protest demonstration—or praise them. In a history class, you might read the "Letter from Birmingham Jail" in which Martin Luther King, Jr., censures eight clergymen who had censured him for his actions on civil rights. Other people have written letters or articles of censure directed at groups who take a position—on civil rights, women's rights, abortion, capital punishment, and so on. You find letters or articles of praise on the opposite side.

People sometimes praise or censure groups of people not for their positions but for what they are. In argument, censure of this type is called *ad hominem,* an attack on the person or persons instead of on the issue. When either praise or censure is directed at a *group* of people, it usually addresses a single issue—for example, their taste in music, the way they dress, the way they talk, and so on. When praise or censure extends beyond the single issue, it is usually a result of *stereotyping,* or treating all members of the group as if they have all the same characteristics. An extreme example would be censuring someone's politics because of his or her taste in music.

Readings

The two next readings are short pieces, one censuring a group of people, and the other praising a group of people. As you read the two, think about the purposes of their writers. What does Tom Wolfe want you to think as you read "The Down-Filled People"? What effect does his brief essay have on you? How does Gretel Ehrlich want you to think about cowboys? Does reading her paragraph change your attitudes? What does "The Down-Filled People" tell you about Wolfe? What does "Cowboys" tell you about Ehrlich?

The Down-Filled People

Tom Wolfe

They wear down-filled coats in public. Out on the ski slopes they look like hand grenades. They have "audio systems" in their homes and know the names of hit albums. They drive two-door cars with instrument panels like an F-16's. They like High-Tech furniture, track lighting, glass, and brass. They actually go to plays in New York and follow professional sports. The down-filled men wear turtleneck sweaters and Gucci belts and loafers and cover their ears with their hair. The down-filled women still wear cowl-necked sweaters and carry Louis Vuitton handbags. The down-filled people strip wood and have interior walls removed. They put on old clothes before the workmen come over. In the summer they like cabins on fresh water and they go hiking. They regard *Saturday Night Live* and Steve Martin as funny. They say "I hear you," meaning "I understand what you're saying." They say "Really," meaning "That's right." When down-filled strangers are at a loss for words, they talk about real-estate prices.

Cowboys

Gretel Ehrlich

A cowboy is someone who loves his work. Since the hours are long—ten to fifteen hours a day—and the pay is $30 he has to. What's required of him is an odd mixture of physical vigor and maternalism. His part of the beef-raising industry is to birth and nurture calves and take care of their mothers. For the most part his work is done on horseback and in a lifetime he sees and comes to know more animals than people. The iconic myth surrounding him is built on American notions of heroism: the index of a man's value as measured in physical courage. Such ideas have perverted manliness into a self-absorbed race for cheap thrills. In a rancher's world, courage has less to do with facing danger than with acting spontaneously—usually on behalf of an animal or another rider. If a cow is stuck in a boghole he throws a loop around her neck, takes his dally (a half hitch around the saddle horn), and pulls her out with horsepower. If a calf is born sick, he may take her home, warm her in front of the kitchen fire, and massage her legs until dawn. One friend, whose favorite horse was trying to swim a lake with hobbles on, dove under water and cut her legs loose with a knife, then swam her to shore, his arm around her neck lifeguard-style, and saved her from drowning. Because these incidents are usually linked to someone or something outside himself, the westerner's courage is selfless, a form of compassion.

Questions

1. Which paragraph do you prefer, Wolfe's or Ehrlich's? Analyze why you prefer one over the other.

2. What purposes other than to praise or to censure might these writers have had?

3. Compare the tone of Wolfe's paragraph with that of Ehrlich's.

Discussion

Both Wolfe and Ehrlich describe a group of people, Wolfe to censure and Ehrlich to praise. Wolfe's piece is complete as it is, Ehrlich's excerpted from a book called *The Solace of Open Spaces.*

Tone

In writing, *tone* is something like the sound of your voice. When you speak, sometimes you sound angry, sometimes gentle, sometimes whining, sometimes sarcastic, and so on. All these tones are truly *your* voice. Even though your voice has its own characteristics, you adjust it to the speaking situation—your subject matter, your audience, your relationship to that subject matter and that audience, and your purpose in speaking. Your tone reflects your attitude. How do you read Wolfe's tone? Is it cynical? sarcastic? demeaning? He probably makes you want to find ways of convincing yourself you're not one of *them*, the down-filled people. Ehrlich's tone is different. In using words like *selfless* and *compassion*, she shows an attitude toward her subject that is caring and respectful.

Multiple Purposes

We've already established that Wolfe's primary purpose is to *censure*, Ehrlich's to *praise*. Ehrlich might also want to *inform*—to set the reader straight on what cowboys and their work are really like, to denounce the "iconic myth," or popular image, of rugged, trigger-happy men who, if they're lucky, ride off into the sunset at the end of the movie. Ehrlich shows that, though they are rugged, cowboys are also tender and compassionate. Wolfe probably has other purposes too—entertainment, or *persuasion*. Do you suppose he wants to make you feel guilty if you wear a down-filled coat or enjoy Steve Martin's humor? Or might he have another point?

EXERCISES

Writers achieve particular tones by conscious use of words and details. In these exercises, you can gain insight into how tone is achieved.

1. Keeping the subject matter of down-filled people, rewrite Wolfe's paragraph to make its tone more like that of Ehrlich's paragraphs. You might begin with a sentence like this:

They wear down-filled coats to protect themselves from the bitter cold winds that blow in the harsh winters of the North Country.

Continue rewriting until you have a paragraph that praises instead of censures.

2. Keeping the subject matter of cowboys, rewrite Ehrlich's paragraph to make its tone more like that of Wolfe's paragraphs. You might begin with a sentence like this:

A cowboy is someone who is obsessively infatuated with his work.

Continue rewriting until you have a paragraph that censures instead of praises.

Writing

Selecting a group of people that you're familiar with, describe them twice—once to censure and once to praise, writing one short essay for each purpose. For each writing, adjust your tone and your treatment of details. Here are some possible topics:

- Customers
- Drivers
- Joggers
- Dog owners
- Cat owners

Praising the Dead

Some people think that any mention of death is morbid. Other people are preoccupied with death. Between these two poles is a healthy acceptance of the fact that life comes to an end. Pets die, grandparents die, parents die, friends die. Somehow the survivors need to accept the fact and go on living.

It is common to praise people who have died. *Obituaries,* a staple of daily newspapers, mainly give the facts about a person's life. *Eulogies* are often spoken at funerals, extolling the virtues of the deceased and overlooking shortcomings.

Reading

Since the death of Marilyn Monroe in 1962, much has been written about her life as sex symbol and movie star of the fifties. The esssay that follows was written shortly after her suicide and appeared in the London *Manchester Guardian*. Its writer, W. J. Weatherby, praises the film star and mourns her passing. As you read it you will encounter some unaccustomed features of style, in part because the article was written in the United Kingdom, in part because it was written nearly thirty years ago.

Marilyn Monroe

W. J. Weatherby

Marilyn Monroe's death at thirty-six is a real Hollywood tragedy, unlike most of those the film studios try to fabricate. It seems now to have the same inevitability as Hemingway's a year earlier, and just as death by shotgun gave his life a classical finish, so an overdose of sleeping tablets seems now the only ending we might have expected to this tragedy. The heartrending fact is that many of the friends of this doomed film actress have been afraid for over a year that something like this might happen and nobody seemed able to help. At least the gossip columnists who had begun to ask "What will Marilyn do when she's middle-aged?" have their answer now.

It is questions like that which help to explain the tragedy of Marilyn Monroe, for it is much more than an unhappy young actress who has died. News of her death will probably reach more people than that of anyone for years because she was an international symbol and, as such, had to bear an appalling burden. This was worth while in the early days of her career, for it was only as a sexual figure, everyone's dream blonde, the world's cover girl, that she could reach stardom in Hollywood. But when she had got there and then had a chance to act rather than pose, she found herself still trapped as a symbol. To understand what this meant you had to go out in public with her. Even a casual drink meant being under the spotlight; to go to a theatre could cause a riot. It was as though she had to help to pay for every sexual frustration in our kind of society, every neurotic that clutches at such symbols and has helped to create the Hollywood dream factory. In that sense many people had a hand in her death.

Many a Hollywood actress would have revelled in this rôle, but it was the elusiveness of Monroe—a quality that reflected the shy, sensitive side of her—that helped to make her into this sex symbol, probably the most famous ever created by Hollywood with the possible exception of Valentino (and in the last year or two of his short life he felt the pressures on him to be unbearable). But she was a Hollywood symbol in a much deeper sense than that, for she was born in Los Angeles in the Hollywood shadow, her mother worked—as a negative cutter—in one of the film studios, and she grew up brainwashed, as it were, into the belief that the dream of every girl should be to become another Mary Pickford. And she had plenty of outside incentives to escape into such a dream world. Her parents were not married and she never knew her father; when she was a child her mother had to go into a mental hospital, and she had to go the round of foster parents. It is hardly surprising that she got married as soon as she could—at sixteen—though she was divorced by the time she was twenty. By that time she had seen more of the grey side of life than most people ever do. What an escape to a Technicolor view Hollywood must have seemed. She had committed herself to it long before she ever learnt the price she would have to pay.

Model, bit player, larger rôles, fledgling star—it was a fairly conventional route to Hollywood fame. But she had a quality that made her stand out in the crowds of equally pretty girls competing for attention and this gave her the advantage she needed—though it was years before anyone ever suggested that quality might be talent. Those years—when she was a star but not credited with anything but symbolism—were the critical ones. By the time she had a chance to make use of the acting lessons she took so earnestly, it was as if her experiences had split her personality too much for her ever to feel secure. She had a distressing habit of discarding people after a few years as if she could never count on loyalty or trust. It seems true to say that she was by then a schizophrenic—part of her still the innocent girl next door in her Hollywood dreamland and part of her the career woman, the woman who had decided to accept life as a jungle and live in it on those terms. This was revealed in her attitude towards her position as sex symbol. There were times when she seemed to enjoy it, to make the most use of it she could, and then suddenly you would see the other side of her which had to pay for it—the very attractive mixed-up girl clinging to her pills and her psychoanalysis. 4

There was, of course, a history of mental disorder on her mother's side—both maternal grandparents were committed to mental institutions and an uncle killed himself. Some will try to explain away her problems in terms of heredity. But the influence of this on Marilyn Monroe was rather a fear that she might have inherited something than any sign that she had. But an unbalanced personality like that should never have had to endure the pressures firstly of her rootless early years, an introduction to sex as a child that amounted to rape, and then the Hollywood symbolism. She must in fact have been an extraordinarily strong person to have pulled herself up from such beginnings and to have endured so long and to have continued to grow as an actress. 5

It was Sybil Thorndike who made the shrewdest remark about her talent when they worked together (with Sir Laurence Olivier as fellow star) in *The Prince and the Showgirl*. "You watch her do it in the studio and it doesn't seem much—too vague and underplayed," said Dame Sybil. "But when you see it on the screen, her performance seems perfect. She really opens 6 out. It is as if she were made for the cinema." The same elusive quality that made her such an extraordinary sex symbol also gave her a unique comic style. By *The Seven Year Itch* and *Some Like It Hot,* she had developed a style of her own, a style of wit and charm that was laced together with a very effective off-beat timing that could sometimes madden directors in rehearsals. In her last film, *The Misfits,* written by her third husband, Arthur Miller, she tried to adapt this technique to serious drama and, though not wholly successful, gave a performance in much greater depth than ever before. She had hoped it would justify all her claims to being a serious actress, not a symbol, and so she took the poorish reviews very much to heart.

"Heart" is the word that comes to mind in trying to describe her as a   7
person—she perhaps responded and felt too much for her own good. When she was truly herself she could have an afternoon spoilt by seeing a passing cruelty—such as a fish caught and dangling—that the rest of us would hardly notice. Her marriages reflected her. Not for her those inbred Hollywood marriages. She married Joe Di Maggio, the baseball star and American hero, and then, going to the opposite extreme of American heroes—from sport to the intellectuals—she married Arthur Miller. This seemed to be the perfect complementary marriage—the marriage of beauty and brains. It bewildered those who thought of her as a sex symbol. It delighted those who knew the real Marilyn Monroe—as it saddened them when the marriage broke up over a year ago. Norma Jean Baker (her mother's name was Baker and her father's Mortenson and so she took her mother's) then seemed alone in the crowd—the crowd of Hollywood symbols (and symbols of our society?) bearing down on her.

Questions

1. What does the essay tell you about Weatherby's attitude toward Monroe?
2. Are there any clues in the essay to the writer being a man or a woman? Does it matter whether you know?
3. What does Weatherby tell you about Monroe? Name some facts that interest you.

Discussion

Weatherby eulogizes Marilyn Monroe by praising her virtues and excusing her weaknesses in this brief biography. After an introductory paragraph, Weatherby seems to answer a series of questions:

1. Who was Marilyn Monroe?
2. Why did she become a film star?
3. How did she become a sex symbol?
4. How did being a symbol affect her?
5. Was she a good actress?
6. Why did she die?

The thesis that ties all the questions together is stated in the second paragraph: "for it is much more than an unhappy young actress who has died." Questions are often helpful in deciding what to write, and when we have a controlling idea—a thesis—to hold the answers together, questions can assist us in organizing our writing.

Purpose

Weatherby praises Monroe so that readers may know this film star better and appreciate her talents. Eulogies are usually written at or near the time of someone's death, but when they are written and published they reach not only the present audience but future audiences as well. Even though this essay was written in 1962, it still praises Monroe. Eulogies, perhaps more than most other types of praise, are meant for future audiences as well as present ones.

Weatherby seems to have known Monroe well. It is not clear, however, whether this knowledge was personal or drawn from public documents. The details are treated sensitively and sympathetically. Reread the essay and mark any words that indicate the writer's attitude toward the subject— words like *tragedy* and *heartrending*.

EXERCISE

Writing style is a little different in the United Kingdom than it is in the United States. Spelling is one readily apparent difference. Read Weatherby's essay again and note all the words that are spelled differently than they would be in an American newspaper, like theatre, *for instance.*

Writing

Write a eulogy, an essay in praise of someone who has died, someone you knew either publicly or privately. Concentrate on the good that person did while alive, the positive effects of that person's life, perhaps why that person was the kind of person he or she was. To help you discover ideas and arrange them, you might think of questions like those answered in the Monroe essay. Don't focus on the person's death; write about his or her life—in a positive way. As another example of a eulogy, refer to the one about James Baldwin at the end of this chapter.

Praising the Living

Perhaps we don't praise the living often enough. How often do we miss opportunities to say something really complimentary—sincerely—to someone we know? We probably *think* thoughts like "Didn't he do a great job of washing that car?" or "That was a really great idea" but let the opportunity for saying those words of praise pass by. Sometimes parents forget to praise their children, and sometimes children overlook opportunities to compliment their parents. Teachers may forget to praise their students, and students may forget to praise their teachers. We all know people who are doing ordinary things extraordinarily well or extraordinary things that we never expected to see done. These are things to praise.

Praise, unlike flattery, is genuine. Praise takes note of a person's accomplishments or admirable characteristics, and it is not given on a quid pro quo basis; praise doesn't expect something in return.

Reading

Here Beth Zamzow, a student writer, praises an elderly farmer, the "Pumpkin King," in an article for a local newspaper. This is an item of good news to balance what is often bad news. Notice how Zamzow enters the essay. Where does she appear? This essay is actually the report of an interview. As you read, try to imagine the writer interviewing the "special kind of king."

A Special Kind of King

Beth Zamzow

Long ago in the southwestern corner of Minnesota, a young man   1
planted a small pumpkin patch behind an old white barn. He carefully hoed away each weed around the sensitive vines and watched as the sun and rain transformed small green knobs into wondrous, golden pumpkins. He saw the vines wither and shrivel in the cool September air, leaving the heavy orange pumpkins behind. With his strong back, the man easily carried his produce into the old barn. He cut open two of the tough rinds and pulled away creamy seeds from the stringy mass inside, saving them for the following spring. He then gifted his friends with the best of his harvest.

Word soon spread about these pumpkins and the man who grew them.   2
Some even called him the Pumpkin King. The next year children and their parents traveled from miles away to the rutted, washboard drive leading to his realm, hoping to receive some of his gifts. The king would take the children's hands and lead them into his palace, the old barn. Sheets of

plastic covered large gaps in its walls, and on windy days the children would laugh as corn husks whirled and danced on the dirt floor.

A dusty red carpet running through the palace's center was littered with seed pails. The children gazed with amazement at the huge piles of golden pumpkins and yellow squash lining the walls. They would touch the bumpy, strangely shaped gourds and marvel at the purple and red colors of the Indian corn. They created clouds of dust as they ran from pile to pile, selecting their pumpkins. 3

Each fall the people would return with their children to the land of the Pumpkin King, and each year he expanded his patch to meet the needs of the ever-increasing number of customers. 4

The cycles of planting, harvesting, and giving continued for more than fifty years. As the Pumpkin King neared his eightieth birthday, his patch had grown to a sizable two acres to accommodate the wishes of more than 240 visitors. 5

One day in mid-October, the elderly king sat on an overturned pail in his quiet palace. Most of the people had already come and gone, and the piles of produce were greatly diminished. Only one visitor remained, a young woman who had returned home from college to receive some pumpkins to decorate her room at school. She remembered being in that barn years before, and the Pumpkin King remembered her also. 6

The woman sat on a straw bale next to the short, thin man and listened to his story. His back was no longer strong or straight. His white hair was crowned with a red seed cap, and his eyes seemed to smile behind thick glasses. 7

"Some people found out about my patch, and things just got out of hand. It was wonderful," he said. 8

He told the woman how the town church that year was decorated with eighty-five of his pumpkins and that numerous other schools and businesses were adorned with his produce. "A school teacher from Kansas City took thirty-five pumpkins back for her students," he said, nodding his head to confirm the fact. Other pumpkins traveled to Alaska and Texas that year. 9

The king's hands fingered his grey beard as he told the story of a certain woman from Texas who once forgot his name and printed "Pumpkin King" on the envelope. The letter traveled to his home without incident. Each year he received gifts of pumpkin bread and pumpkin pie. 10

"Some people call me by name, and I don't even know them," the man proudly said. "That's the Pumpkin King, they say." The college student learned that he had been in ten parades and had received the Good Neighbor Award from Northwest Airlines. 11

The king explained to her how, each year, he ordered seed and planned his special garden in the beginning of February, planting right before Memorial Day. His seeds came from seventeen different companies, and he grew nine kinds of pumpkins. Several years ago the king grew his most wondrous pumpkin of them all. It weighed more than 235 pounds. 12

There were years when the spring rains didn't come very often, but the man never worried. "I didn't do anything to the pumpkins. I didn't feed 13 them or water them. I let the Lord take care of it." Some days he worked up to eighteen hours, harvesting from his fields and arranging produce in his barn. "I was out there Sunday mornings before church, but I loved every bit of it," he said. "If I died doing this, I wouldn't die in a happier place."

The king told the young woman that his heart was not working as well   14 as it used to, and he realized that his days of hoeing in the windy, sunny fields were over. "I sat down this spring and told myself that I'm not going to be able to do this much longer," he sadly admitted. His face brightened, though, when he remembered all the laughing children who had visited his palace. "I've gained so many friends and have made a lot of people happy," the king said. "I know I'll never be lonely."

The woman left the palace of the Pumpkin King with her car trunk full   15 of miniature gourds, purple Indian corn, and some very special pumpkins. She realized that the old white barn would be empty next year, but the Pumpkin King's heart was filled with treasures of friendships and happiness.

Questions

1. Who is the "Pumpkin King"? What does the essay tell you about him? Where does he live? What does he look like? Do you know what his real name is?

2. What makes the Pumpkin King special?

3. What does the essay reveal about the writer of this essay? Where do you first encounter her?

4. Using the statements of the old man, try to reconstruct Zamzow's interview questions. For example, when he says, "Some people found out about my patch, and things just got out of hand," you might guess that the writer has asked, "How did raising pumpkins get to be such a big thing with you?"

5. What is Zamzow's attitude toward her subject? What words tell you how she feels about the old man?

6. What purpose might Zamzow have other than to praise?

Discussion

Some people might think that devoting one's life to raising pumpkins is a senseless thing to do and that there's nothing special about being known as the "Pumpkin King." But Zamzow praises an elderly man for just that. He takes an ordinary thing, raising pumpkins, and does it in such an extraordinary way that people for miles around affectionately call him the "Pumpkin King." Zamzow takes time out from school to visit the old man, asking questions about why he makes such a big thing of raising pumpkins and how much longer he thinks he can continue, then writing a report of her interview so that others can know about him too.

Zamzow does not explicitly state her thesis. Her title, however, makes clear what she wants to say about this man: "A *Special* Kind of King."

Style

Words that evoke specific, concrete images make writing vivid. Zamzow uses such words to represent things that can be identified concretely by the physical senses—by sight, hearing, smell, taste, or touch. When she describes the barn, she refers to "a dusty red carpet" that was "littered with seed pails," and you can see the incongruity of a carpet in a barn. Along the walls you can see the "golden pumpkins" and the "yellow squash," and you can imagine the feel of the "bumpy, strangely-shaped gourds." In addition to being concrete, Zamzow's words and phrases are specific, as opposed to general. Instead of identifying the time of year as "fall," she says "mid-October"; instead of saying that "many visitors" came, she accounts for "more than 240 visitors." Find other instances of concrete and specific words that help to make this description vivid.

EXERCISE

Do a focused freewriting (see Chapter 3) on pumpkins. If you can't get started, just write "pumpkins, pumpkins, pumpkins . . ." until you think of something else to say. Something else will *come. Write for five minutes without stopping and without making corrections or revisions. Then exchange papers with someone else in your class. Read your classmate's freewriting while he or she reads yours; respond with questions or comments that might lead to further exploration of the topic. After you receive your freewriting back and read your classmate's comments on what you've written, write for another five minutes.*

Writing

Think of an interesting person you know, and ask that person for an interview. Once you get permission, jot down what you know about that person and write some questions about what else you would like to know. When you do your interview, be courteous, be considerate, and be informed. Ask questions that show a real interest in your interviewee. If your questions lead in some unexpected directions, don't be afraid to depart from your notes and prepared questions. But do remain in charge; you are the interviewer. Take notes. If your interviewee doesn't mind, you might tape your interview; but even if you do tape it, take notes too. (For more information about conducting interviews, see "Recording Interviews" in Chapter 9.)

Then write your essay. Your primary purpose is to praise this individual. Like Zamzow, you might think of submitting your essay to a local newspaper. In that case, consider the people who read the paper, and write accordingly. Like Zamzow, use specific, concrete words—short, simple ones that reveal the subject of your interview; don't eclipse her or him with long, heavy words. If it's appropriate for your essay, you might start as Zamzow does, with a narrative that introduces your subject. Either state your thesis or leave it unexpressed but implied; whether you imply it or express it, be sure *you* know what it is. Then make sure you have a title that shows your point.

ADDITIONAL READINGS FOR DISCUSSION

Reading

The following paragraphs are the conclusion of historian Samuel Eliot Morison's biography of Christopher Columbus, *Admiral of the Ocean Sea*. In them Morison praises the seaman whose travels changed the course of history and gives skeptics some reasons for why Americans celebrate October 12 as Columbus Day, the day Columbus first set foot on the "New World" in 1492.

Death of the Admiral
Samuel Eliot Morison

So died the man who had done more to direct the course of history than any individual since Augustus Caesar. Yet the life of the Admiral closed on a note of frustration. He had not found the Strait, or met the Grand Khan, or converted any great number of heathen, or regained Jerusalem. He had not even secured the future of his family. And the significance of what he had accomplished was only slightly less obscure to him than to the chroniclers who neglected to record his death, or to the courtiers who failed to attend his modest funeral at Valladolid. The vast extent and immense resources of the Americas were but dimly seen; the mighty ocean that laved their western shores had not yet yielded her secret.   1

America would eventually have been discovered if the Great Enterprise of Columbus had been rejected; yet who can predict what would have been the outcome? The voyage that took him to "The Indies" and home was no blind chance, but the creation of his own brain and soul, long studied, carefully planned, repeatedly urged on indifferent princes, and carried through by virtue of his courage, sea-knowledge, and indomitable will. No later voyage could ever have such spectacular results, and Columbus's fame would have been secure had he retired from the sea in 1493. Yet a lofty ambition to explore further, to organize the territories won for Castile, and to complete the circuit of the globe, sent him thrice more to America. These voyages, even more than the first, proved him to be the greatest navigator of his age, and enabled him to train the captains and pilots who were to   2 display the banners of Spain off every American cape and island between Fifty North and Fifty South. The ease with which he dissipated the unknown terrors of the Ocean, the skill with which he found his way out and home, again and again, led thousands of men from every Western European nation into maritime adventure and exploration. And if Columbus was a failure as a colonial administrator, it was partly because his conception of a colony transcended the desire of his followers to impart, and the capacity of natives to receive, the institutions and culture of Renaissance Europe.

Columbus had a proud, passionate, and sensitive nature that suffered   3
deeply from the contempt to which he was early subjected, and the envy, disloyalty, ingratitude, and injustice which he met as a discoverer. He wrote so freely out of the abundance of his complaint, as to give the impression that his life was more full of woe than of weal. That impression is false. As with other mariners, a month at sea healed the wounds of a year ashore, and a fair wind blew away the memory of foul weather. Command of a tall and gallant ship speeding over blue water before a fresh trade wind, shaping her course for some new and marvelous land where gold is abundant and the women are kind, is a mariner's dream of the good life. Columbus had a Hellenic sense of wonder at the new and strange, combined with an artist's appreciation of natural beauty; and his voyages to this strange new world brought him to some of the most gorgeous coastlines on the earth's surface. Moreover, Columbus had a deep conviction of the immanence, the sovereignty, and the infinite wisdom of God, which transcended all his suffering, and enhanced all his triumphs. Waste no pity on the Admiral of the Ocean Sea! He enjoyed long stretches of pure delight such as only a seaman may know, and moments of high, proud exultation that only a discoverer can experience.

One only wishes that the Admiral might have been afforded the sense   4
of fulfillment that would have come from foreseeing all that flowed from his discoveries; that would have turned all the sorrows of his last years to joy. The whole history of the Americas stems from the Four Voyages of Columbus; and as the Greek city-states looked back to the deathless gods as their founders, so today a score of independent nations and dominions unite in homage to Christopher the stout-hearted son of Genoa, who carried Christian civilization across the Ocean Sea.

Questions

1. What does Morison name as some of Columbus's greatest contributions to Western civilization?

2. What were some of Columbus's disappointments? How does Morison view these disappointments?

3. Characterize Columbus from this brief description.

4. What is Morison's attitude toward his subject?

5. Compare Columbus's "discovery" of the New World with a current event.

Reading

The recommendations that follow are copies of real summary remarks on a standard placement service recommendation form; only the names have been changed. As you read, determine which letter is the most likely to get a job for the applicant.

Two Letters of Recommendation

I. Toni Prescott is one of the best students I've known. She is studious, bright, well-read. She meets challenges with enthusiasm; she deliberately takes on the more difficult project. She seems to know her abilities and capabilities and appears unwilling to engage in either the easy task or the one that demands more time or ability than she can bring to it. She doesn't hesitate to speak out when something needs to be said, yet she is a highly personable young woman, pleasant and cheerful with a positive nature.

I know Toni from two of my classes: Freshman Composition and The Rhetoric of Writing. In both classes her work was superior in every way. She participated intelligently and readily in class discussions, attended class regularly, and completed her work on time. Her writing was always well done, revealing the work of a thoughtful mind engaged in a particular problem.

I am confident that Toni Prescott will succeed in whatever endeavor she takes on.

II. Ted Grange was an asset to my business writing class: always sitting in the front row, always prepared, always a willing participant in class discussions, always alert. I was glad to have him there. He worked well in various modes: individually, in groups, or in pairs.

Questions

1. Which of the two recommendations would you rather have in your file?

2. Writers of letters of recommendation try to be as positive as they can about the person recommended. Prospective employers, by contrast, try to read between the lines to determine what has not been said. Reread Ted Grange's letter and try to discover what the writer is *not* saying.

3. Toni Prescott's letter is highly positive. Can you detect any omissions that a prospective employer or graduate school might wonder about?

Reading

The following short piece is an obituary from *The New York Times*. Notice that it states facts, not opinions, about Margie Inman; it neither praises nor censures.

Margie Inman Is Dead at Seventy-six; Walked on Wings of Planes

Davie, Fla., October 7 [1987] (AP)—Margie Lynn Inman, who per-   1
formed on the wings of airplanes in her youth and later battled local officials
for the right to live in a lean-to with a menagerie of pets, has died at the age
of seventy-six.

Mrs. Inman died September 30, the day she was to have entered a   2
nursing home after weeks of failing health, friends said.

She performed as a wing-walker in the 1920s and '30s in the Inman   3
Brothers Flying Circus with her husband, Rolley Roger Inman, a pilot. He
died in a crash in 1944.

Mrs. Inman began living in a lean-to on her property near Fort Lau-   4
derdale after her house collapsed in 1976. She spent much of her Social
Security checks on food for her pet cats, dogs, and rats, which she called "my
kids." Her disputes with neighbors and local officials over the animals
ended when local people pitched in to help her clean up the property.

Questions

1. In chronological order, list the facts this obituary gives about Margie Inman.
2. What do these facts tell you about Inman's character?
3. Compare this obituary with the eulogy for James Baldwin that follows.
4. How could you use the facts in this obituary to write a *eulogy* praising Margie Inman?

Reading

As opposed to the factual, objective obituary, a eulogy includes praise of
the virtues and accomplishments of the deceased person. An obituary is a
brief biography, a eulogy an article of praise. A eulogy includes biographical
information, but from the writer's point of view. The following eulogy for
James Baldwin appeared in *The New York Times* on December 1, 1987. As you
read it, try to distinguish between facts and the writer's opinions.

James Baldwin, the Writer, Dies in France at Sixty-three
Lee Daniels

James Baldwin, whose passionate, intensely personal essays in the   1
1950's and 60's on racial discrimination in America helped break down the
nation's color barrier, died of cancer last night at his home in southern
France. He was sixty-three years old.

Mr. Baldwin's brother, David, was with him at his home in St. Paul de Vence when he died, according to Cynthia Packard, a friend and former assistant to the author, who said she talked with David by telephone last night. Mr. Baldwin died at 6:15 P.M. New York time, according to Ms. Packard.

At least in the early years of his career, Mr. Baldwin saw himself primarily as a novelist. But it is his essays that arguably constitute his most substantial contribution to literature.

Mr. Baldwin published his three most important collections of essays— *Notes of a Native Son* (1955), *Nobody Knows My Name* (1961), and *The Fire Next Time* (1963)—during the years when the civil-rights movement was exploding across the American South.

Some critics said his language was sometimes too elliptical, his indictments sometimes too sweeping. But then Mr. Baldwin's prose, with its apocalyptic tone—a legacy of his early exposure to religious fundamentalism—and its passionate yet distanced sense of advocacy, seemed perfect for a period in which blacks in the South lived under continual threat of racial violence and in which civil-rights workers often faced brutal beatings and even death.

Mr. Baldwin had moved to France in the late 1940's to escape what he felt was the stifling racial bigotry of America.

Nonetheless, although France remained his permanent residence, Mr. Baldwin in later years described himself as a "commuter" rather than an expatriate.

"Only white Americans can consider themselves to be expatriates," he said. "Once I found myself on the other side of the ocean, I could see where I came from very clearly, and I could see that I carried myself, which is my home, with me. You can never escape that. I am the grandson of a slave, and I am a writer. I must deal with both."

Despite the prominent role he played in the civil-rights movement in the early 1960's—not only in writing about race relations but in organizing various sorts of protest actions—Mr. Baldwin always rejected the labels of "leader" or "spokesman."

Instead, he described himself as one whose mission was to "bear witness to the truth."

"A spokesman assumes that he is speaking for others," he told Julius Lester, a faculty colleague at the University of Massachusetts at Amherst, in an interview in *The New York Times Book Review* in 1984. "I never assumed that I could. What I tried to do, or to interpret and make clear, was that no society can smash the social contract and be exempt from the consequences, and the consequences are chaos for everybody in the society."

This serene sense of independence was not simply a political stance, but an intrinsic part of Mr. Baldwin's personality.

"I was a maverick, a maverick in the sense that I depended on neither the white world nor the black world," he told Mr. Lester. "That was the only way I could've played it. I would've been broken otherwise. I had to say, 'A curse on both your houses.' The fact that I went to Europe so early is probably what saved me. It gave me another touchstone—myself."

Mr. Baldwin did not limit his "bearing witness" to racial matters. He   14
opposed American military involvement in Vietnam as early as 1963, and in the early 1960's he began to criticize discrimination against homosexuals.

Mr. Baldwin's literary achievements and his activism made him a world   15
figure and to the end of his life brought him many honors in this country and abroad. The French Government made him a Commander of the Legion of Honor in 1986.

Yet, Mr. Baldwin was also clearly disappointed that, despite his undeniable   16
powers as an essayist, his novels and plays drew decidedly mixed reviews.

Go Tell It on the Mountain, his first book and first novel, published in   17
1953, was widely praised. Partly autobiographical, it tells of a poor boy growing up in Harlem in the 1930's under the tyranny of his father, an autocratic preacher who hated his son.

Mr. Baldwin said in 1985 that in many ways the book remained the   18
keystone of his career.

"*Mountain* is the book I had to write if I was ever going to write anything   19
else," he remarked. "I had to deal with what hurt me most. I had to deal, above all, with my father. He was my model. I learned a lot from him. Nobody's ever frightened me since."

Questions

1. This eulogy is considerably longer than the obituary for Margie Inman. What kinds of facts does the eulogy contain that the obituary does not?

2. What words of Daniels tell you he admires Baldwin?

3. Name some of Baldwin's accomplishments that Daniels seems to admire.

4. Daniels quotes Baldwin on writing and on his civil rights activities. Which of these quotations most significantly tells you what kind of man Baldwin was?

5. Compare the Baldwin eulogy with the Marilyn Monroe eulogy by W. J. Weatherby. What kinds of information do you learn about the subjects? What attitudes do the writers have toward their subjects?

CHAPTER 15

To Summarize and Respond: Writing with Emphasis on the Subject

> *Writing is thinking made tangible, thinking that can be examined because it is "on the page" and not all "in the head," invisibly floating around.*
>
> —*John T. Gage*

Much academic writing is done in response to other writing: you summarize an assigned chapter, analyze and respond to an article or book you have read, or answer an essay question on an exam. In each case, you show what you know about a subject. To get along in school, you must be able to summarize and respond and to ask and answer questions. There are good reasons why such seemingly routine writing is so common in instruction. First, writing of this type assists learning: by summarizing and responding and by asking and answering questions, you read more actively and understand more thoroughly. Moreover, such writing is common in the professional world—summarizing reports, answering inquiries, responding to a colleague's proposal, and so on—so this kind of school writing not only assists learning but also prepares you for writing on the job.

This nuts-and-bolts academic writing has much in common with other kinds of writing. Even though emphasis is usually on the subject, you still must consider the entire rhetorical situation: the purpose, the audience, and your own role—as well as the subject. The purpose of academic writing is usually to show that you understand the material or to assist you in learning and examining the material. By covering the material thoroughly and thoughtfully, you establish your role as a knowledgeable student.

The audience is almost always the teacher and must be considered when you write. Be sure you know what your teacher is looking for, and don't expect one teacher to have the same expectations as another. (This, again, is good preparation for the job, because supervisors don't all have the same expectations either.) ...preferences, and emphasis ...ers will not accept writing ...s want you to use *I* and *we*, ...references varies by disci- ...o requests MLA (Modern ...eacher has specified APA ...g else. If your teacher asks ...n if you think you know a ...bserve that length (within ...ter may be a result of your ...ol as in the world of work, ...d their appropriateness is

...her chapters. Its opening ...hool writing: summaries, ...s. This discussion will be ...sional writing, concluding ...with a variety of writing assignments. Exercises will be interspersed throughout.

Summaries

Summarizing is an essential skill for academic writing. You summarize lab or lecture notes, reading assignments, articles you've read in your library research, and individual or group activities. Summaries often accompany other kinds of writing: essay exams, critiques, and reports, to name a few. This discussion concentrates on summaries that may stand alone or be a part of a larger piece of writing.

A **summary** presents in condensed form the substance of another piece of writing. It usually begins with a *nutshell* statement, or overall summary, then presents the essential points of the writing, not necessarily in the same order as in the original. Related to the summary is the **abstract,** or précis, which gives a concentrated essence of the larger piece of writing. An abstract generally covers the main points in the same order as the original and usually does not begin with a nutshell statement. An abstract is usually written from the same perspective as the original, whereas a summary is often written from the perspective of the summarizer.

Compare these brief examples of a summary and an abstract of Judith Viorst's essay "Friends, Good Friends—and Such Good Friends" in Chapter 12:

Summary

In "Friends, Good Friends—and Such Good Friends," Judith Viorst classifies women's friends according to varieties and levels of intensity. She identifies eight varieties of friends: convenience friends, special-interest friends, historical friends, crossroads friends, cross-generational friends, part-of-a-couple friends, men who are friends, and best of friends. Only best of friends share total trust and love and are completely honest with one another. All other varieties of friendships are at a lower level of intensity.

Abstract

The varieties of women's friendships are convenience friends, special-interest friends, historical friends, crossroads friends, cross-generational friends, part-of-a-couple friends, men who are friends, and best of friends. Only best of friends, at the highest level of intimacy, share total trust and love and are completely honest with one another.

—Judith Viorst, "Friends, Good Friends—and Such Good Friends"

The *summary* is written from the perspective of the summarizer: "Judith Viorst classifies," "she identifies." The *abstract,* by contrast, does not refer to Viorst; rather it reports the content of the essay as if Viorst were writing. Also, the summary begins with a nutshell statement, whereas the abstract begins with Viorst's first classification, the varieties of friendships. Notice too that the nutshell statement of the summary names the source of the summary but that such information is outside the abstract. (An alternative in the abstract would be to include the source in parentheses at the end of the first sentence, as in the example on page 433.) Neither summary nor abstract expresses opinions of the summarizer or abstractor.

Whether you write a summary or an abstract depends on your purpose. As a part of a larger piece of writing, such as a report, summary is more effective. One reason is that stylistically a summary is written from the same point of view as the rest of the report, and as the writer you can select as much information from the original as you need for your purpose. Abstracts usually stand alone—at the beginning of a report, for example—to give readers a quick view of the entire entity. If you were writing a report, then, you would *summarize* other pieces of writing that support your points and provide the necessary background, and you would *abstract* your own report. Both summaries and abstracts should accurately reflect the meaning and sense of the original. Summaries, however, can be more selective, concentrating on particular aspects of the original rather than giving a complete overview.

Among the ways in which summaries and abstracts gain conciseness, coordination and subordination are the most useful. *Coordination* relates two or more ideas at an equivalent level, often using the coordinating conjunctions (*and, but, or, nor, so, for, yet*); commas separate items in a series, and semicolons sometimes separate equivalent clauses. Here is an example of coordination in the Viorst summary: "Only best of friends *share total trust and love and are completely honest with one another.*" This sentence has two coordinate pairs. "Trust" and "love" combine the ideas of what best of friends share, and "share total trust and love" and "are completely honest with one another" make assertions about the same subject, "best of friends," joined by the connecting *and*. The summary paragraph has other instances of coordination; notice especially the parallel list of varieties of friends.

Subordination relates ideas that are not equivalent, making one idea dependent on another. The following sentence from the Viorst abstract illustrates how an idea composing several sentences in the original is compressed into a subordinate portion of a sentence: "Only best of friends, *at the highest level of intimacy,* share total trust and love and are completely honest with one another." In this sentence, "at the highest level of intimacy" has become a modifying phrase, set off by commas.

Writing a Summary

To write a summary, you must understand the original and your purpose for summarizing it. Sometimes we summarize a complete article and sometimes only a portion of it. The instructions here are for summarizing an entire article, though you can apply them also to summarizing a portion of an article or a book.

1. *Read.*   First read the article through to get its gist; make no notes or marks at this time. After you've finished reading, write in a single sentence what you think is the main point. Then look for a thesis sentence in the article and underline it; does it agree with the nutshell statement you wrote? Make sure your view of the article isn't slanted toward a minor point.

2. *Underline.*   Once you have a clear understanding of the writer's main point, read the article again, this time underlining major points in support of the thesis and transitional phrases that show how parts are connected. Omit specific details, examples, description, and unnecessary explanations. Go through the article another time if necessary.

3. *Write.*   Now begin writing your summary. Open with your nutshell statement, including a reference to the writer and the title of the article (as in the preceding Viorst summary). Then write your summary, using your underlines as a guide, writing with your own words and phrases, not those of the original. This is one place where many people go wrong in summarizing: they lift a series of sentences from the original instead of writing in their own words. In a summary you can use phrases like "Viorst classifies" and "Burgess describes," but be careful not to include your own opinions or thoughts. For now, don't worry about length; you can cut later. To conclude, make a final statement that reflects the significance of the article from the original writer's view.

4. *Revise.*   Read your summary for accuracy; if it doesn't make the same point as the article or if you have omitted something important, revise. Read your summary for coherence; if it doesn't read smoothly, with all parts clearly related, refer to the transitional phrases you marked in the original and use them or others to relate your sentences. Read for length; if your

summary is more than one-fourth the length of the original, start cutting, using subordination and coordination to compress ideas, deleting all repetitious and unnecessary words. Write another draft and ask someone else to read it for sense and comprehensibility. Ask for criticism and accept it graciously.

5. *Edit.* Correct spelling and punctuation errors, and look for other errors, especially those that you know commonly occur in your writing. Write a clean draft and proofread for copying errors.

Writing an Abstract

Writing an abstract is similar to writing a summary. First read the article for comprehension, then begin marking key points. In writing your abstract, you may find it helpful to draft a summary sentence for *each paragraph,* combining all your single sentences with appropriate connecting words or phrases. Try to end up with a shortened version of the larger whole, omitting nothing important. To keep your abstract in the original writer's perspective, avoid words such as "Viorst classifies" and "Burgess describes"; refer to the preceding Viorst abstract and the abstract that follows.

Sample Summary and Abstract
(original essay appears in Chapter 11)

Summary

In "Senses," physicist George R. Harrison discusses a physical feature common to all people, their senses, focusing primarily on one of the senses, vision, to show the complexity of all of them. The eye, he says, is so sensitive that it can detect light from a candle at a distance of many miles. Yet the eye is limited as to the wavelengths of light it can see, and the lens frequently becomes deformed and clouded, further limiting vision. Science, however, has invented ways for extending the capabilities of the eye by means of magnification and other methods. As with vision, science has extended and transformed the capabilities of the other senses, expanding the understanding and use of the external world.

Abstract

The five senses enable people to connect with the world (George R. Harrison, "Senses"). Each sense, however, has more than one type, so that the number is actually more than five. The eye has four types of vision. Extremely sensitive retinas receive light through a focusing lens that is adjusted by a diaphragm called a pupil and is shielded by a shutter called an eyelid. Vision is supported by the other senses, allowing a person to sense an object by touching it, hearing it, smelling it, or tasting it. The eye is limited by the wavelengths it can detect and its own deformities. Scientists, however, have invented means for overcoming these limitations, utilizing magnification and other methods. Scientists have also extended and transformed the capabilities of the other senses, enabling people to better know their world.

EXERCISE

Contrast the summary and abstract of Harrison's "Senses." Find examples of how they differ in perspective and content and how they both use coordination and subordination. If necessary, refer to the original essay in Chapter 11.

Essay Examinations

Essay examinations are a specialized type of writing for which answering questions is the major purpose. You write an essay exam to show what you know about a given subject, not to inform someone about that subject. It goes without saying, then, that all the advice in the world about writing the exam is of no use unless you know the material.

Preparing for an Essay Exam

Cramming for an essay exam will help only if you have kept up with your reading and note taking throughout the term. Students who are experienced at preparing for college essay exams advise that you read your assignments when you receive them and review your notes frequently. For particularly difficult material, they recommend summarizing both your reading and your notes. (For tips on efficient note taking, refer to Chapter 9, where experienced student note takers share some advice.)

Close to exam time, review your notes and summaries. Study your assigned readings, picking up points that your teacher covered in class. To aid your review, use one of the methods of invention described in Chapter 3. The classical probes might be especially helpful, or the more visually oriented cubing. Apply them to your subject: identify it, classify it, compare and contrast it, analyze it, use it, give some examples of it. Aim for a broad understanding of the subject, but also try to file away a number of important details; it is mainly for drilling yourself on details that cramming can be useful. To aid your broad understanding, write some questions that you could expect to find on the exam and then work out answers to them.

And get sleep, and food. A rested and alert mind is better able to meet the challenge of utilizing your knowledge of the subject in response to a difficult question. Then go to class confident that, even though you may not know all the material, you know enough of it to answer most questions.

Writing an Essay Exam

Don't panic. Take time to read the exam carefully and to determine what is required. If you have several questions to answer, budget your time according to the percentage points of the questions—half of your time for a 50 percent question, for example. If you have one question, allow some time for planning, most of it for writing, and some for revising and editing. Here are some tips for managing the condensed writing process.

1. *Prewrite.*   Read each question carefully, letting key words tell you what the examiner expects. If the question asks for causes and effects, for example, a listing of examples will not do the job. If it asks for a list, several paragraphs on one item will not do. Study the following key words and see how they differ in their instructions.

Key Words in Essay Exams

Analyze	Separate the subject into its parts and examine each part, relating each to the whole and to each of the others.
Compare	Show similarities.
Contrast	Show differences.
Define	Give the meaning, keeping in mind the class of the thing and how it differs from others in its class.
Describe	Give physical and factual characteristics.
Discuss	Give a complete and detailed answer by examining, analyzing, defining, and doing anything else appropriate.
Enumerate	List concisely the points required.
Evaluate	Make a judgment, either pro or con, and explain your decision.
Explain	State the *how* and *why*, clarifying and interpreting the material.
Illustrate	Explain or clarify by means of examples or diagrams.
Outline	In a concise and systematic form, give main ideas and important supporting material.
Summarize	Give the material in a condensed form.

If you draw a blank while reading the question, try stimulating your mind with the same invention questions you used for studying (classical probes or cubing, for example). Jot down ideas as they come to you. Even though you think you will remember your good ideas, they probably will slip away. Make a list of topics you want to cover. But work quickly. Spend about 10 percent of your time prewriting.

2. *Write.*   When you're ready to start writing, use your prewriting list as a guide. Make your first sentence a rephrasing of the question: "Explain several ways in which science and transportation are related" becomes

"Science and transportation are related in several ways." This sentence then serves as your thesis. Write an organized essay, the method of organization determined by the key words of the question, and include specific details wherever appropriate. Make sure that you don't get off your topic and that all your paragraphs follow your thesis. Save about 10 percent of your time for revising and editing.

3. *Revise.*   An essay exam is necessarily a quick process. But it's amazing how much better you can make your essay in only a few minutes. There are mainly two things you must do in revision:

a. Make sure that all your paragraphs relate to your thesis and that the end of your essay makes the same point you began with. If one of your paragraphs is widely off the topic, you may have to scrap it; *X* it out and write "omit" in the margin. But the paragraph may be salvageable—by adding a topic sentence that relates the paragraph to your thesis and/or by rewriting your thesis to encompass the paragraph. If your ending makes a point different from your thesis, adjust either the end or the thesis. It's extremely important that all parts of your essay be related. Don't skip this step in your revision.

b. Check for errors and make corrections. Look for the kinds of errors you commonly make, because you probably have some in this essay. Cross out the error, and make the correction neatly above it or in the margin. Don't write over the error, because your correction will probably be illegible. This step is extremely important too. It can make the difference of a full letter grade or more.

One final point: for writing essay exams, use a pen, not a pencil. Penciled writing may seem easier to erase and revise, but it usually ends up smudged. Even under the best of conditions, penciled writing is harder on the reader's eyes; ink is brighter and clearer.

EXERCISE

With your classmates, discuss the following essay question to determine (1) what it is asking, (2) what the first sentence of an answer might be, and (3) how the answer would be developed. Use blank spaces for items of subject matter you don't know.

Analyze three forms of fossil fuel, comparing their methods of formation, the extent of existing resources, their roles in meeting energy needs, and their roles in future energy needs.

Critiques and Responses

A **critique** is an analysis of and a commentary on another piece of writing; it generally focuses on technique as well as on content. A **response** is a commentary on another piece of writing that may address technique but generally focuses on content. Book reviews are a type of critique, analyzing both technique and content; book reports tend to be in the response category, focusing more on content. In school writing, both critiques and responses are common. Their subject matter is another piece of writing; they usually show that the writer has read and understood the work. Both critique and response may include summary, analysis, interpretation, and evaluation. Expressions of personal disagreement are uncommon in critiques but may be found in responses, especially if the writer can back them with evidence.

Whether you write a critique or a response depends on your purpose. It's important that you find out precisely what the assignment calls for. A literature assignment may ask you to write a critique of a short story, and a freshman composition assignment request a response to a newspaper commentary. The critique assignment calls for analysis of the story's theme, form, characters, and plot, plus interpretation and evaluation. The response may look for analysis of the purpose in the newspaper commentary and evaluation of the validity of the writer's position plus a statement of supporting or opposing position. But critiques are not restricted to literature, nor responses to newspaper commentaries. If you were to write a critique of a newspaper commentary, you would address such rhetorical concerns as the writer's sense of audience, attainment of purpose, authority on the subject, and accuracy and sufficiency of evidence. And if you were to write a response to a short story, you would react particularly to the content, perhaps relating it to your own experience, perhaps noting the validity of the theme and realism of the characters, perhaps commenting on the value of the piece. As you can see from the sample essays in this chapter, the distinction between critique and response is frequently blurred.

Writing a Critique or a Response

To write either a critique or a response, you must be informed, having carefully read the piece in question and having enough experience in the subject matter to determine your criteria for analysis. The process is in some ways similar to summarizing, since both deal with another piece of writing, but the critique and response require the additional measures of analyzing and evaluating.

1. *Read.* First read the piece through just for enjoyment and information, making no notes. Read actively and thoughtfully, seeking answers for such active reading questions as "What is the writer's main point?" and

"What is the writer's attitude toward the subject?" (refer to the Questions for Active Reading on page 6.) Upon completing your first reading, write a brief reaction.

2. *Analyze.*   Read a second time, trying to be more thorough, more analytical of both detail and technique, making notes now and underlining details you may want to remember. Try to answer the Questions for Active Reading on Page 6, plus the Questions about Audience for Reading on page 25. To heighten your understanding of the piece, apply one of the invention methods in Chapter 3—the classical probes, the journalist's questions, or cubing, perhaps. Determine your specific criteria for analysis, such as

    a. Does the writer appear to be informed about the subject?

    b. Is the writer's purpose clear?

    c. Does the writer appear to understand the audience?

    d. Does the writer's technique support the purpose?

        (1) How is the essay organized?

        (2) How are the major points supported—with examples, observations, quotations, statistics, and so on?

        (3) What are the major features of sentence structure in terms of length, pattern, and variety?

        (4) How does word choice relate to subject, purpose, and audience?

        (5) What is the tone of the piece? Is it consistent?

If necessary for an informed reaction, read related materials.

3. *Evaluate.*   Step back from your work now to allow yourself time and space to ruminate on what your analysis means, how the piece you've read relates to your knowledge and experience, how you feel about what the writer has said. Determine your specific criteria for evaluation based on your purpose. You might consider these questions:

    a. How informed is the writer about the subject?

    b. Is the writing appropriate for the time and environment when the piece was written?

    c. How competent is the writer's technique?

    d. How well does this piece compare with similar writings?

    e. How thoroughly does the writer support the major points?

Write another reaction, and discuss your thoughts with other people. Make a working outline of how you plan to proceed. Here's a basic structure that you might be able to adapt:

    a. Introduction: title, author, preliminary information, summary, your main point

    b. Background: facts, issues, biographical data, essential definitions

    c. Strengths of the writing

    d. Weaknesses of the writing

    e. Conclusion: final statement reinforcing your main point

4. *Write.* Using your notes, reactions, and working outline, begin writing a draft. As in summary, begin with an introduction that states your thesis and names the author and title of the work you are writing about. Here's an example:

> During my twenty-five years of experiencing life, I don't believe a woman has ever called me for a date. Granted, the first fifteen years or so didn't really hold much potential, but the last ten have failed to produce also. Therefore, I've decided that women just don't call men for dates. In his July 31, 1989, *Newsweek* "My Turn" article, "Women, Pick Up the Phone!" Gerald Nachman has come to the same conclusion.
>
> —Peter E. Dulgar

In this introduction to an essay that appears later in this chapter, Dulgar names the author, the title, the magazine, and the point of his response—that he and Nachman agree.

As with most of your writing, in your critique or response you have a thesis and major supporting points. These points may be derived from your analysis of the work and the writer's credentials for writing it, your interpretation of the work and its implications, and your evaluation of its worth.

Critiquing and responding require abundant support from the work itself. This support may be in the form of summary, paraphrase, and direct quotation. The amount of *summary* you use depends on whether your reader has read the work or not; the more familiar the reader, the less summary needed. **Paraphrase** is similar to summary in that you put the writer's ideas in your words; it is different from summary in that it is not condensed, sometimes it is even longer than the original. Observe in the following paraphrase how the original idea is stated in different words:

Original

Certainly more people fail because they do not know the requirements of being an employee than because they do not adequately possess the skills of their trade; the higher you climb the ladder, the more you get into administrative or executive work, the greater the emphasis on ability to work within the organization rather than on technical competence or professional knowledge.

> —Peter F. Drucker, "How to Be an Employee"

Paraphrase

According to Peter F. Drucker, an essential job requirement is knowing how to be an employee. More people fail on the job, he says, because they don't know how to work within a firm's organization than because they don't have the skills or knowledge of their trade. The ability to work in the employ of a company becomes especially necessary as one is promoted to higher levels of responsibility.

—"How to Be an Employee"

Paraphrase and summary sometimes utilize **direct quotation.** Quotation ought to be used sparingly, but it is appropriate when the writer's words are especially apt, highly technical, or strongly opinionated. In the preceding paraphrased sentence, for example, Drucker uses the term "being an employee" in a specialized way, and the paraphrase might quote it directly, as this revision of the first sentence illustrates:

> According to Peter F. Drucker, knowing "the requirements of being an employee" is essential to job success.

When you are critiquing or responding, the bulk of your support will come from the piece you are working with. Naming it once at the beginning may be the only documentation necessary, with the possibility of a work cited notation at the end. If you refer to other sources, however, you will need to name them. A works cited entry includes the name of the author, the title of the work, and publishing information. Here are two examples:

> Drucker, Peter F. "How to Be an Employee." *Fortune* May 1952: 74–76.
> Brill, Steven. *The Teamsters.* New York: Simon, 1978.

(See also how Tracy Wallack, on page 452, documents the article she responds to and the additional article she has read.)

Throughout your writing, strike a tone that is courteous, serious, and respectful. Avoid sarcasm, anger, and pathos. Think of yourself as a scholar writing for other scholars.

5. *Revise.* Read your draft through to remind yourself of what you have said. Then reread the work you are responding to; you may discover new ideas or find out you were off base somewhere along the line. Ask yourself if you need new evidence. Check your tone for an appropriate level of courtesy and seriousness. See if you use present tense verbs whenever you refer to what the other writer says, for example:

> Gore *writes* with urgency and conviction as he *explains* the consequences of our misuse of the earth.

But use past tense verbs when referring to your own reading:

> Its content was so riveting that it brought me to deep introspection as I read.

Have a friend read your essay and give you critical comments: Is it clear? Is it fair? Is it accurate?

6. *Edit.* As with all your writing, look for the kinds of errors that you normally make and correct them. Write a clean draft and proofread for copying errors.

EXERCISE

Write a paraphrase of the following paragraph. Keep the meaning the same, but use your own words and writing style. Begin by referring to the author. Since this is not a summary, your paraphrase may be as long as, or longer than, the original.

Generally speaking, people can be grouped into two categories of intellectual preference. The first group prefers explorations which require a precision of logical processes. These are the people who become interested in the natural sciences and mathematics. They do not become scientists because of their education, they choose a scientific education because it gratifies their scientific mental set. The second group prefers explorations which involve the intellect in a less logically rigorous manner. These are the people who become interested in the liberal arts. They do not have a liberal arts mentality because of their education, they choose a liberal arts education because it gratifies their liberal arts mental set.

—Gary Zukav, *The Dancing Wu Li Masters*

Reading

Critiques analyze and comment on another piece of writing, generally focusing on technique as well as on content. Responses comment on another piece of writing, generally focusing on content and how it agrees with the responder's own experience and knowledge. Given these definitions, read student writer Peter E. Dulgar's essay to determine whether it is a critique or a response to the *Newsweek* article that follows it. (The title of Nachman's article is the original; the one in parentheses is the title *Newsweek* used.)

Please . . . Pick Up the Phone!

Peter E. Dulgar

During my twenty-five years of experiencing life, I don't believe a   1
woman has ever called me for a date. Granted, the first fifteen years or so

didn't really hold much potential, but the last ten have failed to produce also. Therefore, I've decided that women just don't call men for dates. In his July 31, 1989, *Newsweek* "My Turn" article, "Women, Pick Up the Phone!" Gerald Nachman has come to the same conclusion.

It seems as if I've made an infinite number of calls to women I've been interested in—although I'm sure that in reality the total was somewhere under a million. I'm not an especially brave person when it comes to that type of thing, but I think I've been making a pretty good effort. It usually takes me about a day to work up the nerve to actually make the call. In the meantime I experience a full range of nervous side effects, from pseudo-ulcers to a peculiar arm spasm which causes me to repeatedly pick up the phone and then slowly place it back in its cradle.   2

Society's recipe for men must have something to do with these feelings. It's written somewhere in the rulebook for Western Civilization that men will be confident and commanding. Someone must have edited out the sections on fear and rejection.   3

I can't imagine true equality for women until they have experienced the thrill of making *the* call. This is the "final secret barrier to true equality," as Nachman describes it. Women can have all the equality they want, but they also have to assume their share of the telephone burden.   4

I'm sure women are afraid of rejection too, but the only way to achieve equality is to take risks. I can honestly say that calling a woman on the telephone—actually picking up the phone, dialing, and talking to a woman I don't really know—is about the riskiest thing I've done as a man.   5

This transition could benefit the equality of men too. We'd learn what it's like to have three grandmothers die in the same week, and our hair would have to suffer an unnatural amount of washing.   6

So pick up the phone, women! We'll pick it up too, and the combination should keep us all happy.   7

Warm Hearts, Cold Feet
(Original *Newsweek* title: "Women, Pick Up the Phone!")

Gerald Nachman

The last sexual taboo—yes, it appears there's still *one* left—is the brazen hussy who calls a man for a date.   1

High up on the roster of things that single women hate most about men they've just met is the lout who promises he'll call and doesn't. This is a horrid and thoroughly ungentlemanly practice, to be sure, but I have a radical solution that seems not to have occurred to any females I know, otherwise fearless and resourceful creatures: why don't women call the men who don't call them?   2

Well, I know why and I'll tell you. It's because they can't. They're simply incapable, as in psychologically paralyzed. The very thought terrifies most women and turns their dialing fingers to stone. The females I've talked   3 to—modern in every politically correct way—don't quite know why, either, but each concedes, almost shamefully, that she can't bring herself to do it. Few women seem not even to have seriously entertained such an outrageous concept. I would wager that Gloria Steinem has never called a man she met at a party and might like to see again.

What gives here, female persons? 4

A good deal of grief could be avoided—misunderstandings, miscalculations, and just plain misery—if women awaiting that all-important ring could pick up the phone and call the man who seems, for his own vague and snarled reasons, unable to call her. I don't mean women in relationships, or those who have been out once with someone. No, I mean telephone virgins who have never, you know, done *it*: called a guy cold. 5

One reason for the reluctance to use the phone, undoubtedly, is that women assume that the lack of a call equals rejection. But permit me to reassure them that when a man does not call, usually it isn't that at all. 6

Part of the time it's sloth or indecision. Part of the time it's good old cowardice. Part of the time he loses the number (never write anything crucial on a cocktail napkin). Part of the time he can't quite remember what the woman looked like and why he wanted her phone number in the first place. Part of the time he just forgets. Part of the time he lets so much time pass that he's afraid the woman will forget *him*. And yes, OK, part of the time he changes his mind. 7

But in this one silly little convention, it remains forever 1959. Despite a generation of feminist thought and deed, there is still this archaic unwritten hush-hush ladies-and-gentlemen's agreement, this final secret barrier to true equality, this quaint vestige of dainty telephone etiquette. 8

Women will still ask men to dance and buy them drinks and take them to dinner; they will even start conversations with them on street corners and in grocery stores; they will wink and carry on in a semiscandalous manner at cocktail parties—but they will not telephone them first. 9

For whatever reasons of propriety, rather than make a direct call, a woman can much more readily write a man a note, suggesting ever so nonchalantly (the deftly placed "P.S.," the coy parenthetical aside) that they "get together sometime." I have done a little research in this field (and for the purposes of today's study, specifically polled a dozen certifiably advanced females), and the results reveal that a woman would sooner ask a guy to marry her than telephone a man she met at dinner the night before. 10

Hey, I'm a sensitive guy and I'm aware of their worries, but the basic reason for all the fear and trembling seems to be based on antiquated teenage training, the old mom's tale that maintains: *It's the gentleman's place to call, dear.* 11

Perhaps one way to get the ball rolling here is for women to ask for a man's business card. Not, mind you, merely as a sly ploy, a coquettish flutter of interest—the dropped hanky of networking—but for the avowed purpose of actually putting it to use. 12

The proffered card even provides a built-in safety catch: a man who hands out a card to a woman he's unsure about (or hasn't the foggiest 13 interest in) at least has been warned and can begin rehearsing his excuse should she indeed phone: "Of course I remember you, Gloria, and you're *real* sweet to call, but, well, I'm sort of involved with someone right now . . ."

Quite apart from the very real fear of being considered a bimbo or wacko, a woman understandably is hesitant to call a man due to possible rejection, one she's brought on herself—that hollow hello at the other end of the line, the halfheartedly cheery *"Oh . . . hi"* that men have had to endure since the invention of the telephone. Having been the recipients of such calls, women are all too aware of the little deceptions that can occur at the receiving end.

Female fears are not altogether groundless. Women are afraid that if they do muster the courage to dial first, the man will be so mortified he won't know what to say. Many men—indeed, even the most technically liberated and right-thinking ones—are likely to be struck mute when women begin calling for dates, but we'll get over it, I feel certain, and, in no time, learn to perfect a flirtatious titter and say, "Why, hello there. What a surprise!"

If the caller turns out to be someone the man had an inkling he just *might* call himself but was worried that she wouldn't be interested or had forgotten him, he is going to be one happy boy. If the hoped-for female call fails to materialize, it's probably a good thing for men to learn what it's like to watch a silent telephone.

I concede it's going to be rough sledding for these bold pioneer women who make those first intrepid calls. And until we get used to the idea, men are bound to sound baffled and weird for a while. Once the concept catches on, though, as I'm sure it will with a little courage on each side, it could revolutionize the women's movement (at least the single women's movement) and free both sexes from the manacles of rampant phoneism.

Questions

1. Is Dulgar's essay a critique or a response? Support your answer with evidence from his essay.
2. Reconstruct Dulgar's criteria for analyzing Nachman's essay.
3. What purpose does Dulgar achieve with "Please . . . Pick Up the Phone!"? Who do you think is his intended audience?
4. Characterize the tone of Dulgar's essay and, with a classmate, analyze the essay for details and words that contribute to that tone.
5. Notice how Dulgar cites the Nachman article. Does he give you enough information for locating the article if you needed to?

Reading

"Latin America from the Bleachers" reviews a book about baseball in Latin America. The reviewer, Tom Miller, has written books about Latin America himself. The review appeared in *The New York Times Book Review* in

1989. Read the review to determine what Miller's criteria for analysis might have been and what his evaluation of *El Beisbol* is.

Latin America from the Bleachers
Tom Miller

El Beisbol: Travels through the Pan-American Pastime.
By John Krich.
272 pp. New York: The Atlantic Monthly Press. $18.95.

One day last fall I was talking with the groundskeeper at the baseball   1
stadium in Agua Prieta, a Mexican border town joined at the navel with
Douglas, Arizona. Just beyond the ball park's outfield wall stand two parallel
fences separating the United States from Mexico. A gully runs between the
two. In the early 1970's, according to the custodian, a player for the home-
town Vaqueros named Montoya slugged a homer out of the park all the way
to the United States. "There've been five home runs into the ditch," the
fellow said, waving a hand, "but this was the only one over the second fence.
We call it 'the international home run.' "

The notion of baseball as an international sport is a comforting one; it   2
is our most benevolent, least expensive, and most accessible export. It is
neutral but not neutered, peaceful but not passive. John Krich has taken
this idea and headed south with it into Mexico, the Caribbean, Central
America, and all the way to South America to determine the influence our
benign pastime holds on Latin America.

Mr. Krich, a Sunday morning softball player, seems well suited for the   3
task. One previous book, *Music in Every Room,* gained acclaim for its offbeat,
sly travel writing. Another, *A Totally Free Man,* is an energetic fictionalized
autobiography of Fidel Castro.

In *El Beisbol,* Mr. Krich juggles no fewer than five hardballs at once—   4
the sport, the lands he visits, international relations, the players he encounters, and himself. While it seems obvious early on that he has difficulty
keeping them all in the air simultaneously, I wanted to cheer him on anyway, all
the way to Venezuela, secure in the knowledge that something new would be
revealed and hopeful that his strong writing would rise to the task.

Mr. Krich becomes a wandering sports fan, full of genuine curiosity and   5
patronizing good will as he zigzags from ball park to ball park, country to
country: "To carry an American passport in the Americas is to follow a trail
cleared by the Marines. What a set of groundskeepers!"

Baseball, not New York schooling, taught him about countries to our   6
south. "My first inklings of our continental neighbors," Mr. Krich writes, "came
from the glorified seasonal workers who traveled North following the summer
game, the migrant *braceros* who helped pick crops in green outfields."

In his first stop searching for the source of these seasonal workers,   7
hoping to blend the symbolic with the historical, he finds the spot where
Columbus landed in the Dominican Republic. He stays only long enough to

get bored by a local freelance historian and note that the Indians Columbus encountered were probably the first to yell, "We wuz robbed!" He also begins the unfortunate habit of quoting innumerable cabdrivers.

In Puerto Rico almost everybody claims Roberto Clemente as having   8 been his closest friend, and *El Beisbol* overflows with stories about the Pittsburgh Pirate who went down with a planeload of goods destined for earthquake relief in Nicaragua on New Year's Eve, 1972. A visit to the Roberto Clemente Sports City near San Juan ends up with its director suggesting the island prepare for independence. On a ride across Puerto Rico Mr. Krich argues about the Cuban revolution with his driver. In Ponce on New Year's Eve his "search for authenticity" caves in, and he joins some youngsters on a family back porch as they watch videos of Sting. Interviews with Vic Power and Ruben Gomez, who starred with the Cleveland Indians and the New York Giants, respectively, make the author's visit to Puerto Rico worthwhile, as they describe major league racism from teammates, cops, and circumstances in the 1950's and 60's.

Back in the Dominican Republic, a "country disguised as a tryout   9 camp," he makes it to San Pedro de Marcorís, the port city whose welcoming billboard claims it has "given the most major leaguers to the world." Mr. Krich observes: "All roads in this republic lead to baseball—no matter how rutted or circuitous, no matter how many times you get stopped. . . . This is one Latin country where the suspects dragged from their homes in the dead of night are usually coveted shortstops."

The heart of *El Beisbol* thumps in Nicaragua, where the author is part   10 of a good-will group of Americans touring that beat-up country to play sloppy baseball and give away bats, balls, and gloves. The "Baseball for Peace" team plays clubs organized by a Nicaraguan farmers' union, and loses its opener, 14–0. The fields are pretty terrible; at one, oxen graze in left field, and "the right field line is your basic malarial swamp. . . . The infield is rutted, the bases wherever we imagine." The author, who warms the bench for most of the tour, finally pinch-hits. He gets hit by a pitch just above the elbow and ends up on the disabled list. But the most profound injury to these merry peaceniks schlepping through enemy territory comes not from the pitcher's mound but from the mouth of a *campesino:* "Why do you bring us baseballs when we need spare parts for our Italian tractors? Do you know we haven't been able to lay irrigation ditches in a year? What good are bats and balls to people who are starving?" The questions go unanswered.

It is in Venezuela that Mr. Krich, by now apparently tiring of his own   11 mission, rebounds as he searches for "the end of baseball." "Who's to say that going from ballpark to ballpark is an any less edifying form of tourism than traipsing from battlefield to battlefield, cathedral to cathedral?" he asks. Indeed, if his quest wears thin at times, it never wears out, and at Ciudad Piar, 325 miles southeast of Caracas as the ball flies, he finds what he takes to be the southernmost baseball diamond in the Americas: "I spring from the cab and do a lap around the bases. . . . I find safety tagging first, second, third, home." *El Beisbol* closes with a terrific fantasy of the baseball-ization of the Americas.

But something is troubling here. Throughout his journey the author   12
never seems uncomfortable with his bare-bones Spanish, yet he mocks
Spanish speakers' limited English. "Gringo," he writes, "have no fear that
you can't speak the language." A disturbing pattern of superficial observation occasionally surfaces and comes across as condescension. Mr. Krich
writes: "Latin culture looks remarkably, distressingly homogeneous"; and,
"I still don't know what to make of this culture that is not very efficient at
anything except song, color, commotion." Shallow perceptions like these
tarnish what is otherwise a book of integrity and pleasure. Did the author
learn nothing more from his exceptional odyssey than coups may come and
coups may go, but baseball lives forever?

Questions

1. Miller opens his review with a personal experience. Do you regard this as an
   effective beginning? In which paragraph of his several-paragraph introduction
   does he state his thesis—his reaction to Krich's book? In addition to a personal
   experience and a statement of thesis, what does Miller include in his introduction?

2. Notice the newspaper format for a book review. Set off at the head of the review
   is the book title, the author's name, the number of pages, the place of publication, the publisher, and the price. How does this information differ from the last
   entry shown in the works cited example on page 451?

3. With a classmate, discuss Miller's credentials to write an informed review of
   Krich's book. Locate evidence of his authority.

4. How does Miller use quotations and summaries in his review?

5. On what criteria does Miller criticize Krich's book? What does he like about the
   book? What does he regard as its weaknesses?

6. What is Miller's overall evaluation of the book?

Reading

In the following essay, student writer Traci Teas responds to a newspaper article by Al Sicherman, "Be Scared for Your Kids" (see Chapter 8). Teas
relates Sicherman's column to her own experience.

Fatal Trip
Traci Teas

Minneapolis *Star Tribune* columnist Al Sicherman usually brightens   1
Sunday mornings with his off-the-wall humor and witty, albeit zany, interpretations of everyday occurrences. On Sunday November 15, 1989, however, his column had a serious tone. The subject, his son's fatal LSD-induced

fall, had so much emotional appeal that it made the front page as a human-interest story. Its content was so riveting that it brought me to deep introspection as I read. Though Sicherman's focus is to warn parents to "be scared for [their] kids," the column does hold a vital message for us as college students as well. This message, of the devastating effect upon unsuspecting parents when they find that their otherwise bright college student's death was due to recreational drug use, is one that should teach all of us to look at what our drug or alcohol use is doing to others.

College students before us were destroying themselves and their fruitful futures by allowing their drug use to take over, or at least hinder, their judgment. Still the message has not sunk in. Not until we are smacked in the face with an incident such as Joe Sicherman's death do we realize the impact that it would have on our parents and others who love us if we were to die because of a mind-altering substance.   2

Sometimes we forget why we are in college. We hurry through classes, homework, and studying to go out, socialize, and experience life independent from our parents. Though making new friends, experiencing new things, and enjoying the newfound privileges of adulthood are all a part of college life, so are advancing ourselves, excelling, and broadening our horizons. How can we do these things when we are drunk at the bar most nights of the week, stoned in class, or flying out a window on an acid trip?   3

Perhaps Joe Sicherman lost his focus and found himself imbibing too much in the recreational side of college life. Evidently, he was enjoying himself as a freshman at a Wisconsin college. He was an extremely funny, bright kid who, like his father, had the potential to be an excellent journalist. Humorous anecdotes displaying his sense of humor decorate his father's article. These asides make the piece all the more tragic as we realize that this humor no longer will be created to brighten the lives of those around him. Moreover, Joe's death has put a damper on his father's light, funny writing style: "I probably won't be writing a humor piece for a while," he says. For that reason, all of us who are fans of Sicherman are losing out because of Joe's fatal experimentation with LSD. This should make us both angry with Joe for causing so much pain in his father's life and aware of the large number of people affected by the careless death of a young adult.   4

Should college students never take drugs or drink alcohol? Should they always act in a mature, responsible way and constantly avoid inappropriate behavior? No. No one can put those restrictions on young adults, and we do have to learn from our mistakes. Should college students be aware of the ramifications of their behavior on others? Very definitely. That is the essence of Sicherman's message to college students. He wants us to realize that "it is parents' worst fear that something terrible will happen to their kids; it is kids' constant struggle to be free of the protection of their parents" (10).   5

Something terrible happened to Sicherman's child. Sicherman had dreams for his son that will never be realized. Now he has only memories of an eighteen-year-old son who thought it would be all right to try LSD, a son   6 who plunged through a seventh-story dorm window to his death. Meanwhile, the father is left feeling guilty, as if he had somehow caused, or could have prevented, his son's death. Is that fair? Is the father to blame, or is it we, the younger, college-aged generation, who perpetuate the idea once again that it is cool to take drugs until we pass out or vomit—or die? Let's take a good, hard look at our behavior, and let's not take from our parents what they have given us, our lives.

Work cited

Sicherman, Al. "Be Scared for Your Kids." *Star Tribune* [Minneapolis, MN] 5
 Nov. 1989: Al, 10.

Questions

1. Although Teas responds mostly to the content of Sicherman's article, she does refer also to his technique, commenting, for example, on the serious tone, so unusual for Sicherman's columns. Name one or two other comments on technique.

2. What is Teas's thesis?

3. A key word in Teas's thesis is *should*. What influence does this thesis have on the tone of the essay? Characterize the tone.

4. Is Teas convincing? What else might she have done to lend additional support to her thesis?

Reading

Student writer Renee Walsh writes about a short story, "I Stand Here Ironing" by Tillie Olsen. As you read, try to determine Walsh's criteria for analysis and evaluation. What is her evaluation of the story?

Ordinary Heroes
Renee Walsh

A friend of mine approached me the other day, discouraged by life's 1
trials. She was looking for something to admire, something or someone to look up to. She said there weren't any heroes anymore. Looking around at the modern world, I had to agree with her.

Shortly thereafter, I read something that made me change my mind. 2
That something was the story "I Stand Here Ironing" by Tillie Olsen. When I first read it, it struck so many familiar chords in my own life that I had to read it a second time. Olsen writes with an imagery and sensitivity that is rare, with an honesty that is almost never seen. Through her story she showed me that there are plenty of heroes today.

The character of the mother in the story is not the stereotypical hero 3
that most people would think of. She has made mistakes, she has done the

wrong thing, even when she knew it was wrong, and she has not always been there for herself or her children. A stereotypical hero would always do the right thing and would always, unlike real people, know what that was. In this story, however, there is considerable evidence that both mother and daughter are real heroes.

It has always been my opinion that if something feels right at the time, or if it is all you can do, then it is right. If something is true in your heart, then it will be true to your life. Critic Joanne Frye says in her essay about this story that Olsen writes of "the problems of selfhood in the modern world" (287). The character of the mother has difficulty finding and holding on to her "self" largely because of external events such as the war, the depression, and her abandonment by her husband. These are events beyond her control, yet she perseveres, and survives with her "self" intact. If this were not so, she would not be able to come to the conclusions that she does at the end of the story. She comes away from all of it a little wiser and a lot stronger. Despite the mistakes she may or may not have made, she is a hero.   4

In the story, the mother speaks of when she had to send her daughter Emily away to nursery school. She realized at the time that this was probably not the best thing for Emily, but at the same time she knew that it was the only thing available to her. As the mother states: "It was the only way we could be together, the only way I could hold a job" (Olsen 812). It truly was the only way, and, as one source says, "gauging the hurts and needs of one human being against the hurts and needs of another: this is the pattern of parenthood" (Frye 288). The mother balanced their need to stay together with the pain of being separated by the nursery school for part of the time, and decided to go with the latter for as long as they could. Both mother and daughter survived this pain: survival of pain is what makes heroes.   5

Another way the mother acts heroically is using her insight toward the end of the story to see into Emily's life and make a beneficial decision. Ann Charters says that by saying to the counselor "Let her be," when the counselor says that Emily needs help, the mother is recognizing that Emily will be better off finding her own way than receiving the type of "help" they have thus far received (141). I agree with Charters; the help they have received has seldom benefited them. The mother sets a good example of caring and understanding by letting Emily help herself without interference.   6

Emily has more of a parallel to the typical hero than her mother does. Emily has largely overcome the events of her past and used them to find herself and her talents. According to one source, Olsen "presents a convincing case for the influence of external circumstances on human achievement" (Yalom 59). In her character of Emily, Olsen also shows us how one particular person overcame and went beyond those circumstances.   7

There is a point in the story where the mother says she doesn't recognize her daughter. Emily is on stage performing, and what the mother sees is someone confident, commanding, and strong. Emily is there behind the act, and the mother should recognize her, because Emily has many of the   8 same qualities that she herself has. Both have overcome great difficulty, both have seen and survived great pain, and both have gone beyond their external circumstances to become more than what the world would have them be.

By yesterday's standards, they are anti-heroes. They are not Superman or Superwoman, but super women. I applaud Tillie Olsen for showing us what largely goes unnoticed. Olsen shows us that we are all heroes, that we all have worth, despite hardship, despite flaws, despite mistakes. "I Stand Here Ironing" is a story which, while forcing the reader to see, also comforts and soothes. My reaction to this story cannot be totaled, because that reaction is still happening. The story has made me look inside myself and answer questions I never knew I had; it has also made me question answers I thought I was sure of. It is a story I will always think of as the one that made me look around and see people for what they really are . . . and can be.

9

Works cited

Frye, Joanne S. "'I Stand Here Ironing': Motherhood as Experience and Meta-
phor." *Studies in Short Fiction* 18 (Summer 1981): 287–92.
Olsen, Tillie. "I Stand Here Ironing." *The Story and Its Writer: An Introduction
to Short Fiction.* Ed. Ann Charters. 2nd ed. New York: St. Martin's, 1987.
811–17.
Charters, Ann, William E. Sheidly, and Martha Ramsey. Instructor's Manual
to Accompany *The Story and Its Writer: An Introduction to Short Fiction.* New
York: St. Martin's, 1987.
Yalom, Marilyn, ed. *Women Writers of the West Coast: Speaking of Their Lives and
Careers.* Santa Barbara: Capra, 1983.

Questions

1. What criteria does Walsh use for evaluating Olsen's story "I Stand Here Ironing"?

2. Walsh uses present tense verbs to describe actions in the story except for actions that occurred before the time of the story. How does she use verbs to describe her own reactions to the story? Locate verbs at several points in the essay. What effects do these variations in tense have on reading the essay?

3. What is Walsh's thesis? How does she develop her essay in support of her thesis?

4. Show how Walsh's conclusion reiterates and reinforces her thesis.

Reading

This student essay responds to a *Time* magazine article by Senator Albert Gore entitled "What Is Wrong with Us?" (see Chapter 7). The writer also refers to a second article in the issue, and both articles are named in her works cited list at the end.

An Urgent Need

Tracy Wallack

The *Time* magazine article "What Is Wrong with Us?" (66) by Senator   1
Albert Gore expresses the global need for environmental action to save our
earth from humanity's own destruction of it. Gore writes with urgency and
conviction as he explains the consequences of our misuse of the earth.
Gore's active participation in making the public aware of the approaching
environmental crisis is a good example of quality leadership and should be
credited as such.

Gore discusses five political barriers that must be overcome before   2
political action is warranted. He says the first barrier is psychological; people
are unwilling to accept the fact that the earth, because of people, has been
and continues to be severely damaged. In a desperate plea for help, Gore
bluntly states, "We are at an environmental boiling point" (66). Gore feels
that a change in political thinking is required to save the earth.

Skeptics like Kenneth E. F. Watt, professor of environmental studies at   3
the University of California at Davis, call the greenhouse effect "the laugh of
the century" (Sancton 28). Thomas A. Sancton, on the other hand, agrees
with Senator Gore: "The skeptics could be right, but it is far too risky to do
nothing while awaiting absolute proof of disaster" (28).

Other experts, such as Harvard biologist E. O. Wilson, have compared   4
humanity's destruction of the earth to the great mass extinction of the
dinosaurs (Sancton 28). Sancton, like Gore, states that humanity is in a war
for survival and that this war can be won only if all nations become one and
attack the problems globally (30).

Senator Gore is rightfully concerned about the earth. After all, the   5
future generations of all living things depend for their survival on the
continued health of the earth. The threat our environment is facing is real
and will not go away. As Sancton says, "Now, more than ever, the world
needs leaders who can inspire their fellow citizens with a fiery sense of
mission, not a nationalistic or military campaign but a universal crusade to
save the planet" (30). Sancton's statement is true, but I also agree with Gore that
resolving our environmental problems will be "unimaginably difficult" (66).

Works cited

Gore Albert. "What Is Wrong with Us?" *Time* 2 Jan. 1989: 66.
Sancton, Thomas A. "What on Earth Are We Doing?" *Time* 2 Jan. 1989: 24–30.

Questions

1. Direct quotations are effective in critiques and responses when the words of the
    original are particularly apt, highly technical, or personal opinions. Wallack has
    several quotations in her essay. Analyze the effectiveness of each one on the basis
    of these criteria. Would the essay be improved if any of the statements were
    paraphrased instead of quoted?

2. In what ways does Wallack use the Sancton article to support her response to Gore's article? Do you think this is an appropriate use of a second article?

3. What do you learn about Wallack in her essay?

4. What assumptions does Wallack make about her audience?

Writing

Following the steps outlined under "Writing a Summary," write a summary of the following essay by Peter F. Drucker, known for his writings as an economist, management consultant, and teacher. (This article comes from the May 1952 issue of *Fortune* magazine.) Read the essay before beginning to make notes. Open your essay with a nutshell statement, and support that statement with the major ideas of Drucker's essay. Write from your perspective, not Drucker's, but do not express your opinions. Conclude with a reinforcing statement. Make your summary approximately one-fourth the length of the original. Use coordination and subordination to compress ideas and reduce wordiness.

How College Helps You Be an Employee

Peter F. Drucker

What can you learn in college that will help you in being an employee? 1 The schools teach a great many things of value to the future accountant, the future doctor, or the future electrician. Do they also teach anything of value to the future employee? The answer is: "Yes—they teach the one thing that is perhaps most valuable for the future employee to know. But very few students bother to learn it."

This one basic skill is the ability to organize and express ideas in writing 2 and in speaking.

As an employee you work with and through other people. This means 3 that your success as an employee—and I am talking of much more here than getting promoted—will depend on your ability to communicate with people and to present your own thoughts and ideas to them so they will both understand what you are driving at and be persuaded. The letter, the report or memorandum, the ten-minute spoken "presentation" to a committee are basic tools of the employee.

If you work as a soda jerker you will, of course, not need much skill in 4 expressing yourself to be effective. If you work on a machine your ability to express yourself will be of little importance. But as soon as you move one step up from the bottom, your effectiveness depends on your ability to reach others through the spoken or written word. And the further away your job is from manual work, the larger the organization of which you are an employee, the more important it will be that you know how to convey your thoughts in writing or speaking. In the very large organization, whether it is the government, the large business corporation, or the Army, the ability to express oneself is perhaps the most important of all the skills a man can possess.

Of course, skill in expression is not enough by itself. You must have something to say in the first place. The popular picture of the engineer, for instance, is that of a man who works with a slide rule, T square, and compass. And engineering students reflect this picture in their attitude toward the written word as something quite irrelevant to their jobs. But the effectiveness of the engineer—and with it his usefulness—depends as much on his ability to make other people understand his work as it does on the quality of the work itself.

Expressing one's thoughts is one skill that the school can really teach, especially to people born without natural writing or speaking talent. Many other skills can be learned later—in this country there are literally thousands of places that offer training to adult people at work. But the foundations for skill in expression have to be laid early: an interest in and an ear for language; experience in organizing ideas and data, in brushing aside the irrelevant, in wedding outward form and inner content into one structure; and above all, the habit of verbal expression. If you do not lay these foundations during your school years, you may never have an opportunity again.

Writing

Following the guidelines under "Writing a Critique or a Response," write a critique of "A 'Simple' Behavioral Problem" by Marston Bates, a biologist noted for his knowledge of mosquito behavior. The essay is excerpted from his book *The Forest and the Sea,* first published in 1960. After reading the essay for the first time, establish your criteria for analysis and evaluation, considering such aspects as purpose, intended audience, writing style and technique, and use of terminology. As you write your critique, support your thesis with evidence from Bates's essay, using summary, paraphrase, and quotation as appropriate. You may want to relate the content of the essay to your own experience or other material you have read on the subject.

A "Simple" Behavioral Problem
Marston Bates

I have spent many hours of my life trying to understand the world in which mosquitoes live by trying to look at the world from the mosquito point of view. It is not easy and I can't report much progress. It is a world that I can know only indirectly through inferences from the way mosquitoes act; from experimentally altering the environment to see what happens; and through trying to measure things I can't perceive directly with various sorts of instruments.

I go on the assumption that the mosquito's world is made up of the same general sort of elements that my world is. If I study the sense organs of a mosquito, I can presume from the way they are made that they serve for perceiving light, odors, tastes, and vibrations, though I can't always be really sure of the functions of the sense organs that I find. Their sensitivity is clearly quite different from the sensitivity of my sense organs, and when I try to make mosquitoes carry out the normal process of living—bite, mate, lay eggs—under laboratory circumstances, I frequently end up completely frustrated. I've overlooked some factor that is essential before the mosquito will carry out that particular activity.

Sometimes I've thought about abandoning mosquitoes, taking up instead the study of mice or monkeys. With a fellow mammal I might have some chance; we would have, essentially, the same kind of eyes, ears, noses, touch perception. I might have a chance at understanding the world of a mouse. But I never have made any serious study of the behavior of mammals. It wouldn't be any easier than the study of insects, I am sure; though I suspect the difficulties would be of a different kind. I think I could do a better job of reconstructing the perceptual world of a mouse, but there would always be the danger of interpreting the mouse's behavior in terms of my own feelings and reactions—the danger of anthropomorphizing: attributing human emotions and feelings to other animals. There is no danger whatever of anthropomorphizing when you are studying mosquitoes—human reactions just won't fit at all in the insect world. Since in many cases you can't even figure out what the mosquito is reacting to, there is little likelihood of sympathizing with the reaction.

What makes a mosquito bite, for instance? Or perhaps I should say, how does a mosquito locate a suitable host? Quite a few scientists have fussed with this question for quite a few years, but the answer still is far from clear. One would first suspect smell. Insects in general have an extraordinarily keen sense of smell; the paired, plumed antennae are primarily organs of smell because apparently insects live in a sort of three-dimensional world of odors hard for us to imagine. Some male moths can locate a female of their own species a mile or so away and fly directly toward her. Butterflies locate the proper species of plant on which to lay their eggs by smell. Insect behavior, over and over again, appears to be governed by odor gradients in the environment.

But efforts to explain the behavior of a biting mosquito by smell have generally failed. Sweat, blood, feces, all efforts to abstract the smell of an animal from the living animal itself have failed to arouse mosquito interest, or have aroused reactions no different from those aroused by a slice of apple or a wad of cotton moistened with perfume.

Several different people who have worked with the problem have found that a hungry female mosquito will react to warmth or moisture or both. A Dutch scientist discovered some years ago that mosquitoes would persistently try to bite a glass tube covered with wet filter paper and kept warm by circulating warm water. But it hardly seems possible that this attraction could operate at any distance. A bit of "dry ice" (frozen carbon dioxide) introduced into the cage would increase the frenzy of the mosquitoes trying to bite the "artificial arm." Many sorts of experiments show that hungry mosquitoes react positively to an increase in the carbon dioxide in the air (every animal constantly breathes out a higher concentration of carbon dioxide than it breathes in) but again it is difficult to imagine this attraction operating at any distance from the animal.

During the Second World War, I was involved in a great deal of work on mosquito repellents. Certain plastic solvents were discovered to be quite effective in inhibiting mosquitoes from biting, and much of the work was a simple sort of experimentation aimed at trying to find out which of these were most effective and for how long. I have no idea how they worked—why they stopped the mosquitoes from biting—and I don't think anyone does. One of the most effective of these substances is di-methyl-phthalate. I remember once working in a flooded tropical river valley where mosquitoes were incredibly abundant. I was stripped to the waist, but I had smeared myself with di-methyl-phthalate. Swarms of mosquitoes would hover around me, coming within an inch of my skin, but never lighting, never trying to bite. What had attracted the mosquitoes to me—and what stopped them an inch away?   7

Here is a simple behavior problem which I have outlined in some detail just because it is simple, and yet exasperatingly difficult. I am sure this aspect of mosquito behavior can be "explained." There are endless ideas to be tested, and I have probably overemphasized our present ignorance. It isn't one problem, it is a series of problems: the problem of the factors, physiological and environmental, that put a mosquito into a state where it is ready to bite; the problem of factors in host location that operate at a distance; and the problem of factors operating in the immediate vicinity of the host. And every behavioral problem seems to be similarly complex, composed of a series of subproblems that have to be teased out and analyzed separately.   8

Writing

Select one of your courses, particularly one for which you are likely to be required to write an essay exam, and prepare for an exam according to the guidelines under "Essay Examinations." Write several questions that could be asked on the exam, then write an essay on one of them, again following the guidelines.

Glossary

Abstract a condensation of another piece of writing, similar to **summary,** usually written from the same perspective and in the same order of development as the original.

Active reading a way of reading which seeks answers to questions and interacts with the text.

Active voice see **Passive voice.**

Addition a form of **revision** in which a writer inserts in an earlier draft explanations, illustrations, transitions, and so on as words, punctuation, sentences, or paragraphs.

Agreement a principle of grammar that verbs correspond to their subjects, singular verbs for singular subjects ("A *record is* sometimes *revised* as a report") and plural for plural ("*Records are* sometimes *revised* as reports"), and that pronouns correspond to the words they stand for ("When a *writer* proofreads, *he or she* [not *they*] reads for errors" or "When *writers* proofread, *they* read for errors").

Analogy a means of developing and arranging ideas that explains one subject through references to a second subject ("Writing is like growing a plant").

Answering questions a common type of academic writing in which the audience usually knows more than the writer and the writer shows what he or she knows about the subject, as in **essay examinations.**

Appeal of character (*ethos*) an aspect of **persuasion** which presents the **writer** as informed, respectable, and trustworthy.

Appeal of logical reasoning (*logos*) an aspect of **persuasion** in which a writer presents a well-reasoned argument based on **facts (examples, testimony, statistics, and historical evidence)** and relevant **opinions.**

Appeal to the minds and emotions of the audience (*pathos*) an aspect of **persuasion** in which the writer identifies with the **audience** and calls on its needs and interests.

Arguable proposition a stance on an undecided issue, one that can be argued on the basis of **facts** and relevant **opinions.** An arguable proposition can serve as the **thesis** of a **persuasive essay.**

Audience a component of a **rhetorical situation.** Depending on the other components, the writer adjusts discourse to a particular audience. See also **purpose, subject,** and **writer.**

Brainstorming see **Listing or brainstorming.**

Cause and effect analysis a means of developing and arranging ideas that examines causes or effects of particular circumstances.

Censure See **Praise or censure.**

Chronology a means of developing and arranging ideas according to the sequence of events; simple time order.

Citation of sources See **Documentation.**

Classical probes a means of **invention** related to the mental processes. Ideas are discovered and explored by identification, comparison, classification, cause and effect analysis, process analysis, and exemplification. As a method for **revision,** the classical probes can assist a writer in discovering undeveloped ideas in a draft.

Classification a means of developing and arranging ideas according to their categories.

Clustering see **Mapping or clustering.**

Coherence the aspect of a composition in which all parts relate and are connected to one another. Coherence is achieved by a clearly stated **thesis sentence,** repetition of **key words,** review of **old information** before statement of **new information,** insertion of **transitional expressions,** and other devices.

Comma splice an error in punctuation that joins two sentences with a comma ("Sometimes freewriting is used without a focusing topic, you begin writing whatever is on your mind"). A writer can correct a comma splice by replacing the comma with a period or a semicolon, or by adding a conjunction after the comma. Fused sentences are similar except that in them two sentences are joined without any punctuation between.

Comparison a means of developing and arranging ideas by comparing them to one another and showing how they are similar and different; contrast is a type of comparison that focuses mainly on differences.

Conclusion the end of a composition, often reiterating the main idea.

Connotations the associations conjured up by a word that, in addition to its explicit meaning, make up an audience's understanding of what a writer is saying.

Contrast see **Comparison.**

Critical reading **active reading** directed either to the meaning of a text or to its **style** and structure.

Critique an analysis of and commentary on another piece of writing. The critique usually focuses on technique as well as on content.

Cubing a means of **invention** allowing a writer to visualize a subject enclosed in a cube whose six sides require the writer to examine the subject by classifying it, analyzing it, describing it, differentiating it, locating it, and using it.

Dangling modifier a modifying phrase, usually at the beginning of a sentence, that does not modify the word the writer intended ("*Studying humorous essays,* they often have breaks in the humor"). This syntactic error can usually be corrected by revising the sentence to make its subject the same as the implied subject of the phrase ("*Studying humorous essays, you* find that they often have breaks in the humor").

Definition a statement of meaning, or the characterization of a class of something, for instance, an essay explaining taste or endometriosis.

Deletion a form of **revision** in which a writer removes words, punctuation, sentences, or paragraphs to make the composition clearer and more concise.

Development methods of expanding and arranging ideas, occurring often during **drafting** but also during **prewriting** and **revising.** See also **Chronology, Space, Classification, Comparison, Analogy, Cause and effect, Exemplification, Definition, Question and answer, Answering questions,** and **Problem and solution.**

Documentation references to sources of information, such as books and journal articles. Scholarly courtesy requires showing sources of **quotations, paraphrases,** and **summaries,** usually by naming the author, title, page numbers, and publishing information—sometimes parenthetically following the reference and sometimes in footnotes or endnotes. A list of works cited or references usually follows a paper that borrows words and ideas from other writers.

Drafting the act of putting words on the page or word processor screen, often preceded by **prewriting** and followed by **revising.**

Editing the act of removing errors in a draft, usually in words and punctuation, ordinarily following **revision.**

Emphasis a method of arranging ideas that places the most important at the beginning or the end of a composition. Also, the focus of a piece of writing: the **writer,** the **audience,** or the **subject.**

Entertain a **purpose** for writing that appeals to the emotions of the audience to create pleasure.

Essay a composition that expresses the views of a **writer** on a single **subject.** The essay usually consists of an **introduction** to the subject, a **thesis sentence** that expresses the writer's position on the subject, and several **paragraphs** of thesis development, often concluding with a reiteration of the main idea.

Essay examinations a **subject**-emphasis form of writing in which the writer shows an **audience** who already knows the subject matter that the writer also is informed about it.

Ethos see **Appeal of character.**

Exaggeration a stylistic feature common in humor and writing that **appeals to the emotions of the audience,** found notably in parody, sermonic addresses, and satire.

Example a type of **fact,** or support for an opinion, that may be drawn from personal experience, experience of others, reading, or observations.

Exemplification a means of developing and arranging ideas in which **examples** illustrate and explain statements.

Explain a **purpose** for writing in which the **subject** is emphasized, telling the **why** and **how** of something.

Facts verifiable statements that are true and therefore inarguable. Types of facts are **examples, testimony, statistics,** and **historical evidence.**

Fallacies errors in logic, such as broad generalization, oversimplification, question begging, either-or reasoning, post hoc cause, and ad hominem.

Feedback response from readers on how they perceive a composition, useful in **revision** for telling where the draft needs to be improved.

Fragment an incomplete sentence, lacking a subject, a verb, or both ("Applying Bradley's words to the present context"). A fragment can be corrected by adding the missing part or by attaching the fragment to a nearby sentence ("Senator Gore applies Bradley's words to the present context" or "Senator Gore quotes General Omar Bradley, applying Bradley's words to the present context").

Freewriting a means of **invention** in which a subject is explored by means of preliminary writing done rapidly and without concern for **style** or correctness.

Fused sentence see **Comma splice.**

General to specific and specific to general related methods of arranging ideas. General to specific begins with a statement of thesis or topic followed by specific explanations and **examples,** and specific to general first accumulates illustrations and explanations and concludes with a generalized statement.

Historical evidence a type of **fact,** or support for an opinion; verifiable occurrences.

Imitation a means of **invention** that enables a writer to discover new ideas while copying the **style** of other writers.

Inform a **purpose** for writing in which the **subject** is emphasized and the **audience** is assumed not to know the information conveyed.

Instruct a **purpose** for writing in which the **subject** is emphasized, telling **how** something is done.

Introduction the beginning of a composition, establishing the **subject,** the **writer**'s relationship to the **audience** and to the subject, the **thesis** and **purpose** of the composition, the **tone,** and usually some means of heightening audience interest.

Invention methods of discovering and exploring ideas and how to express them (Chapter 3). See also **Classical probes, Cubing, Freewriting, Imitation, Journalist's questions, Listing, Mapping, Outlining, Questions about audience,** and **Reading.**

Journal a record of personal experiences and impressions for purposes important only to the **writer**; sometimes, as an academic journal, a record of school-related analyses, **summaries,** insights, and so on.

Journalist's questions a means of **invention** in which ideas are discovered and explored by questions beginning *who, what, where, when, why, and* how. *As a method for* **revision,** the questions can assist a writer in discovering undeveloped ideas in a draft.

Key words a **coherence** device that links ideas by repeating words that are significant in expressing those ideas.

Listing or brainstorming as a means of **invention,** a rapid itemized recording of thoughts related to a particular subject.

Logos see **Appeal of logical reasoning.**

Mapping or clustering as a means of **invention,** an itemized recording of thoughts on a particular subject which are then related by connecting lines. As a reading technique, mapping can assist a reader in understanding what has just been read. As a method of **revision,** mapping can reveal irrelevant information or undeveloped ideas.

Move a **purpose** for writing that appeals to the emotions of the audience to bring aout action or to engender compassion, anger, or other feelings toward others.

Narration storytelling by means of **chronological** development. Narration is used to introduce a composition, to illustrate a point, and to compose an entire essay.

Old information/new information a **coherence** device based on the principle that new ideas build on ideas already expressed. A writer recaps an idea already stated before making a new statement.

Opinion a position on an issue that if supportable by facts is arguable and thus can be stated as a **thesis.** Relevant, fact-based opinions can serve as support for arguments.

Outlining a means of organizing one's thoughts in a conventional format. An outline can serve as a guide for writing; as a means of **invention** or **revision** it can show up gaps in the development of ideas.

Paragraphs divisions of prose compositions that develop single aspects of the subject; units of writing of unspecified length.

Paraphrase a rewording of another piece of writing. Unlike **summary,** a paraphrase is usually not a condensation.

Passive voice a sentence arrangement in which the subject does not perform the action of the verb ("Events were described by an observer"). Usual sentence arrangement would be active voice, with the subject performing the action of the verb ("An observer described events").

Pathos see **Appeal to the minds and emotions of the audience.**

Persuasion writing for the **purpose** of moving an **audience** to action or changing the audience's views on an issue, accomplished with three appeals: **appeal of the writer's character (***ethos***), appeal to the minds and emotions of the audience (***pathos***), and appeal of logical reasoning (***logos***).**

Praise or censure a **purpose** for writing in which the **subject** is a person who receives approval or disapproval.

Prewriting a period of thinking that precedes **drafting,** usually to explore the subject, how to approach it and organize it, what **style** and **tone** the writer should assume, how to phrase sentences, and so on.

Problem and solution a means of developing and arranging ideas in which a writer describes a perplexing situation and then proposes a way or ways of remedying it.

Pronouns words that stand for nouns. To have meaning, pronouns' relation to their antecedents must be clear (examples of pronouns that are not clear: "All *this* led Timex to look around for new worlds to conquer." "We entered the lower-price watch market to convince buyers that *they* don't have to be expensive"). If the reference of the pronoun is not clear, it may be necessary to substitute a noun ("All *this success* led Timex to look around for new worlds to conquer." "*Timex* entered the lower-price watch market to convince buyers that *good watches* don't have to be expensive").

Proofreading the act of correcting typing or scribal errors in a composition, usually the final step in preparing a manuscript.

Purpose the determining factor in how the other three components of the **rhetorical situation (writer, audience,** and **subject)** relate to one another.

Question and answer a means of developing and arranging ideas in which a writer asks a question and then answers it.

Questions about audience a means of **invention** in which ideas are generated by the writer's knowledge of the **audience.** As a method for **revision,** the questions can assist a writer in seeing whether a draft has adequately considered the needs and interests of the intended audience.

Quotation an exact copy from another piece of writing, enclosed in quotation marks to show that it is borrowed.

Reading as a means of **invention,** a major source of ideas for writing.

Reading as a reader a method of **revision** that puts the writer in the **audience's** place to see whether the writing is clear and understandable.

Reading as a writer **active reading** directed to the **style** and structure of the text rather than its meaning.

Rearrangement a form of **revision** in which a writer rearranges the words, punctuation, sentences, or paragraphs of an earlier draft.

Record a **purpose** for writing in which the **subject** is emphasized and which coincides with the occurrence of an event.

Reflective writing a **purpose** for writing in which the **writer** is emphasized and which derives from the writer's own thoughts and perceptions.

Repetition a stylistic feature common in writing that **appeals to the emotions of the audience,** drawing on a sense of rhythm.

Report a **purpose** for writing in which the **subject** is emphasized; objective writing that is usually done after an event occurs.

Response impressions and interpretations of another piece of writing. See also **Critique.**

Revision the act of reconsidering what one has written and making changes in the form of **addition, deletion, substitution,** or **rearrangement.**

Rhetoric the principles of communication, balancing the relations among **writer, audience, subject,** and **purpose.**

Rhetorical situation an occasion for communication, in which **writer** (or speaker), **audience, subject,** and **purpose** are the principal components.

Space a means of developing and arranging ideas according to placement—vertically, horizontally, or circularly.

Statistics a type of **fact,** or support for an opinion; relevant data.

Style the distinctive way a writer uses words and their combinations to convey a particular **purpose,** persona, and **audience** relationship. See also **Tone** and **Voice.**

Subject a component of a **rhetorical situation.** Other components influence the writer's attitude toward and coverage of the subject. See also **Audience, Purpose,** and **Writer.**

Substitution a form of **revision** in which a writer substitutes words, punctuation, sentences, or paragraphs for those in an earlier draft.

Summary the key points of a piece of writing, reduced for another writer's purposes.

Testimony a type of **fact,** or support for an opinion; a quotation from an expert on the issue.

Thesis sentence the main idea of an **essay,** stated in a single sentence that expresses the subject and makes an assertion about it. The thesis sentence may also state the essay's method of development.

Title the name of a composition, identifying and describing it, often written to attract **audience** interest.

Tone an aspect of writing that is roughly comparable to the sound of one's voice. It reflects a **writer**'s attitude toward the **subject,** for instance objective, cynical, or humorous. See also **Voice.**

Transitional expressions coherence devices that connect thoughts by relational words, such as *however* and *but* showing contrast, *therefore* and *so* showing result, and *moreover* and *and* showing addition. Transitions are sometimes better achieved by an entire sentence or even a paragraph.

Unexpressed assumptions underlying suppositions of a **thesis** that may or may not require support.

Voice that which makes a person's writing individual, comparable to the sound of a person's voice in speech. While each **writer**'s voice is individual, it can be varied depending on the writer's attitude toward the **subject** and the **audience** (for instance, an angry voice or a friendly voice). See also **Tone.**

Writer a component of a **rhetorical situation.** A writer may project various roles depending on the other components. See also **Audience, Purpose,** and **Subject.**

Index

Credits *(continued)*

Pages 388–389. Suzette Haden Elgin, "Telephone Listening," from *The Last Word on the Gentle Art of Verbal Self-Defense* © 1987. Used by permission of the publisher, Prentice Hall Press, a division of Simon & Schuster, Inc., New York.

Pages 391–393. Tom Bodett, "Ditch Diving,"from pages 22–24 of *Small Comforts*, © 1987 by Tom Bodett. Reprinted by permission of Addison-Wesley Publishing Co., Inc., Reading, Massachusetts.

Pages 395–397. David D. Burns, "Ten Things You Should Know About Your Anger," from *Feeling Good*. Copyright © 1980 by David D. Burns, M.D. Reprinted by permission of William Morrow & Co.

Pages 397–400. John Irving, "How to Spell" advertisement in *Power of the Printed Word*. Reprinted by permission of International Paper.

Pages 400–402. Marya Mannes, "How Do You Know It's Good?," *Glamour*, November 1962. Excerpt from *But Will It Sell?*, published by J. B. Lippincott Company. Courtesy *Gourmet*. Copyright © 1962 by The Condé Nast Publications Inc.

Page 412. Tom Wolfe, "The Down-Filled People" from *In Our Time*. Copyright © 1961, 1963, 1964, 1965, 1968, 1971, 1972, 1973, 1975, 1976, 1977, 1978, 1979, 1980 by Tom Wolfe. Reprinted by permission of Farrar, Straus and Giroux, Inc.

Page 412. Gretel Ehrlich, "Cowboys," from *The Solace of Open Spaces*. Copyright © 1985 by Gretel Ehrlich. Reprinted by permission of Viking Penguin, a division of Penguin Books USA Inc.

Pages 415–417. W. J. Weatherby, "Marilyn Monroe," from *The Bedside Guardian 1952–1963*. Published by Collins Publishers. Copyright © 1963 by the Manchester Guardian and Evening News Ltd.

Pages 423–424. Samuel Eliot Morison, "Death of the Admiral," from *Admiral of the Ocean Sea: A Life of Christopher Columbus*. Copyright © 1942, 1970 by Samuel Eliot Morison. By permission of Little, Brown and Company.

Page 426. Associated Press, "Margie Inman Is Dead at 76," *New York Times*, October 6, 1987, p. 85. Copyright © 1987 by The New York Times Company. Reprinted by permission from Associated Press.

Pages 426–428. Lee Daniels, "James Baldwin, the Writer, Dies in France at 63," *New York Times*, December 1, 1987. Copyright © 1987 by The New York Times Company. Reprinted by permission.

Pages 442–444. Gerald Nachman, "Warm Hearts Cold Feet," original title: "Women, Pick Up the Phone!" from "My Turn" column, *Newsweek*, July 31, 1989, p. 8. Reprinted by permission of the author.

Pages 445–447. Tom Miller, "Latin America from the Bleachers," from *New York Times Book Review*, June 4, 1989. Copyright © 1985/89 by The New York Times Company. Reprinted by permission.

Pages 453–454. Peter F. Drucker, "How College Helps You Be an Employee," *Fortune* magazine, May 1952. Copyright Peter F. Drucker 1952. Reprinted by permission of the author.

Pages 454–456. Marston Bates, "The Problem with Mosquitoes," excerpt from *The Forest and the Sea: A Look at the Economy of Nature and the Ecology of Man*. Copyright © 1960 Marston Bates. Reprinted by permission of Random House, Inc.